COLOR PLATE 3

An example of colors arranged in a color solid

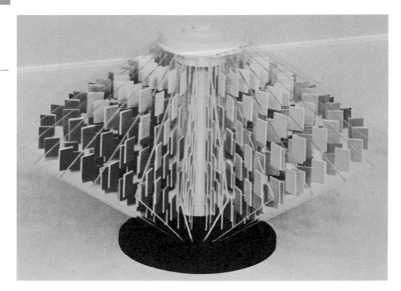

Courtesy of Inmont Corporation.

COLOR PLATE 4

An example of pointillism by Georges Seurat

Georges Seurat, French, 1859–1891, *Sunday Afternoon on the Island of La Grande Jatte,* oil on canvas, 1884–86, 207.6 × 308 cm, Helen Birch Bartlett Memorial Collection, 1926.224. Photograph © 1991, The Art Institute of Chicago. All Rights Reserved. Detail (left) from Georges Seurat, French, 1859–1891, *Sunday Afternoon on the Island of La Grande Jatte,* oil on canvas, 1884–86, 207.6 × 308 cm, Helen Birch Bartlett Memorial Collection, 1926.224. Photograph © 1991, The Art Institute of Chicago. All Rights Reserved.

Sensation and Perception

FOURTH EDITION

Sensation and Perception

Margaret W. Matlin
State University of New York
at Geneseo

Hugh J. Foley
Skidmore College

Allyn and Bacon
Boston ◆ London ◆ Toronto ◆ Sydney ◆ Tokyo ◆ Singapore

Senior Editor: Carolyn O. Merrill
Editorial Assistant: Alyssa Dorrie
Marketing Manager: Joyce Nilsen
Production Administrator: Elaine Ober
Editorial-Production Service: Sally Stickney
Manufacturing Buyer: Megan Cochran
Cover Administrator: Linda Knowles
Cover Designer: Susan Paradise

Copyright © 1997, 1992, 1988, 1983 by Allyn and Bacon
A Viacom Company
160 Gould Street
Needham Heights, Mass. 02194-2310

Internet: www.abacon.com
America Online: Keyword: College Online

Library of Congress Cataloging-in-Publication Data

Matlin, Margaret W.
    Sensation and perception / Margaret W. Matlin, Hugh J. Foley. --
4th ed.
      p. cm.
    Includes bibliographical references and indexes.
    ISBN 0-205-26382-8 (alk. paper)
    1. Perception. 2. Senses and sensation. I. Foley, Hugh James.
II. Title.
BF311.M4263   1997
152.1—dc20   96-38560
                                                  CIP

Printed in the United States of America

10 9 8 7 6 5 4 3 2 1   01 00 99 98 97 96

Credits begin on page 553, which constitutes a continuation of this copyright page.

For Arnie Matlin
Mary Ann Foley

Contents

Preface

We find sensation and perception fascinating, so from the very beginning we were motivated to write a textbook that reflected our enthusiasm for the subject matter. At the same time, the richness of our perceptual experiences arises from the operation of extraordinarily complex mechanisms. How could we accurately portray such complexity without dampening our reader's enthusiasm? The tension implicit in that question was always at the forefront of our thoughts as we worked to revise the textbook. We have tried to write a book that is interesting, student oriented, comprehensive, and current, while requiring no specialized background in physiology, mathematics, or experimental psychology. Not a simple task!

However, any textbook should be viewed as a work-in-progress. Given the opportunity, dedicated authors continually strive for improved clarity in their prose. Furthermore, the research community generates new and exciting work at a pace that seems to increase annually. When we completed the third edition of this textbook late in 1991, we had worked hard to produce a textbook that would be readable, yet would reflect much of the current research in the field. However successful we may have been at those tasks, we both leapt at the opportunity to collaborate on a fourth edition of the textbook. Like returning to visit an old friend, neither of us could resist trying to capture in words some of the progress being made in understanding perceptual processes.

We have been working for the past couple of years to produce the book you now hold in your hands. In fact, we could work continually on polishing our prose and including the new research that crosses our desks daily. However, the good people at Allyn and Bacon know academics well enough to foresee that we are quite capable of puttering away in such a fashion *ad infinitum*. Thus, the "dreaded" deadline brings our work to a close for now. We'll plan to continue this particular work-in-progress in a fifth edition.

For those of you who are unfamiliar with the earlier editions of this textbook, the next section provides an overview of the organization of the book. Those of you who are familiar with the third edition may want to skip to the following section, which covers some of the changes we have introduced in this new edition.

TEXT ORGANIZATION AND FEATURES

Sensation and Perception is intended as an introduction to these topics for use in courses in perception or in sensation and perception. Although primarily a textbook for undergraduates, graduate students seeking an overview of the discipline of of perception may also find the textbook useful.

This fourth edition is organized in four major parts. The first part consists of an introductory chapter and a chapter on the methodologies used to study perception; the second part contains six chapters on vision; the third part contains three chapters on audition. The final part includes the skin senses, the chemical senses, and perceptual development.

Four major themes are introduced in Chapter 1 and are woven throughout the book to provide the reader with a sense of continuity across many diverse topics:

1. The senses share some clear similarities and interact with one another.
2. The stimuli themselves are rich with information and are found in a rich context.
3. The human sensory systems perform well in gathering information about stimuli but can occasionally be led astray.
4. Prior knowledge and expectations help shape our perceptions.

This edition also includes the following general features:

- Clear, straightforward writing style with numerous examples to illustrate how the sensory systems and perception operate in everyday experience
- Applications in areas such as art, education, and other professions throughout the text
- Many brief, small-scale demonstrations for students to try by themselves, using minimal equipment
- Thirteen In-Depth sections focusing on recent research on selected topics and providing details on research methods
- A chapter outline at the beginning of each chapter
- New terms introduced in boldface italics, with their definition in the same sentence
- A summary at the end of each major section of a chapter to provide frequent opportunities for review

- Review questions, a new term list, and an annotated list of recommended readings at the end of each chapter
- A glossary, at the end of the book, containing a definition of every new term introduced in the book and a phonetic pronunciation for terms with potentially ambiguous pronunciations

WHAT'S NEW IN THIS EDITION?

We approached this new edition armed with input from a number of sources. Students (our own and those at other institutions) helpfully pointed out areas of the earlier edition that they thought merited revision. Faculty who used the earlier edition were also generous with their advice about potential revisions. A select handful of reviewers also provided detailed feedback on the third edition. This input from our readers was extraordinarily helpful. Thus, we would really appreciate hearing about your reactions to this new edition.

In addition to responding to suggestions prompted by the third edition, we updated the research covered in the textbook. We made extensive use of PsycLIT searches and pursued relevant books reviewed in *Contemporary Psychology*. In addition, we wrote to numerous researchers in the discipline, requesting reprints and preprints. Other researchers generously sent us copies of their work as it was published. As a result of our efforts, you will find that about 600 of the 1300 sources we used were published after 1990.

Professors and students who used previous editions of this text responded enthusiastically to the clarity of writing, the interest level, and the student-oriented features. We have retained those features in this new edition and have made some additions and changes.

Because the third edition of this textbook was substantially reorganized, we decided to minimize the structural changes in this edition. Although we reorganized the presentation of material within several chapters, the only structural change you will find is in the relocation of the motion chapter. We decided to focus our attention on the visual perception of motion. In doing so, we moved the chapter on motion perception (Chapter 8) earlier in the textbook to make it contiguous with the other chapters on vision.

As we mentioned earlier, much of our focus was on integrating new material into the textbook. For instance, we completely changed eight of the In-Depth sections and updated the remaining five. Each chapter received extensive attention, resulting in several changes:

- In Chapter 2, we revised the section on signal detection theory. In addition, the new In-Depth section discusses signal detection in the context of face perception and eyewitness identification.

- Chapter 3 includes an updated discussion of the parvo- and magnocellular systems. The new In-Depth section focuses on the role of areas of the visual cortex beyond the primary visual cortex. Damage to those areas leads to interesting disorders such as agnosia and prosopagnosia.

- Chapter 4 begins with a discussion of prerequisites for vision, with the addition of a discussion of the role of higher-order processes. Recent work on the filling-in processes that occur at the blind spot illustrates the role of such higher-order processes. We also review case studies of people whose sight was restored after they had been blind for many years, to underscore the important role of experience for visual perception.

- Portions of Chapter 5 were reconfigured for clarity and cohesion. A new In-Depth section discusses contemporary Gestalt research—especially some interesting controversies that have arisen regarding the role of figure–ground organization in form perception.

- The close relationship between distance and size perception is the focus of Chapter 6. Portions of this chapter were also reorganized. The new In-Depth section focuses on binocular cues to depth.

- Chapter 7 includes a new In-Depth section on how color information is coded beyond the retina. In that context, we discuss a recent theory of color vision proposed by Russell and Karen DeValois.

- Chapter 8 focuses entirely on visual motion perception. We substantially updated the In-Depth section on the perception of biological motion. We also added more detail about the physiological bases of motion perception.

- The discussion of the auditory system begins in Chapter 9. The In-Depth section discusses recent research on the functioning of the hair cells of the inner ear, including the importance of the motility of outer hair cells. We also added detail about the treatment of hearing impairments.

- Within Chapter 10 we added a great deal of information about the impact of visual information on auditory localization. In these latter chapters, we make every effort to emphasize the integration of the senses (Theme 1 of the textbook).

- Chapter 11 includes a new In-Depth section that focuses on interactions between auditory and visual stimuli. We also added new information about music and speech perception.

- We made substantial changes to our discussion of pain perception in Chapter 12. The topic of the new In-Depth section is phantom limb pain. Recent work by Ronald Melzack and Vilayanur Ramachandran uses the experience of phantom limbs to make important contributions to our understanding of brain functioning.

- In Chapter 13, we added new information about the impact of olfactory information on behavior. We also added information on odor identification and odor memory.

- Chapter 14 was substantially reorganized in conjunction with Margaret Matlin's G. Stanley Hall invited address at the American Psychological Association convention in 1995. The new In-Depth section focuses on how infants coordinate vision and audition, consistent with Theme 1 of the textbook.

ACKNOWLEDGMENTS

We would both like to thank a number of people whose contributions to the fourth edition of *Sensation and Perception* have been invaluable. First, we are absolutely delighted to report that Sally Stickney again served as Editorial-Production Coordinator. Her intelligence, expertise, good judgment, and professional skills remain extraordinary! We simply cannot offer sufficient praise for her superb work on our book.

Elaine Ober, Editorial-Production Supervisor at Allyn and Bacon—a longtime favorite since her wonderful help with the first edition of this book—exemplifies what every author hopes for in an editor: extensive knowledge, conscientious concern, and top-notch editorial ability. Deborah Brown performed an exemplary job as the production editor in the final phase of this fourth edition, and Karen Mason was a superb designer and compositor. We would be blissfully happy authors if all our future editors were as skilled as Sally, Elaine, Deborah, and Karen!

Several others at Allyn and Bacon also deserve special acknowledgment. Bill Barke, who is now the president of the company, originally suggested writing the first edition; we appreciate his continued support for our book. Laura Pearson, Sean Wakely, and Carolyn Merrill have all offered their editorial expertise to help us shape this fourth edition. Jennifer Normandin and Alyssa Dorrie were exceptionally skillful editorial assistants. Finally, we would like to thank the many Allyn and Bacon sales representatives who have given us feedback over the years.

We also want to thank the reviewers who provided numerous useful suggestions for improving both factual and stylistic aspects of the manuscript. For help with this fourth edition, we would like to thank Mark Fineman (Southern Connecticut State University), W. Lawrence Gulick (University of Delaware), Lawrence Guzy (State University of New York, Oneonta), Richard H. Haude (University of Akron), Morton Heller (Winston-Salem State University), Gloria Leventhal (William Patterson College), and Benjamin Wallace (Cleveland State). Reviewers who helped on the previous three editions also deserve our continuing appreciation: Douglas Bloomquist (Framingham State College), Tom Bourbon (Steven E. Austin State University), James Craig (Indiana University at Bloomington), Susan E. Dutch (Westfield State College), David Emmerich (State University of New York, Stony Brook), Phyllis Freeman (State University of New York, New Paltz), Larry Hochhaus (Oklahoma State University), David Irwin (Michigan State University), Lester Lefton (University of South Carolina), Mary Peterson (University of Arizona), Janet Proctor (Purdue University), Alan Searleman (St. Lawrence University), William Tedford (Southern Methodist University), Dejan Todorovic (Boston University and University of Beogradu, Belgrade, Yugoslavia), Lyn Wickelgren (Metropolitan State College of Denver), and James Windes (Northern Arizona University).

PERSONAL ACKNOWLEDGMENTS

I would like to acknowledge several professors who inspired my interest in perception. These include Leonard Horowitz, who is responsible for my switching from a major in biology to a major in psychology, Douglas Lawrence, and Eleanor Maccoby of Stanford University. Grateful appreciation is also due to my professors in graduate school who provided me with a very solid background in sensation and perception: Daniel Weintraub, Richard Pew, Irving Pollack, and W. P. Tanner at the University of Michigan.

Additional thanks go to people who supplied useful information and reviewed portions of the book in which they are experts. I would particularly like to thank Nila Aguilar-Markulis, Kathy Barsz, John Foley, Morton Heller, Peter Lennie, Daniel Levin, Arnold H. Matlin, Ray Mayo, George Rebok, Lanna Ruddy, John Sparrow, David Van Dyke, Susan K. Whitbourne, and Melvyn Yessenow. Three members of Milne Library at State University of New York at Geneseo also deserve special thanks: Paula Henry, Judith Bushnell, and Harriet Sleggs.

Once again, I want to thank my husband, Arnie, and my children, Beth and Sally, for their continuing encouragement, optimism, appreciation, and helpful suggestions. Their enthusiasm and support are inspiring!

M. W. M.

First of all, I'd like to thank three teachers who have had a tremendous influence on me. Julian Granberry was the first person to get me excited about the possibility of studying human beings in an empirical fashion. He was also the best teacher I had as an undergraduate and is largely responsible for my choice of profession. As my graduate advisor, Dave Cross taught me virtually everything I know about psychophysics. Finally, Dave Emmerich introduced me to his fascination with sensation and perception. I owe a great deal of my thinking about this area (and the structure of my own course) to his course in sensation and perception. Dave is the quintessential gentleman-scholar and an inspiration to students fortunate enough to have made his acquaintance. If one day my students think of me as I now think of Dave, then I will be a happy person.

The primary contributors to the text, however, were my students. Students in my perception course at Skidmore College have brought great enthusiasm and energy to the course, which encourages me to do everything I can to teach them well.

The process of completing the current edition was greatly facilitated by some wonderful students—especially Michael Ippolito, Sarah Kelly, Sarah Smith, and Melissa Wyman. Mike and the two Sarahs helped out in ways too numerous to mention. Those of you who are familiar with the third edition might remember Melissa Wyman's name. Although she is wrapping up her graduate studies at the University of Minnesota, she has been kind enough to help out with revisions to the text and the instructor's manual over the past two summers.

Finally, I must thank my wife/colleague Mary Ann Foley. Now that I've joined her at Skidmore College, I can more fully appreciate all that she does. What an inspiring teacher and supportive colleague! And what a wonderful person with whom to share one's life! I could never fully express all that I feel about her, but she knows . . . she knows.

H. J. F.

Sensation and Perception

CHAPTER

1 Introduction

Oops! Okay, now we're on track. As you read this text, you are demonstrating extraordinary sensory and perceptual abilities. Once we oriented the text properly, your eyes could move along this page at a steady pace, identifying letters and words so fast as to defy explanation. If you're like most people, you tend to take sensation and perception for granted because you see, hear, touch, smell, and taste so naturally and automatically. You open your eyes and see text, people, plants, and parrots. You open your mouth, insert a morsel of food, and taste tomatoes, cheesecake, curried goat. What could be simpler? Perception, however, is a complex puzzle that has intrigued philosophers and psychologists for centuries.

One important goal of this textbook is to teach you about the many subtle processes that underlie perception. Just as the beginning of the first paragraph probably brought you to an abrupt halt, we hope to challenge your assumptions about the simplicity of perception. Think about your experience as you started to read the first paragraph. Why did the unusual orientation of the text make reading so difficult? What does your difficulty tell you about the nature of perception? Throughout this textbook, we hope to present you with similar intriguing perceptual experiences that will help you explore the complexities of perception.

The title of this textbook is *Sensation and Perception*. Before going any further, we should define these terms. **Sensation** refers to immediate and basic experiences generated as stimuli fall on our sensory systems. **Perception** involves the interpretation of those sensations, giving them meaning and organization. Psychologists acknowledge a fuzzy boundary between these two terms. However, in practice we cannot easily determine a clear-cut distinction between sensation and perception. We interpret the incoming stimuli so rapidly that sensations become perceptions almost immediately.

A fuzzy boundary also exists between perception and cognition. **Cognition** involves the acquisition, storage, retrieval, and use of information. The boundary between perception and cognition blurs because many theorists believe that perception also involves the acquisition, storage, retrieval, and use of information. For example, learning and memory play important roles in cognition, but they also play important roles in perception. If you reflect on your experience as you read the opening paragraph, you should acknowledge that your past reading experience did not prepare you for text in an unusual orientation. You might also imagine that with additional experience, you could become equally adept at reading text in an unusual orientation. Your appreciation of the complexities of perception will be enhanced by learning more about cognition. We certainly encourage you to take a course in cognition if you have not already done so. Several cognition textbooks are available, should you be interested in exploring this area (e.g., Anderson, 1995; Matlin, 1994; Solso, 1995).

Sensation, perception, and cognition work together to create in our heads impressions of the qualities of objects that exist in the world. To examine how they do so, let's consider an example. Figure 1.1 shows an ordinary scene. As you look at the figure, each structured segment is broken up by sensory receptors and the nervous system into a series of impulses. As Gregory (1974a) notes, "All of the rich information about perceptual structure which we take for granted has somehow dissolved into a series of yes or no electrical blips moving along some tiny, poorly insulated fibers" (p. 76). Nonetheless, our nervous system manages to reconstruct the image you perceive from this series of electrical blips. Our perceptions are neatly organized, and they are a reasonably accurate mirror of the real world. Your knowledge of the world lets you perceive the structures as windows, doors, steps, and columns. In fact, your experience would probably lead you to doubt that this is a picture of someone's house. Moreover, you'd recognize that the lower windows probably open onto rooms whose floors are below ground level. You might also see how the picture looks if you turn the page upside down, to examine the role of experience in aiding your perception of the building.

FIGURE 1.1 An example of organization in perception.
(Photo by Ron Pretzer/LUXE)

Why should you study sensation and perception? We can think of five reasons, although others may occur to you as you explore the topic more thoroughly. The first concerns philosophy. We mentioned the challenge of re-creating the qualities of objects, of bringing the outside world to the inside mind. A branch of philosophy called *epistemology* concerns how we acquire knowledge, including knowledge of the properties of objects. One intriguing concern of epistemology is whether we require experience with the world before we can perceive it accurately. Can your 2-month-old niece have accurate knowledge, for instance, about how far away the side of the crib is from her nose, or must she learn about distance through repeated experiences of reaching, grasping, and bumping?

Other philosophical questions are equally intriguing. For instance, you might consider the central role that perception plays in your experience of who and where you are. Think of what your life would be like if you had absolutely *no* perceptual experience. You might also find Daniel Dennett's (1978) essay "Where am I?" to be informative about the important role of perceptual experience.

The study of sensation and perception has played a pivotal role in the history of psychology. Thus, in learning about sensation and perception, you will also be learning about some of the early research in psychology (which often appears as questions on the Graduate Record Examination in psychology). Exploring sensation and perception also provides a background for other areas of psychology. As we've already mentioned, these two areas are closely associated with cognition—a vital topic in psychology in the last half of the 20th century. Knowledge in sensation and perception would be helpful in other representative areas:

- Motivation—An important topic is eating and weight control, and essential background for this topic might include taste perception and the perception of the shape of one's body.
- Psychology of language—Any attempt to explain comprehension of spoken language must begin with sound perception.
- Nonverbal behavior—This topic involves sending and receiving information about body position, facial expressions, and intonation—all perceptual attributes.
- Gerontology—We can more readily understand the isolation that many elderly people experience if we know about visual and auditory impairments that may accompany aging.

In fact, if you have an introductory psychology textbook handy, turn to the table of contents and notice how each of the major topics is related to sensation and perception.

Sensation and perception also have numerous practical applications in schools, occupations, and industries. Reading teachers can apply what psychologists have learned about eye movements (Chapter 4) and letter identification (Chapter 5). Physicians can use information about reducing pain (Chapter 12). Environmental scientists should be aware of research on excessive noise levels (Chapter 10).

Another reason for reading this book is more personal. You own some exceptional equipment. Your eyes, ears, skin, nose, tongue, and nervous system are extremely skilled and efficient. Nonetheless, you may know more about how a vacuum cleaner or an automobile works. You'll be living the remainder of your life with your sensory systems, so it should be both interesting and useful to know them more intimately.

Finally, you should study perception because it's fun. Okay, maybe we're a bit biased, but if we do our jobs properly, we will convey to you the pleasure we experience when studying the fascinating topics that we're about to cover. In the next section, we'll highlight some of the topics that we're about to explore.

PREVIEW OF THE BOOK

This book examines how we take in information about the outside world and how the world appears. It will consider the anatomy and physiology of the sensory systems, how energy from stimuli in the outside world is conveyed to the brain, and how sensory information is interpreted to form perceptions. Chapter 1 outlines the scope of the book, summarizes the major theoretical approaches to sensation and perception, presents several themes that will be traced throughout the text, and offers hints on how to use the book.

Chapter 2 discusses methodologies employed in the study of perception. This chapter is focused primarily on psychophysics, the study of the relationship between physical stimuli and our psychological reaction to them. For example, we will discuss why you are more likely to "hear" a subway coming (even if it hasn't left the previous station) when you've been waiting a long time. We will also address why you can notice a 5-pound weight loss more easily for Pat, who weighs 100 pounds, than for Chris, who weighs 200 pounds.

Chapter 3 provides an overview of the visual system, because we need to know the structure of the visual equipment before proceeding to other topics. In this chapter, we examine the anatomy of the eye, discuss how visual information travels to the brain, and explore how the visual information is processed in the brain. The topics considered in this chapter address several aspects of the visual system. What medical problems, typically uncovered in an eye examination, affect visual perception? If you are driving at night and look at the headlights of an oncoming car, why do you have trouble seeing afterward? What role does the brain play in processing visual information?

Chapter 4 discusses the prerequisites for vision and several basic abilities of the visual system that enable us to see clearly. In this chapter, we introduce the important concept of a constancy, which provides stability to our changing perceptual experience. The chapter also addresses questions such as (1) How important is change or contrast for vision? (2) How does our visual system enhance these changes? (3) What does 20/20 vision mean? and (4) How do you keep a ball in focus as it moves toward you?

Chapter 5 considers more complex visual processing, particularly the perception of shapes. Our perception of shape also shows impressive organization; a door seems to have a shape that sets it apart from the surrounding building. We also recognize patterns; we identify a curved line as part of a tree, not a cat's tail. Three issues discussed include the following: What principles have psychologists identified as important to perceiving shapes? Do we recognize a letter more quickly if it is part of an English word than if it appears by itself? Also, why is it more difficult to identify a person whose face is presented upside down?

Chapter 6 is concerned with size and distance. Somehow, we manage to perceive objects as three-dimensional and as residing in three-dimensional space, even though our eyes can represent only two dimensions. Three questions answered in this chapter are (1) When are your two eyes useful for perceiving depth? (2) How do artists represent three-dimensional space on a two-dimensional canvas? and (3) Why do we experience illusions of size and depth?

Chapter 7 examines color vision, including color vision deficiencies and theories about color perception. It also discusses how we can perceive colors even in simple black-and-white designs. Some questions answered include these: Why do we get green if we mix yellow and blue paints but gray if we mix yellow and blue lights? Why is the term *color-blind* incorrect? How can we continue to see a shirt as blue, even under a red light?

Chapter 8 investigates the visual perception of movement. In Chapter 6, you will learn about how the visual system encodes three-dimensional space. In Chapter 8, we will discuss how people perceive the movement of objects through that three-dimensional space. One topic addressed in that chapter is how we perceive motion when we are presented only with a series of still photographs. Another topic addressed is how we can sometimes perceive ourselves to be in motion while we are in a stationary car or train.

Chapters 3 through 8 concern visual perception only. As you will soon see, however, the senses share many commonalities. In the remaining chapters, you will see that several principles found in vision are also found in the other senses. Our discussion of hearing in Chapters 9, 10, and 11 parallels the discussion of vision in Chapters 3, 4, and 5. We first discuss the anatomy and physiology of audition, then basic auditory processes, then more complex auditory processes.

Chapter 9 focuses on the physical apparatus necessary for hearing. We discuss the structures in the ear that process the physical stimulus, as well as the neural sites that are involved in auditory perception. Two questions the chapter answers are (1) How does the auditory system analyze the various sounds that might come to it simultaneously from a singer, guitarist, and drummer in a band? and (2) What commonalities emerge in a comparison of the auditory and visual systems?

Chapter 10 examines basic aspects of hearing. It considers topics such as pitch and loudness perception, auditory localization, and the perception of sound combinations. Some issues addressed include the following: How does the ear manage to record the pitch of a train squeaking to a halt, Placido Domingo singing a Verdi aria, and your uncle snoring? Why do some tone combinations sound pleasant, whereas others are unbearable? How do humans and animals decide that a sound is coming from the left side rather than from another direction?

Chapter 11 discusses more complex aspects of hearing, including music and speech perception. After first discussing complex sounds in general, we turn our attention to pitch, loudness, timbre, and tone combinations as they relate to music. We provide examples of organization and pattern in music as well as musical constancy and illusions. The speech perception section begins with a description of the sounds in speech; other topics include how thought processes influence speech perception and theories of speech perception. The following questions are addressed: How can you recognize a tune, even if it is played in an unfamiliar key? How do we manage to hear speech accurately when so much of it is fuzzy or distorted?

In the remaining chapters of the book, we examine the skin senses (Chapter 12), the chemical senses (Chapter 13), and, finally, the development of perception (Chapter 14).

Chapter 12 examines the senses related to the skin. Objects and people in the world touch us, and we touch them back. We also perceive pain and warmth and cold, and we know the positions of our body parts and whether we are standing upright or tilted. Some of the topics covered are (1) Why were you aware of your wristwatch pressing against your skin when you put it on this morning, although you hadn't noticed it again until now? (2) Why do people have to feel pain to survive? and (3) Why do you sometimes have difficulty deciding whether water is warm or cold?

Chapter 13 deals with the chemical senses— smell and taste. We discuss sensitivity to smells, how smells become less noticeable as we are exposed to them, recognition of smells, and constancy and illusions related to smell. We also discuss sensitivity to taste, how tastes become less noticeable as we are exposed to them, and how smell interacts with taste. Some issues we will examine include these: Why don't you smell the perfume or shaving lotion you applied this morning, although a friend who joins you for lunch notices it immediately? Can parents recognize their children on the basis of smell alone? Why was the information incorrect that your junior-high science teacher told you about the regions of the tongue? Why does water taste vaguely sweet after your morning grapefruit?

Chapter 14 is concerned with the development of perception. You will learn that the perceptual skills are rather well developed in infancy. These skills become even more sophisticated during childhood. Elderly people sometimes

have impaired vision or hearing, but most people do not experience major perceptual disabilities as they grow older. One issue discussed in this chapter is whether babies can hear the difference between some sounds that adults think are identical. Another issue addressed is whether most elderly people experience severe visual deficits.

OVERVIEW OF THEORETICAL APPROACHES TO SENSATION AND PERCEPTION

This section outlines some major approaches to sensation and perception. It provides a background for several theoretical topics that are discussed more completely in other chapters.

A thorough review of theories of sensation and perception would probably begin with theories of perception proposed by Greek philosophers more than 2,000 years ago; it would also include the early explorations of the physiology of the eye and the physics of light. Our survey will be limited to the more recent past and will examine six approaches: empiricist, Gestalt, behaviorist, Gibsonian, information-processing, and computational. Other sources can be consulted for details on the early history of perception (e.g., Boring, 1942; Hochberg, 1988).

The Empiricist Approach

In the early 1700s, George Berkeley struggled with a basic problem: How can we perceive objects as having a third dimension, depth, if our eyes register only height and width? We consider this important question again in Chapter 6 when we discuss the perception of distance and depth. Berkeley (1709/1957) was influential in developing *empiricism*, which states that basic sensory experiences are combined through learning to produce perception. We do not know how to perceive depth when we are born; instead, we must acquire this perceptual ability by learning (Hochberg, 1979; Uttal, 1981).

A relatively modern empiricist, William James (1842–1910), has often been called America's greatest psychologist. James created the phrase "blooming, buzzing confusion" to describe the perceptual world of the newborn infant. He proposed that babies live in a confusing world that, through learning, becomes relatively orderly.

The empiricist explanations for topics such as distance perception and size constancy are still popular today, as we will see in later chapters. Developmental psychologists, however, have discovered that babies have better perceptual capacities than James described. Their perceptual worlds are not so orderly as they will become in adulthood, but they are far from random, as we will explore in Chapter 14.

The Gestalt Approach

A number of German Gestalt psychologists in the first part of this century objected to the empiricist approach to perception (Koffka, 1935; Köhler, 1947; Wertheimer, 1923). They argued that the empiricists' approach was too artificial and that it did not pay enough attention to the relationship among the various parts of a stimulus (Hochberg, 1979; Rock & Palmer, 1990). *Gestalt* can be translated as "configuration" or "pattern," and the

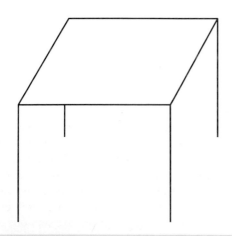

FIGURE 1.2 A well-organized configuration; the whole is perceived as more than the accumulation of isolated parts.

Gestalt approach emphasizes that we perceive objects as well-organized, whole structures rather than as separated, isolated parts (Palmer, 1991). Thus, the shape that we see is more than an accumulation of its individual elements. For example, the design you see in Figure 1.2 is more than the simple combination of eight separate lines; the well-organized configuration suggests a table.

The Gestalt approach developed many principles to account for the organization of shapes. The empiricists emphasized the contribution of learning and experience to perception, whereas Gestalt theorists discussed but did not stress these factors. Instead, they emphasized humans' inborn ability to perceive form. In Chapter 5 we will see that the Gestalt principles still play an important role in several theories of shape perception.

The Behaviorist Approach

Behaviorism stresses the objective description of an organism's behavior. Strict behaviorists are uncomfortable with the area of perception, which examines how the world appears rather than how people behave. Because behaviorism was the dominant psychological theory in the United States from the 1930s to the 1960s, research in the more complex areas of perception declined significantly during those years (Hochberg, 1979; Uttal, 1981).

The area least influenced by the behaviorists' bias against perception was psychophysics. Psychophysics uses clearly defined methods to assess people's reactions to physical stimuli. This objective, quantitative approach was compatible with behaviorism and therefore survived its reign well.

The Gibsonian Approach

James J. Gibson, a Cornell University psychologist who died in 1979, approached perception differently from the empiricists or Gestaltists. The *Gibsonian approach* emphasizes that our perceptions are rich and elaborate because the stimuli in our environment are rich with information, rather than because our thought processes or experiences provide that richness

(Michaels & Carello, 1981; Reed, 1988). For example, Gibson proposed that we perceive objects as having a third dimension because of information about qualities such as their surface texture. The empiricists argued that we need to learn to perceive depth, whereas Gibson stressed that all the information we need is in the stimulus itself. As Neisser (1981) remarked in an obituary about Gibson, "Gibson begins not with the sense organs or even with organisms but with the environment that is to be perceived" (p. 215). We consider the Gibsonian approach to perception in some detail in several chapters.

Indirect perception approaches assume that stimuli do not provide accurate, complete information about objects or events (Michaels & Carello, 1981). In contrast, Gibson described a *direct perception approach* in which we can directly perceive our environment from the information in the stimulus; we do not need memories or reasoning processes. Gibson believed that when we can adequately describe the features of environmental stimuli, we do not need to devise elaborate theories to explain the psychological processes that might underlie perception.

Gibson (1979) also emphasized that our investigation of perception should concentrate on real-world perception. He saw little value in perceptual experiences found only in laboratories, such as looking at a white bar on a black screen in a darkened room while your head movements are minimized because you have been strapped into a head vise.

The Information-Processing Approach

Information processing was developed by people who were interested in computers and communication science, and the approach is a dominant area in psychology today. In the *information-processing approach*, researchers identify psychological processes and connect these processes together by proposing specific patterns of information flow (Uttal, 1981). For example, one influential model proposed that information from our sensory receptors passes through a series of stages: brief sensory storage, short-term memory, and long-term memory (Atkinson & Schiffrin, 1968). After one stage performs its specified operations, the information passes on to the next stage for another kind of processing.

As Uttal (1981) points out, the information-processing approach is not really a theory: "In fact, in its current form, it is far from a theory at all, but instead should be considered to be a particular language and orientation toward psychological processes" (p. 117). For example, the information-processing approach usually provides a description of the phases of psychological processes but does not specify whether these phases were acquired by learning or inborn ability. In contrast, the four theories previously discussed are more likely to focus on explanations for psychological processes, such as the origin of perceptual ability.

Information-processing models typically stress that humans have limited capacities. Thus, we cannot perceive too many items at one time. If we are paying close attention to one message, we must ignore another message.

Information-processing psychologists urge us not to divide sensation, perception, memory, and other processes into isolated compartments. Instead, we must realize that each process depends on others. Earlier psychologists, such as those who favored the empiricist approach, often made distinctions among several areas of experimental psychology. For example, *sensation* referred to the immediate contact between stimuli and the sensory receptors. The term *perception* referred to adding meaning and interpretation to these basic sensations. Thus, these psychologists believed that sensations were pure and were not influenced by previous learning and experience. Perceptions, they believed, were very different from sensations because they were influenced by learning and experience. Information-processing psychologists, however, stress that sensation, perception, and higher mental processes—such as memory—must all be treated within a single system (Haber, 1974). As we'll see throughout this book, memory often helps to shape our perceptions.

The Computational Approach

The *computational approach* is similar to Gibson's direct perception approach, because it acknowledges the richness of the visual stimulus. Unlike the direct perception approach, however, and more similar to the indirect perception approaches, the computational approach proposes that perception requires solving problems. The computational approach differs from the information-processing approaches, though, because it attempts to solve perceptual problems with general physical knowledge rather than with specific knowledge about the objects you are currently seeing.

David Marr (1982) was an extremely influential researcher in this area before his untimely death. In work that typifies the computational approach, Marr attempted to develop mathematical models through which human vision could be explained. These models were created so that they were consistent with physiological information, and consequently they were not only possible but also plausible. For instance, the change represented by an edge or boundary is very important to the visual system, as you will see in Chapter 4. Marr demonstrated a mathematical filter, shaped like a Mexican hat, that not only works to perceive edges but also is consistent with what we know about the physiology of the visual system (Chapters 3 and 5).

We have reviewed six approaches. Each has had a substantial impact on the discipline. Because this textbook is eclectic, it borrows elements of all six frameworks.

SECTION SUMMARY

Overview of Theoretical Approaches to Sensation and Perception

1. Empiricism, which was developed primarily by Berkeley, proposes that all information is derived from sensory perceptions and experience. Similarly, William James argued that babies' early perceptual experiences are random and disorganized.

2. The Gestalt approach emphasizes that we perceive objects as well-organized wholes instead of separate parts. The Gestalt approach proposes that shape perception is inborn and that learning is relatively unimportant.

3. The behaviorist approach stresses the objective description of behavior. Consequently, behaviorists have not been very interested in the psychological processes underlying perception.

4. The Gibsonian approach points out that stimuli in the environment are rich with information. Perception is thought to be direct; we do not need to perform calculations and interpretations in order to perceive.

5. The information-processing approach maintains that information is handled by a series of stages. This approach stresses that sensation, perception, and other higher mental processes are interconnected rather than isolated.

6. The computational approach demonstrates mathematical mechanisms that perceptual systems might use to process stimuli. The stimuli are thought to be sufficiently rich that they provide a great deal of information, but higher-level processes involving general physical principles are also thought to operate in perception.

THEMES OF THE BOOK

Four themes woven throughout this textbook are intended to provide some additional structure for the material and to encourage you to find patterns and relationships among areas that may initially seem unrelated. Incidentally, the themes reflect the eclectic theoretical orientation of this textbook. For example, the second theme is based on Gibson's theories, whereas the fourth theme is consistent with the empiricist approach.

1. *The senses share some clear similarities and interact with one another.* Naturally, tasting is not identical to seeing or hearing, but all have important commonalities. Some of the commonali-

ties among perceptual systems presumably arise from the need to solve similar problems. Sensation in any system begins with a form of physical energy that stimulates the sensory receptors. This energy is converted into a form that can be transmitted along the neurons, and the stimulation ultimately reaches the brain. Differences in the forms of physical energy processed by the various senses lead to differences among them, but similarities emerge because all the information is processed by a single brain.

One commonality among the senses is the importance of change. As you will soon see, changes in the physical stimulus are crucial for all the senses. As a corollary, when a stimulus continues unchanged, this stimulus often becomes less important to the senses. For example, it would be inefficient and disadvantageous for us to continually perceive the presence of some stimuli. Just as habits free our minds from concentrating on repetitive tasks, the senses adapt to a stimulus that is presented continuously—its perceived intensity tends to decrease. For instance, the odor in a "fragrant" locker room fortunately seems less overpowering after several minutes. Similarly, you feel the pressure of your watch on your wrist when you first put it on in the morning, but moments later you no longer notice it. On the other hand, we exhibit far less adaptation to continuous painful stimuli, which is as advantageous as the adaptation displayed in other senses.

Another reason for commonalities and interactions among the senses is the fact that objects in the world typically affect more than one sense. For example, food cooking on the stove can be simultaneously seen, heard, felt, touched, and tasted. We perceive each aspect of the food not as coming through a separate sensory channel but as an integrated whole. Our perceptual systems have evolved to provide us with a unified sense of the world, which means that they must interact with one another.

2. *The stimuli themselves are rich with information and are found in a rich context.* Clearly, this second theme is based on the Gibsonian approach to sensation and perception. For exam-

ple, compare the surface texture of the rug or flooring surrounding your feet with the surface texture several yards away. The texture becomes denser as the distance increases, and this information about the stimulus is useful when you want to judge distance. Now take your book and move it from left to right, then toward you and away from you. Notice that it systematically covers up part of the background and uncovers another part as you move it. The rich context in which the book is perceived (the texture of the floor, the source of light and shadows it creates, etc.) provides us with a great deal of information about the book's appearance.

One indication of the richness of the stimulus emerges in our discussion of auditory phenomena. Although much of the early research in audition is based on simple pure tones, complex tones are *much* more common outside the laboratory. When researchers began to use these complex, real-life tones in their research, they found that humans were better able to process these stimuli along a number of dimensions. Can't you just hear Gibson saying, "I told you so!"

3. *The human sensory systems perform well in gathering information about stimuli but can occasionally be led astray.* Stimuli in the outside world may be rich with information, yet all of that richness would be wasted if our sensory systems were not so well adapted to picking it up. A bat, for example, would be unlikely to appreciate a Rembrandt painting, and the subtleties of a fine burgundy would be lost on a chicken. The more subtle, cognitive aspects of appreciation aside, these organisms do not have adequate sensory systems to encode stimulus attributes. Consider, for instance, how our visual system can encode the attributes of an apple. Obviously, it can register information about the apple's color, shape, size, and distance. However, it can also detect more subtle qualities, such as whether it has been polished, whether it has a bruise on one side, and how much the stem area is indented. The sheer number of attributes is impressive.

The sensory systems are also impressive because of the range of environments in which they can operate. You can see in extremely bright sunlight and also in a darkened room, for instance. Furthermore, your sensory apparatus can be exquisitely sensitive. For example, a certain chemical can be detected when less than 0.0000036 milligram of it is spread through a cubic meter of air (Cain, 1988). The range from the smallest to largest perceivable visual or auditory stimulus is equally impressive. We can see in daylight and, to a degree, in moonlight, even though the light from the noonday sun is almost 100 million times brighter than the light from the moon!

Our sensory systems seem to be particularly well adapted to humans' specific needs. For instance, our visual system is especially competent in detecting motion by other humans (see Chapter 8). Our hearing apparatus is particularly sensitive to the frequency range of the human voice (see Chapter 10). Newborns arrive with their senses in reasonably good order: they can follow movement, hear distinctions between sounds,

and recognize the odors of familiar people (see Chapter 14).

Our sensory systems are sensitive and flexible enough to provide very good "bottom-up" processing, which we discuss in more detail in Chapter 5. In brief, **bottom-up processing** (or **data-driven processing**) explains how the sensory receptors register the stimuli. The information flows from this "bottom" level upward to the higher, more cognitive levels. We begin with the data and transform and combine them until we have perceptions and cognitions.

As good as our senses are, they can occasionally be led astray by particular stimuli. For example, look at Figure 1.3. Do the two lines appear to be equal in length, or is one longer than the other? We can learn about the functioning of the senses in several ways, one of which is to examine cases in which they fail to provide us with accurate information. Throughout the text we

FIGURE 1.3 Are the two lines (AB and AC) equal in length or is one line longer than the other? If your visual system is ordinarily so accurate, why is it misled by this drawing? (From Gardner, 1988)

will provide illustrations of illusory perceptions—inaccurate perceptions that enlighten us about the functioning of the senses.

4. *Prior knowledge and expectations help shape our perceptions.* Perception involves more than the combination of data from the sensory receptors. As emphasized by the empiricists, sensory information is supplemented and transformed by higher, more cognitive processes. The bottom-up, or data-driven, approach can be contrasted with ***top-down processing*** (or ***conceptually driven processing***), which emphasizes the importance of observers' concepts in shaping perception. According to this view, observers have accumulated ideas about how the world is organized. On a Nevada ranch, for example, that four-legged creature on the horizon is more likely to be a horse than a zebra. We will perceive that creature as a horse unless the "data" provide us with very clear information about stripes. You may *hear* your friend mutter as you leave a test, "How did you like the exam?" although the data in that stimulus were really, "Howja like thuzamm?" Once again, your knowledge and expectations, combined with the context, allowed you to interpret some potentially ambiguous data.

Our knowledge and expectations also lead us to try to "make sense" of ambiguous stimuli by exploring them further until our perceptions are clearer. Humans are active and inquiring organisms who are typically not satisfied with uncertainties. If you are groping for your bathrobe in a dark room and you're not certain whether you grabbed a shirt by mistake, you actively explore the fabric until you find a button, a familiar feel to the material, or a belt. If you can't read the bumper sticker on the car in front of you, you creep forward until you can. If you can't hear the operator on the telephone, you ask for the message to be repeated. Thus, our concepts about the world help to clarify many ambiguities, and they guide us in active efforts to clarify many other ambiguities.

It is pointless to argue, incidentally, about which approach is correct, the bottom-up or the top-down. Clearly both processes are necessary to explain how we manage to perceive so quickly and so accurately. These two approaches, representing the third and fourth themes of this book, combine with the second theme—about the wealth of information available in the stimulus—in order to help answer the mystery of perception. Our perceptions are a reasonably accurate mirror of the real world for three reasons: (1) stimuli are rich with information; (2) human sensory systems are effective in gathering information; and (3) concepts help shape our perceptions.

HOW TO USE THIS BOOK

Several different features in this book have been included to help you understand, learn, and remember the material. This section tells you how to use these features most effectively.

Each chapter begins with an outline. Inspect the outline before you read a new chapter and pay particular attention to the structure of the topic. For example, notice the two major sections in Chapter 2 ("Research Methods"): "Measuring Responses to Low-Intensity Stimuli" and "Measuring Responses to More Intense Stimuli." Subsections and In-Depth sections are also included in these outlines to give you a sense of what the chapter covers.

This textbook stresses applications. The first kind of application of perception research involves professions such as medicine, consumer psychology, and gerontology. These applications are frequently discussed because it is useful to know how theoretical research can be applied to solve real-life problems. This material may also help you learn more effectively, because concrete material is typically more memorable than abstract material.

A second application involves recalling phenomena from your own experience. Psychologists concerned with human memory have demonstrated that we recall material better if we ask ourselves whether it applies to us (e.g., Rogers et al., 1977). Therefore, take advantage of your experience! Don't read the chapters passively, but continually try to examine how the information applies to your own perceptual processing.

The third application consists of informal experiments labeled "Demonstrations." Each requires only a short time commitment and no equipment more exotic than flashlights, paper and pencils, and glasses of sugar water. You can perform most of these demonstrations by yourself. These demonstrations should also help to make the material more concrete and easy to relate to your own experiences.

Chapters 2 to 14 each have an "In-Depth" section, which examines recent research on a selected topic relevant to the chapter. These sections focus on experimental methodology and the outcome of experiments.

Throughout each chapter, new terms are introduced in boldface italics (e.g., *empiricism*), and their definition appears in the same sentence. These terms also appear in the list of new terms at the end of each chapter in the order of their occurrence. Check the glossary at the end of the book, which contains all the new terms, if you are uncertain about their meaning. The glossary definitions include a phonetic pronunciation for potentially ambiguous terms. These pronunciations are intended not to insult your intelligence but to aid you in learning. Furthermore, you can ask a question in class more easily when you know that the superior colliculus is a "kole-*lick*-you-luss" and not a "kole-like-*you*-loos."

You will notice that an unusual feature of this textbook is a summary at the end of each of the major sections in a chapter rather than at the end of the entire chapter. We chose to include frequent small summaries, rather than a single lengthy summary, for two reasons: (1) you can review the material more often, and (2) you can master small segments before you move on to unfamiliar material. You can take advantage of this feature by testing yourself when you reach the end of a section. Read the summary and notice which items you didn't remember. Test yourself once more, rechecking your accuracy. Some students report that they prefer to read only one section at a time rather than the whole chapter. Then when they begin a study session in the middle of a chapter, they reread the previous section summaries before reading the new material.

Each chapter also includes review questions. The review questions may ask you to apply your knowledge to a practical problem or to integrate material from several parts of the chapter or even across chapters.

The final feature of each chapter is a list of recommended readings intended to supply you with resources if you want to write a paper on a particular topic or if the area is personally interesting. In general, the books, chapters, and articles provide more than an overview of the subject yet are not overly technical.

REVIEW QUESTIONS

1. What are sensation and perception, and why have they been particularly difficult to differentiate? Return to Figure 1.1 on page 3. Turn the page upside down. How might this new orientation allow you to distinguish between sensation and perception? Would you think that the new orientation would have a greater impact on sensation or perception?

2. How do sensation and perception differ from cognition? How might sensation and perception be related to cognition? The information-processing approach stresses the interrelationship between sensation, perception, and cognition. Use the example of reading text to point out how the boundaries among the concepts must be fuzzy rather than precise.

3. This introduction stressed that sensation and perception have applications to numerous professions. Contemplate the profession you would like to enter and inspect the preview of the book, considering how some of the topics might be relevant to it.

4. Imagine yourself eating a piece of pizza. Review the preview of the book and illustrate how some aspect of the mundane act of eating pizza can be related to each chapter. Would you think that visual perception would have much of an impact on the taste of the pizza?

5. Use one or two sentences to describe each of the major approaches to perception. Explain briefly how each of these approaches would account for your perception of the picture in Figure 1.1. Why would you expect that a picture might be a particularly difficult stimulus from a Gibsonian perspective? (*Hint:* Compare the richness of the stimulus of the actual building to the richness of the picture of the building.)

6. How much would each of the theoretical approaches emphasize learning in connection with perception? (In at least one approach, it may be difficult to determine.)

7. Which of the theoretical approaches most closely fits your current ideas about sensation and perception? Which of them seems the least likely to you?

8. Review the first theme of the book, similarities among the sensory processes. Think about different kinds of adaptations you have noticed. Have you noticed any other kinds of similarities among the processes?

9. Review the last three themes of the book. Now describe how each explains why you are able to read this question at a fairly rapid rate.

10. To help you prepare to read this book more effectively, look at Chapter 2 and plan how you can apply the features discussed in the "How to Use This Book" section when you read about research methods in perception.

NEW TERMS

sensation (2)
perception (2)
cognition (2)
epistemology (3)
empiricism (6)
Gestalt (7)
Gestalt approach (7)

behaviorism (7)
Gibsonian approach (7)
indirect perception approaches (8)
direct perception approach (8)
information-processing
    approach (8)

computational approach (9)
bottom-up processing (11)
data-driven processing (11)
top-down processing (12)
conceptually driven
    processing (12)

RECOMMENDED READINGS

Boring, E. G. (1942). *Sensation and perception in the history of experimental psychology*. New York: Appleton-Century-Crofts. This classic book will provide a good introduction to empiricism and Gestalt psychology, as well as to earlier approaches to perception.

Hochberg, J. (1979). Sensation and perception. In E. Hearst (Ed.), *The first century of experimental psychology* (pp. 89–142). Hillsdale, NJ: Erlbaum. Hochberg, a well-known researcher in the area of perception, wrote this chapter as part of a volume commemorating the 100-year birthday of Wundt's psychology laboratory. The chapter offers a concise introduction, including a summary of several theories not considered in this book.

Reed, E. S. (1988). *James J. Gibson and the psychology of perception*. New Haven: Yale University Press. If you are interested in a readable introduction to Gibson's theories, presented in a chronological and biographical fashion, you will find this book invaluable. Reed does an excellent job of presenting complex details in a clear fashion, with the added bonus that you can learn about the life of a great psychologist.

Uttal, W. R. (1981). *A taxonomy of visual processes*. Hillsdale, NJ: Erlbaum. Chapter 2 of Uttal's book, "Theories of Perception," is particularly useful because it attempts to classify the major theories of perception according to dimensions such as holistic–elementalistic and nativistic–empiricistic.

CHAPTER

2 Research Methods

How bright does the light seem to be as you are reading this book? How loud do you think the sounds are around you? (Is there music playing? Are people talking?) Over the course of hundreds of years, scientists and technicians have developed very accurate instruments for quantifying the physical properties of such stimuli. You could walk into a camera shop today and buy a photometer to measure the amount of light energy reflected from an object or go to Radio Shack and buy a sound-level meter to measure the loudness of a sound.

Psychologists, however, are less interested in the physical properties of the stimuli around you. They are more interested in your psychological experience of those stimuli. How can we possibly measure your inner experience of brightness or loudness? This task is especially challenging because perception is a private activity. To experience the difficulties involved in this enterprise, stop reading for a moment and try to think of some ways to tell a friend who is on the telephone how bright a light appears to you or how loud a sound seems.

Given the complexity of the problem, you might be tempted, initially, to think that we could just measure the physical properties of stimuli and be done with it. Can't we simply equate the physical stimulus with the psychological experience of the stimulus? A few examples should convince you that such an approach cannot work.

Have you ever started your car and discovered that you've left the radio on? What seemed a perfectly reasonable loudness when you were listening to your music over the background of road noise is now extremely loud, so you quickly turn it down. (Similarly, an alarm-clock radio sounds louder when it goes off in the morning than it did when you set it the night before.) Notice that the energy coming from the radio doesn't change; the volume knob remains in the same position. However, your perception of loudness does change. In other words, two identical physical stimuli can produce different perceptions.

Furthermore, two different physical stimuli can produce identical perceptions. For example,

one brand of bacon may have a trace more salt than another; these two *physical* stimuli are different. But you might be unable to detect this difference, thereby indicating that the two brands are *psychologically* identical.

These few examples should convince you that the relationship between the physical properties of stimuli and a person's psychological experience of those stimuli is complex. The same physical stimulus might produce very different perceptions, or different physical stimuli might produce the same perception. The study of the relationship between properties of physical stimuli and psychological reactions to those properties is called **psychophysics**. This term was coined over a hundred years ago by Gustav Theodor Fechner (1801–1887).

According to legend, Fechner awoke on the morning of October 22, 1850, with the basic ideas that gave birth to psychophysics, and so psychophysicists celebrate that date annually as Fechner's Day (Boring, 1961; Rosenzweig, 1987). Fechner outlined several basic methods to investigate the psychological experience of physical stimuli, and they have remained essentially unchanged to this day. In fact, one could argue that Fechner's ideas marked the beginning of an experimental approach to psychology, because he was the first person to espouse a rigorous systematic approach to the study of psychological experience. Others, such as Ebbinghaus, were influenced by Fechner's approach and applied it to human memory and other areas of psychology beyond perception.

Figure 2.1 illustrates the relationship between a physical dimension and perceptions of stimuli along that dimension. It also indicates the complexity of the problems confronting a psychophysicist. At the bottom of the figure is the physical dimension. A major advantage in psychophysical research is that the physical dimension can be easily quantified.

The impact of the physical stimulus on the observer is labeled "subjective experience" (Figure 2.1b). This dimension is largely unobservable to the outside world. What we mean by subjective experience is the person's perceptual experience

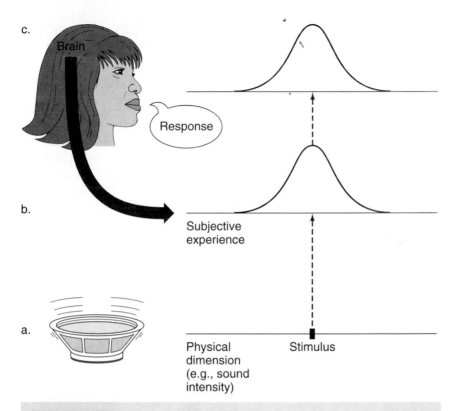

c.

Brain

Response

b.

Subjective
experience

a.

Physical
dimension
(e.g., sound
intensity)

Stimulus

FIGURE 2.1 Psychophysics is the study of the relationship between a physical stimulus and our psychological reaction to it. The physical dimension (a) is easily measured. However, the psychological reaction or subjective experience (b) is unique to each individual and can't be universally quantified like the physical dimension. The only way to find out about b is to have a person report what he or she is experiencing (c). Notice that there is not a one-to-one relationship between these dimensions. The bell-shaped distributions for b and c suggest that on different occasions the same stimulus can produce different subjective experiences and different responses. For instance, in the car radio example in the text, the same physical stimulus (sound energy) can seem louder on one occasion than another.

and the brain-cell activity produced by the stimulus. Fechner was actually most interested in studying the two components that we have lumped together as subjective experience, characterized as the mind–body relationship (the relationship between perceptual experience and brain activity).

Although we can measure the physical stimulus with great precision (illustrated by a single point along the dimension), its effect on the observer is not so simple. In Figure 2.1, the physical stimulus causes a range of subjective experience. This is intended to illustrate that many factors (such as inner "noise," wandering attention, differing contexts, etc.) can lead the same stimulus to be perceived differently on different occasions—producing a distribution of different levels of subjective experience over time. (Remember the car radio anecdote.) So one of the first problems confronting the psychophysicist is that the relationship between physical energy and subjective experience is not one-to-one, but one-to-many. Psychophysicists presume that many contextual factors may lead a person to respond differently on different occasions to the identical level of subjective experience (e.g., Poulton, 1989). The problems don't stop there, however.

The subjective dimension portrayed in Figure 2.1 is largely unobservable and hypothetical. Because the perceptual experience is essentially private, the only way an outsider can get any idea of the inner experience of another person is to have that person engage in some behavior. Thus, the final dimension illustrated in Figure 2.1 is the response dimension. The best possible response, for a scientist attempting to peer into the inner dimension, is some quantifiable behavior. From Fechner's era to now, researchers have been devising methods of measuring these private perceptions by having people engage in behaviors that allow the researcher to derive numbers from the behaviors.

The purpose of this chapter is to explore some of these measurement techniques and the nature of the relationship between physical stimuli and psychological responses. If you're like most people, you are unlikely to find the material in this chapter wildly exciting. As Suzanne McKee (1993) points out, "As any American undergraduate will attest, perception is entertaining and stimulating, while psychophysics is boring and incomprehensible. Who cares about four methods for measuring something you can't see?" But she goes on to say that "In all honesty, I love psychophysics."

Now we can't guarantee that you'll come to love psychophysics, but we'll try to make your excursion through it as painless as possible. We do think that it's a trip you should take. (And we can assure you that you should find much of the rest of the material throughout the text to be very "entertaining and stimulating.")

Why are we so interested in psychophysics? One answer is that psychophysics is important as a self-sufficient area of inquiry. If we are concerned about how the mind works, then we should be curious about how the mind processes physical stimuli from the environment.

Psychophysics is also an essential tool for studying sensation and perception. For example, if you have ever had your hearing tested, the test involved one of the psychophysical methods. Some areas of sensation and perception may initially seem to be unrelated to psychophysics, until someone points out a connection. For instance, in Chapter 4 we will discuss acuity, the ability to see fine details. As Benzschawel and Cohn (1985) argue, acuity is really like a detection task from psychophysics. To tell the difference between a *P* and an *R* on an eye chart on your doctor's wall, you need to decide whether you detect an extra little bar in the lower right-hand corner of the letter.

In addition, psychophysical techniques have been adapted for use in other areas of psychology. One technique has been applied to the field of personality psychology, measuring stress and anxiety (Dawson, 1982). Cognitive psychologists have used another psychophysical method to examine why older people are less accurate than younger people on certain memory tasks (Grossberg & Grant, 1978). Finally, social attitudes, such as opinions about the prestige of various professions, have been examined with psychophysical tools (Stevens, 1986; Wegener, 1982).

Applied psychologists also use psychophysics. An environmental psychologist may want to determine whether people who live along a busy highway detect less traffic noise when the highway is bordered by huge concrete blocks. A drug company may hire a psychophysicist to see whether its new analgesic increases tolerance for pain. A syrup company may conduct psychophysical tests to see whether customers can detect that their new, low-calorie syrup is substantially thinner than the sugar-laden version.

In summary, then, psychophysical methods are important because they serve as the basis for much of the research presented throughout this text. Further, these methods allow us to learn about areas of psychology beyond sensation and perception, including practical applications to problems in everyday life. Let's now turn our attention to these psychophysical techniques.

The discussion is divided into two sections. In the first section we will describe how people respond to low-intensity stimuli that are difficult to detect. We will discuss the methodologies of both classical psychophysics and some newer methods. The second section examines how people respond to more intense stimuli, which are easily detectable. We will look at the classical psychophysical methods for measuring discrimination and at the nature of the relationship between physical intensity and psychological response.

MEASURING RESPONSES TO LOW-INTENSITY STIMULI

You are standing on the subway platform, gazing down the dark tunnel to your right. Is that a faint light that you see, signaling the arrival of your train? Do you hear a distant rumble, assuring you that the Lexington Avenue Express is on its way? These are questions involving detection. In *detection* studies, we provide low-intensity stimuli and notice whether people report them.

Classical Psychophysical Measurement of Detection

One application of Fechner's psychophysical methods has been in the measurement of absolute thresholds. Much as the threshold of a house marks the transition from being outside the house to being inside the house, people thought of an *absolute threshold* as an abrupt change from not being able to detect a stimulus to just being able to do so. This approach is illustrated in the results displayed in Figure 2.2.[1] Imagine an experiment in which 70 trials are

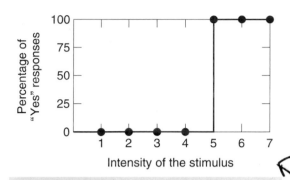

FIGURE 2.2 Incorrect conception of a threshold, showing abrupt change. The threshold clearly falls between 4 and 5, because a person shifts from reporting no stimulus (0% "Yes" responses) to reporting the presence of the stimulus (100% "Yes" responses).

presented, with each of the 7 intensity levels presented to a person 10 times, but in a random order. On each trial, the person is told to respond "Yes" when he or she can see the stimulus and "No" when he or she can't see the stimulus. Thus, that person might respond "No" whenever the stimulus intensity is 1, 2, 3, or 4 (and therefore says "Yes" 0% of the time). However, at a stimulus intensity of 5 or above, the person consistently reports "Yes" (and therefore says "Yes" 100% of the time). Thus, this person's threshold lies somewhere between an intensity of 4 and 5 units. For simplicity, we call it 4.5.

When people started to do actual detection experiments, however, their results did not look at all like those shown in Figure 2.2. Instead they looked much more like those displayed in Figure 2.3. Notice that the observer shows a gradual increase in the percentage of "Yes" responses. On 2 of the 10 trials on which a stimulus of intensity 3 was presented, this person responded "Yes." (Thus, 20% on the vertical axis corresponds to a 3 on the horizontal axis.) On the remaining 8 trials she reported that she could not see the stimulus. The threshold must lie somewhere between a stimulus intensity of 2 (never say "Yes") and 7 (always say "Yes"), but where? Psychophysicists typically define the absolute threshold as the smallest

[1]Note that the horizontal axis presents the intensity of the physical stimulus (lower intensities to the left and higher intensities to the right) and the vertical axis presents the perceptual response (0% reports of seeing the stimulus to the bottom and 100% reports of seeing the stimulus to the top). So the graph itself represents the essential psychophysical relationship between physical stimuli and perceptions of them.

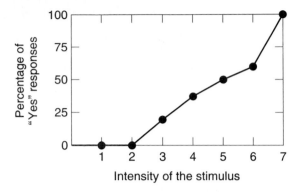

FIGURE 2.3 Results of a typical threshold study, showing gradual change. The threshold is the point at which 50% of the stimuli are reported as being present (50% "Yes" responses). In this case, the threshold would be 5.

intensity required for the stimulus to be reported 50% of the time. The threshold for the person represented in Figure 2.3 would be at a stimulus intensity of 5.

Why does the same stimulus sometimes produce different responses? If you remember the car radio example, such results should make sense. Remember, the same physical stimulus can produce one subjective experience on one occasion and a different subjective experience on another (the distribution of subjective experience in Figure 2.1b). So if the stimulus produces a relatively large subjective experience, the observer is more likely to respond "Yes." On occasions when the same stimulus produces a relatively small subjective experience, the observer is more likely to respond "No." Beyond that, as illustrated by Figure 2.1c, the same subjective intensity can yield a range of responses. Of course, the larger the amount of physical energy in the stimulus, the higher the level of subjective intensity, and the greater the probability of a "Yes" response.

Table 2.1 provides some illustrations of absolute thresholds in humans. These thresholds are only meant to give you a feeling for typical findings of detection experiments. The research

has not really been done with bee's wings or candle flames over long distances at night.

In his classic text, *The Elements of Psychophysics*, Fechner (1860) described three different methods that can be used to determine absolute thresholds: the method of limits, the method of adjustment, and the method of constant stimuli. We will describe each of them in turn.

Method of Limits

Before reading any further, try Demonstration 2.1, which is an example of how the method of limits can be used to measure a detection threshold. In the **method of limits**, you might begin with a stimulus that is clearly noticeable (e.g., the observer can always taste the sugar), and then present increasingly weaker stimuli until the observer reports, "No, I can't detect it." This is referred to as a **descending series** of trials. Next, you might begin with a stimulus that is clearly below threshold (e.g., the observer can never detect the sugar), and then present increasingly stronger stimuli until the observer reports, "Yes, I can detect it." This would be an **ascending series** of trials. In a typical psychophysical experiment using the method of limits, the observer would be presented with several alternating ascending and descending series.

TABLE 2.1

Some Approximate Detection Threshold Values

Sense Modality	Detection Threshold
Light	A candle flame seen at 30 miles on a dark clear night
Sound	The tick of a watch under quiet conditions at 20 feet
Taste	One teaspoon of sugar in 2 gallons of water
Smell	One drop of perfume diffused into the entire volume of a three-room apartment
Touch	The wing of a bee falling on your cheek from a distance of 1 centimeter

Source: Adapted from Galanter (1962).

Demonstration 2.1

Using the Method of Limits to Measure Absolute Threshold

In this demonstration you will use the method of limits to measure an observer's ability to detect sweetness. First, take 1 teaspoon of table sugar and dissolve it in one 8-oz. glass of cool tap water; stir to dissolve. Line up five empty glasses and fill them as indicated:

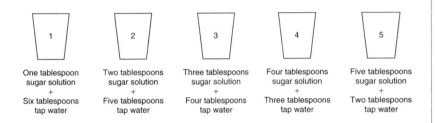

1	2	3	4	5
One tablespoon sugar solution + Six tablespoons tap water	Two tablespoons sugar solution + Five tablespoons tap water	Three tablespoons sugar solution + Four tablespoons tap water	Four tablespoons sugar solution + Three tablespoons tap water	Five tablespoons sugar solution + Two tablespoons tap water

Now you may begin the trials. Blindfold your observer and present a solution (as specified below). The observer tastes a small sip and says "Yes" if sweetness is detected and "No" if sweetness is not detected. Then the observer spits out the solution, rinses with tap water for about 20 seconds, and repeats the procedure with the next trial in the series. Continue a series until your observer shifts responses from "Yes" to "No" or from "No" to "Yes." When the shift occurs, begin the next series.

The table below indicates the order in which you should present the solutions. For example, begin the first series with solution 1 because this has an asterisk. Begin the second series with solution 4, follow with solution 3, and so on. We have recorded our observer's responses; record your observer's responses next to ours. (Incidentally, save any remaining solution for Demonstration 2.2.)

				Series Number			
		1	2	3	4	5	6
Not very sweet	1	*No *				*No *	
	2	No	No	*No *	No	No	No
	3	No	Yes	No	Yes	Yes	Yes
	4	Yes	*Yes *	Yes	Yes		Yes
Very sweet	5				*Yes *		*Yes *
Threshold for each series		3.5__	2.5__	3.5__	2.5__	2.5__	2.5__

The overall threshold equals the average of the midpoints (thresholds) calculated for the individual series. The overall threshold for our observer was 2.8. What is the average of the thresholds for your observer?

When using the method of limits, we need to use both ascending and descending series because we can obtain a different value for the threshold, depending on which series is used. This difference in thresholds has some practical applications. For example, suppose that someone is playing a radio in the room in which you are studying. You could turn down the volume, using a descending series, until you think that the intensity is appropriate. However, you may discover that the final sound intensity is lower if you first turn down the volume until you cannot hear it and gradually make it louder, using an ascending series.

These two sets of series also correct for two other kinds of tendencies. Some people make *errors of habituation*; they operate on the principle that "the stimulus is likely to be the same as last time, so I'll keep giving the same answer." Thus, they tend to keep saying no on ascending series and to keep saying yes on descending series for some time after they should have changed their response. Other people make *errors of anticipation*; they operate on the opposite principle, that "the stimulus is likely to be different from last time, so I'll change my answer." As a result, they "jump the gun." On ascending series they claim that they can detect the stimulus when in fact they can't. On descending series, they claim that they can no longer detect the stimulus when in fact they still can.

How can we correct for errors of habituation and errors of anticipation? If we assume that a person who makes errors of habituation is just as likely to make them on ascending series as on descending series, the errors will cancel each other out. The threshold we obtain will be too high on ascending series, but it will be too low on descending series. If the two are averaged, therefore, we should end up with an accurate threshold. The same kind of cancellation of errors will work for errors of anticipation.

One other human factor can contaminate the method of limits and produce an inaccurate threshold, unless it is controlled. Suppose that every ascending series in Demonstration 2.1 started with Cup 1. Tasters might notice on the first series that the sugar is detectable by the third cup. If every series began with that same stimulus, then tasters might simply shout "I taste it" when they reach the third cup, without even paying attention to the taste. If we are inconsistent about the starting point for each series, however, the participants in a psychophysics study cannot get away with simply counting trials. Thus, the ascending series sometimes begins with Cup 1 and sometimes with Cup 2, and the descending series begins with either Cup 4 or Cup 5.

Demonstration 2.1 shows only six series of trials. A formal psychophysics experiment would be more likely to have dozens of series. The method of limits is an appropriate name because a series of trials stops when the observer reaches a limit and changes the responses either from yes to no or from no to yes.

Method of Adjustment

In the **method of adjustment**, the observer—rather than the experimenter—adjusts the intensity of the stimulus. Typically, the observer makes adjustments that are continuous (e.g., by adjusting a knob) rather than discrete (e.g., by tasting separate solutions containing different amounts of a substance).

This method can be used to obtain a threshold very quickly, and so it may be used to locate an approximate threshold. However, observers may be less careful when they use this method, leading to great variation from one observer to the next. Consequently, psychophysicists use it less than other methods. Notice, though, that you often use the method of adjustment in everyday life, for example, when you adjust the knob on your radio so that the sound is barely audible.

Method of Constant Stimuli

In the **method of constant stimuli**, the stimuli are presented in random order, as in Demonstration 2.2. The experimenter usually selects between five and nine stimuli, such that the weakest stimulus is clearly below threshold and the strongest stimulus is clearly above threshold. (As you can imagine, these values must be chosen after pretesting with a speedy method such

Demonstration 2.2

Using the Method of Constant Stimuli to Measure Absolute Threshold

In this demonstration you will use the method of constant stimuli to measure the ability to detect sweetness. Use the solutions from Demonstration 2.1 or mix up more according to those instructions. Blindfold an observer. The observer will sip, report, spit, and rinse as in Demonstration 2.1. However, you will present the solutions in random order, as indicated below. Again record your observer's responses next to our observer's responses.

Trial	Solution Number	Response	Trial	Solution Number	Response
1	2	No	11	5	Yes
2	5	Yes	12	4	Yes
3	4	Yes	13	1	No
4	1	No	14	2	No
5	3	Yes	15	3	Yes
6	2	No	16	2	Yes
7	4	Yes	17	5	Yes
8	1	No	18	1	No
9	5	Yes	19	4	Yes
10	3	No	20	3	Yes

Summary Table

Solution Number	Number of "Yes" Responses	Proportion of "Yes" Responses
1	0	.00
2	1	.25
3	3	.75
4	4	1.00
5	4	1.00

Now plot the proportion of "Yes" responses below, as we have done. Notice where the horizontal line corresponding to .50 "Yes" responses crosses the line you make to connect the plotted proportion. This is the threshold.

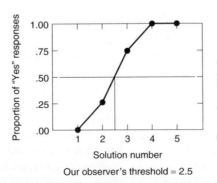

Our observer's threshold = 2.5

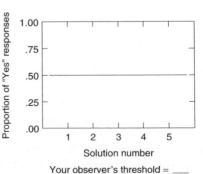

Your observer's threshold = ____

as the method of adjustment.) Notice that the name *constant stimuli* is appropriate because researchers select a constant set of stimuli before the testing begins, and they present these stimuli a constant number of times during testing.

In Demonstration 2.2, each of the five solutions is presented four times. In contrast, in a formal psychophysics experiment each stimulus would be presented more often (Gescheider, 1985). The method of constant stimuli is extremely time-consuming, particularly because the stimuli must be pretested. However, this method is preferred when psychophysicists want to obtain a careful measurement of a threshold, because it eliminates some biases found in the other two methods.

How do experimenters decide which method to use? The method of constant stimuli provides the most reliable data, and it is relatively free of biases. However, a disadvantage is that the experimenter needs to pretest the stimuli at near-threshold levels. The method of adjustment produces errors and is typically used only for stimuli that are continuously adjustable. Nonetheless, it may be useful for pretesting the stimuli that will be used with the method of constant stimuli. The method of limits requires less planning than the method of constant stimuli and may be the choice of an experimenter who wants fairly reliable thresholds without too much investment of time.

Although our discussion has been oriented toward thresholds, some psychophysicists speak of measuring *sensitivity*. The technical use of the term closely parallels the common use of *sensitivity*. When you describe people as highly sensitive, you typically mean that they are capable of detecting minor (usually emotional) changes in those around them, or that they have a low threshold for detecting change. Insensitive people have such high thresholds that a major emotional upheaval is necessary for them to detect a change.

In other words, sensitivity is inversely related to thresholds. When you have a low threshold for a stimulus, that means that only a low intensity of that stimulus is required for you to say, "I perceive it." In other words, you are sensitive to that stimulus. Thus, the *lower* the threshold,

the *higher* the sensitivity. Conversely, the *higher* the threshold, the *lower* the sensitivity. For example, when you have been out in the bright sunshine and first enter a dark room, you have a high threshold for perceiving a dim light; your sensitivity is low. After you have been in the dark room for 20 minutes, however, you have a low threshold for perceiving a dim light; your sensitivity is high. Because the terms *threshold* and *sensitivity* are potentially confusing, you should inspect graphs of psychophysical functions carefully to see whether large numbers reflect a high threshold or a high sensitivity.

The original versions of these classical psychophysical methods presented a stimulus on every trial. However, psychophysicists were perplexed by the fact that the same stimulus would be detected on some trials and not on others. Thinking that the observers might be using some sort of guessing strategy, researchers began to insert "catch trials"—trials on which no stimulus at all was presented. They found that people would often report the presence of a stimulus on catch trials. These results could not be easily explained within the framework of threshold theory. However, many years later signal detection theory was developed to explain why observers reported a stimulus on a catch trial. Although Fechner's psychophysics differs from signal detection theory, signal detection theory actually shares many theoretical underpinnings with Fechner's psychophysics (Link, 1994).

Signal Detection Theory

The three classical methods of psychophysics that we have examined have a common goal: locating a threshold. The implication is that a certain stimulus intensity can be determined that constitutes a borderline between detectable stimuli and those that cannot be detected. Signal detection theory, on the other hand, criticizes the very notion of a fixed threshold.

Signal detection theory, or *SDT*, argues that the thresholds obtained by classical psychophysical methods are composites of two separate processes: (1) the observer's sensitivity to the stimulus, and (2) the observer's decision-making strategy or criterion (Green & Swets, 1966; Macmillan & Creelman, 1991). Using SDT, researchers can separate sensitivity from criterion by examining the observer's responses to trials containing a *signal* (where a weak physical stimulus is present) and trials containing only *noise* (where no physical stimulus is present, only background noise). Consistent with one of the themes of this book, signal detection theory stresses the importance of top-down processing. Thus, the physical stimulus alone is not sufficient to determine perception—mental factors are also critical.

To clarify how these two processes function, let's consider an anecdotal example of detection provided by a student (Edington, 1979). Suppose that you were just puttering around your room. How likely are you to incorrectly report that you hear your phone ringing? Pretty unlikely, right? Now suppose that you decide to take a shower. Don't you occasionally think that you hear the phone ringing while you're taking a shower, but find that it isn't ringing? The difference between these two situations is one of sensitivity. In the first instance, the signal (phone ringing) would be superimposed upon a very low level of noise (background activity, etc.), so you would be unlikely to miss hearing the phone ring. Nor would you report that it was ringing when it was not. In the second instance, however, the noise level is considerably higher. Thus, you are more likely to report hearing a nonexistent ring or to actually miss hearing a ringing phone. So the signal-to-noise (S/N) ratio is much lower when the shower is running. (If you have purchased a stereo system, you are probably already somewhat familiar with this notion. Most stereo components report sensitivity in terms of the S/N ratio, with higher numbers indicating increased sensitivity.)

Now, let's suppose that you've just been interviewed for an important job, and the person who interviewed you told you to expect a call sometime between 3:30 and 5:00 on a particular afternoon. The one thing you *don't* want to do is to miss that phone call. Under these circumstances, you might actually think that you hear the phone ringing as you go about your business

in your room. (After all, you can't just sit there and stare at the phone for an hour and a half!) You would be even more likely to think that you heard the phone ringing if you had to take a shower during that time period. Compared to the earlier examples, what has changed in this situation to make you much more likely to report hearing the phone ringing? Your sensitivity hasn't changed, because the signal-to-noise ratio is equally high (working in your room) or equally low (taking a shower). Your expectations, however, have changed substantially. In the earlier examples, you had no real expectations that the phone would ring, and not much was riding on the possibility that you might miss a phone call. However, when you expect a phone call, you shift your *criterion*, or your willingness to say that you detect a stimulus.

We will now examine a typical SDT experiment to illustrate how you might measure an observer's sensitivity and criterion, using a methodology that is not much different from that used by classical psychophysicists. Not only will you learn some specifics about SDT, but you will also see why such experiments call into question the very notion of a threshold.

Design of a Signal Detection Experiment
Let's discuss a hypothetical experiment in which an observer is asked to listen for a weak tone. (Although this experiment involves hearing, SDT can be applied equally well to all the senses.) Out of 100 trials, we will randomly select 50 trials on which no tone is presented (normal background noise only). On the remaining 50 trials, a *very weak* tone is presented, essentially added to the noise. We refer to these trials as *signal + noise* trials. (The + is read as "plus.") In trying to conceptualize this experiment, you should realize that the perceived difference between the two types of trials must be very small. In other words, if observers could always tell that a tone was present on a trial, we could not obtain a good estimate of their detection abilities. So each trial represents a difficult decision for the observer.

Table 2.2 illustrates four possible outcomes that can occur on each trial of this experiment.

TABLE 2.2   Four Possible Outcomes of a Signal Detection Trial

		What Did the Observer Respond?	
		"Yes, I hear it"	"No, I don't hear it"
Was the signal present or absent?	Present	Hit (correct)	Miss (mistake)
	Absent	False alarm (mistake)	Correct rejection (correct)

What should happen on the noise-only trials (i.e., catch trials)? A perfectly accurate observer would always respond "No," to indicate that no stimulus is present. This would be a ***correct rejection***. What happens occasionally, however, is that the observer incorrectly responds "Yes," which is a ***false alarm***. When a stimulus is actually present (a signal superimposed upon background noise), a perfect observer would always respond "Yes," which we call a ***hit***. In reality, however, the observer occasionally will respond "No," which we call a ***miss***.

In analyzing the data from our experiment, we will determine the proportion of trials on which each of these four outcomes was obtained. Notice, however, that a complementary relationship exists between hits and misses, and between correct rejections and false alarms. Thus, in our hypothetical experiment, on the 50 noise trials an observer who gets 40 correct rejections (proportion = .80) must also get 10 false alarms (.20). On the 50 signal + noise trials an observer who gets 45 hits (.90) will get 5 misses (.10). Researchers can therefore analyze the results of a signal detection experiment by ignoring correct rejections and misses and looking only at hits and false alarms.[2]

---

[2]Those of you who have had a statistics course should also note the similarity between Table 2.2 and the hypothesis testing table showing Type I errors (saying that a difference exists, when in actuality there is no difference) and Type II errors (saying that no difference exists, when in fact there is a difference). So a Type I error is essentially a false alarm, and a Type II error is a miss.

Results of a Signal Detection Experiment

We can now examine the results of our hypothetical experiment for a single observer, expressed as a proportion of hits and false alarms obtained during the 100 trials of the experiment. First, let's consider the noise trials (illustrated in Figure 2.4a), which are the source of our false alarm data. The horizontal axis represents the subjective intensity the observer is experiencing on any given trial, measured in arbitrary units. The vertical axis represents the probability of a particular subjective intensity arising for the observer. So from looking at Figure 2.4a, we could determine that on most noise trials, our observer would experience a subjective intensity of 3 (high point of the distribution). On other trials, however, the subjective intensity could go lower than 1 or higher than 5, but the probability of these extreme subjective intensities is fairly low (low points of the distribution).

What produces the probability distribution of subjective intensities shown in the figure? After all, no tone is presented on noise trials. As we will see in later chapters, brain cells are always firing—even in the absence of stimulation. We refer to this as a *background rate of firing*. So we could think of the distribution as arising from differing levels of spontaneous brain cell activity in the parts of the brain that deal with audition. On some noise trials, this activity is so low that the subjective intensity on that trial is very low (around 1). On other trials, this activity is quite high, leading to a high subjective intensity (near 5). However, the brain cell activity is rarely at either extreme, and for most trials

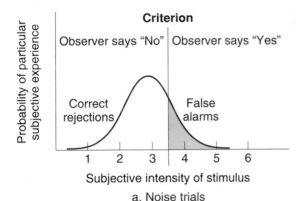

a. Noise trials

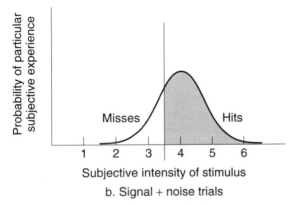

b. Signal + noise trials

FIGURE 2.4 A figure representing the possible outcomes of a signal detection experiment. The observer establishes a subjective intensity as a criterion for reporting the presence of a stimulus. When a stimulus produces a subjective intensity that exceeds the criterion, the observer says that a stimulus is present ("Yes"). Part a illustrates trials on which only noise (no actual signal) is presented. The observer reports either hearing a signal (false alarm—shaded area) or not (correct rejection—unshaded area). Part b illustrates trials on which a signal is presented in addition to the noise, which increases the subjective intensity and shifts the distribution to the right. The observer reports either hearing the noise (hit—shaded area) or not (miss—unshaded area).

the subjective intensity is centered around a score of 3.

Next, let's examine the signal + noise trials (Figure 2.4b), from which we derive the propor-

tion of hits. Even though the signal + noise distribution is shown separately from the noise distribution, you should realize that the horizontal and vertical axes are identical. In other words, the subjective intensity units shown on the horizontal axis are the same in Figures 2.4a and 2.4b. The probability distribution illustrated in the signal + noise figure is essentially the same as that for noise trials, with the important exception that the distribution is shifted to the right, in the direction of greater subjective intensity. In fact, you could think of the addition of the tone energy on a signal + noise trial as adding a constant amount of subjective intensity to each of the points in the noise-only distribution. You should also note the similarity in representation and interpretation between Figure 2.1 and Figure 2.4b.

Because the subjective intensity units on the horizontal axes of Figures 2.4a and 2.4b are identical, we can actually place the noise distribution and the signal + noise distribution on the same horizontal axis, as is done in Figure 2.5. Even though the two distributions are being shown on the same horizontal axis, don't lose sight of the fact that they represent the responses to two distinctly different types of trials in the SDT experiment.

Distinguishing between Sensitivity and Criterion

Remember, one of the benefits of SDT is that we can determine both the observer's criterion and sensitivity. We will use d' (or d-prime) as an index of sensitivity and the Greek letter β (beta) to indicate the position on the two curves determined by the observer's criterion. How can we determine these two measures from our data? Figure 2.5 helps illustrate the origin of the measure of sensitivity (d'), which is basically the distance between the peaks of the two distributions. With increasing amounts of energy in the tone, the signal + noise distribution will move further to the right of the noise distribution. If the energy in the tone is minuscule, the noise and the signal + noise distributions would be almost on top of one another.

Figures 2.4 and 2.5 also show the observer's criterion (β) as a vertical line passing through the horizontal axis. You can think of the criterion as

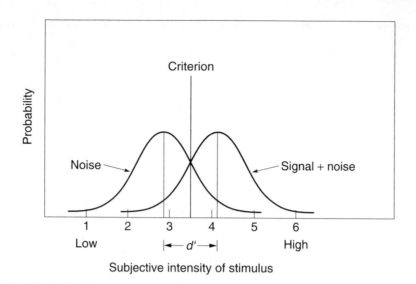

FIGURE 2.5   A graph representing the results of a signal detection experiment. The graph contains data from two different types of trials: for one type of trial, only noise was presented; for the other type of trial, a signal was added to the noise. Notice that this graph is the same as the one in Figure 2.4, but with the two distributions shown on the same horizontal axis.

representing the observer's decision that if a particular trial produces a subjective intensity greater than β, the observer will respond "Yes." If the subjective intensity on a trial falls below β, the observer will respond "No." Looking at the noise distribution, you can see that the area of the distribution to the right of β represents the proportion of false alarms for this observer (saying "Yes" when no tone was present). The area of the noise distribution to the left of β represents correct rejections (correctly reporting that no tone was present). In the signal + noise distribution, the area to the right of β represents the proportion of hits (saying "Yes" when a tone was present) and the area to the left of β represents the proportion of misses (saying "No" when a tone was present). Notice that representing β with a single line implies that an observer has a fixed criterion, which remains constant throughout the experiment.

Experimenters use an observer's proportion of hits and false alarms to determine β and d'.

The procedure is actually fairly simple, but computation of d' requires some background in statistics.[3] We will try to provide you with an intuitive understanding of the process without reference to statistics. To do so, consider five hypothetical participants in our experiment (Aaron, Beth, Chris, Diane, and Eric), whose data are displayed in Table 2.3.

First of all, notice that Aaron and Diane obtained the identical proportion of hits (.50), but did so with different proportions of false alarms (.16 for Aaron and .31 for Diane). Also, notice that Beth and Diane got an equal proportion of false alarms (.31), as did Chris and Eric (.40).

[3]Assuming that the noise and signal + noise distributions are normal allows one to make use of the properties of the normal curve. Thus, one could determine the distance in standard deviation units from the mean of the noise distribution to β, and from β to the mean of the signal + noise distribution. The separation between the peaks of the two distributions, d', is just the sum of the two distances.

TABLE 2.3

Outcome of Hypothetical SDT Experiment

Participants	p (hit)	p (false alarm)
Aaron	.50	.16
Beth	.69	.31
Chris	.77	.40
Diane	.50	.31
Eric	.60	.40

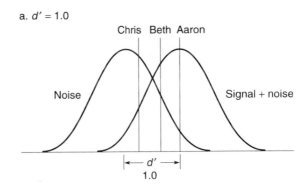

a. $d' = 1.0$

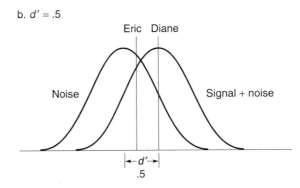

b. $d' = .5$

FIGURE 2.6 A graph of the results of a signal detection experiment that explores the distinction between sensitivity and criterion. A larger d' indicates greater sensitivity, so the three people indicated in part a are more sensitive than the two people indicated in part b. Aaron's criterion is more conservative than Chris's, and Diane's is more conservative than Eric's. Beth and Diane have similar criteria, but because Beth is more sensitive ($d' = 1.0$), she will make more hits and fewer false alarms than Diane.

However, in both cases their proportions of hits differed. When observers obtain similar proportions of hits—yet their proportions of false alarms are not similar—we can conclude that their sensitivities (measured by d') differ. A comparison of Figures 2.6a and 2.6b illustrates why this must be the case.

Let's look at Figure 2.6a first, where the noise and the signal + noise distributions are separated by a certain amount ($d' = 1.0$). If observers with this sensitivity, such as Aaron, establish a criterion (β) by which they obtain .50 hits, their false alarm rate is fixed at .16. The only way to obtain the same hit rate and a false alarm rate of .31 (as Diane did) is for the observer to be less sensitive. That would imply a d' less than 1.0, which means that the two distributions are closer together, as illustrated in Figure 2.6b. On the other hand, with the same sensitivity as Aaron—but with less conservative criteria—Beth and Chris obtain greater proportions of hits and false alarms. Be sure that you can look at Figure 2.6a and identify the portions of the two distributions that indicate hits and false alarms.

How can we be sure that Aaron, Beth, and Chris all have the same sensitivity? The two distributions in Figure 2.6a are identical in shape but fixed at a specific distance from one another. Therefore, when an observer decides on a criterion, the position of the criterion will determine a particular combination of proportion of hits and false alarms. Knowing what proportion of hits and false alarms an observer obtained, we could determine the specific sensitivity that must have produced the two proportions. The specific proportions of hits and false alarms produced

by Aaron, Beth, and Chris are all consistent with an equivalent sensitivity ($d' = 1.0$), but with differing criteria. Try Demonstration 2.3 to illustrate this principle to yourself.

Beth and Diane obtained identical proportions of false alarms (.31), as did Chris and Eric (.40). However, Beth and Chris obtained a larger proportion of hits than their counterparts. How can two people achieve identical proportions of false alarms but different proportions of hits?

Demonstration 2.3

Signal Detection Theory

To illustrate this process for yourself, make two photocopies of the curve shown here. Label one distribution "Noise" and the other "Signal + Noise." With a pencil, draw a vertical line through the noise distribution wherever you want, to represent a criterion. Now shade the area to the right of the line to indicate the proportion of false alarms. Can you see why that area represents false alarms? Right, that area represents saying "Yes" to a stimulus that contained no stimulus.

Now draw a vertical line anywhere in the signal + noise distribution. If you shade in the area to the right of the vertical line, you've indicated the proportion of hits. Because the vertical line on each distribution simply indicates the observer's criterion, you can superimpose the two vertical lines. When you do so, you fix the distance between the two distributions *(d')*.

Photocopy a new noise distribution but draw a vertical line farther to the right of the distribution than the line in your original noise distribution. The area to the right of the criterion is smaller, so false alarms are less frequent. Align the criterion of your new noise distribution with the criterion drawn on the original signal + noise distribution. Notice that the two distributions are farther apart than they were originally; *d'* is larger.

Now erase your vertical lines and draw in new ones, and again align the vertical lines. By repeating this process, you should get an intuitive feeling for how researchers determine *d'* from proportions of hits and false alarms. If you can estimate the proportions of the distributions accurately, you would find that the proportions of hits and false alarms produced by Aaron, Beth, and Chris are all consistent, with the same separation of the noise and signal + noise distributions.

Such discrepancies can be found only with differences in sensitivity. It should be clear to you that Diane and Eric are less sensitive than Beth and Chris. As seen in Figure 2.6b, the proportion of hits and false alarms obtained by Diane and Eric are consistent with a signal + noise distribution that is much closer to the noise distribution. Why might Diane and Eric have lower sensitivity than Aaron, Beth, and Chris? This could happen for any of a number of reasons, including some hearing loss resulting from attending loud concerts or playing music too loud through headphones. You should also see that Diane is more conservative than Eric, with a β farther to the right, and fewer hits and false alarms.

Factors That Influence Criteria

As seen in our example, people may come to an SDT experiment with differing criteria. Presumably, observers' past histories incline some to be more conservative ("I won't say that I hear the tone unless I'm absolutely certain") and some to be more liberal ("Maybe the tone was there, so I guess I'll report that I heard it"). Is it possible to encourage a person to change his or her criterion for an experiment? Given the earlier anecdote about waiting for a phone call, you should anticipate that a person's criterion could be manipulated during an experiment. We will discuss two ways in which researchers have manipulated criteria.

One important determinant of the criterion is the *payoff*, the rewards and punishments associated with a particular response. From the beginning of SDT, researchers have assumed that observers can be persuaded to adjust their criteria to earn more money (von Winterfeldt & Edwards, 1982). For example, suppose we say that we will pay you 50¢ every time you correctly report seeing a light (hit) and that you will pay us 10¢ every time you incorrectly report seeing a light (false alarm). You would calculate the payoff and say "Yes, I see it" if there were any chance at all that the light was present. You would have adopted a liberal criterion.

Contrast this pattern of responding with your behavior if we tell you that we will pay you 10¢ every time you correctly report seeing a light (hit) and you will pay us 50¢ every time you incorrectly report seeing a light (false alarm). Wouldn't you shift your criterion to be more conservative so that you would say "Yes, I see it" only if you were certain that the light had been presented? Notice that the criterion is determined by your strategy in making decisions, rather than your sensitivity, which has remained unchanged.

A second important factor is the probability that the signal will occur. In our hypothetical experiment, the probability of a trial being just noise was equal to the probability of a trial being signal + noise. Not all experiments have 50% noise trials and 50% signal + noise trials. Table 2.4 illustrates how the probability of a signal influences the proportion of hits and false alarms in a completely hypothetical experiment. Notice that when few of the trials are signal + noise trials (probability of a signal = .10), the observer appears to develop a

TABLE 2.4

Probability of a Hit or a False Alarm, as Signal Probability Increases from .10 to .90 (Hypothetical Experiment)

Probability of a Signal	Probability	
	Hit	False Alarm
.10	.32	.08
.20	.42	.12
.30	.52	.17
.40	.62	.25
.50	.70	.32
.60	.78	.41
.70	.84	.50
.80	.90	.61
.90	.93	.73

tendency to become more conservative—to become reluctant to report the presence of the tone. On the other hand, when most of the trials are signal + noise trials (probability of a signal = .90), the observer becomes more liberal and produces more hits *and* false alarms.

Receiver Operating Characteristic Curves

The data from signal detection experiments are often depicted in a *receiver operating characteristic curve* (*ROC curve*), which shows the relationship between the probability of a hit and the probability of a false alarm (Swets, 1986a, 1986b). Figure 2.7 shows a typical ROC curve. Notice that the vertical axis indicates the probability of a hit and the horizontal axis indicates the probability of a false alarm. How is the ROC curve determined? Imagine two distributions separated by a particular d' (e.g., the d' illustrated in Figure 2.5). Suppose you take β and place it to the far left of the two distributions, and then determine the proportion of hits (about 1.0) and the proportion of false alarms (also about 1.0). Then you could plot one of the points on the ROC curve. By moving β a bit to the right, plotting the new proportions of hits and false alarms, and then repeating the process, you would eventually produce the

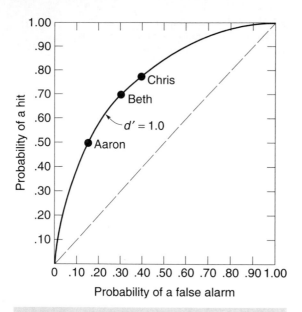

FIGURE 2.7 The results of a signal detection experiment can be shown using a receiver operating characteristic (ROC) curve, which plots the probability of a false alarm against the probability of a hit. Because Aaron, Beth, and Chris all have the same sensitivity, they fall along the same line. However, because Aaron is the most conservative, he falls to the left of the ROC curve (fewer hits and fewer false alarms). Chris is more liberal than Aaron, which leads to a larger proportion of hits—accompanied by an increase in the proportion of false alarms.

entire curve. Data from observers with that particular d' must fall at some point along the curve.

For any given ROC curve, the sensitivity is constant; that is, the tone does not increase or decrease in intensity and the observer does not change in perceptual ability. The observer's *criterion* changes within an ROC curve, however, usually due to some of the reasons we have just discussed. Each point along a given ROC curve represents a different criterion. Figure 2.7 shows an ROC curve for a $d' = 1.0$. This ROC curve is consistent with the results shown in Table 2.4 and also with the sensitivity of Aaron, Beth, and Chris

(Figure 2.6a), whose criteria are plotted on the graph. In the SDT experiment, the probability that Aaron obtained a hit was .50 (proportion of signal + noise trials on which he responded "Yes") and his probability of a false alarm was .16. The intersection of these two probabilities determines the location of Aaron's point on the ROC curve.

The left-hand portion of any ROC curve represents a strict (conservative) criterion in which the observer is very likely to say "No, I don't hear it" and is very unlikely to say "Yes, I hear it." In contrast, the right-hand portion of any ROC curve represents a liberal criterion in which the observer is very unlikely to say "No, I don't hear it" and is very likely to say "Yes, I hear it." The criterion becomes increasingly liberal as the curve moves from left to right (just the opposite of the situation in politics). Thus, Aaron is a more conservative observer than Chris.

Suppose the signal detection experiment is repeated with a more intense tone (or a more sensitive observer). In this case, the resulting ROC curve might resemble Curve A in Figure 2.8. For comparison's sake, Curve B is taken from Figure 2.7. Curve C represents either a weaker tone or a less sensitive observer. In fact, the results from Diane and Eric (Figure 2.6b) would fall along Curve C. When d' is 0, the observer is forced to simply guess; hits and false alarms occur equally often. In fact, when d' is 0, the ROC curve is a straight line. Compare the four ROC curves. Notice that for any given false alarm rate, the curves differ enormously with respect to the probability of a hit. For example, when the probability of a false alarm is .20, Curve A has a very high hit rate (.88), Curve B has a medium hit rate (.53), Curve C has a low hit rate (.32), and Curve D has only as many hits as false alarms (.20).

Psychologists calculate the proportion of hits and false alarms obtained in an experiment and plot them on a graph. Then they calculate d' from formulas or by comparing their ROC curves with published curves (e.g., Baird & Noma, 1978; Gescheider, 1985). Clearly, the graphical comparison of hits and false alarms is useful, because the single graph allows the researcher to examine an observer's criterion *and*

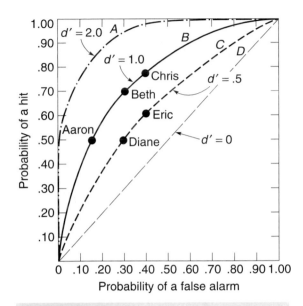

FIGURE 2.8 Four ROC curves. (A straight line is one type of curve, so the "curve" for a *d'* of 0 is a straight line.) Notice that at any point along one line, sensitivity is the same but the criterion changes (the left portion of each curve represents conservative criteria and the right portion represents liberal criteria). Also notice that as the curves move up and to the left, sensitivity is increasing.

sensitivity simultaneously. Try Demonstration 2.4 to make certain that you know how to plot and interpret an ROC curve.

What kind of observer is best with respect to sensitivity and criterion? Clearly, it is best to have a large *d'*—that is, noise and signal + noise curves as separate as possible. With a large *d'*, the ratio between the hit rate and the false alarm rate is large. Often, however, this is not under our control. Some people are simply more sensitive than other people; they see better, hear better, and so forth. The only practical way to increase *d'* is to increase the intensity of the signal. Given a particular sensitivity, is it better to set your criterion high or low? This question has no easy answer because you must consider the payoff—the relative advantages and disadvantages—of each outcome. The

advantage of a low, or liberal, criterion is a high hit rate, which is good. The high hit rate, however, will be coupled with a high false alarm rate, which is bad. You can lower the false alarm rate by setting a higher, or more conservative, criterion. Now, however, your hit rate will decrease. It may be helpful to think of various situations (e.g., detecting a tumor in an X-ray image, detecting a whiff of smoke in a building, detecting an incoming plane on radar) and decide whether a low or a high criterion would make more sense.

IN-DEPTH **Signal Detection Theory Applied to Face Recognition**

So far, we've been discussing signal detection theory in the context of simple perceptual stimuli, such as low-intensity sounds and lights. However, as Macmillan and Creelman (1991) note, we can make use of our knowledge of signal detection theory to study more complex processes such as face recognition. Faces are very complex stimuli, and being able to recognize faces is an important human capability. Therefore, psychologists are very interested in the processes involved in face perception and recognition. One important application of face recognition is in the identification of criminals by eyewitnesses.

Can you apply what you know about signal detection theory to a situation in which you have witnessed a crime? Think in terms of Figure 2.4. The horizontal axis might be relabeled "Similarity to your memory of the criminal's face." The actual criminal would be the signal. However, at a later time (say, in a lineup), the criminal might not look exactly like your mental image. As a result, there is some variability in the similarity of the criminal to your mental image, which creates a signal + noise distribution. All other people's faces would represent noise. Some of them look like your mental image of the criminal (the upper end of the noise distribution), and others look very different from your mental image of the criminal (the lower end of the noise distribution).

Suppose that you were asked to pick the criminal out of a lineup of six potential perpe-

Demonstration 2.4

Understanding ROC Curves

The purpose of this demonstration is to make certain that you know how to plot and interpret ROC curves. Suppose that you have gathered the data shown below at the left from an observer by varying the probability of a signal's occurrence. Plot the data in the figure, and then answer the questions below (the answers are at the bottom of the demonstration).

Probability of a Hit	Probability of a False Alarm
.52	.05
.71	.15
.82	.30
.90	.42
.92	.58

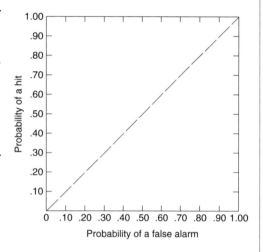

1. Comparing your curve with the curves in Figure 2.8, what would you estimate is your *d'*?
2. What method, other than changing the probability of the signal, could also have been used to get your observer to change his or her criterion?
3. Notice the diagonal line in the figure. If an observer had that kind of performance, would this person be more or less sensitive than your observer?
4. Is there any point along the curve at which the false alarm rate is higher than the hit rate?
5. Does your observer's sensitivity vary from one situation to the next for the points you have plotted in the figure? If not, what does vary?
6. As the probability of a hit increases, does the probability of a false alarm increase, decrease, or stay the same?

Answers: 1. The *d'* is approximately 1.5.   2. You could pay money for hits and/or subtract money for false alarms.   3. Less sensitive; in fact, this person would be responding at a chance level.   4. No, the hit rate is always higher.   5. No, the sensitivity does not vary; the criterion varies.   6. The probability of a false alarm increases.

trators in which Person #4 is the actual criminal. If you identify Person #4 as the perpetrator, you have made a hit. If you say that Person #4 is not the perpetrator, you have made a miss. If Person #2 looked so much like your mental image of the perpetrator that you picked that person out of the lineup, you have made a false alarm. Finally, if you say that Person #2 is not the perpetrator, then you have made a correct rejection.

According to signal detection theory, what leads you to make a decision ("That person's the criminal!") is that the person exceeds your criterion for similarity to your mental image of the criminal. At the same time, the other people in the lineup fall below your criterion. You should also understand how picking a person out of a lineup might lead you to establish a very conservative criterion, knowing that the person you identified would be incarcerated for a long time.

On a less somber note, suppose that you were simply walking along a busy street on the way to a movie. You might think you see a friend and wave, only to discover on closer inspection that the person is a total stranger. When deciding simply whether to wave to someone you think is an acquaintance, you are likely to establish a much more liberal criterion. After all, in this example, little cost is involved other than the risk of embarrassment.

As will become increasingly clear in later chapters when we compare our visual sense with other senses, people tend to rely heavily on visual input in making sense of the world. Even the most skeptical people are inclined to believe what they see. In the courtroom, an eyewitness to a crime is considered crucial, whereas other evidence is referred to as circumstantial—often with disdain. Given our reliance on visual input, and the importance of faces as stimuli in our environment, wouldn't you think that people would be able to make eyewitness identifications with great accuracy?

ACCURACY OF EYEWITNESS TESTIMONY

You may be surprised to learn that, in fact, witnesses are not particularly good at identifying perpetrators of crimes. In one particularly no-

table instance, a priest named Father Pagano (see Figure 2.9a) was mistakenly charged with the crimes committed by another man (see Figure 2.9b), based on the testimony of *seven* witnesses. The instructions to the eyewitnesses were probably flawed in this instance. However, you might question how a person could confuse these two men. How similar do they look to you? Clearly, a false alarm in eyewitness testimony is a very serious mistake that can result in the arrest of an innocent person such as Father Pagano (Loftus & Ketcham, 1991; Rodgers, 1982).

Obviously, researchers who are interested in the factors that influence eyewitness identification are not able to make use of actual criminal situations. Instead, they often try to develop a controlled laboratory or field study that resembles the situations in which people serve as eyewitnesses. Such studies are almost always pale reflections of criminal situations, often showing a number of photographs to people and then testing to see how well those people could later pick out the originally presented pictures from a set containing those pictures and several distractor pictures.

First, try to imagine yourself in the position of a person in such an experiment. Then imagine yourself as an eyewitness to an actual crime. How would your experiences differ? A number of distinctions should come readily to mind: (1) If you observed an actual crime, you probably would have experienced a great deal of emotion as you observed the crime (fear, anger, etc.). (2) Some emotion is also likely when you select the perpetrator from a lineup or an array of photographs. After all, your decision might help put a person in prison. (3) In witnessing a crime, you are observing a real person who is moving and talking, rather than a static, two-dimensional photograph. You can certainly think of several other differences. Nonetheless, it should be clear to you that failures in eyewitness identification present researchers with a significant problem. In spite of the artificiality of the experimental setting, we can learn some valuable lessons from experiments that address factors that might influence eyewitness testimony.

Experiments that use the signal detection approach have an important advantage: Com-

FIGURE 2.9   On the left is Father Pagano, who was identified as a thief by seven witnesses. On the right is the actual criminal, who ultimately confessed to the crimes of which Father Pagano stood accused. Do you think you could confuse these two people?

puting d' allows researchers to determine an observer's ability to accurately distinguish between faces they've seen before (the "perpetrators") and new faces ("innocent people"). If d' is near 0, then an eyewitness is unable to identify a perpetrator reliably. As d' increases, people become more capable of distinguishing between the guilty and the innocent faces. We'll now take a look at some studies that have used a signal detection approach and see what they tell us about eyewitness identification.

A valuable place to begin is a review of facial identification studies provided by Shapiro and Penrod (1986). They looked at over a hundred studies on eyewitness identification to see how a variety of factors might influence d' and β. For instance, some studies investigated the effect of the instructions given to the people

studying the pictures. One group, for example, might be told to look for distinctive facial features, whereas another group might be told to make inferences about some personality traits of the people portrayed in the pictures. The differing instructions did appear to affect d'; however, they did not influence β. In fact, for a range of independent variables (e.g., tested on face memory immediately versus at some later point, short versus long amount of time to study the face stimuli, no training versus training in facial recognition) β is little affected by the factor, but d' often is. Interestingly, over the range of factors summarized by Shapiro and Penrod (1986), the average d' is rarely above .80—for the experimental group that performs better. Such low values of d' indicate that eyewitness identification is a difficult task.

NUMBER OF ITEMS, DELAY, AND d'

As a representative example of a face recognition study, consider the experiment reported by John Podd (1990). Podd showed people pictures of faces created by a device (Photofit) used by the police to create composite pictures of suspects. Podd was interested in the impact of the number of faces that a person had to recognize, so people in Group 1 studied 20 faces, those in Group 2 studied 35 faces, and people in Group 3 studied 50 faces. Photofit produces full-face (front view) pictures, and each picture was presented for five seconds. Podd was also interested in the effect of the length of time between seeing the faces and being asked to pick out the faces. To test this factor, a third of the people in each group were tested 10 minutes after seeing the pictures, a third were tested one week later, and a final third of the people were tested two weeks later. For the test, each person was shown a series of faces, half of which were new and half of which were old. Therefore, people in Group 1 saw 40 faces, people in Group 2 saw 70 faces, and people in Group 3 saw 100 faces.

Podd found that people became slightly less sensitive with the passage of time. The value of d' for people tested right after initially viewing the faces was 1.47. After one week d' was 1.34, and after two weeks d' was 1.21. The decrement in d' over time is largely due to an increase in the number of false alarms, which rose from about .20 to .30. The hit rate was roughly constant over time. People also became much less sensitive with increasing numbers of faces to remember. If a person had studied 20 faces, d' was 1.55. For people who studied 35 faces, d' was 1.32, and for people who studied 50 faces, d' was 1.16. For this factor, the decrement in d' was largely due to a decrease in hits; false alarms remained roughly constant.

These data should suggest the importance of arranging police lineups as quickly as possible after a crime, because eyewitnesses might well become increasingly likely to choose the wrong person with the passage of time. Eyewitnesses to crimes with many perpetrators seem to face a more difficult identification task than people who observe a crime committed by a single person or a small number of perpetrators. ◆

Two-Alternative Forced Choice Procedure

In a signal detection experiment, an observer is asked to respond to each of a series of trials, with each trial either a noise or a signal + noise trial. Observers' criteria determine, in part, how they will respond on each trial—either "Yes" or "No."

Is it possible to minimize the impact of an observer's criterion? One approach that attempts to do so is the two-alternative forced choice procedure (Macmillan & Creelman, 1991). In the ***two-alternative forced choice procedure (2AFC)***, a trial consists of two presentations—one that contains the target stimulus and one that does not. The observer's task is to indicate which of the two presentations is the target. Because one of the two presentations contains the target, the effects of expectations and criteria are minimized.

As you might well imagine, the 2AFC task is easier than the signal detection task. In an SDT experiment, for example, four trials in a row might be noise trials. Thus, on any particular trial the observer isn't aided by knowing what occurred on the previous trial. In a 2AFC procedure, however, the observer is presented with a pair of stimuli. To use SDT terminology, the observer *knows* that one of the stimuli is noise and the other is signal + noise. So the observer can compare the two stimuli and report that the "stronger" one contains the signal. If neither stimulus appears stronger, she or he will be reduced to guessing, and the hit rate (naming the presentation that correctly contains the target stimulus) will be at the chance level, or .50. As the target becomes more easily perceived, the hit rate will approach 1.0.

Researchers can adapt the 2AFC procedure to include more than two presentations on each trial (i.e., 3AFC, 4AFC, etc.). Further, the 2AFC procedure can be combined with adaptive procedures, in which the level of the stimulus used is varied on the basis of the observer's earlier responses (Stillman, 1989). For instance, the stimulus level would be continually reduced as long as the observer was correctly indicating the presentation containing the target. When the observer makes an error, the level of the stimulus would be raised on the next trial (e.g., Simpson, 1989).

The 2AFC procedure can be used effectively in many areas of perception. However, even the 2AFC procedure might be susceptible to errors, particularly when only a small number of trials is used in the experiment (O'Regan & Humbert, 1989).

SECTION SUMMARY

Measuring Responses to Low-Intensity Stimuli

1. Psychophysics is the study of the relationship between physical stimuli and the psychological reactions to them.
2. The classical psychophysics methods measure absolute thresholds, the smallest amount of energy required for the stimulus to be reported 50% of the time. The transition between nondetection and detection is gradual rather than abrupt.
3. The method of limits involves presenting systematically increasing or decreasing amounts of a stimulus. It provides a fairly reliable threshold without too much time investment.
4. The method of limits can use both ascending and descending series to correct for errors of habituation and errors of anticipation. The series do not begin with the same starting point every time; this precaution guards against observers' merely counting trials before reporting detection.
5. The method of adjustment involves the observer's adjusting the intensity of the stimulus until it is barely detectable. It provides a threshold very rapidly, but errors are more likely than with the other two methods.
6. The method of constant stimuli involves presenting near-threshold stimuli in random order. It provides a highly accurate threshold, but it is time-consuming and requires that the researchers already have a good idea of where the threshold lies.
7. Signal detection theory disputes the very notion of a threshold, because classical psychophysical techniques hopelessly entangle two factors—sensitivity and criterion. Sensitivity depends upon stimulus intensity and the sensitivity of the observer. The criterion, which measures willingness to report the stimulus, depends upon factors such as probability of stimulus occurrence and payoff (rewards and punishments).
8. The outcome of a signal detection trial can be a hit, a correct rejection, a false alarm, or a miss. The probability of each of these four outcomes depends on the sensitivity measure, d', and the criterion measure, β.
9. Signal detection theory can also be represented in terms of probability distributions for trials in which signal + noise occurred and for trials in which only noise occurred.
10. As an observer, it is best to have a large d', but the criterion is determined by several factors, including payoffs for particular responses.
11. ROC curves can be used to plot the proportion of hits and false alarms. Each separate ROC curve represents a different d'.
12. Signal detection theory has been used in research on eyewitness identification. Research suggests that false alarms increase with delays between viewing a face and being given a recognition test on the face.
13. The two-alternative forced choice procedure (2AFC) is often used because it minimizes the influence of the observer's criterion. Even this procedure might produce biased estimates of thresholds if only a small number of trials is used.

MEASURING RESPONSES TO MORE INTENSE STIMULI

So far the discussion of psychophysics has focused on how people respond to low-intensity stimuli such as dim lights and weak tones. In this section, we turn our attention to the measurement of stimuli that can easily be detected. These more intense stimuli play a prominent role in everyday experience. We usually have no trouble detecting the vinegar in the hot-and-sour soup at a Chinese restaurant. Instead, the question is whether the Pink Pearl Restaurant uses more vinegar than the Chinese Bowl Restaurant, and if so, is that difference just barely noticeable or very clearly noticeable? In this section we will examine the classical psychophysical measurement of discrimination of stimuli that are above threshold (suprathreshold). We will also look at the more modern approach to psychophysics introduced by S. S. Stevens, in which psychophysicists examine the relationship between the physical magnitude of a stimulus and the observer's estimation of that magnitude.

Classical Psychophysical Measurement of Discrimination

In *discrimination* studies, researchers try to determine the smallest amount that a stimulus must be changed to be perceived as different. Observers' discrimination ability is measured by a *difference threshold*, defined as the smallest change in a stimulus that is required to produce a noticeable difference 50% of the time. For example, suppose you manufacture candy bars and you want to produce a new version of a popular favorite that is noticeably larger. However, you don't want it to be too big because of the expense. You could ask people to make judgments about a range of sizes to determine what size is perceived to be larger than the original bar 50% of the time. You would then know that your new candy bar would have to be at least that big.

In a discrimination experiment, the *standard stimulus* remains constant, whereas the *comparison stimulus* varies. In general, the comparison stimulus changes according to a specified schedule, and the experimenter records how much change is necessary before the observer notices that the comparison stimulus is different from the standard stimulus. The term *difference threshold* was introduced in the previous paragraph, and it can be used in defining another important term. A difference threshold is the amount of change in a physical stimulus required to produce a *just noticeable difference (jnd)* in the psychological sensation. For example, suppose that the

intensity of the physical stimulus is 10 units. If the stimulus has to be increased to 12 units to produce a just noticeable change in the sensation, the difference threshold of 2 units would correspond to one jnd (Gescheider, 1985). Notice that the term *difference threshold* refers to the physical stimulus, whereas the term *jnd* refers to the psychological reaction.

The phrase *just noticeable difference* or its abbreviation, jnd, can be useful in everyday life. If your college installs new lights on campus but the change in apparent brightness is only minimal, you could describe the situation as being one jnd brighter. You might notice that when you use premium gasoline rather than regular gasoline your car runs about one jnd more smoothly.

One additional term should be mentioned before discussing the measurement of discrimination. The *point of subjective equality* is the value of the comparison stimulus the observer considers equal to the value of the standard stimulus. As the name implies, it is the point where the two stimuli are subjectively equal (Baird & Noma, 1978).

Each of the three classical psychophysical methods for measuring absolute thresholds can also be adapted to measure discrimination. We will describe these methods briefly; more complete descriptions are available elsewhere (Baird & Noma, 1978; Engen, 1971).

In the *method of limits for measuring discrimination*, the standard stimulus remains the same, and the comparison stimulus is presented in alternating ascending and descending series. For example, suppose you want to examine the discrimination of pitch. Specifically, you want to determine how much change you can make in a comparison stimulus before the observer notices that it is different from a 1000-Hz standard stimulus. For instance, on some ascending series of trials you begin with a tone clearly perceived as lower in pitch (e.g., 950 Hz) and present comparison stimuli that increase in frequency. On some descending series of trials, the comparison stimuli might decrease from 1050 Hz. Your observer must judge whether the comparison stimulus is a higher pitch, a lower pitch, or the same pitch as the standard stimulus. The just noticeable difference is determined by the frequency of the comparison stimulus at which the judgments change from "higher than" to "same as" or from "same as" to "higher than."

In the *method of adjustment for measuring discrimination*, the observer adjusts the comparison stimulus until it seems to match the standard stimulus. The comparison stimulus is set at the beginning of a trial to a level either above or below the standard stimulus. The observer is asked to make this adjustment many times. Consequently, we have a large number of selections of comparison stimuli that the observer believes are equivalent to the standard stimulus. For example, suppose you want to examine discrimination for tones of different frequencies and the standard stimulus is a 1000-Hz tone. An observer might set the comparison stimulus to 995 Hz on one trial, 1003 Hz on another trial, and so forth. (Notice, again, the discrepancy between physical stimuli and perceptions, because the observer might think that all the different tones are equivalent.) The method of adjustment yields several measures of discrimination, but a common approach is to measure the variability of the comparison stimuli thought to equal the standard stimulus.

In the *method of constant stimuli for measuring discrimination*, the experimenter presents the comparison stimuli in random order and asks the observer to judge whether each comparison stimulus is greater than or less than the standard stimulus. (In some variations the observer can also say that the two stimuli are the same.) In a study of tone discrimination, for example, comparison tones of 1010, 1005, 1000, 995, and 990 Hz might be presented 20 times each for comparison with the 1000-Hz standard stimulus. The just noticeable difference is the size of the difference between the standard stimulus and the comparison stimulus that can be discriminated half the time.

Thus, each of the three classical psychophysical techniques can be used to measure discrimination as well as detection. The advantages and disadvantages of each method were discussed earlier, and the three methods may yield somewhat different results (McKelvie, 1984).

Relationship between Physical Stimuli and Psychological Reactions

Suppose you add 1 ml of vinegar to one glass of water and 2 ml of vinegar to a second glass of water. Does the second solution taste twice as sour? Similarly, does a room that has four candles burning seem four times as bright as a room with only one candle? In this section, we will discuss the relationship between the intensity of the physical stimulus and the magnitude of the observer's reaction. For example, what is the relationship between the amount of vinegar in a solution and how sour the solution seems? Also, what is the relationship between the intensity of the light in a room and how bright the light seems? This is a crucial problem for psychophysicists, and we will discuss the conclusions reached by three prominent researchers.

Weber's Law

In the early 1800s, Ernst Weber examined the relationship between physical stimuli and psychological reactions by focusing on the just noticeable difference. Consider the following problem. Suppose that you can discriminate between the brightness of a room in which 60 candles are lit and the brightness of a room in which 61 candles are lit. (Surprisingly, most people can.) Now suppose that 120 candles are lit in a room. Can you discriminate between the brightness in that room and a room in which 121 candles are lit? After all, we have added the same one candle to make the room brighter. However, Weber found that the important determinant of observers' psychological reaction was not the *absolute* size of the change (e.g., one candle). Instead, the important determinant was the *relative* size of the change. Specifically, we require one additional candle for *each* 60 candles if we want to notice a difference. If the standard stimulus is 60 candles, we notice the difference when one candle is added. If the standard stimulus is 120 candles, we require 122 candles in the comparison stimulus to notice a difference.

Weber's law states that when *I* represents stimulus intensity,

$$\frac{\Delta I}{I} = k$$

Verbally, Weber's law states that if we take the change in intensity (Δ, or delta, is the Greek letter used to symbolize change) and divide it by the original intensity, we obtain a constant number (*k*). The constant, *k*, is called the **Weber fraction**. With candlelit rooms, *k* equals $\frac{1}{60}$. Notice how you can obtain a *k* of $\frac{1}{60}$ by dividing the jnd of 2 by an *I* of 120. Notice also that the jnd for 300 candles would be 5.

We have seen that the Weber fraction is $\frac{1}{60}$ when people judge the brightness of a candlelit room. However, this fraction varies widely from one judgment task to another. For example, the Weber fraction for judging the pitch of pure tones is $\frac{1}{333}$ (Engen, 1971). That means that we need to change a tone's pitch by only 0.3% ($\frac{1}{333}$) for the difference to be noticeable. In contrast, we are much less competent in noticing changes in taste and smell. For example, the Weber fraction is generally about $\frac{1}{5}$ for judging taste (McBurney, 1978), and it is about $\frac{1}{14}$ for judging smells (Cain, 1977). If a particular solution contains 5 ml of vinegar, we would need to add 1 ml to the solution for the change in taste to be detectable. Notice, incidentally, that smaller fractions indicate better discrimination abilities.

In summary, Weber did *not* find a one-to-one correspondence between physical stimuli and psychological reactions. The same stimulus that was sufficient to produce a noticeably brighter room in one situation (1 candle added to 60 candles) was not sufficient to produce a noticeably brighter room in another situation (1 candle added to 120 candles).

Weber's law is nearly two centuries old. How well does it predict the results of psychophysical studies? Research has demonstrated that Weber's law holds true for a variety of psychophysical judgments (Laming, 1985). However, it is more successful in the middle ranges than in predicting discrimination ability for high-intensity or low-intensity stimuli.

Fechner's Law

Gustav Fechner used Weber's law to derive a scale that related the size of the physical stimulus to the size of the observer's psychological reaction (e.g., Murray, 1993). He assumed that jnd's were equal, and plotted these psychological units as a function of the physical units that gave rise to them. From Weber's law, you should be able to figure out that jnd's from the upper end of the scale actually require larger increases in physical stimulation compared to jnd's from the lower end of the scale. (Remember, $\Delta I/I$ is constant, so as *I* increases, ΔI must also increase.) The relationship, therefore, is not linear, but curvilinear. According to **Fechner's law**, the relationship is logarithmic (Baird & Noma, 1978). The formula

$$S = k \log I$$

claims that the magnitude of the sensation (*S*) is equal to a constant (*k*) multiplied by the logarithm of the intensity of the physical stimulus (*I*). In other words, Fechner's law states that the psychological magnitude is proportional to the logarithm of stimulus intensity.

As you may recall, the common **logarithm** of a number equals the exponent, or power, to which 10 must be raised to equal that number. As a result, a logarithmic transformation shrinks large numbers more than small numbers. In other words, as *I* grows larger, *S* grows larger; however, *S* does not grow as rapidly as *I*. For example, suppose that *k* has a value of 1. If the intensity of the stimulus is 100 units, then *S* = 2 (because the logarithm of 100 is 2; $10^2 = 100$). Now, if we double the intensity of the stimulus to 200 units, then *S* = 2.3 (because the logarithm of 200 is 2.3; $10^{2.3} = 200$).

Notice that a doubling of the intensity of the physical stimulus does *not* lead to a doubling of the psychological response. As *I* grows from 100 to 200, *S* grows only from 2 to 2.3. Once again, the correspondence between physical stimuli and psychological reactions is not one-to-one. Incidentally, Fechner's law is reasonably accurate in many situations, but—like Weber's law, on which it is based—it is inaccurate in others.

Stevens's Power Law

More recent research by S. S. Stevens (1962, 1986) provides an alternative view of the relationship between stimulus intensity and psychological reaction. According to **Stevens's power law**,

$$S = kI^n$$

Verbally, Stevens's power law says that the magnitude of the sensation (*S*) is equal to a constant (*k*) multiplied by the intensity (*I*) of the stimulus, which has been raised to the *n*th power.[4] In general, psychophysicists find Stevens's power law to be more useful than Fechner's law. However, Stevens's law is somewhat controversial (e.g., Krueger, 1989, 1991; Murray, 1993).

The size of the exponent has a major effect on the nature of the relationship between the intensity of the stimulus and the magnitude of the psychological reaction. If the exponent is exactly 1, a linear relationship exists between the intensity of the stimulus and the magnitude of the psychological reaction. The graph of this relationship is a straight line, such that an increase in the intensity of the stimulus is accompanied by a regular and consistent increase in the magnitude of the psychological reaction. When the exponent is greater than 1, increases in the intensity of the stimulus are accompanied by increasingly larger psychological reactions; the graph of this relationship curves upward. The steepness of the curve is determined by the size of the exponent. Finally, if the exponent is less than 1, increases in

the intensity of the stimulus are accompanied by increasingly smaller psychological reactions; the graph of this relationship curves downward. In fact, with exponents less than 1, the power law relationship is very similar in shape to the relationship depicted by Fechner's law.

Figure 2.10 illustrates three curves, one for each kind of relationship. Notice that when people are making judgments about the apparent length of a line, the correspondence is generally one-to-one—as the magnitude of the line grows, so does an observer's impression of length. When people are supplying their responses to electric shock, with each modest increase in stimulus magnitude they perceive that the magnitude of the shock is growing rapidly. With a fairly small physical intensity of electric shock, people judge the intensity to be extremely large. For brightness, though, beyond the lowest magnitudes, the experimenter must increase the stimulus by tremendous proportions before the observer shows even a modest increase in psychological reaction.

Electric shock has a large exponent, although it may not be as large as 3.5 (Cross et al., 1975; Price et al., 1992) , and brightness has a small exponent. Table 2.5 illustrates several other kinds of physical dimensions that psychophysicists have investigated. It's interesting to note, for example, that taste does not have a stable exponent; it's less than 1 in the case of saccharine and more than 1 in the case of salt. Furthermore, the specific exponent also depends on how the concentration of these solutions is measured (Myers, 1982). Researchers have also found the exponent to be influenced by a number of other methodological factors (e.g., Foley et al., 1990; Kowal, 1993).

A technique that Stevens frequently used to obtain judgments is called magnitude estimation. In the **magnitude estimation** technique, the observers are asked simply to give numbers to match (estimate) their impression of psychological magnitude. People are remarkably adept at making such judgments. Usually, only a small number of observations are taken from each observer, and the data of all observers are averaged (Falmagne, 1985).

---

[4]As you may remember, the power to which a number is raised indicates the number of times that a number should be multiplied by itself. For example, 10^3 equals $10 \times 10 \times 10$. Furthermore, powers less than one involve taking the root of the number. For example, $9^{.5}$ or $9^{1/2}$ means that you must take the square root of 9, which is 3.

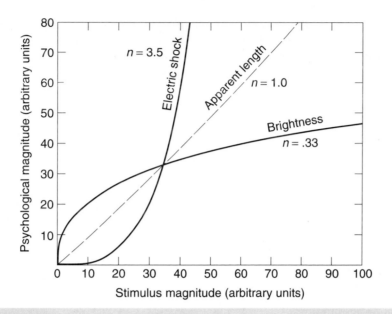

FIGURE 2.10 The relationship between stimulus intensity and magnitude of psychological response based on Stevens's power law ($S = KI^n$ where n is the value of the exponent). When n is 1, a linear relationship exists (apparent length). When the exponent is greater than 1, the psychological reaction is increasing more rapidly than the stimulus magnitude (electric shock). If the exponent is less than 1, the psychological response is increasing less rapidly than the stimulus magnitude (brightness).

Stevens also used a ***cross-modality matching*** procedure. In this method, observers are asked to judge one stimulus modality (loudness of a sound) with another modality (brightness of a light). At first, this method seems somewhat bizarre; "You want me to turn up this light so it is as bright as the sound is loud?" Again, however, people take naturally to such an experimental task. Try it

TABLE 2.5 Representative Examples of Physical Dimensions, Their Measured Exponents in Power Functions, and How They Were Measured

Physical Dimension	Measured Exponent	How Measured
Brightness	.33	Small target in the dark
Loudness	.67	Sound pressure of a high tone
Taste	.8	Saccharine
Length	1.0	Projected length of line
Taste	1.4	Salt
Heaviness	1.45	Lifted weights
Warmth	1.6	Metal contact on arm
Electric shock	3.5	Electric current through fingers

yourself. First turn the volume on your radio to a normal listening level. Next, tune your radio to a position that is between stations. The noise you hear is similar to the white noise often used in psychophysical experiments. Now draw a line so that your impression of the length of the line matches your impression of the loudness of the noise. Then try adjusting the volume to other positions and drawing new lines to represent these loudnesses. Although you might not feel confident in your judgments, there will be a reasonably good relationship between the lengths of the lines you have drawn and the loudnesses to which they were matched.

When the method of cross-modality matching is used, observers are actually telling the researcher about their perception of two modalities simultaneously. In other words, you were setting the sensation magnitude (S) for loudness equal to the S for line length, which equates two power functions (Luce & Krumhansl, 1988). In fact, the cross-modality matching relationship is readily described by a power function, and the exponent of this function is a ratio of the exponents of the two modalities. Although the power function is only an approximation of the relationship between the physical stimulus and perception, its common occurrence indicates that it is a reasonable approximation (Krueger, 1991).

In this section, we have examined the relationship between the intensity of physical stimuli and the magnitude of psychological reactions. In some cases the relationship is linear, but more often it is curvilinear. Thus, a change in the physical stimulus is translated into either a magnified or diminished change in psychological reaction. Because we can undergo only a modest range of physical shock intensity before doing harm to our bodies, only a small change in electric shock intensity is necessary to elicit a fairly large psychological reaction (so the exponent is greater than 1). However, as we will see in later chapters, we can perceive a tremendous range of loudness and brightness, which would produce compression (and exponents less than 1) if these ranges were mapped onto a magnitude dimension common to electric shock. If we assume that our perceptual systems map a wide range of sound and light intensities onto the same common dimension of magnitude as a narrow range of electric shock, then the characteristic power function exponents make sense (Teghtsoonian, 1973).

SECTION SUMMARY

Measuring Responses to More Intense Stimuli

1. Discrimination studies examine how much a stimulus must be changed to be perceived as just noticeably different.

2. Discrimination studies ask people to compare a standard stimulus with a comparison stimulus. These studies typically calculate the just noticeable difference.

3. In the method of limits for measuring discrimination, the comparison stimulus is systematically increased or decreased.

4. In the method of adjustment for measuring discrimination, the observer adjusts the comparison stimulus.

5. In the method of constant stimuli for measuring discrimination, comparison stimuli are presented in random order.

6. Three researchers—Weber, Fechner, and Stevens—have been primarily responsible for formulating equations to describe the relationship between physical stimuli and psychological reactions.

7. Ernst Weber found that observers require larger changes in the stimulus to notice a difference if they are discriminating between intense, rather than weak, stimuli.

8. Gustav Fechner proposed that as stimulus intensity increases, the magnitude of the psychological response increases, but not as dramatically. Fechner's law states that the magnitude of the psychological response is related to the logarithm of the intensity of the physical stimulus.

9. Using magnitude estimation and cross-modality matching techniques, S. S. Stevens proposed that the magnitude of the psycho-

logical response is related to the intensity of the stimulus, raised to a certain power, n. In general, Stevens's predictions are more accurate than Fechner's.

REVIEW QUESTIONS

1. Describe how psychophysics might be relevant if you wanted to examine low-intensity stimuli in each of the following areas: vision, hearing, touch, temperature perception, pain, smell, and taste. In each case, briefly describe how you would use the method of limits (or an appropriate modification) to measure a detection threshold.

2. Why do we need both ascending trials and descending trials in the method of limits? Why don't we need to worry about the two kinds of trials in the method of constant stimuli? Similarly, why do we need to vary the stimulus with which we begin using the methods of limits, and why is this precaution unnecessary when using the method of constant stimuli?

3. Return to Question 1 and describe how you would use the method of adjustment and the method of constant stimuli to measure detection thresholds in each of the areas listed.

4 Describe the advantages and disadvantages of each of the three classical psychophysics methods, illustrating each method with an example from vision.

5. Suppose you are standing near an electric coffee urn, waiting for the red light to turn on to indicate that the coffee is ready. Apply signal detection theory to the situation, describing aspects of sensitivity and criterion. Now describe the four possible outcomes in this situation with respect to the occurrence of the signal and your response.

6. The following questions apply to ROC curves:
   a. If d' is large, is the probability of a hit larger or smaller than if d' is small?
   b. What does d' measure?
   c. Suppose that Tuan has a d' of .5 and Ramón has a d' of 1.5. If they have the same hit rate, which of them has the higher false alarm rate?
   d. How is a particular point on an ROC curve related to the location of the criterion line in the probability distributions in Figure 2.5?

7. Why might signal detection theory be useful for research on eyewitness testimony? What would be the likely effect on d' of creating a lineup of people who were very similar in appearance? Suppose that the typical d' for eyewitness identification is 1.0. What would be the impact on hits and false alarms if you set a very conservative criterion?

8. Describe how you could use each of the three classical psychophysics methods to measure color discrimination. Then discuss how psychophysics might be relevant if you wanted to examine high-intensity stimuli in each of the areas mentioned in Question 1 (in addition to color discrimination). Mention both discrimination studies and studies concerning the relationship between physical stimuli and psychological responses.

9. Which is heavier, a pound of iron or a pound of feathers? Younger children might pause before answering, and might even answer incorrectly. Why? They are probably thinking which would feel heavier, rather than which would be heavier. How would you determine the Weber fraction for the weight of iron and for feathers? What would it mean if they are different?

10. The section on the relationship between physical stimuli and psychological reactions ended with a statement that a change in the physical stimulus is typically translated into either a magnified or a diminished change in the psychological reaction. Discuss this statement with reference to Fechner and Stevens.

NEW TERMS

psychophysics (16)
detection (19)
absolute threshold (19)
method of limits (20)
descending series (20)
ascending series (20)
errors of habituation (22)
errors of anticipation (22)
method of adjustment (22)
method of constant stimuli (22)
sensitivity (24)
signal detection theory
　(SDT) (24)
signal (25)
noise (25)
criterion (25)
signal + noise (25)

correct rejection (26)
false alarm (26)
hit (26)
miss (26)
d' (27)
β (27)
payoff (31)
receiver operating characteristic
　curve (ROC curve) (31)
two-alternative forced choice
　procedure (2AFC) (37)
discrimination (39)
difference threshold (39)
standard stimulus (39)
comparison stimulus (39)
just noticeable difference
　(jnd) (39)

point of subjective equality (39)
method of limits for measuring
　discrimination (39)
method of adjustment for
　measuring discrimination (40)
method of constant stimuli for
　measuring discrimination (40)
Weber's law (41)
Weber fraction (41)
Fechner's law (41)
logarithm (41)
Stevens's power law (42)
magnitude estimation (42)
cross-modality matching (43)

RECOMMENDED READINGS

Gescheider, G. A. (1985). *Psychophysics: Method, theory, and application* (2nd ed.). Hillsdale, NJ: Erlbaum. Although intended for an advanced-level course, this textbook is generally clear. A positive feature is that each chapter is accompanied by psychophysics problems to be solved by the student; the answers are in the back of the book.

Link, S. W. (1992). *The wave theory of difference and similarity.* Hillsdale, NJ: Erlbaum. Parts of this book might be too mathematical for the typical reader, but it contains a wealth of information. Link has a fairly unusual perspective on psychophysics, which permeates the book. However, his detailed unfolding of the historical developments in psychophysics is extraordinarily useful for integrating different theories.

Luce, R. D., & Krumhansl, C. L. (1988). Measurement, scaling, and psychophysics. In R. C. Atkinson, R. J. Herrnstein, G. Lindzey, & R. D. Luce (Eds.), *Stevens' handbook of experimental psychology: Vol. 1. Perception and motivation* (2nd ed., pp. 3–74). New York: Wiley.

In spite of the complexity of the material, this chapter manages to provide a readable overview of many of the methodologies employed in the study of perceptual processes.

Macmillan, N. A., & Creelman, C. D. (1991). *Detection theory: A user's guide.* Cambridge: Cambridge University Press. Although we've provided a brief introduction to the topic of signal detection theory, you would really benefit from working through this book if you want to become proficient in the use of the theory. Macmillan and Creelman do a good job of covering a range of applications of signal detection theory, offering the reader a number of exercises to insure mastery of the material.

Stevens, S. S. (1986). *Psychophysics: Introduction to its perceptual, neural, and social prospects.* New York: Wiley. Published after Stevens's death, this book is a readable summary of his theories and research. However, it does not cover additional topics, such as signal detection theory, as do other books.

The Visual System

lthough the human eye is about the size of a jumbo olive, it performs impressive tasks. The eye can handle information about colored and uncolored objects either near or far away and can work when lighting is dim or glaring. This chapter focuses on the structure of the eye, how it encodes information about the visual stimulus, and how this information is passed on to various areas of the brain for analysis.

VISUAL STIMULUS

We would not be able to see the world around us without light—but what is light? Light is one kind of electromagnetic radiation. ***Electromagnetic radiation*** refers to all forms of waves produced by electrically charged particles. As Figure 3.1 illustrates, the visible light that humans see occupies only a small portion of the electromagnetic radiation spectrum. Some of the light that reaches our eyes comes directly from a light source, such as the sun, a light bulb, a computer screen, or a candle. Such light sources typically emit radiation over a wide portion of the spectrum. Other light reaches our eyes indirectly, after light from a source is reflected off a surface, such as paper, fabric, or skin. Such surfaces tend to reflect selected portions of the spectrum, while absorbing others, a topic that we will explore in the chapter on color perception (Chapter 7).

Although humans respond to one portion of the spectrum, other organisms respond to other parts. For example, pit vipers and boa constrictors have sensory organs that are sensitive to infrared rays, which are to the right of the visible spectrum. These animals can therefore form heat-sensitive images of their potential prey (Sinclair,

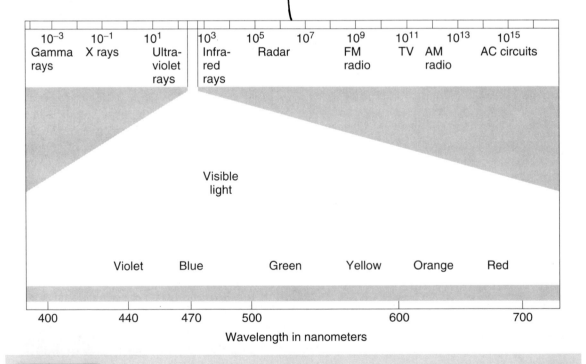

FIGURE 3.1 The electromagnetic radiation spectrum, a continuum of all forms of waves produced by electrically charged particles. Notice the tiny area between 400 and 700 nm (expanded in the lower part of the figure and also seen in Color Plate 1 inside the front of this text). This is the visible light spectrum, the only part that humans can see.

a. Example of long wavelength

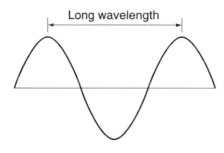

b. Example of short wavelength

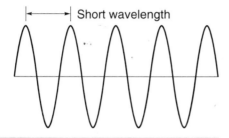

FIGURE 3.2 Examples of light waves varying in wavelength. Wavelength refers to the distance a wave travels during one cycle (or the distance between two peaks).

1985). The human visual system cannot detect wavelengths as long as those in infrared rays.

Our visual system also cannot detect short wavelengths, such as the ultraviolet rays that give you a suntan and the X rays used by radiologists. However, some animals are sensitive to these wavelengths, and they can more readily see clothing after it has been washed with detergents containing "whiteners" because the clothing reflects increased amounts of ultraviolet light (Associated Press, 1990).

Light is made up of waves. We can describe light in terms of its **wavelength,** which is the distance the light travels during one cycle, that is, the distance between two peaks, as illustrated in Figure 3.2. The light wave in Figure 3.2a has a longer wavelength than the one in Figure 3.2b.

Wavelength is typically measured in nanometers. A **nanometer** (nm) equals 1 billionth of a meter. The shortest wavelengths that we can see are represented by violet, which has a wavelength of about 400 nm. The longest wavelengths are represented by red, which has a wavelength of about 700 nm. Color Plate 1, inside the front cover of this book, illustrates the spectrum between violet and red. In summary, then, **light** is the portion of the electromagnetic radiation spectrum made up of waves that range from about 400 to about 700 nm.

We have talked about the length of light waves. As we will discuss in the chapter on color vision (Chapter 7), the length of light waves is related to the hue of a visual stimulus. **Hue** refers to the psychological reaction of color produced, in part, by the wavelengths in the light. Light waves have two other characteristics, purity and amplitude. **Purity,** the mixture of wavelengths in the light, is related to the perceived saturation of a visual stimulus. Finally, **amplitude,** the height of the light wave, is related to the brightness of a visual stimulus. Figure 3.3 shows how light waves can differ in the height of their peaks. Notice that Figure 3.3a has greater amplitude than Figure 3.3b; its peaks are higher. Light waves that have greater amplitude are perceived as brighter.

You may have noticed that we mentioned three *pairs* of attributes: (1) wavelength and hue, (2) purity and saturation, and (3) amplitude and brightness. The first member of each pair describes a characteristic of the physical stimulus, whereas the second member describes what we perceive, a psychological reaction. For example, large-amplitude wavelengths in a physical stimulus will usually be perceived by humans as bright.

SECTION SUMMARY

Visual Stimulus

1. Light is part of the electromagnetic spectrum; wavelengths for light (measured in nanometers) range between 400 nm (roughly violet) and 700 nm (roughly red). Other organisms are sensitive to different portions of the electromagnetic spectrum, but these

a. Example of a bright-looking light, with light waves of a greater amplitude

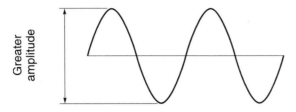

b. Example of a dim-looking light, with light waves of a smaller amplitude

FIGURE 3.3 Examples of light waves varying in amplitude. You can think of amplitude as the amount of light energy present in the stimulus.

wavelengths are either too long or too short for the human visual system.

2. Light can also be described in terms of its purity and its amplitude, as well as its wavelength.

3. Wavelength, purity, and amplitude describe physical stimuli, whereas hue, saturation, and brightness describe perceptions.

STRUCTURE AND FUNCTION OF THE EYE

The purpose of the visual system is to transform the electromagnetic energy in the visual stimulus into neural energy. *Transduction* is the process of converting one form of energy into another, and so the sensory organs serve as transducers. We will now trace the pathway along which the energy in the visual stimulus is processed.

Cornea, Sclera, and Anterior Chamber

The eyeball is a slightly flattened sphere. Its shape is maintained by the pressure of the internal fluids on the white external membrane, the *sclera* (Fatt & Weissman, 1992). Muscles that allow us to move our eyes are attached to the sclera (Riordan-Eva, 1992a).

At the front of the eyeball is the *cornea,* a clear membrane that joins with the sclera and bulges out slightly. If you look at someone's eye from the side, you can see both the cornea and the sclera (as illustrated in Figure 3.4). The incoming light from the visual stimulus must be brought into focus on the rear surface of the eyeball, and the cornea begins this process. In fact, about two-thirds of the bending of incoming light energy takes place at the cornea.

The sclera and cornea are made up of the same fibers, so why do they look so different? The sclera is not transparent because the fibers are interwoven to provide strength. In contrast, the cornea is transparent because the fibers are distributed uniformly (Biswell, 1992; Fatt & Weissman, 1992). The situation is similar to what happens in a hot sugar solution, which can be spun to make an opaque cotton candy that

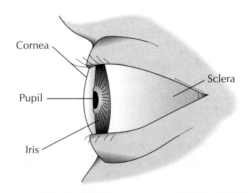

FIGURE 3.4 The cornea, a clear protective membrane in front of the pupil and iris, as seen from the side. The cornea helps to bend incoming light rays so that they fall directly on the back surface of the eyeball.

light could not easily pass through (analogous to the sclera) or cooled down carefully to form clear candy such as lollipops (analogous to the cornea).

When the cornea is misshapen, producing an *astigmatism,* a person will experience a blurring of some of the incoming light. An astigmatism can be corrected by an external lens. However, pediatricians have become increasingly sensitive about detecting astigmatisms early. Abnormal neural development can occur if an astigmatism goes undetected, and external lenses (glasses) will be less effective.

Other problems with the cornea occur because of its location at the front of the eye. The cornea can be damaged accidentally—through trauma, abrasion, or the introduction of foreign particles into the eye (Asbury & Sanitato, 1992). In addition, many diseases can affect the cornea (Biswell, 1992). If sufficiently damaged, the cornea may be surgically replaced. Unlike many other transplant operations, corneal transplants have a high success rate. Corneas lack blood vessels, which helps make them transparent and also reduces the risk of tissue rejection (Biswell, 1992; Riordan-Eva, 1992a).

If the cornea lacks blood vessels, how does it receive nourishment? Many parts of the body are nourished by blood vessels—but blood vessels in the cornea would block the incoming light. Instead, the cells in the cornea receive nutrients and oxygen from the *aqueous humor* (humor means fluid), a watery liquid that resembles the cerebrospinal fluid surrounding the brain. Blood plasma is transformed into aqueous humor through several stages of filtration (Fatt & Weissman, 1992). This fluid fills the *anterior chamber* immediately in back of the cornea.

The aqueous humor is continually being recycled, but the canal through which the aqueous humor leaves the anterior chamber can become blocked, particularly in older people. This blockage can lead to a buildup of pressure called *glaucoma*. The increased pressure can eventually damage the sensitive nerve cells at the back of the eyeball.

About 2 million Americans have glaucoma, and about 80,000 of them become blind as a result

(Vaughn & Riordan-Eva, 1992). Because of the seriousness of glaucoma, several tests have been developed to detect its presence. Most eye examinations include a tonometry test. *Tonometry* uses a special instrument to measure the pressure inside the eye (Chang, 1992).

If glaucoma is detected in time, the outlook is usually good, because special drugs can be prescribed to reduce the pressure inside the eye (Vaughn & Riordan-Eva, 1992). To detect glaucoma as early as possible, researchers are making use of the fact that a loss of peripheral vision is characteristic of glaucoma in its early stages. Recently developed tests can detect the early stages of glaucoma by assessing the extent of loss of peripheral vision (P. Brown, 1990, 1991). If the increased pressure is not detected in time, surgery is necessary to allow the aqueous humor to drain (Beard, 1991; Vaughn & Riordan-Eva, 1992).

Pupil and Iris

Most organisms must function under a wide range of lighting conditions. The illumination from the noon sun is about 100 million times as intense as the illumination from the moon (Hood & Finkelstein, 1986). As we will see, our visual system is amazingly sensitive to light energy. Thus, we can detect very small amounts of light, such as those occurring in the evening. Nocturnal animals, such as the cat, are even more adept at detecting low levels of light than are humans. However, what happens in bright sunlight? Is it possible to have too much of a good thing? Apparently so! You will not see clearly when excess light is scattered through the eyeball. If you've ever been out on a bright beach without sunglasses, you've probably tried squinting or shielding your eyes with your hand because you could not see clearly otherwise. Thus, the eye needs to minimize the amount of light bouncing around in the eyeball.

How does the visual system deal with the wide range of lighting conditions under which it operates? The opaque sclera ensures that most light can enter only through the transparent cornea. However, the cornea lets in far too much

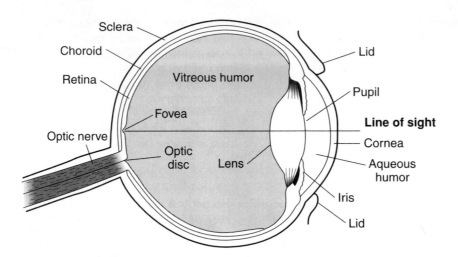

FIGURE 3.5 Structure of the human eye. The cornea and lens serve to focus the incoming light on the retina, particularly the fovea. Notice that the pupil itself is not an actual structure but rather a hole in the iris.

light under extremely bright conditions. So the visual system needs a variable mechanism that can admit maximal light energy under dimly lit conditions and minimal light energy under brightly lit conditions.

The mechanism that has evolved to fulfill this function is a ring of pigmented muscles collectively called the *iris* (see Figure 3.5). The pigmentation is important in restricting the incoming light, and darker pigmentation (e.g., brown) is actually more effective in this regard than lighter pigmentation (e.g., blue). *Albinos,* who

are born without pigmentation in the iris, are beset with a range of visual problems, and they must wear tinted external lenses to restrict the amount of incoming light.

The *pupil* is actually just the hole in the middle of the iris through which light information passes. The iris has two kinds of muscles, one to make it *constrict* or close (making the pupil smaller) and one to make it *dilate* or open (making the pupil larger). When the lights are bright, the iris closes up; when the lights are dim, it opens. Try Demonstration 3.1 to illustrate this process.

Demonstration 3.1

Iris and Pupil Size

Go into a dark room or closet with a door that can be opened to let in a little light. Take a mirror and a flashlight with you. Open the door just enough so that your left eye (next to the door) can see your right eye (away from the door) in the mirror. Notice the size of your pupil. It should be relatively large because the iris is open. Now turn on the flashlight so that it beams directly upon your right eye. Watch how rapidly the pupil shrinks in size because the iris is closing up. Turn off the flashlight and watch the pupil dilate.

The primary advantage of a small pupil is not the restriction of light but the increased distance over which objects will be in sharp focus. Although the visual system is unlike a camera in many ways, a camera uses a similar principle. You can think of the aperture setting on a camera as analogous to the iris/pupil. When you select a larger *f-stop*, you are making the *aperture* (i.e., opening) smaller. This will work fine when sufficient light is present, or with sufficiently "fast" film. However, in dimly lit settings you must use a smaller f-stop. When you can use a smaller aperture, your picture will be in focus over a greater distance, or *depth of field*. With a larger aperture, the background will be out of focus because it is beyond the depth of field. Thus, the broader range of clarity that results from using a smaller aperture is a benefit similar to that gained by the human eye when the pupil is at its smallest.

In humans the pupil is round. The next time you look at a cat, however, notice that its pupils are not round. In fact, the pupils become thin vertical slits when the lights are bright. Similarly, the harbor seal has adapted to searching for food in dark murky water and to caring for its young on the land in bright sunlight (Renouf, 1989). When underwater, the harbor seal's pupil is wide open. When in bright sunlight, however, the pupil is a narrow vertical slit.

Why does the pupil look black? Why can't you look into the pupil and see the eye's internal structure? To illustrate the problem, place a small object on a table and then stand a roll of paper towels over the object. Now, try to see the object by looking down through the tube in the middle of the roll. This task is difficult for a couple of reasons. First, most of the light that enters the tube is absorbed. Second, as you peer into the tube, you will be blocking the source of light. On the other hand, if you stand to the side, you cannot see the bottom of the tube. A real Catch-22! A similar problem faces us as we attempt to look into another person's eye.

Ophthalmologists—doctors specializing in eye diseases—and other physicians use a special tool called an *ophthalmoscope* to look inside the eye (Chang, 1992). The ophthalmoscope is

equipped with a special mirror and lens so that the light from a person's eye *can* be reflected back to the observer. Instead of the black pupil we ordinarily see, the physician can see structures inside the eye.

Lens

The *lens* is a transparent structure located directly behind the pupil. The center of the lens is harder than the exterior, which contains elongated fibers arranged like the layers of an onion (Koretz & Handelman, 1988). We noted earlier that the cornea bends light rays as they enter the eye. The lens completes the task of bringing light waves into focus on the photoreceptors that line the rear of the eye (Fatt & Weissman, 1992).

The lens can focus light rays from both nearby and faraway objects through a process called *accommodation*. The mechanism by which it does so was first described by Hermann von Helmholtz, a 19th-century German physiologist. (Remember his name; it will recur throughout this text.)

The *ciliary muscle* surrounds the lens and is attached to it by means of tiny fibers called *zonules* (see Figure 3.6). When you are looking at a distant object (20 feet away or more), the ciliary muscle relaxes, which causes the muscle to expand and pull on the zonules. In this unaccommodated state, the lens is pulled out to its flattest shape, so the incoming light is bent the least (see Figure 3.6a). When you are looking at an object that is nearer, the ciliary muscle contracts, causing the lens to become thicker (see Figure 3.6b). In this accommodated state, the lens will bend light the most (Koretz & Handelman, 1988). Thus, objects appear sharp, rather than blurry, regardless of the distance of the objects.

As we grow older, however, the lens loses its ability to accommodate—a condition called *presbyopia*. Because the lens cannot bend the incoming light as well as it should, we find it difficult to focus on nearby objects. Presbyopia is caused by several factors. The lens actually continues to grow throughout our lifetime, so older people have thicker lenses (Fatt & Weissman,

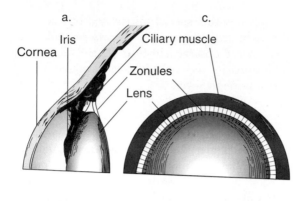

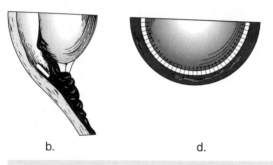

FIGURE 3.6 Detailed cross section of the front of the eye, showing changes in lens shape with accommodation. Parts a and b show the lens from the side, and parts c and d show the lens from the front. In parts a and c, the ciliary muscle is relaxed. When the ciliary muscle relaxes, it also expands, pulling on the zonules and flattening the lens (unaccommodated—for viewing distant objects). In parts b and d, the ciliary muscle is contracted. When contracted, the ciliary muscle does not pull the zonules as much, and the lens becomes fatter (accommodated—for viewing nearby objects). (From Koretz & Handelman, 1988)

1992). As a result, the angle at which the zonules meet the lens is different. Contraction of the ciliary muscle has little effect on the shape of the lens, so the lens stays relatively flat (Koretz & Handelman, 1988). Thus, nearby objects are harder to see, leading people with presbyopia to read by holding a book at arm's length. To correct for this deficit, people have to wear reading

glasses, or bifocals if their vision needed correction prior to the onset of presbyopia.

It is crucial that the lens be clear so that light can pass through it. A *cataract* is a cloudy lens, which can happen as a result of injury or disease (Shock, 1992). You really need special equipment to detect a cataract in someone else—unless the disease is fairly advanced. In its advanced stages, the lens will appear to be a milky white color. Luckily, cataracts can be detected with an ophthalmoscope, even in the early stages. Most cataracts are found in elderly people, occurring in over half of Americans over the age of 65 (Shock, 1992). Cataracts account for at least half of the blindness in the world (Riordan-Eva, 1992b). When cataracts develop, the clouded lens can be surgically removed. A substitute lens, called an *intraocular lens,* is typically implanted after the defective lens has been removed (Shock, 1992).

The various structures we have discussed so far, from the cornea through the lens, serve to bring images into focus on the eye's photoreceptors. The actual transduction of light energy takes place in the retina, and we now turn our attention to this crucial component of the visual system.

Retina

The *retina* is the layer of light receptors (or *photoreceptors*) and nerve cells at the rear of the eye. The photoreceptors absorb light rays and transform them into information that can be transmitted by the *neurons,* or nerve cells. This extremely important part of the eye is only about as thick as a page in this book. The retina contains photoreceptors called cones and rods and different kinds of nerve cells, which are discussed in greater detail shortly.

Locate the portion of the retina called the fovea in Figure 3.5. The *fovea* is a region smaller than the period at the end of this sentence. Because the photoreceptors are most densely packed within the fovea, this portion of the retina produces clearest vision. In fact, as you are reading this paragraph, your eyes are jumping along the page to register new words on your fovea. All the words on the page may appear to be clear and readable. However, if you focus on a single word on the page, words more than 3 cm away will be blurry and difficult to read. Those words are reaching areas of the retina outside the fovea, where the vision is substantially less clear.

Humans have a single fovea located in the center of each retina, but we should not assume that this arrangement is common. Many mammals lack foveas, and some animals (horses and birds) have two foveas in each eye. In horses this is a marvelous evolutionary adaptation, because the horse can see directly ahead at the same time that it sees the ground at its feet!

Figure 3.7 shows a sketch of a cross section of the retina in the area of the fovea. Notice that the upper layer of cells is much thinner in the central, fovea region. As you have probably come to expect about the anatomy of sensory processes, this arrangement is not accidental. Instead, light can pass through the cells much more readily to reach the region of the retina so critical for most of our vision.

Now return to Figure 3.5 and notice the area of the retina labeled "optic disc." At the **optic disc** the optic nerve leaves the eye. The **optic nerve** is the bundle of neurons that carries information away from the retina. The optic disc has no photoreceptors, so you cannot see anything that falls on this part of the retina. The optic disc therefore creates a **blind spot**. We will have more to say about the blind spot in Chapter 4. Try Demonstration 3.2 to illustrate the presence of a blind spot.

Posterior Chamber

Between the retina and the lens is a compartment called the posterior chamber. This compartment contains **vitreous humor**, a jellylike substance that helps maintain the shape of the eyeball and supplies some nutrients to the retina (Fatt & Weissman, 1992). The pressure from the vitreous humor keeps the eyeball almost spherical, in spite of external pressures. Some solid matter, called **floaters**, may be suspended within the vitreous

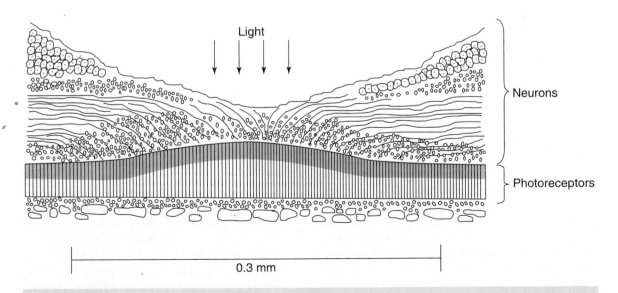

FIGURE 3.7 Cross section through the fovea. Notice that the layer of neurons is much thinner in the midfoveal area, facilitating the passage of light rays to the photoreceptors in this region so important for vision.

Demonstration 3.2

Blind Spot

Close your left eye and use your right eye to look at the X. Gradually move this page toward your eye and then away from it, keeping the distance in the range of 4 to 16 inches. At some point you will reach a distance at which the dot seems to disappear. At this distance the dot is falling upon the blind spot. In the blind spot, the nerve fibers gather together and leave the eye. There are no light receptors at this point, so there is no way to register the spot on the retina here. In Chapter 4 we discuss how our visual system compensates for the blind spot.

X   ●

---

humor. You may actually be able to see floaters drift across your own eyes, especially as you look at uniform bright white surfaces. Floaters become increasingly common as people age.

Figure 3.5 also shows the choroid, which is on the back of the eye just inside the sclera. The *choroid* is a web of many small arteries and veins behind the retina. The choroid provides nutrients and oxygen for the retina in front of it. In addition, because of its dark brown color, the choroid absorbs extra light that the photoreceptors did not pick up. Acuity is improved by eliminating the stray light that would bounce around the interior of the eye. In nocturnal animals, such as the cat, the choroid is replaced by a reflective surface—the *tapetum*—so that the organism has a greater chance of detecting small amounts of light. When driving at night, you will occasionally surprise some nocturnal creature in the headlights of your car, and its eyes will appear to glow. You are actually seeing the reflections of your headlights off the tapetum. As you would imagine, the tapetum actually works against seeing clearly in bright light.

SECTION SUMMARY

Structure and Function of the Eye

1. Parts of the eye visible from the outside are the sclera, the cornea, the iris, and the pupil.

2. The cornea, a clear membrane in front of the iris, bends light rays to bring them into focus on the retina. A misshapen cornea results in astigmatism.

3. The shape of the lens changes to bring both near and distant objects into better focus through a process called accommodation. A cataract is a cloudy lens.

4. The eye has two chambers, each filled with a different material. The anterior chamber contains aqueous humor, and the posterior chamber contains vitreous humor. Both materials supply nutrients, and the vitreous humor helps maintain the eyeball's shape.

5. The choroid layer contains arteries and veins, and it absorbs extra light.

6. The retina absorbs light rays and changes the electromagnetic information into information that can be transmitted by the neu-

rons. The retina contains the fovea, where vision is sharpest, and the optic disc, where a blind spot is created because of the absence of light receptors.

STRUCTURE AND FUNCTION OF THE RETINA

Because the retina is extremely important in vision, we will consider the kinds of cells in the retina in some detail. Figure 3.8 shows six kinds of cells. Cones and rods are the two kinds of photoreceptors that transduce the light information into neural information. *Cones* provide our perception of color under well-lit conditions. *Rods* allow us to see under dimly lit conditions, but they provide only black-and-white perception. The information from the cones and rods is transmitted through the other cells toward the visual area of the brain. This information is passed along through the *bipolar cells* to the next level in the chain, the ganglion cells. *Ganglion cells* take the information from the bipolar cells and bring it toward the brain. Notice in Figure 3.8 that the light must pass through the web of nerve cells to reach the photoreceptors. These photoreceptors are pointed toward the choroid at the back of the eye.

You can think of the chain of interconnections from the photoreceptors to the bipolar cells to the ganglion cells as a vertical chain. However, the information also travels horizontally across the retina through horizontal cells and amacrine cells. We will have more to say about these horizontal interconnections later in this chapter and in Chapters 4 and 5. For now, you should understand that *horizontal cells* allow communication among photoreceptors. They also interconnect bipolar cells. Furthermore, horizontal cells communicate with one another. *Amacrine cells* allow communication between bipolar cells and also between ganglion cells. Finally, amacrine cells are interconnected by means of other amacrine cells.

We will now examine some of these cells in greater detail, beginning with the photoreceptors. Then we will consider the other kinds of cells that permit both vertical and lateral communication at the retinal level.

Photoreceptors

How, exactly, do the cones and rods perform their transduction function? How do they convert light energy into a form of energy that can be transmitted through the visual system?

Notice the portion of the cones and rods at the top of Figure 3.8, specifically the horizontal disclike structures within the photoreceptors. A rod holds between 2,000 and 3,000 of these discs. The discs contain chemical substances called *photopigments* that accomplish the transduction of light. Each disc may contain as many as 3 billion photopigment molecules (Beatty, 1995).

In humans, the photopigments have two components, a large protein called opsin and an organic molecule called retinal (Stryer, 1987). The retinal component is the same for all photopigments. Because retinal is derived from vitamin A, depletion of this important vitamin has an adverse effect on vision—especially night vision. Although retinal is found in all photopigments, the exact form of opsin varies from one photopigment to the next. Like other higher primates, humans have four kinds of photopigments, one for rods and three for cones.

Each photopigment absorbs much more light in one portion of the electromagnetic spectrum than in any other portion. For example, Bowmaker and Dartnall (1980) studied material in the retina of a man whose eye had been removed because of a tumor in the choroid layer. They discovered that the photopigment in the rods was particularly responsive to a wavelength of 498 nm. Keep in mind that rods give rise to black-and-white vision, so even though 498 nm is in the area of the spectrum called blue-green, rods would interpret this wavelength as a shade of gray. The three photopigments found in the cones were each particularly responsive to one

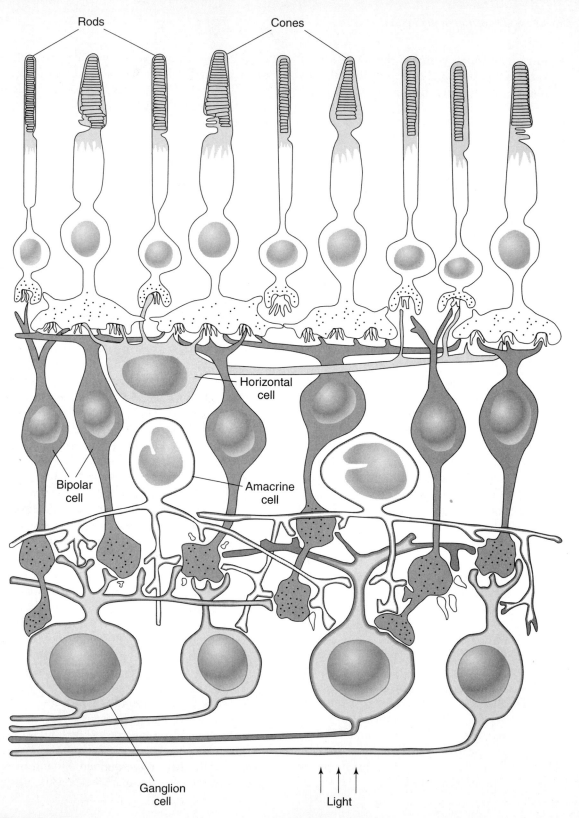

Rods

Cones

Horizontal cell

Bipolar cell

Amacrine cell

Ganglion cell

Light

specific wavelength: one to 420 nm, another to 534 nm, and the last to 564 nm. (The significance of the three cone photopigments will be discussed more completely in Chapter 7.)

When you are in a completely darkened room, the two components of each photopigment are stable and do not separate. However, when light hits a photopigment molecule, the molecule becomes unstable, and a rapid series of changes take place. In fact, the reaction of photopigments to light energy is among the fastest chemical reactions recorded (Pinel, 1993).

For example, consider *rhodopsin,* which is the photopigment found in rods. The process involved in breaking down rhodopsin has been investigated in great detail (and is thought to be similar for the photopigments in cones). After light hits rhodopsin, retinal and opsin are separated and retinal is transformed (McNaughton, 1990). The process begins with the activation of a G-protein, which initiates several rapid intermediate steps (Beatty, 1995). (These G-proteins also play a major role in taste and smell perception, so they will reappear in Chapter 13.)

Ultimately, the breakdown of photopigments results in hyperpolarizing the photoreceptor (Stryer, 1987). *Hyperpolarization* is the change in the electrical potential of the photoreceptor from its negative resting state to a more negative state. In other words, the sign of the voltage ("polarization") becomes even stronger (*hyper* means "extra"). This change in electrical potential tells the interconnected nerve cells that light energy has struck the photoreceptor. First, light produces hyperpolarization in photoreceptors. Activity in the photoreceptors then pro-duces hyperpolarization in the connected bipolar cells and horizontal cells.

Hyperpolarization is an unusual response to stimulation. Most neurons respond to stimulation by changing from a negative state to a more positive state—a process called *depolarization.* However, exposing a photoreceptor to light hyperpolarizes the receptor to a negative potential (–70 millivolts) common to the resting state of most neurons (Beatty, 1995). So, you could think of the hyperpolarization of photoreceptors as an unusual response, or you could think of the "normal" state of photoreceptors as being bathed in light. When "stimulated" by darkness, the potential of the photoreceptor becomes more positive, as with most neurons.

In order to respond to further stimulation, a photoreceptor must regenerate its photopigments. In rods, for example, vitamin A and other substances work to regenerate rhodopsin from retinal and opsin. Under brightly lit conditions, rods are continually bleached, meaning that they cannot regenerate rhodopsin. Thus, in daylight we are using only our cones to see.

Part of the rod itself also regenerates periodically. Recall the disclike structures in the outer portions of the rods illustrated in Figure 3.8. Researchers have discovered that new discs are formed at the base of the stack, and the stack moves away from the base. Early in the morning, the oldest discs at the outer part of the stack are cast off, a process known as *disc shedding.* Additional studies on cone renewal have demonstrated that a similar process occurs for cones, except that cones shed their discs at night (O'Day & Young, 1978). In other words, each system renews itself after the period during which it is likely to have been active.

Duplicity Theory

Differences in photopigments and in the timing of disc shedding are only two of many differences between cones and rods. *Duplicity theory,* an approach to vision formulated more than a century ago, proposed two separate kinds of photoreceptors in humans, each with different characteristics. Later research confirmed that duplicity

FIGURE 3.8 A diagram of the kinds of cells in the retina. Notice the intricate connections among these cells, and that incoming light must pass through the layers of ganglion, bipolar, amacrine, and horizontal cells before reaching the rods and cones. (Adapted from Dowling & Boycott, 1966)

TABLE 3.1 Comparison of Cones and Rods

Characteristic	Cones Photopic (color)	Rods Scotopic (black and white)
Shape	Tapered tip	Blunt tip
Number	5 million in each eye	100 million in each eye
Distribution	Throughout retina, but most densely concentrated in fovea	Not in fovea
Lighting conditions required for best functioning	Well-lit	Dimly lit
Relative number of receptors for each ganglion cell	Few	Many
Acuity	Excellent	Poor
Sensitivity	Poor	Excellent
Disc shedding	Evening	Morning
Photopigment	Three types	Rhodopsin
Dark adaptation	Rapid, but high threshold	Slow, but low threshold

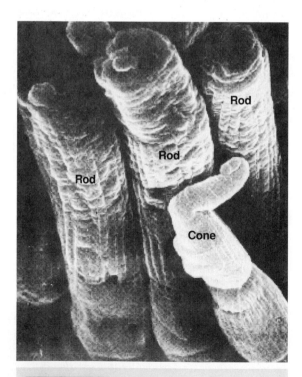

FIGURE 3.9 An electron microscopic view of rods and cones. (Photo courtesy of Dr. Frank Werblin)

theory was correct—humans have two extremely different systems within each eye. We will now examine these two types of photoreceptors in greater detail. Table 3.1 provides an overview of some of the differences we will be discussing.

Shape and distribution differences. Researchers have identified three types of cones, which are typically tapered toward their tips (see Figure 3.9). In contrast to the cones, the rods are relatively blunt-tipped photoreceptors.

In humans, each eye has approximately 100 million rods and "only" about 5 million cones. As seen in Figure 3.10, the cones are most densely concentrated in the center of the retina, near the fovea. The fovea itself contains over 30,000 cones and no rods (Beatty, 1995). In contrast, rods are found nearly everywhere *except* the fovea. The highest concentration of rods is in a circular region with a radius of about 7 mm from the center of the fovea. Notice that the rod density in this region is about the same as the cone density in the fovea.

Dark adaptation differences. Not only are the cones and rods differentially sensitive to light, but

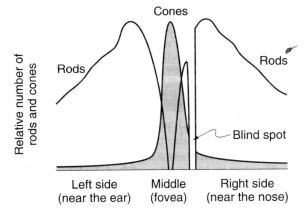

FIGURE 3.10 The distribution of rods and cones in the retina of the left eye. Cones are concentrated in the fovea and rods in the area outside the fovea. Notice that no photoreceptors are in the blind spot, which is produced by the optic disc where the optic nerve leaves the eye.

they also differ in the speed with which they adapt to changes in illumination. Let's explore how cones and rods differ in their adaptation. *Adaptation* is a change in sensitivity to a particular light intensity (Cohn & Lasley, 1986; Lamb, 1990). *Dark adaptation* is an increase in sensitivity as the eyes remain in the dark. *Light adaptation* is a decrease in sensitivity as the eyes remain in the light (Watson, 1986). The two kinds of adaptation can be remembered in terms of the *present* lighting conditions, either dark or light.

In nature, the transition from light to dark takes place slowly. Presumably, our species has evolved in that context. However, as a result of technological innovation, we can greatly speed up the transition from light to dark (or vice versa) at the flick of a switch. If you've gone to a matinee after the movie has already begun, you've probably been struck by the fact that dark adaptation is not an instantaneous process. Entering the darkened theater from the bright sunlight leaves you temporarily blinded, and only

after you've been in the theater for a while can you determine the wide range of behaviors in which your fellow moviegoers are engaging. (Some might even be watching the movie!)

Many laboratory studies have been conducted to investigate dark adaptation. In these studies, the observer is first exposed to an intense light, called the *adaptation stimulus,* for several minutes. Then the observer is placed in total darkness and the threshold for detecting a small spot of light is measured; this spot of light is called the *test stimulus.* The threshold is measured using an ascending series. The experimenter presents a low-intensity light and slowly increases the intensity. The experimenter records the intensity at which the observer reports seeing the test stimulus—the threshold. The experimenter then repeatedly measures the threshold after different time periods until complete dark adaptation is achieved. The curve shown in Figure 3.11 schematically illustrates the typical adaptation curve for one eye.

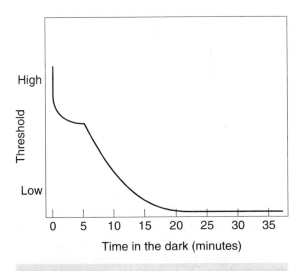

FIGURE 3.11 A dark adaptation curve, showing the relationship between time in the dark and the intensity of light that can be detected (threshold). Keep in mind that a low threshold is indicative of high sensitivity. Notice the kink in the curve at about 6 minutes of dark adaptation, which is clarified in Figure 3.12.

Demonstration 3.3

Dark Adaptation

Find a flashlight that is opaque on all sides except where the beam of light shines through. Take about 15 index cards and the flashlight and go into a dark room where you can stay for 15 to 20 minutes. Place all the index cards over the beam of light. Remove the cards one at a time until you can barely see the light. Calculate the number of cards remaining on the flashlight. After a few minutes, the light will look brighter to you. Add a card and see whether you can still see the light. If not, wait another minute and try again. Keep repeating the process for 15 more minutes. Notice that as you spend more time in the dark, you can detect an increasingly dim light.

Try Demonstration 3.3 to illustrate dark adaptation for yourself.

In Figure 3.11, look at the portion of the curve for a few minutes after the light has been turned off. The light must be relatively intense before a person can detect it. After about 30 minutes, however, dark adaptation is nearly complete; sensitivity is high and threshold is low (i.e., low-intensity light can be detected). In fact, the eye is now about 100,000 times as sensitive as it was in the bright light. A ***dark adaptation curve*** such as the one in Figure 3.11 shows the relationship between time in the dark and threshold, or the intensity of light that can barely be detected.

Why are we talking about dark adaptation in the context of cones and rods? The results of a typical dark adaptation experiment (Figure 3.11) are obtained by shining the test stimulus on the retina where it might fall on both cones and rods. Notice the kink in the curve that occurs after about 5–10 minutes in the dark. The first part of the curve represents the activity of cones, and the second part represents the activity of rods.

How were researchers able to map the differential dark adaptation of cones and rods? First of all, let's consider the cones. If you wanted to look at the dark adaptation of cones, what could you do? Right, go to the one place on the retina where only cones are found—the fovea! If you used a very small test stimulus, and ensured that it fell only on the fovea, you would obtain results such as those illustrated in Figure 3.12a. Notice that the threshold drops quickly during the first few

minutes. Sensitivity levels off at this point, however, and the threshold remains relatively high.

Testing dark adaptation for rods is a bit more difficult. Ideally, you could locate and test a person who has only rods in her or his retina (a ***monochromat***). Only about one person in 33,000 is a monochromat (Angier, 1992). Alternatively, you could minimize the presence of cones by shining the test stimulus only on the periphery of the retina—about 20° out from the fovea—where many rods but few cones are found. In either case, you would obtain a dark adaptation curve similar to the one shown in Figure 3.12b. Initially, the threshold is extremely high; then it decreases sharply, and later levels out at a very low threshold.

Dark adaptation is usually complete after about 30 minutes, but a number of factors influence its rate. These factors include the size and shape of the test stimulus and whether it is exposed continuously or in a flashing on-and-off pattern. Other factors include the size of the pupil and the intensity, color, and duration of the adaptation stimulus. For example, an intense adaptation stimulus may prolong the dark adaptation process to 40 minutes (Hood & Finkelstein, 1986; Reeves, 1983).

So the process of dark adaptation actually involves two stages. In the early stage, cones adapt rapidly to the change in lighting conditions. However, because they are not as sensitive as rods, we would not be able to detect weak light stimuli. The rods also begin adapting to the change in

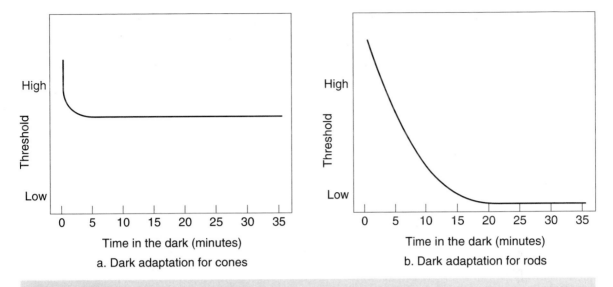

High

Threshold

Low

0   5   10   15   20   25   30   35

Time in the dark (minutes)

a. Dark adaptation for cones

High

Threshold

Low

0   5   10   15   20   25   30   35

Time in the dark (minutes)

b. Dark adaptation for rods

FIGURE 3.12 Dark adaptation curves for (a) the area in the fovea having only cones and (b) the area in the periphery having only rods. Notice that in part a, adaptation occurs quickly and the threshold is relatively high, whereas in part b, adaptation occurs at a slower rate but the threshold is much lower.

lighting conditions, but they are slower to adapt than cones. Luckily, they are more sensitive, so we are able to function in relatively low levels of illumination. Remember that rods provide us with noncolored or **achromatic** vision, rather than color vision. You may have heard the saying, "In the night, all cats are gray." To humans, a marmalade-colored cat indeed looks orange in daylight, when cones can be used. At night, after dark adaptation has taken place and the rods are functional, that cat can only look gray.

How does the eye become more sensitive to light as time passes in darkness? The complete answer to this question is not known. Let's consider several factors. First of all, as we have mentioned, when you move from an intense light into darkness, your pupil dilates, or widens. When the pupil of the human eye is fully dilated, it lets in about 16 times as much light as when the pupil is small. The human eye can increase its sensitivity somewhat, then, by letting in more light. (For the sake of comparison, you should notice the much more dramatic pupil size

changes in a cat. In intense light the cat's pupils are tiny slits; at night the cat's pupils are huge.) Pupil size changes can increase the eye's sensitivity to light in a limited way. However, the dark-adapted eye is about 100,000 times more sensitive than the light-adapted eye. Pupil dilation is thus only a small part of the story.

A second factor that permits the eyes to be more sensitive in the dark is that dark-adapted eyes have a higher concentration of rhodopsin. As we've mentioned, rhodopsin is broken down in the presence of intense lights. When the lights are turned off, the level of rhodopsin rises again. The concentration of pigment available in the photoreceptor is a major determinant of the level of dark adaptation (Pugh, 1988). A dark-adapted eye may well respond to the smallest unit of light energy.

The third factor involves brain input (Frumkes, 1990). Recent research suggests that circadian rhythms may lead some species to become more sensitive to light at night (Barlow, 1990; Barlow & Kaplan, 1993). Thus, horseshoe crabs may see as well at night as they do during the day, allowing them to find mates in the darkness (Brody, 1993). Such circadian rhythms have been found in other species, including humans. Brain input must also be important for human dark adaptation, but the details are not yet known.

Our discussion of dark adaptation has highlighted important differences between cones and rods. Cones adapt more rapidly than rods but are ultimately far less sensitive. Rods adapt more slowly than cones, but they provide us with better vision under dimly lit conditions such as those you find in a movie theater. Later, when you leave a matinee on a brightly lit day, you initially find the daylight to be extremely bright. However, through light adaptation, you quickly adapt to the sunlight. This process illustrates another difference between cones and rods.

Light adaptation differences. Dark adaptation takes about 30 minutes. In contrast, light adaptation takes about 1 minute (Hood & Finkelstein, 1986). During light adaptation, the pupils reflexively become smaller, allowing less light to enter the eyes. Shortly after the change from dark to bright light, the rods become bleached (i.e., the rhodopsin is broken down) and no longer function. However, sufficient light now exists for the cones to become fully functional. Just as the processes underlying dark adaptation are complex, so too are the processes that underlie light adaptation (Shapley et al., 1993).

As we mentioned earlier, we are less sensitive to light when we are light adapted. However, at the levels of illumination typically present during the day, we do not need to be light sensitive. Instead, we would rather see clearly, and the cones allow us to do so.

Differences in photopigment sensitivity. As we mentioned earlier, the cones and rods differ in the types of photopigments they contain. The photopigments are maximally sensitive to different portions of the spectrum, as illustrated in Figure 3.13. To simplify matters, the three types of cones are considered together in this figure to clarify the difference between cones and rods. Remember,

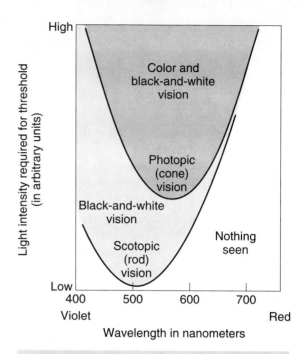

FIGURE 3.13 Photopic (cone) and scotopic (rod) threshold curves. The photopic curve represents the average sensitivity of the three cone systems. Once again, notice that rods are much more sensitive (have a lower threshold) than cones. In the area above the photopic curve, we can see stimuli as colored as well as black and white. Stimuli that fall between the scotopic and photopic curves can be seen but would appear to be black, white, or gray (regardless of wavelength). Stimuli below the scotopic curve could not be seen at all. Thus, a stimulus at 600 nm could not be seen until its intensity was increased to the point that it crossed the scotopic line. However, even though a wavelength of 600 nm would ordinarily produce a sensation of orange, it would appear only as a shade of gray until its intensity was higher than the photopic curve. (Adapted from Chapanis, 1949)

even though the rods are maximally sensitive to a portion of the spectrum that we would ordinarily associate with a color, the rods provide us with only black-and-white vision.

Notice in the figure that the rods are relatively insensitive to long-wavelength light (the red end of the spectrum). This insensitivity has very practical implications. If your eyes are dark adapted and you wish them to remain so, you should be exposed to only red light. For example, an amateur astronomer could orient herself by looking at a star map under red light. The red light would provide sufficient stimulation for the cones but would not affect the rods. Thus, she would maintain her dark adaptation. Then, her rods would be maximally sensitive when looking through her telescope for dim celestial bodies.

Acuity, sensitivity, and color vision differences. Cones are best suited for seeing in well-lit conditions, and they allow us to see in color. Vision that uses cones is called *photopic vision,* from the Greek stem *phot,* which means "light," and *opia,* which means "eye." The rods allow us to see in dimly lit conditions, but they provide us with only black-and-white vision. Vision that uses rods is called *scotopic vision,* from the Greek stem *skot,* which means "darkness." Given that rods are used in poorly lit conditions and that no rods are found in the fovea, then vision should be poor for objects registered on the fovea at night. Astronomers have learned to use "averted vision," or looking just to the side of the astral object they want to see. You can learn this technique for yourself by trying Demonstration 3.4.

All the information collected by the roughly 105 million photoreceptors in each eye is transmitted away from the retina through approximately 1 million ganglion cells. As a consequence, many photoreceptors have to "share" each ganglion cell. As it turns out, however, the sharing is unequal. Greater pooling of information, or *convergence,* is found for rods than cones. In the fovea, which contains only cones, a ganglion cell would receive information from a very small number of cones. Toward the edge of the retina, which is rich with rods, a ganglion cell will likely receive information from more than 100 rods.

The amount of convergence of information has an impact on *acuity,* the precision with which we can see fine details. When you want to see fine details of a picture, for example, you would like the information from each receptor on the retina to keep its information separate from the information that neighboring receptors have. If you pooled the information from a group of receptors, acuity would be reduced. Suppose, for example, that a design consisting of narrow black-and-white stripes is falling on an area in which 100 receptor cells share a single ganglion cell. All the information about black and white would be combined at the ganglion, which would pass along information consistent with a uniform gray stimulus.

Convergence explains why acuity is lower in the rod region than in the cone region; convergence reduces acuity. Convergence also helps explain why sensitivity is better in the rod region than in the cone region. *Sensitivity* is our ability

---

Demonstration 3.4

Night Vision and the Fovea

Choose a clear night and find a place with no bright lights nearby. Look up at the stars and locate a dim star slightly to the right or left of the point at which you are gazing. If you shift your focus to gaze at this star, however, it seems to disappear. In dim light, rods operate but cones do not. If an object is registered on the areas of your retina rich with rods, you can see it; that is, you can see objects best on the areas slightly outside the fovea. If an image of an object falls on the area of your retina rich with cones, you cannot see it. Consequently, at night you will not see an image that falls precisely on the fovea.

to detect small amounts of light. Because a single rod needs somewhat less energy than a single cone to be active, rods already have a "head start" (Figure 3.13). Rods have an additional advantage because convergence allows them to pool information. Each signal may be weak, but when the individual signals are pooled, the cumulative effect may be strong enough to stimulate the ganglion cell. In contrast, a weak signal from a cone, which may be the only receptor "assigned" to a particular ganglion cell, will probably not be sufficient to stimulate the ganglion cell.

So cones and rods differ in their contributions to acuity and sensitivity. Cones provide us with greater acuity and rods with greater sensitivity, partly because of differences in convergence. With greater convergence comes greater sensitivity, but at the expense of acuity. With lesser convergence comes lesser sensitivity, but greater acuity. The next stages in the vertical chain we are tracing are the bipolar and ganglion cells.

Vertical Connections: Bipolar and Ganglion Cells

Photoreceptors pass their information to bipolar cells. Our retina contains at least two different types of bipolar cells (Beatty, 1995). *Midget bipolar cells* tend to connect to a single cone or a small number of cones. Some of the convergence of information in the visual system begins with the bipolar cells. *Diffuse bipolar cells* make several connections with different photoreceptors, typically rods, initiating the convergence process (DeValois & DeValois, 1993; Rodieck et al., 1993). The bipolar cells pass their information to the ganglion cells, which collectively form the optic nerve as they convey the information from the eye toward the brain.

When properly stimulated, a ganglion cell generates an action potential. An *action potential* is a swift change in the potential of a nerve from a negative resting state (usually around –70 millivolts) to a positive state (usually around +50 millivolts). Notice that this process is depolarization. These changes in voltage allow researchers to ob-

serve the activity of these cells with recording techniques we will describe shortly. After the cells generate an action potential, they take a break, called a *refractory period*. During this refractory period, the cells return to their resting potential.

In the absence of a visual stimulus, the ganglion cell fires at a relatively low rate, referred to as spontaneous or *maintained activity* (Enroth-Cugell, 1993). Some activity occurs, then, even when the cell is receiving no stimulation. The information from the bipolar cells can result in excitation or inhibition of the ganglion cell. *Excitation* occurs when the incoming information leads to an increased firing rate in the ganglion cell. *Inhibition* occurs when the incoming information leads to a decrease in the firing rate of the ganglion cell.

To understand how researchers have studied ganglion cells (and most of the neural functioning we are about to discuss), an overview of single cell recording is necessary. *Single cell recording* is a research technique in which an extremely small *microelectrode* (about 0.01 mm in diameter) is used to measure the activity of a single neuron. Researchers operate on an experimental animal, such as a monkey or a cat, to place the microelectrode in an exact location in the visual system. To study ganglion cells, for example, the microelectrode can be placed within the optic nerve after it leaves the eye. Small spots of light are then presented on a screen in front of the animal (whose head movements are restrained), and the ganglion cell's responses to these stimuli can be recorded. The portion of the retina that, when stimulated, produces a change in the activity of the ganglion cell is called the ganglion cell's *receptive field.*

What does the receptive field of a ganglion cell look like? In mammals, these receptive fields are circles or ovals (Beatty, 1995; Pinel, 1993). They generally come in one of two varieties: (1) on-center, off-surround, or (2) off-center, on-surround. The surrounds of these receptive fields are often referred to as *antagonistic surrounds,* because they respond to light in a fashion opposite to (antagonistic to) that of the center. For example, if a ganglion cell has an on-center, off-surround receptive field, shining a light in the center of the receptive field will produce a burst of electrical activity in the ganglion cell. That is, the cell will show activation. However, if light shines in the surrounding, outer portion of its receptive field, the ganglion cell will show inhibition. If no light reaches any portion of the receptive field, the ganglion cell will fire spontaneously at a low rate, as mentioned earlier. Furthermore, if light shines on the entire receptive field, the activation in the center will be only slightly greater than the inhibition in the surround. The result will be a low rate of firing—only slightly higher than when no light is present. (So you see why the size of the light stimulus used is crucial. Too large a stimulus could cover the entire receptive field, and the researcher could easily miss the change in firing rate.) Figure 3.14 illustrates how an on-center, off-surround ganglion cell would respond in these four situations.

The second type of receptive field responds in exactly the opposite fashion. This receptive field has an off-center and an on-surround arrangement. Ganglion cells with this type of receptive field fire more often if the surround receives light and less often if the center receives light. Spend a moment figuring out how these cells would react to the four stimulus situations illustrated in Figure 3.14.

From this brief overview, you might think that using single cell recording to determine receptive fields is an easy process. We are glossing over several details, which actually make the process fairly arduous. Keep in mind that the microelectrode is recording from a ganglion cell that might be connected to *any* area of the retina. So the researchers must move their stimulus around over the whole field of vision until they find just the right location. Not only is the location crucial, but the size, shape, and direction of movement of the stimulus might also be crucial for some cells. The process is a painstaking one, and discovering the receptive field for a particular cell can take several hours. David Hubel, who is well known for research on the visual system, likens the process to mowing a lawn with nail scissors (Hubel, 1990). (Apparently he has some

experience in these matters, because not only has he done an enormous amount of single cell recording, but he also actually did mow his lawn using scissors when he was a graduate student.)

In addition to differences in receptive fields, ganglion cells differ in their function and the way they connect with bipolar cells. On this basis, we can distinguish at least two different types of ganglion cells. We will have more to say about bipolar and ganglion cells when we begin to discuss the pathways leading from the retina to the visual cortex. For now, we will turn our attention to the horizontal connections in the retina.

Lateral Connections: Horizontal and Amacrine Cells

With only vertical connections in the retina, one would not find the receptive fields for ganglion cells that we have just described. The presence of a surrounding region of a receptive field that responds differently to light from the center region is presumably due to the activity of the horizontal cells (Masland, 1986).

Amacrine cells are of several different types, determined by both shape and the neurotransmitters they contain. Presumably, the different amacrine cells serve different functions (Rodieck et al., 1993). One type of amacrine cell (containing the neurotransmitter acetylcholine) functions to enhance the responses of certain ganglion cells. These amacrine cells have widely branching dendrites and are probably the most common in the retina. Another type of amacrine cell serves as an interconnection between rod-activated bipolar cells and ganglion cells. As a result, this type of amacrine cell transmits information over a range of lighting conditions (Masland, 1986). A third type of amacrine cell (containing the neurotransmitter dopamine) only connects other amacrine cells. To date, however, we know a good deal more about anatomical differences among amacrine cells than we do about their functions (Hubel, 1988).

Every process discussed so far occurs within the paper-thin retina. Even at this relatively

Stimulus situation   **Ganglion cell firing rate**

a. White stripe on a
   dark background

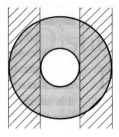

Activation

b. Dark stripe on a
   white background

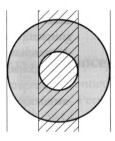

Inhibition

c. Completely dark
   field

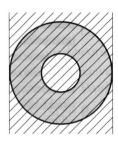

Only spontaneous firing

d. Completely light
   field

Slight activation

FIGURE 3.14 Electrical activity produced by an on-center, off-surround ganglion cell in response to four stimulus situations. Stimulation of the receptive field on the retina can lead to excitation of the ganglion cell when the on-center is primarily stimulated (a), or inhibition of the ganglion cell when the off-surround is primarily stimulated (b). When no light falls on the receptive field (c), the ganglion cell fires irregularly (spontaneous firing). When light completely covers the receptive field (d), the ganglion cell is slightly activated.

primitive level of visual processing, however, information is registered about color, contrast, and movement. In the next section, we will trace the pathways from the retina to the visual cortex.

SECTION SUMMARY

Structure and Function of the Retina

1. The cells in the retina are the photoreceptors, bipolar cells, ganglion cells, horizontal cells, and amacrine cells.

2. Light energy breaks down the photopigments found in rods and cones. This process causes the photoreceptor to become hyperpolarized, which is the neural signal that initiates the sensory experience of vision.

3. Cones and rods differ in their reaction to a change from brightly lit to dimly lit conditions (dark adaptation). Cones adapt rapidly but are relatively insensitive. Rods adapt more slowly but allow us to see in very dimly lit conditions. The eyes require about 30 minutes to dark adapt.

4. Cones and rods also differ in their reaction to a change from dimly lit to brightly lit conditions (light adaptation). Cones adapt rapidly, allowing us to see clearly. Rods rapidly become bleached and are not functional under brightly lit conditions.

5. Cones allow color vision in well-lit, or photopic, conditions. They are located throughout the retina but concentrated in the fovea, and very few cones share each ganglion cell. As a result, acuity in cones is excellent but sensitivity is poor.

6. Rods, which allow black-and-white vision in dimly lit, or scotopic, conditions, are in the part of the retina outside the fovea, and many rods share each ganglion cell. As a result, acuity in the rod region is poor but sensitivity is excellent.

7. Ganglion cell electrical activity is studied by inserting a microelectrode near a ganglion cell, using single cell recording techniques. The receptive fields of ganglion cells are either on-center, off-surround or off-center, on-surround.

8. Amacrine cells and horizontal cells provide lateral connections within the retina to influence the activity of the cells providing vertical connections (i.e., the photoreceptors, bipolar cells, and ganglion cells).

PATHWAYS FROM THE RETINA TO THE VISUAL CORTEX

Increasingly, neuropsychological evidence points to the specialization of the brain for particular functions. Thus, one area of the brain seems specialized for speech perception and another for speech production. Of course, we are normally unaware of such specialization. We don't think, "Okay, now I need to activate the speech perception area of my brain." On the other hand, damage to that area of the brain will immediately highlight the specialization. With localized damage, a person may have difficulty speaking, while other functions remain normal (but see Farah, 1994a).

Such specialization is also found within the visual system. Toward the end of this chapter, we will discuss evidence that a particular area of the brain is specialized for processing facial stimuli. However, even at the earliest stages of processing, our visual system shows signs of specialization. In fact, information leaving the retina has already been segregated into two different channels. Apparently, each channel is specialized to process a particular type of information. Furthermore, each channel is presumed to operate independently, processing its unique information in parallel with the other channel.

The visual pathways are likely to be more complex than our description may lead you to believe (Breitmeyer, 1992; Merigan & Maunsell, 1993). Even when researchers have a clear notion of the physiological properties of cells, their perceptual roles may not be clear (Lennie, 1993). However, most research suggests that two channels actually do exist. Future studies should clarify the exact roles of the channels and the extent to which they function independently of one another. We will now return to a discussion of the retina to examine the origins of these two channels.

Retinal Origins of Two Parallel Visual Pathways

The two visual pathways have their origins in the bipolar cells. Midget bipolar cells feed information to *midget ganglion cells.* Midget ganglion cells are the most common ganglion cells, representing about 80% of all ganglion cells (Lennie, 1993). These cells conduct information at a relatively slow rate (about 6 m/sec). When presented with a stimulus, midget ganglion cells continue to fire in a sustained fashion while the stimulus is present.

Midget ganglion cells are predominantly connected to cones and thus are particularly important for the perception of color (DeValois & DeValois, 1993). Because cones are concentrated in the fovea, midget ganglion cells are also concentrated in the fovea. The fovea is crucial for acuity, so the midget ganglion cells provide information about the details of stimuli. Based on the relative insensitivity of cones to light, you should correctly predict that the midget ganglion cells are also relatively insensitive (Lennie, 1993).

Because of the size of these midget ganglion cells, the pathway they initiate is called the parvo pathway (parvo means "small"). The *parvo pathway* is predominantly responsible for carrying information about the color and detail of stimuli, as well as slowly moving stimuli (Merigan & Maunsell, 1993). This pathway is sometimes called the parvocellular pathway or shortened to the P pathway. We will have more to say about the parvo pathway later in the chapter and in the chapters that follow. For now, however, we will turn our attention to the other pathway.

The second pathway begins with diffuse bipolar cells, which feed *parasol ganglion cells.* With their widely spread dendrites, these ganglion cells look a bit like a parasol with the fabric stripped away. Parasol ganglion cells are less common, making up about 10% of all ganglion cells (Lennie, 1993). These cells conduct information at a relatively fast rate (about 15 m/sec). The parasol ganglion cells respond with quick bursts of action potentials when they are stimulated, and then they return to their previous firing rate.

Parasol ganglion cells are predominantly connected to rods, which typically exhibit greater convergence. Therefore, parasol cells have larger receptive fields and are unlikely to provide us with the sort of detail provided by the midget cells. Because the parasol cells do not differentiate among the cone inputs they might receive, they are thought to be relatively insensitive to color information. On the basis of the relative sensitivity of rods to light, you should correctly

TABLE 3.2   Characteristics of Ganglion Cells

Characteristic	Type of Ganglion Cell	
	Midget Cell	**Parasol Cell**
Nature of receptive field	Center-surround	Center-surround
Ganglion cell size	Small	Large
Percent of ganglion cells	80%	10%
Kind of response	Sustained	Quick bursts at onset
Speed of conduction	Slower	Faster
Sensitivity to light	Lower	Higher
Color sensitivity	High	Almost none
Pathway	Parvo	Magno
LGN connection	Top (dorsal) layers	Bottom (ventral) layers

predict that the parasol ganglion cells are also relatively sensitive to light (Lennie, 1993).

The pathway that begins with these parasol ganglion cells is called the magno pathway (magno means "large"). Increasing evidence suggests that the ***magno pathway*** is involved in the perception of illumination differences and moderate or rapid movement (Merigan & Maunsell, 1993; Shapley, 1992; Wandell, 1995). In some texts, this pathway may be called the magnocellular pathway or shortened to the M pathway.

Table 3.2 summarizes the characteristics of the midget and parasol ganglion cells. Together, they represent about 90% of the ganglion cells leaving the retina. (The remaining 10% of the ganglion cells are still being investigated, but they don't fall neatly into either of these two categories.) The pathways that begin with these ganglion cells are definitely vital to vision. For example, when both the parvo and magno pathways are destroyed, little vision remains (Merigan & Maunsell, 1993). We will now continue to trace these two pathways, including a brief detour to the superior colliculus.

Initial Stages of the Visual Pathways

The ganglion cells leaving the eye are bundled together into the optic nerve, which is almost as big around as your little finger. Figure 3.15 shows the optic nerve and other structures in the visual pathway to the brain. The information

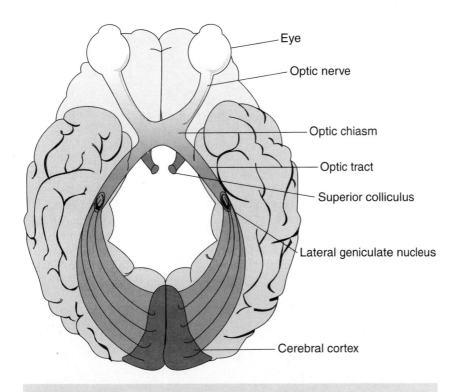

— Eye

— Optic nerve

— Optic chiasm

— Optic tract

— Superior colliculus

—Lateral geniculate nucleus

— Cerebral cortex

FIGURE 3.15   The visual pathway from the eye to the brain. The first synapse of the majority of the ganglion cells in the optic nerve is at the lateral geniculate nucleus. The next synapse in the visual pathway occurs in the occipital lobe of the cerebral cortex.

traveling along the optic nerve has already un- dergone a good deal of processing within the retina. As we have already seen, interconnec- tions between neurons serve as a means of pro- cessing information. The processing takes place

at a *synapse,* the space between two neurons over which information is transmitted. Neurons can be very long, so you shouldn't think of a synapse as a means of keeping neurons short. In looking at Figure 3.15, keep in mind that the

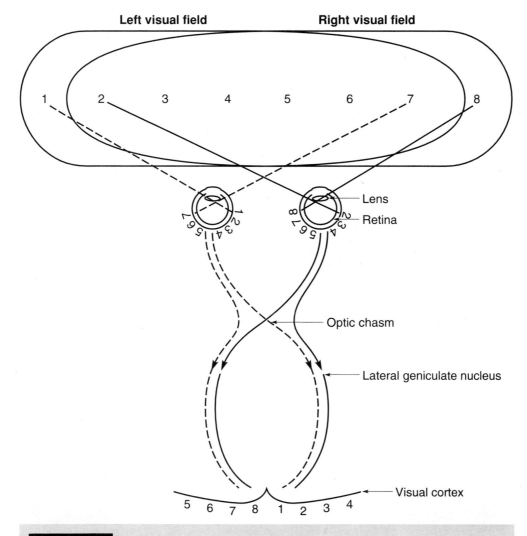

FIGURE 3.16 Schematic diagram of visual processing, showing two kinds of crossings, one at the retina and the other at the optic chiasm. The optics of the eye cause informa- tion from the right visual field to fall on the left side of the retina. The crossings at the optic chiasm ensure that information from the same side of each eye reaches the same brain hemisphere for processing (i.e., information from the left side of each eye goes to the left hemisphere, and likewise with the right).

first synapse of the ganglion cells in the optic nerve is either in the lateral geniculate nucleus or in the superior colliculus. So the first opportunity for further processing of visual information occurs in these two locations.

Optic Chiasm

The visual system actually provides two kinds of crossovers. The first "crossover" occurs before the image is formed on the retina. Because of the optics of the eye, the external image is reversed and upside down on the retina. Suppose you are looking at a series of numbers from 1 to 8. Notice that the numbers are reversed and upside down on the retina in Figure 3.16. As you look at the world, something on the left-hand side (*left visual field*) is registered on the *right*-hand side of each retina. In contrast, something on the right-hand side (*right visual field*) is registered on the *left*-hand side of each retina.

Most of the ganglion cells in the optic nerve terminate in the lateral geniculate nuclei (Figures 3.15 and 3.16). However, before they do, half of the ganglion cells cross over to the other side of the brain. In Figure 3.15 notice the *optic chiasm*, where the two optic nerves come together and cross over. The name *optic chiasm* makes sense because optic means "having to do with the eye" and chiasm is based on the Greek letter χ (*chi*); the shape of the χ corresponds to the crossover in the optic chiasm. No synapses are found in the optic chiasm; it is merely the location where the portions of each optic nerve cross over to the other side of the brain. Therefore, the chiasm serves no function in terms of processing the visual stimuli.

The ganglion cells from the left half of the left eye do not cross over at the optic chiasm. Instead, they continue back to the left lateral geniculate nucleus. Likewise, the ganglion cells from the right half of the right eye remain on the right side of the brain. However, the ganglion cells from the right half of the left eye cross over to the right side at the optic chiasm. The ganglion cells from the left half of the right eye cross over to the left side of the brain. As a result, information from the left visual field (the numbers 1, 2, 3, and 4) of both eyes is carried to the lateral geniculate nucleus and the visual cortex on the right of the brain. Right visual field information (5, 6, 7, and 8) is carried to the left lateral geniculate nucleus and left visual cortex. Because this arrangement is potentially confusing, study Figure 3.16 carefully.

Why does this complex crossing pattern exist? As we will see in Chapter 6, part of the reason humans are able to see the world as three-dimensional is slight differences in the images formed on the two retinas. The crossover that takes place at the optic chiasm brings the crucial information from each retina to the same region of the visual cortex. Look straight ahead and notice some object in the left visual field. Although this object is being registered on both the right and left retinas, information from both sources will end up on the right side of the visual cortex, where the information can be combined.

In Figure 3.15 notice that the bundle of ganglion cells is called the *optic tract* after it crosses the optic chiasm. Groupings of ganglion cells are first called the optic nerve. Then after passing through the optic chiasm, the cells are regrouped and called the optic tract. Keep in mind, however, that no synapse has yet occurred, and so the information from the retina remains intact and untransformed. So the change in name reflects the fact that the optic tract contains information from half of each eye. However, those two sources of information are kept separate until later in the visual system. The optic tract fibers travel to two areas. Some of the fibers go to the superior colliculus, but most go to the lateral geniculate nucleus.

Superior Colliculus

The *superior colliculus* is a relatively primitive part of the midbrain that in humans is important for eye movements (Sparks & Mays, 1990). For example, cells in the monkey's superior colliculus respond more strongly to a spot of light when the animal has moved its eyes to look at that spot of light (Wurtz et al., 1982).

Two superior colliculi are found in the visual system, one for each optic tract. Recall that the parvo and magno systems occupy about 90%

of the ganglion cells leaving the retina. Most of the remaining 10% of the ganglion cells continue to the superior colliculi. Some of these are parasol ganglion cells, which are more sensitive to movement than details about shape. The rest of the ganglion cells going to the superior colliculus are not yet classified. The pathway of visual processing continues from the superior colliculus to the LGN and to the secondary visual cortex (Van Essen et al., 1992).

Visual ganglion cell input is not the only input received by the superior colliculus. In fact, the superior colliculus receives information from the auditory system as well as information from the skin senses (e.g., touch). This nonvisual information is arranged to coincide spatially with the organization of the visual input. In the snakes we discussed at the beginning of this chapter, the information from their infrared-detecting pit arrives in the superior colliculus and is also arranged to coincide with the visual input. Thus, the superior colliculus probably helps to integrate information from various senses (Stein & Meredith, 1993).

Furthermore, the superior colliculus receives input from the visual cortex, which serves to modulate the activity of the superior colliculus. In fact, research has suggested a range of inhibitory inputs to the superior colliculus. Monkeys that have had their visual pathways severed at the lateral geniculate nucleus are unable to see. However, when the inhibitory inputs to the superior colliculus are removed, partial vision is restored in these monkeys. Thus, these animals have some visual function even without the rich source of retinal information moving through the lateral geniculate nucleus to the visual cortex. They are able to see using the information passing through the superior colliculus (once the inhibitory inputs are removed).

In fish and amphibians, the superior colliculus is crucial to vision—remove it and they are virtually blind! In monkeys, the removal of the superior colliculus primarily affects spatial vision and eye movements, and the effects are most obvious immediately after the operation. However, they ultimately recover. In fact, they eventually recover so completely that researchers began to doubt the importance of the superior colliculus for generating eye movements. As it happens, though, two different systems control eye movements in monkeys, one involving areas of the brain referred to as frontal eye fields and one involving the superior colliculus. When the superior colliculi *and* the frontal eye fields are removed, monkeys can no longer generate eye movements, although they can still see clearly and discriminate among visual stimuli (Schiller, 1986).

Lateral Geniculate Nucleus

The **lateral geniculate nucleus (LGN)** is a part of the thalamus—found in the midbrain (see Figure 3.15). The ganglion cells of the parvo and magno systems have their first synapse at the LGN. From the LGN, the two pathways continue to the visual cortex.

Jargon shock may have reached an advanced state when you first encountered the name of this section, but the name "lateral geniculate nucleus" makes sense. Lateral means "on the side," and one LGN is found on each side of the thalamus. Geniculate means "bent like a knee," and this description is also accurate (see Figure 3.17). Nucleus means "little nut." So a lateral geniculate nucleus looks like a little nut that is bent like a knee, located on the side of the brain.

Because the ganglion cells entering the LGN have passed through the optic chiasm, input to the LGN comes from both eyes. However, input from the two eyes is kept separate in the LGN in a layered, or laminated, fashion. In fact, the LGN contains six layers, three from each eye, as seen in Figure 3.17.

Why six layers? Why not just two, if the purpose of the layers is to keep the information from each eye separate? In fact, the six layers presumably arise from keeping the parvo and magno channels from each eye separate. Four layers of the LGN contain parvo pathway information—two layers of midget-cell input from the left eye, and two layers of midget-cell input from the right eye. The remaining two layers contain magno pathway (parasol-cell) input, one layer from each eye.

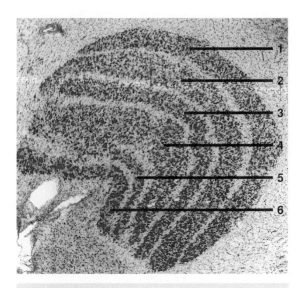

FIGURE 3.17 The lateral geniculate nucleus. Note the six layers that keep separate the parvo and magno pathways from the two eyes. (Photograph courtesy of Dr. Joseph G. Malpeli and Dr. Frank H. Baker)

Not only are the parvo and magno pathways arranged in layers within the LGN, but within each layer the cells also have a particular order. The order is called **retinotopic** because the location of cells in the LGN has an approximately maplike correspondence to the location of cells on the retina. So cells near one another in the LGN receive information from photoreceptors near one another on the retina.

Because they receive their input from ganglion cells, LGN cells function much like retinal ganglion cells. In other words, LGN cells have circular receptive fields, with on- or off-centers and antagonistic surrounds (as in Figure 3.14). However, the antagonistic surrounds of LGN receptive fields are more powerful than the surrounds of ganglion cells. Thus, light that stimulates the surround of an LGN cell with an on-center, off-surround receptive field would cause the LGN cell to fire far less than a similar ganglion cell. Furthermore, the LGN cells generally fire at a slower rate than ganglion cells (Kaplan et al., 1993).

Why do the LGN cells differ from the ganglion cells? As it happens, the ganglion cells aren't the only inputs to the LGN. Input to the LGN comes not only from the retina but also from other parts of the brain. In fact, up to 90% of the synapses in the LGN are nonretinal (Kaplan et al., 1993). Presumably, these inputs have a modulating effect on LGN functioning.

So the LGN is not simply a relay station designed to keep the ganglion cells to a manageable length. Instead, it is a location where information is processed. The inputs from other areas of the brain are crucial to the LGN, enabling it to function as a gate or a filter (Kaplan et al., 1993). The rest of the pathway from the LGN to the visual cortex is relatively straightforward, with no other crossovers or synapses.

Visual Cortex

The **visual cortex** is the part of the **cerebral cortex**, or outer part of the brain, concerned with vision. The visual cortex is in the rear part of the brain (occipital lobe), as seen in Figure 3.18. If you place your hand on the back of your head, just above your neck, the visual cortex will be immediately in front of your hand.

The cerebral cortex consists of many other parts—in addition to the visual cortex—and it is vital for human functions. In animals other than mammals, the cerebral cortex is either extremely tiny or nonexistent. In some primates such as monkeys and chimpanzees, the cerebral cortex is important, but in humans it is almost essential.

The entire cerebral cortex is only about 2 mm thick. In other words, the cover on your textbook is thicker than the covering on your brain! This covering is elaborately folded. If we could spread it out, the total area would be about 1,400 cm^2, about the size of the screen on a 21-inch (53 cm) television. As Hubel and Wiesel (1979) note, the folding probably occurs because this extensive structure has to be packed into a box the size of a human skull.

The visual cortex is subdivided into the primary and secondary visual cortex (see Figure 3.18). Neurons from the lateral geniculate nuclei

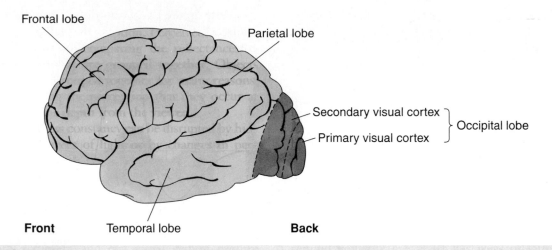

Frontal lobe

Parietal lobe

Secondary visual cortex
Occipital lobe
Primary visual cortex

Front   Temporal lobe   **Back**

FIGURE 3.18 The visual cortex, located in the occipital lobe of the cerebral cortex.

terminate in the ***primary visual cortex,*** which is also referred to as ***Area 17*** of the visual cortex or the ***striate cortex.*** Striate means "striped": a microscopic investigation of this area of the cortex reveals pale stripes. As early as 1776, Francesco Gennari suggested that anatomical differences in this area of the cortex might lead to differences in function (Glickstein, 1988). The importance of this area for vision was firmly established by the mid-1800s.

By convention, the layers within the primary visual cortex are identified by Roman numerals. The outer layer next to the skull is layer I, and the innermost layer is layer VI. In this numbering system, the cells from the LGN terminate in the region at the bottom of layer IV, which is called layer IVc. All those neuronal messages traced from the photoreceptors in the retina, through the bipolar cells, through the ganglion cells, and through the LGN ultimately pass through layer IVc of the primary visual cortex.

As was true in the LGN, the inputs from the parvo and magno systems are kept separate at this level of the visual cortex. The retinotopic organization of the LGN is also maintained in layer IVc of the visual cortex. Do not take this retinotopic arrangement too literally, however.

When you look at a picture of the Mona Lisa, for instance, a perfect picturelike representation of her (complete with smile) is *not* found in your visual cortex.

Many factors make the representation less than perfect. For example, about half the neurons in the visual cortex receive information from the fovea, which is an extremely small area of the retina. Thus the part of a picture registered on the fovea will be represented by more than its normal share of space in the visual cortex. The overrepresentation of information from the fovea with respect to the cortex is called ***cortical magnification.*** Furthermore, your perception of the Mona Lisa is actually a composite of several fixations of your fovea on different parts of the picture.

Incidentally, the cells in layer IVc have the same kind of center-surround receptive fields as ganglion and LGN cells. Other neurons in the visual cortex have very different receptive fields, as we will now explore.

Neurons in the Visual Cortex
Our understanding of the visual cortex can be attributed to a number of diligent researchers, of whom two of the most prominent are David

Hubel and Torsten Wiesel. They first began reporting their research in the late 1950s and shared the 1981 Nobel Prize in physiology with Roger Sperry. Hubel and Wiesel initially used the single cell recording technique to determine the characteristics of cells in the visual cortex. Their findings were particularly exciting to psychologists because they suggested a way in which the visual system could analyze the parts of a pattern.

Hubel and Wiesel (1965, 1979) isolated two kinds of neurons, each with response patterns different from the center-surround patterns found at earlier stages of visual processing. Their names are impressively straightforward: simple and complex cortical cells.

1. *Simple cells* are found in layer IVb of the primary visual cortex, and they receive input from layer IVc neurons directly underneath. Neurons in the earlier stages of visual processing have roughly circular receptive fields, but the simple cells respond most vigorously to lines and to edges (Wandell, 1995). As is often the case in research, this finding was made serendipitously. Hubel and Wiesel were investigating a cell in the striate cortex by presenting all sorts of stimuli that had been found to elicit responses from optic nerve cells in the cat. The striate cortex cell remained unresponsive until Hubel and Wiesel inserted a new glass slide into their stimulus-presentation device, and the inadvertently cast shadow of the slide caused the cell to fire (Schiller, 1986). Hubel and Wiesel quickly switched to presenting lines to the cat's visual field and found that cells in layer IVb were extremely responsive to these stimuli.

These cells are fairly selective. First of all, the light must fall on a particular part of the visual field. Diffuse illumination of that area will not work, although the cells might give a sputter of activity to small spots of light. Also, the lines must be in the correct orientation for the cells to respond *enthusiastically*. The most effective line orientation depends upon which cell you are examining. Furthermore, these cells are so picky that a change of about 15° may cause them to stop responding. For example, a cell that would respond

optimally to the small (hour) hand of a clock that reads 12:00 would stop responding if that hand advanced a mere 15° to its position at 12:30!

Figure 3.19a illustrates the electrical activity that might be generated if this cell were to respond to several different orientations of a line. Notice that the cell produces only a low level of spontaneous firing if the line is horizontal. Somewhat more firing is found if the line is close to vertical. But a maximum firing rate occurs only when the line is perfectly vertical. These firing rates can be used to construct a graph illustrating the relationship between the angular orientation of the line and the cell's response rate; this graph is known as an *orientation tuning curve*, and it is illustrated in Figure 3.19b. Similar tuning curves can be constructed for other cells, which might be optimally responsive to other orientations such as diagonal or horizontal lines.

2. *Complex cells* are usually found in layers II, III, V, and VI of the cortex (but not in layer IV, where simple cells are found). Complex cells respond best to moving stimuli (Lennie, 1980). We saw that simple cells respond best to lines registered in a specific portion of the retina. In contrast, complex cells respond to a larger receptive field. Some complex cells respond with particularly vigorous bursts of electrical activity when a line moves in a particular direction, for example, when a vertical line moves to the left (but not to the right). Other complex cells respond to movement in both directions.

Some simple cortical cells and some complex cortical cells are referred to as end-stopped cells. *End-stopped cells* will respond most vigorously if the stimulus ends within the cell's receptive field (Beatty, 1995). Because a line or edge that extends beyond the receptive field of an end-stopped cell would produce less firing, these cells are particularly useful for detecting corners and other boundaries.

A consistent trend emerges in moving toward higher levels in the visual processing system; cells become more selective. Photoreceptors respond when the light reaches them. Gan-

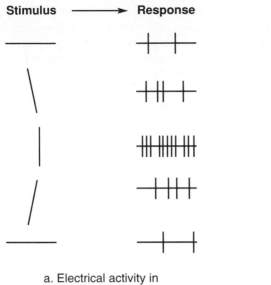

Stimulus ⟶ Response

a. Electrical activity in
   response to lines

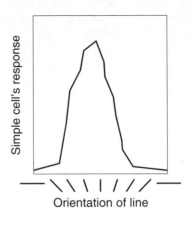

b. An orientation
   tuning curve

FIGURE 3.19 A simple cell's response to lines of different orientations. These cells are very selective—notice that maximum firing occurs when the stimulus is vertical and activity drops significantly when the stimulus is rotated just a few degrees (a). This selectivity is apparent in the orientation tuning curve shown in part b. The peak response of the simple cell occurs when the line is oriented vertically.

glion cells and LGN cells respond more strongly if stimulation of the center of the receptive field contrasts with the surrounding area. Simple cells require lines, and complex cells require moving lines. End-stopped cells require that the lines end within their receptive fields.

Hubel and Wiesel and their coauthors, as well as other research groups, have conducted more recent research that provides additional details about the structure of the visual cortex. In particular, their explorations have revealed that the primary visual cortex is arranged in a series of columns.

Cortical Architecture

When Hubel and Wiesel were exploring the properties of individual cells, they became intrigued with a feature that they refer to as "architecture" (Hubel, 1982). When one lowers a microelectrode through layers of the cortex, all

the cells have the highest response rate to a line of one orientation. This vertical series of cells responding to stimuli with a particular orientation is referred to as a ***column*** (Mountcastle, 1978). Figure 3.20 illustrates how a microelectrode inserted perpendicular to the surface of the cortex might pass through a large number of cells, all of which produced the highest response rate when a line was presented in the visual field at a 45° angle. Hubel and Wiesel inserted the microelectrode through the 2-mm thickness of one point in the primary visual cortex, tested the animal, and recorded the orientation the cells in that column preferred. Then they moved on to a new location a fraction of a millimeter away and tested again.

Hubel and Wiesel discovered that by moving the microelectrode as little as 0.05 mm—literally a hairbreadth—from its previous location, they found a column of cells that no longer re-

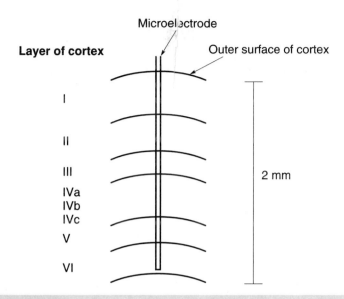

FIGURE 3.20 Research has shown that if a microelectrode is inserted through the visual cortex, all the cells through which it passes respond maximally to a line of one particular orientation. This vertical series of cells is called a column.

sponded so enthusiastically to a line of the previously tested orientation. Instead, the preferred orientation had shifted to a line that had rotated by about 10°. For example, if cells in the previously tested column had produced the highest response rate to a line at a 45° angle, the cells in the column 0.05 mm away would be likely to produce the highest response rate to a line at a 55° angle.

Hubel and Wiesel repeatedly moved the microelectrode a distance of 1 mm along the cortex. They encountered a series of columns in which the preferred stimulus had changed from a perfectly horizontal line to a vertical line and completed the cycle by returning to a perfectly horizontal line. Figure 3.21 illustrates these results schematically. (Because layer IVc has cells with center/surround preferences rather than orientation preferences, a blank space is found at that layer.) Because 18 to 20 adjacent columns are re-

quired to complete a full cycle of stimulus-orientation preferences, Hubel and Wiesel called this sequence of columns a *hypercolumn.*

Notice that Figure 3.21 is a three-dimensional diagram. The third dimension is labeled "right-eye ocular dominance" and "left-eye ocular dominance." Cells in the cortex receive information from both eyes, but they usually have a higher response rate to one eye, a tendency called *ocular dominance.* The clump of cells nearer to the viewer would be more responsive to stimuli from the left eye. The next clump of cells would be more responsive to stimuli from the right eye.

It might be tempting to believe that all the columns are similar as long as they share a given preference for stimulus orientation and a given ocular dominance. Within each set, however, each column corresponds to a particular location in the visual field. Thus, within every tiny patch in Area 17 of your visual cortex—a patch no bigger

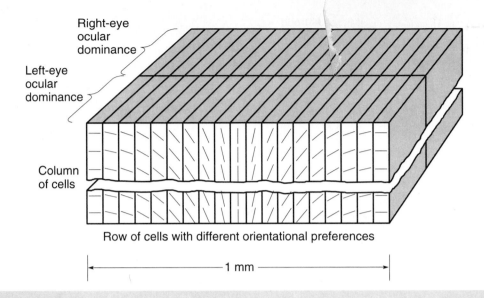

Right-eye ocular dominance

Left-eye ocular dominance

Column of cells

Row of cells with different orientational preferences

|← 1 mm →|

FIGURE 3.21 Schematic diagram of a hypercolumn. Note that the hypercolumn includes cells from all layers of the cortex (I through VI), cells with all orientation preferences, and cells with both right- and left-eye ocular dominance. The break in the middle of the figure indicates layer IVc, where the cells are not sensitive to orientation. Interspersed within the hypercolumns are blobs, which convey information about color. As indicated in the figure, any vertical column contains cells sensitive to only one orientation. However, as the microelectrode is inserted at different horizontal locations, the orientation of the receptive field changes in a systematic fashion.

than 1 mm² and 2 mm deep—your visual system encodes a variety of stimulus-orientation preferences, two kinds of ocular dominance (right-eye and left-eye), and a variety of locations.

Later research in Area 17 uncovered patches of neurons that were *not* sensitive to orientation. These neurons, seen in Figure 3.21, were referred to by the delightfully straightforward name "blobs." (Actually, their full name is "cytochrome oxidase blobs," but "blobs" will suffice.) The **blobs** supplement the spatial orientation information found in the hypercolumns by providing color information (Beatty, 1995). Given the color information in blobs, you should realize that the parvo system provides the input to the blobs (Zeki, 1993).

The blobs within a column are not joined, and the space between blobs is filled with cells called **interblobs.** Interblobs are more like other cells in the column, because they are sensitive to orientation and not to wavelength. The interblobs also receive their input from the parvo pathway.

With the development of new technologies, researchers are now able to study the functioning of blobs and columns in living organisms, using relatively noninvasive techniques. Daniel Ts'o and his colleagues used an optical imaging system to confirm the presence of blobs and columns in the primary visual cortex and beyond (Ts'o et al., 1990). They also were able to confirm the presence of orientation preference and ocular dominance in the primary visual cortex. However, they found no ocular dominance beyond the primary visual cortex. We will now turn our attention to those areas beyond Area 17.

Beyond the Primary Visual Cortex

Early research on cortical processing in vision concentrated on the primary visual cortex (Area 17). Recently, however, important findings have emerged from studies of areas beyond the primary visual cortex. As Figure 3.18 illustrated, other regions at the back of the brain are also concerned with vision. Collectively, these regions are called the ***secondary visual cortex*** (as opposed to the primary visual cortex) or the ***extrastriate cortex*** (where *extra-* means "beyond," as in "extraterrestrial"). These areas were mentioned in the discussion of the superior colliculus because the superior colliculus sends information to the secondary visual cortex, rather than to the primary visual cortex. The secondary visual cortex also re-ceives information from the primary visual cortex, so the information coming into this area has already been processed.

In all, at least 30 different regions of the brain are involved in processing visual information (Cowey, 1994). The additional visual areas generally occupy the secondary visual cortex, as well as the lower region of the cortex in front of the secondary visual cortex (see Figure 3.18). In this section of the chapter, we will briefly explore the contributions of some of these areas that extend beyond Area 17.

AREAS V2 THROUGH V5

As we have noted, the primary visual cortex is organized into six layers noted by the Roman numerals I through VI. The primary visual cortex is

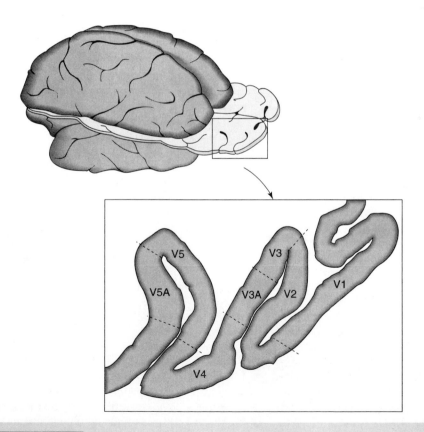

FIGURE 3.22 Area VI (primary visual cortex) and Areas V2–V5 (secondary visual cortex). (From Zeki, 1993)

also called V1. (Thus, area V1 contains layer VI.) As you can see in Figure 3.22, several visual areas are located in front of the primary visual cortex. Each of these areas plays an important role in visual processing. Area V1 sends a great deal of its output to V2. Thus, you shouldn't be surprised to learn that the separation of function found in V1 is also found in V2 (Zeki, 1993). For instance, the blobs of V1 connect with thin stripe regions in V2. The interblobs of V1 connect with interstripes in V2. The thin stripe and interstripe cells of V2 then connect with V4.

Determining the role of V4 is difficult. Because of the input it receives from the blobs, you should expect that V4 is important for color perception. Some portion of V4 might well be the center for color perception, but V4 must play other roles in visual perception as well (Schiller, 1994, Schiller & Lee, 1991; Zeki, 1993). For example, the interblob input to V4, as well as input from other cortical areas, suggests that some form and motion perception take place in V4. In fact, recent research suggests that many neurons in V4 have complex orientation-sensitive receptive fields (Gallant et al., 1993). We will have more to say about the role of V4 in Chapter 7.

The orientation-sensitive cells of V1 connect to thick stripe regions in V2 and then continue to V3 and V3a. As you can see in Figure 3.22, V3 and V3a are located in the fold of the cortex, so they are not actually visible when looking at the brain. These areas seem to be important for form perception. Information is passed from V3 and V3a indirectly to V4 and directly to V5.

Area V5, also called MT, seems to be crucial for motion perception (Albright, 1992; Movshon & Newsome, 1992; Schiller, 1994; Zeki, 1993). V5 receives its input from V1, V2, and V3, as well as other areas of the visual cortex. Because of its importance for motion perception, we will have more to say about this area in Chapter 8.

We can trace the parvo and magno pathways through V1 and V2. However, the extensive communication between areas found in the extrastriate cortex argues that the separation between the two pathways begins to break down (Merigan & Maunsell, 1993; Van Essen et al., 1992). Although the parvo and magno pathways may no longer be distinguishable, the concept of specialization of function in the cortex remains. Thus, V4 may contain the center for color vision and V5 may be the center for motion perception. In addition, a stream of information that codes for spatial location goes from the primary visual cortex through V5 to the parietal lobe (Horwitz et al., 1992). A second stream that codes information about the shape of objects goes from the primary visual cortex through V4 to the inferior temporal cortex (Merigan & Maunsell, 1993). We will now turn our attention to this area.

THE INFERIOR TEMPORAL CORTEX

The *inferior temporal cortex (IT)* is located on the lower part of the side of the cortex and is important for object perception (Horwitz et al., 1992; Miyashita, 1993). As seen in Figure 3.18, the temporal lobe occupies the lower part of the brain in front of the occipital lobe.

Thompson (1985) provides a particularly vivid account of research in this area of the cortex. Charles Gross and his colleagues at Harvard University were using the single cell recording technique to map the receptive field of a cell in the IT. They presented the usual visual stimuli, including spots of light, bars, and other stimuli, to one monkey. The neurons responded weakly to these stimuli, but they did not provide any enthusiastic bursts of electrical activity. The researchers had been studying a particular cell for an extended time, but the response had been so minimal that they decided to move on to another cell.

One whimsical experimenter bade that cell a symbolic farewell by waving good-bye. The cell immediately began to respond rapidly to the moving hand. Serendipity had struck once again! As you can imagine, the researchers did *not* proceed to the next cell, but instead began cutting out hand-shaped stimuli and waving them in front of the monkey's eyes. Their inquiry demonstrated that the stimulus that produced the most vigorous response from the cell was an upright hand shaped like a monkey's paw.

Such specificity of response led researchers to speculate jokingly about a "grandmother cell." A grandmother cell would be one that responds most rapidly to a *very* specific stimulus—as specific as your grandmother's face (Cowey, 1994).

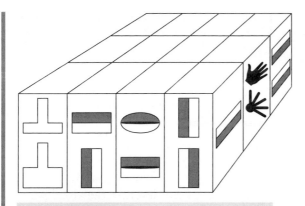

FIGURE 3.23 Columnar organization found in inferior temporal cortex. Note the features to which cells in the columns are sensitive. (From Stryker, 1992)

Although researchers have not identified cells with such specificity, the cells in IT do have very specific receptive fields. In fact, some of the cells are most responsive to facial stimuli (Desimone, 1991; Perrett & Mistlin, 1990; Young & Yamane, 1992, 1993).

The IT contains neurons sensitive to particular shapes that may well form the basis of complex object perception (Brody, 1993; Fujita et al., 1992; Stryker, 1992). As we will discuss in greater detail in Chapter 5, many theories of object perception hypothesize that we piece together unique features or components of complex objects in the process of recognizing them. Researchers were able to identify the nature of the receptive fields of these IT cells by first presenting a wide array of toy animals, vegetables, and other objects. Ultimately, the researchers were able to identify the basic features that stimulated a particular IT cell. Not only are neurons sensitive to such basic features found in the IT, but they are also arranged in a columnar fashion, as seen in Figure 3.23 (Fujita et al., 1992).

The pathway from the primary visual cortex to the IT seems vital for object perception. As you might expect, disruption of the information in this pathway leads to problems in the perception of objects. In the final part of this section, we will turn our attention to problems in object perception that emerge as a result of damage to parts of this pathway.

DISORDERS OF OBJECT AND FACE PERCEPTION

Damage to the temporal lobe often results in visual agnosia. In **visual agnosia** a person with intact basic visual abilities cannot identify a picture of an object. For example, when asked to draw pictures of objects from memory, patients with agnosia could do so (see Figure 3.24). Thus, they *know* what a pencil, an umbrella, or a pair of glasses looks like. People with agnosia can copy, match, and draw objects after very brief presentations, which shows that they can see clearly. However, people with agnosia are typically incapable of identifying pictures of such objects—even ones they have just drawn (Farah, 1990; Humphreys et al., 1994; Jankowiak et al., 1992; Riddoch & Humphreys, 1992).

An even more startling disorder is prosopagnosia. People with **prosopagnosia** are incapable of identifying faces (Campbell, 1992a; Damasio

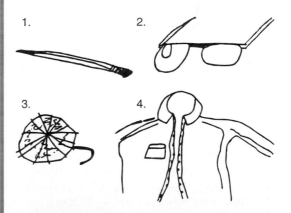

FIGURE 3.24 Drawings of a pencil, a pair of glasses, an umbrella, and a shirt made by a person with agnosia. After drawing these objects from memory, the person would be unable to identify the objects depicted. (From Jankowiak et al., 1992)

et al., 1990; Farah, 1994b; McNeil & Warrington, 1991). Thus, a man with prosopagnosia could look at the very familiar face of his wife and not recognize her. In fact, he could not identify his own face. An early report of prosopagnosia concerned a gentleman in a club who was annoyed by another man who kept staring at him. Such rude behavior was actually produced by a mirror—the gentleman was seeing his own reflection!

Faces are full of details, making them extremely complex objects. One possible interpretation of prosopagnosia *is* that the disorder is not specific to faces but is simply agnosia for very complex objects. Given what you know about the specificity of cells in the temporal cortex, you can imagine that damage to those areas might lead to a face-specific disorder. However, faces are full of details, making them extremely complex objects. One possible interpretation of prosopagnosia is that the disorder is not specific to faces but is simply agnosia for very complex objects.

Recent evidence strongly supports the notion that prosopagnosia is specific to faces. For instance, consistent with the Gestalt approach mentioned in Chapter 1, faces appear to be processed as a whole, rather than as an assemblage of parts. People with prosopagnosia can see all the parts of a face clearly. However, they appear to be unable to integrate the parts into a whole (Farah, 1994b; Tanaka & Farah, 1993). Other evidence comes from a person with prosopagnosia who is a sheep farmer. He is capable of recognizing and naming his sheep by seeing their faces, but he cannot recognize human faces (McNeil & Warrington, 1993).

Other areas of the brain are also involved in visual perception. For instance, the IT is connected to the limbic system, which is important for emotion. Although we would not ordinarily think of the limbic system as having a function in face perception, recent evidence illustrates the importance of this linkage. For example, one woman suffered damage to a structure in her limbic system (the amygdala), which rendered her incapable of feeling fear (Allman & Brothers, 1994). Not only could she not feel fear, but in addition she could not perceive fear on the faces of others! Clearly, visual perception is a complex process that involves a wide array of brain structures. ◆

Concluding Remarks about the Visual System

The majority of this chapter has emphasized a bottom-up, or data-driven, approach to perception. Data gathered from the receptors are passed up to higher levels in the visual processing system. Consistent with Theme 3 of this book—that human sensory systems perform well in gathering information—the chapter has emphasized that our visual systems are impressively designed to pass information through increasingly sophisticated kinds of processing.

We have not yet mentioned Theme 4—that prior knowledge and expectations help shape our perceptions. However, these learning experiences do appear to be relevant in the higher areas of visual processing. Thus, a recent review article on the inferior temporal cortex (IT) is subtitled "Where visual perception meets memory" (Miyashita, 1993). Throughout this text, we will highlight the importance of top-down, or conceptually driven, processes. Our discussion of the role of the higher levels of visual processing, such as IT, illustrates the origins of such top-down processes.

In this chapter, we have focused on the specialization of function within the visual system. Our discussion should lead you to pose an important question. If our visual system is made up of so many independently functioning areas, how do we arrive at the unitary, integrated perception of the world that we all share? We don't have an answer to this question, though the answer may lie in the common firing rhythm of neurons in different locations of the cortex (Blakeslee, 1992b; Jagadeesh et al., 1992; McClurkin et al., 1991). The ultimate answer to the question will be important not only for visual perception but also for the very nature of consciousness (Wandell, 1995).

SECTION SUMMARY

Pathways from the Retina to the Visual Cortex

1. The visual system has two kinds of crossovers: (1) visual material is reversed by the lens onto the retina, and (2) at the optic chiasm, half of the fibers in each optic nerve cross over. As a result of these crossovers, everything from the left side of the visual field ends up on the right-hand side of the head, and everything from the right side of the visual field ends up on the left-hand side of the head.

2. The optic tract, as the optic nerve beyond the optic chiasm is called, travels to the superior colliculus, which is important in the detection of movement, and to the lateral geniculate nucleus.

3. The lateral geniculate nucleus is organized into six layers that keep separate the information from the two eyes; cells in the LGN function like ganglion cells.

4. The visual cortex, which is responsible for higher levels of visual processing, is divided into the primary visual cortex (also called Area 17, striate cortex, and V1) and the secondary visual cortex (also called the extrastriate cortex).

5. Neuronal messages from the lateral geniculate nucleus arrive in layer IVc of Area 17, which has a retinotopic arrangement.

6. Outside of layer IVc, the primary visual cortex has two basic kinds of neurons: simple cortical cells (responding to lines and edges) and complex cortical cells (responding to movement). Some of both types of cells are end-stopped, which means that they prefer lines that end within their receptive fields.

7. Neurons in Area 17 are arranged in columns. In each column, neurons have the highest response rate to a line of one particular orientation. Cells in an adjacent column have the highest response rate to a line whose orientation has shifted by about 10°.

8. A hypercolumn is a series of columns that covers a full cycle of stimulus-orientation preferences. Cells in the cortex are arranged according to ocular dominance and location, as well as to their preferences with repect to stimulus orientation.

9. Located within a hypercolumn are regions of cells that are not orientation sensitive. These regions are called blobs, and they are important for color perception. Between blobs is a region of neurons called interblob cells.

10. The secondary visual cortex receives information from the primary visual cortex. Within the secondary visual cortex are areas that are important for color (V4) and motion (V5) perception.

11. A pathway that is important for spatial location runs from the primary visual cortex through the secondary visual cortex to the parietal lobe. A pathway that is important for object recognition runs from the primary visual cortex through the secondary visual cortex to the temporal lobe.

12. People with agnosia have basic visual abilities, but cannot recognize objects. Thus, they can see all the detail in a picture and draw a clear picture of the object they are looking at, but cannot recognize the object depicted in their own drawing. People with prosopagnosia have a specific agnosia for faces.

REVIEW QUESTIONS

1. The beginning of the chapter discussed the visual stimulus. List the three pairs of attributes that are concerned with light, specifying which member of the pair concerns the physical stimulus and which concerns the psychological reaction. What psychological reaction do we have to (a) short wavelengths, (b) long wavelengths, (c) low-amplitude wavelengths, and (d) high-amplitude wavelengths?

2. Discuss the portion of the electromagnetic radiation spectrum that humans can see. Discuss differences among species with respect to (a) the part of the spectrum to which they are sensitive; (b) the nature of the photoreceptors—cones and rods; (c) the crossover pattern at the optic chiasm; and (d) the superior colliculus.

3. Review the location and the function of the following: sclera, iris, pupil, cornea, and lens. Describe how light is focused on the retina.

4. What is the fovea, and where is it? How is the distribution of cones and rods relevant to a discussion of the fovea? Compare acuity in the fovea and nonfovea regions of the retina. Then compare sensitivity in these two regions, noting how the issue of convergence is relevant.

5. Rods and cones differ in a number of ways. List as many differences as you can. Compare the process of dark and light adaptation for cones and rods. Try to think of practical applications of both processes (devising brightness and color spectrum of lights along highways, preserving dark adaptation for drivers, etc.).

6. Ganglion cells in the retina were discussed in some detail. Can you describe the differences between midget and parasol ganglion cells? Ganglion cells are similar in their receptive fields. How do their receptive fields differ from cells later in the visual pathway?

7. The arrangement of the neurons in the lateral geniculate nucleus and in layer IVc of the visual cortex were described as retinotopic. Discuss this term in relation to those two areas.

8. What is the function of neurons in the remaining layers of Area 17, above and below layer IVc? How could such simple and complex cortical cells arise from the input found in layer IVc? How do end-stopped cells differ? How do the blobs differ?

9. Damage to particular areas of the visual pathway is often instructive about the function of a particular area. Try to imagine the impact of damage to the following areas: the parvo pathway, the magno pathway, both the parvo *and* magno pathways, the ganglion cells going to the superior colliculus, V1, V4, V5, the pathway from V1 to the parietal lobe, or the pathway from V1 to IT. (See Chapters 7 and 8 for a discussion of damage to V4 and V5, respectively.)

10. Try to imagine and then describe the perceptual experience of a person with agnosia or prosopagnosia. Why would such people be capable of seeing detail? What does agnosia or prosopagnosia tell us about the organization of our visual systems?

NEW TERMS

electromagnetic radiation (48)
wavelength (49)
nanometer (49)
light (49)
hue (49)
purity (49)
amplitude (49)
transduction (50)
sclera (50)
cornea (50)
astigmatism (51)
aqueous humor (51)
anterior chamber (51)
glaucoma (51)

tonometry (51)
iris (52)
albinos (52)
pupil (52)
constrict (52)
dilate (52)
f-stop (53)
aperture (53)
depth of field (53)
ophthalmologists (53)
ophthalmoscope (53)
lens (53)
accommodation (53)
ciliary muscle (53)

zonules (53)
presbyopia (53)
cataract (54)
intraocular lens (54)
retina (54)
photoreceptors (54)
neurons (54)
fovea (54)
optic disc (55)
optic nerve (55)
blind spot (55)
vitreous humor (55)
floaters (55)
choroid (56)

RECOMMENDED READINGS

Beatty, J. (1995). *Principles of behavioral neuroscience.* Dubuque, IA: Brown & Benchmark. Intended as an introduction to the field, this recent text is easy to read and contains beautiful graphics. One chapter is devoted to vision and another chapter is devoted to other senses.

Pinel, J. P. J. (1993). *Biopsychology* (2nd ed.). Boston: Allyn & Bacon. This text is well written and contains excellent illustrations. The chapters on the visual system and the mechanisms of perception are particularly relevant.

Vaughn, D., Asbury, T., & Riordan-Eva, P. (Eds.) (1992). *General ophthalmology* (13th ed.). Norwalk, CT: Appleton & Lange. Most ophthalmology textbooks require an extensive medical background. In contrast, this book is clearly written and well organized. Many different authors contributed the 24 chapters in the text, which has a decidedly clinical orientation. Thus, for example, the chapter on the lens will tell you more about what can go wrong with the lens than it will tell you about how the lens works.

Wandell, B. A. (1995). *Foundations of vision.* Sunderland, MA: Sinauer. Wandell's recent textbook provides much greater detail on the topics in this and later chapters. If you are interested in reading material beyond that found in most introductory-level perception texts, Wandell's text is a fine resource.

Zeki, S. (1993). *A vision of the brain.* Oxford: Blackwell. This book does for perception what George Johnson's wonderful *Palaces of Memory* does for memory, making the underlying physiology interesting to a layperson. In spite of the fact that Zeki's book contains much more technical detail than Johnson's book, it is extraordinarily readable and interesting. Although the focus is on processing of color information, this book is actually a good introduction to visual neurophysiology, presenting the history (and important people) of neurophysiology while also exploring and unraveling profound mysteries.

CHAPTER

4

Basic Visual Functions

In Chapter 3 we provided a basic introduction to the anatomy and physiology of visual perception. Although you might have found the discussion to be extremely detailed, trust us when we tell you that we covered only the essential principles. Surely, you must have come away with the sense that our visual system is extremely complex. In this chapter we begin to address why this complexity is necessary, as we explore the ways in which our visual system attempts to interpret the simplest visual stimuli.

What do we need to see the world around us? Obviously, we need visual stimulation (energy from a small segment of the electromagnetic spectrum) brought into focus on our receptors (retinas) by our cornea/lens system. So far, the process may seem much like that in a camera, which also uses a complicated set of lenses to bring light into focus on film. Soon, however, we will provide many examples that illustrate the sharp differences between the human visual system and a camera.

In this chapter, we first highlight some very basic visual processes that indicate major differences between our visual system and even the most sophisticated cameras. Next, we will examine the way we perceive the lightness of surfaces around us and the processes by which we see clearly. Finally, we will briefly survey the types of eye movements that keep objects in clear focus.

PREREQUISITES FOR NORMAL VISION

You should recognize that we are discussing normal vision and not the visual experience that one might have in dreams or hallucinations. As we discussed in Chapter 3, normal vision requires sufficient light energy from the range of electromagnetic radiation to which a person's eyes are sensitive. However, what we mean by "sufficient" is not constant—more light energy is necessary when a person's eyes are light adapted.

Humans also need an intact system for processing the energy, and we have discussed disruptions of the system that have an important impact on the ability to process stimuli. Basically, the cornea and lens bring the light energy into focus on the retina, which transduces the light energy into neural energy. The neural impulses are then further processed as they move through the visual pathway. As you will now see, visual perception depends on several other factors that we have not yet addressed.

We will first examine some prerequisites for vision beyond light energy and a receptor system—specifically, the need for edges and change. Next, consistent with Theme 4 of this text (see page 12), we will show that visual perception is an extremely active process involving central processes. At the end of this section, we will emphasize the importance of central processes and experience for visual perception.

Edges Are Important

An *edge*, or *contour*, may be thought of as a location where a sudden change in color, brightness, or lightness occurs. The distinction between these last two characteristics, brightness and lightness, may not be that obvious, but it is very important (Arend & Spehar, 1993; Gilchrist, 1994a; Schirillo et al., 1990; Sewall & Wooten, 1991). *Brightness* refers to the perceived intensity of light energy. For instance, a light source (such as a light bulb or the sun) might be bright or dim, but would not be black, white, or gray. *Lightness* refers to the perceived *achromatic* (noncolored) reflectance of the surface—whites, blacks, and shades of gray. Surfaces appear to have lightness as an inherent property, depending on the proportion of light they reflect. We will discuss lightness perception later in this chapter, and color perception in Chapter 7.

To illustrate edges, draw a line with a colored marker on a white sheet of paper. You will see an edge on one side of the mark as you go from white to color, and then another edge as you go from color back to white. If you look around for a moment, you will notice the many edges around you.

What would happen if you were to stare at a scene without edges, such as a uniform red field?

a. Light presented only at Point 1

Light at Point 1

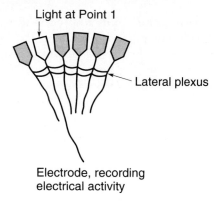

Lateral plexus

Electrode, recording
electrical activity

Electrical activity
from cell at Point 1

b. Light presented at Point 1 and Point 2

Light at Point 1   Light at Point 2

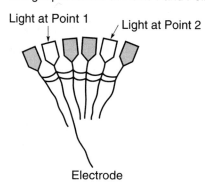

Electrode

Electrical activity
from cell at Point 1

c. Light presented at Point 1 and
   intense light presented at Point 2

Light at Point 1   Intense light at Point 2

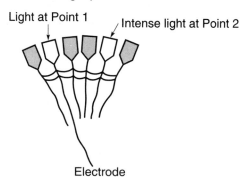

Electrode

Electrical activity
from cell at Point 1

FIGURE 4.1 Illustration of a lateral inhibition study using the compound eye of the horsehoe crab (Limulus). In part a, the light presented to the photoreceptor at Point 1 causes an increase in electrical activity of that photoreceptor. In part b, even though the photoreceptor at Point 1 is receiving the same stimulation, it fires less because of the inhibition sent over the lateral plexus from Point 2, where another light is stimulating that photoreceptor. By increasing the intensity of the light at Point 2, the firing from the photoreceptor at Point 1 can be further inhibited (c).

Initially, you would see a uniform red field. After 10–15 minutes, however, your experience would have changed radically, and you would be seeing a uniform gray field! Regardless of the color of the field, after a period of time you would perceive the same uniform gray field.

How can you demonstrate this to yourself? As Coren and his coauthors (1994) have suggested, you can create a uniform white field by placing white plastic spoons in front of your eyes. You will look fairly ridiculous, so you might want to do this in private—a classroom demonstration with everyone in class equipped with plastic spoons is a sight to behold! To make the field colored, simply tape colored cellophane to the back of the spoons, or color them with a marker, being sure not to create any visible lines or marks on the spoons. You might as well sit down, and then all you have to do is look toward a source of light and wait. After about 10 minutes, regardless of the color of light striking your retina, you will experience a uniform dark gray field—much like what you would experience with your eyes closed on a very dark night. In fact, your visual experience is similar to having your eyes closed. People who have been trapped outdoors in a severe snowstorm also report a similar experience, which, as you might imagine, is quite disorienting.

What you have created is a low-budget *Ganzfeld* (German for "whole field"), a visual field with no edges. More important, you have demonstrated a central visual principle: Without edges we could not see! Even though light energy is falling on a fully functional receptor system, a person would see nothing unless the stimulus has edges (Gur, 1991).

What happens if you introduce an edge into the Ganzfeld? You can have a friend place a piece of paper in front of your eyes so that a shadow falls over one of the spoons, or raise your foot until it comes between your light source and your spoons. You will immediately see the field in its original color, but now with an edge falling across it. As soon as you provide the visual system with a single edge, the uniform gray field disappears. In our everyday experience, edges are everywhere, which is why we rarely have an experience similar to the Ganzfeld.

Lateral Inhibition

Given the importance of edges, you should not be at all surprised to learn that our visual system is equipped to highlight edges. This process is called *lateral inhibition*, where lateral means "sideways": Whenever a light reaches one point on the retina, the neural activity for nearby points is inhibited. The more intense the light, the greater the inhibition.

Lateral inhibition was studied initially in the compound eye of Limulus, the horseshoe crab (Hartline et al., 1956). In the Limulus, each photoreceptor registers light independently and is attached to its own "private" neural cell. (In contrast, recall from Figure 3.8 that the human retina is arranged so that several photoreceptors "share" each neuron.) Each photoreceptor in the Limulus's eye is relatively large. Consequently, researchers can easily stimulate a single photoreceptor without scattering the light to adjacent photoreceptors. Researchers can also select the neural cell corresponding to that photoreceptor, and they can record the electrical activity from that neural cell.

Figure 4.1 illustrates a prototypical study of lateral inhibition. Hartline and his colleagues presented light to a photoreceptor at Point 1. The recording of the electrical activity at the corresponding neural cell is illustrated in Figure 4.1a. As you can see, the electrical activity is strong. Then these researchers presented simultaneous lights to photoreceptors at Points 1 and 2, as illustrated in Figure 4.1b. Notice that the electrical activity from the neural cell corresponding to Point 1 shows a clear *decrease*. When the intensity of the light at Point 2 was increased, the electrical activity from the critical neural cell decreased even further, as illustrated in Figure 4.1c.

Thus, the electrical activity of a Limulus photoreceptor depends not only on that photoreceptor's level of stimulation but also on the level of stimulation of nearby photoreceptors. The more these neighboring photoreceptors are

a. Light intensity

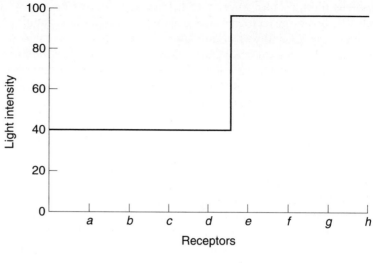

b. Original electrical activity

40	40	40	40	100	100	100	100

c. Inhibition from left-hand neighbor

	−4	−4	−4	−4	−10	−10	

Inhibition from right-hand neighbor

	−4	−4	−10	−10	−10	−10	

d. Total output (original activity *minus* inhibition)

	32	32	26	86	80	80	

e. Perceived brightness

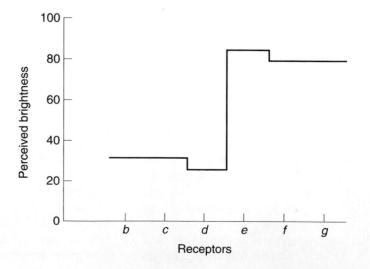

stimulated, the lower the electrical activity of the neural cell. In other words, lateral inhibition is present. The mechanism for lateral inhibition in the Limulus is the lateral plexus, a primitive net that connects the photoreceptors and allows them to influence each other's electrical activity.

The human retina is much more complex than the visual system of the Limulus. However, it has a system of connections among photoreceptors that operates in a somewhat similar fashion. Turn back to Figure 3.8 and examine the horizontal cells, which connect the photoreceptors. At a somewhat more advanced stage of visual processing, you can see that the amacrine cells connect the ganglion cells with one another and also connect bipolar cells with one another. Thus, the cells in the human retina can communicate and potentially inhibit each other's electrical activity, demonstrating lateral inhibition.

Lateral inhibition might seem like an inefficient process. After all, what purpose could be served by inhibiting the firing of adjacent receptors? Actually, lateral inhibition can serve to enhance our perception of edges, and we have already discussed the importance of edges. Figure 4.2 illustrates how lateral inhibition might serve to highlight edges.

As seen in Figure 4.2a, the physical stimulus is an edge produced by a change from lower- to higher-intensity light. Let's say that the light source produces 40 units of electrical activity on the dark side and 100 units of electrical activity on the light side (Figure 4.2b). Keep in mind that we are discussing the physical stimulus, so these are the sorts of measurements you might make with an instrument such as a photometer.

Suppose that the horizontal cells transmit inhibition from each receptor to its neighbor and that this inhibition equals 10% of the "sender's" electrical activity. Thus, a receptor that produces 40 units of electrical activity transmits 4 units of inhibition to each of its neighbors, and a receptor that produces 100 units of electrical activity transmits 10 units of inhibition to each of its neighbors. Figure 4.2c shows how much inhibition each receptor receives from each of its two neighbors. (We will not discuss receptors *a* and *h* because, for simplicity, the activity of their outside neighbors is not illustrated.) The numbers in Figure 4.2d show the total output after subtracting the inhibition. A graph of the total output appears in Figure 4.2e.

Thus, our visual system improves on the information arriving at the retina. Objects in our world are typically defined by reasonably clear boundaries or edges. Consistent with Theme 2 of the book, the visual stimulus is rich with information. However, our visual system takes those reasonably clear boundaries and exaggerates them so that the dark side is even darker and the bright side even brighter. Some of this enhancement occurs at the retinal level due to lateral inhibition. Objects are therefore more conspicuous because their edges are intensified. Consistent with Theme 3 of the book, the perceptual systems are extremely well designed to provide optimal perceptual experiences.

Lateral Inhibition and Mach Bands

Lateral inhibition can explain a perceptual phenomenon known as Mach bands, after Ernst

FIGURE 4.2 Schematic diagram of the way in which lateral inhibition can serve to highlight edges. The change in light intensity is abrupt between receptors *d* and *e* (a), resulting in differences in firing rates from 40 (for receptors *a* through *d*) to 100 (for receptors *e* through *h*), shown in part b. Because of the inhibitory lateral connections between receptors, firing in neighboring receptors is reduced by 10% of the original electrical activity (c). (The firing rates and inhibitory percentage are arbitrarily chosen numbers to illustrate the point.) The net effect of the lateral inhibition is illustrated numerically (d) and graphically (e). Without lateral inhibition, the change in electrical activity would be a step function just like that seen for the physical stimulus. With lateral inhibition, the change in electrical activity is more abrupt at the transition point (between *d* and *e*) than between other points away from the transition point.

Demonstration 4.1

Mach Bands

a. Find a light bulb in a lamp where the shade can be removed. Turn on the lamp, turn off all the other lights in the room, and close the curtains. Move the lamp so that it is about 1 foot from the wall. Use one hand to shade your eyes from the glare of the lamp, and use the other hand to hold up your closed textbook about 3 inches away from the wall—between the wall and the lamp. Observe the area surrounding the book's shadow. Notice how the edge of the shadow looks particularly dark and how the edge of the well-lit part of the wall nearest the shadow looks particularly light. Although we seldom notice them, Mach bands are actually common in everyday life.

b. Now look at the figure below, focusing on the region just to the right of the arrow. Find another shade of gray in a different stripe that seems to match that shade as closely as possible.

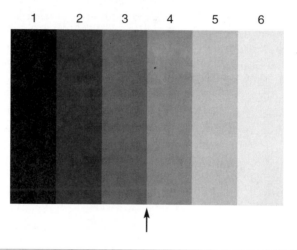

Mach, an Austrian physicist and philosopher who described them in 1865. In a **Mach band,** people perceive bright and dark bands within a single stripe, even when the physical distribution of light does not vary (Ratliff, 1984). You can illustrate Mach bands for yourself in Demonstration 4.1.

The five interior edges of Demonstration 4.1b all seem to be distinct and appear to have a faint lighter border to the right and a faint darker border to the left of each edge. As a result, you might be inclined to match the faint border to the right of the arrow with the gray stripe to the right of the next edge. However, all parts of each

gray stripe are actually uniform throughout. You can prove this to yourself by placing a white piece of paper on each side of a gray stripe, isolating that stripe from the surrounding stripes. All of a sudden, the light border on the left of the stripe and the dark border on the right of the stripe disappear. In fact, each stripe has uniform lightness!

Mach bands are an example of lateral inhibition because the physical contrast that already exists is exaggerated still further. Figure 4.3a represents the actual intensity of the stripes at each position. Each step is flat, representing a uniform intensity at every point within each stripe. Figure 4.3b is a schematic representation

a.

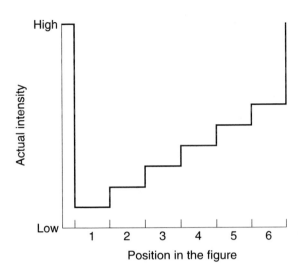

b.

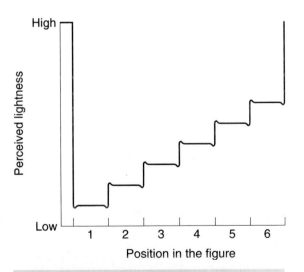

FIGURE 4.3 Graphic illustration of Mach bands. Part a represents the lightness of the stripes seen in Demonstration 4.1b. (Note that there is no physical stimulus corresponding to the observed Mach bands.) Part b represents the perceptual experience of Mach bands seen in Demonstration 4.1b. Compare part b to Figure 4.2e to see how lateral inhibition can produce Mach bands.

of the perceived intensity of the stripes. The perceived reflected intensity, or lightness, depends not only on an area's lightness but also on the lightness of the surrounding areas.

The similarity between Figure 4.2e and Figure 4.3b should be readily apparent. As seen in Figure 4.2e, lateral inhibition serves to sharpen an edge by making the darker side of the edge just a bit darker and the lighter side of the edge just a bit lighter. Lateral inhibition serves not only to enhance edges but also to create Mach bands—the borders to the sides of edges seen in Demonstration 4.1b (and illustrated in Figure 4.3b). Keep in mind the distinction between physical stimuli and perceptions of those stimuli. Mach bands do not exist in the physical world, so a photometer would never detect their presence. Instead, Mach bands are perceptual phenomena, with no real counterpart in the physical world.

Change Is Important

In order to see, we need sufficient light energy falling on our receptors, and at least one edge must be present. Is that all that we need? Actually, another component is crucial to visual perception, and that is *change over time*. Even if all the other conditions are present, we would be unable to see without change. An edge represents a change in lightness or color of the visual stimulus, so the overall importance of change for perceptual experience should be clear to you.

Luckily, the human visual system is constantly producing change by means of ***involuntary eye movements***—spontaneous, unconscious, and unavoidable minor movements and tremors made by our eyes when we look out at the world (Ditchburn, 1981). In one type of movement, the eye drifts a small amount—equivalent to about 10 to 20 cones—and the muscles give a tiny jerk to bring it back. Your eye also makes miniature trembling motions—perhaps equivalent to 1 to 2 cones—but they are continuous. Both of these involuntary eye movements serve to sweep edges back and forth over the photoreceptors, creating constant change. Figure 4.4 illustrates the sorts

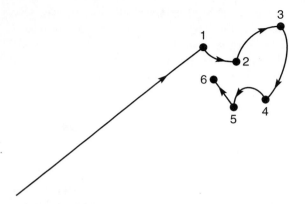

FIGURE 4.4 Example of involuntary eye movements. Numbered dots show the order of eye fixations. The time interval between dots is about 0.2 second. The distance between dots 1 and 2 is about 4 cones. The direction of involuntary eye movements is random.

of motions typically produced. Notice that the direction, curvature, and length of these movements are random. So even if you try to hold your gaze steady on a single point in the visual field, involuntary eye movements guarantee that change will still be present.

As you look out at the world, you are totally unaware of these involuntary eye movements. Apparently, your lack of awareness is partly due to the richness of the typical visual experience. In fact, early astronomers were among the first to notice the effects of involuntary eye movements (Hochberg, 1971). The stars appeared to move around as the astronomers viewed them! A visual field of scattered points of light is sufficiently impoverished that these astronomers perceived their own involuntary eye movements as small tremors in the stars. You can experience your own involuntary eye movements with Demonstration 4.2. We will return to a discussion of the motion perceived in the demonstration when we examine motion perception in Chapter 8.

To illustrate the importance of change for vision, we must eliminate the changes due to involuntary eye movements. But how can we do this? Researchers have developed several means of creating a ***stabilized retinal image,*** where an image always falls on exactly the same retinal location (Riggs et al., 1953). With technological advances, stabilization is now accomplished by means of a computer-controlled display coupled to an eye-movement detector. When eye movement is detected, the computer shifts the image so that it remains at exactly the same location on the retina. With this approach, involuntary eye

---

Demonstration 4.2

Involuntary Eye Movements

Make a very small point of light by covering the lens of a flashlight with a piece of heavy cardboard through which you've punched a very small hole. Take the flashlight into a completely dark room and stand about 10 feet away from the point of light. After you have watched the light for a brief while, it will appear to move around slightly. Without other surrounding stimuli to serve as points of reference (which would all shift simultaneously with involuntary eye movements), the visual system interprets the shifting position of the light on the retina as being caused by movement of the light rather than movement of the eyes. Presumably, the perceived motion is due to unconscious inferential processes; because we are typically unaware of involuntary eye movements, any changes in retinal position are most likely due to changes in the environment.

movements continue, but the image keeps the same position on the retina.

Another (more dangerous) approach is to stop involuntary eye movements by injecting someone with a muscle paralyzer. Stevens underwent such paralysis (1976), except for one arm used to signal the researchers about what he was experiencing (including a signal that meant "Stop the experiment and get me out of here."). The near-total paralysis required the use of an artificial respirator—indicating the extremes to which some researchers will go to collect data. When using this approach, the image is stabilized because the eye no longer moves at all.

Using either method, what happens once the image has been stabilized? Gradually, the borders of the target fade, and then the entire object disappears. Temporary blindness results. Thus, not only does the visual system require edges, but the position of the edges on the retina must change over time. Keep in mind that sufficient light is falling on an intact receptor system—and that edges are present. Nonetheless, without change in the position of the edges, a person experiences the lack of stimulation similar to the Ganzfeld phenomenon.

Higher-Level Processes Are Important

As Richard Gregory (1991) notes, "The classical notion of how we see things is that perception is passive—that the eyes are windows, and in floods reality" (p. 328). If you reflect on your own perceptual experience, you might also think of perception as passive. After all, you seem to look out and effortlessly perceive all the richness of the world that surrounds you. However, researchers emphasize the "organic machinery that hums continuously below the threshold of visual consciousness" (Brown & Thurmond, 1993, p. 200). These unconscious processes are essential to our perceptual experience—perception is a very active process (Churchland et al., 1994). We will have more to say about these processes in later chapters. For now, we will focus our attention on a process referred to as completion or filling in (Ra-

machandran & Gregory, 1991). Keep these completion processes in mind when we discuss phantom limbs in Chapter 12.

As we pointed out in Chapter 3, each retina has a blind spot. Why are people unaware of their blind spots? The primary reason is that we spontaneously tend to complete objects that are interrupted by the blind spot. Such completion processes suggest higher-level processes—consistent with Theme 4 of this text (see page 12).

If you review Demonstration 3.2, you should note that the black dot disappeared for two reasons. First, it was placed at the blind spot, so no photoreceptors were stimulated by the dot. Second, it was surrounded by white space. If you move your eye over the page so that the blind spot is centered over text, you will notice that the blind spot is not at all obvious, and you do not see a hole in the page of print. Your visual system has filled in the area of the blind spot with letters just like those that are registered on your retina surrounding the blind spot!

Recently, researchers have investigated how the visual system "fills in" the blind spot (Brown & Thurmond, 1993; Ramachandran, 1992a, 1992b, 1992c; Sergent, 1988). The complexity of these processes seems to require the operation of higher visual centers. Try Demonstration 4.3 to illustrate the complexity to yourself. Notice that you fill in the blind spot quite differently, depending on how you've interpreted the stimulus.

Another example of completion processes is found in people with a *scotoma* (blindness due to damage to the visual system). Pinel (1993) points out the interesting case of a scotoma experienced by the eminent psychologist Karl Lashley. Lashley (1941) described a situation in which his scotoma, which affected vision near his fovea, obliterated the head of a friend. As Figure 4.5 shows, Lashley did not see a hole in his visual field; instead, the area affected by the scotoma was filled in. In the absence of edges, the visual system is capable of "filling in" an area with very complicated patterns.

Krauskopf (1963) used stabilized retinal images to demonstrate an important completion process involving colored images. First, he pre-

Demonstration 4.3

Filling in the Blind Spot

As you did in Demonstration 3.2, close your left eye and use your right eye to look at the X. Gradually move this page toward your eye and then away from it, keeping the distance in the range of 4 to 16 inches. Note that in the first display, you complete the horizontal black line through the blind spot. However, in the second display, rather than completing the horizontal black line, you complete the vertical "white" line. Your visual system had to first organize the stimulus before it could determine how to complete the area of the blind spot. (Based on Ramachandran, 1992a)

sented a green ring with a red disc inside it. Krauskopf then had people view the display while he stabilized the red inner disc. Because the outer ring was not stabilized, people continued to see the green ring. What happened to the red disc? It was stabilized, so it disappeared (as expected). But did people see a green ring with a hole in it? No, they just saw a solid green disc—in spite of the fact that the photoreceptors for the inner part of the disc were receiving red

light. Keep this result in mind when we discuss color perception (Chapter 7).

Krauskopf's results further highlight the importance of edges. Apparently, the visual system is very efficient, because it looks only at points of change (edges) and then "fills in" the areas between edges with the color found on that side of the edge. Can you see why this process is more efficient than determining the color of every unique point in a scene? If you've ever used the

a. Lashley's scotoma

b. What Lashley saw

FIGURE 4.5   Illustration of the effects of Lashley's scotoma. The left side of the figure shows the position of Lashley's scotoma as he looked at his friend. The right side of the figure shows what Lashley actually saw. Notice that the completion processes filled in the area occupied by the friend's head with the pattern of the wallpaper behind the friend.

fill function in typical computer paint programs, you'll understand why this process is efficient. Because the only edge seen by the people in Krauskopf's study appeared between the green outer disc and the surround, they unconsciously "filled in" the entire disc with green.

Not everyone believes that Krauskopf's results illustrate completion processes (Gilchrist, 1994a). However, all current explanations emphasize the active nature of perception and the role of higher-level processes. Some of these processes are influenced by experience, so we will now examine how experience influences visual perception.

Experience Is Important

Imagine a person who was born blind and had lived that way for 30 years. What would that person see if you could restore her or his sight? A variant of this question was first posed by the 17th-century philosopher William Molyneux. With the advent of modern medicine, we actually have some evidence with which to address the question.

Two case studies of restored vision provide us with important insights into the role of experience. The first person, studied by Richard Gregory and Jean Wallace, is called S. B. (Gregory, 1974b). The second person, studied by Oliver Sacks, is called Virgil (Sacks, 1995). In both cases, the men lost their sight at an early age and then had their vision restored after about 50 years of blindness.

Striking similarities emerge in reviewing these two cases. The first visual experience for both men was probably the face of the person who removed their bandages after the restorative surgery—and both were very confused about what they were seeing. Neither was able to tell that a face was in front of him until the person spoke. Both men had a difficult time perceiving even very simple objects such as blocks or spheres, though they were able to learn to see most of these objects over time. Finally, both men were transformed from competent blind people into tentative and confused sighted people.

These cases provide several kinds of evidence for the importance of experience. First of all, because they had no visual experience over many years, both S. B. and Virgil were unable to see clearly immediately after their sight was restored—they had to learn to see. Secondly, one might argue that the lack of visual experience over years influenced the organization of the visual cortex. Increasingly, researchers are learning about the impact of experience on neural organization (Barinaga, 1992; Gilbert & Wiesel, 1992; Wiesel et al., 1992). Finally, both men *were* able to develop visual skills over time with experience, but it was a slow and difficult process.

Another way to examine the role of experience in visual perception is to alter the visual input. As you know, the optics of the eye create an image on the retina that is upside down and reversed in relation to the object in the world. In the late 1800s, George M. Stratton wore lenses that inverted the image on the retina. Stratton experienced all sorts of difficulties initially. However, after experience with the inverted input, he began to adapt. Many studies have examined adaptation to rearranged visual input, and they have all stressed the importance of interactive experience (e.g., Held, 1965, 1980). We will have more to say about this research in Chapter 14.

Have you ever noticed how hard it is to "read" a photographic negative? Do you think that you could adapt to a world that appeared as a negative? Stuart Anstis has tried to adapt to such a visual world, where colors appeared as their complements (e.g., blacks appeared as whites). Anstis either looked through a camera viewfinder (monocularly) when mobile or he looked at a television monitor (binocularly) when stationary. Neither Anstis, who adapted to the negative input for three days, nor one of his graduate students, who adapted for eight days, became thoroughly adept at perceiving the negative world. They both became more adept at reading facial expressions,

for instance, but they still had great difficulty identifying faces (Anstis, 1992; Grady, 1993). Adaptation to color inversion seems a much more difficult task than adapting to inverted images.

In this section we have attempted to convince you that a person's visual experience is the result of much more than light energy falling on photoreceptors. Vision is a very active process that requires edges, change, higher-level processes, and experience (Churchland et al., 1994; Hochberg, 1994). We will now turn our attention to a very basic visual process—determining which parts of the visual field are lighter and darker.

SECTION SUMMARY

Prerequisites for Normal Vision

1. In order to see, we require a physical stimulus and an intact visual system (as discussed in Chapter 3).

2. A Ganzfeld is a uniform visual stimulus that lacks edges. People who look at a Ganzfeld long enough report seeing a uniform gray field, regardless of the color of the light entering the eyes. Edges are therefore extremely important for our visual system.

3. Lateral inhibition, due to the lateral connections among photoreceptors, serves to enhance edges and to produce Mach bands.

4. Research on stabilized retinal images shows that edges are important and that the visual system requires changes in the position of the edges on the retina. Even when we try to hold our gaze steady, these changes are brought about through involuntary eye movements.

5. Vision is an active process involving higher-level processes, illustrated by the completion processes found at the blind spot.

6. Case studies of both restored vision and adaptation to rearranged visual input show us that experience is vital for visual perception.

PERCEIVING LIGHT ENERGY

As we discussed in Chapter 3, light energy falls on retinal receptors and is transduced into neural energy. Neurons fire at a greater rate when more light falls on the photoreceptors. Apparently we have a simple explanation for lightness perception: When more light energy falls on photoreceptors, we perceive that area as lighter; and when less light energy falls on photoreceptors, we perceive that area as darker. We could refer to this explanation as the photometric approach—lightness perception as analogous to measurement by an instrument such as a photometer. This simplistic notion of the relationship between light energy and perceived lightness is far from accurate, as you will see when we discuss the factors that influence lightness perception. Instead, we will argue that lightness perception is due to relational processes that require higher-level functions (Gilchrist, 1994a; Whittle, 1994).

Lightness Perception

Light energy can reach our eyes directly from a source, such as the sun, or indirectly, as reflected off a surface. Lightness, as we mentioned earlier, refers to our perception of the achromatic characteristics of a surface (whites, grays, and blacks). The term *albedo* refers to the proportion of light reflected by an object. Albedo is a property of an object that stays the same, even when the amount of light falling on the object changes. An object with a high albedo (such as the moon or white paper) reflects a large portion of the light energy that falls on it. An object with a low albedo (such as the print on this page or a dark suit) reflects a small portion of the light energy that falls on it.

Strangely, a black object can sometimes reflect more light than a white object, illustrating that perception of lightness is not strictly dependent on the amount of light energy reflected off a surface and into your eyes. Consider how the amount of light falling on an object changes from one situation to the next. For example, as you move a white piece of paper from a dimly lit interior to the bright outdoors, more light energy falls on the paper. Figure 4.6 illustrates how a constant proportion of light can be reflected in

different lighting situations. The black print on the paper may reflect only 10% of the light falling on it, whereas the white paper may reflect 90% of the light falling on it.

For example, suppose you are reading this book on a sunny day, when the illumination is 1,000 units (in some unspecified light measurement system). If the black print has an albedo of

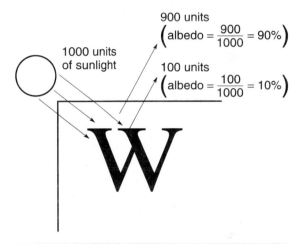

FIGURE 4.6 Illustration of the physical stimuli involved in lightness perception. The black letter *W* has an albedo of 10% and therefore reflects only 100 of the hypothetical 1,000 units of light produced by the sun. The white paper on which the letter is printed has an albedo of 90% and therefore reflects 900 units of light. Lightness constancy is apparent when the page is moved indoors under 10 units of light produced by a lamp. Under the reduced-intensity light, the black letter would reflect 1 unit and the white page would reflect 9 units of light. The white page reflects a smaller amount of light energy into the eye indoors than the black letter outdoors (9 units of light compared to 100 units of light). Nonetheless, we readily see the page as white and the letter as black under both lighting conditions. The absolute amount of light energy cannot be the sole determinant of lightness perception!

10%, the letters will reflect 10% of the 1,000 units, or 100 units. In contrast, suppose you are looking at the white page indoors, where the illumination is 10 units. If the page has an albedo of 90%, it will reflect 90% of 10 units, or 9 units. Your eye receives 100 units from the black print outdoors and 9 units from the white page indoors. In spite of the fact that the page indoors reflects less light energy into your eyes, you would certainly say that the white page looks lighter than the print. Thus, we do not make lightness judgments solely on the basis of the absolute amount of light reflected into our eyes.

Instead, our perception of the lightness of an object remains constant despite changes in illumination; we refer to this phenomenon as ***lightness constancy.*** Lightness constancy provides us with our first example of a constancy—a concept considered throughout the textbook. A ***constancy*** is a tendency for qualities of objects to stay the same despite changes in the way we view the objects. This is certainly an important tendency! Try to imagine a visual system that allowed qualities of objects to change whenever you changed the viewing conditions. A piece of paper might appear to be white under some lighting conditions, gray under other conditions, and black under still other conditions. Living in this world with such a visual system would certainly be a challenge.

We need to have some vocabulary to refer to objects "out there" and the objects as they are registered on the retina. The term ***distal stimulus*** refers to the objects "out there" in the world, such as a page of print. The term ***proximal stimulus*** refers to the representation of objects in contact with a sense organ. You can remember which term is which by thinking of distal as "in the distance," because for visual stimuli the distal stimulus makes no contact with the retina. In general, then, a constancy occurs when our sense of the distal stimulus remains roughly the same in spite of changes in the proximal stimulus. Constancies have been observed for several qualities of objects, including lightness, size, shape, and color. In subsequent chapters, we will address other constancies, but for now, we will explore lightness constancy in greater depth.

IN-DEPTH   Lightness Constancy

The preceding section introduced the notion of lightness constancy, which means that an object seems to stay the same lightness despite changes in the amount of light falling on it. For example, the white paper on this page continues to appear to be white whether you are reading in dim light or bright light. Similarly, the letters on this page remain black, whether you are reading in dim light or bright light. We can continue to make these discriminations even when the amount of light falling on the page is very low (Arend, 1993). Try Demonstration 4.4 to show how objects appear to be equally light under different illuminations.

This section emphasizes the observation that the physical stimuli falling on our receptors (proximal stimuli) differ from our psychological reactions to them. We can describe the visual properties of objects in terms of the intensity or amplitude of light waves. In contrast, we describe our psychological reactions in terms of lightness.

The physical property of objects that corresponds most closely to lightness is albedo. Objects with a very low albedo are seen as black, objects with intermediate albedos are seen as grays, and objects with high albedos are seen as white. The high correlation between albedo and perceived lightness is not very informative, however, because we cannot directly assess albedo. For instance, if you could see an isolated piece of paper but nothing else (including the source of light falling on the paper), you could not tell its albedo. The paper might appear to be gray because it really *is* gray, or it may be a white piece of paper in very dim light. Further, as you will see, perceived lightness depends on factors in addition to the physical properties of the stimulus, such as albedo.

EXPLANATIONS FOR LIGHTNESS CONSTANCY

An early theory of lightness constancy was proposed by Hermann von Helmholtz (1866), the 19th-century German physiologist we first mentioned in Chapter 3. Helmholtz proposed that we take illumination into account when we

---

Demonstration 4.4

Lightness Constancy

Take a piece of cardboard or some other thin object that light will not shine through. Place one edge of the cardboard upright on the dotted line. Orient your book near a desk lamp so that the lamp is in the direction indicated. Place your head so that your nose touches the top edge of the cardboard. Your left eye should see the one gray patch and your right eye should see the four comparison patches. Which of the four patches most closely matches the true shade of gray that your left eye is looking at? Now remove the cardboard so that both sides have the same illumination and see whether you still choose the same match.

←———— Lamp

                                 1   2   3   4

---

judge lightness. In other words, the print on this page stays black outdoors because we are sensitive to the fact that the sunlight is very bright. The page remains white indoors because we are sensitive to the fact that the indoor light is much less intense.

Notice that Helmholtz's theory involves a large amount of mental activity. The information is not directly available in the stimulus. Instead, we judge lightness by first figuring out the illumination. Then we assess how much light an object reflects onto our retina and take illumination into account to calculate lightness. One reason that Helmholtz's explanation is not widely accepted today is that people are not very accurate in judging how much light an object reflects onto their retinas (Beck, 1974). Without that information, we could not calculate lightness very accurately.

The most prevalent explanation for lightness constancy is based on the ratio principle. The ratio principle was developed by Hans Wallach (1948) of Swarthmore College. (Wallach's is another name that will recur throughout this text.) According to the **ratio principle**, the important factor that determines how light an object appears is the stimulus intensity of that object in comparison to other objects in the scene. Thus, this page looks white because it reflects relatively more light energy than the print under all illuminations.

Wallach's principle grew out of an experiment in which observers looked at two discs, each surrounded by a ring. As illustrated in Figure 4.7, Wallach set the intensity levels of the standard disc and ring, as well as the ring around the variable disc. An observer was instructed to adjust the intensity of the variable (second) disc so that it matched the intensity of the standard disc. Wallach found that the observer's match was influenced by the intensity of the ring surrounding the variable disc. Basically, the results showed that the observer varied the disc's intensity so that the ratio between the variable disc and ring was the same as the ratio between the standard disc and ring. Keep in mind that all the observer was trying to do was to make the two discs appear to be equal in lightness (e.g., the same shade of gray).

According to the ratio principle of lightness perception, observers pay attention to the relative intensity of the stimuli rather than the ab-

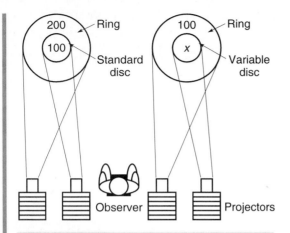

FIGURE 4.7 Illustration of Wallach's (1948) experiment underlying the ratio principle. Observers were presented with a standard ring and disc and asked to match the lightness of the standard disc with the variable disc. Wallach controlled the lightness of the standard ring and disc as well as the ring around the variable disc. Observers set the lightness of the variable disc so that the ratio of the right-hand ring to the variable disc was the same as the ratio between the left-hand ring and standard disc. In this case, the ratio for the standard is 2:1, so the observer would set the variable disc to 50.

solute intensity. An object may reflect very little light. However, it will appear light as long as it is lighter than other objects in the scene. The objects need not be next to each other, because we appear to integrate information about the light reflected off many objects in the scene (Arend, 1994; Bergström, 1994; Gilchrist, 1994a).

Lightness constancy occurs because the relative intensity of an object remains the same, even when illumination varies. Thus, the ratio of light reflected off the white page to the light reflected off the print remains 9:1 regardless of viewing conditions. Your white shirt therefore looks light in the moonlight because it is the lightest object in sight. Your dark shoes look dark in the noonday sun because they are the darkest objects in sight.

Research suggests that the ratio principle holds over an extremely wide range of illumination (Gilchrist & Jacobsen, 1989; Jacobsen & Gilchrist, 1988a, 1988b). For example, Alan Jacobsen and Alan Gilchrist (1988b) varied the reflected light energy over a range of 1 million to 1, and they found that observers' responses were consistent with the ratio principle. To date, then, we can explain much of lightness constancy by means of the ratio principle. However, not everyone agrees that the ratio principle sufficiently explains lightness perception (Arend & Spehar, 1993; Heinemann, 1989; Jameson & Hurvich, 1961). As the next sections illustrate, lightness perception is too complex a process to be completely explained by the simple ratio principle, although a more general relational approach may suffice (Gilchrist, 1994a).

PERCEPTUAL ORGANIZATION PRECEDES LIGHTNESS PERCEPTION

Although you might think that lightness perception is a fairly primitive perceptual ability, evidence suggests that you must organize the visual scene before you can perceive the lightness of objects in the scene (Agostini & Proffitt, 1993; Bergström, 1994). In other words, you must first decide which objects go together, and then you can determine their lightness. The situation is complicated by the fact that lightness itself might serve as an organizational cue (Rock et al., 1992b). We will have more to say about these organizational principles in Chapter 5.

Objects might go together because they are similar or because they are located at the same distance from you. For example, suppose that a gray dot appears to be grouped with a set of black dots because it is moving with them, or because it is aligned in a column with the black dots. Suppose that another gray dot of equal lightness appears to be grouped with a set of white dots. The gray dot will *appear* to be lighter when it is grouped with the black dots than when it is grouped with the white dots (Agostini & Proffitt, 1993). Note that the lightness is not determined by the absolute amount of light reflected from the gray dot but by the relationship between the gray dot and the other dots in its group.

Objects can also be grouped together because they appear to be at the same depth from the observer. The lightness of objects appears to be determined in comparison to other objects at the same depth (coplanar). For example, experiments by Gilchrist have shown that lightness judgments depend on the relative intensity of objects perceived to be the same distance from the viewer (Bergström, 1994; Gilchrist, 1977, 1980). In contrast, the relative intensity of objects merely next to each other in the retinal image (but perceived to be at different distances from the viewer) is less important. In other words, viewers must make depth perception judgments before they make lightness judgments. Lightness judgments therefore involve more than simple contrast of adjacent retinal stimulation. Interestingly, perceived depth information may influence lightness judgments but not brightness judgments (Schirillo et al., 1990).

EXCEPTIONS TO LIGHTNESS CONSTANCY

Lightness constancy is a fairly robust phenomenon, holding up over a wide range of conditions (Sewall & Wooten, 1991). Although lightness constancy is robust, it can still be disrupted. One way we can fool the visual system is to manipulate the lighting conditions in unusual ways. Another way we can fool the visual system is to manipulate depth information. Situations in which lightness constancy fails are actually very useful, because they enable us to develop more complete theories of lightness constancy.

Gelb (1929) conducted a classic study in which a black object appeared to be white. To achieve this transformation, he created an unusual situation. Observers sat in a dark room and looked at a disc made of black velvet. From a hidden projector, Gelb projected a bright beam of light that fell precisely on the black velvet disc, as seen in Figure 4.8. The observers reported that they saw a white disc. Then Gelb placed a little slip of white paper in front of the disc, so that the light was shining on the piece of white paper as well as the black disc. Presto! Observers suddenly reported that the disc was black.

Now that the observers knew that the disc was truly black, they would certainly remain convinced that it was black, wouldn't they? Actually, Gelb found that when he removed the slip of white paper, people again reported seeing a white disc. In social psychology, we are accustomed to thinking that we cannot fool a person twice; once someone is aware of a deception, he or she will not fall for the same trick again. However, Gelb's demonstration was so convincing that the observers were willing to ignore what they knew and report only what they saw. Gelb's study is a convincing demonstration of the point we made earlier—people do not perceive albedo directly. If they did, they would not have been fooled by the hidden light.

Can you see how Gelb's results are actually consistent with the ratio principle? Because the observers could not detect the presence of the hidden light source, they could only assume that illumination was constant throughout the room. The illuminated black disc was reflecting much more light than any other objects in the room, so the observers were forced to infer that it must have a very high albedo. Thus, according to the ratio principle, it must be a white disc! Once the white piece of paper was also placed in the light from the hidden projector, the proportion of light reflected from the black disc became small in comparison to that reflected from the white paper. Again, the ratio principle would predict that the disc would appear to be black, because it is reflecting a much smaller percentage of the hidden light than the white piece of paper.

Ernst Mach developed another illustration of the operation of depth cues, which also illustrates the operation of unconscious inferences. Try Demonstration 4.5 to experience Mach's book for yourself. The impact of prior information on perception again seems a plausible explanation for Mach's book. People are very much aware of the location of a light source, such as the lamp in a room. As is the case for corners in the room, the light source will differentially illuminate surfaces in the room—with some surfaces in shadow. When you mentally invert the index card, the reflected light from the surfaces of the card is no longer consistent with the location of the light source. If you were holding an actual open book in your hand, with the light source off to the right, the left side of the book would be lighter and the right side of the book would be in shadow.

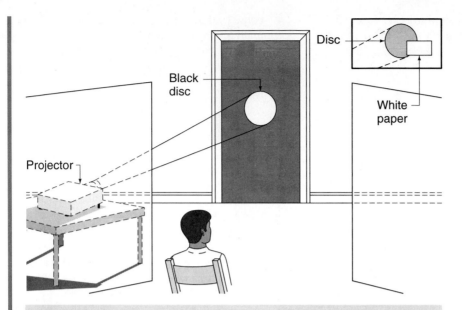

FIGURE 4.8   Gelb's (1929) experiment. The projector was hidden from the observer's view so that the observer would assume that there was no additional illumination in the room. The light from the projector fell only on the rotating velvet disc, which then appeared to be white to the observer. When a piece of white paper was placed in the path of the light from the hidden projector, the observer saw the disc as black and the paper as white. In spite of this information, when the piece of white paper was removed, the observer again saw the disc as white.

How does your visual system treat this novel situation? Apparently, it infers that the left side of the "book" must be a very black material that absorbs the light coming in from the right. It also infers that the right side of the "book," which should be in shadow, must be a light source itself. The physical stimuli remain constant throughout the demonstration, with the only change being a mental inversion of depth information. However, your perceptions are markedly different in the two conditions. Such is the power of higher-order processes.

So how can we explain lightness constancy? No current theory can adequately explain it! Consistent with three of the themes of this book, the stimulus, the perceptual processing system, and complex mental processes are all involved. In the case of lightness constancy, we must consider the contrast in the stimulus, physiological processes at the level of the retina, and perceivers' knowledge about distance, illumination, grouping, and other important factors that are relevant in making decisions about an object's lightness. ◆

Now that you have a better idea of various factors that influence the perception of simple achromatic light, we will turn our attention to other basic visual processes. In our discussion of the visual system in Chapter 3, you saw that the fovea was crucial for seeing detail in the visual stimulus. We will first review the notion of acuity raised in Chapter 3, as well as factors that influence acuity. We will also discuss the ways people maintain acuity as an object moves around them.

Demonstration 4.5

Mach's Book

First, fold an index card in half so that it looks like the roof of a house, as seen in the illustration below. Then orient the card so that one surface is directed toward the light source and the other is in shadow. For our purposes, we will assume that the light source is to the right of the card—so the left side is in shadow and the right side is illuminated. Close one eye, and when you look at the card you will see a lightness difference between the two surfaces.

Now try to mentally invert the index card, so that it is more like an open book than a roof. Looking with only one eye removes some depth cues, making it somewhat easier to mentally invert the card. This does take a bit of practice, and you'll actually get better at this mental manipulation over time. When you are able to invert the card, you will have created Mach's book. What do you see? The lightness of the two surfaces should have changed substantially. The left surface (in shadow) should appear to be much darker, and the right surface (in light) should appear much lighter, almost glowing. Keep in mind that the stimulus energy falling on your eyes is the same whether or not you've mentally inverted the card.

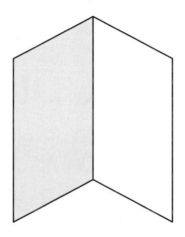

SECTION SUMMARY

Perceiving Light Energy

1. Objects vary in their albedo, or percentage of light reflected. Lightness constancy occurs when low-albedo objects are seen as dark under widely varying illuminations and high-albedo objects are seen as light under widely varying illuminations.

2. Several theories of lightness constancy have been proposed, but Wallach's ratio principle serves as the basis for most current theories. According to the ratio principle, perceived lightness is determined by the relative amounts of reflected light from surfaces in the scene. Objects in the visual field that reflect relatively little light are seen as dark, and objects that reflect relatively large amounts of light are seen as light.

3. Perceptual organization is very important for lightness perception. Perceived lightness emerges by comparing the reflectances of objects that are grouped together. Objects may be grouped together for many reasons, including the perception that they occur at the same depth from the viewer.
4. Lightness constancy can be disrupted by hidden sources of light or by changes in perceived depth.

ACUITY

Both a camera and our visual system require sharp focus. If you've ever had a roll of film developed, only to discover that several of the shots are out of focus, then you know how important it is to bring the image into focus on the film. Likewise, your visual system requires sharp focus on the retina.

Visual acuity is the ability to see fine details in a scene. More formally, "Acuity measures the resolution capabilities of the visual system in terms of the smallest high-contrast detail to be perceived at a given distance" (Olzak & Thomas, 1986, p. 7.45). With good acuity, for example, we can discriminate two black dots placed close to each other on a white background as two separate objects rather than one blurred object. Good acuity allows us to notice, for example, that a friend has a rash—rather than a mild sunburn—before the friend comes close. With good acuity, we can read a road sign announcing the name of the next exit in enough time to move into the right-hand lane.

Acuity is concerned with discriminations between stimuli in space. For example, an acuity task might involve judging whether a white region separates two black areas. Several methods of measuring acuity are available. All involve a description of the amount of space occupied by the target, called visual angle. Because acuity tests are easy to administer, they have become the standard procedure for assessing visual capability (Olzak & Thomas, 1986). In everyday life, we think of "good vision" as equivalent to "good acuity."

Other visual abilities, such as rapid dark adaptation, color vision, and the speed of eye movements, are either secondary or irrelevant to our intuitive concept of visual ability. In this section, we address several concerns related to acuity.

Measuring Acuity

Acuity can be measured in many different ways. The most common means for measuring acuity is the Snellen eye chart, devised by Hermann Snellen (1834–1909), a Dutch oculist, in 1862. The Snellen eye chart is a standard screening test in many doctors' offices. As Figure 4.9 will remind you, the eye chart has rows of letters ranging from large to small. The observer is instructed to say the names of the letters in each row. The tester notes the row with the smallest letters that the observer can name correctly.

Acuity on the Snellen chart is typically measured by comparing your performance with the performance of a normal observer. Suppose that you stand 20 feet from the chart. If you can read the letters that a person with normal sight can read at 20 feet, then you have 20/20 vision. If your acuity is poor, however, you would have to stand closer to read the letters. If you need to stand 20 feet from the chart to see the letters clearly that a normal person could see at 40 feet, then you would have 20/40 vision. In some states, a person with 20/200 vision after correction is declared "legally blind" (Schiff, 1980). This person would need to stand 20 feet from the chart to read the letters that a person with normal vision could read at 200 feet.

The Snellen eye chart has some problems, though. Some letters, like Y and V, are easily confused with each other. Other letters, like T, are easy to recognize. In most cases, the observer arrives at the correct response with the aid of several letter features. Consider the big *E* at the top of the chart, for instance. The straight horizontal line on the top tells us that the letter cannot be a C, D, G, H, and so on. The straight vertical line on the left tells us that the letter cannot be an A, C, G, J, and so on. Another disadvantage is that the chart does not include enough

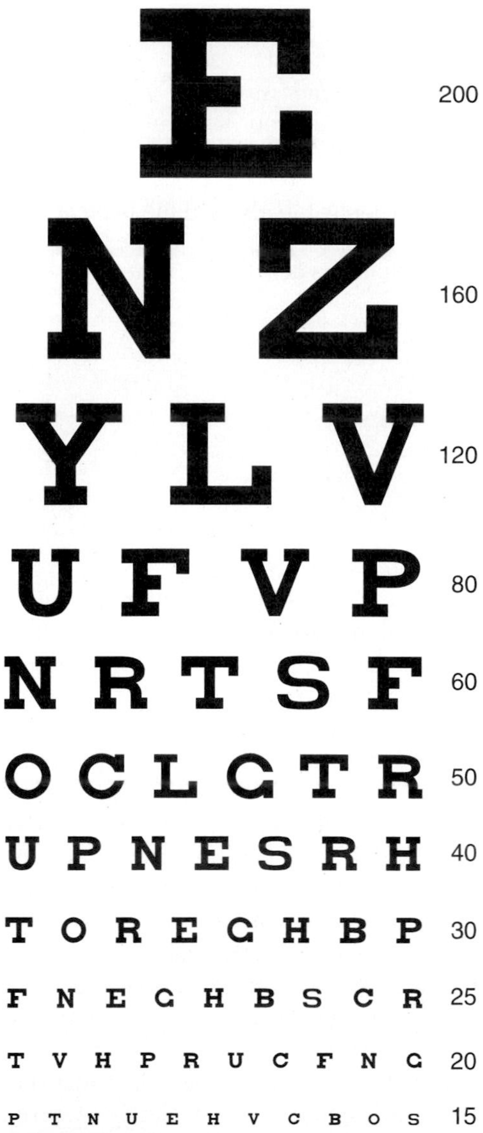

E	200
N Z	160
Y L V	120
U F V P	80
N R T S F	60
O C L G T R	50
U P N E S R H	40
T O R E G H B P	30
F N E G H B S C R	25
T V H P R U C F N G	20
P T N U E H V C B O S	15

FIGURE 4.9 Snellen chart. The size of the chart is reduced in this figure. On a full-sized chart, someone with 20/20 vision would be able to recognize letters in the next-to-last line at a distance of 20 feet. On this substantially reduced chart, someone with 20/20 vision should be able to read the last line at about 30 inches (roughly arm's length). If you can only read the line labeled 30, then you have 20/30 vision. (You would have to be at 20 feet to read what a person with normal vision could read at 30 feet.)

letters on the top two lines to provide an accurate test for people with severe visual impairment (Sloan, 1980).

Because of these drawbacks, the Snellen chart has often been replaced by other acuity measures. In its defense, however, the Snellen chart has practical significance. In real life, we need to identify letters at a distance, and the Snellen chart does measure letter identification.

Factors Affecting Acuity

Characteristics of the Eye

The focus of the eye is one obvious factor influencing acuity. Some people have spectacular acuity, perhaps as good as 20/10. In contrast, other people have poor acuity; remember that people with vision worse than 20/200 after correction may be classified as legally blind. We will consider eyesight problems and their correction when we discuss accommodation in the next section.

Try Demonstration 4.6 to illustrate another important influence on acuity, position on the retina. We discussed this issue briefly in Chapter 3; now let's consider the details. You can see the letters at the bottom of Demonstration 4.6 clearly only when they are registered on the fovea. The fovea occupies approximately 1° in the center of the eye. This area is so small that if you are holding your book roughly 18 inches away from you, only about six letters of the text will fall on the fovea. Just a short distance from the center, acuity drops off rapidly. Look at Figure 4.10, which illustrates the relative acuity at various points on the retina. As the figure illustrates, 10° away from the center, the relative visual acuity is only about 30% of the acuity found at the fovea. Notice the relative acuity for different parts of your eye as you look at this sentence in your book. The letters you are looking at right now are clear and sharp, but the letters on either side are blurry.

You may recall the explanation for the tremendous increase in acuity at the fovea. Look back at Figure 3.10, which shows the distribution of cones across the retina. Clearly, this

Demonstration 4.6

Retinal Location and Acuity

Place this book flat on your desk and move your head away until it is about 6 inches away from the book. Cover your left eye with your left hand. Look directly at the plus sign on the right-hand side of the figure below, just above the 0° mark. Keep your eye on this fixation point. Notice that you can see the letter at 0° quite clearly, and the letter at 5° is also fairly clear. However, the letters at 10°, 20°, and 30° are fuzzy. You will probably be unable to read the letters at 40° and 50°.

D	P	N	A	B	Q	W
+	+	+	+	+	+	+
50°	40°	30°	20°	10°	5°	0°

figure is similar to Figure 4.10. In the fovea, where cones are abundant, acuity is excellent; in the periphery, where cones are few and far between, acuity is poor.

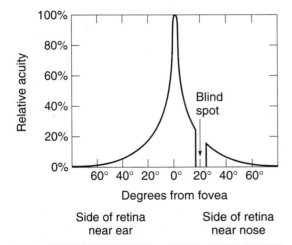

FIGURE 4.10 Relative visual acuity as a function of position on the retina. As discussed in Chapter 3, greatest acuity is achieved at the fovea (set to 100%), and it declines on either side of the fovea. Note that at the blind spot (about 20° to one side of the fovea) relative acuity is negligible.

Accommodation

As Chapter 3 discussed, light entering the eye is first bent by the cornea, then it is bent still further by the lens. The cornea bends the light rays by a constant amount, but the shape of the lens changes according to the distance of an object from the retina. More specifically, *accommodation* is a change in the shape of the lens that is necessary to keep an image in proper focus on the retina. When the retinal image is blurred, the visual system attempts to increase acuity by accommodation. In other words, accommodation is crucial to maintain acuity for objects that vary in their distance from the observer.

Suppose that the lens were rigid and could not change its shape. Suppose also that the curvature of the lens were designed so that objects at a distance could be seen clearly. A problem would arise if you wanted to look at a nearby object. The light rays from that object would be focused on a point behind the retina rather than on the retina itself. The image of the object would be blurred. Fortunately, however, the lens is flexible, changing shape so that the light rays are focused on the retina, and the image of the object is sharp.

We have seen that accommodation occurs with changes in distance of the object being viewed. Furthermore, an object that comes closer to us also takes up an increasingly larger portion of our retinas. As a consequence, changing size (or looming) might also be a stimulus to accommodation. McLin and his colleagues (1988) asked people to watch a cross as it changed size on a computer screen in a dark room. Although the image was actually at a constant distance, this simple stimulus was sufficient to cause people to accommodate. When the looming cross was also blurred, however, accommodative changes were more rapid. Thus, size changes and blurring of the stimulus appear to be important cues to the visual system that accommodation might be necessary.

Normal focusing. Let us first consider focusing in eyes with normal accommodation ability. Imagine that a normal eye is looking at a white disc on a dark background. If that disc is far away, the light rays going from the disc to the eye are parallel—that is, they are the same distance apart. If the disc is close, however, the light rays are not parallel; instead, they diverge as they approach the eye. (The physics explanation underlying this phenomenon is beyond the scope of this book.)

Look at Figure 4.11. Let's first consider two situations in which the disc is far away and the light rays are parallel. If the light rays enter a thick lens (4.11a), the thick lens bends them too much, and they gather in focus at a point in front of the retina. If the lens flattens (4.11b), however, the light rays are bent just the right amount so that they gather in focus right at the retina.

Now consider two situations in which the disc is near and the light rays are not parallel. If the light rays enter a thick lens (4.11c), the thick lens bends them substantially, enough so that they gather in focus at the retina. If the light rays enter a thin lens (4.11d), however, the thin lens does not bend them enough; if light could pass through the retina, the rays would focus at a point behind the retina. As a result, the rays would not be in focus on the retina. Now try Demonstration 4.7, which illustrates accommodation.

Accommodation is performed by the **ciliary muscle,** a tiny muscle attached to the lens, to which you were introduced in Chapter 3. When this muscle contracts, the lens becomes thicker,

and you can see things nearby. When this muscle relaxes, the lens becomes thinner, and you can see things far away. For young adults, adjustment to changes in viewing distance through accommodation takes about 0.4 second.

Notice that accommodation involves a muscle inside the eye. The involuntary eye movements talked about earlier in the chapter, as well as the eye movements discussed in the next section, involve muscles outside the eye.

A normal eye can bring into focus a point far away. The farthest point that you can see clearly is referred to as the **far point.** Nearby objects can be kept in focus until they are just a few inches away from the eye, but then the curvature of the lens has reached its limits. Try bringing your finger close to your eye to determine the limits of accommodation. The closest point at which you can see your finger clearly is referred to as the **near point.**

What happens to the lens when lighting conditions are poor? In the dark, the ciliary muscles relax and the lens reaches an intermediate resting focus referred to as the **dark focus.** Several studies support the theory that dark focus is the result of a balance between inputs from the sympathetic and parasympathetic systems. For instance, even though people are in a totally dark room, their lens will change shape with changes in arousal. Increased arousal (sympathetic system activation) leads to a decrease in dark focus, and the lens becomes thinner. In contrast, decreased arousal (parasympathetic system activation) leads to an increase in dark focus, and the lens becomes thicker (Miller & Takahama, 1988). These results suggest that accommodation under brightly lit conditions might also be influenced by nonvisual factors such as arousal. In fact, several researchers have reported changes in accommodation as a result of test anxiety, viewing gruesome slides, and other arousing manipulations (Miller & LeBeau, 1982; Miller & Takahama, 1987).

Focusing problems. We have been discussing the capabilities of the normal eye. Unfortunately, the shapes of many people's eyeballs and lenses do

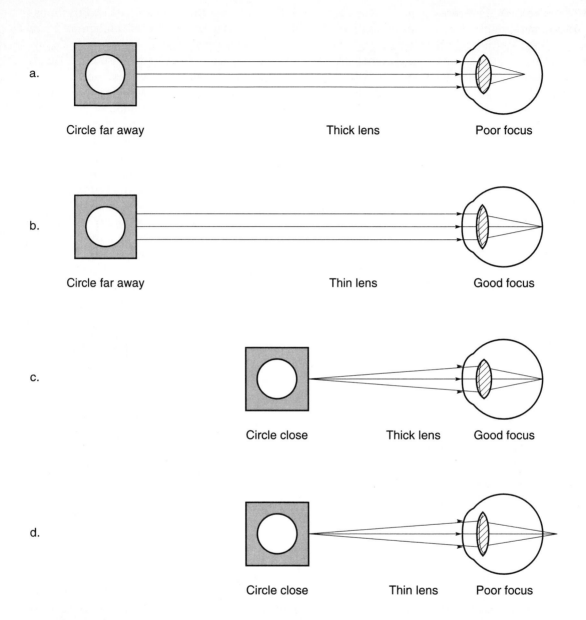

a.

Circle far away   Thick lens   Poor focus

b.

Circle far away   Thin lens   Good focus

c.

Circle close   Thick lens   Good focus

d.

Circle close   Thin lens   Poor focus

FIGURE 4.11   Illustration of accommodation. For distant objects, if the lens is thick it will bend the incoming light too much, causing the image to be in focus ahead of the retina rather than on the retina (4.11a). As a result, the image will be blurred when the light reaches the retina. To produce good acuity, the lens must be relatively thin for looking at distant objects (4.11b). For close objects, if the lens is thick it will bend the incoming light sufficiently to bring the image into focus on the retina (4.11c). If the lens is thin, however, the image will be brought into focus behind the retina, leading to a blurred image on the retina (4.11d).

Demonstration 4.7

Accommodation   First, close your left eye, using only your right eye for this demonstration. Next, stand in front of a window and hold a finger about 8 inches in front of your eyes. Focus on your finger, which will force your lens to become thicker. Notice how blurry all the distant objects become. With your thickened lens, light rays from distant objects focus on a point in front of your retina.

Now focus on a distant object, which will force your lens to become thin. Now your finger will look blurry. With a thin lens, light rays from nearby objects focus on a point that would be in back of the retina (if it were transparent, just as in the diagram in Figure 4.11).

If you have ever taken photographs, you know that it can be difficult to obtain clear images of both nearby and distant objects. The left picture below shows a clear image of a nearby object (but a blurry distant object). The right picture below shows a clear image of a distant object (but a blurry nearby object). (Photos by Ron Pretzer)

not allow them to bring an image into clear focus on the retina. Vision for a dot at a certain distance may therefore be blurred rather than crisp. People who are ***myopic,*** or ***nearsighted,*** can see objects nearby but cannot see objects clearly that are far away. They cannot focus on a point far away; in fact, they may not be able to see clearly any object farther than a yard away. Relative to people with normal vision, myopes have closer far points and closer near points. The increased ability to see ob-

jects near one's nose does not compensate for the loss of ability to see distant objects clearly, so most myopes choose to wear corrective lenses.

Nearsighted people typically have eyeballs longer than normal, although myopia can arise from other causes (Pugh, 1988). Figure 4.12 shows the situation in which the eye is too long. Notice that without correction, the image of distant objects is focused in front of the retina for nearsighted people—even with the lens as thin

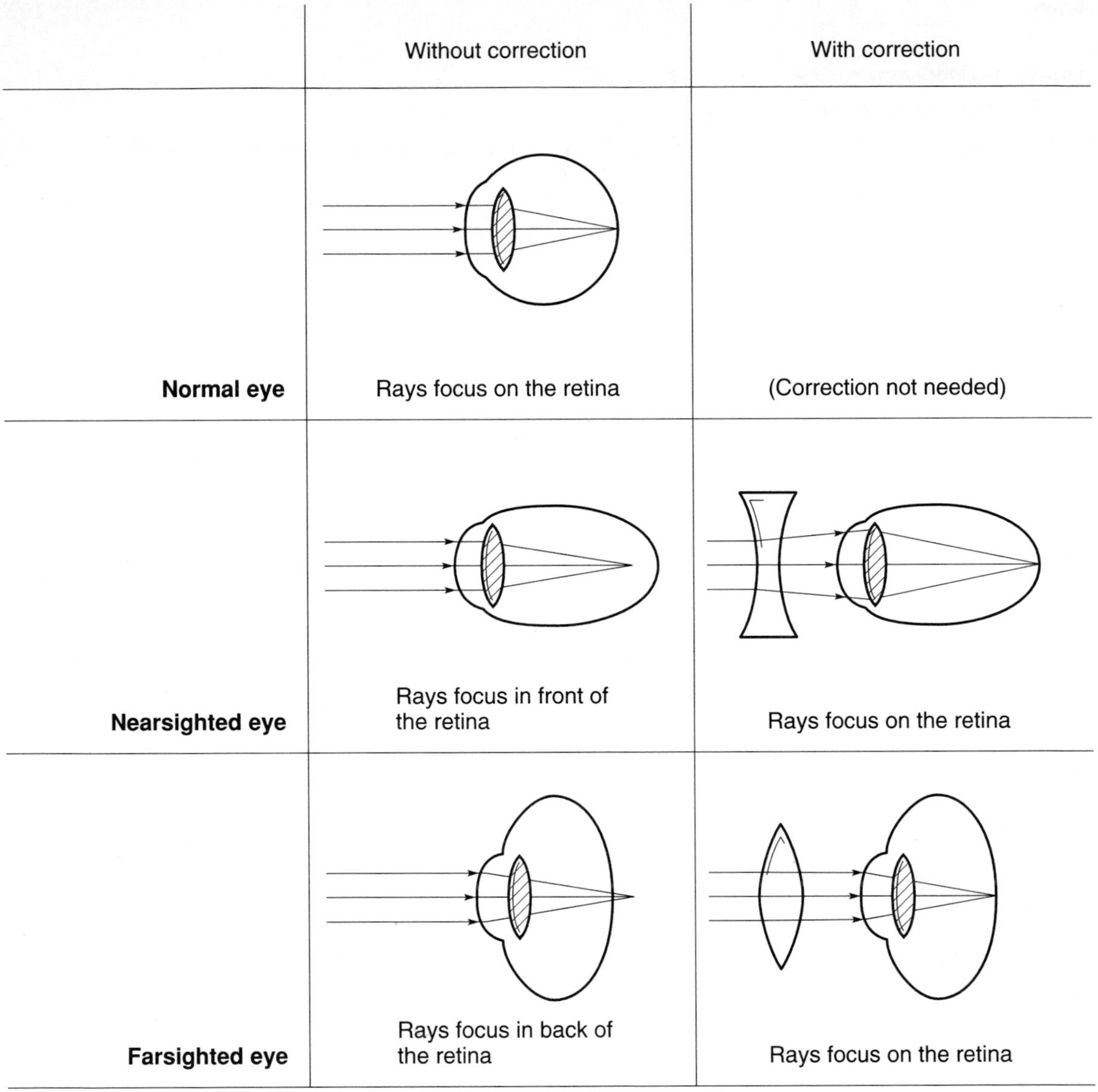

	Without correction	With correction
Normal eye	Rays focus on the retina	(Correction not needed)
Nearsighted eye	Rays focus in front of the retina	Rays focus on the retina
Farsighted eye	Rays focus in back of the retina	Rays focus on the retina

FIGURE 4.12 Comparison of visual abilities of normal, nearsighted, and farsighted eyes. For distant objects, the normal eye makes the lens thin, bringing the image into focus on the retina. The nearsighted eye, on the other hand, cannot focus on distant objects. If the lens were to be made thicker, it would just bend the light to a greater extent, causing the image to focus even farther in front of the retina. Instead, an external lens must be placed between the object and the eye. By using the external lens, light can now be brought into focus on the retina. A different problem confronts the farsighted eye. Now the image is brought into focus in back of the retina. The farsighted eye can bring the object into focus by thickening the lens, enabling it to focus on distant objects (hence the term *farsighted*). For nearby objects, however, the farsighted eye would be unable to thicken the lens sufficiently to bring the objects into focus, so a corrective external lens is necessary. Corrective external lenses allow both nearsighted and farsighted people to use their internal lenses to accommodate in a fashion similar to that used by people with normal vision.

as possible. For nearby objects, however, myopic people can see clearly. Look at Figure 4.11d and you'll see why. If the lens is thin in a normal eye, a nearby object would be brought into focus behind the eye. Because of the elongated eyeball of myopic people, nearby objects can be brought into focus with the lens made thin. So people with normal vision look at a nearby object through a thick lens. In contrast, myopes look at a nearby object through a thin lens. Remember, then, that *nearsighted* (myopic) people can see things *nearby*, and images of distant objects are focused in *front* of the retina.

Nearsightedness can be corrected by wearing corrective lenses, as illustrated in Figure 4.12. Notice how this lens makes the light rays diverge more, so that after passing through the lens of the eye the rays end up exactly on the retina. The vision of a myopic person, when corrected, resembles the vision of a person with normal vision (Westheimer, 1986). Incidentally, the corrective lens is intended to correct vision for distant objects, but vision for nearby objects is also affected. Nearsighted people wearing corrective lenses cannot focus on objects as close to their eyes as they could without corrective lenses. If you are nearsighted and wear glasses or contact lenses, see how close you can bring your finger to your eye and still keep it in focus, both with and without corrective lenses.

Why is myopia a problem for so many people (up to 20% of the population)? Although myopia is thought to have a hereditary component, several lines of research suggest that myopia may also be the consequence of experience (Wiesel & Raviola, 1986). For instance, the amount of time spent reading is fairly strongly correlated with amount of myopia (Young, 1981). Young pursued this intriguing correlation by studying the development of myopia in monkeys. Instead of inducing myopia in monkeys by teaching them to read, Young provided them with extensive experience with close objects by raising them in conditions where nothing was more than 20 inches from their eyes. After 3 years, the monkeys had become myopic. Presumably, the strain on the various ocular muscles

from doing close-up work is a contributing factor in myopia.

People who are **hypermetropic,** or **farsighted,** can see objects far away, but they cannot see nearby objects clearly. They have eyeballs shorter than normal, or their lenses are too thin. People with normal vision would look at distant objects with their lens as thin as possible, but if hypermetropes looked at a distant object through a similar thin lens, the object would be out of focus on the retina. As Figure 4.12 shows, if the light rays could go through the eye, they would come into focus behind the eye. The hypermetrope can bring the object into focus, however, by further bending the light rays with a thickened lens. Although a person with normal vision and a hypermetrope can see distant objects clearly, the person with normal vision is using a thin lens and the hypermetrope is using a thick lens. People with normal vision can shift to looking at nearby objects by making their lens thicker, but hypermetropes already have their lens thickened, so they cannot thicken it further to see nearby objects. With the use of an external corrective lens, hypermetropes (and myopes) are able to accommodate to nearby and distant objects in a fashion similar to that of people with normal vision.

Characteristics of the Stimulus

If you have ever struggled to read a map in the car at night, you know one stimulus characteristic that influences acuity: luminance, or the amount of light that enters the eye (MacLeod et al., 1990). That map would be perfectly legible in the daytime, but you will not find the street you are pursuing if you have to rely on occasional light from dim street lamps. Riggs (1971) notes that in starlight (luminance of about 0.0003 cd/m^2) we can see the white pages of a book but not the writing on them. In moonlight (luminance of about 0.03 cd/m^2) we can notice separate letters but cannot read the text. (In other words, if you plan to read poetry by moonlight, take a flashlight.) We require a luminance of about 30 cd/m^2 before we feel comfortable

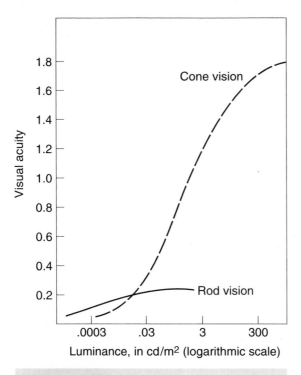

FIGURE 4.13 Figure showing visual acuity as a function of luminance for both rod (scotopic) and cone (photopic) vision. Acuity is never very high with rods, but in low levels of lighting, the rods can outperform cones. For light intensities above about 0.03 cd/m², however, cone vision is increasingly better than rod vision.

about reading. The recommended luminance standard in measuring acuity is 85 cd/m² (Olzak & Thomas, 1986). Acuity continues to increase as luminance increases until it levels off at about 3,000 cd/m². Figure 4.13 illustrates the relationship between luminance and acuity.

Notice that Figure 4.13 actually consists of two curves. With low levels of luminance, only the rods are able to function. Acuity is poor at these low levels because rods are interconnected to a greater extent than the cones in the fovea; rods show greater convergence. As you know, rods are concentrated in the outer portion of the retina.

Now notice the curve that represents vision with cones. With increases in luminance, the fovea can now be used effectively. The higher acuity in the foveal region is responsible for the dramatic improvement in acuity as the luminance increases. Now try Demonstration 4.8 to illustrate the relationship between luminance and acuity for yourself.

We have seen that luminance is one stimulus factor that influences acuity. You will not be surprised to learn that a related factor, glare, is also relevant. Under conditions of glare, acuity is substantially reduced (Finlay & Wilkinson, 1984). Many of the problems attributed to prolonged use of computers are actually caused by glare off the monitor screen, rather than the monitor itself.

Demonstration 4.8

Relationship between Luminance and Acuity

Identify five different levels of luminance that you encounter in a typical day, for example: (1) outside in the intense sunlight at noon; (2) your room in the late afternoon, with all the lights turned on; (3) your room at night, with one overhead light turned on; (4) your room at night, with just one desk lamp turned on, far away from you; and (5) your room at night, with no lights on but with some light coming in the window. In each of these conditions, turn to the Snellen eye chart in Figure 4.9, prop the book up, and move about 10 feet away. On which line can you successfully identify all the letters accurately? Does your acuity decrease as the luminance decreases?

SECTION SUMMARY

Acuity

1. Visual acuity is the ability to see fine details, or the resolution capacities of the visual system.

2. The Snellen chart measures acuity by asking observers to identify a target letter.

3. Acuity is influenced by several factors, including the person's ability to focus an image, the position of the image on the retina, and the lighting conditions under which the object is viewed.

4. Accommodation is the process whereby the ciliary muscles change the shape of the lens to keep an image in proper focus on the retina. Without accommodation, the light rays from an object would often be focused on a point either behind or in front of the retina rather than on the retina.

5. People who are nearsighted (myopic) and cannot see distant objects have eyeballs longer than normal or lenses that are too thick; the image of a distant object is focused in front of the retina.

6. People who are farsighted (hypermetropic) and cannot see nearby objects have eyeballs shorter than normal or lenses that are too thin; the image of a distant object would be focused behind the retina if light could pass through the retina.

EYE MOVEMENTS

Think about the number of different reasons you may have for moving your eyes. You watch a kite as it trembles and jerks on its way to a crash landing. You trace the smooth course of a robin as it approaches its nest. You move your eyes in small jumps along the page as you read this paragraph. You rotate your eyes inward to focus on a fly landing on your nose.

Both accommodation and eye movements are related to acuity. Accommodation allows us to focus on both near and distant objects. Eye movements allow us to keep moving objects on our foveas—the part of the retina that provides the greatest acuity. Because we rarely look at stationary objects, we must be able to track a moving object.

To appreciate eye movements more thoroughly, imagine how your life would be limited if your eyes were "glued" in a stable position in your head. Suppose that you could change the direction of your gaze only by moving your entire head. This kind of system would be extremely awkward, inefficient, and time-consuming for most tasks. Fortunately, however, our eyes are attached to muscles that can move them independent of head movement.

The accuracy, speed, and complexity of our eye movements are indeed amazing, giving further evidence for the impressive capabilities of our perceptual systems (Theme 2, see page 10). Llewellyn-Thomas (1981) marvels about the performance of the visual system in connection with one representative task, keeping track of a fast-moving baseball:

> It's astounding that any of us can hit [a baseball] at all. A ball is travelling a hundred miles an hour. A visual sample is taken from a bad angle in a single fixation from which the batter has to compute and extrapolate the ball's trajectory while initiating the voluntary muscle movements to guide a round club along a convoluted curve so it impacts the ball hard at a unique point in time and space! Impossible—all those differential equations to solve, and curves to plot in milliseconds! (pp. 318–319)

When you consider how often novice baseball players can make contact with the ball, even when thrown at speeds well under 100 miles an hour, you cannot help but be impressed by our visual systems. These are not unique human abilities—think of the success of winged predators, such as hawks, or of monkeys swinging along vines. Movements such as these all require coordination of motion with input from eye movements.

Eye movements can be classified in two basic groups, according to whether the angle between the lines of sight for the two eyes remains constant or changes as the eyes move. Before we discuss the classifications, take a moment to appreciate this distinction. First, look up at a boundary between a distant wall and a ceiling. Let your eyes trace along this line and notice how they move as a pair in the same direction. If you were to draw a line from each eye to the spot on which it was focusing, the angle between the two lines would remain roughly constant as you moved your eyes. *Version movement* is the term used for eye movement in which the angle between the lines of sight remains relatively constant and the eyes move in the same direction. We use version movements to track an object moving sideways at a distance from us.

In contrast, stretch a finger out in front of you and focus on the tip of the finger as you bring it toward your nose. The angle between the lines of sight changes drastically as you perform this eye movement. When you are looking at the outstretched finger, the lines of sight form an acute angle. When you are looking at the finger on your nose, the lines of sight form a wide angle. *Vergence movement* is the term used for eye movement in which the angle between the lines of sight changes and the eyes move toward or away from each other.

More specifically, the eyes *converge,* or move together, to look at nearby objects. The eyes *diverge,* or move apart, to look at distant objects. (*Convergence* and *divergence* are the nouns corresponding to those verbs; they refer to the act of moving together or moving apart. Notice that you can remember the general term *vergence* because it is a part of those two words.)

Version Movements

Several kinds of version movements depend on the nature of the task that must be performed; in all cases, however, the two eyes move in the same direction. We will consider two important kinds of version movement: saccades and pursuit movements.

Saccadic Movements

When you look out at the world, you see a fairly wide visual field, but only the part falling on the fovea is seen clearly. In order to capture as much information in the field as possible, you move your eyes in a series of jumps (Findlay, 1992; Irwin, 1992, 1993; Rayner, 1992a). *Saccadic movement* is the term used to refer to these rapid movements from one fixation point to the next. These movements are necessary to bring the fovea into position over the objects of interest. During the *saccade,* the eye moves from one location to the next, but you don't "see" during a saccade; otherwise you'd perceive only a blur (Irwin, 1993). Instead, you see during the *fixation pause*—the pause between saccades. Next, you knit together a clear composite view of a larger portion of the visual field based on several different fixations. Note how you are largely unaware of any of these processes.

Characteristics. Saccadic movement has some important attributes. First, saccades are probably the most frequent kind of eye movement. You make over 100,000 saccades in a day (Irwin, 1993). Second, saccades are jerky, rather than smooth. Third, saccades are rapid—much faster than the relatively leisurely eye movements used in pursuing the flight of a bird or in vergence movement.

Let's look at the timing of the phases in saccadic movements. To plan a saccade requires about 0.20 second (200 milliseconds). For example, if participants in a study are instructed that they must execute a saccade each time they see a specified signal, a delay of about 0.20 second occurs after the signal before the eye begins to move (Abrams, 1992). This delay is longer than the time required for the saccade itself, which ranges from 0.02 to 0.10 second, depending on the distance the eyes move (Findlay, 1992). The eye travels at an amazing speed during this brief saccade, reaching a velocity up to 600° per second (Hallett, 1986). The final stage of a saccade is the fixation pause, which lasts about 0.20 second before the eye begins another cycle.

The fourth characteristic of saccadic movements is that the eye muscles do not tire substantially during them. Fuchs and Binder (1983) asked several stalwart observers to make large (60°) saccades at the rate of 1 saccade per second for 31 minutes—close to 2,000 saccades. The velocity of these saccades had decreased only 10% by the end of this tortuous session, and some hearty encouragement from the experimenter brought the velocity back to normal.

In summary, then, the eye movements that you are executing as you read this sentence are frequent, jerky, and rapid. Furthermore, the movements produce little fatigue.

Pursuit Movements

You use the version movement called pursuit movement when you watch a bird fly through the sky, a baseball being hit out of the ballpark, and a child gliding by on a bicycle. *Pursuit movements* are required to track something moving against a stationary background. We need pursuit movements because we want to keep objects on our fovea in order to provide the greatest acuity.

Pursuit movements have several important characteristics. They are relatively slow, with velocity typically ranging between 30° and 100° per second, substantially slower than the 600° per second velocities that saccadic movements can reach (Hallett, 1986). A second attribute of pursuit movements is that they are smooth, in contrast to the jerky saccades. In fact, they are often called "smooth pursuit movements" to emphasize this important characteristic.

A third attribute is that they attempt to match a target's speed, although they have a general tendency to "underpursue" because the eyes cannot move as fast as the target (Hallett, 1986).

As a result of underpursuit, the object's image on the retina moves rather than remaining in a constant position. This movement of the retinal image makes it difficult to see details on moving objects. Details will be particularly blurry if the object is moving rapidly (Murphy, 1978).

Vergence Movements

So far, we have been considering version movements, the kinds of eye movements that keep the same angle between the lines of sight during eye movement. In contrast, recall that vergence movement involves eye movement in which the angle between the lines of sight changes.

The purpose of vergence movements is to allow both eyes to focus on the same target—which is crucial for maintaining acuity. Try Demonstration 4.9, which shows how you would have double vision if you avoided vergence movements.

Vergence movements are relatively slow; their velocities rarely exceed 10° per second (Hallett, 1986). The average vergence movement lasts about 1 second, a relatively long time in comparison to the saccadic eye movements. Vergence movements are also slower than accommodation (which uses muscles inside the eye), even though both operations are used in shifting fixation between far objects and near ones. Demonstrate the speed of vergence movements to yourself by changing your fixation point from a nearby object to a distant object and back to the nearby object.

Demonstration 4.9

Convergence   Hold both index fingers together as far away as possible from your body, and fixate both your eyes on your fingers. Continue to focus on your right index finger, while slowly bringing your left finger in toward your nose. Do not use convergence to keep your left finger in focus. As you move your left finger inward, stop about 4 inches from your nose. Notice that you will have double vision for your left finger. Now converge on your left finger, bringing it into focus. Notice that now you will have double vision for your right finger.

In Chapter 6 we will talk about vergence movements in connection with distance perception. Under some circumstances, we may use the degree of convergence as one cue to the distance of an object. When both eyes are looking straight ahead, we are focusing on a more distant object. When our eyes are rotated inward, we are focusing on a nearer object.

SECTION SUMMARY

Eye Movements

1. Version movements of the eyes occur when the angle between the lines of sight remains constant; version movements include saccadic movements and pursuit movements.

2. Saccadic movements are the rapid movements of the eye from one fixation point to the next. They are frequent, jerky, and rapid. Saccadic movements do not produce substantial fatigue.

3. Pursuit movements are used to track moving targets; these movements are slow and smooth, and they attempt to match the speed of a target.

4. Vergence movements occur when the angle between the lines of sight changes. The eyes converge to look at nearby objects and diverge to look at distant objects. Vergence movements are slower than version movements.

REVIEW QUESTIONS

1. What are the prerequisites for vision, and how do they illustrate clear differences between our visual system and the functioning of an automatic camera?

2. Review the connection between lateral inhibition and Mach bands. Then try to integrate the information on lateral inhibition with information from Chapter 3 on receptive fields. How might receptive fields give rise to lateral inhibition?

3. A frog does not have involuntary eye movements. Discuss the implications of this deficit for the frog's visual perception. What would you predict would happen if a frog's head were immobilized?

4. Discuss theoretical approaches to lightness constancy. What role does albedo play in determining lightness constancy? Describe several instances in which constancy appears to fail, and indicate how each of these instances might be addressed by one of the theories of lightness constancy.

5. Many of your friends may think of perception as a passive process. Using information from different sections of this chapter, construct an argument for the active nature of perception.

6. Think about all the characteristics of the visual system and of a stimulus that could influence acuity. Combining all these factors, describe a situation in which acuity would be the best possible. Then describe a situation in which acuity would be the worst possible.

7. What are the four kinds of eye movements discussed in this chapter? What is their function? Identify the kind of eye movement(s) represented in each of these situations: (a) You watch a bird fly away from you in a diagonal direction, so that its flight is also from right to left. (b) You are staring into someone's pupils, but your eyes move slightly. (c) You are carefully examining a painting in art class.

8. In Chapter 3 we discussed many of the structures that are important for visual perception. Draw on that information to discuss various topics from this chapter. Here are some questions you might try to answer: (a) How does your knowledge of the retina, particularly the fovea, help you to understand saccades? (b) What area of the visual cortex would process information important to directing pursuit movements? (c) What visual pathway would be important for lightness perception?

9. Describe the accommodation process that takes place in normal eyes when viewing a *nearby* object, and then summarize how this focusing is abnormal in nearsightedness and farsightedness. How can each of these disorders be corrected?

10. Contrast the focusing performed by the eye muscles during accommodation with the other eye movements mentioned in this chapter. Be certain to mention location of the muscle and speed of the movement.

NEW TERMS

edge (89)
contour (89)
brightness (89)
lightness (89)
achromatic (89)
Ganzfeld (91)
lateral inhibition (91)
Mach band (94)
involuntary eye movements (95)
stabilized retinal image (96)
scotoma (97)
albedo (101)
lightness constancy (102)

constancy (102)
distal stimulus (102)
proximal stimulus (102)
ratio principle (103)
visual acuity (108)
accommodation (110)
ciliary muscle (111)
far point (111)
near point (111)
dark focus (111)
myopic (113)
nearsighted (113)

hypermetropic (115)
farsighted (115)
version movement (118)
vergence movement (118)
converge (118)
diverge (118)
convergence (118)
divergence (118)
saccadic movement (118)
saccade (118)
fixation pause (118)
pursuit movements (119)

RECOMMENDED READINGS

Boff, K. R., Kaufman, L., & Thomas, J. P. (Eds.). (1986). *Handbook of perception and human performance* (Vol. 1). New York: Wiley. This volume is a necessity for any college library where students and faculty are seriously interested in perception. Chapters relevant to basic visual processes include those on sensitivity to light, the eye as an optical instrument, seeing spatial patterns, and eye movements.

Gilchrist, A. (Ed.). (1994b). *Lightness, brightness, and transparency.* Hillsdale, NJ: Erlbaum. Gilchrist has long been a leader in research on lightness perception, so we recommend that you read his introductory chapter if you want to learn more about his approach. The remaining five chapters in this edited volume might not be as approachable, but each one contains important insights.

Minnaert, M. (1968/1993). *Light and color in the outdoors* (L. Seymour, Trans.). New York: Springer-Verlag. Although this book was written decades ago, it only recently appeared in English. Even in translation, Minnaert conveys his fascination with naturally occurring light phenomena. If you've ever wondered about something you've seen in the outdoors (brightness of stars, complex shadows, rainbows, mirages, etc.), Minnaert probably discusses it in this book.

Rayner, K. (Ed.). (1992b). *Eye movements and visual cognition: Scene perception and reading.* New York: Springer-Verlag. This collection of 28 chapters emerged from a conference on eye movements. The topics are wide ranging, including several chapters on saccades, visual search, perceiving scenes, and reading. A number of chapters are both interesting and accessible, but our favorite was the chapter on the eye movements involved in reading cartoons.

In the two preceding chapters we examined some of the more basic aspects of the visual system. In Chapter 3 we studied the mechanisms that transduce light energy into the energy required by our neural processing apparatus. Chapter 4 outlined some of the prerequisites for vision, with an emphasis on the importance of edges and change. In this chapter we examine the more complex aspects of visual functioning and address a central question in perception: How do we extract pattern and shape from the welter of edge information?

Although you may not be consciously aware of edges, you certainly can notice them when we call your attention to them. For instance, as you look at your textbook, you can readily perceive the letters on the page as patterns of edges. Your book's cover forms edges against a background that is itself filled with edge information. Edges abound, yet you do not see edges—you see objects! You see letters, books, faces, tables, chairs, and bookbags.

How you do so remains something of a mystery, but in this chapter we examine several attempts to unravel that mystery. After examining different approaches to the perception of objects in the world, we will turn our attention to illustrations of the complexities involved in shape perception—illustrations that pose challenges to the approaches discussed.

APPROACHES TO SHAPE AND PATTERN PERCEPTION

Objects in the world have their distinctive shapes or forms, so you might think that we could define shape or form with little difficulty. Unfortunately, a precise definition is extremely problematic (Uttal, 1988). For our purposes, we can simply consider *shape* or *form* to be an area set off from the rest of what we see because it has an edge or adjoining edges. Thus, the shape of your book is determined by a particular arrangement of edges.

How does your visual system determine that particular edges go together to form your book?

Any approach to shape perception must uncover the processes that enable you to integrate the edges of an object, such as your book, to arrive at the perception of that object. As we explained in Chapter 4, people perceive lightness as the end product of a number of processes, including one that determines depth. Similarly, you should expect that a number of processes underlie the perception of shape. Some of these processes may occur sequentially, with the output of one process providing the input to another process. Other processes may occur simultaneously, in parallel.

As we mentioned in Chapter 1, some processes are considered data-driven (bottom-up processes) and other processes are considered conceptually driven (top-down processes). The very earliest stages of visual experience, which analyze data from the sensory receptors, must involve *data-driven processing*. The data arrive and set into motion the process of recognizing various shapes. You should recognize that this process echoes Themes 2 and 3 of this text, which emphasize the importance of the stimulus and the sensory systems.

Conceptually driven processing emphasizes the importance of the observers' concepts in determining perception. In conceptually driven processing, observers have expectations and concepts about how the world is organized. They believe that certain objects are likely to be found in certain situations. These expectations and concepts set into motion the process of recognizing various shapes. You should recognize that this process emphasizes Theme 4 of this text (see page 12), which highlights the importance of knowledge and experience.

Data-driven processing can be called *bottom-up processing*. You recognize simple, low-level features, and the combination of these simple features allows you to recognize more complex, complete shapes. Conceptually driven processing, on the other hand, can be called *top-down processing*. Using knowledge you have about the world, you recognize a form, which may be quite complex. Context, expectancies, knowledge, and memory—concepts that you have as an observer—"drive" the recognition process. Recognition of the whole then allows us to identify the simpler elements that are present in the whole.

The earliest stages of processing are likely to be data driven, and the latest stages of processing are likely to be conceptually driven (Tversky, 1991). Data-driven processes allow you to extract edges without requiring a great deal of prior knowledge. On the other hand, knowledge *can* play a role in some of the very earliest stages of perceptual processing (Weisstein & Harris, 1974). Conceptually driven processes are necessary for you to recognize any object—whether it is a book, a letter, or a person. Recognition requires you to compare your perception to a pre-existing memory. Ultimately, your perceptual experience is bound to involve interactions of these two types of processes.

We will now examine several approaches to shape perception. As you read about each approach, try to identify whether it emphasizes bottom-up or top-down processes.

Spatial Frequency Analysis Approach

According to the *spatial frequency analysis approach,* the visual system breaks down the stimulus into a series of narrow light and dark stripes. This approach to visual stimuli has been useful in research on visual sensitivity. It has also been applied to shape perception, though this application has been criticized (e.g., Pinker, 1984).

Fourier Analysis

Jean Baptiste Joseph Fourier (1768–1830) made several mathematical contributions that form the basis of spatial frequency analysis (Davis & Hersh, 1981). His work can also be applied to the analysis of sound waves, as you will see in Chapters 9 and 10, but we are now concerned with the analysis of visual stimuli. *Fourier analysis* involves analyzing a stimulus into its component sine waves (Graham, 1992; Weisstein, 1980). If you have taken a trigonometry course, you may recall that a *sine wave* is a smooth wave pattern resembling the light waves discussed in Chapter 3. As you can see in Figure

5.1a, the wave pattern is repeated at regular intervals, fluctuating from high intensity to low intensity and back. This sine wave corresponds to a narrow horizontal segment taken from Figure 5.1b. Figure 5.1b shows a *sinusoidal grating,* a set of blurry stripes that alternate between dark and light. (The dark stripes represent the low-intensity areas of the sine curve; the light stripes represent the high-intensity areas.)

Figure 5.1a shows a single sine wave and how it corresponds to a stimulus that is a blurry set of stripes. As we said in the preceding paragraph, Fourier analysis proposes that any visual stimulus can be analyzed into many component sine wave gratings. So let's consider the kind of sine waves that might be the components for a horizontal strip taken from a set of stripes. Suppose that we add together a series of sine waves, a process known as *Fourier synthesis.* (We perform a Fourier *analysis* to analyze a stimulus into

Location in diagram below

a. Sine wave

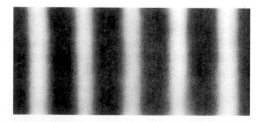

b. Sinusoidal grating

> **FIGURE 5.1**   A sine wave (a) and its corresponding sinusoidal grating (b). Notice that the darker stripes in the grating correspond to the low points on the sine wave and the lighter stripes in the grating correspond to the high points on the sine wave.

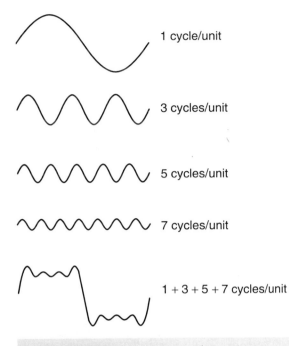

1 cycle/unit

3 cycles/unit

5 cycles/unit

7 cycles/unit

1 + 3 + 5 + 7 cycles/unit

FIGURE 5.2 The complex wave produced by adding four sine waves resembles a square wave. Fourier analysis would involve going from the complex wave to the four constituent since waves. Fourier synthesis would involve adding the four waves to produce the complex wave.

its component sine waves; we perform a Fourier *synthesis* for the reverse process of combining sine waves to represent the pattern in the stimulus.) We could select a series of sine waves that have 1, 3, 5, and 7 cycles within the same horizontal distance, as shown in Figure 5.2. If we add these waves together, this Fourier synthesis results in the figure at the bottom of the diagram. You'll notice that it is similar to a segment of the square wave shown in Figure 5.3a. As seen in Figure 5.3b, a square wave corresponds to a series of regularly repeating dark and light stripes that have crisp—not blurry—edges.

In short, Fourier analysis provides the tools for analyzing any pattern, regardless of its complexity, into component sine wave gratings.

Through Fourier synthesis, we can construct the complex patterns that might be found in a typical black-and-white photograph (Graham, 1981).

Spatial Frequency

How can we describe a sinusoidal grating so that it is most useful in relation to visual processes? The grating in Figure 5.1b has a spatial frequency of about 2 cycles per inch. However, this system of measurement will not be useful when we want to discuss visual processes. If that pattern is presented 4 inches from your nose, the stripes are relatively broad; at a distance of 4 feet, the stripes are relatively narrow. Because of this ambiguity, spatial frequency is typically measured in terms of the number of cycles in each degree of visual angle.

Visual angle means the size of the angle formed by extending two lines from your eye to the outside edges of the target. (Consult Demonstration 5.1 as we discuss this term.)

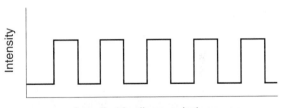

Location in diagram below

a. Square wave

b. Intensity distribution for a square wave

FIGURE 5.3 A square wave (a) and its corresponding intensity distribution (b). Compare this figure to Figure 5.2, particularly noting that the smooth transitions from lighter to darker areas in Figure 5.2 are replaced by more abrupt transitions in this figure.

Demonstration 5.1

Visual Angle

Hold this book up in front of you, with your elbows bent at 90° angles; if you have a ruler, measure 35 cm (about 14 inches) away from your eyes. Look at the 1.2 cm diameter circle below. This circle occupies a *visual angle* of about 2°. The diagram beneath the circle illustrates this relationship schematically. Many other circles could produce a visual angle of 2°, including a circle with 2.4 cm diameter at a distance of 70 cm. Note, also, that the 1.2 cm diameter circle would have a visual angle of 1° if moved back to 70 cm.

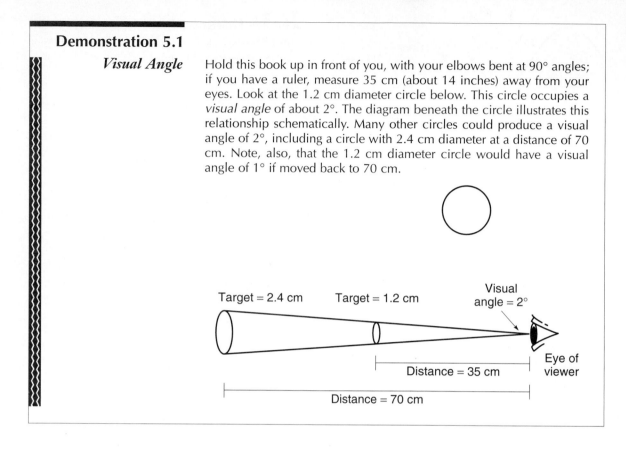

The visual angle is measured in degrees, minutes, and seconds. A circle has 360 degrees (symbolized °). However, because your eyes cannot see in back of your head or even straight above your head, visual angles are always much smaller than 360°. Just as an hour is divided into minutes and seconds, a degree in space is divided into minutes and seconds. Each degree has 60 minutes (symbolized '), and each minute has 60 seconds (symbolized ").

The size of the visual angle depends on the size of the target and the distance of the target from the eye. In Demonstration 5.1, you are looking at a circle 1.2 cm across. Larger circles at the same distance would occupy larger visual angles. The size of the visual angle also depends upon the distance of the target from the eye. As you move the circle away from you, it occupies an increasingly smaller visual angle. As seen in Demonstration 5.1, a circle 2.4 cm across viewed

from a distance of 70 cm would occupy the same visual angle as a circle 1.2 cm across viewed from a distance of 35 cm.

Look again at Figure 5.1b and hold the book 24 inches from your eyes. Figure 5.1b shows a 1-cycle grating at that distance. In other words, one complete cycle, including a dark and a light phase, is found within 1 degree of visual angle. Incidentally, if you move the book to a distance of 48 inches (twice as far away), you will achieve a 2-cycle grating. You could also create a 2-cycle grating by making twice as many stripes in the same horizontal distance of Figure 5.1b, and then viewing the figure from 24 inches.

Contrast Sensitivity Functions

The patterns you have seen so far have shown high-contrast stripes of black and white. The contrast can be reduced by alternating black and *gray* stripes. The contrast between the two kinds of

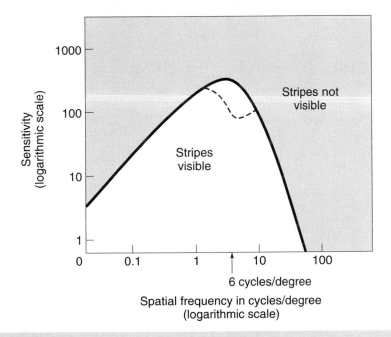

FIGURE 5.4 The solid line represents a typical contrast sensitivity function for an adult human. Most adults are maximally sensitive to a spatial frequency of about 6 cycles/degree, which is roughly the high point of the function. The stripes in high spatial frequency stimuli, such as those above 100 cycles/degree, are not visible to most adults. The dotted line represents the results of selective adaptation to a grating of 7.5 cycles/degree (to be discussed on page 129).

stripes can be decreased even further until an observer cannot distinguish between the stripes and a uniform gray patch. For example, a researcher might take the 1-cycle grating shown in Figure 5.1b and gradually lower the contrast until the observer reports, "I can't distinguish that figure from the gray patch." (You may recognize this psychophysical technique as the method of limits.) This procedure could be repeated with a variety of gratings, perhaps representing spatial frequencies between 0.1 cycle and 50 cycles/degree.

Figure 5.4 shows a typical ***contrast sensitivity function,*** a diagram that illustrates the relationship between spatial frequency and sensitivity. Notice that the y-axis is labeled "Sensitivity." As you'll recall from Chapter 2, high sensitivity corresponds to low threshold. The sensitivity is highest for gratings with spatial frequencies of 6

cycles/degree. That means that observers are particularly good at discriminating between this particular grating and a gray patch. In fact, they are so good with this grating that the contrast between the black and gray stripes can be low. Spatial frequencies of 1 cycle/degree or less and spatial frequencies of 10 cycles/degree or more require much higher contrast between the two kinds of stripes. The visual system simply does not process those gratings as well. Incidentally, if you want to know just what the grating that you can see so well looks like, turn back to Figure 5.1b, prop up your book, and back up about 12 feet.

In the 1960s, two British researchers, Fergus Campbell and John Robson, suggested that pattern perception could be described in terms of spatial frequency (Campbell & Robson, 1964, 1968). They proposed that our visual system has several sets of neurons, each of which responds best to a particular spatial frequency. These neurons, located in area V1 of the visual cortex, are sensitive to particular spatial frequencies—due to the size of their receptive fields (Graham, 1992; Wandell, 1995). The sensitivity of these neurons to particular spatial frequencies creates multiple ***spatial frequency channels***. These multiple analyzers can explain most of the research on pattern perception, particularly for near-threshold stimuli (Graham, 1992).

How do the differences in receptive field size give rise to neurons tuned to particular spatial frequencies? As you will recall, in Chapter 3 we discussed tuning curves, which demonstrate that simple cells in the visual cortex respond better to some orientations than to others. Similarly, tuning curves can be derived for particular spatial frequencies.

For example, let's consider a particular cell that has an on-center, off-surround arrangement, as shown in Figure 5.5a. If a sinusoidal grating is presented so that the white portion stimulates the center and the gray portion stimulates the surround, the cell will respond at a high rate. However, if the sinusoidal grating shows wide stripes (i.e., low spatial frequency), the strong excitation of the center is canceled by the strong in-hibition of the surround; this situation is shown in Figure 5.5b. Finally, if the sinusoidal grating shows narrow stripes (i.e., high spatial frequency), the moderate excitation of the center is canceled by the moderate inhibition of the surround; this situation is shown in Figure 5.5c.

Naturally, however, we manage to perceive sinusoidal gratings that have either higher or lower spatial frequencies than the one in Figure 5.5a. For example, one set of neurons with wide receptive fields might respond best to a spatial frequency of 0.5 cycle/degree. Another set of neurons might respond best to 1 cycle/degree, and other sets to frequencies such as 6, 10, and so on. As seen in Figure 5.4, the ideal combined frequency is 6 cycles/degree, based on the contrast sensitivity functions of all the component neurons that make up the visual system.

The theory of spatial frequency analysis is complicated. Let's briefly review before we consider the experimental evidence for this theory. By means of Fourier analysis, any complex scene can be broken down into its component sine waves, each of which corresponds to a set of blurry black-and-white stripes known as a sinusoidal grating. This grating is measured by the number of cycles of grating included in 1 degree of visual angle. In general, people are most sensitive to

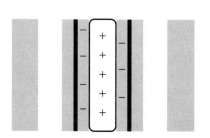

a. High response rate

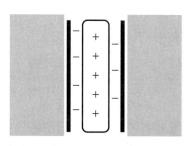

b. Low response rate

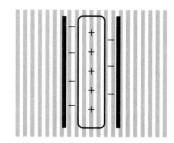

c. Low response rate

FIGURE 5.5   An illustration of how an on-center, off-surround simple cortical cell would be stimulated by three different spatial frequencies. The spatial frequency in part a would produce the highest response rate because the high intensity of the stimulus falls on all of the on-center (and only a little of the off-surround). In part b, the on-center is also stimulated, but the inhibition caused by stimulating the off-surround would result in a reduced rate of firing. In part c, the spatial frequency is so high that again both the on-center and the off-surround would be stimulated, resulting in a lower firing rate.

gratings with spatial frequencies of 6 cycles/ degree. However, each spatial frequency channel in the visual system seems to respond best to a different spatial frequency. Neurons with narrower receptive fields create channels for frequencies higher than 6 cycles/degree, whereas neurons with wider receptive fields create channels for lower frequencies.

Evidence for the Operation of Spatial Frequency Analysis

We have discussed how spatial frequency analysis *could* account for pattern perception. Now we need to consider whether the research suggests that this kind of sine-wave analysis actually *does* occur. A number of studies of spatial frequency have been summarized elsewhere (Graham, 1989).

One of the earliest studies on spatial frequency analysis is also one of the most convincing. Blakemore and Campbell (1969) calculated the kind of contrast-sensitivity function illustrated by the solid line in Figure 5.4. Then the observer looked at a 7.5 cycles/degree grating for 1 to 2 minutes, and the researchers again calculated a contrast-sensitivity function. Intriguingly, the sensitivity to spatial frequencies decreased substantially around 7.5 cycles/degree. This decrease is represented by the dotted line in Figure 5.4. In other words, continuous exposure to a particular stimulus produces "fatigue" in the neurons that respond to spatial frequencies in the region of 7.5 cycles/degree. Other studies have used this *selective adaptation procedure* to demonstrate that continuous exposure to one spatial frequency decreases later sensitivity to that particular frequency. Incidentally, this is one example of a general phenomenon called *adaptation* that we will examine in other sensory systems later in the book. As Theme 1 proposes, the sensory systems share numerous similarities.

However, researchers have expressed some objections to the spatial frequency approach. For example, as Cutting (1987) points out, the spatial frequency approach guarantees that everything in the stimulus will be analyzed into sine waves; Fourier analysis is so unselective that even meaningless, unimportant, and irrelevant parts will be included in the analysis. Real perceivers, in contrast, appear to be more selective; they can ignore the irrelevant portions of a pattern. Nonetheless, most modern theories of visual perception acknowledge that spatial frequency analysis plays an important role. We will now turn our attention to the equally influential Gestalt approach.

Gestalt Approach

We provided a brief introduction to Gestalt psychology in Chapter 1. In this section, we will first describe the major principles that characterized the original Gestalt approach. At the end of the section, we will discuss problems with the original Gestalt approach and some modern derivatives of the Gestalt approach.

The **Gestalt approach** emphasizes that we perceive objects as well-organized "wholes" rather than separated, isolated parts. Such an emphasis epitomizes a **holistic orientation** to perceptual processing. Thus, the perceptual whole that we experience is not simply the sum of its parts (Kimchi, 1992; Palmer, 1992b). For example, consider an experiment by Pomerantz and his colleagues (1977). A modified version of their study appears in Demonstration 5.2. Notice that the diagonal lines in part a are also found in part b. Although the deviant feature is identical in both part a and part b, you probably noticed the deviant region much more quickly in part b than in part a. In fact, Pomerantz and his colleagues found that people took more than twice as long to identify the deviant region for the simple figures in part a as for the more complex figures in part b. This study suggests that we process more than simple isolated features. The triangle created in part b is a real figure, not just a diagonal line added to a right angle.

The holistic Gestalt approach is distinctly different from a more analytical orientation, such as spatial frequency analysis. An **analytical orientation** emphasizes the importance of the components that combine to form our perceptu-

Demonstration 5.2

Identification of Features in Simple and Complex Figures

Inspect the two diagrams below. In each diagram one region is deviant because the figure is different from the other three. Do you identify the deviant region faster in part a or part b?

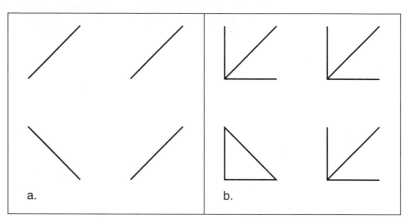

a.   b.

al experiences. However, you should think of these two general orientations as complementary, because perception relies on both holistic and analytic processes (Prinzmetal, 1995).

The three psychologists most closely associated with the classical Gestalt approach—and whose work forms the basis for most of this section—are Max Wertheimer (1923), Kurt Koffka (1935), and Wolfgang Köhler (1947). Gestalt psychologists investigated three areas that we will consider here: the laws of grouping, the "goodness" of figures (known as the law of Prägnanz), and figure–ground relationships. We will see that many of their ideas are still considered central to understanding shape perception, although their theories have certain limitations.

These Gestalt principles remain influential because they provide a means for organizing the edges extracted in the early stages of visual processing. For instance, Gestalt principles might provide a means for interpreting the output of spatial frequency analysis (Palmer, 1992b). We'll now discuss some of the Gestalt principles that allow us to group together visual elements.

Laws of Grouping

Five major *laws of grouping* describe why certain elements seem to go together rather than remaining isolated and independent:

1. The *law of proximity* states that objects near each other tend to be seen as a unit.
2. The *law of similarity* states that objects similar to each other tend to be seen as a unit.
3. The *law of good continuation* states that objects arranged in either a straight line or a smooth curve tend to be seen as a unit.
4. The *law of closure* states that when a figure has a gap, we tend to see it as a closed, complete figure.
5. The *law of common fate* states that when objects move in the same direction, we tend to see them as a unit. Because this law involves movement, we cannot truly illustrate it on a motionless page.

These laws are illustrated in Figure 5.6.

Incidentally, you can see each of the designs in Figure 5.6 another way, if you make a great effort. For example, when looking at Figure 5.6b, you

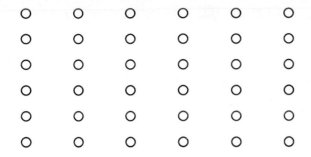

a. The law of proximity. You will see this arrangement as a set of columns—not a set of rows. Items that are near each other are grouped together. Now notice the typing in this book. You see rows of letters rather than columns because a letter is closer to the letters to the right and left than it is to the letters above and below.

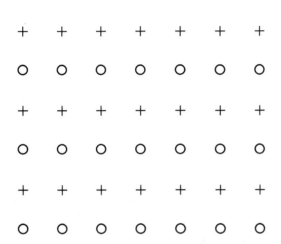

b. The law of similarity. You will see this arrangement as a set of rows rather than columns. Items that are similar to each other are grouped together. Now look at the two words at the end of this sentence that are in **boldface type.** Notice how these two words in heavier print cling together in a group, whereas the words in regular, lighter print form their own separate groups.

c. The law of good continuation. You will see a zigzag line with a curved line running through it, so that each line continues in the same direction it was going prior to intersection. Notice that you do not see the figure as being composed of the two elements below:

Look out the window at the branches of a tree, and focus on two branches that form a cross. You clearly perceive two straight lines, rather than two right angles touching each other.

d. The law of closure. You will see a circle here, even though it is not perfectly closed. A complete figure is simply more tempting than a curved line! Now close this book and put your finger across one edge, focusing on the shape of the outline of your book. You will see a rectangle rather than a bent line with four angles.

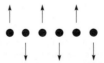

e. The law of common fate. If dots 1, 3, and 5 suddenly move up and dots 2, 4, and 6—at the same time—suddenly move down, the dots moving in the same direction will be perceived as belonging together. The next time you look at automobile traffic on a moderately busy street, notice how clearly the cars moving in one direction form one group and the cars moving in the opposite direction form another group.

FIGURE 5.6 Five of the Gestalt laws of grouping.

can force yourself to see seven columns, rather than seven rows. Nonetheless, an arrangement of rows is the pattern that emerges most readily.

Sometimes we can create a contest between two of the laws to see which is "stronger." For example, try opposing the law of proximity and the law of similarity. Make a row of plus signs and circles fairly close to each other. Underneath, at a distance greater than the distance between the pluses and circles, make another identical row of pluses and circles. Continue this process until you have six rows. Do you see rows or columns? You may be able to create a design in which no law of grouping is the clear-cut winner. The grouping will be unstable, and it will shift from one moment to the next. In contrast, try combining the laws of proximity and similarity. The grouping will be nearly permanent, and it will be extremely difficult to disrupt.

Max Wertheimer (1923) was the first to describe these laws of grouping. The grouping laws may be most obvious for visual perception (and that is why they are discussed in this chapter). However, Wertheimer noted that the laws of grouping occur with the other senses as well. For example, tap on your desk three times, pause, and tap again three times. The taps organize into groups on the basis of proximity. Now alternate soft and loud tapping; the loud taps will group together, and the soft taps will group together. Or suppose you are listening to a duet in which the singers at one point hit the same note and cross over; the law of good continuation may operate. Can you think of examples from nonvisual systems of the laws of closure and common fate?

Law of Prägnanz

As Kurt Koffka described the *law of Prägnanz,* "Of several geometrically possible organizations the one will actually occur which possesses the best, simplest and most stable shape" (Koffka, 1935, p. 138). For instance, the law of Prägnanz predicts that some geometric figures are "better" than others. Thus, simple 90° angles, perfect circles, and perfect squares are good figures, in contrast to 80° angles, lopsided circles, and tilted squares (Arnheim, 1986).

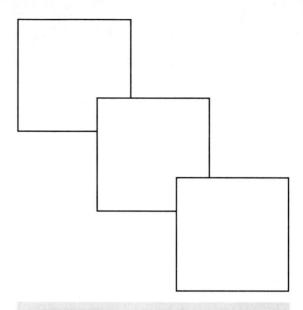

FIGURE 5.7 An illustration of the law of Prägnanz, which predicts that you will see this figure as three overlapping squares because that is the simplest interpretation of the figure.

Figure 5.7 shows a design that could be interpreted in at least two ways. It could represent three squares, two of which have small squares cut out of the lower right corner, or it could represent three squares overlapping each other. The law of Prägnanz predicts that you will see three overlapping squares.

How would Gestalt theory predict, in advance, what you would perceive in displays such as Figure 5.7? Devising a coding scheme for simplicity is quite difficult, though some researchers have been working on this problem (Leeuwenberg & Boselie, 1988; Pomerantz & Kubovy, 1986). Part of the problem surely resides in the fact that simplicity, or Prägnanz, can arise from a number of different sources.

For instance, Gestaltists thought that the preferred interpretation would be the one that is the most efficient and the most economical (Attneave, 1982; van Tuijl, 1980). We might also refer to this preference as the minimum principle

FIGURE 5.8 Two stimuli that can be formed by placing five dots within an invisible 3 × 3 grid. Which of the two patterns seems simpler to you? The symmetry of the left pattern is thought to make it simpler, indicating that symmetry may underlie Prägnanz. (From Garner & Clement, 1963)

(Leeuwenberg & Boselie, 1988). Thus, simpler representations would require fewer cognitive resources (Hatfield & Epstein, 1985). As a result, we could more easily encode good figures into memory. In fact, a number of studies indicate that people are better able to remember good figures (Howe & Brandau, 1983; Howe & Jung, 1986).

Another source of simplicity is symmetry. Wendell Garner (e.g., 1974; Garner & Clement, 1963) contributed a great deal to our understanding of the importance of symmetry for pattern goodness. If you look at Figure 5.8, which of the two objects strikes you as the simpler? Both are made up of five dots, but do they seem equally simple? Garner's research predicts that the more symmetrical figure will be perceived as simpler.

More recent research has confirmed the importance of symmetry for figural goodness (Palmer, 1991, 1992b). Other research has shown that people have a perceptual bias toward symmetry (Tversky, 1991). For example, people remember the alignment of countries in maps as being more symmetrical than the actual alignment.

Whatever the mechanisms that give rise to Prägnanz, most researchers would agree that our perceptual experience is driven by simplicity. In fact, we could consider the law of Prägnanz as a general principle that encompasses all other Gestalt laws (van Tuijl, 1980). In the last section we looked at the laws of grouping. These laws—proximity, similarity, good continuation, closure, and common fate—encourage the formation of good, simple, and stable shapes. Similarly, the law of Prägnanz encompasses figure–ground relationships, which are considered in the next section. Unfortunately, however, the law of Prägnanz is rather vague. Pomerantz and Kubovy (1981) point out the irony that Prägnanz—the law of simplicity—is not really as simple as it seems.

Figure–Ground Relationship

In the section on the laws of grouping, we saw that perceivers group parts of a design according to certain rules. In the section on the law of Prägnanz, we saw that people tend to organize forms to produce a simple interpretation, such as three overlapping squares. Organization is not random; we perceive patterns in the world around us. Parts of a design are also organized with respect to figure and ground. When two areas share a common boundary, the ***figure*** is the distinct shape with clearly defined edges. The ***ground*** is what is left over, forming the background. Look, for example, at a book (the figure) lying on your desk (the ground). The figure–ground relationship was one of the most important contributions of Gestalt psychologists.

Edgar Rubin (1915/1958), a Danish psychologist, was one of the first to try to clarify what constitutes the figure, as opposed to the ground. He reached four conclusions about figure and ground:

1. The figure has a definite shape, whereas the ground appears to have no shape. The figure is a "thing," whereas the ground is only a substance.
2. The ground seems to continue behind the figure. For example, try Demonstration 5.3.
3. The figure seems closer to us, with a clear location in space. In contrast, the ground is farther away and has no clear location in space; it is simply somewhere in the background.
4. The figure is more dominant and more impressive than the ground; it is also remembered better. As Rubin states, the figure seems to dominate consciousness. The ground, on the other hand, seems to become part of the general environment.

Demonstration 5.3

Ground Continuing Behind Figure

Which is figure and which is ground in this picture? Probably, the cross with the radial marks looks like the figure, and the one with concentric circles looks like the ground, continuing behind the figure. With some effort you can force the radially marked cross to become the ground and the concentrically marked cross to become the figure. This is difficult, however, because the radial marks do not seem to continue behind the new figure.

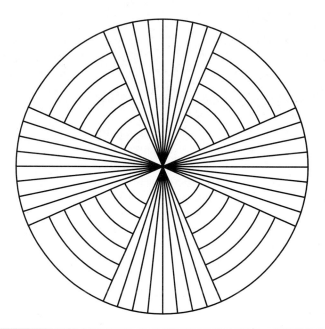

As you stare at some figures against certain backgrounds, you may notice that an interesting reversal begins to occur. In Demonstration 5.3, for example, you probably began by seeing the radially marked cross as the figure. Perhaps, though, after a few seconds of looking at the figure, the concentrically marked cross popped out, forcing the radial markings into the background.

Ambiguous figure–ground relationships are situations in which the figure and the ground reverse from time to time, the figure becoming the ground and then becoming the figure again. These reversals often appear spontaneously, although you can also force the reversals to occur

if you concentrate upon seeing a prominent shape in the ground. Figure 5.9 shows the vase–faces problem, one of the most famous examples of the ambiguous figure–ground relationship. You can see either a white vase or two outlined faces. However, you cannot see both the vase and faces at the same time.

The Dutch artist M. C. Escher enjoyed playing perceptual tricks on his viewers. You will find several examples of ambiguous figure–ground relationships in Escher's (1971) work. In one picture, for example, light-colored horsemen and dark-colored horsemen take turns becoming figure and ground.

FIGURE 5.9 The vase–faces figure illustrates the potential ambiguity of figure–ground relationships. You can see the white vase against a dark ground or you can see the black faces against a white ground. Notice how difficult it is to see both the faces and the vase simultaneously.

In everyday life we do not see many examples of ambiguous figure–ground relationships. Sometimes, however, we find it difficult to detect an animal concealed against a background of a similar pattern and design. We may even be unaware of the animal's presence until it suddenly scurries off. This protective coloration offers animals an advantage over potential predators. Regan and Beverley (1984) studied camouflaged figures in the laboratory and discovered that many could not be distinguished from the ground until the figure moved.

Problems with the Gestalt Approach

As Grossberg and Mingolla (1985) observe, one of the great accomplishments of Gestalt psychologists was to suggest a short list of rules for perceptual organization. However, "as is often the case in pioneering work, the rules were nei-

ther always obeyed nor exhaustive" (p. 142). Let us consider some of the problems:

1. The major method in Gestalt psychology was phenomenological observation, a phrase clearly related to the more common word *phenomenon*. **Phenomenological observation** means that observers must look at their immediate experience and attempt to describe it completely, with as little bias or interpretation as possible (Lindauer, 1984; Metelli, 1982; Pomerantz & Kubovy, 1981). However, modern experimental psychologists tend to mistrust phenomenological observations because they doubt that observers really are providing unbiased observations.

2. Gestalt theorists proposed a neurological explanation for their principles that involved electromagnetic fields in the brain. Research has not supported this explanation, and the original neurological aspects of the theory have been discarded (Hatfield & Epstein, 1985; Rock & Palmer, 1990).

3. The Gestalt laws are vague, and experts have not come to a clear-cut agreement as to the exact list of laws. In fact, counts of the number of laws range between 1 and 114 (Pomerantz, 1986; Pomerantz & Kubovy, 1986).

4. Hints and suggestions can have an enormous influence on figure–ground perception. For example, Kennedy (1974) suggests that you think of the figure in Demonstration 5.3 as a beach ball rather than a cross. Probably you have no difficulty doing this. If conceptually driven processes can influence perception so strongly, argues Kennedy, then figure–ground perception cannot be very basic or primitive.

Despite these objections, Gestalt psychology has clearly *not* been abandoned by psychologists interested in perception. Since its introduction by Wertheimer in 1912, Gestalt psychology has continued to have a considerable impact on several areas of psychology, particularly on the perception of form (Pomerantz & Kubovy, 1981, 1986; Rock & Palmer, 1990). In the next section, we will discuss some current research that clearly follows in the Gestalt tradition.

IN-DEPTH Modern Gestalt Research

Some researchers are so closely affiliated with the Gestalt approach that they consider themselves neo-Gestaltists. Many more researchers are still investigating areas studied by the Gestalt theorists. For example, Michael Kubovy (1994; Kubovy & Wagemans, 1995) has contributed greatly to our understanding of the role of proximity in grouping. In this section, we will sample from some recent research that will illustrate the vitality of the Gestalt tradition.

Although the Gestalt psychologists espoused many principles of perceptual organization, new principles have emerged over time. Recently, Stephen E. Palmer (1992a) has proposed a new principle of organization called **common region.** According to the principle of common region, we tend to group together stimuli that appear to occur within the same region. For instance, looking at a map of the United States, would you group Pittsburgh, PA, with Harrisburg, PA, or with Columbus, OH? Although Pittsburgh is actually closer to Columbus, people tend to group it with Harrisburg—another city within the bounds of Pennsylvania. As you can see in Figure 5.10, in spite of identical arrangements of the words on the two placards, the message is changed radically by changing the regions that bound the words. Do you get the impression that far too many people are adhering to the message of the lower placard?

As we mentioned early in this chapter, researchers have become increasingly interested in determining the processes or stages that underlie object perception. If we assume that the Gestalt laws of grouping are necessary for linking the edges extracted by very early processes, then the Gestalt laws must operate fairly early in the process of object perception.

However, Koffka (1935) pointed out that before the laws of grouping could be applied, a more primitive operation must occur. Palmer and Rock (1994a, 1994b) have elaborated on Koffka's ideas and called the operation uniform connectedness. According to the principle of **uniform connectedness,** we organize input as a single unit when we perceive a connected region of uniform visual properties, such as lightness, color, and so on (Palmer & Rock, 1994b). Figure 5.11 illustrates

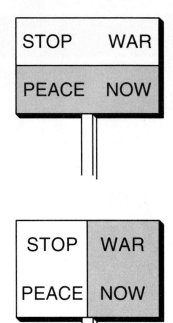

FIGURE 5.10 These two placards demonstrate the importance of common region. Changing the regions that are common to two of the four words alters the message of these two placards dramatically. (From Palmer, 1992a)

the operation of uniform connectedness. Notice how easily this principle overrides the laws of proximity and similarity.

Uniform connectedness may arise as edges are connected. As you will recall from our discussion in Chapter 4, edge detection is crucial for vision. When edges unite to bound an area of the visual field, the area within the edges will be uniform, because of the absence of edges. Krauskopf's (1963) experiment on stabilized retinal images provides an important illustration of the way the visual system connects the area bounded by edges. As you may recall, when Krauskopf stabilized the inner red circle, people

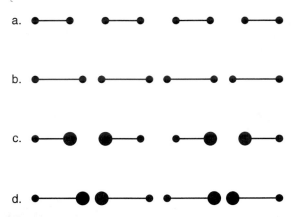

FIGURE 5.11 Four patterns that illustrate the principle of uniform connectedness. In all four patterns, each line creates a pattern connecting the two dots. Notice that the line forms such a strong connection that this unit is able to override the Gestalt grouping laws of proximity (in b), similarity (in c), and even proximity and similarity together (in d). (Palmer & Rock, 1994b)

perceived a uniform green circle. Presumably, the interior was filled in because the receptors on the inside of the circular edge were all receiving green light.

Palmer and Rock (1994b) propose an ordering of perceptual processes in which uniform connectedness occurs at the beginning to organize the visual scene, followed next by figure–ground organization. These and other intermediate processes create object perception as a final product. Many researchers agree with Palmer and Rock that figure–ground organization occurs as a fairly early process—certainly preceding object recognition.

However, not everyone agrees with the ordering of the processes proposed by Palmer and Rock (Peterson, 1994b). For example, Mary Peterson and her colleagues argue that some form of object recognition must *precede* figure–ground organization (Peterson, 1994a; Peterson & Gibson, 1993, 1994a, 1994b; Peterson et al., 1991). Consider Figures 5.12a and 5.12b. How easily could you maintain the symmetrical black area in the middle of the two figures as figure? Most people find it easier to see the black area as figure in Figure 5.12a than in Figure 5.12b. Why?

Presumably because they notice that the white space in Figure 5.12b could be seen as two half-silhouettes of standing women. As soon as that perception emerges, it's more difficult to see the black area as figure. The "trick" is that the two stimuli are identical, except that one is the other turned upside down. Because the two stimuli are identical, except for orientation, you should see the black area as figure with equal ease in both cases, if Palmer and Rock are correct.

Peterson and her colleagues argue that because people have more difficulty seeing the inner black area of Figure 5.12b as figure, they must be perceiving the objects (the white silhouettes) prior to organizing the stimulus into figure and ground. Peterson and her colleagues find similar results in other experiments. For example, people are shown stimuli like those in Figures 5.12c and 5.12d. On some trials the stimuli are in the present, upright position and on other trials the stimuli are upside down. People can perceive the silhouettes as figure more readily in the "upright" orientation, and they find it harder to see the remainder of the stimulus (the left side in this orientation) as figure. However, they can see more easily that

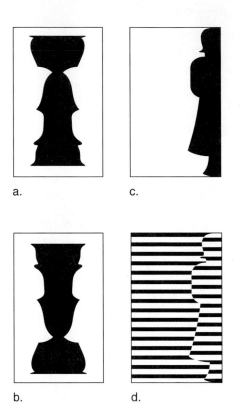

a.

c.

b.

d.

FIGURE 5.12 Four patterns used by Peterson and her colleagues to illustrate the precedence of object perception over figure–ground organization. Figure 5.12a is simply Figure 5.12b upside down. You should find it fairly easy to see the middle black area in Figure 5.12a as figure. However, because you can more easily see the white area in Figure 5.12b as two white silhouettes of women, you should find it more difficult to perceive the black middle area as figure, compared to Figure 5.12b. For Figures 5.12c and 5.12d, you can perceive the silhouette as figure more readily when the stimuli are in this position. Turn your book upside down and you should find it more difficult to maintain those areas as figure. (From Gibson & Peterson, 1994; Peterson & Gibson, 1994; Peterson et al., 1991)

portion of the stimulus as figure when the stimulus is shown in the upside-down orientation.

Because they believe that figure–ground separation must precede object perception, Palmer and Rock (1994a) disagree with Peterson's interpretation of her results. Thus, this healthy controversy is likely to continue until more research clarifies the processes that underlie object perception.

Such attempts to identify the ordering of processes in shape perception should ultimately prove fruitful. For example, previous researchers had thought that Gestalt principles were applied very early in the processing of visual stimuli. However, recent research indicates that attention is crucial for the operation of Gestalt principles (Mack et al., 1992; Rock & Mack, 1994). People simply do not see background textures full of Gestalt cues when they are attending to a stimulus in the foreground (Mack et al., 1992). On the other hand, aspects of the stimuli that presumably contribute to uniform connectedness—such as color—operate at some preattentive stage (Rock et al., 1992a).

This brief review of some current research should make clear that many of the questions that stimulated the Gestalt psychologists continue to generate research. We will now turn our attention to a recent approach that makes use of both spatial frequency analysis and Gestalt organizational principles—the computational approach. ◆

Computational Approach

As we mentioned in Chapter 1, the *computational approach* tries to formally define the visual processes necessary to represent the world. Any one of several different programs or algorithms might actually produce these processes. A computational theorist is often interested in developing programs that can take in the sort of information falling on the human retina and process the information to yield representations of the world. Although even the simplest organisms seem to accomplish this task quite easily, computational theorists find it difficult to program artificial systems to accomplish the task (Ullman, 1993).

When a program or algorithm is ultimately developed, the theorist must then determine the extent to which the proposed program or algorithm is similar to the actual algorithm found in our visual systems (Richards, 1988).

Much of the work emphasizing the computational approach has focused on the early stages of visual processing, or what might be referred to as low-level scene analysis. However, these theorists explicitly acknowledge the operation of higher-level processes (Fischler & Firschein, 1987). For instance, recognizing an object as a house requires that we know what a house is (Barrow & Tenenbaum, 1986). Nevertheless, the computational approach tends to rely on the application of general knowledge about physical principles rather than on specific information about the world (Wagemans, 1988).

The late David Marr and his colleagues at the Massachusetts Institute of Technology, especially Ellen Hildreth and Shimon Ullman, have had a tremendous influence on the computational approach. The influence of these researchers will be reflected in this section, which draws heavily on their work.

Marr (1982) analyzed the perceptual process into three different levels: (1) the computational theory, (2) representation and algorithm, and (3) the hardware implementation. The computational theory is relatively abstract and most closely related to the perceptual problem being solved. One such problem might be, Why do we see the world as unchanging in spite of retinal changes?

Such a problem might be solved in potentially different ways (algorithms) using different hardware. The distinction between algorithms and hardware roughly resembles the distinction between software and computer. To solve the problem of writing a paper, you might choose one of several different word-processing programs. Versions of the chosen program might have been implemented for totally different brands of computers, so you next choose the hardware to solve your problem. You should note that the actual program, or code, used to invoke the algorithms of the word processor could differ substantially within and between types of computers.

The neuroanatomy and neurophysiology of vision are mostly involved with the level of hardware implementation (Plaut & Farah, 1991). Marr was not confident that we would learn much about the process of vision by studying the hardware of vision—he likened that approach to learning about bird flight by studying feathers. Instead, we should study aerodynamics, which would lead us to a better understanding of birds' wings. Likewise, if we learn about the principles necessary to solve the problem of edge detection, we would have a better understanding of the nature of the algorithms and hardware involved in vision.

From Edges to Shape Perception

In Chapter 4 we discussed the importance of edge detection. The computational approach also emphasizes the importance of edge detection for early stages of visual perception. Marr (1982) offered the notion of a zero-crossing as the starting point in edge detection. A *zero-crossing* is the point at which a function changes from positive to negative and occurs when there is an intensity change in the visual field. Mathematically, a particular filter—called a *Mexican-hat filter*—can detect a zero-crossing. A cross section through the center of the function is seen in Figure 5.13. You will see the origin of the filter's name when you look at the three-dimensional representation in Figure 5.14b.

What happens when we pass an image through this filter? In part, it depends on the size of the filter used. In Figure 5.14, the original picture (a) was analyzed by both a wide and a narrow Mexican-hat filter to produce the two pictures seen in part c and part d, respectively. Notice that in both cases, edges and blobs are extracted from the original image, with the narrower filter producing greater detail.

If you recall the receptive fields we discussed in Chapter 3, you will see the close connection between the Mexican-hat filter and the "hardware" that appears to produce the filter. A ganglion cell's on-center, off-surround receptive field is much like the Mexican-hat filter shown in Figure 5.14 seen from overhead. In other words, the horizontal interconnections among

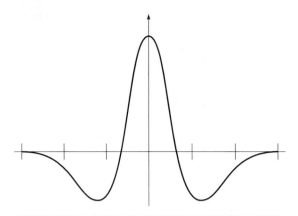

FIGURE 5.13 A cross section through the center of a Mexican-hat filter. The *x*-axis represents area and the *y*-axis represents intensity.

our photoreceptors produce receptive fields that can function as edge-producing filters.

The computational approach contains elements of the spatial frequency approach. Recalling the information in the earlier section, you should see that the width of the receptive field (filter) would determine the spatial frequency to which the neuron is most sensitive (Stillings et al., 1987). Narrower filters would be more sensitive to higher spatial frequencies. Presumably, the visual cortex receives zero-crossing "maps" of input from the multiple spatial frequency analyzers and combines them into a representation of the original image (Hildreth & Ullman, 1989).

According to Marr (1982), the information from the filters leads to the primal sketch. The raw *primal sketch* is like "a map specifying the precise positions of the edge segments, together with the specifications at each point along them of the local orientation and of the type and extent of the intensity change" (Marr, 1982, p. 71). Organizing principles, such as the Gestalt principles discussed previously, operate on the elements of the raw primal sketch to group the elements together and produce the full primal sketch.

These organizing principles become apparent when you look at the pattern in Figure 5.15,

designed by Marroquin. Notice how your visual system continually offers different organizations for the elements in the figure. Your system seems to be trying to organize the display into "objects" that may even appear to be defined by *virtual lines*—lines that aren't really there! These virtual lines play an important role in the theories of Marr and others (Earle, 1991). Keep these virtual lines in mind when we discuss illusory contours.

How we extract three-dimensional (3-D) information from two-dimensional (2-D) retinal input is a topic we will explore in great detail in Chapter 6. At this point, you should realize that the ability to do so is crucial for the rich sense of depth that we experience as we look out at the world. One step in the process will likely be the determination of figure and ground, for which some computational theorists have already developed algorithms (Grossberg, 1993a, 1993b).

Marr proposes that we achieve a three-dimensional representation in two stages. The first stage, called the *2.5-D sketch,* is a representation of the visible surfaces in the visual field from the viewer's perspective. The sketch is labeled 2.5-D to indicate that it does not fully capture all of the 3-D information, nor is it completely two-dimensional. The 2.5-D sketch is built up from the full primal sketch along with information derived from motion and differences between the images on the two retinas (Bruce & Green, 1990; Marr, 1982).

Some theorists argue that the viewer-centered representation remains crucial for object recognition (Tarr & Pinker, 1990). Others believe that, because we are capable of recognizing objects when viewing them from several different perspectives, we are unlikely to rely on a viewer-centered representation for object recognition (Corballis, 1988; Marr, 1982). Corballis (1988) argues that object recognition may precede—and aid—the determination of an object-centered representation. On the other hand, Marr and Nishihara (1978) propose that prior to recognizing an object, we transform the 2.5-D sketch into a representation that is object-centered. This object-centered *3-D sketch* represents depth more accurately than the 2.5-D

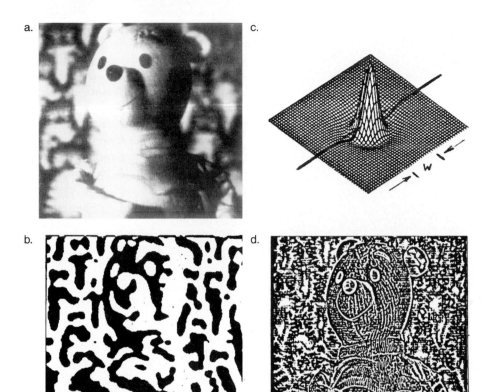

FIGURE 5.14 The analysis of a photograph using a Mexican-hat filter. Part a shows the original photograph. Part b captures the three-dimensionality of the Mexican-hat filter, with the dark line through the center yielding Figure 5.13. Analyzing part a with a wide filter (W in part b is large) yields part c. Analyzing part a with a narrow filter (W is small) yields part d. (From Richards, Nishihara, & Dawson, 1988)

sketch. You might be able to imagine how a person could construct a 3-D sketch by mentally combining various cylinders or cones—like a sculpture made from clay.

Suppose that you had a bunch of cylinders of various sizes. As you can see in Figure 5.16, combining these cylinders in various ways allows for a fairly flexible representation of objects. Construction of objects from such cylinders is useful because it allows us to predict the parts of the objects that would be visible from a particular perspective and the parts that would be hidden (Paap & Partridge, 1988). In order to create such representations, people must be able to mentally attach the cones or cylinders to one another at different positions and different angles (Hummel, 1994; Hummel & Biederman, 1992). Put the six cones together one way and you have

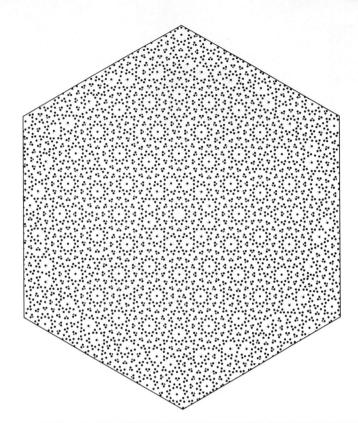

FIGURE 5.15 An illustration of the operation of organizing principles in the visual system. As you stare at this figure, you will see several circles of different sizes emerge. Sometimes an element of the figure is part of one circle, and at other times that same element is part of another circle. (From J. L. Marroquin, as seen in Marr, 1982)

a roughly human form. Shorten the two leg cylinders and lengthen the two arm cylinders, and you now have a roughly simian form. Change the orientation and size of the six cylinders, and you now have an ostrich.

Biederman's (1987) *recognition-by-components approach* is similar to that taken by Marr and Nishihara. Biederman refers to the basic shapes from which objects are constructed as *geons* (short for "geometric icons"). Biederman proposes 36 different geons, from which a vast array of objects could be constructed. For instance, more than 150

million possible objects could be constructed from various combinations of 3 geons. Recognition does not require that all of the component geons be processed, however. For instance, in Figure 5.17 you can recognize a stylized penguin composed of just a few geons as easily as you can recognize a more completely drawn penguin—a fact that eases the task of a cartoonist.

Sources of Shape Information

As we emphasize in Theme 2 (see page 10), natural stimuli are rich sources of information. Part

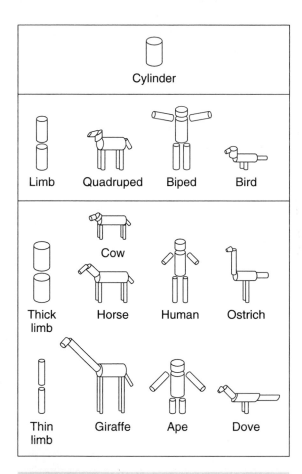

FIGURE 5.16 A figure that illustrates the flexibility of a cylinder in constructing various shapes. For instance, only six cylinders are needed to capture a basic biped. Manipulating the dimensions of the six cylinders could produce a recognizable human form or ape form. (From Marr & Nishihara, 1978)

FIGURE 5.17 A penguin is distinguishable in either drawing, even though only a few geons are present in the drawing on the left. In order to recognize shapes, we need not analyze all of the constituent geons. (From Biederman, 1987)

of the task confronting a computational theorist is to identify the types of information in natural stimuli that might be used to derive an object's shape. Computational theorists have identified a number of different aspects of stimuli that aid in the perception of shape. These theorists tend to identify the aspect of the stimulus that gives rise to shape information as "shape from _____,"

where the blank is filled in with the crucial aspect of the stimulus. We will now review some of these sources of information about shape.

Shape from motion indicates that we gain a good deal of information about an object's 3-D shape when it is in motion (e.g., Norman & Todd, 1993; Pollick, 1994; Tittle & Braunstein, 1993; Tyler, 1991b). As we will discuss in Chapter 6, when you look at the shadow of a 3-D object projected onto a 2-D surface, you have no sense at all that the object has any depth. However, when the object is placed into motion, so that the 2-D shadow moves, the object immediately becomes three-dimensional (Wallach & O'Connell, 1953). Because the image cast on our retinas is 2-D, computational theorists have developed algorithms that derive 3-D shape from moving 2-D images (Norman & Todd, 1993). Neurophysiological research also supports our ability to extract shape from motion (Siegel & Andersen, 1991).

Computational theorists have determined that the way that light falls on an object provides important cues called *shape from shading* and *shape from highlights* (Bülthoff, 1991; Bülthoff & Mallot, 1988; Churchland & Sejnowski, 1992; Ramachandran, 1988). Look around you and notice that the curvature common to many objects—like faces—tends to create areas that receive less light than other areas. Notice how an overhead light creates shading under a person's nose and chin. These shadows attached to the object provide important information about the shape of the object. We will have more to say about the role of shadows in depth perception in Chapter 6. Notice also that shiny surfaces, like some people's foreheads, may also reflect the light source more directly, creating a bright highlight. Such highlights are also important cues to an object's shape (Bülthoff, 1991).

Computational theorists have identified other aspects of the stimulus that give rise to shape information. For now, however, we will turn our attention to other approaches to shape and pattern perception.

Feature-Integration Approach

The previous approaches to shape perception have made little specific mention of the role of attention. Attention is a word with varied meanings. We define **attention** as the focusing or concentration of mental activity. The role of attention in shape or form perception is highlighted in the **feature-integration approach** developed by Anne Treisman and her colleagues. Treisman (1986) writes,

> Some simple generalizations about visual information processing are beginning to emerge. One of them is a distinction between two levels of processing. Certain aspects of visual processing seem to be accomplished simultaneously (that is, for the entire visual field at once) and automatically (that is, without attention being focused on any one part of the visual field). Other aspects of visual processing seem to depend on focused attention and are done serially, or one at a time, as if a mental spotlight were being moved from one location to another. (p. 114B)

The first stage in this model, **preattentive processing,** involves the automatic registration of features, using parallel processing across the vi-

sual field. A **parallel process** is one that allows all the targets to be processed simultaneously. You should note the similarity between this stage and the primal sketch of the computational approach.

The second stage of this model, **focused attention,** involves the identification of objects by serial processing. A **serial process** requires the targets to be processed one at a time. Focused attention is described as the "glue" that binds the separate features into a unitary object.

Treisman and Gelade (1980) examined these two kinds of processing approaches by studying two different kinds of stimulus situations, one that used isolated features and one that used combinations of features. These researchers proposed that if isolated features are processed automatically in preattentive processing, then a target should be located rapidly if it differs from its neighboring, irrelevant items. It should seem to "pop out" of the display automatically. In a series of studies, Treisman and Gelade discovered that if a target feature differed from the irrelevant items with respect to a simple feature such as orientation or color or curvature, observers could detect the target just as fast when it was presented in an array of 30 items as when it was presented in an array of three (Treisman, 1986; Treisman & Gelade, 1980).

In other research, Treisman and Souther (1985) found that people use preattentive processing when a simple feature is *present* in a target, but they use focused processing when that same feature is *absent* from the target. Figure 5.18 shows displays similar to the ones people examined in Treisman and Souther's study. In Figure 5.18a people searched for a circle with a line; in Figure 5.18b they searched for a circle without a line. As you can see, the circle with a line "pops out" in the upper display, but you must inspect the display on the bottom more closely to determine that it contains the target.

Feature-integration theory suggests that when attention is either overloaded or distracted, features can be combined inappropriately in perception; an inappropriate combination is called an **illusory conjunction.** When the circumstances prevent us from looking at an object

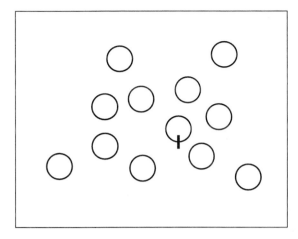

a.

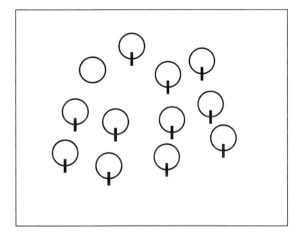

b.

FIGURE 5.18 Stimuli used in Treisman and Souther's (1985) study. Do you find the different stimulus more easily in part a or in part b?

with focused attention, we jumble together the features in an attempt to perceive the object (Intraub, 1985, 1989; Treisman & Schmidt, 1982). The illusory conjunctions may occur because of difficulties integrating information in the visual cortex about objects and spatial location (Cohen & Rafal, 1991).

Most experiments that create illusory conjunctions use very brief exposures. For example, people were asked to report the presence of a plus sign in brief exposures of the three displays seen in Figure 5.19. When the plus sign was not present, people were more likely to report that it was present in displays like 5.19b than in displays like 5.19c. Notice that Figure 5.19b contains both of the components of the plus sign, which are then placed into an illusory conjunction (Prinzmetal, 1995). More recent experiments show that illusory conjunctions can occur with exposure times as long as 1.5 seconds (Prinzmetal, 1995).

Why don't we experience illusory conjunctions more frequently? Gestalt principles may play a role in the process, because people are more likely to produce illusory conjunctions between objects in close proximity to one another. Illusory conjunctions are less likely when objects are distant from one another (Prinzmetal, 1995). Treisman (1986) suggests that top-down processing helps to screen out inappropriate combinations. For example, people are less likely to experience illusory conjunctions between color and shape when such a conjunction would lead to an inappropriate combination, such as a purple carrot. Thus, prior knowledge and expectations help people to use attention efficiently (Treisman, 1986). Consistent with Theme 4 of this book, cognitive processes aid perception.

Prototype-Matching Approach

So far, we have examined four approaches to shape and pattern perception: spatial frequency analysis, the Gestalt approach, the computational approach, and the feature-integration approach. According to the fifth perspective, the ***prototype-matching approach,*** we store abstract, idealized patterns in memory. When we see a particular object, we compare it with a ***prototype,*** or an ideal figure. If it matches, we recognize the pattern. If it does not match, we compare it with other prototypes until we find a match. For example, you have probably developed a prototype

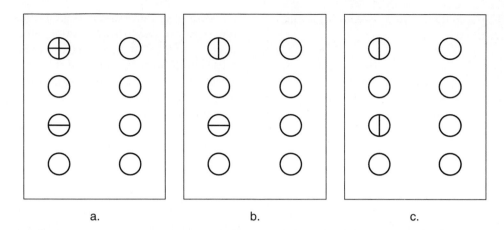

a.   b.   c.

FIGURE 5.19 An example of stimulus arrays used to create illusory conjunctions. If people are asked to search for a plus sign (as in part a), they are more likely to report incorrectly that they have seen a plus sign in part b than they are to report a plus sign in part c. (From Prinzmetal, 1995)

for your college's president. This prototype represents a person of a certain height and body build and certain facial features. This prototype does not need to specify a particular facial expression or a particular kind of clothing—after all, a prototype is abstract. When you see the president, recognition occurs because the person in front of you matches the prototype.

The prototype-matching view is flexible. The prototype is a general pattern, not a specific one with every feature well defined. After all, we can recognize a letter even when it is distorted. Consider the letter M, for example. Look at the assorted M's in Figure 5.20. You recognize those letters as M's even though they are all different. You can also recognize an M in various orientations like M and M and in various sizes like M and M.

You might wonder where prototypes come from. A good deal of research suggests that we extract prototypes from repeated exposures to different exemplars (e.g., Barsalou, 1990; Posner & Keele, 1968; Solso & McCarthy, 1981). Thus, once you know that all the letters in Figure 5.20 are M's, you can extract the essential characteris-

tics that determine M-ness. Your prototype might be something like "roughly vertical stroke up, stroke down and right, stroke up and right, stroke down." If you know about the work of the devel-

FIGURE 5.20 The fact that you can readily recognize all of these stimuli as M's is an indication of the flexibility of your visual system. Such flexibility is inconsistent with a template-matching approach to shape or form perception.

opmental psychologist Jean Piaget, you might also relate the formation of prototypes to his concept of assimilation.

Do not confuse the prototype-matching view with an earlier approach that was similar but much less flexible—template matching. According to the ***template-matching approach,*** we have many templates, or specific patterns, stored in memory. When we see a letter, for example, we see whether it matches one of the templates. If it matches, we recognize the letter. If it does not fit the template, we search for another template. In a way, the template is like a lock, and a letter is like a key. As you know, a key may be only a tiny bit different from the appropriate shape, yet that difference is sufficient to prevent the key from opening the lock.

The idea of each pattern fitting into an appropriate template sounds interesting, but it has a clear drawback: We would need literally millions of templates to be able to recognize all the variations of all the letters and shapes. The system would have to be overwhelmingly bulky to store all the templates. Furthermore, it would be overwhelmingly time-consuming. To recognize a letter, we would have to compare the letter with numerous templates. How could you ever read at an average rate of more than 200 words per minute if you had to struggle with dozens of templates for each letter?

Clearly, the prototype-matching approach is more likely to underlie shape perception than the restrictive template-matching approach. However, both the prototype- and template-matching approaches are useful because they emphasize the distinction between the percept and the mental representation to which it must be compared in order for us to recognize an object (Quinlan, 1991). Any approach to object recognition must at some point hypothesize such an operation.

SECTION SUMMARY

Approaches to Shape and Pattern Perception

1. A shape or form is determined by particular arrangements of edges. How we perceive shapes is determined by a combination of bottom-up and top-down processes.

2. The spatial frequency analysis approach proposes that Fourier analysis can be used to break a complex scene into its component sine waves, each corresponding to a different sinusoidal grating. People have multiple spatial frequency channels, each with a different ideal frequency determined by the receptive fields of its neurons. Overall, however, people are most sensitive to gratings with spatial frequencies of 6 cycles/degree.

3. The Gestalt approach emphasizes that we see objects as well-organized "wholes" rather than separate parts. The perception of objects arises through the organization of elements according to the laws of grouping, which include the laws of proximity, similarity, good continuation, closure, and common fate.

4. The law of Prägnanz refers to the tendency to perceive figures as good, simple, and stable. Thus, some figures are "better" than others and are easier to encode into memory than poor figures.

5. In figure–ground relationships, the figure has a definite shape with clearly defined contours, in contrast to the ground, or background. The figure also seems closer and more dominant. In ambiguous figure–ground relationships, the figure and the ground reverse from time to time.

6. The principle of uniform connectedness, whereby similar areas of the visual field are linked together, appears to operate at very early stages of visual perception. Figure–ground relationships are thought by some researchers to be determined fairly early in visual perception, but other researchers argue that some form of object perception actually precedes figure–ground organization.

7. According to the computational approach, we build up our perception of shapes through a series of processes. Edge information is extracted through the Mexican-hat filter provided by the receptive fields and combined into a primal sketch. The primal sketch, combined with other information, produces the 2.5-D

sketch. The completed representation, the 3-D sketch, emerges from the combination of the 2.5-D sketch with other information.

8. A number of factors aid in our perception of shape, including shape from motion, shape from shading, and shape from highlights.

9. The feature-integration approach emphasizes the importance of attention. This approach proposes that shape perception emerges from two processes—one parallel (preattentive processing) and one serial (focused attention).

10. The prototype-matching approach proposes that people recognize an object by comparing its percept with an ideal figure or prototype stored in memory.

INFLUENCE OF CONTEXT ON SHAPE AND PATTERN PERCEPTION

Context plays an important role in many areas of psychology, although not everyone would agree about the pervasiveness of its importance (Capaldi & Proctor, 1994; Grossberg, 1995). As an example of the importance of context, consider the difference between yelling "Fire!" in a theater and yelling "Fire!" on a shooting range (Capaldi & Proctor, 1994). On some occasions, context is crucial! We believe that context plays a very important role in perception generally, but particularly in shape perception.

You can think of context in at least two ways. First, you can think of context as the stimuli that surround (and potentially influence the perception of) a target stimulus. Thus, when looking at Figure 5.21, you will read the same stimulus as B in the top array and as 13 in the bottom array. Second, you can think of context as existing in the mind of the perceiver. Have you noticed how your own experience, your mood, or your state of arousal can influence your perception of events? Top-down processing emphasizes the role of the perceiver's knowledge in creating a context within which stimuli are interpreted. Thus, an expert

computer programmer will perceive flaws in code to which a neophyte would be oblivious.

Obviously, these two types of contexts are interrelated. If you know what kind of scene you are examining, you can rely upon important information about the kinds of objects you are likely to find in that scene. For example, if you are looking at a scene we could call "Psychology Building on a Tuesday Morning," you know that you are more likely to find your perception professor there than, say, Meryl Streep or William Shakespeare. The contextual stimuli evoke a set of mental expectations, which, in turn, provide a context that aids you in identifying the people you see in that context.

In this section, we will review some of the ways in which context influences perception. We will first focus on the perception of visual scenes in general, then on the perception of letters. Next, we will examine how context can give rise to illusory contours and can lead us to misperceive stimuli.

Perceiving Objects in the Context of Scenes

Before we begin, you should recall our discussion of the computational approach to shape perception. Marr, Biederman, and other computational theorists we mentioned emphasize how shapes can be perceived without recourse to knowledge about the context within which they appear (De Graef, 1992). Thus, an object-centered 3-D shape can be extracted by binding cones, cylinders, or geons with orientation information. Other theorists take a more strongly top-down approach, in which mental structures or schemas are important for the perception of objects (e.g., Grossberg, 1995; Hochberg, 1979, 1994). In this section, we will selectively review some work that emphasizes the importance of context for object recognition.

Stephen E. Palmer (1975b) provides a useful example of the importance of context. Look at each line fragment in Figure 5.22b. Each squiggle by itself is meaningless and unrecognizable. However, when each squiggle is placed within the

BRONZE

B60428

An illustration of the role of context in object perception. Note that the initial parts of the two lines are identical but will be perceived as a B in the top line and as 13 in the bottom line. Note, also, that the same symbol is perceived as an O in the top line and as a zero in the bottom line.

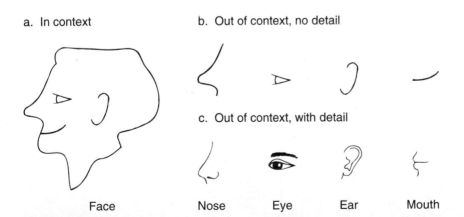

a. In context

b. Out of context, no detail

c. Out of context, with detail

Face   Nose   Eye   Ear   Mouth

FIGURE 5.22 Facial features in context (a) and out of context (b and c). Notice that the ambiguous features in part b are unambiguous when seen in part a. With greater detail, even component features of a face are recognizable out of context, as seen in part c. (From Palmer, 1975a)

context of a face—as in Figure 5.22a—the irregular bump is suddenly, unmistakably, a nose. In context, then, primitive, unrealistic lines can be recognized as features. Convince yourself of this by drawing a variety of lines to represent a mouth. Almost any segment of a reasonable length could pass for a mouth in the context of a face. Such shapes can be recognized in context, although they would be meaningless out of context.

Although we *can* recognize features out of context, the features must be more detailed. If we supply internal structure for each feature by adding realistic details, then the angular bump is clearly a nose, as in Figure 5.22c.

Another experiment by Palmer (1975a) explored the influence of "world knowledge" on recognition. You know that you are likely to find bread in a kitchen, a mailbox in a front yard, and a drum in a band. Palmer showed his observers scenes such as the one on the left in Figure 5.23. Then he very briefly showed them figures such as in parts a, b, and c. In some cases, the figure was appropriate for the scene (such as the bread in part a). In other cases it was inappropriate, but its shape was similar to that of an appropriate figure (such as the mailbox in part b). In still other cases, the figure was inappropriate, and the shape was different from the appropriate figure (such as

the drum-shaped item in part c). In a final condition, observers did not see any contextual scene; they were asked to identify the figure without any context. In each condition, they were asked to name the object and to rate their confidence that their identification had been correct.

When the figure was appropriate for the scene, such as a loaf of bread in a kitchen, the observers were 84% accurate in their identification. They were substantially less accurate when they had no contextual scene. However, they were even less accurate when the figure was inappropriate for the scene, such as the mailbox or the drum in the kitchen.

Susan Boyce and Alexander Pollatsek used a similar approach (Boyce & Pollatsek, 1992a, 1992b; Boyce et al., 1989). People saw several related objects within a scene that provided an appropriate context, an inappropriate context, or no context. As people looked at the scene on a computer screen, one of the objects wiggled. As soon as the object wiggled, the person named the object as quickly as possible. People were quicker to identify the object when it occurred within an appropriate context.

Think about how you may have noticed the effect of appropriate context in your past experience. A friend whom you would recognize

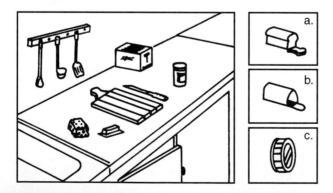

FIGURE 5.23 Context scene and target objects used in Palmer's experiment. People are more accurate in recognizing briefly presented objects (such as the bread in part a) when seen in an appropriate context. (From Palmer, 1975b)

readily in an appropriate setting, such as a college classroom, is suddenly unrecognizable in your hometown supermarket or a New York City art gallery.

Helene Intraub and her colleagues have taken a different approach to show that people make use of context in perceiving a scene (Intraub, 1992; Intraub et al., 1992; Intraub & Bodamer, 1993). When people are shown a tightly framed picture of an object, such as a person's head or a basketball, they later remember seeing more of the scene than was actually present in the picture (Intraub & Richardson, 1989). Intraub refers to this tendency to report seeing more of the scene than was present as *boundary extension.*

The original research used pictures tightly cropped around an object, with the person asked to draw the picture after a long delay. Subsequent research indicates that boundary extension occurs when closely cropped pictures are used but not when wide-angle pictures showing lots of background are used (Intraub et al., 1992). Other research shows that boundary extension can also occur when people are forewarned about its existence and when they are tested more immediately after seeing the original pictures (Intraub & Bodamer, 1993).

Intraub interprets her results as indicating that people activate a schema based on the information in the original picture. However, the activated schema contains elements not actually in the original picture. So when people later attempt to replicate the picture, they draw on their schemas in addition to the actual picture. Note that this process is similar to the Gestalt notion of closure, or object completion, in that boundary extension goes beyond the actual information present in the original stimulus. Boundary extension differs from closure because it goes beyond completing an object to adding information that surrounds an object.

Numerous other experiments have been conducted to illustrate the importance of context in pattern perception. Perhaps the most extensive research on this topic involves the word-superiority effect, which is discussed in the next section.

Perceiving Letters in the Context of Words

Among the many shapes that are particularly salient to humans are the letters of the alphabet. As you read through this book, you are constantly processing these unique shapes and extracting meaning from them. The processes by which you do so represent an area of intense research at this time. We will focus our attention here on research related to one particular finding—context has an impact on letter perception. This research is particularly important to our contention that context plays a major role in perception (Theme 1, pages 9–10).

The finding we are primarily interested in is referred to as the word-superiority effect. According to the *word-superiority effect,* letters are perceived better when they appear in words than when they appear in strings of unrelated letters (Taylor & Taylor, 1983). For example, the letter R is easier to perceive when it appears in the word TIGER than when it appears in the nonword GIETR. The word-superiority effect, also known as the *word-apprehension effect,* was first demonstrated more than 100 years ago by Cattell (1886). He presented series of letters for 10 milliseconds and asked observers to report as many letters as they could. When random letters were presented, the observers usually reported only about four or five individual letters. However, if English words were presented, the observers usually reported three or four complete words, that is, several times as many letters as in the random-letter condition.

The word-superiority effect was generally ignored for several decades, until Reicher (1969) revived interest in the phenomenon. In his study, observers first saw a stimulus, such as a four-letter word (e.g., WORK) or a four-letter nonword (e.g., ORWK) that was both meaningless and unpronounceable. This stimulus was presented for 50 milliseconds. Immediately afterward, a visual mask was presented that covered the four letters. At the same time, off to one side, two letters appeared. These letters were placed in one of four letter positions, and the observers were asked to report which of the two letters had actually appeared in the stimulus.

For example, the word WORK might be followed by the display

$$- - - \frac{\text{D}}{\text{K}}$$

Observers had to specify whether they had seen a D or a K in the fourth position of the earlier stimulus. Notice that both letters form an acceptable English word. Thus, an observer could not receive a high score simply by guessing at a letter that would complete an English word. Furthermore, this experiment eliminated an accusation that could have been applied to Cattell's study: Perhaps observers can *perceive* the letters equally well in words and in isolation, but they *remember* the words better and therefore report more items. Reicher's experiment did not rely on observers' memories, however, because they simply chose between two alternatives. Thus, Reicher's study was designed to test whether the word-superiority effect would persist, even when two important advantages for words (guessing and memory) had been eliminated. The results showed that accuracy was between 65% and 77% higher when the stimuli were words, clearly strong support for the word-superiority effect.

After Reicher reopened the mystery of the word-superiority effect, many researchers investigated aspects of the effect. Much of the research indicated that the effect is not influenced by the visual characteristics of the letters in the word (Krueger, 1992). Instead, the effect appeared to be due to the phonological aspects of the words, i.e., how the letters in the word sound. However, because the word-superiority effect occurs even for letters that aren't pronounced (e.g., the silent *s* in *island*), the effect cannot be due to phonological information alone (Krueger, 1992).

Illusory Contours

An *illusion* is an incorrect perception. In an illusion, what we see does not correspond to the true qualities of an object. Illusions are interest-

ing phenomena, but they are particularly important for what they can tell us about perceptual processes. We will now examine a class of illusory stimuli that is problematic for many theories of shape perception.

Sometimes we can see a shape against a background, even when no concrete contour or edge can be seen between the shape and the background. In *illusory contour* figures, we see edges even though they are not physically present. In other words, context alone is sufficient to give rise to the perception of edges or contours. Notice, for example, that Figure 5.24 seems to show a white triangle against a background of three circles and an outline triangle. Each side of the white triangle appears to be a continuous line, even though the true contour is less than 1 inch long at each corner of the figure. Imagine the problems that these apparent edges present for most of the approaches to shape perception that we have discussed.

Illusory contour figures have contextual elements with true contours known as *inducing areas*. In Figure 5.24 the inducing areas include

FIGURE 5.24 An example of illusory contours producing a triangle.

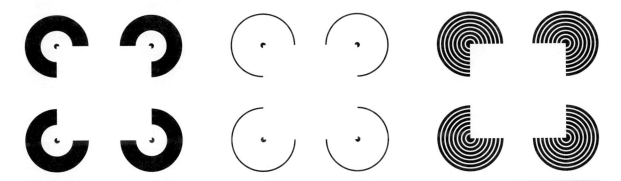

FIGURE 5.25 Three examples of illusory squares formed by different inducing areas. Notice how the inducing areas influence both the perceived lightness of the illusory squares and the distinctness of their edges. (From Lesher & Mingolla, 1993)

the boundary between the white and the black in the three black figures. Similarly, ***inducing lines*** are lines that encourage illusory contour. In Figure 5.24 the three V-shaped elements are inducing lines. The mystery, however, is that the contour of the illusory figure appears to extend between the inducing areas. Incidentally, another term that is frequently used as a synonym for illusory contour is ***subjective contour.***

Illusory contour figures have three important attributes (Meyer & Petry, 1987). First, a distinct surface appears to be present. Frequently, the surface seems to be lighter than the background, even though the intensity registered on the retina is identical (Kanizsa, 1976). The enhanced lightness may well be due to lateral inhibition (Coren, 1991). Second, there appears to be a distinct edge or contour around the surface. As seen in Figure 5.25, both the distinctness of the edge and the lightness of the illusory figure are diminished when the inducing figures are thinner, or have fewer lines (Lesher & Mingolla, 1993). Third, the edge and surface appear to continue beyond the inducing elements of the figure.

Why do we see subjective contours? Explanations range from the physiological to the more cognitive (Lesher, 1995). Relatively recent evidence suggests that physiological processes offer at least a partial explanation for illusory contours.

Researchers have found cells in areas V1 and V2 that respond to illusory contours (Treisman et al., 1990; Winckelgren, 1992). Rüdiger von der Heydt and his colleagues (Peterhans & von der Heydt, 1989; Peterhans et al., 1986; von der Heydt & Peterhans, 1989; von der Heydt et al., 1984), who found the cells in V2 that respond to illusory contours, propose that two paths of information give rise to illusory contours.

As you will recall from our discussion of the visual cortex, researchers have identified simple and complex cortical cells. Some of these simple and complex cortical cells are end-stopped. According to von der Heydt, in one path the "regular" simple and complex cortical cells provide information about edges. In the other path, the end-stopped cells group information about object boundaries. Thus, the end-stopped cells might also be very important for detecting ordinary occlusions that occur when one object covers part of another. Although a good deal of evidence supports such low-level explanations of illusory contours (Dresp & Bonnet, 1991; Siegel & Petry, 1991), other researchers hypothesize the need for higher-level processes (e.g., Grossberg & Mingolla, 1987).

Some researchers explain illusory contours with Gestalt principles. From the principle of Prägnanz, they argue that we create subjective contours because we see simple, familiar figures in preference to meaningless, disorganized parts (e.g., Coren, 1972; Coren & Porac, 1983). Notice that in Figure 5.24 we could see three circles with wedges sliced out, alternating with three V-shaped lines. However, this interpretation of the picture is unnecessarily complicated. Instead, we use depth cues (described in detail in Chapter 6) to sort out the picture, placing a simple white triangle in front of the background. This interpretation "explains" why we see peculiar gaps in the three circles—the triangle is merely hiding portions of them.

However, when a simpler explanation is that the wedges are part of the circles themselves, the illusory figure is often minimized (Parks, 1993). One way to make the wedges appear to be part of the circles is to make the circles three-dimen-

sional, like pies with a slice removed (Parks & Rock, 1990). Sometimes, even with 3-D inducing areas, illusory contours emerge (Purghé, 1993).

Some researchers take a more cognitive approach. They suggest that illusory contours arise because the visual system tries to solve a mystery or a problem as it attempts to sort out figure and ground (Parks, 1984, 1986; Rock, 1986, 1987; Rock & Anson, 1979). Thus, we use top-down processing, consistent with Theme 4 of the book (see page 12), to make sense of an otherwise puzzling and disorderly jumble. When you look at Figure 5.26, such cognitive processes seem important in producing the illusory contours that appear to be supporting the people (Bonaiuto et al., 1991).

Needless to say, illusory contours present a real problem to the various approaches to shape perception. As a result, illusory contours represent a rich research area for the foreseeable future (Lesher, 1995).

Distortions of Shape Due to Context

Context can often help us to arrive at an accurate representation of an object in the world. However, context can also mislead us, as we saw in the section on illusory contours. Context can also produce distorted shapes. For instance, Demonstration 5.4 shows two examples of the twisted-cord illusion, produced by designs that involve a twisted black-and-white cord. Notice how the context leads us to misperceive the orientation and shape of the figures.

The illusions in Figure 5.27 demonstrate the operation of angular induction, whereby the orientation of a test line is affected by an inducing line or lines (Greene, 1993a, 1993b, 1994; Greene & Levinson, 1994). As in the twisted-cord illusion, the orientation of the lines or the shape of the geometric figures is distorted by the context. For instance, as you can determine with a ruler, the lines in Figure 5.27a are parallel to each other, even though they appear to bulge outward in the middle. In contrast, the parallel lines in Figure

a.

b.

FIGURE 5.26 An example of illusory figures that emerge from the positioning of human figures. (From "Visual Illusory Productions with or without Amodal Completion" first published in *Perception,* 1991, 20, pp. 243–257, fig. 6, by Bonaiuto et al. Reprinted by permission of Pion Limited, London. Bonaiuto et al., 1991)

Demonstration 5.4

Twisted Cord Illusions

In illustration a, convince yourself that the letters are oriented straight up and down. Either measure the distance of the top and bottom of a letter from one of the sides or notice that the top and bottom of each letter are located along the same column of dark diamonds in the checked pattern. In b, place your finger at any point along the "spiral" and trace around, trying to reach the center of the design.

a.

b.

5.27b appear to be closer to one another in the middle. Parts c and d show a circle and a square that are distorted by the surrounding lines. Keep Figure 5.27d in mind when we discuss the Ponzo illusion in Chapter 6.

SECTION SUMMARY

Influence of Context on Shape and Pattern Perception

1. Research has supported the importance of context in determining pattern recognition.

Context can be helpful, but it can also be misleading.

2. The computational approach tries to explain object perception based on information in the stimulus itself. However, a good deal of research shows that the context, or scene, within which we view an object is important. For example, an object is perceived more rapidly when seen in an appropriate context.

3. According to the word-superiority effect, letters are perceived better when they appear in words than when they appear in strings of unrelated letters. The effect was

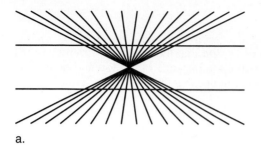

a.

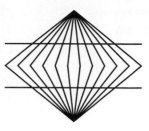

b.

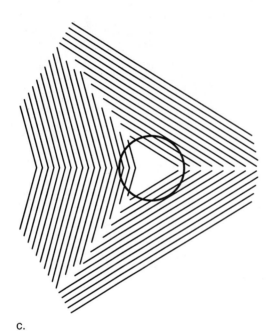

c.

d.

FIGURE 5.27   Four examples of shape distortions produced by context. Ordinarily, context is helpful to perception, as in Figure 5.23. In these figures, however, the context distorts the two parallel lines seen in parts a and b and the circle and square seen in parts c and d, respectively.

first demonstrated in 1886 and has been supported in numerous subsequent studies using a wide variety of experimental conditions and stimuli.

4. In illusory-contour figures, we see contours even though no edge appears between the shape and the background. Several explana-

tions have been proposed for the illusory contours, some with a more physiological, bottom-up orientation and others with a more top-down orientation.

5. Although context usually improves shape perception, both illusory contours and other illusions—such as the twisted-cord illu-

sions—demonstrate that context can occasionally lead to misperceptions.

SELECTED TOPICS IN SHAPE AND PATTERN PERCEPTION

The Role of Time in Shape Perception

Shape perception does not occur instantaneously but requires a certain amount of time. Remember that the foveal region of the retina produces high visual acuity. However, the fovea can take in only a small portion of the visual field. This causes a problem when we want to look at an object that is so large that it cannot fit on the fovea, so it must be perceived as the result of several eye movements (Hayhoe et al., 1991; Irwin, 1992, 1993). Thus, we might argue that object perception is based less on the retinal image, per se, and more on the integrated image that occurs later in processing (Rock & Linnett, 1993).

In the "Eye Movements" section in Chapter 4, we discussed these saccadic movements. We mentioned that an important characteristic of saccadic movements is the suppression of vision as the eyes leap from one location to the next. Such suppression is also evident in a phenomenon called backward masking. In ***backward masking,*** "the accuracy for reporting a visual target is reduced by following the target with a spatially overlapping mask" (Liss & Reeves, 1983, p. 513). Notice that the second figure masks the first figure and that masking therefore works backwards.

Suppose that someone presented very briefly a black square, as in Figure 5.28a. Then that square disappeared and was quickly replaced by the square-outline shape in Figure 5.28b, the shape being carefully constructed so that the square fits neatly inside its inner boundary. Under appropriate conditions, you might not perceive the square that was initially presented.

Werner (1935) was the first to demonstrate backward masking, a phenomenon that has important implications for the perception of contours. Werner found that if he presented the black square very briefly, then a gray screen for

a.   b.

FIGURE 5.28 Shapes used in a masking study. If the black square in part a is presented briefly and followed rapidly by the black square outline in part b, people will not report seeing the original black square.

about 0.15 second, then the square-outline shape, observers failed to see the first square.

Werner did not find forward masking, the tendency for the first figure to mask a second figure. When he presented the square-outline shape (Figure 5.28b) and then the black square (Figure 5.28a), observers perceived both figures. In vision, backward masking is easier to produce than forward masking.

Masking has been demonstrated by using other figures in addition to ones in which an inner contour of one shape matches the outer contour of another. For instance, backward masking can occur with flashes of light. The important attribute of masking is that when another stimulus interferes with the formation of a contour, the shape will not be seen.

The research on backward masking demonstrates the importance of time factors in perception. Shape perception can be influenced by other shapes presented immediately afterward. Specifically, a shape's contour may not be perceived if another shape is presented too soon after the original one.

Effects of Stimulus Orientation

The importance of experience, stressed in Theme 4 of this text, becomes evident when we view the world from an unusual orientation. You need go no further than a mirror to determine the difficulty

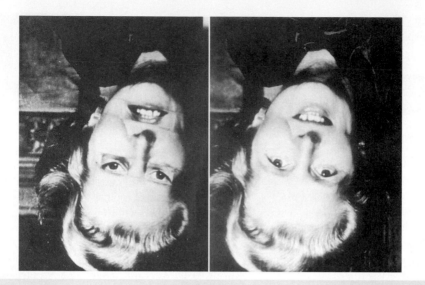

FIGURE 5.29 The role of experience in shape perception is illustrated in this figure. Because we are used to seeing faces in an upright orientation, we do not detect any major difference in the two pictures of Margaret Thatcher. In the left figure, however, Mrs. Thatcher's eyes and mouth have been kept in an upright orientation—even though the rest of her face has been inverted. Although you will see little difference between the two pictures in this orientation, turning your book over will lead you to see the two pictures as distinctly different. (From Thompson, 1980)

of reading this text in an unusual orientation. Although you can easily read this text directly, your task becomes more difficult when you try to read mirror-reflected words. Mirror-reflected objects of various types pose serious perceptual challenges (Cooper, 1994; Cooper & Schacter, 1992; Ilan & Miller, 1994; Ittelson et al., 1991).

Consider another unusual orientation, such as a 180° rotation. Because we are accustomed to looking at upright faces, faces seen in this unusual orientation are much more difficult to process (Rock, 1988). Evidence for this effect is found in Figure 5.29. Two pictures of former British Prime Minister Margaret Thatcher's face have been inverted, but for the picture on the left, her eyes and mouth have been kept in the upright position. When we view the inverted pictures, we see little or no difference between the two pictures. However, when we turn the book over to view the two pictures in the normal, upright orientation, the pictures are decidedly different (Sjoberg & Windes, 1992; Thompson, 1980).

This effect is not restricted to pictures, as Figure 5.30 illustrates. We are accustomed to seeing text in one particular orientation. When text is inverted, we are less able to detect disparities than when the text is perceived in its normal orientation (Rock, 1988).

The impact of inverting an image is not restricted to the difficulty of noting discrepancies. In fact, with some shapes, an inversion yields a totally different interpretation or meaning. For example, one hallmark of a normal person is the ability to distinguish between fantasy and reality. Do you see fantasy or reality in Figure 5.31? What do you see when you invert the figure?

As we will see in Chapter 6, inversions can even lead to a reversal of depth information. Look

Ygolohɔʏƨꟼ

Ygolohɔʏƨꟼ

FIGURE 5.30 Orientation also affects our perception of letters. At first glance you might see little difference between these two strings of inverted letters. However, when you turn your book over, the discrepancies between the two strings will be readily apparent. (From Rock, 1988)

at Figure 5.32 and determine if the dotted lines fall on the peaks of the figure or in the valleys. Now invert the figure and determine where the dotted lines fall.

Note that in each of the figures, the physical stimulus remains unchanged except for its orientation. In other words, the image falling on our retinas is identical, yet we find it difficult to detect discrepancies in one orientation that are readily apparent in another (Figures 5.29 or 5.30) or we see only one of two possible forms when viewing the figure from one particular orientation (Figures 5.31 or 5.32).

When we see objects in unusual orientations, we are capable of mentally rotating them until they are in their normal orientations (Cooper & Shepard, 1984; Murray, 1995). Recent evidence suggests that in order to perceive objects that are in unusual orientations, we may first have to mentally rotate their images until they match a familiar representation (Gibson & Peterson, 1994; Johnson, 1991; Tarr & Pinker, 1990, 1991). Certainly, the effects of unusual orientation argue for the importance of top-down processing in object perception. In the next section we will examine some figures that can be seen in two different ways without inverting the figure.

Ambiguous Figures

You might well argue that an image rotated 180° is radically different from the nonrotated image. As you might imagine, theories of shape perception have trouble explaining stimuli that can be interpreted in different ways without any inversion at all. Figure 5.33 is the classic illustration of an ambiguous figure. Do you see the old lady or the young woman? Can you switch to the other perception?

As Hoffman and Richards (1984) point out, in shape perception we seem to analyze the whole shape into constituent parts. For instance, notice that when the ambiguous figures in Figure 5.34 reverse, the dots attached to them become parts of different parts of the figure. Thus, when

FIGURE 5.31 Orientation can lead us to see the same stimulus in completely different ways. Can you distinguish between fantasy and reality? Turn the book over and see if you still see fantasy.

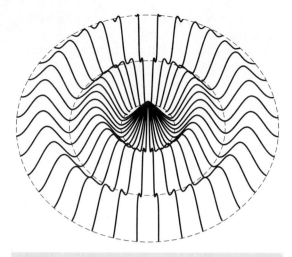

FIGURE 5.32 Another example of the effects of changes in orientation on perception of a stimulus. The dotted lines are in the valleys of the sine function in this orientation. What happens when the book is inverted? (From Hoffman & Richards, 1984)

FIGURE 5.33 A figure that can be seen in two different ways without inversion. Do you see the young girl or the old woman?

viewing the Schroeder staircase (Figure 5.34a) as stairs seen from above, the dots are both attached to the second stair up. However, when viewing the same stimulus as if from a basement looking up at the stairs from below, one dot is attached to one stair and the other dot is attached to the stair above. Similarly, the three dots in Figure 5.34b could all decorate one single cube or—when the design reverses—three adjacent cubes.

Ambiguous stimuli such as these are particularly compelling. How can a single stimulus lead to two such radically different interpretations? Why should the visual system shift from one interpretation to the other? Some researchers believe that the shifts can be better explained by low-level processes such as satiation (e.g., neural fatigue), but others invoke cognitive factors (Horlitz & O'Leary, 1993). The answers to such questions require that we learn much more about the processes involved in shape perception. However, the fact that the same stimulus can yield such different perceptions suggests that factors beyond the stimulus alone must be involved.

Shape Constancy

We introduced the notion of a constancy in Chapter 4. Remember that a perceptual constancy occurs when we perceive a distal stimulus as remaining roughly unchanged in spite of changes in the proximal (retinal) stimulus. *Shape constancy* means that an object appears to stay the same shape despite changes in its orientation. In reality, the proximal shape of an object is the same as the distal shape only if the object is *exactly* perpendicular to your line of view. In all other cases, the proximal shape is distorted.

Get up from your chair and walk around the room. Look at a particular object, such as a window, and view it from different angles. Notice

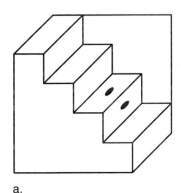

a.

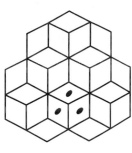

b.

FIGURE 5.34 Two ambiguous figures. The Schroeder staircase in part a can be perceived as stairs seen from above or below. In part b you might see six cubes or seven cubes. (If you have difficulty seeing seven cubes, it might help to turn the page over.) In both parts, notice how the spots become attached to different parts of the figure when you switch perceptions. (From Hoffman & Richards, 1984)

that the shape registered on your retina is a trapezoid from every orientation except when you are facing it directly. Observe how the rim of a cup usually forms an ellipse rather than a perfectly round circle. Nevertheless, the window seems to stay rectangular and the rim of a cup seems to stay circular. Objects do not grow distorted and then normal-shaped again as we change our orientation to them.

What factors appear to produce shape constancy? Memory for the shape of the object, for example, might have a role in shape constancy (Hochberg, 1971). Because you know that a compact disc is round, you know that the true shape of the disc is circular, even when it is seen at a slant and may be producing an ellipse on the retina.

According to Rock's (1983) unconscious-inference interpretation of shape constancy, we arrive at shape constancy by a reasoning-like process in which information about an object's retinal image shape and depth is combined in the same fashion as two premises in a logical proof. Thus, when a compact disc is slanted away from the observer, he or she infers that the true shape has not changed.

In Chapter 4 we saw that depth information influences lightness perception. Similarly, we make use of depth information to determine the degree to which an object is being viewed at an angle. According to the ***shape–slant invariance hypothesis,*** a viewer calculates objective shape by combining information about an object's retinal shape and its slant. The compensation process by which slant is taken into account has been found to explain several instances of shape constancy (Wallach & Marshall, 1986a, 1986b).

SECTION SUMMARY

Selected Topics in Shape and Pattern Perception

1. Shape perception is typically built up over time, based on the integration of images that are the end products of several saccades.

2. Masking is an example of a more general phenomenon in which one stimulus cannot be completely processed because of interference from a second stimulus. In backward masking, a second figure can mask a first fig-

ure. Visual backward masking is easier to demonstrate than forward masking.

3. The role of learning in shape perception becomes apparent when we view familiar objects, such as faces or letters, from unusual perspectives.

4. Ambiguous figures illustrate the operation of higher-level processes, because a single stimulus is capable of giving rise to totally different perceptions.

5. Shape constancy is thought to arise because of prior knowledge about an object or because we take the slant of the object into consideration when determining its shape.

REVIEW QUESTIONS

1. Describe data-driven (bottom-up) processing as if you were talking to a student studying introductory psychology. Use your own words in this description, and use examples from the material in this chapter. Which approaches to shape perception seem most dependent on data-driven processes? What role do these processes play in the particular approaches?

2. The importance of conceptually driven (top-down) processing is emphasized throughout this book. What *is* conceptually driven processing? Which approaches to shape perception seem most dependent on these processes?

3. In Chapter 3 we examined the anatomical and physiological bases for visual perception. Evaluate each of the approaches to shape perception in terms of the extent to which it is consistent with our knowledge of the anatomy and physiology of vision.

4. Theme 2 of this text (see page 10) emphasizes the importance of the rich context within which objects are perceived. Use several examples from this chapter to support the importance of context in shape perception, such as: (a) the study by Pomerantz and his colleagues, shown in Demonstration 5.2, on identifying lines that either had or did not have a surrounding context; (b) the study by Palmer on object recognition; (c) the research on the word-superiority effect; (d) illusory contours; and (e) ambiguous figures.

5. The Gestalt laws of grouping apply in architecture, a topic discussed by Prak (1977). Examine the architecture and organizational structure of buildings nearby and try to find examples of as many of these laws as possible.

6. You are driving along a country road. Next to a farmhouse you see a crude hand-lettered sign, "EGGS FOR SALE." Describe how the following approaches account for your recognition of letters in that sign: the spatial frequency analysis approach, template-matching approach, prototype-matching approach, computational approach, and feature-integration approach. Do you think you would find it more difficult to read the sign if you saw it in front of an urban apartment?

7. Think of yourself as you are reading this book. How does the word-superiority effect facilitate reading? How does context facilitate reading? How are saccades involved in reading?

8. Draw an example of a figure with a subjective contour. What are the explanations for the subjective contour in your drawing? What problems does a subjective contour pose for the various approaches to shape perception?

9. What factors appear to be involved in shape constancy? Given the distortions of shape induced by some contexts, why do you think that we normally perceive shapes accurately? What might these shape distortions and illusory conjunctions have in common?

10. Given all that you've learned up to this point, provide your own description of the processes involved in shape perception. Start with a distal stimulus in an unusual orientation, such as a person swinging upside down on some monkey bars. Because of the swinging, that person's face will not fall on one spot on your retina. What approaches do you think would be most useful in explaining how you come to recognize the person?

NEW TERMS

shape (123)
form (123)
data-driven processing (123)
conceptually driven
processing (123)
bottom-up processing (123)
top-down processing (123)
spatial frequency analysis
approach (124)
Fourier analysis (124)
sine wave (124)
sinusoidal grating (124)
Fourier synthesis (124)
visual angle (125)
contrast sensitivity function (127)
spatial frequency channels (128)
selective adaptation
procedure (129)
Gestalt approach (129)
holistic orientation (129)
analytical orientation (129)
laws of grouping (130)
law of proximity (130)
law of similarity (130)
law of good continuation (130)

law of closure (130)
law of common fate (130)
law of Prägnanz (132)
figure (133)
ground (133)
ambiguous figure–ground
relationships (134)
phenomenological
observation (135)
common region (136)
uniform connectedness (136)
computational approach (138)
zero-crossing (139)
Mexican-hat filter (139)
primal sketch (140)
virtual lines (140)
2.5-D sketch (140)
3-D sketch (140)
recognition-by-components
approach (142)
geons (142)
shape from motion (143)
shape from shading (143)
shape from highlights (143)
attention (144)

feature-integration
approach (144)
preattentive processing (144)
parallel process (144)
focused attention (144)
serial process (144)
illusory conjunction (144)
prototype-matching
approach (145)
prototype (145)
template-matching
approach (147)
boundary extension (151)
word-superiority effect (151)
word-apprehension effect (151)
illusion (152)
illusory contour (152)
inducing areas (152)
inducing lines (153)
subjective contour (153)
backward masking (157)
shape constancy (160)
shape–slant invariance
hypothesis (161)

RECOMMENDED READINGS

Ballesteros, S. (Ed.). (1994). *Cognitive approaches to human perception*. Hillsdale, NJ: Erlbaum. This collection of 11 chapters reflects a very cognitive orientation to perception, with several chapters addressing issues in shape perception and perceptual organization. The chapters in the sections on attention and visual perception and on form perception are particularly relevant to issues raised in this chapter. You should also find Julian Hochberg's chapter to be a strong argument for the need for mental structures or schemas in object perception.

Bruce, V., & Green, P. (1990). *Visual perception: Physiology, psychology, and ecology* (2nd ed.). Hove, UK: Erlbaum. Dr. Bruce has made a number of important contributions to the study of visual perception—including her book and articles on face perception. In this textbook, she and Patrick Green have written a very clear overview of many areas of visual perception. Of particular importance for the topics of this chapter are the chapters on Marr's computational approach, perceptual organization, and object recognition (Chapters 4, 5, and 7).

Solso, R. L. (1994). *Cognition and the visual arts*. Cambridge, MA: MIT Press. Solso provides a very readable summary of a wide range of topics. He reviews the biological underpinnings of visual perception before discussing processes involved in form perception. The chapters on perspective are particularly relevant to our discussion of depth perception in Chapter 6.

Uttal, W. R. (1988). *On seeing forms*. Hillsdale, NJ: Erlbaum. Uttal has written a series of books related to visual perception. This addition to the series is particularly useful because of the overview of theories of form perception that Uttal provides. The book reflects a somewhat unusual perspective, but Uttal offers useful criticisms of several theories of form perception.

CHAPTER

6

Distance and Size Perception

Before beginning this chapter, let's review where we have been. First, we looked at the biological underpinnings of vision. Then we examined some basic visual processes, such as edge detection and lightness perception. Then we looked at more complex visual processes, such as how we organize edges into shapes and how patterns emerge in looking out at the world.

Hopefully, with each chapter you have come to take your visual perceptions less and less for granted. Even the simple detection of edges should now seem to you an extraordinarily complicated process. Human visual abilities should strike you as nothing less than minor miracles.

One of those miracles is our ability to see the world as three-dimensional. Our visual system has evolved to provide a vivid sense of depth from retinal input that is itself two-dimensional. The retina in each eye can encode information directly only in a two-dimensional fashion (up-down and left-right), yet we see some objects as near us and others as far away. We alluded to the importance of depth information when we discussed lightness perception in Chapter 4 and figure–ground distinctions in Chapter 5. Thus, you should realize that the processes are strongly interrelated, even though we've explored them in a linear order.

In the first part of this chapter, we will explore some of the processes that must underlie the miracle of depth perception. If you are like us, however, your sense of wonder will be further increased, rather than diminished, by learning about how the visual system works to provide a sense of depth.

Closely tied to the perception of depth, as you will soon see, is the perception of the size of objects. Because of this close relationship, after discussing depth perception we will turn to the perception of size. Our discussion of size perception will also enable us to explore another important constancy—size constancy.

Finally, in keeping with Theme 3 of this text (see page 10), you will see that our remarkably capable visual system can sometimes be led astray. Some of the most fascinating visual illusions involve the processes that underlie depth and size perception, so we will examine several of those illusions. As we mentioned in Chapter 5, the illusions are intrinsically interesting, but their major importance lies in what the illusions tell us about how the visual system must be functioning.

We will begin our discussion by addressing the principles that give rise to the perception of depth or distance. Like most of your other perceptual experience, depth perception seems automatic, even unavoidable. Because of the immediacy of your experience of depth, you seldom think about the processes that might underlie the perceptual experience.

Before you begin reading the next section, take a few minutes to look around you as if you were seeing for the first time. Note the vivid impression of depth that emerges and try to determine how you are able to see in depth. How can you tell which of two buildings or people is nearer to you? How can you catch a ball thrown at you, or judge the distance (or size) of a bird in flight? By taking a more analytic approach to the perception of depth, as a psychologist might, you may discover many of the principles for yourself before we describe them to you.

DISTANCE PERCEPTION

How many cues to depth did you identify? We will now begin a systematic investigation of the major cues to depth or distance. First, however, let's be a bit more specific about what we mean by distance perception.

Distance perception (or *depth perception*) refers to your ability to perceive the distance relationships within the visual scene. We can think of three different types of distance or depth relationships. *Egocentric distance* refers to the distance of an object from you, the observer. (You can remember the word egocentric because it literally means "self-centered.") When you estimate how far you are from the finish line in a race, you are judging egocentric distance. *Relative distance* refers to how far two objects are from each other. When you decide that the library looks farther away than the gym, you are judging relative distance. Finally, you perceive objects as three-dimensional; objects have depth or thickness in addition to height and width. Thus, some parts of an object look farther away than other parts. Distance is involved in all three kinds of situations, and psychologists do not emphasize the differences among these situations when they theorize about distance.

Distance perception was one of the first topics to be studied by people interested in perception. Artists in the Renaissance faced a practical problem: How could they portray three-dimensional depths and distances on a two-dimensional canvas? Later, in the 17th century, philosophers wondered how humans come to know about the world: How do we know that the world

is three-dimensional if the eye appears to represent only two dimensions? We will return to the ideas of philosophers and painters later in this section when we examine theories and applications of distance perception. Let's begin our discussion of distance perception by examining the sources of information about an object's distance.

Although other factors surely influence depth perception, we will concentrate our attention on 12 sources of information. First, we will examine 10 monocular cues to depth. Next, we will see how these cues can be used to give a sense of depth to two-dimensional representations. Then, we will provide some detail about cues to depth that emerge from the fact that we use both of our eyes to see the world. Figure 6.1 provides an overview of the cues to depth we will describe.

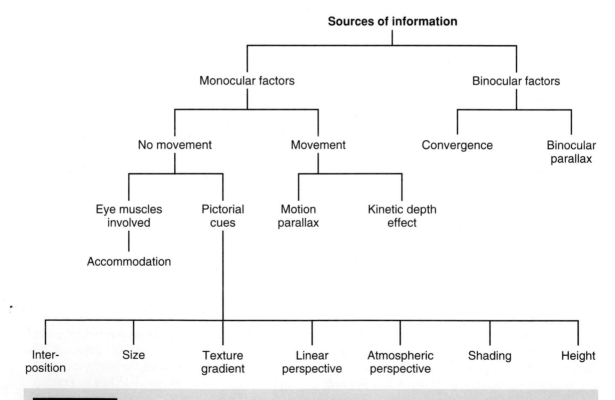

FIGURE 6.1 A classification scheme for information about depth and distance. As the text indicates, all the cues shown in the hierarchy are not equally effective; cues lower in the hierarchy are not inferior sources of information compared to cues higher in the diagram.

Monocular Cues to Distance Perception

Most of our sources of information about distance are monocular. ***Monocular factors*** require only one eye to provide us with distance information. Although we typically see the world through two eyes, monocular cues would be effective if we were to view the world through one eye. Lest you think of these monocular factors as "second-class citizens," keep in mind that we all rely solely on monocular cues when judging distant objects. And consider Wesley Walker, who was able to function as a wide receiver with the New York Jets with vision in only one eye. Even though he was running, Walker was able to follow the path of the football and catch it—surely a complex visual task! If a person can accomplish such a difficult task with vision in only one eye, monocular factors must be central to depth perception. Let's first consider eight of these factors that require no movement of either the object or the observer.

Perceiving Depth without Motion Cues

1. ***Accommodation,*** as you recall from earlier chapters in this book, is the change in the shape of the lens in your eye as you focus on objects at different distances. When you look at distant objects, the lens is relatively thin. When you look at nearby objects, the lens is relatively thick. Eye muscles that control lens shape therefore respond differently to objects at different distances. However, we may not pay attention to the information that these muscles provide about distance. Some time ago, Hochberg (1971) concluded that accommodation is, at best, a rather weak cue to distance, even when the distance is less than 10 feet. That conclusion still seems valid.

Accommodation involves information provided by your eye muscles. As Figure 6.1 shows, the remaining seven monocular, nonmovement cues have been called pictorial cues. ***Pictorial cues,*** or static cues, are cues that artists can use to represent distance in a picture. A ***cue*** is a factor that lets you make a decision automatically and spontaneously. Notice that we do not use the phrase "pictorial *clues*," because clues are factors that provide information but require a great amount of thought. (Sherlock Holmes discovered clues—not cues—and then sat down with his pipe and thought before reaching a decision.) When you see a pictorial cue, you automatically make a distance judgment. In fact, some of these cues may provide depth information at such an early age that they are likely to be innate (Gunderson et al., 1993; Yonas et al., 1985, 1986).

2. ***Interposition,*** or overlap, means that one object overlaps or partly covers another. When interposition occurs, we judge the partly covered object to be farther away than the object that is completely visible. For example, your textbook looks closer to you than the desk that it partly covers. This cue is one of the most important monocular cues. Furthermore, it plays an important role in the binocular disparity process we will discuss later (Anderson & Nakayama, 1994; He & Nakayama, 1994; Nakayama & Shimojo, 1990).

3. ***Size cues*** refer to the influence of an object's size on distance estimates. If two similar objects are presented together, the object that occupies more space on the retina is judged to be closer. In a classic experiment, Ittelson and Kilpatrick (1951) asked people to judge which of two balloons was closer. The two balloons were actually the same distance away, and their size could be controlled by inflating them with bellows. Furthermore, the room was dark, so other distance cues were missing. People reported that the larger balloon appeared to be closer. As a balloon was inflated, it seemed to zoom forward in space. As the air was let out, the balloon seemed to zoom backward. Thus ***relative size***—an object's size relative to other objects—can be a helpful cue in telling us which of two objects is closer.

The ***familiar size*** of an object can also be a helpful cue, because some objects are normally found in standardized sizes (Sedgwick, 1986). For example, you know how big this textbook is. If it occupies a tiny space on your retina, you judge it to be far away. Of course, someone might be able to fool you by showing you a giant-sized version of this book in a room with no other distance cues. You would probably judge the book

FIGURE 6.2 A photograph illustrating several cues. Changes in texture gradient are evident when you look at the rocks closer to you (larger and more distinct) compared to the rocks farther away (smaller and less distinct). Linear perspective is evident in the vanishing point to which the parallel railroad tracks recede. The ties are clearly below the tracks because the tracks cover the ties (interposition). Objects lower in the visual field appear to be closer, and objects nearer the horizon appear to be farther away (height cues). Knowing that the railroad ties are the same size also helps us to see the ties that produce a smaller retinal image as farther away (size cues). (Photo by Ron Pretzer)

to be the normal size and closer than it truly is, rather than larger than it normally is.

People who have participated in perception experiments have seen a wide variety of objects of abnormal sizes, all designed to test the effectiveness of size cues. For example, people were shown photographs depicting three coins simultaneously—a dime that was the size of a quarter, a normal-sized quarter, and a 50-cent piece the size of a quarter. Viewers judged the dime, which was bigger than normal, to be closer than the quarter. In contrast, the 50-cent piece, which was smaller than normal, was judged to be farther away (Epstein & Franklin, 1965).

Familiar size may not be as helpful a cue as you might think. One reason is that people may be equally accurate in their judgments of the size of familiar and unfamiliar objects (Predebon, 1992). A second reason is that other cues are more helpful. This might strike you as strange, because most people without a background in perception think that size cues are a major factor in distance estimates. In fact, other factors that *seem* much more subtle and unimportant—such as motion cues—are really more helpful. Perceived size and motion are somewhat related, however, because moving objects will typically change size on the retina. Just as an inflating balloon will appear to

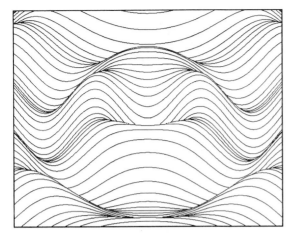

a.

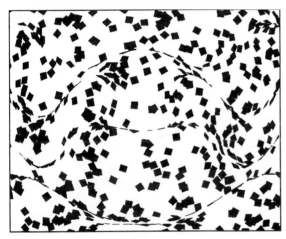

b.

c.

come closer in the absence of other depth cues, moving objects in the world loom as they approach us. These changes in size may be useful cues for judging the path and velocity of moving objects, such as thrown balls (Peper et al., 1994).

4. *Texture gradient* refers to the fact that the texture of surfaces becomes denser as the distance increases, if we are viewing those surfaces from a slant. Texture gradients can be illustrated in a picture, but this source of information has not been appreciated by psychologists until relatively recently (Gibson, 1979; Hagen, 1986; Neisser, 1981). You can also see an example of a texture gradient in the rocks in Figure 6.2. Notice that the nearby rocks surrounding the tracks appear to be larger and more detailed. In the distance, the rocks appear to be smaller and less detailed.

Texture gradients are such powerful cues to depth that even simple schematic representations are sufficient to produce a clear sense of depth. For example, all three parts of Figure 6.3 clearly illustrate the same complex three-dimensional shape. Notice that Figure 6.3a contains shading information in addition to the texture gradient information. Although parts b and c of the figure contain *only* texture gradient information, the shape of the object is readily apparent. Thus, the depiction of this extremely complex object appears to be taking place at a fairly global level of analysis, because the actual texture used seems to be unimportant (Todd & Akerstrom, 1987; Todd & Reichel, 1990).

Simply attending carefully to the ground around you will make you more aware of texture

FIGURE 6.3 A complex three-dimensional figure represented in two dimensions. In part a the shape is represented by contour lines, and some shading is evident. In part b the same shape is represented by a texture gradient. In part c a different texture is used, and shading information is minimized. Notice the effectiveness of texture gradients in capturing the object's shape—even without shading information. (Parts a and b from Todd & Akerstrom, 1987; part c from Todd & Reichel, 1990)

gradients in your visual world. The units that make up the texture (e.g., floor tiles or stones) are the same size throughout the scene, yet they look smaller and closer together in the distance than in the foreground.

James J. Gibson (1950) was among the first psychologists to emphasize texture gradients. In a way, the texture gradients provide a kind of scale by which we can measure objects. Thus, a nearby object that hides three texture units is the same size as a distant object that also hides three texture units—whether the texture units are floor tiles, strands of rug yarn, or pebbles. Natural textures that are both irregular (e.g., pebbles and grass) and regular (e.g., paving stones and tiles) provide useful distance and size cues (Newman et al., 1973). As useful as texture gradients may be, adding natural objects—such as trees—to the visual scene enhances the accuracy of such judgments (Bingham, 1993a).

5. *Linear perspective* means that parallel lines appear to meet in the distance. Look at Figure 6.2 for one example of linear perspective. The true distance between the railroad tracks remains constant, yet this distance occupies an increasingly smaller part of the retina as we see portions that are closer to the horizon.

Cutting (1986) points out that linear perspective depends on your point of view. If you stand on the ground and look toward the horizon, railroad tracks show linear perspective but telephone poles are parallel. Now imagine that you are in a low-flying airplane, looking down at the ground. From this different perspective, the railroad tracks are now parallel as you look straight down. However, the telephone poles now demonstrate linear perspective. The tops of the poles appear far apart, yet their bases appear close together.

6. *Atmospheric perspective,* or aerial perspective, refers to the observation that distant objects often look blurry and bluish, in contrast to nearby objects. This is because the air between you and the distant objects may not be perfectly clear. Thus, atmospheric perspective resembles interposition (Deregowski, 1984). In interposition, a tree may cover part of a dog that

is farther away from the viewer. In atmospheric perspective, the objects that are performing this "covering" are tiny particles in the air. These accumulated particles partially obscure your view of a distant object.

Furthermore, the particles in the air slightly change the light reflected from objects, so that they appear bluish. Thus, compared to nearby objects, distant objects appear to be blurrier and bluer. Color Plate 2 inside the front cover is an illustration of atmospheric perspective. Notice that the distant mountains are softly blurred and faintly blue. If you look at realistic paintings of hills, you will see that they are also blue. Painters have used this distance cue for centuries. For instance, Leonardo da Vinci (1452–1519) discussed adding blue when painting distant objects.

We use atmospheric perspective as an informal scale to judge the distance of faraway places. Furthermore, we acquire a scale that is appropriate to the region in which we live. Easterners who live in humid areas and city dwellers who live in smoggy atmospheres develop a scale that does not work in the Rockies, for example. A mountain that looks blurry and blue enough to be 30 miles away by their scale might really be 50 miles away!

7. *Shading* is a cue provided by the pattern of light and shadows. Look at any object on your desk and notice how the lighting is definitely not uniform and constant across the entire surface. As we mentioned in Chapter 5, shading helps define the shape of objects, because it provides information about parts of an object that stick out or cave inward and also about flat or curved parts (Ramachandran, 1988). This effect is particularly true when the shading information presented to each retina is different—as a binocular cue (Bülthoff & Mallot, 1988). Use of this cue emerges fairly early, because children as young as 3 use information about shadows when they judge depth (Yonas et al., 1978).

We are accustomed to seeing shadows produced by overhead lighting. Except for rare examples, such as the floor lights in theaters, have you ever seen lighting from below? Observers looking at a picture typically assume that the lighting is from overhead (Berbaum et al., 1983a,

Demonstration 6.1

Shading and Depth Perception

Look at this picture and decide which surface is closer to you (the observer). Now turn the picture upside down and decide which surface appears closer to you. (Reprinted with permission from the cover of *Science,* 169, July 31, 1970. Copyright 1970 American Association for the Advancement of Science)

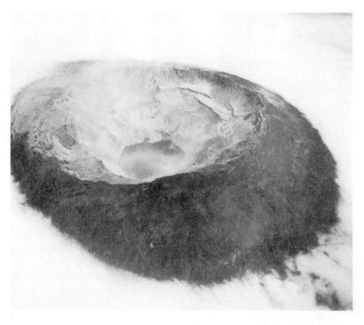

1983b, 1984). The assumption of overhead lighting can produce some intriguing results. Try Demonstration 6.1, for example, which illustrates the importance of shading in depth perception. When the picture is right side up, we see what appears to be a lake nestled in a volcano. When the picture is turned upside down, the dark shadowy area doesn't make sense as a convex shape if the lighting is from overhead. That assumption of overhead lighting is so strong that it forces the volcano to turn inside out. The shadowy area is now a concave shape from which a new, tiny volcano pops out, topped by a lake at its crest. Compare this result with the effects of inversion on shape perception discussed in Chapter 5.

Just as we typically assume that light comes from above, we also assume that faces are convex (pushed out toward us). In fact, we tend to see

objects as convex until we acquire cues to the contrary (Cohen, 1992). What happens when you are presented with hollow-mask (concave) faces lit from above? As Ramachandran (1988) points out, the faces appear to be convex and the lighting appears to come from below, as seen in Figure 6.4. The effects of experience certainly operate here (Theme 4)! We have almost no experience with hollowed-out faces, and only slightly more experience with lighting from below (maybe from Halloween), so the visual system interprets this figure in a fashion most consistent with experience.

Shading is an important cue to depth, but the depth inversion seen in Demonstration 6.1 need not be solely due to the assumption of overhead lighting. A more general explanation might be that our visual system has a bias to perceive

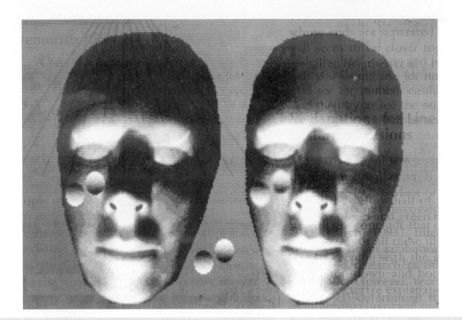

FIGURE 6.4 What happens when an unusual object is lit from the normal overhead position? The two faces shown here are actually hollowed-out masks seen from the inside, with the noses pointing away from rather than toward you. The impact of experience is evident, because your perception is likely that of protruding faces lit from below. In other words, your visual system prefers to see the faces as normal, even if it means seeing the light source as coming from an unusual position. If you focus only on the two discs between the faces, the one on the left will appear to be concave and the one on the right, convex—with both lit from above. When the discs are simply pasted on the left face, it becomes difficult to interpret their depth. When the discs are shaded into the right face, they both appear to be lit from below, like the face, and the one on the left now appears to be convex. (From Ramachandran, 1988)

surfaces as slanted backward (Reichel & Todd, 1990). Rarely is an object in nature farther away from us at the base of the visual field and closer to us at the top of the visual field. Most objects are straight up and down (like a wall) or else slanted away from us. Even in the absence of shading information, depth reversals occur when stimuli are viewed upside down (Reichel & Todd, 1990).

Just as we interpret shadowy regions as far away from a light source, we interpret highlighted areas as closer. For example, apparent depth within a picture increases as the contrast between highlights and shadows increases (Berbaum et

al., 1983b). If you see a bright, gleaming area in one part of a figure and dark shadow in another part, you interpret that figure as having depth. In fact, with all other depth information constant, highlights are sufficient to cause a picture to appear to be either convex or concave (Blake & Bülthoff, 1990).

8. **Height cues,** or elevation cues, refer to the observation that objects *near* the horizon appear to be farther away from us than objects *far* from the horizon. This statement may seem initially confusing, so look at Figure 6.5. Because the line represents the horizon, we interpret the

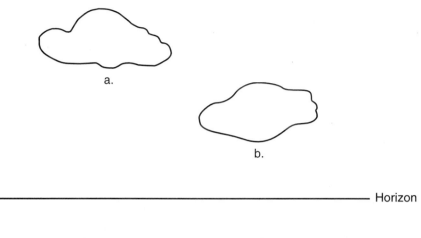

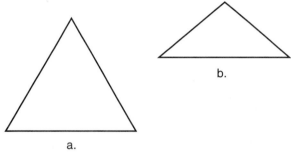

FIGURE 6.5 Depiction of height cues. Objects "attached" to the ground are farther away when higher in the visual field. Objects "attached" to the sky are farther away when lower in the visual field.

triangles as resting on the ground. Notice that triangle b is nearer the horizon, so we interpret it as being farther away from us than triangle a. The same closeness-to-the-horizon rule applies to the clouds. Cloud b is nearer the horizon, so we interpret it as being farther away from us than cloud a. Verify that this relationship holds true in "real life" by looking out a nearby window. Notice that objects near the horizon are far away, whereas objects far from the horizon (either at the top or bottom of your visual field) are nearby.

We discussed earlier that psychologists began examining the texture-gradient cue relatively recently. The height cue, in contrast, is literally as old as the Greeks. In fact, the first de-

scription of height cues can be traced to Euclid, a mathematician living in Greece about 300 B.C. (Cutting, 1986). Euclid is better known for developing the principles of geometry that you probably studied in high school.

Before we move on to other monocular sources of distance information, let's review the monocular/no-movement factors. These eight factors are accommodation, interposition, size, texture gradient, linear perspective, atmospheric perspective, shading, and height. Accommodation differs because it is a muscular cue, whereas the other seven are pictorial cues. Interposition is perhaps the most basic of the pictorial cues.

The next three factors are somewhat related to each other; faraway objects are smaller (size cue), faraway surfaces have smaller distances between the texture elements (texture gradient), and faraway objects represent a fixed distance—such as the distance between railroad tracks—with a smaller space on the retina (linear perspective). Atmospheric perspective and shading are both factors that involve lighting. Finally, height cues involve the placement of objects in the visual field. This observation brings us full circle to the first of the pictorial cues, interposition, which also involves placement in the visual field.

Perceiving Depth with Motion Cues

All the depth-perception factors discussed so far involve rigid head positions and stable objects. In reality, most of our visual experience involves moving objects or moving retinas, as we turn our heads and move our bodies past objects. In Chapter 5, we saw that motion is an important factor in perceiving an object's shape (e.g., Tittle & Braunstein, 1993; Van Damme et al., 1994). Central to our concerns in the present chapter, motion is also an extremely important source of information about distance and depth (e.g., Mershon et al., 1993; Ramachandran, 1990; Williams, 1992). Two kinds of distance cues involve motion: motion parallax and the kinetic depth effect.

You may not have been aware of motion cues to distance because they do not seem as important to nonpsychologists as some of the factors just discussed. Perhaps they are relatively unknown because they cannot be represented in a picture, and the only formal training most of us receive regarding depth perception is likely to be in elementary school art. Although the motion cues are less well known than the pictorial cues, they are probably more important to accurate depth perception. For example, the ability of flying insects to navigate through space is largely due to motion cues (Srinivasan, 1992).

9. *Motion parallax* refers to the fact that as you move your head sideways, objects at different distances appear to move in different directions and at different speeds. *Parallax* means a change

in position, so motion parallax is a change in the position of an object that is caused by motion.

Motion parallax is an excellent source of both shape and distance information (Cutting et al., 1992; Johansson, 1974; Rogers & Collett, 1989). For example, organisms can discriminate distances accurately using only the parallax caused by moving their heads (Srinivasan, 1992; Wallach & O'Leary, 1979). Furthermore, we rely heavily on such motion parallax information as we maneuver through a complex environment (Cutting, 1992).

However, you may never have noticed how much information these head movements provide. Go to a window and focus on a part of the window frame. Hold your hand in front of your eyes. Now move your head to the left and notice that your hand seems to move in the opposite direction, to the right. In contrast, objects you can see out the window, which are farther away than the window frame on which you are focusing, appear to move to the left. Thus, they seem to move in the same direction as your head.

Notice that the direction in which objects appear to move is related to the fixation point, the part of the scene registered on your fovea. Objects closer to you than the fixation point seem to move in a direction opposite to your own movement. In contrast, objects farther away than the fixation point seem to move in the same direction as your own movement. When you were a child, did you ever notice that the moon seemed to be following you? Like other distant objects, the moon often seems to move in the same direction as your own movement.

The next time you ride in a car or bus, fixate a point in the distance out one of the side windows. Notice how the speed of motion—as well as the direction of motion—depends on distance. Posts on a highway that are relatively close to you seem to whiz past, whereas a billboard that is farther back—just in front of your fixation point—seems to move more slowly.

As mentioned earlier, the monocular factors that involve movement cannot be represented in a picture. Spectators tend to move about in front of a painting (Pirenne, 1975). When they move, the various objects in the picture do not move in different directions at different speeds, as the objects in a real-life scene would. When you walk past a still-life painting, for example, the bowl of fruit does not move to the left and the distant curtains do not move to the right. Because a static picture cannot represent motion parallax, no artist can make a picture look perfectly three-dimensional to a roving spectator. The sense of depth generated by holograms is due, in part, to the fact that they can represent motion parallax.

James J. Gibson (1966, 1982) proposed that motion parallax is part of a more general motion pattern that he calls motion perspective. According to Neisser (1981), Gibson had developed an appreciation for perceptual information by the age of 8. His father worked on the railroad, so the future perceptual theorist observed with interest that the world seemed to flow inward when seen from the rear of the train, whereas it seemed to expand outward when seen from the locomotive.

Motion perspective, which serves as an important component to Gibson's theory, refers to the continuous change in the way objects look as you move about in the world. As you directly approach a point straight ahead, objects on all sides seem to move away from that point. For example, as you walk between the rows of books in the library, staring straight ahead, you should have the sense of motion perspective illustrated in Figure 6.6. The importance of motion perspective in depth perception has been demonstrated experimentally (e.g., Braunstein & Andersen, 1981). Furthermore, a computational approach has been implemented that can actually measure optic flow (Bülthoff et al., 1989).

In Chapter 4, we mentioned the difficulties people face in attempting to track a moving ball. Keeping your eye on the ball is a sufficiently difficult task (Watts & Bahill, 1990). How do you judge how far away it is, how quickly it's moving, and how you have to move to catch or hit the ball? Such questions have motivated a good deal of recent research (e.g., Bahill & Karnavas, 1993; Bootsma & Peper, 1992; Bootsma & Van Wieringen, 1990; Peper et al., 1994). As we mentioned earlier in the chapter, changes in the size of the

ball can serve as an important cue to distance. The effects of gravity on the moving ball also aid in the determination of distance (Watson et al., 1992). The dynamic aspects of hitting or catching a moving ball highlight the importance of motion cues in distance perception. Even though the hitter or catcher may not perceive distance, per se, spatial analysis is certainly involved.

10. The second monocular-movement factor involves the motion of objects rather than observers. In the *kinetic depth effect,* a figure that looks flat when stationary appears to have depth once it moves. Try Demonstration 6.2 to illustrate the kinetic depth effect with a rotating figure. The kinetic depth effect was first demonstrated with the shadows of rotating objects and has been explored in many other studies. In one well-known set of experiments, Wallach and O'Connell (1953) found that the two-dimensional projection of solid blocks, wire figures, straight rods, and other figures looked flat when the objects were stationary but looked three-dimensional when they rotated. Similarly, a transparent sphere with dots on its surface looks solid when rotated (Braunstein & Andersen, 1984).

Notice that most other depth cues are missing in Demonstration 6.2. For example, cues such as interposition, shading, and texture gradient do not appear on the paper. Nonetheless, once the figure moves, you notice that some parts move faster than others and that they also move in different directions. This kind of movement forces you to conclude that the object casting the shadow must be three-dimensional. Once the movement stops, however, the object can be interpreted as two-dimensional.

The kinetic depth effect can also be illustrated on a computer display. For instance, Sperling and his colleagues (1989) asked people to identify shapes solely on the basis of moving dot patterns. The shapes were surfaces (similar to Figure 6.3) that varied in their depicted height. Each shape was presented with varying densities of dots, which did not appear to be strongly three-dimensional when stationary. Imagine that Figure 6.3b were composed of small dots instead of squares. The researchers represented the shapes with 20,

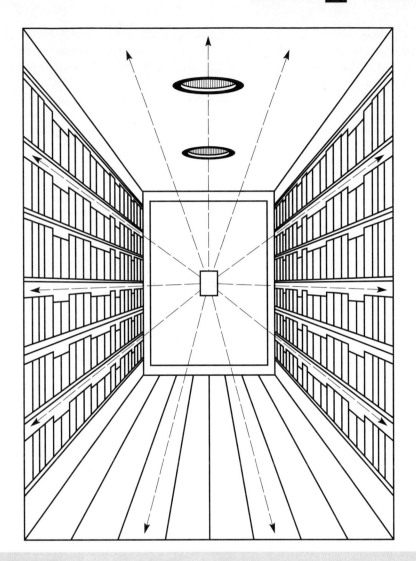

FIGURE 6.6   An attempt to provide a static illustration of optic flow. If you pay attention to the relative motion of objects as you walk along, you'll get a better idea of the notion of optic flow. As you focus on an object ahead of you and move toward it, notice that objects nearer to you flow past rapidly, whereas objects near the point of fixation move little, if at all.

80, or 320 dots. When the dots were rotated, consistent with the underlying shape, a clear impression of three-dimensionality emerged for the displays with more dots. As you might imagine, then, people were better able to identify the target shapes when viewing moving representations with a greater number of dots. People were also more accurate when the target shape had greater depth.

Now that you have been introduced to all the monocular sources of information about depth, try Demonstration 6.3. Next we'll con-

Demonstration 6.2

Kinetic Depth Effect — Take a pipe cleaner or a paper clip and bend it into a clearly three-dimensional figure. Find a piece of paper and a lamp. Place the figure between the lamp and the paper and notice that the figure, as seen through the paper, looks flat and two-dimensional. Now rotate the figure and notice how it suddenly appears to have a third dimension.

sider how artists represent these monocular depth cues, and then we'll explore the binocular sources of information about depth.

Representing Three-Dimensional Space in Two Dimensions

You should have found Demonstration 6.3 informative. Even if you aren't a great artist, you were probably able to provide a reasonable representation of three-dimensional space on a two-dimensional piece of paper. As you have surely noticed, accomplished artists can use the monocular depth cues very effectively.

People—particularly in our culture—have a tendency to perceive two-dimensional drawings as representing three-dimensional space. Such a tendency may give rise to many illusions, such as

Demonstration 6.3

Monocular Sources of Information about Depth — Draw a picture to illustrate the pictorial distance cues. You should show a total of seven. Which monocular/no-movement source of information cannot be represented in this drawing? Then turn on the television when a cartoon show is featured. Which pictorial distance cues are represented and which are not? Which monocular-movement sources of information are represented and which are not?

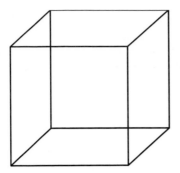

FIGURE 6.7 The Necker cube. This ambiguous figure was first described in 1832 by the chemist Louis Albert Necker.

those we will discuss at the end of this chapter. Some two-dimensional drawings resemble the ambiguous figures discussed in Chapter 5 and can be seen as either two-dimensional or as three-dimensional. The Necker cube, seen in Figure 6.7, is probably the best known of these figures. You will most likely perceive the Necker cube as representing a three-dimensional object, but you can also see it as two-dimensional. As with the ambiguous figures in Chapter 5, as you look at the Necker cube, you should see it change orientations spontaneously—all the while remaining three-dimensional.

Another example of such an ambiguous figure is quite old. Figure 6.8 is a rendering of a hexagon from the floor of Arena Chapel, built in Padua, Italy, in 1306. The entire floor is filled with this hexagonal pattern! Notice how you can perceive the figure as a flat white six-pointed star on a shaded background. You can also see the pattern as three cubes in depth. In fact, you can see three cubes in two different ways. As with the Necker cube, you should find yourself spontaneously seeing first one set of three cubes and then another set of three cubes.

Paintings, Drawings, and Photographs

Most two-dimensional art uses the pictorial depth cues we have been discussing to create a clear

sense of three-dimensionality. As we noted earlier in the chapter, artists in the Renaissance studied depth cues to help them portray distance on a flat canvas. For example, Leonardo da Vinci was aware of practically all the depth cues available to the painter (Hochberg, 1971). Some artists, like Leonardo, use these cues extensively in their paintings. Other artists, however, have ignored them—either intentionally or unintentionally.

Traditional paintings take advantage of the seven pictorial cues summarized in Figure 6.1. Distance or depth can be portrayed quite effectively using only these cues. Figure 6.9 provides the clear impression of raised surfaces appropriate for crumpled paper. Shading is the only depth cue shown, yet it provides the illusion of depth. In fact, you can buy stationery at The Museum of Modern Art in New York that looks just like Figure 6.9. The stationery is an example

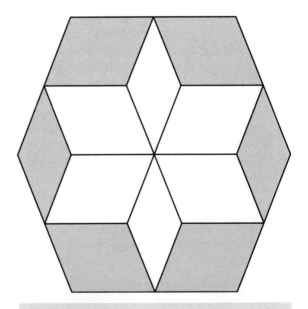

FIGURE 6.8 This figure illustrates a hexagonal section of the floor of Arena Chapel, in Padua, Italy. The chapel was constructed in 1306. Note that you can perceive the figure as purely two-dimensional and also as a two-dimensional representation of three-dimensional space.

FIGURE 6.9 Shading information alone is a powerful cue to depth. Using the whole range of depth cues available allows an artist to create trompe l' oeil art—fooling the eye into seeing depth in a two-dimensional painting. (Photo by Ron Pretzer)

of trompe l'oeil art. ***Trompe l'oeil*** is French for "fool the eye," and such art fools the eye by creating an impression of depth when the surface is really just two-dimensional.

Now notice the portrait in Figure 6.10 by Constance Marie Charpentier (1767–1849), a French painter. This portrait uses a number of cues: size (the distant people are small), linear perspective (the lines on the distant building converge), shading (depth information can be seen in the woman's dress), interposition (her left arm covers part of the window and part of her body), and height cues (the distant couple is higher on the page than the woman). The full-sized painting may also show texture gradient

and atmospheric perspective, but they are not obvious in this reproduction.

Of course, because the picture actually *is* two-dimensional, your visual system has a number of cues that work against seeing the picture as three-dimensional. You can enhance the sense of depth by viewing the picture monocularly through a reduction screen, so that your visual field is limited to the picture.

Other painters are not concerned about the representation of distance. Consider American folk artists. You are probably familiar with the work of Grandma Moses. Figure 6.11 is a painting by Helen Fabri Smagorinsky, a 20th-century painter whose style resembles that of Grandma Moses. The painting shows impressive vitality and activity, but no attempt is made to accurately portray depth. For example, Smagorinsky chooses not to fully use the following cues: size (notice that the people in the background are the same size as those in the foreground), texture gradient, linear perspective, and atmospheric perspective. Shading is used to some extent. However, notice that interposition and height are clear distance cues.

Still other artists use the pictorial depth cues to create two-dimensional representations of objects that would be impossible to construct (Molins, 1991). Such impossible figures are common in the works of M. C. Escher, the Dutch artist we mentioned in Chapter 5. For example, Figure 6.12 is an impossible figure. Did the figure strike you as impossible when you first saw it? Notice that the figure is only impossible when considered as a whole. If you restrict your vision to small portions of the figure, each portion could be readily rendered in a three-dimensional world. Furthermore, the figure would be possible if you could perceive it as a flat pattern—a random assortment of lines and curves. However, people find it difficult *not* to interpret the figure as representing a three-dimensional object (Deregowski, 1980). The three-dimensional object represented in the figure is truly impossible.

Movies

The origins of the modern motion picture are to be found in the 1800s, when several people

FIGURE 6.10 *Mlle. du Val D'Ognes* by Constance Marie Charpentier. Can you spot the several cues that give rise to the perception of depth in viewing this painting? Close one eye and look at the painting again through your cupped hand so that you see little or nothing of the surrounding page. Does the painting take on greater depth? Why?

developed devices that produced the illusion of movement. Although stationary pictures are limited to the pictorial cues, moving pictures can take advantage of the monocular depth cues that involve motion.

For example, the camera can duplicate your head movements to create motion parallax. This is accomplished by a tracking shot, a special film technique in which the camera moves sideways along a track (Hochberg & Brooks, 1978). Figure 6.13 illustrates three representative shots from a series of frames that could be taken as the camera moves sideways. If the camera is focused on the man, the child in front of him seems to move to

FIGURE 6.11 *Genesee County* (1981) by Helen Fabri Smagorinsky. Identify the depth cues that are present and the depth cues that are absent. How powerful an impression of depth does the painting produce?

the left as the camera moves to the right. On the other hand, the picture on the wall seems to move to the right as the camera moves to the right.

The kinetic depth effect is the second monocular factor involving movement, and it can also be illustrated in movies. The kinetic depth effect is most impressive when an object or a person looks two-dimensional, but then movement reveals the third dimension. In movies the picture seldom looks two-dimensional. Occasionally, however,

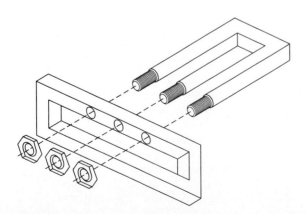

FIGURE 6.12 The three-pronged, one-slot widget, the frame, and the nuts are all impossible figures. As a simple two-dimensional line drawing, this figure is unremarkable. However, when we view it as a two-dimensional representation of three-dimensional objects, we see the difficulty of constructing such objects from this "blueprint." (From Gardner, 1988)

FIGURE 6.13 Example of a tracking shot used in moviemaking. Notice how the changing interposition cues provide a sense of the relative depth of the child, man, and picture as the camera moves from left to right.

you may see a shadow or a figure in an unlit corner that looks flat until it moves or rotates. Watch for this effect, especially in horror movies.

Although they are not common, you are probably aware of 3-D movies. In fact, such movies are experiencing a resurgence in popularity with the IMAX theaters, such as the one in Manhattan (Biancolli, 1995). The film and goggles used to create the IMAX effects differ from those used in earlier films, but the basic principles remain unchanged. In the next section, we will explore binocular cues, including one that produces the sense of depth in 3-D movies.

IN-DEPTH   Binocular Cues to Distance Perception

We have discussed 10 monocular cues to depth, as well as their application in creating the sense of three-dimensionality from two-dimensional representations. Because they are monocular cues, a person who is blind in one eye or who has lost one contact lens can perceive depth using these factors to the same extent as a person with binocular vision. However, two binocular factors contribute to depth perception of nearby objects: convergence and binocular disparity. In this section, we will first describe how convergence and disparity give rise to depth. Then we will briefly

examine the physiological processes that seem to underlie binocular disparity. We will then show how disparity can make two-dimensional representations appear to have depth. Finally, we will discuss situations in which the information on the two retinas does not produce disparity.

CONVERGENCE

As you may recall from Chapter 4, **convergence** means that the eyes converge, or move together, to look at nearby objects. Demonstrate convergence for yourself by looking at a distant object on the horizon and then shifting your focus to the tip of your finger placed on the end of your nose.

If you had to design a visual system to extract as much information about depth as possible from visual experiences, shouldn't the system use convergence information? Perhaps, for example, we could calculate the distance of a particular object once we knew the distance between the eyes and the angle formed at the intersection of the two lines of sight—a wide angle for nearby objects and a narrow angle for distant ones. High school students calculate distances like these when they study trigonometry. Does your visual system calculate an object's distance in a similar fashion, although more automatically?

Actually, the answer to this question is not yet clear. Some evidence suggests that observers can use the information from convergence some of the time (Chung & Berbaum, 1984; Hochberg, 1971; Yellott, 1981). Other evidence suggests that convergence is of little use in determining distance (Arditi, 1986). In any case, convergence information is not useful for judging objects that are far away. When you are looking at an object that is about 10 feet away, your eyes are not converged—neither of your eyes is rotated inward. Furthermore, the position of your eyes does not change as you change your fixation from an object 10 feet away to one 9 miles away. In contrast, the degree of convergence does change impressively when you change your fixation from an object 10 feet away to one 10 inches away. In summary, convergence may sometimes act as a depth cue, particularly when other, more helpful, cues are absent.

BINOCULAR DISPARITY AND STEREOPSIS

Your eyes are roughly 2.5 inches apart, certainly not a tremendous distance. Nevertheless, this distance guarantees that the two eyes will have slightly different views of the world whenever nearby objects are at different distances. ***Binocular disparity*** refers to the different information that arises at the two eyes.

You can illustrate binocular disparity by holding your left thumb about 6 inches from your eyes and to the left. Hold your right thumb about 2 feet directly ahead of you. Focus on your right thumb. Keep your head stable, close your left eye, and open your right eye. What happens to your right thumb? Does it appear to stay in the same position? Now close your right eye and open your left eye. Does your left thumb appear to jump back and forth? Your right thumb is creating no disparity, but your left thumb is creating disparity. Binocular disparity is important because it provides the information needed to judge depth binocularly, an ability known as ***stereopsis*** (Anderson & Nakayama, 1994).

Let's examine the concept of binocular disparity in more detail and introduce a concept called the horopter. Figure 6.14 shows a schematic example of two different disparity situations. In both cases, the eyes are focused on an object at point F. Using a focal point at location F, an imaginary curved line called the ***horopter***

can be drawn to represent all the points that are equally distant from the observer. For example, position your thumbs as you did earlier. Imagine a curved line passing through your right thumb and continuing on either side—but always 2 feet away from your eyes; this curve is the horopter. Objects on the horopter and near the horopter, in an area called ***Panum's area,*** can be fused into a single image (Tyler, 1991c). Outside Panum's area, objects will typically produce double images. When you are looking at your right thumb, your left thumb appears as two thumbs.

In Figure 6.14a, an object at point A would be the same distance from the observer as the focal object, F. As you can see in the figure, the focal object will create images that fall at the same relative location on each retina (labeled f and f' for the left and right eyes, respectively). Because the object at point A is equidistant from the focal object (i.e., on the horopter), its image will also fall at the same relative location on each retina. However, because the object at point A is to the right of the focal object, its image will fall to the left of the focal object on each retina. For objects at both A and F, no disparity is found on either retina. As a consequence, the objects would appear (accurately) to be equidistant.

What about the object at point B in Figure 6.14a? As you can see, the object at B is in front of the horopter. Therefore, its image will fall at different locations on the two retinas (labeled b and b'). Objects in front of the horopter create ***crossed disparity,*** because the image crosses to the outside of the focal point on each retina. Notice that b is to the left of f, but b' is to the right of f'. Thus, crossed disparity is a cue that objects are near us (relative to the focal object).

In Figure 6.14b you see a different situation illustrated. Here, an object is located at point C, which is beyond the horopter. Notice that disparity still arises—the images of this object will fall at different locations on the two retinas (labeled c and c'). However, in this case, the image in both eyes falls to the inside of the focal object. Objects behind the horopter create ***uncrossed disparity,*** which is a cue that objects are far from us (relative to the focal object).

Both Figure 6.14a and Figure 6.14b illustrate a relatively large degree of binocular disparity, one that corresponds to a difference of

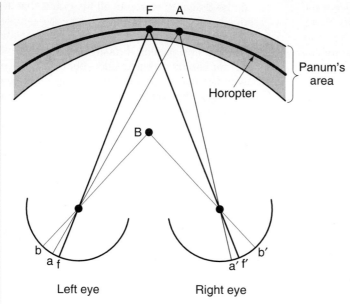

a.

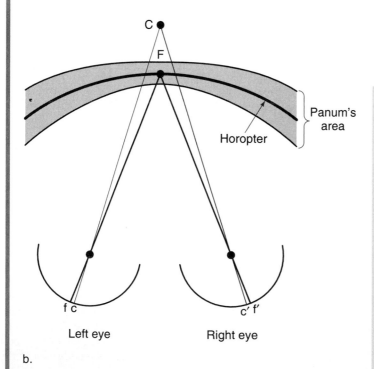

b.

FIGURE 6.14 These figures illustrate binocular cues to depth. In both a and b, the eyes are focused on an object at point F. Another object is equidistant to the focal object, located at point A. In both cases, the retinal images fall on the same part of both retinas. Objects that are equidistant to the focal object fall along the horopter, which means that each object will cast an image on the same part of both retinas. Objects that do not fall on the horopter create binocular disparity, because the images fall on different areas of the two retinas. Part a illustrates crossed disparity, created by objects that are nearer than the focal object. Part b illustrates uncrossed disparity, created by objects that are farther than the focal point.

several millimeters along the retina. Impressively, our visual system can detect differences in depth of two objects that correspond to a difference of 1 micrometer (μm) along the retina (Yellott, 1981). A micrometer is 1 one-thousandth of a millimeter, and a millimeter is approximately the thickness of the wire on a paper clip. One micrometer is therefore an impressively small difference, yet we can detect binocular disparity of 1 μm. Furthermore, Wallach (1985a) argues that depth perception based on binocular disparity is innate—we are born with visual systems predisposed to perceive depth.

Binocular disparity is primarily effective for determining the depth of nearby objects. Research shows that people perform significantly more accurately in judging the distance of nearby objects when they use binocular information rather than just monocular information. However, even when people have binocular information, they are not completely accurate. Specifically, people estimate nearby objects as being farther away than they really are (J. Foley, 1980, 1985, 1991). Interestingly, people estimate distant objects as being nearer than they really are.

Are binocular cues useful in judging such distant objects? In one test of this question, researchers compared the accuracy of monocular and binocular depth perception by testing airplane pilots (Grosslight et al., 1978). Pilots landed their planes with either normal binocular vision or monocular vision (enforced by wearing an eye patch). The researchers offered prizes of up to $200 to encourage the pilots to be particularly accurate. Objective measurements of the landings showed that monocular landings were just as accurate as binocular ones.

As Figure 6.14 illustrates, binocular disparity exists at the retinal level. Given all that you know about our visual system, you should be wondering about how our visual system can combine information that falls on different parts of the retina. We'll now briefly review some of the physiological underpinnings of stereopsis.

PHYSIOLOGICAL BASIS FOR STEREOPSIS

At what point in the human visual system do we find neurons receiving information from both eyes? If you remember the discussion from Chapter 3, you know that the answer lies beyond the lateral geniculate nucleus (LGN). Recall that at the LGN, the input from each eye is kept separate.

Some researchers have suggested that the magno pathway is crucial for stereopsis (Livingstone & Hubel, 1988). Although the magno pathway may be important for some coarse form of stereopsis, the parvo pathway is probably responsible for fine-grained stereoscopic vision (Patterson & Martin, 1992; Tyler, 1991a). Ultimately, our stereoscopic vision is likely to be the product of the interaction of both the magno and parvo pathways (Weisstein et al., 1992; Williams, 1992).

Studies of cells in V1 and V2 of the visual cortex uncovered cells that are sensitive to binocular disparity (Patterson & Martin, 1992; Regan et al., 1990). A subset of complex cortical cells seems to be ideally suited for encoding disparity (Ohzawa et al., 1990). As their name implies, *disparity-selective cells* have high rates of electrical discharge when stimuli are registered on different (disparate) areas of the two retinas. Some cells respond most to low levels of disparity, whereas other cells "prefer" high levels of disparity. Some of these cells respond more strongly to crossed disparity; other cells respond more strongly to uncrossed disparity (Tyler, 1991a). As you might expect, the response rate of disparity-selective cells is quite low when they receive input from only one eye (Bruce & Green, 1990).

As we will discuss later in this section, the purpose of stereopsis and other depth cues is to give rise to an accurate representation of space and the location of objects within that space. The neural site that determines the location of objects probably occurs at a higher level than the visual cortex, possibly the hippocampus (Wilson & McNaughton, 1993).

USING BINOCULAR DISPARITY TO CREATE DEPTH IN PICTURES

The stereoscope was invented by Charles Wheatstone in 1838, and this instrument has contributed greatly to our knowledge about depth perception (J. Foley, 1980; Mitchison & Westheimer, 1984; Ross, 1976). A *stereoscope* is a piece of equipment that presents two photographs of a scene taken from slightly different

Demonstration 6.4

Stereoscopic Pictures   Take a blank piece of cardboard about 20 cm (8 inches) wide and line it up along the dotted line in the figure below. Rest your nose on the cardboard edge closest to you. Each eye should stare at the figure on the appropriate side of the cardboard. Try to fuse the two separate images into a single, unified image. You may find it helpful to try converging your eyes by looking slightly cross-eyed. When you achieve a single image, it should look three dimensional.

viewpoints. Typically these viewpoints are separated to the same extent as human eyes.

A **stereoscopic picture** consists of two pictures, one for the right eye and one for the left eye. When the two pictures are seen at the same time in the stereoscope, they combine to make a three-dimensional scene. Stereoscopes became popular in the 19th century, and you might have used a modern version of the stereoscope, called a Viewmaster.

Notice how the two pictures in Demonstration 6.4 are slightly different. When each eye looks at the appropriate view and you manage to fuse the two images, you should have a sensation that one rectangle floats in front of the other.

Stereoscopes also have a number of practical uses. For instance, aerial surveys use stereoscopic pictures to give a more accurate depiction of depth. In these cases, the two cameras used to make the pictures are typically mounted quite far apart to emphasize the apparent depth of ground surfaces. Stereoscopic displays are being devel-

oped to provide pilots with three-dimensional information about the terrain and cockpit information (Patterson et al., 1992b). Researchers have also developed three-dimensional mammography to make it easier for physicians to detect breast tumors (May, 1994).

Astronauts used a technique for photographing moonscapes stereoscopically—one that you can use to create your own stereoscopic pictures. They shifted all their weight onto one foot and took one picture of a scene, then they shifted all their weight to the other foot and took another picture of the same scene. Shifting their weight actually had the effect of displacing the pictures by just the right amount (about 2.5 inches). Using the two pictures produced by this technique, you should be able to create your own stereoscopic pictures that you could then view in a stereoscope.

One problem with using stereoscopic pictures to study stereopsis is that they often incorporate pictorial depth cues, in addition to binocular disparity. Thus, you could not know for sure

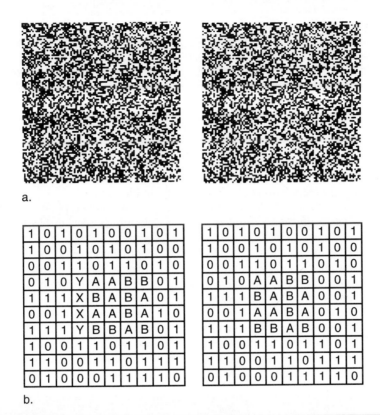

a.

b.

FIGURE 6.15 An example of Julesz's random-dot stereograms. The two fields are identical random displays of dots except for the central area. As seen in the lower part of the figure, a square section is displaced in the two views. In the left view, the "square" begins in the fifth column. In the right view, the "square" begins in the fourth column. The square is labeled with A's and B's instead of 1's and 0's to make it stand out from the rest of the figure, but think of the A's as black dots and the B's as white dots. When the "square" is shifted to the right (in the left figure), the uncovered space is filled with a random pattern of dots (indicated by X's and Y's). The shift in the two patterns represents the binocular disparity that would arise if a square were floating above a random-dot background. When viewed stereoscopically, as in Demonstration 6.4, a perception of depth will emerge. Because no monocular depth cues are present, the sense of depth must come solely through binocular disparity. The square might not appear immediately, but continue to look at the patterns and it should eventually emerge.

that the sense of depth emerged solely from the binocular information. To counteract this problem, Bela Julesz (1971, 1977, 1995) developed random-dot stereograms. In Figure 6.15a, neither of the images makes any "sense" when viewed alone—no picture emerges. No pictorial distance cues are present in the random-dot stereogram. Thus, only stereopsis can explain the apparent depth that emerges when the two images are fused. Because of this fact, random-dot stere-

ograms have become the favored tool of researchers interested in stereopsis.

Initially, you might find it difficult to fuse the random-dot stereograms. Evidence suggests that people become increasingly adept over time at fusing random-dot stereograms (O'Toole & Kersten, 1992). Don't give up; the ultimate perception of depth will be quite rewarding—and fusing the images will be easier the next time!

Closely related to random-dot stereograms is a class of illusory depth experiences. When presented with a repetitive pattern—such as a repeating wallpaper pattern, or rows of tiny dots on ceiling or floor tiles—people often report that part of the pattern seems to pop out toward them! This phenomenon can be traced to a mismatching in the two retinas of repeating elements in the pattern (Mitchison & McKee, 1985, 1987a, 1987b).

Essentially, the sense of depth that emerges from such stimuli arises because the visual system devises an inappropriate solution to the correspondence problem (Frisby & Pollard, 1991; Wildes, 1990). The **correspondence problem** is the difficulty our visual system can face in linking the input from the two retinas. Ordinarily, the input from the two retinas is so distinctive that the solution to the correspondence problem is relatively simple. Thus, as you look at your textbook with first your left eye and then your right eye, you should get the sense that the two images are fairly similar. The upper left corner of the book in the left-eye image would combine naturally with the same corner in the right-eye image,

even though the location of the corner may not be identical on both retinas.

When you look at a repetitive pattern, such as that found in some floor and ceiling tiles, you should recognize that your visual system faces a more serious correspondence problem. Which pattern of three little dark spots in the left-eye image should combine with a pattern of similar dark spots in the right-eye image? If your visual system links the "wrong" portions of the two images, you may perceive depth that is not present in the stimulus.

A related phenomenon is the autostereogram, as seen in Figure 6.16. An **autostereogram** is a single image that contains binocular depth information when viewed appropriately (Tyler & Clarke, 1990). The popular *Magic Eye* books are filled with these images. Your visual system can solve the correspondence problem of the autostereogram in at least two ways. One solution gives rise to a flat random pattern, which you will see if you just glance at the figure. In another solution, you seem to be looking through the page, as though into a window. When you

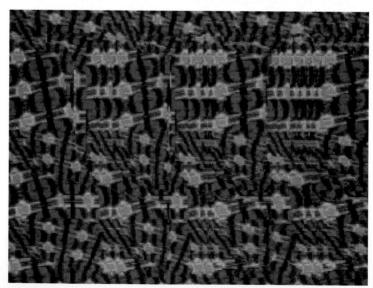

FIGURE 6.16   An autostereogram created by Hugh Foley using pointillist. You might not be able to see this image as three-dimensional initially. Try bringing your nose right up to the page and then slowly moving your head back from the page while keeping your eyes looking straight ahead. In other words, try *not* to bring the page into focus. The simple image should eventually emerge. The hidden image is the Greek letter psi (Ψ).

are able to take this perspective, the dots that are linked together differ from those that you linked when you saw the autostereogram as a flat figure. Autostereograms are probably more difficult to perceive than random-dot stereograms, so don't give up easily if the image doesn't appear.

BINOCULAR RIVALRY

The different images presented to the two eyes are typically fused into a single image containing depth information, leading Julesz (1971) to refer to the percept as *cyclopean*. (Remember the one-eyed Cyclops monster from Greek mythology.) If the images presented to the two eyes are too different, however, they cannot be fused into a single percept. When the images cannot be fused, a situation called **binocular rivalry** exists. Typically, your visual system perceives the image from one eye, and it suppresses portions of the image from the other eye. Then, after a few seconds, the situation reverses and you now perceive the image from the suppressed eye.

Binocular perception ultimately involves both rivalry and stereopsis (Blake, 1988; Blake et al., 1991; Wolfe, 1986). Objects that are located far from the object of focus will fall on such different areas of the two retinas that they cannot be fused. Because objects that fall outside Panum's area cannot be fused, rivalry is a common aspect of binocular perception. However, notice that you are rarely aware of the lack of fusion. Thus, the tendency toward stereopsis is so strong that it typically overpowers rivalry (Harrad et al., 1994).

Using a stereoscope, you can create rivalry that you will notice readily. In fact, people make use of this rivalry to detect counterfeit money. A real dollar bill can be presented to one eye, and a dollar bill suspected of being counterfeit can be presented to the other eye. Even the tiniest difference in detail between the two bills can be detected immediately. Thus, our visual system is acutely sensitive to differences in binocular input. ◆

Now that we have discussed all 12 sources of information about distance and depth, turn back to Figure 6.1 and review these 12 factors briefly.

We began with the 10 monocular factors, 8 of which involved no motion (accommodation plus the 7 pictorial cues) and 2 of which involved motion. We ended with the 2 binocular factors, the relatively unimportant factor called convergence and the much more important factor called binocular disparity.

Theories of Distance Perception

We can identify three major theoretical approaches to distance perception: the empiricist position, the Gibsonian position, and the computational approach. As you will see, the emphases of these three theories are different. The empiricist position stresses the contribution of memory and cognitive processes, which corresponds to Theme 4 of this book (see page 12) but also acknowledges the contribution from the visual system, or Theme 3 (see page 10). The Gibsonian position stresses the richness of environmental input, which corresponds to Theme 2 (see page 10). The computational approach, as we have discussed previously, grew out of attempts to develop programs that would enable machines to perceive the world in depth (Marr, 1982). Essentially, the computational approach asks what "knowledge" and what "perceptual abilities" are required to enable a computing machine to extract depth from a rich environment. Let's examine these three approaches in more detail.

The Empiricist Position

As discussed in Chapter 1, *empiricism* is a philosophical approach stating that all information is derived from sensory perceptions and experiences. For example, we are not born knowing how to perceive distance; we must acquire this skill by learning.

The empiricist position was outlined by George Berkeley in 1709 in an essay entitled *An Essay Towards a New Theory of Vision*. Basically, the problem that Berkeley tackled was this: The stimulus registered in the eye has only two dimensions, height and width. Nonetheless, we also see depth or distance. How can we judge how far away an object is if "we cannot sense distance in and of itself . . . " (Berkeley, 1709/1957, p. 13)? We do have retinal size information—the amount of space an object occupies on the retina—but distance cannot be registered on the retina in an equivalent way. Still, we do perceive depth, so where does this perception come from?

Berkeley proposed that we come to perceive distance by learning and experience. Specifically, we learn to associate various cues for distance with kinesthetic information about distance. ***Kinesthetic information*** is nonvisual information that includes all the muscular information we receive as we interact with objects. For example, we might feel a certain amount of muscle strain in our eyes as we look at an object close to our eyes. We receive muscular information as we reach out for an object a certain distance from our bodies or as we walk toward a distant object. Thus, we know about distance indirectly because we link up kinesthetic information with various kinds of visual distance cues (e.g., the pictorial distance cues). Notice that kinesthetic information is primary in Berkeley's theory, and vision is secondary.

As you might imagine, accommodation and convergence are important sources of distance information if kinesthetic information is basic to distance perception. The pictorial cues, such as interposition and linear perspective, are important cues that may have to be learned. Familiar size, as we suggested earlier, is particularly relevant for the empiricist approach because of the importance of learning and experience.

According to the empiricist tradition, then, the retinal image alone is *not* sufficient for depth perception—it is limited to two dimensions. Only with the enhancement of retinal information through experience can we come to see the world in depth. As Michaels and Carello (1981) summarize empiricism, "Traditional theory belittles the input, but at the same time praises the quality of the product. In such an analysis, the quality of the percept must come, in part, from the perceiver" (p. 5).

Hochberg (1988, 1994) has added to the depth-perception theories developed by the empiricists. His approach stresses the perceiver's active role in interpreting the visual world.

Hochberg argues that we constantly interact with objects around us. As a consequence, we develop certain expectations. When we encounter a new scene, we perceive what we expect to perceive. That is, we construct the most reasonable interpretation of the evidence before us, and this interpretation is what we actually see.

Many modern-day perceptual theorists who have borrowed from the empiricist tradition prefer to call their approach a ***constructivist theory***. According to the constructivist theory, the perceiver has an internal constructive (problem-solving) process that transforms the incoming stimulus into the perception (Cutting, 1986; Rock, 1983). Basically, constructivist theory proposes that the stimulus is often ambiguous, with no clear-cut interpretation. The perceiver's task is to solve the problem: What arrangement of objects in the environment is most likely to produce the stimulus registered on my retina? In Chapter 5 we saw that some theorists suggest that people "solve" illusory contour figures such as Figure 5.24 by reasoning that the most probable explanation is that a white triangle is covering the background figures. Similarly, constructivist theory proposes that people use their experience with objects at different distances to solve problems about depth perception.

Constructivist theory suggests a time-consuming process, which is occasionally true. However, as Rock (1983) explains, adult perceivers can solve perceptual puzzles rapidly because of their experience. Thus, a 4-year-old may have trouble tying shoelaces, but an adult does not. Similarly, adults can readily solve most puzzles involving distance.

In summary, the empiricist position—in both its original and modern form—emphasizes that the visual stimulus on the retina does not provide adequate depth information. Other kinds of cues and sources of information must be added for accurate distance perception.

The Gibsonian Position

According to James J. Gibson, the visual stimulus that reaches the retina is rich and full of information. Cutting (1986) summarizes the ***Gibsonian*** *approach,* or *direct perception approach:* "Direct perception assumes that the richness of the optic array just matches the richness of the world" (p. 247). Gibson argued that the stimulus contains sufficient information to allow for correct perception. Visual information does not involve internal representations or mental processes (Greeno, 1994; Nakayama, 1994).

Gibson argued that most traditional cues—such as linear perspective, size, overlap, and atmospheric perspective—are not relevant for depth perception in real-world scenes (Gibson, 1979). He arrived at this conclusion after inspecting research on student pilots: Tests based on the cues for depth did not predict their success or failure. Therefore, Gibson suspected that the traditional list of cues for depth was not adequate.

Gibson's early writing emphasized the importance of texture gradients as a source of information about distance (Gibson, 1950). As discussed earlier, texture gradients provide a scale whereby we can measure objects' distances from us.

Gibson's emphasis on texture gradients is part of his more general ground theory. According to *ground theory,* distance perception depends on information provided by surfaces in the environment. The ground, floors, and building walls are all examples of surfaces that provide information. In the real world, these surfaces help us know the distance of objects. As you look out your window, the objects you see do not float in air. Instead, the ground serves as their background, so distance can be seen directly (Gibson, 1979).

Gibson's early theories stressed the importance of texture gradients. His later work (e.g., Gibson, 1966) pointed out the importance of *motion perspective,* or the change in the way things look as we move through space. As we will note in Chapter 8 on motion perception, either observers or objects are likely to be moving. This movement provides rich information about objects' depths and distances. Because of his orientation, Gibson would have little interest in the perceptual experience of organisms forced to perceive the world in a completely stationary fashion—with their heads immobilized in some device. He would also have little interest in the perception of images on a television monitor, which humans have surely not evolved to perceive (Cutting, 1993).

Gibson emphasized the concept of *affordances,* or actions one could perform with objects (Cutting, 1993; Greeno, 1994). Thus, a large tree might be climbable, huggable, or a perfect back support, but would not be throwable or easily leapt over. Some objects, such as a sheet of paper, have a wealth of affordances (Cutting, 1993). When you are writing, paper might be a vehicle for containing perfectly lucid prose. All too often, however, the affordance is compactibility, prior to throwing the wadded paper toward the circular file!

As we have seen, a sheet of paper can also contain a picture that portrays a rich sense of depth. In some natural, evolutionary sense, pictures or photographs are surely novel items, much like television pictures. Nonetheless, Gibson attempted to explain how we *could* perceive depth in pictures, which he called indirect perception. In fact, Gibson's attempts to explain how we perceive depth in pictures may well have contributed to the development of his broader theories (Cutting, 1993). One weakness in his approach is that he tried to do so without recourse to the pictorial depth cues.

We have discussed the empiricist position on depth perception, which stresses how we enrich the visual stimulus with associations and expectations. This view proposes that perception involves thought, that it may occasionally be slow, and that it involves learning and awareness (Cutting, 1986). In contrast, the Gibsonian position stresses that the visual stimulus contains a wealth of information. This approach proposes that perception does not rely heavily on thoughtlike processes, that it is fast, and that it involves innate factors—but not awareness. Watching the acrobatics of a fly or a bee, we cannot help but be struck by the possibility that Gibson is correct.

However, it seems likely that these two approaches can be at least partly compatible, rather than mutually exclusive (Ramachandran, 1986). Indeed, the objects we see in natural environments probably contain abundant information about depth—more information than the empiricists originally envisioned. On the other hand, humans are thinking perceivers who use their associations and expectations to further enrich the visual stimulus, especially if it is ambiguous. Moreover, both theories need to acknowledge the contribution from the visual system, as Theme 3 of this book stresses. For example, depth perception is enhanced by the cortical cells that are sensitive to binocular disparity. Depth perception therefore involves a visually rich environment, a visual system that is well equipped to register information about distance, and a thinking, problem-solving perceiver.

The Computational Approach

We began discussing the computational approach in the context of edge and shape perception (Chapter 5). The *computational approach* is characterized by an attempt to develop a set of rules and procedures that could give rise to the perception of complex stimuli. The computational approach shares many characteristics of the constructivist approach and the direct perception approach. Thus, the computational approach states that knowledge is crucial for perception. However, that knowledge is of a more general nature than the constructivist approach might utilize (Wagemans, 1988). For instance, Marr (1982) used the research of Warrington and Taylor (1978) to show that humans can perceive an object without specific knowledge of that object's name or function. Thus, according to a computational approach, we should be able to perceive a telephone on top of a desk without using any specific knowledge we might have about the likelihood that a small black object on top of a desk might be a telephone.

The computational approach makes use of only general knowledge (e.g., laws of physics and geometry) in analyzing a complex scene into separate objects and shapes—rather than specific knowledge. Unlike the direct perception approach, then, the computational approach recognizes the importance of prior knowledge for perception. Furthermore, researchers with the computational orientation are not content simply to identify factors that might give rise to depth perception. Computational researchers also mimic those factors in programs to see if computers could then extract depth information from visual input.

Like the direct perception approach, the computational approach recognizes the richness of the visual input. However, the computational approach does not state that perception is direct. Instead, it invokes the simultaneous operation of several perceptual modules for low-level processing of input. A *module* is a distinct processor that has a limited function, performs its function rapidly, has a specific neural architecture, and is not accessible to central processes (Fodor, 1983; Marr, 1982). For example, in our discussion of the importance of shading, we might see the operation of a shape-from-shading module. A direct perception theorist would argue that the stimulus itself contains sufficient information for perceiving depth. In contrast, the computational approach theorist would argue that, although the stimulus is rich in information, the final perception arises from the combination of input from experience and from several different processing modules.

As we have discussed earlier, the computational approach attempts to develop computer programs that are capable of processing visual input. Because the orientation of the computational approach is so technical, we cannot adequately describe the approach in an introductory-level perception textbook. However, you have already been exposed to some aspects of the modules being investigated. For instance, as we have already mentioned, motion is extremely important for depth perception. You should not be surprised that the computational approach recognizes the importance of motion in proposing a shape-from-motion module. As you have already learned, researchers are in the process of developing computational representations of optical flow (Bülthoff et al., 1989). Furthermore, the computational approach to stereoscopic vision acknowledges the importance of binocular input (e.g., Frisby & Pollard, 1991; Wandell, 1995; Wildes, 1990).

Overall, then, you should not think of the computational approach as being vastly different from the constructivist or direct perception approaches in terms of the factors that are important for depth or distance perception. Instead, the computational approach differs in terms of the extent to which mental operations are involved (more than the direct approach allows) and the extent to which specific knowledge is involved (less than the constructivist approach might allow). The computational approach appears to influence the kind of research done in the other two camps, so the three approaches may become increasingly similar.

Perceiving a Three-Dimensional World

Regardless of the approach to distance perception you might find most appealing, the perceptual problem you face should be clear. You live in a three-dimensional world, and you must have a means of representing that space. Although Gibson would likely dismiss the very concept of space perception (Cutting, 1993), we see it as the ultimate purpose of depth perception.

Given our emphasis on the distinction between the perceptual world and the physical world, we certainly recognize that the correspondence between the two is never exact. Instead, what we perceive has been likened to the opening statement of a district attorney: "a carefully constructed story, part fact, part supposition, clearly biased, sometimes downplaying or ignoring evidence to the contrary" (Albert & Hoffman, 1995, p. 95). So, our perceptual systems may have evolved to provide us with a sense of space that is not totally accurate but accurate enough to allow us to navigate the world successfully. In fact, because blind people share the same navigational problem, they also develop a sense of spatial organization based on nonvisual cues (Haber et al., 1993).

Gogel (1990, 1993) refers to the perceptual experience of space as phenomenal geometry. To accurately locate objects in the environment requires information about the egocentric distance of the object, the direction of the object relative to the observer, and whether or not the observer is in motion (Gogel, 1993). In this chapter, we've focused almost exclusively on how people determine egocentric distance. We will have more to say about the impact of observer motion in Chapter 8, especially how we come to perceive a stable world as we move through it.

The importance of knowing the direction of an object should be obvious to you. Knowing that food is about 100 yards away would do you little good if you had no idea of which direction you should set out in to get the food. Imagine how difficult your life would be if you confused direction, so that the food appeared to be 100 yards to your left when it was actually 100 yards to your right!

A. H. is an undergraduate student with a localization deficit of this sort (McCloskey et al., 1995). When an object is to her left, she will often reach out to her right to grab the object! In her daily life, A. H. is able to correct herself, because she can see that her hand is getting farther away from the object. Because she could compensate, her deficit was not identified until A. H. was an undergraduate. However, several tests show that the localization deficit is a real one, particularly for stationary objects.

At the same time, A. H. has no difficulty localizing with her other senses. She also has no difficulty with other visual tasks, such as identifying objects. When we discussed illusory conjunctions in Chapter 5, we mentioned that shape information was processed separately from location information. Thus, A. H.'s deficit seems to be specific to the visual localization mechanisms. Future research with A. H. will likely clarify the nature of her spatial experience, as well as the source of her deficit.

SECTION SUMMARY

Distance Perception

1. Of the factors influencing distance perception, eight monocular factors do not require movement.
   a. Accommodation, or a change in lens shape, is probably not an important factor.

b. Interposition means that we judge a partly covered object to be farther away than the object that covers it; it is a primary source of distance information.

c. Size (either relative or familiar) is important in laboratory studies of distance perception, but it is not vital.

d. Texture gradient, or the increase in surface density at greater distances, was emphasized by Gibson; its importance has been experimentally demonstrated.

e. Linear perspective, which means that parallel lines seem to meet in the distance, is an important pictorial cue.

f. Atmospheric perspective means that distant objects often look blurry and blue.

g. Shading conveys depth information, because the lighting is not uniform across a surface and because objects far from a light source are more shadowy.

h. Height cues tell us that objects near the horizon are farther away from the observer.

2. Two monocular factors involve movement.

a. Motion parallax means that as you move your head sideways, objects at different distances seem to move in different directions.

b. Because of the kinetic depth effect, the two-dimensional projection of an object seems to have depth when the object rotates.

3. Paintings can illustrate seven of the monocular/no-movement factors: interposition, size, texture gradient, linear perspective, atmospheric perspective, shading, and height cues.

4. In addition to the pictorial cues, movies can make use of motion parallax (and its more general form, motion perspective), and the kinetic depth effect.

5. Convergence is a binocular cue in which the eyes move together to look at a nearby object. Convergence might sometimes be a helpful source of depth information, at least for nearby objects.

6. Binocular disparity, in which the two eyes present two slightly different points of view, is an important source of information about the distance of nearby objects. Stereopsis is the sense of depth that emerges from binocular disparity cues. Complex cells in the visual cortex are probably important for stereopsis.

7. Binocular disparity can be represented in stereograms, random-dot stereograms, and autostereograms.

8. The empiricist position on depth perception states that we perceive distance by associating various cues for distance with kinesthetic information; the visual stimulus itself is inadequate. Modern variations of empiricism, including constructivist theory, stress the importance of our expectations and problem-solving abilities in determining what we perceive.

9. Gibson's direct theory of depth perception argues that the visual stimulus is rich with information; texture gradients and motion perspective are particularly important.

10. The computational approach blends aspects of constructivist theory and Gibson's direct perception theory. Researchers in this interdisciplinary field have developed mathematical models that can be used by computers to perceive depth and distance.

11. Through the various depth cues, people are able to represent the three-dimensional world in which we live. However, some people cannot easily determine the location of objects.

SIZE PERCEPTION

You perceive the world so effortlessly that you might be inclined to think that perception is simple. As we become more analytical of our experience, however, we realize that the processes underlying our perceptual abilities are exceedingly complex. You look out at the world and see that one bird is far away, whereas another bird is close. You are typically unaware of any computations involved in judging those distances, yet now you have been exposed to a long list of factors that affect distance perception.

Likewise, you look out at the world and see some objects as large and others as small. The perception seems immediate and effortless, yet from the other topics we have discussed, you should expect the underlying processes to be fairly complex. We will first explore the factors that influence size perception, and then we will turn our attention to another important constancy—size constancy.

Factors Influencing Size Perception

As we stated at the beginning of this chapter, the perception of distance and the perception of size are interrelated. In the preceding section, for example, you saw that the known size of various objects could serve as a cue to the distance of those objects. To simplify matters, we will first examine factors influencing the perception of the size of objects that are equidistant from us. Next, we will examine how the perceived distance of an object is important in determining its perceived size.

Determining the Size of Objects at the Same Distance from the Observer

When two objects are the same distance from you, how do you determine which of the two is larger? Intuitively, you might think that one of the objects would take up more space on your retinas, and that would be sufficient to allow you to determine which of the two is larger. Review the notion of visual angle presented in Chapter 5, particularly Demonstration 5.1 (page 126). If two objects are the same distance from the observer, the one with the larger visual angle is the larger object.

Of course, size perception is not that simple. Several factors influence the perception of size, so that visual angle cannot be the only factor involved in perceiving the size of equidistant objects. Furthermore, we cannot assume that people perceive visual angle accurately. Although two objects may have identical visual angles, one might be perceived as having a larger visual angle (McCready, 1985). If two objects are equidistant, the one with the larger *perceived* visual angle will appear to be larger.

One factor that influences size perception is shape. As Anastasi (1936) demonstrated, a square or a circle appears to be smaller than a star or diamond of equal area. Several other investigators have demonstrated that shape influences size perception. In general, the results suggest that more elongated objects appear to be larger than equal-size objects that are more compact.

Characteristics of the stimulus, such as its shape, certainly have an influence on the perceived size of the stimulus. However, consistent with Theme 2 (page 10), the context in which the stimulus is viewed is also crucial. For example, the perceived size of an object is influenced by the size of the object's background (Rock & Ebenholtz, 1959). An object viewed against a large background will appear smaller than an object of equal size viewed against a small background. Note the similarity between these context effects on size perception and Wallach's ratio principle of lightness perception (discussed in Chapter 4). Furthermore, the perceived size of many letters of the alphabet is influenced by the organization of surrounding letters (Carrasco & Sekuler, 1993).

Other factors can also influence size perception. Perceived velocity influences size perception, because a slower-moving object will appear to be larger than a faster-moving object of equal size (Kaneko & Uchikawa, 1993). Perceived lightness can also influence size perception. For example, a light square presented against a dark background appears to be larger than an equal-sized dark square against a light background (van Erning et al., 1988). Furthermore, either square appears to be larger when viewed against a highly contrastive background (e.g., white against black) compared to a less contrastive background (e.g., white against light gray).

Determining the Size of Objects at Varying Distances from the Observer

The perceived size of an object is influenced by its shape, by the context within which the object is viewed, and by other factors. In addition to all these factors, perceived size is also influenced by the perceived distance between an object and the viewer. The egocentric distance between the viewer and an object is crucial for determining the perceived size of the object. Thus, perceived distance and perceived size are inextricably linked.

Demonstration 6.5

Emmert's Law   Attach a piece of white paper to a surface several feet from where you are sitting. Now fixate the center of the circle below for about a minute, making certain that your eyes do not move significantly. Then look at the white space to the right of the circle; you should see a bright-looking afterimage. Note the size of the afterimage. Now transfer your gaze to the white paper and note whether the afterimage seems to have grown. Incidentally, if the afterimage seems to fade during this demonstration, a rapid blink will restore it.

Look again at Demonstration 4.5 on page 107. Notice that two very different distal objects can cast the same proximal image. Thus, an object could be twice as large as another object but twice as far away. The two objects, therefore, would have the same visual angle and their images would cover the same area of the retina. If we were unable to determine that the objects were at different distances, we would have a difficult time deciding that their sizes differed.

We can illustrate the relationship between size and distance by exploring Emmert's law, named after the man who discovered it in 1881. First, try Demonstration 6.5 to experience the principles underlying Emmert's law. You'll notice that this demonstration uses a negative afterimage. Staring at the circle in Demonstration 6.5 leads to adaptation; as you look away from the black circle, a white circle appears. However, the perceived size of the circle depends on the background against which it is viewed. ***Emmert's law*** states that an afterimage projected on a more distant surface appears bigger than the same afterimage projected on a nearby surface (Boring, 1942). In terms of an equation, Emmert's law can be stated as

Perceived size = *K* (Retinal image size ×
Perceived distance)

This equation, in which *K* represents a constant, says that the perceived size is a function of both the size of the retinal image and the perceived distance of the object. Notice how this equation explains Demonstration 6.5. The afterimage has a constant retinal image size (and *K* is a constant), so both those values remain the same under all viewing conditions. The only terms that change when you look from a nearby surface to a faraway surface are perceived size and perceived distance. Specifically, an increase in the perceived distance (when you look off at the faraway surface) means that the perceived size must increase as well. As a consequence, perceived size is larger on the faraway surface.

Although Emmert's law deals with afterimages, it reveals the crucial relationship between perceived size and apparent distance. Changes in the size of the retinal image (the proximal stimulus) that are accompanied by corresponding changes in the perceived distance of the object (the distal stimulus) would lead us to perceive the object as having constant size. We now direct our attention to this important constancy.

Size Constancy

Size constancy means that an object seems to stay the same size despite changes in the object's

---

Demonstration 6.6

Size Constancy Take your pen and hold it about 3 cm (1 inch) in front of your eyes. Notice the size of the visual angle that it occupies and think about how big the retinal size must be for a pen held this close. Now move the pen out to 30 cm (12 inches). Notice how the visual angle is much smaller; the retinal size is also much smaller. Now prop up the pen and walk across the room. The visual angle is now extremely small, and the retinal size is also extremely small. Think about how the pen looked to you. Did it seem to shrink to doll-sized proportions as you walked away from it? In fact, it seemed to stay a constant size, despite the fact that the retinal size was much, much smaller when the pen was viewed from across the room.

---

retinal image (e.g., McKee & Welch, 1992; Morgan, 1992). Notice, then, that the proximal (retinal) size of the object can shrink and expand, depending on how far away it is, yet the distal size of the object stays the same. Try Demonstration 6.6 to help you notice how the visual angle and retinal size change as an object moves away from your eye. Visual angle, a term introduced in Chapter 5, means the size of the arc that an object forms on the retina. Retinal size refers to the amount of space the object occupies on the retina. Visual angle and retinal size are closely related terms.

Think about how size constancy operates in the real world. As your professor steps forward to make a particularly important point, he or she does not expand magically before your eyes (although the retinal image does). As a car drives away from you, you don't see it shrink to matchbox size. Similarly, a dog playing "fetch the stick" with you does not appear to expand and contract. The next time you get up from reading this book, notice how objects seem to stay the same size as you move away from them. Obviously, size constancy plays an important adaptive role.

You might argue that you have size constancy because you know how big your professor, a car, and Rover are. Yes, familiarity may help to preserve size constancy (Leibowitz, 1971), but size constancy operates for unfamiliar objects as well, as long as distance information is present. Thus, a random shape cut out of white paper

would seem to stay the same size as you changed your distance from that unusual shape.

Distance Information and Size Constancy

In everyday life you have substantial information about distance that can tell you how far away an object is. Theoretically, you could combine knowledge about an object's distance and knowledge about its retinal size to determine how big an object "really" is—that is, its distal size.

A classic experiment demonstrated the importance of distance information in determining size constancy (Holway & Boring, 1941). As Figure 6.17 shows, observers were seated so that they could look down either of two darkened hallways. Down the right-hand hallway, a test stimulus could be placed at any distance from 10 to 120 feet. The test stimulus was a circle whose size could be systematically varied to produce a visual angle of 1° regardless of its distance from the observer. (Consequently, the circle was 12 times as large at the 120-foot distance as at the 10-foot distance.) Down the left-hand hallway, 10 feet away, was a comparison circle, which observers were instructed to adjust until it matched the size of a particular test stimulus.

This study had four experimental conditions:

1. Normal, binocular viewing with all distance information present
2. Monocular viewing with all other distance information present

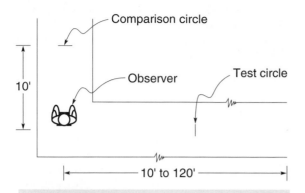

FIGURE 6.17 Setup for the Holway and Boring experiment (looking down on the hallways). The observer would view the test circle at varying distances so that the visual angle was constant. The observer viewed the test circle under four different conditions and adjusted the comparison circle so that it appeared to be equally large.

3. Monocular viewing through a peephole, which removed the distance information available from motion parallax (the head-movement factor)
4. Monocular viewing through a peephole with drapes along the hallway, which removed almost all distance information.

Notice, then, that the amount of distance information available to observers differed in the four conditions.

Figure 6.18 shows the observers' performance in the four conditions. First look at the two dashed lines, placed on the figure as guidelines. The top dashed line represents how people would perform if they had perfect size constancy and the object seemed to stay exactly the same size, no matter how distant it was. The other dashed line represents how people would perform if they had absolutely no (zero) size constancy—if in judging its true size they considered only retinal size and not the distance of the object.

Now notice how people performed in the four conditions. In the normal viewing condition (1), people showed a little overconstancy;

they overcorrected for distance and actually made overly large estimates for distant objects. The overconstancy results are probably artifacts of the way in which the data were collected (Teghtsoonian, 1974). In the monocular condition (2), people showed almost perfect size constancy. In the monocular/peephole condition (3) and in the monocular/peephole/drapes condition (4), people showed underconstancy; they provided estimates that were too small for distant objects. Without information about distance, people do not show much size constancy.

The role of distance information is complicated by the increasing evidence that judgments of small distances are based on different cues from those used to judge large distances. Size constancy may well depend on the type of information used to judge large distances (McKee & Welch, 1992).

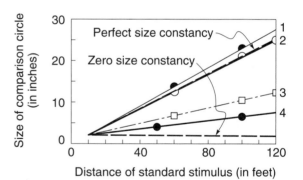

FIGURE 6.18 Results of the Holway and Boring experiment that resulted from the four viewing conditions. The horizontal dashed line indicates no size constancy. Because the visual angle was constant, if the observers could not take distance into account, the test circle should always appear to be equally large. The oblique dashed line indicates perfect size constancy. As the viewing conditions changed from 1 to 4, the observers received increasingly restricted distance cues. In the presence of distance cues, the observers exhibited size constancy. In the absence of distance cues, the observers lost size constancy.

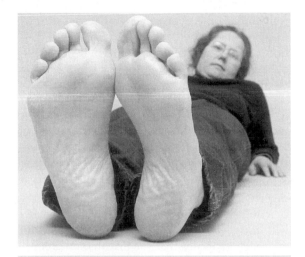

FIGURE 6.19 Although this woman's feet are actually normal size, the unusual angle from which this photograph was taken makes it difficult to maintain size constancy. (Photo by Ron Pretzer)

The impact of distance information on size constancy can also be demonstrated in photographs that reduce distance information. Figure 6.19 is a photograph from an angle highly unusual in Western tradition (Hagen, 1986). Because so little distance information is present, size constancy cannot be preserved, and the feet in the foreground look unusually large.

Explanations for Size Constancy

More research has been conducted on size constancy than on any other constancy (Leibowitz, 1971). Nevertheless, psychologists disagree about what factors are responsible for this phenomenon.

Several factors have been proposed, and it seems likely that each may be involved in some aspects of size constancy. We already mentioned that familiar size may be helpful. If you know how big a pencil is, you can guess its size even when the distance varies. This differentiation must be learned; young children misidentify a man in the distance as a boy and a distant large animal as a dog (Leibowitz, 1971).

A second explanation of size constancy is the size–distance invariance hypothesis. This explanation applies to both familiar and unfamiliar objects. According to the *size–distance invariance hypothesis,* a viewer calculates an object's perceived size by combining an object's retinal size and its perceived distance. This definition is a restatement of Emmert's law. Notice another prediction that can be derived from Emmert's law. If two objects have the same retinal size, the object that appears to be farther away will be perceived as larger. This classic theory was originally proposed by Helmholtz (1866), the empiricist whose views we discussed earlier. Do not take this principle too literally, however. You don't take out a pocket calculator to figure the objective size. In fact, you probably are seldom aware of this process. Even animals seem to be guided by this principle, so it cannot involve elaborate conscious calculations (Gogel, 1977).

The size–distance invariance hypothesis has been updated by Irwin Rock. Rock (1983) uses the term *unconscious inference,* which Helmholtz also used. When we make an inference in logic, we draw a conclusion based on the evidence and we are *conscious,* or aware, of the inferential process. In *unconscious inference,* we arrive at a perception in a somewhat similar fashion, beginning with evidence and arriving at a conclusion. However, in perception the process is not conscious; furthermore, the result is a perception rather than a logical conclusion. For example, an observer might inspect a scene in which the retinal image size of one pencil is roughly twice the size of another pencil. The observer might reason, unconsciously, "The retinal image size for pencil A is twice that of pencil B. However, the distance for pencil A is half that of pencil B. Therefore, their perceived sizes are equivalent."

Some researchers have tried to figure out exactly what distance information people take into account in the size–distance invariance hypothesis. Leibowitz and his colleagues (1972), for example, discovered that the distance factors of accommodation and convergence led to size constancy for objects closer to the eye than about 3 feet. Other researchers have found that the size–distance invariance hypothesis is not perfect-ly reliable (Hubbard & Baird, 1988; Hubbard et al., 1989). For example, when judgment condi-tions vary, so does the relationship between judged size and distance (Vogel & Teghtsoonian, 1972). Thus, the relationship between size and distance is variable rather than invariant.

Another explanation for size constancy con-cerns the relative sizes of objects being judged (Rock & Ebenholtz, 1959). As we mentioned earlier, the size of the frame within which an ob-ject is viewed has an impact on the perceived size of the object. According to this *relative-size explanation,* people notice the size of an object, compared to other objects. For example, look at your pen on the desk. Now get up and walk across the room. The image of the pen grows smaller, but the image of the desk also grows smaller. In fact, the ratio of the retinal sizes re-mains constant. The retinal size for the pen may be one-tenth as long as the retinal size for the desk, whether you are 1 foot or 10 feet away. Thus, objects seem to stay the same size as we move away from them because they keep their same size relative to other objects near them. Notice that in this theory the viewer does not need to take distance into account. All the infor-mation necessary for constancy is present in the relationship among the stimuli.

One other explanation is also concerned with the relationship among stimuli. According to Gib-son's direct perception explanation, mentioned earlier, we can directly perceive the environment from the information in the stimulus (Gibson, 1959). For example, people notice the size of an object by comparing it to the texture of the sur-rounding area. As you saw earlier in this chapter, Gibson emphasized texture in distance percep-tion; texture is equally important in his theory of size constancy. Try Demonstration 6.7 to illustrate the importance of texture in size constancy.

We have mentioned that Gibson's emphasis on the information available in the stimulus pro-vides support for Theme 2 of this textbook (see page 10). The stimulus registered on the retina is not an impoverished representation of reality. Stimuli are rich with useful information about the environment. Most other theories propose that the mechanisms for constancy are located within the viewer, whereas the direct perception approach proposes that the explanation is locat-ed within the stimulus.

An important Gibsonian concept, particu-larly relevant to the constancies, is invariants. *Invariants* are aspects of perception that persist over time and space and are left unchanged by certain kinds of transformations (Epstein, 1977; Michaels & Carello, 1981). For example, in Demonstration 6.7 the relationship between the two sheets of paper and the texture units sur-rounding them provides enough information to establish size constancy. Regardless of distance, the same piece of paper consistently covers an invariant number of texture units. Thus, we can tell that its size must remain invariant.

Our discussion of distance perception con-cluded that explanations from both the empiricist and the Gibsonian traditions are probably valid. By extension, the computational approach also captures many elements of distance perception. We can assess distance relatively accurately be-cause we can take advantage of a wide variety of

---

Demonstration 6.7

Influence of Surrounding Texture on Size Constancy

Select a long, flat area that has noticeable texture patterns, such as a tile floor, a sidewalk, or a rug with a regular geometric pattern. Take two same-sized sheets of paper and place them about 1 foot and 10 feet away from you. Notice how the paper covers the same number of texture units in both cases. For example, it may cover 1 1/4 tiles; this coverage is the same whether the paper is near or far from you.

information sources about distance. Similarly, we will conclude the discussion of size constancy by noting that several factors are probably responsible for our remarkable accuracy in preserving size constancy: Objects seem to stay the same size because of familiarity, the size–distance invariance hypothesis, the relative size of other objects, and the texture of the surrounding areas.

SECTION SUMMARY

Size Perception

1. The egocentric distance of the object is important in the accurate perception of an object's size. Several other factors also influence the perceived size of an object, including shape, background size, and lightness of the object.

2. Emmert's law illustrates the crucial relationship between size perception and distance. Although the law was formulated on the basis of afterimages, it is useful for explaining how size perception generally depends on distance perception.

3. Size constancy arises when the distal size of an object remains constant in spite of proximal changes. Several theories have been proposed to explain size constancy, including the size–distance invariance hypothesis, unconscious inference, the relative-size explanation, and Gibson's direct perception explanation.

ILLUSIONS OF DISTANCE AND SIZE

In our discussion of distance and size perception, we have focused on the many factors that give rise to correct perceptions of the world around us. As we saw with the perception of shape, our perceptions are not always veridical. We would probably not survive for long if the majority of our perceptions were illusory, so part of the charm of illusions is their rarity. For the psychologist, however, illusions are important because they provide clues to the functioning of the visual system. Just as we can learn a great deal about normal perception by

studying people with perceptual abnormalities, we also learn a great deal from studying illusions. Illusions of distance and size are particularly intriguing, as you will soon see.

Illusions Involving Line Length or Distance

Figure 6.20 shows one of the most famous illusions, the Müller–Lyer illusion, first demonstrated in the late 1800s. In the ***Müller–Lyer illusion,*** the two horizontal lines are actually the same length. Nonetheless, the line with the wings pointing outward looks about 25% longer than the line with the wings pointing inward. Thus, if the wings-inward figure were 10 inches long, the wings-outward figure would have to be less than 8 inches for people to consider their lengths equal (Lown, 1988).

Coren and Girgus (1978) estimate that more work has been done on the Müller–Lyer figure than on all other illusions combined. As you would expect, psychologists have tried many variations of the figure, including those in Figure 6.21. Impressively, the illusion remains strong in all these variations.

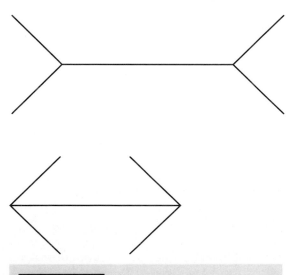

FIGURE 6.20 The Müller–Lyer illusion. Which of the two horizontal lines is longer?

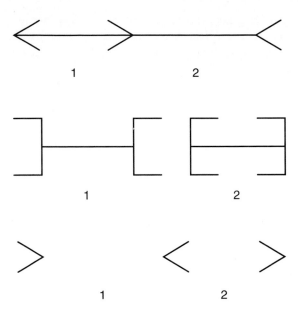

FIGURE 6.21 Several variants of the Müller–Lyer illusion. In each case, segment 1 is equal to segment 2.

izontal lines look longer than when they are presented alone, and horizontal lines look shorter than when they are presented alone (Masin & Vidotto, 1983). Second, when a line is interrupted by another line, we judge the interrupted line to be shorter. To make a "pure" horizontal–vertical illusion, therefore, neither line should be interrupted. If you try drawing an L so that the two lines are of equal length, you will find that you will be more accurate than you were in Demonstration 6.8. An inverted-L form of the illusion reduces the magnitude of the illusion somewhat further. However, some distortion remains (Brosvic & Cohen, 1988; Rowe-Boyer & Brosvic, 1990).

Coren and Girgus (1978) point out other natural occurrences of the horizontal–vertical illusion. People overestimate the height of vertical objects such as parking meters, lampposts, and buildings, often by as much as 25%. Thus, a standing tree looks taller than the same tree after

The Müller–Lyer illusion can also be demonstrated with a variety of psychophysical methods. Although researchers typically employ the classical psychophysical techniques, the Müller–Lyer illusion can be effectively demonstrated using the magnitude estimation technique, which we discussed on page 42 (McClellan et al., 1984).

Another line-length illusion is the **Sander parallelogram,** presented in two versions in Figure 6.22. The distance a_1a_2 (or b_1b_2) is equal to the distance a_2a_3 (or b_2b_3). Nonetheless, the distance a_1a_2 looks much longer than the distance a_2a_3. If you can ignore the inducing parallelogram, you might be able to see the figure $a_1a_2a_3$ as an upside-down isosceles triangle. If you can do that, then you can convince yourself that the line lengths are equal—even without a ruler. However, you'll probably need a ruler to demonstrate that the two distances in Figure 6.22b are equal.

Before reading further, try Demonstration 6.8. This line-length illusion is called the **horizontal–vertical illusion;** it is effective for two reasons. First, vertical lines presented next to hor-

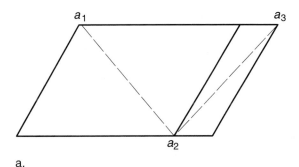

FIGURE 6.22 Two versions of the Sander parallelogram. The distances a_1a_2, a_2a_3, b_1b_2, and b_2b_3 are all equal.

Demonstration 6.8

Horizontal–Vertical Illusion

Extend the vertical line upward until it seems equal in length to the horizontal line. Then measure the two lines and check your accuracy.

FIGURE 6.23 Gateway Arch in St. Louis, Missouri—an example of the horizontal–vertical illusion. (Photo courtesy of St. Louis Regional Commerce & Growth Association)

being chopped down. One of the most famous architectural examples of this illusion is the Gateway Arch in St. Louis (Figure 6.23). Only by measuring can you convince yourself that the height and the width are equal. In reality, both height and width are 630 feet.

The *Ponzo illusion* is shown in Figure 6.24. Notice how the figure in part a creates the impression of linear perspective, even though it is drawn with only a few lines. In part b, additional distance cues convince you that the distant bar must be larger because it has the same retinal size as the closer figure. We can call the figure in part a an illusion. Is the figure in part b an illusion? The field depicted in part b certainly has depth, so size constancy should lead the upper bar to appear larger. As you can see, the boundary between "inaccurate" perception in illusions and "accurate" perception in size constancy is extremely fuzzy. Suppose the observer interprets certain cues in a line drawing to be depth cues, although no instructions specified to do so. In this case, judging two equal figures unequal in objective length is called an illusion. When more depth cues are present, judging two equal figures unequal in objective length is called size constancy. Indeed, the distinction between illusions and size constancy does sound arbitrary!

So far we have considered illusions involving line length. Several similar illusions do not involve estimating the length of an actual line;

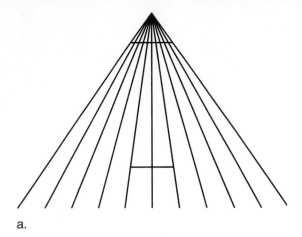

a.

b.

instead, they involve estimating the distance between two objects. For example, in Figure 6.25 you see the *spacing illusion,* in which lines whose ends are separated by a constant amount will seem to be closer together when the lines are tilted (Mather et al., 1991).

Explanations for Line-Length and Distance Illusions

More than 1,000 articles had been written about more than 200 illusions by the late 1970s (Coren & Girgus, 1978). Most of these articles concern the illusions just discussed. As you can imagine, we will not conclude that one simple explanation will suffice for all these illusions.

In keeping with the general distinction between top-down and bottom-up processes, we can characterize explanations for visual illusions as either psychological or physiological (Gordon & Earle, 1992). Psychological explanations for

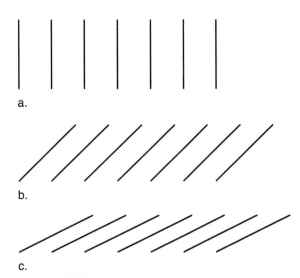

a.

b.

c.

FIGURE 6.24 Ponzo illusion. The two horizontal lines in part a are actually the same length. The two bars in part b are also the same length. The depth cues in both illustrations lead us to see the upper line or bar as farther away. How might the distance information explain the illusion? Notice in part b the power of texture gradients. In the photo, can you point out the dip in the field (just above the upper bar)? (Photo by Ron Pretzer)

FIGURE 6.25 The spacing illusion. Do the distances between the ends of the lines appear to stay constant? In fact, the distances are equal in all three examples. (From "The Spacing Illusion: A Spatial Aperture Problem?" by Mather et al. first published in *Perception,* 1991, 20, pp. 387–392, fig. 1. Reprinted by permission of Pion Limited, London)

illusions emphasize the constructive, hypothesis-testing nature of perception. Physiological explanations emphasize the importance of lower-level processes.

One example of a psychological explanation for illusions involves misapplied constancy. According to the ***misapplied constancy explanation,*** observers interpret certain cues in the illusion as cues for maintaining size constancy. Therefore, they make length judgments on the basis of size constancy, and a line that looks farther away will be judged longer (Gillam, 1980). This explanation is particularly relevant for the Ponzo illusion. Look again at Figure 6.24a and notice how the top line does indeed look farther away. Invoking this explanation, we would conclude that

the top line must be longer because it appears to be more distant.

Many of the illusions we have been discussing can be explained by interpreting the illusory figure as representing three-dimensional space in two dimensions, as a picture does. Gillam (1980) produced an effective demonstration of how this might work. If you look at the room in Figure 6.26, you will see nothing at all unusual. However, the room is filled with illusions! For instance, the length of the front of the carpet is exactly equal to the length of the back wall. If you trace over the edges involved, you will find that each looks like half of the Müller–Lyer illusion with one part of the wing removed. The two dogs are equal in size, although the apparent depth should make the rear

FIGURE 6.26 An illusory room that shows how seeing a two-dimensional illustration as representing three-dimensional space might give rise to illusions. Which is longer: the front of the carpet or the wall at the back of the room? Two other illusions are also present in the drawing. Get out your ruler; you can't trust your eyes! (From Gillam, 1977; photo courtesy of B. Gillam)

dog appear to be larger (as in the Ponzo illusion). Finally, the length from the front to the back of the carpet is equal to the length of the back of the carpet (horizontal–vertical illusion).

The misapplied constancy explanation argues that people are sensitive to distance cues in illusions because they have had experience with cues such as converging lines. People therefore use this experience inappropriately in making judgments about the Ponzo illusion. According to this view, then, *experience* is a crucial factor, and people who have had less experience should be less deceived by the illusion. For example, the Ponzo illusion has little effect on children 5 years of age and younger (Leibowitz, 1971). However, the illusion is as effective for 10- to 15-year-olds as it is for adults.

Perceptual research with other cultures also argues for the importance of experience (Deregowski, 1989). People who have had little experience with pictorial representation of three-dimensional space are becoming increasingly rare. However, past research has supported the important role of experience in determining susceptibility to illusions such as the Ponzo illusion.

In short, the misapplied constancy explanation of illusions emphasizes the contribution of our cognitive processes during perception, an emphasis consistent with Theme 4 of this textbook (see page 12). Thus, visual illusions support the active role of the mind in interpreting the potentially ambiguous retinal images (Hoffman, 1983). Unfortunately, misapplied constancy is an inadequate explanation for a number of visual illusions (Gordon & Earle, 1992; Ward et al., 1977).

The misapplied constancy approach *might* explain some illusions, such as the Ponzo illusion. However, other approaches may be equally effective in explaining these illusions (Day, 1989; Pressey & Epp, 1992). One promising explanation, which we might call the ***incorrect comparison explanation,*** states that observers' perceptions are influenced by parts of the figures that are not being judged. For instance, people's attention may be more easily drawn to the oblique lines when looking at the upper horizontal line in the Ponzo illusion. The oblique lines may be too far away from the lower line to have any influence over its perceived length. Thus, the upper horizontal line would be perceived as longer, regardless of perspective cues (Pressey & Epp, 1992).

In the Müller–Lyer illusion, people's attention may be drawn to the ends of the figures, which would make the arrows-out version appear to be longer (Day, 1989; Gordon & Earle, 1992; Morgan et al., 1990). Thus, observers cannot separate the lines from the wings in this illusion. Experimental evidence supports this explanation. For example, the magnitude of the Müller–Lyer illusion is greatly reduced when the wings are a different color from the lines, so that the wings would be less likely to enter into the comparison (Coren & Girgus, 1972).

The ***eye-movement explanation,*** a somewhat more physiological approach, states that illusions can be explained by differences in actual eye movements or in preparations for eye movements. Eye movements, per se, have been ruled out as explanations for many illusions, such as the Müller–Lyer illusion (Coren, 1986; DeLucia et al., 1994). However, people may *prepare* to make eye movements when inspecting illusions such as the Müller–Lyer illusion. These preparations may partially explain some illusory effects (DeLucia et al., 1994).

Strongly physiological explanations of illusions are becoming more prevalent with the increasing influence of the computational approach (Gordon & Earle, 1992; MacLeod & Willen, 1995). However, the illusions do not appear to originate in the retina (Gillam, 1980). Studies have demonstrated that illusions can still be produced when part of the figure is presented to one eye and another part is presented to the other eye. Therefore, the explanation must originate at a point in the visual system more central than the lateral geniculate nucleus, the earliest step in visual processing at which the inputs from the two eyes first come together. Promising research suggests that the filtering performed by spatial frequency analysis may help to explain some illusions (Gordon & Earle, 1992; Greene & Fiser, 1994).

By itself, none of the approaches we have discussed can fully explain all the line-length illusions. Each illusion probably depends on at least one of these explanations, as well as other factors that no one has yet developed (Beagley, 1985).

Illusions Involving Area

The illusions we have considered so far have focused on linear distance, involving either the length of a line or the distance between two points. Thus, they involve a single dimension. Other illusions involve area, or two dimensions. The book you are holding in your hands right now presents you with an area illusion. What proportion of the book page is taken up by margins? Unless you guessed that about one-third of the page was margin, you fell victim to the *margin illusion*. People typically perceive margins as taking up a much smaller proportion of a page. In a related illusion, a passage of text will appear to be longer when surrounded by wide

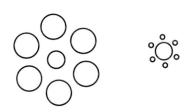

a.

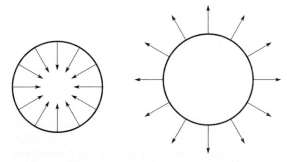

b.

FIGURE 6.27 A couple of examples of area illusions. The two inner circles in part a are equal. The two circles in part b are equal.

margins, compared to the same text with paper cropped around the text (Degoldi & Day, 1992).

Several area illusions are shown in Figure 6.27. Notice the effect of context in each of the illusions. There is the tested element (e.g., the circles in part b) and the inducing elements (e.g., the arrows in part b). You would have no difficulty judging the two circles to be equal if they were presented to you without the inducing elements. As in the case of the distance illusions, the inducing elements produce a misperception.

The Ames Room

Another classic size illusion is the Ames room, named for its creator, Adelbert Ames (1952). The *Ames room* is an unusually shaped room that causes distortions in apparent size because it is perceived as a normally shaped room. Looking through a peephole into an Ames room, such as the one at the Exploratorium in San Francisco, you would see a scene like that in Figure 6.28a. Can you believe that the two girls are the same size?

The Ames room is actually hexahedral in form. Thus, the rear wall is not at all rectangular—the right corner is both much closer and shorter than the left corner. As Figure 6.28b illustrates, the rear wall actually slants away from the viewer. However, when viewed monocularly, it appears to be a normal cube-shaped room.

Let's briefly return to the afterimages used to establish Emmert's law. Emmert's law says that if you project a circular afterimage onto a wall, the size of the afterimage is determined by the distance between you and the wall. Given Emmert's law, what would you predict would happen if you projected a circular afterimage onto a wall that you know is slanted? As you might have guessed, the nearer part of the afterimage will appear to be smaller than the more distant part of the afterimage, distorting the afterimage into an oval shape.

We've already stated that all the points along the rear wall of the Ames room appear to be equidistant from the observer, but the wall is actually quite slanted. Suppose you projected a circular afterimage onto the rear wall of the Ames

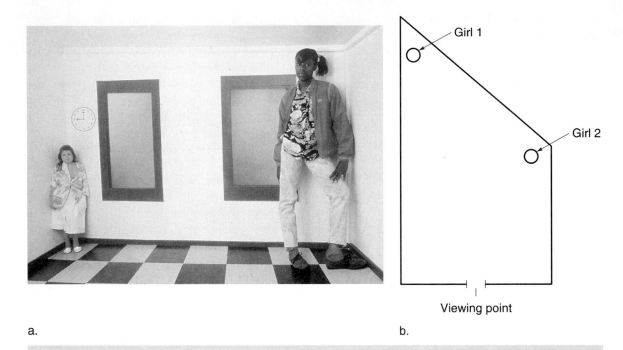

a.   b.

FIGURE 6.28 The Ames room. The girls are actually the same size! Because of the unique construction of the room (see part b), Girl 1 is much farther away from the viewer. Our experience with symmetrical rooms and the construction of the room conspire to deliver an illusory experience.

room. Would the afterimage be circular or oval? As you might have decided, the shape of the afterimage is circular because the shape is determined by the *apparent* orientation of the wall, not its actual orientation (Broerse et al., 1992).

Some people explain the Ames room in terms of experience. After all, you have had a wealth of experience with cubic rooms and virtually none with hexahedral rooms. However, a number of pieces of evidence argue against the role of experience in explaining the Ames room (Day, 1993). Instead, we might more profitably think of the retinal image created by the Ames room. Because of the clever construction of the Ames room, all of the cues present at the retina are consistent with a normally shaped room (Day, 1993). So of course we perceive the room to have a normal cubic shape. Once we do so, the illusory size experiences are inevitable.

The Moon Illusion

If you enjoy moonlit walks, you've probably noticed that the full moon appears to vary in size. Due to the *moon illusion,* observers generally report that the moon at the horizon looks about 30% bigger than the moon at the zenith, or highest position (Baird & Wagner, 1982; Rock & Kaufman, 1962). (A similar illusion is found with the sun, but you should never look at the sun.) Given that both the visual angle and distance of the moon remain unchanged, why should the apparent size of the moon change? This question has intrigued scientists since the origins of scientific thought (Plug & Ross, 1989).

Some researchers have sought a physical explanation for the moon illusion (Plug & Ross, 1989). They thought that the moon appeared to be larger at the horizon because the light rays passed through more of the earth's atmosphere at the horizon. However, such a physical explanation for the moon illusion can be ruled out by taking photographs of the horizon and zenith moon. Measurements of the moon at horizon and zenith are identical, so the moon is not enlarged due to the atmosphere. Further research has ruled out other physical factors, such as differences in color and brightness, as possible explanations for the moon illusion (Hershenson, 1982; Kaufman & Rock, 1962).

We know, then, that the moon occupies the same area on the retina in both its horizon and zenith positions. Although some disagree (Haber & Levin, 1989), most researchers would conclude that the explanation must therefore be psychological. But what *is* the explanation?

Let us first examine an explanation that has experienced widespread popularity. This approach is called the ***apparent-distance theory*** because it argues that the moon seems to be farther from the viewer when it is on the horizon than when it is at the zenith. Thus, as Figure 6.29 shows, the two positions of the moon may differ in their apparent distance from the viewer. An early form of this theory was proposed in the 11th century (Ross &

Ross, 1976), but the modern version was developed by Kaufman and Rock (1962).

If people believe that the sky is shaped like a shallow bowl—as Figure 6.29 shows—then the moon should appear to be larger on the horizon because the horizon sky is so far away. In contrast, when the moon is at the zenith, people should believe the moon is relatively close to them. If the moon is close to them and the retinal size is still the same, then it looks small. Rather than maintaining its horizon size, the zenith moon appears to shrink down to the dotted-moon size shown in Figure 6.29. (Notice that this explanation is similar to Emmert's law, which says that an afterimage will be smaller if you shift your gaze from a far to a nearby background.)

The apparent-distance theory is complicated enough already, but we face an additional problem. When asked to judge which moon appeared to be closer, the horizon or zenith moon, observers typically reported that the horizon moon was closer! How could the horizon moon be larger because it was both farther away than the zenith moon *and* also closer than the zenith moon? One possible explanation is that the visual system unconsciously computes the registered distance to the moon and then derives the perceived size of the moon. When people are later asked to make a conscious judgment of the distance of the moon, they make use of the perceived size (rather than registered distance) and infer that larger objects are closer; therefore, the horizon moon must be nearby (Kaufman & Rock, 1989).

In reevaluating their earlier work after roughly 30 years, Kaufman and Rock (1989) continue to believe in the apparent-distance theory. However, they assert that the terrain below the horizon moon is the major source of the moon illusion. Kaufman and Rock now believe that the flattened sky does not *cause* the moon illusion. Instead, they believe that the terrain factors that give rise to the moon illusion also lead people to perceive a flattened sky.

Other theories also place a great deal of emphasis on the roles of the terrain and the sky; they provide the contexts within which the moon is seen (e.g., Baird, 1982; Restle, 1970). Such theo-

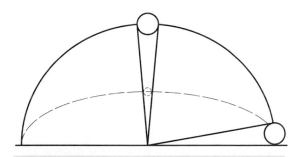

FIGURE 6.29 Effect of apparent distance of the moon on judgments of moon size. The solid curve represents the true path of the moon in the sky; the dashed curve represents the apparent path of the moon against the flattened sky. The solid circles represent the true size of the moon at the horizon and the zenith; the dashed circle represents the apparent size of the moon at the zenith. (At the horizon, apparent size equals true size.)

ries are similar to the theory that size constancy occurs because observers judge an object's size relative to nearby objects (Rock & Ebenholtz, 1959).

John Baird's original (1982) theory, called *reference theory,* proposes that both the sky and the ground are important referents when observers judge the size of the moon. However, unlike Kaufman and Rock, Baird argues that the moon always appears to be equidistant from the observer. When the moon is closer to the horizon, people judge the size of the moon relative to both the sky and the ground. Compared to the retinal sizes of objects on the horizon, the moon looks large. When the moon is overhead, the observer judges the moon's size relative to a huge, uncluttered dome of sky. Compared to that vast sky, the moon looks small.

Baird and his colleagues have continued to develop his theory (Baird et al., 1990; Wagner et al., 1989). They now assume that the actual visual angle of the moon is less important than the perceived visual angle, as McCready (1985, 1986) has suggested. They argue that context influences the *perceived* visual angle, which is smaller in the context of the expansive sky and larger in the context of the horizon. Thus, the zenith moon will appear to be smaller because of its smaller perceived visual angle. The horizon moon will appear to be larger because of its larger perceived visual angle. If the observer assumes that the moon remains the same physical object, with constant size, then the horizon moon (with its larger perceived angle) will appear to be closer than the zenith moon (Baird et al., 1990).

Needless to say, no single explanation has yet received complete acceptance in the scientific community. In the last 20 years alone, at least eight competing explanations have been offered (Hershenson, 1989b). Why have so many different theories been proposed to explain the moon illusion? First of all, celestial objects pose a tremendous challenge to our perceptual system. People have trouble simply judging the size of large terrestrial objects at great distances (Higashiyama & Shimono, 1994). Imagine how much more difficult it is to judge celestial objects. Thus, people significantly underestimate the size of the moon, even at the horizon (Lockhead & Wolbarsht,

1989). None of us looks up at the moon and accurately sees its diameter as equal to the length of the United States!

As intriguing as the moon illusion is, its scientific value lies in what it may tell us about the perception of size. Ultimately, the moon illusion must be understood in the context of a more general theory of size and distance perception (Hershenson, 1989a). Clearly, such a theory has not yet been constructed. Furthermore, the way to construct such a theory is *not* by starting with a phenomenon as complex as the moon illusion. The moon illusion might better serve as the ultimate test of a size/distance theory derived from the study of earthly objects. To try to explain the moon illusion at this stage of the game might well be lunacy.

SECTION SUMMARY

Illusions of Distance and Size

1. The line-length and distance illusions include the Müller–Lyer illusion (and its many variants), the Sander parallelogram, the horizontal–vertical illusion, the Ponzo illusion, and the spacing illusion.

2. A popular psychological explanation for some illusions is the misapplied constancy explanation, in which cues in the illusion are interpreted as cues for maintaining size constancy. Research has demonstrated that experience with depth cues enhances these illusions, a finding that supports the misapplied constancy explanation. However, this theory cannot explain all the illusions.

3. The incorrect comparison explanation proposes that illusions occur when observers base their judgments on the incorrect parts of the figures. Thus, when judging the horizontal lines in the Ponzo and Müller–Lyer illusions, people's judgments are influenced by the inducing elements in the illusions.

4. Although eye-movement patterns seem to be inadequate explanations for most illusions, preparations for eye movements may play a role in some illusory effects.

5. Physiological explanations for illusions are becoming increasingly prevalent. These ex-

planations rely on the filtering performed with spatial frequency analysis to explain several illusions.

6. Two important area illusions are the Ames room and the moon illusion, in which the horizon moon looks about 30% bigger than the zenith moon.

7. Among the competing theories of the moon illusion are the apparent-distance theory and reference theory. However, many theorists believe that the moon illusion is an extremely complex size judgment and that researchers will be able to explain it only when we have a more complete theory of size perception.

REVIEW QUESTIONS

1. Some sources of information about distance, such as size cues, would be included in a "commonsense" list of factors. Other sources of information—such as binocular disparity, convergence, and shading—would be omitted. Describe each of these factors, discuss some supporting research, and point out their importance in theories about distance perception.

2. Many of the distance cues we discussed are referred to as "relative" cues to distance, because they do not seem capable of enabling us to measure distances exactly. Nonetheless, people are quite good at estimating distances with fair precision. Try to figure out which cues, if any, might give rise to absolute, rather than relative, distance perception. Then try to figure out how all the cues to distance might work to provide us with absolute distance information.

3. Summarize the empiricist approach, the direct perception approach, and the computational approach with regard to distance perception. In what ways is the computational approach similar and dissimilar to the other two approaches? Which approach seems best able to explain your experience of depth? Why?

4. One tactic suggested to people trying to lose weight is to put their food on a small plate. What factor in size perception suggests that a person might think that more food was on the plate? What other factors might be used to bias size perceptions?

5. Describe the binocular cues to depth. Why are random-dot stereograms and autostereograms important? Given all that you now know about the cues to depth, how important are the binocular cues relative to the monoc-

ular cues? (Think of the spatial circumstances under which binocular cues are useful.)

6. Why are constancies important, particularly size constancy? To answer this question, imagine trying to move around in our world if constancies did not exist. Try to describe a specific, concrete experience (e.g., catching a ball).

7. What mechanisms seem to be important in maintaining size constancy? How is Emmert's law useful in understanding size constancy? If distance cues were unavailable but other cues were present, do you think that size constancy could be maintained? Why is the size of the moon not constant?

8. Artists interested in realistic portrayals of depth must solve the same problem facing the visual system—they must create a perception of three-dimensionality on a two-dimensional surface. Trompe l'oeil art is particularly effective in this regard. Is trompe l'oeil art illusory? How many of the illusions discussed in this chapter seem to arise from the same principles used to represent depth pictorially?

9. Anastasi found that a parallelogram appears to be larger than a square of equal area. Examine the theories provided to account for visual illusions to see if you can find one that might give rise to the misperceived area of parallelograms. (*Hint:* Look at the top of the Necker cube in Figure 6.7.) Which explanations of visual illusions seem best able to deal with each of the illusions in this chapter? Pay particular attention to the area illusions.

10. How accurate is your representation of space? Close your eyes and try to reach out and grasp nearby objects or point to more distant objects in the room, estimating their

egocentric distance in feet. You should find that you are fairly accurate. What factors give rise to your sense of space? Do you agree with Berkeley that your sense of space emerged from experience, or do you think that space perception is innate? What evidence would you use to support your claim?

NEW TERMS

distance perception (165)
depth perception (165)
egocentric distance (165)
relative distance (165)
monocular factors (167)
accommodation (167)
pictorial cues (167)
cue (167)
interposition (167)
size cues (167)
relative size (167)
familiar size (167)
texture gradient (169)
linear perspective (170)
atmospheric perspective (170)
shading (170)
height cues (172)
motion parallax (174)
motion perspective (175)
kinetic depth effect (175)
trompe l'oeil (179)
convergence (182)

binocular disparity (183)
stereopsis (183)
horopter (183)
Panum's area (183)
crossed disparity (183)
uncrossed disparity (183)
disparity-selective cells (185)
stereoscope (185)
stereoscopic picture (186)
correspondence problem (188)
autostereogram (188)
binocular rivalry (189)
empiricism (189)
kinesthetic information (190)
constructivist theory (190)
Gibsonian approach (190)
direct perception approach (191)
ground theory (191)
motion perspective (191)
affordances (191)
computational approach (192)
module (192)

Emmert's law (196)
size constancy (196)
size-distance invariance
 hypothesis (199)
unconscious inference
relative-size explanation (200)
invariants (200)
Müller–Lyer illusion (201)
Sander parallelogram (202)
horizontal–vertical illusion (202)
Ponzo illusion (203)
spacing illusion (204)
misapplied constancy
 explanation (205)
incorrect comparison
 explanation (206)
eye-movement explanation (206)
margin illusion (207)
Ames room (207)
moon illusion (208)
apparent-distance theory (209)
reference theory (210)

RECOMMENDED READINGS

Julesz, B. (1995). *Dialogues on perception*. Cambridge, MA: MIT Press. This book is as close as most of us will get to having a conversation with Julesz about his work. He provides a very readable retrospective of his research on visual perception, written as a dialogue between Julesz (A) and a questioner (B). The questions Julesz asks himself are always on target, as are his engaging responses. The portions of the book on depth perception are particularly relevant to the current chapter.

Marr, D. (1982). *Vision: A computational investigation into the human representation and processing of visual information*. San Francisco: Freeman. Before his untimely death, David Marr had a tremendous impact on computational approaches to visual perception. Luckily for us, he was able to finish this book, which provides a well-written overview of Marr's approach. There are several sections relevant to depth and distance perception, detailing the computations that could give rise to three-dimensional perceptions from two-dimensional inputs.

Patterson, R., & Martin, W. L. (1992). Human stereopsis. *Human Factors*, 34, 669–692. This review article provides a thorough and clearly written introduction to the principles underlying human stereopsis. The reference section lists a wealth of articles that you could pursue for more detailed information.

Stereogram. (1994). San Francisco: Cadence Books. The *Magic Eye* series from N. E. Thing Enterprises is more widely known for its examples of autostereograms. However, this book also contains some beautiful autostereograms. What makes this particular book a useful source is the accompanying text explaining stereopsis and autostereograms, including an article by Christopher W. Tyler, who first developed autostereograms.

7 Color

Imagine eating dinner tonight and confronting a plate of purple chicken, red corn-on-the-cob, orange lettuce, and blue milk. It would be difficult to finish the meal with your eyes open! Color is such an important part of visual perception that violations of our expectations are overwhelming.

Color has an important impact on the marketing of products. For instance, Eastman Kodak Company spends large sums to make certain that the quality of "Kodak yellow" is controlled within well-defined limits (Boynton, 1971). Detergent boxes must feature bold, primary colors to inspire images of cleanliness and strength (Toufexis, 1983). In fact, when people were tested on their reactions to detergents, they thought that the detergent in a yellow-orange box was too strong, the detergent in a blue box was too weak, and the ideal product came in a blue box with yellow-orange splashes (Kupchella, 1976). Furthermore, when people were asked to judge the capsule colors of drugs, they reported that white capsules suggested analgesic action, lavender suggested hallucinogenic effects, and orange or yellow were stimulants (Buckalew & Coffield, 1982).

Color has enormous social significance as well. Actors and actresses rise to stardom aided by the color of the irises of their eyes. Hair color is even more important; think about the stereotypes we have about blondes or redheads. Skin color, of course, is most important. People have been enslaved, deprived, and killed because of the color of their skin.

The perception of color has been a consistently popular topic for researchers. In fact,

Haber (1992) argues that color is the single most studied topic in vision. Recent evidence certainly suggests that our visual system processes color information better than other features of stimuli (Chaparro et al., 1993). In this chapter, we consider five aspects of color: the nature of color, color mixing, color vision theories, color vision deficiencies, and color phenomena.

NATURE OF COLOR

An object's color, as we typically use the term, has several dimensions. Three primary and interacting dimensions combine to define our perception of color: hue, saturation, and lightness (Melara et al., 1993). Each of these qualities is generally determined by a physical dimension, as discussed in Chapters 3 and 4. As indicated in Chapter 4, when describing colored lights we would replace lightness with *brightness*, which is determined by the intensity of the light source. As illustrated in Table 7.1, an object's hue is primarily determined by wavelength, saturation by purity, and lightness by the amount of light reflected.

Let us first examine *hue*, which is the psychological reaction to wavelengths ranging from about 400 nm (seen as violet) to about 700 nm (seen as red). When we use the word *color* in everyday conversation, we typically mean *hue* instead.

The history of research on color vision might have been different if a plague had not swept through London in the summer of 1666. Isaac Newton escaped this plague by moving to Cambridge that summer, and his major publications on the nature of light were based on his research there (Wasserman, 1978). Newton closed himself in a room that was entirely dark except for a beam of sunlight passing through a small hole in a shutter. Then he took a prism and held it up to the beam of light. The prism refracted, or bent, the white light from the sun into the rainbowlike spectrum you see in Color Plate 1 inside the front cover, with colors ranging from violet to red. Figure 7.1 illustrates how sunlight contains some portion of every wavelength from the visible spectrum. Notice, incidentally, that the

TABLE 7.1
General Relations among Physical and Perceptual Properties of Color

Physical Term	Psychological Term
Wavelength	Hue
Purity	Saturation
Reflectance	Lightness
Intensity	Brightness

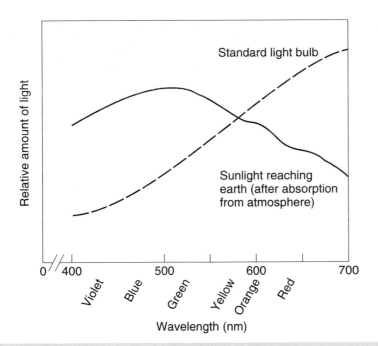

FIGURE 7.1 Wavelength composition of sunlight and light from a light bulb. Both contain all wavelengths of light. However, compared to sunlight, the standard bulb has less energy among the shorter wavelengths and more energy among the longer wavelengths.

light from a standard incandescent light bulb also contains all different wavelengths, but a greater proportion comes from the long wavelengths.

As Newton demonstrated, white light really consists of a combination of different colored lights, an observation that doesn't match our intuitive feelings about light. Another observation that doesn't match our intuitions is the fact that objects *look as if* they are colored, but they are really reflecting light from selected portions of the spectrum. Your jeans may look blue—and blueness seems to be a quality as inseparable from those jeans as their pockets. Nevertheless, the jeans are blue because their surface is absorbing most of the long and medium wavelengths (from the red, orange, yellow, and green portions of the spectrum) and reflecting to your eyes primarily the light from the blue portion of the

spectrum. Similarly, your white shirt is reflecting light to your eyes from the entire spectrum, and your black shoes are reflecting almost no light. So the colors we perceive are partially determined by the nature of the light falling on the surface (the illumination) and the nature of the absorption and reflectance of the surface on which the light is falling.

One common way to organize colors, proposed by Newton in 1704, is in terms of a color wheel. As illustrated in Figure 7.2, a *color wheel* is a circle with all the different wavelengths arranged around the edge. Notice that hues that seem similar to you are located near one another. Yellow is near red and also near green. However, red and green, which seem quite different, are separated on the color wheel. Recent work supports the generally circular organization pro-

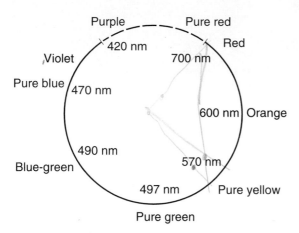

FIGURE 7.2 The color wheel, a method of organizing all the wavelengths of the visible light spectrum. This layout places colors that seem similar (like red and orange) near each other and colors that seem opposite (like red and green) across from each other.

posed by Newton (Izmailov, 1995; Izmailov & Sokolov, 1991, 1992; Shepard, 1993; Shepard & Cooper, 1992).

Next notice the dotted line at the top of the color wheel. This part of the circle represents **nonspectral hues** that cannot be described in terms of a single wavelength from a part of a spectrum. Instead, these hues are produced by combining other hues. Purple is a combination of blue and red. Similarly, studies show that when asked to choose one hue as the best example of red, people choose a red that contains a little touch of blue.

Notice also that some colors are not on the circle. Brown and pink aren't there, let alone the more exotic colors such as silver and gold. In fact, you see on the wheel only a small proportion of the crayons you can buy in the extra-fancy, super-duper collection. Where is burnt sienna or carnation pink or periwinkle or mauve? The outside of the color wheel represents only the **monochromatic colors**—those that could be produced by a single wavelength—plus the nonspectral hues necessary to complete the circle.

In addition to hue, our experience of color is determined by lightness and saturation. Remember from Chapter 4 that objects vary in the amount of light they reflect from their surfaces. Regardless of the intensity of the light shining on an object, we tend to perceive its lightness as constant. Thus, **lightness** is the apparent reflectance of a color; lightness describes our psychological reaction to the physical characteristic, reflectance. Objects run the gamut from very dark (black) to very light (white), with other shades of reflectance in between.

Hue, lightness, *and* saturation cannot easily be represented on a single color wheel. Instead, we require a three-dimensional representation of color as seen in Figure 7.3, which is a picture of a color solid. A **color solid** or **color spindle** represents the hue, saturation, and lightness of all colors. Color Plate 3, inside the front cover, shows one example of a color solid.

The axis along the center of the color solid represents the **achromatic colors** discussed in Chapter 4 (white, grays, and black). You should think of the color solid as a series of color wheels stacked one on top of the other. If you were to take a horizontal section through the color solid at any point, you would see the color wheel associated with a particular lightness. At the top of the color solid are the lighter colors associated with light grays. At the bottom of the color solid are the darker colors associated with dark grays. You could think of Newton's color wheel as the circle formed by taking the horizontal section through the middle of the color solid. The center of Newton's color wheel would be a medium gray.

Figure 7.4 represents one possible section of the color solid. All of the colors within this cross section are equal in lightness. However, the colors vary in purity. The physical **purity** of a color is determined by its location within the cross section. Colors high in purity are arranged around the edge of the circle. As we move toward the middle of the circle, colors become increasingly less pure and more achromatic. The center of the circle represents a shade of gray, an evenly balanced mixture of light waves, with no single wavelength dominant.

Notice that as we move inward from blue to white, we move from a true, deep blue to more "washed out" shades of blue, such as sky blue and baby blue. As we have discussed, the physical characteristic is customarily referred to as *purity*. The *apparent* purity of a color, however, is called **saturation.** Purity is a term from physics, and saturation describes a psychological reaction. Thus, we say that baby blue looks highly unsaturated because we are discussing our psychological reaction. Furthermore, the achromatic colors (grays, black, and white) are all unsaturated.

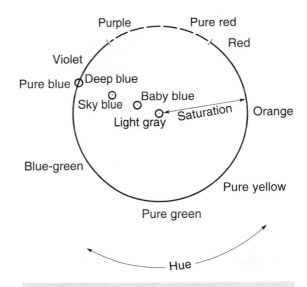

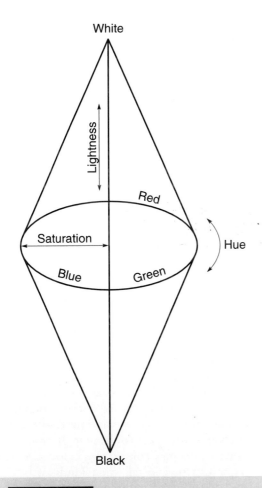

FIGURE 7.3 The color solid, a way to represent all visible wavelengths in terms of hue, saturation, and lightness. Compare this figure with Color Plate 3.

FIGURE 7.4 The color wheel plus saturation, the psychological reaction to the amount of white light added to a hue. A saturated blue lying on the wheel (no white light added) is perceived as a deep hue; an unsaturated blue close to the center (a lot of white light added) is perceived as a much lighter hue (baby blue).

You may wonder why the color solid is pointed at both ends rather than cylindrical. The answer is that some combinations of saturation and lightness are impossible. For example, you cannot have a dark or light color that is highly saturated. As you approach the ends of the color solid, the achromatic light becomes so strong that it overwhelms the monochromatic lights. You might often mistake a dark navy blue sweater for black because the reflectance is so low that the blue in the sweater is harder to detect. In summary, high saturation is possible only when the lightness is intermediate, neither too dark nor too light.

SECTION SUMMARY

Nature of Color

1. Hue corresponds to the length of light waves, and it can be represented by points

along the edge of a color wheel. The color wheel also shows nonspectral hues such as purple and true red.

2. The apparent purity of a color is referred to as saturation. On a color wheel, the saturation of a color is represented by the distance from the center of a circle.

3. A color solid represents hue and saturation on a color wheel. Lightness (which corresponds to the physical term, reflectance) is represented along the vertical dimension. The solid is shaped so that the broadest portion occurs at medium lightness.

COLOR MIXING

What happens when we mix colors? We can actually mix colors in two different ways. The *subtractive mixture* method means that we mix dyes or pigments, or we place two or more colored filters together and shine a light source through them. The *additive mixture* method means that we add together beams of light from different parts of the spectrum. Subtractive mixtures involve only a single light source, whereas additive mixtures combine colors from separate light sources. We will discuss both types of color mixing because they have both had a real impact on the development of theories of color perception. However, keep in mind that the same color perception principles are the basis of both subtractive and additive color mixing (Ratliff, 1992).

Incidentally, you should notice how mixing colors differs from mixing stimuli relevant for some other senses. When you mix red and blue by either the subtractive or the additive mixture method, the result is a color of uniform shade. You cannot detect the separate parts that constitute the mixture because vision is a *synthetic sense* with respect to mixtures. Contrast this situation with the result when we combine two fairly different sounds, say a C and an A on the piano. Here, you can definitely separate the two notes when they are played together because audition is an *analytic sense*. Taste, as well as audition, is typically an analytic sense because we can

detect the separate parts when we taste something. A chocolate mint mousse has two distinct, separable flavors—chocolate and mint. Let's now consider the two kinds of color mixtures.

Subtractive Mixtures

If we were to ask you the color that would result from mixing blue and yellow, and you respond "Green," then you are already familiar with subtractive color mixing. Subtractive mixtures, as we said before, involve mixing pigments or placing colored filters together. They are called *subtractive* because when a beam of white light passes through filters or falls on pigments, parts of the spectrum are absorbed or subtracted. As Figure 7.5 shows, blue paint absorbs the yellow, orange, and red (the long wavelengths) from the white light. Only the light from the violet, blue, and green portions of the spectrum passes on to your eyes. However, yellow paint absorbs violet and blue (the short wavelengths). Consequently, when you mix blue and yellow, the only color *not* absorbed by either of the paints is green (a medium wavelength). You report seeing green because the narrow range of wavelengths entering your eyes comes from the part of the spectrum associated with green.

Remember that we are dealing with subtractive mixtures whenever we mix dyes or pigments. Artists work with subtractive mixtures when they mix pigments on a palette or when they put one color on top of another on the canvas. If you are repainting a room, you will also need to worry about subtractive mixtures, because yellow painted over blue may turn out a sickly green. Anyone who works with colored filters would also be concerned about subtractive mixtures. For example, a window display that uses various colors of cellophane might unintentionally reveal a new color if two colors overlap.

How can people tell what kinds of colors will result from the subtractive mixture technique? Unfortunately, predicting exactly what wavelengths will be absorbed by a particular pigment is quite difficult, and the pattern of absorption may be complex. For example, the light

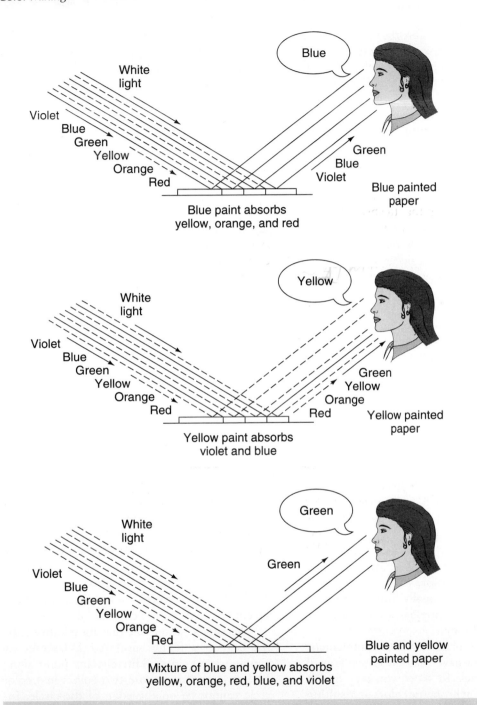

FIGURE 7.5 Subtractive mixtures for blue paint and yellow paint. The final perception, green, results from the only wavelengths not absorbed by the blue or yellow paints. In other words, the subtraction takes place at the level of paints. (From Lindsay & Norman, 1977)

green you see on cabbage absorbs the short and medium-long wavelengths but reflects the light from the medium and very long wavelength portion of the spectrum (Clulow, 1972). If we do not know exactly what wavelengths will be absorbed by the individual pigments, we cannot predict the results of the combination of pigments.

Additive Mixtures

Keep in mind that with an additive mixture of colors, we are adding or combining colored lights and not pigments. The wavelength of each light being combined actually reaches the photoreceptors, which does not occur in subtractive color mixing. After examining how the color wheel can be used to predict additive color mixtures, we will look at instances in which you've probably experienced additive color mixtures. Finally, we will look at the important concept of metameric matching—a topic to which we will return later in the chapter.

Predicting Additive Mixtures Using the Color Wheel

Let's consider the color wheel once more. Look at Figure 7.2 and notice that the wavelengths are not evenly arranged around the periphery of the wheel. The portion of the spectrum from about 420 to about 500 clearly has more than its fair share of the wheel. This unequal distribution is necessary to place complementary hues on exactly opposite sides of the color wheel. *Complementary hues* are those whose additive mixtures make an achromatic color. Notice, then, that when we add together equally intense lights of two highly saturated complementary hues, the result is a shade of gray.

You will have a better sense of complementary hues after you have read the discussion of color vision theories. In short, you may find it helpful to think of achromatic colors as resulting from wavelengths across the whole visible spectrum. As you saw in Figure 7.1, sunlight—which does not appear to be colored—contains energy across the whole spectrum. Each of the complementary hues represents only one portion of the

visible spectrum. However, the additive combination of their wavelengths covers a broader range of the spectrum, leading to the perception of achromatic light.

Figure 7.6 shows how an additive mixture would work if you mixed lights of the two complementary hues blue and yellow. Incidentally, the hues must be carefully chosen or the combination may produce a color other than gray (Jameson, 1983).

If mixing equal amounts of complementary hues produces gray, what do you produce when you mix unequal amounts of other colors? In general, you will produce a color between the two colors and lower in saturation. Here is how you can predict the results:

1. Locate the two colors on the color circle and connect them with a line.
2. Place a dot along the line to represent the relative amount of each light in the combination.
3. Draw a second line from the center of the circle so that it passes through the dot and ends at the edge of the circle.
4. The point at which that line ends on the circle tells you the name of the color; the distance of the dot from the center tells you its saturation.

These predictions will be only rough approximations, and more accurate predictions require using a "color wheel" that is decidedly noncircular (Williamson & Cummins, 1983). For example, the Optical Society of America has produced a three-dimensional color space representation that incorporates current knowledge of color perception (Boynton, 1986; Boynton & Olson, 1987). We have clearly come a long way from the color wheel and the color solid!

We should point out that an additive mixture cannot be highly saturated. Whenever we combine two colors additively, any point along the line connecting those two colors in a color circle cannot lie on the edge of the circle. Instead, it lies in the less saturated region. If the two colors are similar, the additive combination can still be fairly saturated. If the two colors are complementary, however, and if the mixture uses equal quantities of both, the result is an ex-

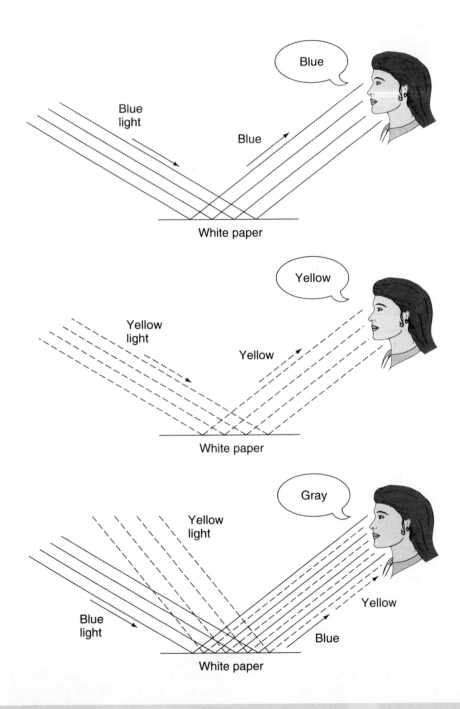

FIGURE 7.6 Additive mixtures for blue light and yellow light. The final perception, gray, results from both the blue and yellow lights reaching the photoreceptors. In other words, the addition takes place at the photoreceptors. (From Lindsay & Norman, 1977)

Demonstration 7.1

Predicting Additive Mixtures

What happens if we make an additive mixture of equal amounts of green and violet? We must place the dot halfway between green and violet. Notice that the result is blue, tending slightly toward green, with intermediate saturation. Try an additive mixture that is mostly violet, with just a little green. To do this, you must place the dot nearer to the violet side. Notice that you get blue. Similarly, try a mixture of mostly orange, with just a little green. Notice that the result is yellowish orange. Finally, try an equal mixture of blue and a slightly orange yellow.

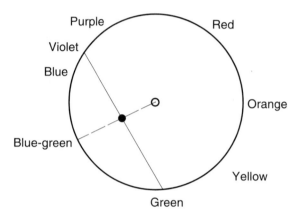

tremely unsaturated mixture. Try Demonstration 7.1 to illustrate additive mixtures and clarify the issue of saturation.

When we mix blue and yellow in a subtractive mixture, we produce green. However, when we mix blue and yellow in an additive mixture, we produce gray. Thus, the two mixture techniques produce different results. The point at which the mixing occurs will help you to keep the two techniques separate. In subtractive color mixing, the combination of pigments takes place *before* the light stimulus reaches the eye, restricting the range of wavelengths reaching our eyes. In additive color mixing, *both* wavelengths reach our eyes—nothing is subtracted. Try Demonstration 7.2 to illustrate the two techniques.

Everyday Examples of Additive Mixtures

In our everyday lives, we do not often see mixed beams of lights of different colors. A more com-

mon way to produce additive mixtures is to place small patches of color next to one another. For example, color television produces its range of colors by using triads of red, green, and blue dots throughout the screen. These dots are very small and closely spaced. Try Demonstration 7.3 to convince yourself that when you watch television, you are really watching spots in front of your eyes. Because of transmission restrictions, the range of colors produced on a television screen is limited relative to the original colors captured by the camera (Williamson & Cummins, 1983).

Of course, ordinarily you don't have your nose pressed up against the television screen. When viewed from a more appropriate distance, the dots are too small to be identified by the unaided eye. Instead, you perceive colors on the screen that arise because of the summation of the wavelengths from a whole bunch of the color

---

Demonstration 7.2

Two Mixture Techniques

First, try making an additive mixture. Take small pieces of blue and yellow paper. Cut the blue paper into narrow strips, then cut these strips into tiny squares. Arrange the squares in random order on part of the yellow paper, so that they cover about half the surface. Tape the squares in place, then tape the yellow paper on a wall at the end of a long hallway. Walk backward down the hallway, looking at the paper, until you can no longer see the individual squares. The combination of yellow and blue should look gray.

To make a subtractive mixture, you might try mixing blue vegetable dye with yellow dye, or blue paint with yellow paint. You might also be able to color a white sheet of paper with both blue and yellow crayons. In each case, the resulting mixture should be green.

---

triads. Suppose that in one part of the screen, all three dots are very bright. What would you perceive? Yes, that portion of the screen would appear to be white. All three wavelengths would reach your retina, and their additive combination would lead to the perception of white.

Artists can also produce additive mixtures with their paints. With a technique called *pointillism,* in which discrete dots of pigments are applied to a canvas, an artist can create the perception of colors that aren't found on the artist's palette. Viewed from a distance, the points blend together, but when viewed closely,

the points become apparent. Another technique, called *divisionism,* is based on the interactive effects of larger patches of colors. We will discuss such effects, called simultaneous color contrast, later in this chapter. Neo-impressionists made use of both these techniques in their paintings (Ratliff, 1992).

Georges Seurat (1859–1891), for example, didn't mix a large number of subtle shades on his palette. In fact, a reconstruction of the palette for his best-known painting contained only about a dozen colors. Some of these pigments were probably mixed in a subtractive fashion, including de-

---

Demonstration 7.3

Additive Mixtures and Color Television

The screen of a color television is like a miniature patchwork quilt consisting of many tiny dots. Typically it has about 1 million dots of three types. When irradiated from behind the screen by a special beam, one type glows blue, another glows green, and another glows red (Boynton, 1979).

How can a patch on the screen look yellow? Take a magnifying glass and notice that a yellow patch is really tiny green and red dots of a carefully chosen hue. The dots are too small to be seen with the unaided eye when you sit at a normal distance from the television, but they are combined by additive mixture. With the magnifying glass, notice other blends of colored dots. See whether you can predict what they would look like from the normal viewing distance.

saturating the pigments by mixing them with white paint (Ratliff, 1992). Yet from this small number of pigments, Seurat was able to produce the wide range of colors seen in *Un Dimanche Après-midi à l'Ile de la Grande-Jatte* (Sunday Afternoon on the Island of the Grand Jatte). Color Plate 4 reproduces this painting, with some unavoidable loss of accuracy in the process. The painting is probably the best exemplar of the neo-impressionist movement, illustrating both the pointillist and the divisionist techniques. In the accompanying detail of the painting, you can see the small dots of pigment used in pointillism. Note that you see none of the individual dots when viewing the entire picture from an appropriate distance.

People who weave or do needlework are also aware of additive mixtures. For example, 19th-century tapestry weavers tried to predict how a given thread would look on a given background (Wasserman, 1978). Observers looking at a tapestry from a distance would see a single color rather than two distinct colors. By choosing the proper blues and yellows (e.g., by using a greenish blue and yellow), they could avoid producing a muted gray. Additive mixtures are also relevant in theatrical lighting. A technician who plans to spotlight an actor by using blue and yellow lights may end up with a dim white light.

We have been discussing mixtures of two colors. When equal parts of *three* colors are mixed together, the color can be predicted by calculating the center point of a triangle produced by connecting the three dots representing each color. When the mixture is unequal, the resulting color shifts toward the color that contributes the largest portion, as you might expect.

Additive Mixtures and Metameric Matching

Early color theorists were greatly influenced by a type of additive color mixing referred to as metameric matching. **Metamers** are pairs of lights that look exactly the same but are composed of physically different stimuli. Imagine two patches of color. The patch on the left is blue-green with medium saturation, and it comes from a single light source. The patch on the right is

created by mixing equal parts of highly saturated violet and green, as represented by the black dot in Demonstration 7.1. Our eyes could not distinguish between these two metamers, even though they are physically different.

In a ***metameric matching*** experiment, an observer is presented with a target color (consisting of a single wavelength of light) and asked to match it by mixing together lights of different wavelengths. An observer with normal color vision can make a metameric match for each color of the spectrum by mixing the correct amount of three different colored lights. Most often, the three colored lights are red (650 nm), green (530 nm), and blue (460 nm). Several resources describe how this procedure works (Mollon, 1982b; Wasserman, 1978; Wright, 1972). A person with normal color vision would not be able to make a match if given only two different colored lights to mix, and this observation led early color theorists to argue that human beings are equipped with three color receptors. In the next section you will see that they were basically correct.

SECTION SUMMARY

Color Mixing

1. The subtractive mixture method means that we mix pigments or we place colored filters together. Parts of the spectrum are subtracted or absorbed by the filters. Predicting the color of the resulting mixture is difficult because the patterns of absorption may be complex.

2. The additive mixture method means that we combine lights of different wavelengths. Imagine a red light and a green light shining on a white piece of paper. We can predict the color of the resulting mixture (yellow) by using the color wheel. Outside the laboratory, additive mixtures can be accomplished by color television and an artistic technique called pointillism.

3. The additive mixture method can produce metamers, pairs of lights that look identical but are physically different. Metameric matching experiments led to theories that

human beings perceive color as the result of three color receptors.

COLOR VISION THEORY

As you have already seen, theoretical arguments are common in many areas of perception. For example, in Chapter 6 we discussed a controversy about distance perception. A group of researchers think that the stimuli reaching the eye are sufficiently rich with distance information. Therefore, little cognitive processing is required, allowing direct perception of depth. Others think that our rich sense of depth can arise only from a great deal of cognitive processing of stimuli, which are essentially ambiguous in terms of depth information. In the early 1970s, an equally fierce argument raged between the supporters of two color vision theories, the trichromatic theory people and the opponent-process people. As Haber (1992) noted, this debate produced most of the excitement in the area of color vision research.

Happily enough, however, the argument has been satisfactorily resolved. Both theories are correct, but they apply to different levels of the visual processing system. Trichromatic theory is correct in terms of the way that input from the receptors is combined (Neitz et al., 1993). Opponent-process theory dominates at the level beyond the receptors.

In this section we will first consider how color is coded by the photoreceptors in the retina. Then we will see how this information from the receptors is interpreted by the neural system. Finally, we will see how this theory of color vision accounts for some color vision facts that were discussed in the first part of the chapter.

Trichromatic Theory and the Photoreceptors

The *trichromatic theory* of color vision assumes that humans have three kinds of color receptors, each differentially sensitive to light from a different part of the spectrum. The precise origins of this theory are not certain (Rushton, 1975;

Wasserman, 1978), but it presumably grew out of some of the research on metameric matching mentioned earlier. The founders of trichromatic theory include Sir Isaac Newton in the 1600s (whose work with prisms we mentioned earlier) and three researchers in the 1800s. These were Thomas Young, an English physician who also achieved fame by translating the Rosetta stone, Hermann von Helmholtz, whose contributions to perceptual research ensure that his name will recur throughout the text, and James Clerk Maxwell, a Scottish physicist who conducted research on electromagnetic radiation. You might see the trichromatic theory referred to as the Young–Helmholtz theory. We will first review the research on cones and then investigate the role that the cones might play in metameric matching.

The Search for Three Types of Cones

In the 1900s, researchers began to produce physiological evidence in support of three kinds of color receptors. You will recall that in Chapter 3 we discussed the two kinds of receptors in the retina. Rods work best in poorly lit environments, where they give rise to the perception of achromatic colors. Cones work best in well-lit environments, where they give rise to the full range of colors (achromatic and chromatic). Only one kind of rod exists, whereas the evidence is now clear that the retina typically contains at least three kinds of cones.

You may also remember from Chapter 3 that the rods contain rhodopsin, which breaks down into retinal and opsin when light reaches the rods. Similarly, the cones contain retinal and a specific opsin that is most sensitive to a particular wavelength (Abramov & Gordon, 1994). Details about the nature of these photopigments and their genetic coding have been identified by Nathans and his colleagues (1989, 1992).

Rushton (1958, 1975) performed a landmark experiment in which he concluded that at least two kinds of cones must be present in the retina. In this study he projected a beam of light into the eyes of human observers. Now when a light is shined on a cat's eye at night, the light reflected back is greenish; the light corresponding to other wavelengths has been absorbed. Similarly, Rushton measured absorption patterns for human eyes by comparing the composition of ingoing and returning light. He found two kinds of color receptors by this process. One kind absorbed mostly long wavelengths, and the other absorbed mostly medium wavelengths. However, Rushton did not discover the proposed third cone system.

Other researchers, such as Marks and his colleagues (1964), discovered the third cone system using a technique called microspectrophotometry. The meaning of this term is suggested by its components: *micro* (small), *spectro* (spectrum), *photo* (light), and *metry* (measurement). More precisely, **microspectrophotometry** is a procedure in which an extremely small beam of light from one limited portion of the color spectrum is passed through individual receptors in retinal tissue that has been freshly dissected. Naturally, the beam of light must be tiny to reach just one receptor. Using special equipment, the researchers can determine how much light is absorbed at each wavelength (Mollon, 1982b).

Research using microspectrophotometry has established that the three kinds of cone pigments have different but overlapping absorption curves. Figure 7.7 is an adaptation of a diagram by DeValois and DeValois (1975). Notice that two of the three curves overlap considerably. In other words, these curves do not differ much in their **spectral sensitivity**, or the region of the spectrum in which they absorb light. Finally, notice that the long and medium curves absorb some amount from nearly the entire spectrum, and the short curve absorbs from almost half the spectrum. We will refer to these three kinds of cones as S (short wavelength), M (medium wavelength), and L (long wavelength), based on the wavelengths to which they are most sensitive.

Incidentally, it seems that the cones sensitive to short wavelengths—the last cones to be discovered—differ from the other two cones because their absolute sensitivity is lower. They are also more vulnerable to disease, and they are almost completely absent in the center of the fovea (Mollon, 1982a, 1982b). DeValois and De-

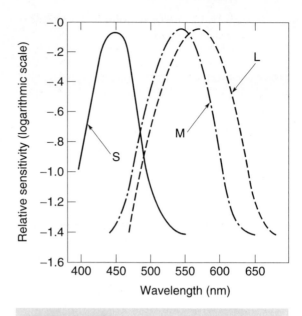

FIGURE 7.7 Absorption curves for the three cone pigments. Each curve is plotted so that its maximum sensitivity is set at –.0, and the other sensitivities are plotted relative to that maximum sensitivity, using a logarithmic scale. For example, the S-cone pigment curve has a maximum sensitivity at about 450 nm; at 400 nm its sensitivity is .1 of maximum (because its logarithmic value is –1.0). Although the three systems overlap considerably, each is maximally sensitive to a different wavelength.

Valois (1993) propose that S-, M-, and L-cones occur in a ratio of 1:5:10. Thus, the retina contains twice as many L-cones as M-cones and 10 times as many L-cones as S-cones.

Recent evidence suggests that some humans have more than three cone systems (Nathans et al., 1992; Neitz et al., 1993). Researchers have identified two different types of M-cones and two types of L-cones. These different cone systems cause a shift in sensitivity of 5–7 nm. As a result of this shift, some people will differ in their color perceptions and in their metameric matches. Even with the evidence that the retina may contain as many as five different cone systems, the input from the cones appears to be combined into three independent channels (Abramov & Gordon, 1994). Thus, we will assume three basic cone systems in investigating the role of the photoreceptors in metameric matching.

Trichromatic Theory and Metameric Matching

By working with Figure 7.7, you are now in a position to better understand the reason that metameric matching works as it does. Remember, the three primaries often given to the observer for adjustment are 650 nm (red), 530 nm (green), and 460 nm (blue). What impact would each of these lights have on the retina? By drawing a vertical line through 650 nm on the horizontal axis of Figure 7.7, you can see that 650-nm light would lead to a low amount of absorption (and firing) in the L system, very little in the M system, and virtually none in the S system. The 530-nm light would lead to a fairly large amount of absorption (and firing) in the L system, a slightly higher amount in the M system, and a small amount in the S system. What about the 460-nm light? Would you agree that it should produce a small amount of absorption in the L system, a bit more in the M system, and a large amount in the S system?

You should now have a good sense of how color information is encoded at the retinal level by means of relative absorption and firing of the three cone systems. Let's consider a metameric matching experiment in greater detail. Suppose that you present a target color of 580 nm (yellow) to an observer. This target should produce a large amount of absorption in both the L and M systems (with slightly more in the L than in the M system) and virtually none in the S system. The observer would be able to produce a fairly close match by mixing large quantities of the 530-nm and 650-nm lights, resulting in a yellow light with a slight bluish tinge. Why? If you add together the absorption patterns for the 530-nm and 650-nm lights discussed above, you will be able to make a fairly good prediction of the result: high absorption in both the L and M systems, but slightly higher for the L system (just what we

want), and a small amount of absorption in the S system (which is not present in the target, so we don't want it). To obtain a perfect match, the third primary (460 nm) must be introduced; but to add it to the existing mixture would further increase the unwanted activity in the S system. Instead, the observer would have to add a small amount of the final primary to the yellow target! It turns out that in metameric matching experiments, the observer often has to add small amounts of one of the primaries to the original target.

What happens to this information about the relative absorption patterns of photoreceptors? How is this information transmitted to the next stage in the visual processing system? Let us proceed to levels beyond the receptors.

Opponent-Process Theory and Mechanisms beyond the Photoreceptors

Trichromatic theory by itself cannot explain all the color phenomena that we will discuss throughout this chapter. Some mechanism beyond the receptor level must combine the information from the cones in a complex way. In particular, the visual system seems to use opponent processes. In its most general form, the ***opponent-process theory*** specifies that cells respond to stimulation by an increase in activity when one color is present and by a decrease in activity when another color is present. For example, the activity rate might increase for a given cell when green is present and decrease when red is present. In other words, cells show activation to some parts of the spectrum and inhibition to other parts.

Ewald Hering, a German physician, developed the earlier work on the opponent-process theme into a formal theory. His work on the subject was published between 1878 and 1920. Hering incorrectly proposed that these opponent processes occurred at the receptor level rather than higher levels in the nervous system. Thus, the *original* version of opponent-process theory was incompatible with trichromatic theory.

Hering was puzzled by certain observations about color. For example, he had noticed that it was easy to report seeing color mixtures such as bluish green or yellowish red, but other color mixtures—such as greenish red or yellowish blue—were impossible. (Try for a moment to picture either of these mixtures.)

Hering proposed six psychologically primary colors, which are assigned by pairs to three kinds of receptors. One type is a white-black receptor whose response rate increases when white light is shown and decreases when no light is shown. Another type is a red-green receptor whose response rate increases to red and decreases to green. Finally, a yellow-blue receptor's response rate increases to yellow and decreases to blue.

Hering's theory did not receive a wide following until Hurvich and Jameson (1957) wrote an article called "An Opponent-Process Theory of Color Vision." The purpose of their psychophysical studies was to determine the amount of light of one color necessary to cancel all perception of the opponent color. For example, they showed a red light and measured the amount of green light that had to be added for observers to report that the light no longer looked red. (Remember from our discussion of additive color mixing that the right amounts of carefully chosen samples of red and green will make a neutral color, one that is neither red nor green, because red and green are complementary colors.) This procedure was repeated with different shades of red and with various shades of green, yellow, and blue.

Hurvich and Jameson therefore made an important contribution to color research by developing a technique that allows us to measure opponent response functions directly (Wasserman, 1978). As we will now explore in some detail, these opponent processes typify the channels that convey color information in the visual system beyond the receptors (Gouras, 1991).

IN-DEPTH Color Coding beyond the Photoreceptors

Much of what we are about to discuss makes reference to information introduced in Chapter 3. You might find it beneficial to review the material on the visual pathways (pp. 69–73) before reading this section. Given its importance for color perception, much of the discussion in this section will deal with the parvo pathway. The topics that we are about to cover will reinforce and extend the information introduced in Chapter 3.

At this point you know that normal color perception requires input from at least three cone systems. The mere existence of three cone systems is not sufficient to yield color perception—especially in light of the criticisms voiced by advocates of an opponent-processing theory. A theory of color perception must incorporate the nature of trichromatic input and also opponent processes. Further, any adequate theory of color processing must deal with several problems (Abramov & Gordon, 1994), including:

1. A neuron in the optic nerve cannot be carrying *only* color information. Because all necessary information about color, lightness, shape, motion, and so on must pass through the optic nerve, each neuron is likely to carry a wealth of information.

2. S-cones are much less common than M- and L-cones. However, the hues to which these cones contribute are psychologically comparable to the hues resulting from the much more numerous M- and L-cones. After all, blue can be just as vivid a color as yellow or red! Thus, at some point the input from the S-cones may need to be amplified.

3. Several pieces of evidence point to the existence of separate mechanisms for red, yellow, green, and blue. How do these four mechanisms arise from only three cone systems?

4. The differential input from the three cone systems must serve as the basis for the color we perceive. On the other hand, the information from three cone systems is not, by itself, sufficient to produce color perception (Zeki, 1993). Thus, our sense of color must arise from additional processing of the input from the three cone systems. Where does such processing occur?

Luckily, sufficient information is now available to allow theorists to propose relatively complete theories of color perception. First, we will summarize (and simplify) a model proposed by Russell and Karen DeValois (1993). Although the model may be incomplete (Abramov & Gordon, 1994), it is a useful summary of what we currently know about the processing of color stimuli.

OPPONENT PROCESSES IN THE RETINA AND LGN

First of all, consider the notion of a circular receptive field, with a center and an antagonistic surround. Imagine that each cone is connected to a midget bipolar cell. Whether the input from that bipolar cell is excitatory (+) or inhibitory (–) determines the nature of the center of the receptive field. Next, imagine that horizontal and/or amacrine cells send opposing input from the surrounding cones to the bipolar cell (DeValois & DeValois, 1993; Kolb, 1991). For instance, assume that the opposing input is collected randomly from nearby cones that differ in the wavelengths to which they are sensitive. Thus, S-cones would receive opposing input from nearby M- and L-cones. M-cones would receive opposing input from nearby S- and L-cones. However, given the scarcity of S-cones, effectively M-cones would receive opposing input only from L-cones. Likewise, L-cones effectively would receive opposing input only from M-cones.

Thus, there would be six different types of opponent mechanisms (DeValois & DeValois, 1993). If the midget bipolar cell is excited by the cone input, three types of opponent mechanisms arise. For instance, one opponent mechanism occurs because of excitation of the bipolar cell by an S-cone and inhibition from the surrounding M- and L-cones (indicated symbolically as +S –ML or as S_o). Another mechanism would occur because of excitation of the bipolar cell by an M-cone and inhibition from the surrounding L-cones (+M –L or M_o). The final mechanism with an excitatory center would be +L –M (or L_o), created by excitatory input to the midget bipolar cell from an L-cone and inhibitory input from the surrounding M-cones.

If the midget bipolar cell is inhibited by the cone input, three different types of opponent mechanisms arise: –S +ML (or $-S_o$), –M +L (or $-M_o$), and –L +M (or $-L_o$). You should be able to

figure out the interconnections thought to underlie each of these opponent mechanisms.

In the early stages of visual processing, several different types of information are being encoded simultaneously. Thus, the opponent mechanisms are recording information not only about wavelength but also about lightness (Zrenner et al., 1990). In terms of lightness (or achromatic light), three mechanisms (S_o, M_o, and L_o) produce on-center, off-surround receptive fields, discussed in Chapter 3. The other three ($-S_o$, $-M_o$, and $-L_o$) produce the off-center, on-surround receptive fields. Figure 7.8 illustrates that white light falling on the middle of the receptive field of an L_o mechanism will produce the typical response we discussed in Chapter 3.

Note, however, that the receptive field has no antagonistic surround in response to the wavelength of light for which the center of the field is tuned. Thus, in the example shown, long-wavelength (red) light falling on the +L portion of the receptive field will lead to excitation. However, the red light falling on the –M portion of the receptive field will *not* produce much inhibition of the ganglion cell. Only wavelengths from the middle of the spectrum (e.g., yellow or green) would lead to a reduction of the firing rate of this cell. What would happen if the light falling on the receptive field were yellow instead of red? As you might have figured, both the +L and –M portions would be stimulated. Now, however, the inhibitory (–M) effects of the surround *would* work against the excitatory (+L) effects of the center of the receptive field. Thus, the L_o receptive field has an antagonistic surround for some lights (e.g., white or yellow), but not for others (e.g., red).

COLOR AND LIGHTNESS CODING IN THE CORTEX

In Chapter 3, we discussed the way in which input from different neurons with circular receptive fields could be added together to yield the edge- and orientation-sensitive simple cortical cells. Suppose the input from the six opponent mechanisms we have been discussing could be added together. Given the proper combinations, their summation would produce the four color perception mechanisms necessary for normal

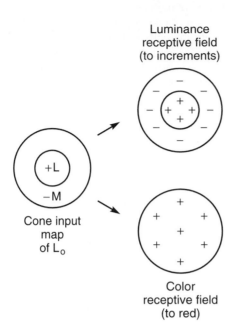

Luminance
receptive field
(to increments)

Cone input
map
of L_o

Color
receptive field
(to red)

FIGURE 7.8 An illustration of the operation of the +L–M (L_o) opponent mechanism. The midget bipolar cell that lies at the heart of the mechanism is excited by input from an L-cone. In addition to that excitatory input, the surrounding M-cones send inhibitory input to the bipolar cell, creating the cone map seen at the left of the figure.

What happens when white light falls on this opponent mechanism? The effect of such broad-spectrum light, to which both M- and L-cones are sensitive, is seen in the top right illustration. You should recognize this as the on-center, off-surround receptive field you learned about in Chapter 3. What happens when red light falls on this mechanism? The effect of such long-wavelength light, to which the L-cones are maximally sensitive, is seen in the bottom right illustration. Because the M-cones are not sensitive to long-wavelength light, there is no inhibitory input to the bipolar cell. Thus, the receptive field for this opponent mechanism differs, depending on the nature of the stimulus. Can you figure out how the L_o mechanism would respond to green (middle-wavelength) light?

color vision, as well as mechanisms for lightness perception (DeValois & DeValois, 1993).

Figure 7.9 illustrates how different summations of the six opponent mechanisms would yield neurons sensitive to red, yellow, green, and blue lights. Thus, a neuron that received input from L_o, $-M_o$, and S_o opponent units would be excited by red light (but would not convey lightness information). A neuron that received input from L_o, M_o, and S_o opponent units would be excited by lightness (but would not convey color information).

One controversial aspect of this model is that the S-cones are not given primacy in producing the yellow-blue opponent channel. As you can see in Figure 7.9, the S-cones contribute to all four color channels. One implication of this model is that our perception of blue might not be totally dependent on the S-cones, as is often proposed. In fact, this aspect of the model was developed because of the scarcity of S-cones and because of evidence that perception of blue depends more on stimulation of M-cones than on S-cones (DeValois & DeValois, 1993). Thus, our perception of vivid blues is not dependent solely on the scarce S-cones but instead on input from the more abundant M-cones modulated by input from S-cones. DeValois and DeValois assume that the function of the S-cones is to modulate the input from the other cone systems. Thus, their theory avoids the need to "amplify" the S-cone signal in the cortex to produce the perception of rich blue hues (see point 2 from Abramov and Gordon's list earlier in this section).

Note also that, according to the DeValoises' theory, these cones yield information about achromatic light, as well as producing the four color channels. Thus, the parvo pathway is important for both chromatic and achromatic information. The magno pathway provides information about lightness and darkness, but it is not the only source of achromatic information.

As we mentioned in Chapter 3, the color pathway goes from the LGN through V1 and V2 before reaching V4—which seems to be vital for color processing. As a final stage of their model, DeValois and DeValois (1993) propose that chromatic input from the simple cortical cells is further combined to produce the color selectivity found in complex cortical cells. Such color-

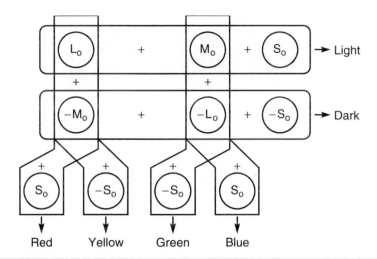

FIGURE 7.9 This figure is a graphic representation of the color perception theory of DeValois and DeValois (1993). Input from the six opponent mechanisms is combined to create cells sensitive to red, yellow, green, blue, light, and dark. When the L_o, M_o, and S_o mechanisms are all stimulated, we perceive the stimulus as very light (white). Therefore, a cell receiving input from all three mechanisms would signal the presence of a light stimulus. Further, combining input from the $-L_o$, $-M_o$, and $-S_o$ mechanisms creates a cell sensitive to a dark stimulus. The figure illustrates that cells signaling the presence of a blue stimulus are created by combining input from the M_o, $-L_o$, and S_o mechanisms. This is a controversial aspect of the theory, because it proposes that our perception of blue is not solely dependent on input from the S-cones but actually involves input from all cones—particularly the M-cones. Note, also, that the S-cones play a role in the perception of all four colors that are crucial to the opponent-process theory. Thus, cells that signal the presence of a green stimulus are identical to those signaling blue, except that they receive input from $-S_o$ instead of S_o mechanisms.

selective cells are thought to be characteristic of those found in the areas beyond V1. Interestingly, the complex cortical cells may not exhibit the opponent processes typical of cells earlier in the pathway.

You should now understand that the theory proposed by DeValois and DeValois addresses many of the problems posed at the beginning of this section. First, the theory shows how both chromatic and achromatic information could be conveyed through identical mechanisms. Second, the theory certainly illustrates how four color mechanisms could arise from three cone systems. Most important, the theory proposes a mechanism whereby short-wavelength colors

can be perceived to be as vivid as other colors even though S-cones are scarce. Time will tell if this theory gains acceptance, but earlier theories proposed by DeValois and DeValois have already been very influential. ◆

Achromatopsia and the Color Center

Achromatopsia is the loss of color vision due to damage to the central nervous system (Abramov & Gordon, 1994). Although other deficits might accompany the damage, the loss of the ability to see colors defines the disorder (Sacks & Wasserman, 1987). Many achromatopsic people have

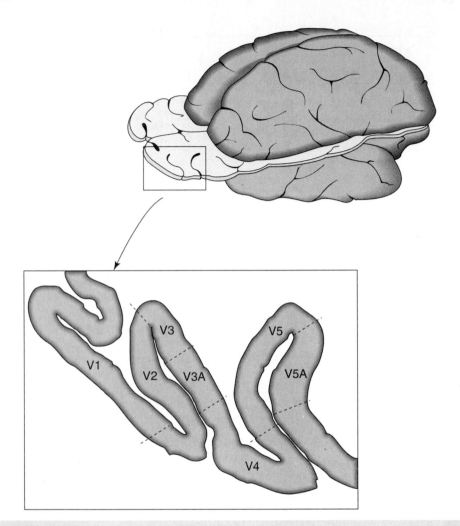

FIGURE 7.10 An enlargement of a section of the cortex. The upper part of the illustration shows the brain, with a horizontal section removed (and slid backward). The area from the occipital lobe that has been enlarged is indicated with a circle. In the enlargement, note the location of V4—the site of the color center.

unaffected form vision, so they see shapes clearly, but everything appears as shades of gray (Zeki, 1993). Surprisingly, people with achromatopsia have fully functional cone systems (Zrenner et al., 1990), which provides further evidence that color perception requires processing of the input from the cones. Where does such processing occur? The damage causing the disorder appears to be localized to area V4 of the brain, which is found in the lingual and fusiform gyri in humans (see Figure 7.10). On the basis of such evidence, Zeki (1992, 1993) argues that at least part of V4 serves as the center for color perception in humans.

In spite of a tradition of localizing functions in particular parts of the brain, for many years researchers were reluctant to consider V4 the center for color perception (Zeki, 1993). A great deal of evidence supports the hypothesis that V4 is the color center. However, even today not all researchers agree (Abramov & Gordon, 1994; Schiller, 1994). Clearly, much remains to be learned in this fascinating area.

Achromatopsia is a severe and relatively uncommon disorder, leading to a complete loss of color vision. We'll now turn our attention to more common—and less severe—instances of disorders to color perception. Note that these disorders often have important implications for theories of normal vision. Achromatopsia may be useful in identifying the center for color perception. The visual deficiencies we are about to discuss inform us about the roles of the cone systems in color perception—especially the importance of opponent processes.

SECTION SUMMARY

Color Vision Theory

1. Until the early 1970s, researchers who supported a trichromatic theory—with three kinds of color receptors—disagreed with those who supported the opponent-process theory, in which cells respond in opposite fashions to the members of a pair of colors. Now researchers generally accept that trichromatic theory describes the way information from the receptors is processed and opponent-process theory applies at levels beyond the receptors.

2. Trichromatic theory was developed in the mid-1800s, and about 100 years later researchers presented physiological evidence to support the theory. This research included absorption patterns for various wavelengths and microspectrophotometry at the level of the individual receptors.

3. Opponent-process theory was originally developed by Hering at the end of the 1800s. According to current theory, opponent processes operate at levels beyond the receptors. Green and red work in opposition, as do blue and yellow and black and white.

4. DeValois and DeValois propose a four-stage model of color perception. They assume that

the S-, M-, and L-cones occur in a 1:5:10 ratio. Lateral inhibitory connections yield six different opponent mechanisms in ganglion cells. Various combinations of these opponent mechanisms yield channels for red, yellow, green, blue, black, and white.

5. A good deal of evidence points to part of V4 as the center for color perception in the brain. Much of this evidence comes from people with achromatopsia, an inability to see colors because of damage to V4.

COLOR VISION DEFICIENCIES

Some people cannot tell the difference between two colors that differ in hue. We often refer to those people as being "color-blind," but that term is much too strong. As you will see, only a few people are totally unable to discriminate colors. We will use the term "color vision deficiencies" instead. People with *color vision deficiencies* have difficulty discriminating different colors.

About 8% of males have some form of red-green color vision deficiency, in contrast to about .4% of females (Birch, 1993). In other words, if you have 250 males and 250 females in a room, approximately 20 males and 1 female will have some trouble discriminating colors. You should think of color deficiencies as more characteristic of males than of females.

We need to discuss color vision deficiencies for two reasons. First, the problem is fairly common. You may be color deficient yourself, and you probably have friends who are color deficient. Second, color deficiencies have important implications for color theories, a topic discussed in the preceding section. In this section we consider the kinds of color deficiencies and their diagnosis.

Kinds of Color Deficiencies

Some kinds of color vision are listed in Table 7.2. If you have normal color vision, you are a normal trichromat. A *normal trichromat* requires three colors, such as red, blue, and green, to match all the other colors. The word trichro-

TABLE 7.2
Kinds of Color Vision, Normal and Deficient

Classification	Cone System Affected	Description
Normal Trichromat	None	Normal color vision
Anomalous Trichromat		
Protanomalous	L-cones	Insensitive to red-green
Deuteranomalous	M-cones	Insensitive to red-green
Tritanomalous	S-cones	Insensitive to blue-yellow
Dichromat		
Protanope	L-cones	Insensitive to red-green
Deuteranope	M-cones	Insensitive to red-green
Tritanope	S-cones	Insensitive to blue-yellow
Monochromat	All	No color vision

mat consists of two parts: *tri*, which means "three," and *chroma*, which means "color."

Researchers can often learn a great deal about the functioning of perceptual systems by studying people with abnormal abilities. Early color theorists were influenced not only by evidence from metameric matching experiments but also by information about abnormal color vision. A very early and influential report came from John Dalton (1798/1948), who studied his own color deficiency using ribbons, flowers, and other objects as stimuli. Dalton found that his brother saw colors in a similar fashion, as did several male members of other families. Such observations led theorists to suggest that color deficiencies were consistent with an abnormality in one of the three cone systems, and that such abnormalities were genetically linked. Subsequent research has confirmed both hypotheses (Nathans, 1989).

A person with the most common form of color deficiency is an **anomalous trichromat**. An anomalous trichromat has all three cone systems, but one of the systems has an abnormal absorption spectrum. As Table 7.2 shows, the cone system that is abnormal determines the three different types of anomalous trichromats (Birch, 1993). Depending on the nature of the abnormality, an anomalous trichromat might experience mild impairment or a more severe impairment in color

perception. About 6% of males are anomalous trichromats, most of whom have an abnormality in the M-cones.

In contrast, a **dichromat** (*di* means "two") is a person who has only two of the three cone systems. As a result, a dichromat requires only two primary colors to match all the colors he or she can see. If you look at Figure 7.7 and imagine that one of the three curves is missing, you will see why the dichromat needs only two colors to match any target color. The dichromat can see colors, but the range is narrow (Paramei et al., 1991). Obviously, this is a more severe color deficiency than that experienced by an anomalous trichromat. Luckily, dichromats are relatively rare (2% of males).

Loss of one of the three cone systems produces each of the three types of dichromats. Protanopes and deuteranopes are the most common dichromats, with each occurring in about 1% of males. Their perception of the world is similar, and both are referred to as being "red-green color blind" because they are likely to confuse red and green. **Protanopes** have no L-cones, and **deuteranopes** have no M-cones. These dichromats have the typical number of cones in their retinas, but protanopes possess only M- and S-cones and deuteranopes possess only L- and S-cones (Carlson, 1991). Recent DNA analyses of samples of Dalton's eyes, which he left for scientific study, reveal that Dalton was a deuteranope (Hunt et al., 1995).

You probably know several protanopes and deuteranopes. The third kind of dichromat is rare. Only about 0.005% (or 1 person in 20,000) of the population are tritanopes (Pokorny & Smith, 1986). *Tritanopes,* who have difficulty seeing blues and yellows, seem to lack the S-cones.

How can we tell what the world looks like to a dichromat? Some evidence comes from a study by Graham and Hsia (1958). They located a woman who, amazingly enough, had normal vision in her right eye but was a deuteranope in her left eye. These researchers presented different hues to each eye and asked the woman to match colors. For example, they showed a red to her color-deficient eye and asked her to adjust the color presented to the normal eye until it seemed to be the same hue. They found that her color-deficient eye saw all the colors between green and violet as blue and all the colors between green and red as yellow.

Some apparent deficiencies in dichromats may be due to the way in which dichromats are tested. As mentioned earlier, the size of color stimuli is crucial. The typical stimuli presented to the dichromat are small enough to fit within the fovea. When larger stimuli are used, however, protanopes and deuteranopes can see red. Even though we think of rods as producing achromatic vision, the evidence suggests that protanopes and deuteranopes are using their rods to see red (Boynton, 1988; Coletta & Adams, 1986; Montag & Boynton, 1987; Pokorny & Smith, 1982)! As surprising as this result might seem, some years ago Edwin Land and his colleagues reported some clever demonstrations showing that people with normal vision could use their rods (and the L-cone system) to see a range of colors (Land, 1977; McCann & Benton, 1969).

We should stress that, aside from their color perception deficiencies, dichromats have normal visual acuity. The retinas of protanopes and deuteranopes have the typical number of cones. In the case of tritanopes, the normal retina has so few of these S-cones that their acuity is not affected. Thus, these dichromats function normally on most visual tasks. In fact, although color is extremely useful for detection and discrimination, color vision is not a crucial ability. Many animals (especially nocturnal ones) do not see the world with the full range of colors perceived by a trichromat. Further, the fact that color deficiencies went virtually unnoticed for many centuries suggests that "color blind" humans were able to function almost flawlessly in their societies. In fact, most dichromats can learn to use a number of color terms accurately—perhaps based on perceived lightness differences—even though they do not see the colors as a normal trichromat would (Jameson & Hurvich, 1978).

On some occasions, however, dichromats face a real disadvantage. For example, isn't it unfortunate that traffic lights are red and green? Until traffic light configurations became relatively standard (vertical lights, red on top), a protanope or deuteranope driving toward an intersection was playing a dangerous guessing game. Now they just have to stop when the top light is lit. The city of Baltimore, taking no chances, adds a vertical stripe through the green light and a horizontal stripe through the red light (Wichman, 1991).

Dichromats also have handicaps in certain professions. For instance, as a medical student taking a course in microbiology, Arnie Matlin was assigned a proctor whose function was to look in the microscope and tell him the color of specified objects. Obviously, dichromat medical students should be discouraged from pursuing specialties such as dermatology, because making precise discriminations about the colors of rashes and other skin problems is an essential ability. Similarly, people with color deficiencies should avoid careers in which colors convey important information, such as airline pilots, train drivers, and electronic engineers (Birch, 1993).

The information on color deficiencies fits the color vision theory discussed earlier. Consistent with the findings at the receptor level, color deficiencies arise from the loss of function in particular cone systems. Consistent with the findings beyond the receptor level, people who cannot see red also have difficulty with green,

---

Demonstration 7.4

Color Deficiency   Turn to Color Plate 5, inside the back cover, and look at it under lighting a little less bright than you would use for normal reading. What number do you see? If you see the number easily, you might make a photocopy of the page and then try to see the number. That will give you a feeling for the difficulties facing a monochromat.

---

and people who cannot see blue also have trouble with yellow.

We have discussed trichromats, who make matches based on three colors, and dichromats, who make matches based on two colors. We now turn to the monochromats. A **monochromat** (*mono* means "one") requires only one color to match perception of all other colors. Every hue looks similar to this person. Fortunately, this disorder is relatively rare, with an incidence of only about one in 33,000. The world of a monochromat is similar to the world of a trichromat when illumination is dim—everything is a different shade of gray (Angier, 1992; Hurvich, 1981). These people are truly color-blind.

Diagnosing Color Deficiencies

Many different ways of diagnosing color deficiency have been developed. One of the most common is the **Ishihara test,** in which the observer tries to detect a number hidden in a pattern of different colored circles (Birch, 1993). Demonstration 7.4 discusses one example from the Ishihara test. A person with normal color vision will see this number as 8. However, a person who has trouble distinguishing reds and greens may read the number as 3. The Ishihara test is often updated, including a version for people who cannot read, with symbols instead of numbers (Birch & McKeever, 1993).

Another common device—an anomaloscope—is based on the principle of metameric matching, discussed earlier. An anomaloscope is used to determine the extent of red-green color deficiency. The person being tested attempts to match the yellow half of a circle by mixing the amount of red and green in the other half of the circle (Birch, 1993). Interestingly, for over 40 years, data from a commonly used anomaloscope convinced researchers that color vision varied seasonally. However, recently Jordan and Mollon (1993) determined that the machine itself varied in its sensitivity, due to heat differences!

SECTION SUMMARY

Color Vision Deficiencies

1. Normal trichromats have normal color vision. They require three colors to match any target color.
2. Anomalous trichromats have an unusual absorption spectrum in one of their three cone systems. As a result, their color matches differ from those of normal trichromats.
3. A dichromat requires only two primary colors to match all other colors because they are missing one of the three cone systems. Protanopes (missing L) and deuteranopes (missing M) cannot see reds and greens. Tritanopes (missing S) cannot see blues and yellows. These color deficiencies are consistent with color vision theories.
4. Dichromats have normal visual acuity and can even make some color discriminations on the basis of lightness differences. Their deficiency can be detected with an anomaloscope or with tests such as the Ishihara test.
5. A monochromat requires only one primary color to match all other colors. These people are truly color-blind.

COLOR PHENOMENA

So far, we have been discussing sensory factors in color perception—how color stimuli are processed from the retina to the cortex. Some of the phenomena we are about to discuss might be explainable in purely sensory (physiological) terms. However, consistent with Theme 4 (see page 12), much of perception involves prior knowledge and expectations. Throughout the book we examine situations in which reality and perception differ. In general, our perceptions are accurate, so occasional discrepancies are particularly intriguing and potentially edifying. In previous chapters we discussed several illusions and also the notion of constancies. In this section we talk about color phenomena. An observer often reports seeing color when the stimulus is truly neutral in hue. Furthermore, an observer may report seeing a color different from that typically reported for the wavelength of light being presented to the subject. These color phenomena make it clear that color is partly determined by factors other than wavelength, the intensity of light, and purity.

Simultaneous Color Contrast

Try Demonstration 7.5, which shows simultaneous color contrast. *Simultaneous* means "at the same time," so **simultaneous color contrast** means that the appearance of the color can be changed because another color is present at the same time. Notice in Demonstration 7.5 that the neutral color gray appears to be slightly yellow when a blue background is present. However, it appears to be slightly blue when a yellow background is present. Thus, "the color seen in a region of space is determined not only by the characteristics of the stimuli in that region, but also by those simultaneously present in surrounding regions" (DeValois & DeValois, 1975, p. 156). This is a principle operating in several works of the artist Josef Albers (1888–1976), an American painter who was born in Germany.

How can we predict which hue a neutral color will adopt? Recall our discussion of complementary hues from the first part of this chapter. Complementary hues are opposite each other on the color wheel—blue and yellow, for example. As it turns out, the neutral color tends to adopt a hue that is the complement of the surrounding hue. Thus, gray will look slightly blue when its background is yellow.

DeValois and DeValois (1975) suggested some time ago that color contrast must be produced at the level of the cortex. However, part of simultaneous color contrast seems to occur prior to the cortex. Boynton (1983) discovered that simultaneous color contrast is stronger when the stimuli are presented to the same eye than to different eyes. Thus, some of the activity probably occurs directly in the retina.

We may not know the precise explanation for simultaneous color contrast. However, the phenomenon itself has been well known for some time. It was first reported by Michel Chevreul in the 1800s. Chevreul was in charge of dyes at the world-famous Gobelins tapestry works in France, and he became interested in special color effects when people began to complain that certain blacks in tapestries lacked

---

Demonstration 7.5

Simultaneous Color Contrast

Turn to Color Plate 6, inside the back cover. Does the gray circle appear to be the same color on both sides of the plate? Against the blue background, the gray circle takes on a yellowish tinge. Against the yellow background, the gray circle takes on a bluish tinge. You can convince yourself that the gray is uniform throughout the circle by covering over the yellow and blue patches.

Demonstration 7.6

Successive Color Contrast

Turn to Color Plate 7, inside the back cover of your text, and place it under a bright light. Stare at the black dot in the center of the plate for 2 to 3 minutes. It will get boring, but don't stop too soon. After the time has passed, quickly transfer your focus to the white area below the color plate. The complement of each color should now appear, and the afterimage will look somewhat like a mirror-image version of the original.

---

depth and strength. Chevreul observed, in fact, that perception is greatly influenced by the surrounding colors (Birren, 1976).

Successive Color Contrast

Demonstration 7.6 illustrates successive color contrast. *Successive color contrast* means that the appearance of a color can be changed because of another color presented beforehand. For example, in Demonstration 7.6 part of the white paper seems to be somewhat yellow because you looked at a blue figure earlier. Thus, staring at a figure of a particular hue produces the complementary hue once that hue is removed.

Successive color contrast is one kind of negative afterimage. The term *negative afterimage* makes sense because the *image* appears *after* the original image. Further, the color of the afterimage is found on the color wheel opposite (*negative* to) the original image. A similar kind of negative afterimage, called an *achromatic afterimage,* involves black-and-white stimuli. For instance, Emmert's law, discussed in Chapter 6, can be studied using a black afterimage of a white circle. In special cases these afterimages may persist for hours and even days (Stromeyer, 1978). In both cases the afterimage is less intense than the original image, it drifts and moves in the same direction the eyes move, and it can be seen in the absence of any illumination.

Successive color contrast can be traced to chromatic adaptation. *Chromatic adaptation* means that the response to a color is diminished after it is viewed continuously for a long time. Adaptation is a general phenomenon found in all

our sensory systems, providing just one example of Theme 1 of this book, that the sensory systems share similarities. In the case of chromatic adaptation, either (or both) of two kinds of mechanisms may be involved. Continuous exposure to a particular color may deplete the photopigments associated with that color, leaving the other photopigment levels relatively high. Or the phenomenon may involve adaptation at the opponent-process level. For example, staring at blue may weaken the blue response, leaving its opponent, yellow, relatively strong. As a consequence, an observer who has been staring at a blue patch will see a yellow afterimage.

Given your knowledge about negative afterimages, what color would you make surgical gowns? White is a pure, clean color, but surgical gowns are not white. Why not? What negative afterimage would a surgeon experience when glancing up after staring into a brightly lit bloody cavity? Green surgical gowns minimize the impact of the afterimage experienced by the surgeon (Wichman, 1991).

Color Constancy

In simultaneous and successive color contrast, a person perceives a particular color in spite of the fact that the wavelengths associated with that color are not falling on the retina. This is also true of color constancy. In *color constancy* we tend to see the hue of an object as staying the same despite changes in the wavelength of the light illuminating the object. Thus, as William James (1890) observed:

The grass out of the window now looks to me of the same green in the sun as in the shade, and yet a painter would have to paint one part of it dark brown, another part bright yellow to give its real sensational effect. (p. 231)

In spite of great differences in illumination of a surface, we tend to use the same color name to describe our experience (Maloney & Wandell, 1986). In Chapter 4 we discussed lightness constancy. You should recognize the common component of the two constancies—the perception of the distal stimulus remains roughly constant in spite of substantial changes in the proximal stimulus.

Accuracy of Color Constancy

Absolute color constancy would be obtained if an object appeared to be the same color regardless of the type of illumination or the colors of nearby objects (Maloney, 1993). For instance, Edwin H. Land (1977) created a demonstration using three stimuli made up of patches of colors. All of the color patches in each stimulus were illuminated by a very different light source. Regardless of the illumination, observers saw the color patches in the three stimuli similarly. In fact, the illuminations were constructed such that the actual wavelengths reflected by the red patch in one stimulus, the blue patch in the second stimulus, and the green patch in the third stimulus were identical. If our sense of color emerged strictly from the physical information we received, an observer should call all three of these patches the same color. However, in spite of the fact that each patch was sending *identical* wavelength information to the observer's eyes, the observer correctly identified each of the three patches. Impressively, they showed strong color constancy. Our perception of color, then, is not dependent on the absolute wavelengths reaching our retinas—but on reflectance relationships among objects in our field of vision (Brou et al., 1986).

On the other hand, color constancy is probably not maintained completely, especially when tested in the laboratory with precise measurements (Brainard et al., 1993; Worthey, 1985). So our color perceptions *are* influenced to a degree by the nature of the illumination. Because of this, makeup mirrors are available with special lighting that duplicates natural sunlight, fluorescent light, and dimly lit rooms. Presumably, an eye shadow that is attractive by candlelight might look quite different in a fluorescent-lit office.

Although color constancy is not exact, color constancy seldom breaks down to the extent that an observer would assign two different color names to the same object just because of changes in illumination (Jameson & Hurvich, 1989). For instance, a blue carpet might look "perfect" under a store's fluorescent illumination. When the carpet is installed in your home, where the illumination is either natural sunlight or incandescent lights, it might look terrible—but you'd still call it blue! To avoid such problems, the best strategy is to view paint or carpet samples at home before making a purchase.

Explanations for Color Constancy

How are we able to maintain color constancy? Helmholtz proposed that after experiencing the same object under a wide range of illuminations, we make an unconscious inference about how the object would appear under white light. Hering thought that the color remained constant because of memory—color and other properties of the object had become permanently fixed. Our current theories are much more complex, but they are more accurate in predicting the evidence that has accumulated over the years.

One early, and still influential, theory was proposed by von Kries. In 1905 he suggested that the illumination causes adaptive changes in our photoreceptors (chromatic adaptation), which then influence our perception of the incoming reflected light (Boynton, 1990). This theory has intuitive appeal, because the illumination falling on the objects also falls on our eyes, affecting them in proportion to the wavelengths present in the light source. The illumination would provide our visual system with a "referent" against which to interpret the incoming reflected light. However, von Kries's theory cannot account for all of the data. In fact, some researchers question the extent to which adaptation to illumination has an impact on color constancy (Brill & West, 1986). For example, Edwin Land proposed the retinex (retina-and-cortex) theory to explain the combined roles of the photoreceptors and higher-level processes in color perception. ***Retinex theory*** seeks to explain color perception and color constancy based primarily on perception of the pattern of reflectances from the stimuli (Land, 1977). Essentially, the visual system determines the lightest part of the stimulus and then seeks to determine if that part could be "white."

In a clever experiment, Uchikawa and his colleagues (1989) illustrated the importance of adaptation to the source of illumination. They simply constructed an observation booth in which the observer sat in a booth separate from the stimuli to be judged and looked through a hole into the room containing the color stimuli (see Figure 7.11). By doing so, the color stimuli could be illuminated by a hidden light source different from the light source falling on the ob-

server. For instance, the observer could become adapted to a red light while the color stimuli were presented under a white light, or the lighting conditions could be reversed. For other phases of the study, both the observer and the color stimuli could be under identical white or red lights. The rooms were designed in such a way that the observer could not tell the type of illumination in the room where the stimuli were presented. Instead, an illuminated square of a particular color appeared to float in space as the person looked through the hole.

Their data showed marked effects when the lighting conditions for the observers and the stimuli they were judging were different. For instance, the observers were much more likely to call a stimulus red, orange, or pink when they themselves were in a room with white light and the stimuli were in a red-lit room. When the observers were bathed in red light, and the stimuli were in a white-lit room, the observers were much more likely to call the colored stimulus green or blue. For color constancy to hold completely, however, no differences should have been found between judgments made when both rooms were red-lit and when both rooms were white-lit. This was not the case, adding further evidence to the notion that adaptation to the illumination is not sufficient for color constancy, although it appears to be necessary.

The computational approaches to vision that have been applied to form perception have also been applied to color perception and color constancy (D'Zmura et al., 1995; Iverson & D'Zmura, 1995; Maloney, 1993; Wandell, 1987). The retinex theory of Land (1983, 1986) represents an early computational approach to color vision. However, retinex theory doesn't accurately predict color constancy because it places too much emphasis on input from distant objects in the scene (Pokorny et al., 1991). Other computational approaches use the von Kries notion of adaptation as a stage in their computational models (Brainard & Wandell, 1992; Dannemiller, 1989, 1991). A later stage is hypothesized to involve the sort of opponent channels we mentioned in our discussion of theories of color

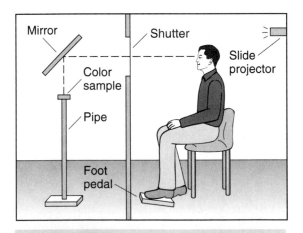

FIGURE 7.11   Schematic view of the experimental arrangement in Uchikawa et al. (1989). This arrangement allowed the researchers to vary the light in the room with the observer independently of the light in the room with the color sample being judged.

Demonstration 7.7

Benham's Top (Subjective Colors)

Make a good photocopy of the design below. Cut it out and glue it to a piece of cardboard. Punch a hole in the center at the + spot, and place it on the end of a pencil or ballpoint pen. Hold the pencil with one hand and spin the edge of the circle with the other. When the speed is just right—neither too fast nor too slow—you should see pastel colors. If the top is turning clockwise, the bands should look somewhat blue (outside band), green, yellow, and red (inside band). If the top is turning counterclockwise, the bands should seem to be in the reverse order: red, yellow, green, and blue.

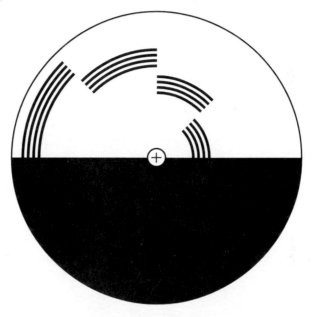

processing beyond the retina. The profusion of computational models indicates the extent of interest in the area of color constancy, as well as the inadequacy of any of the proposed models.

Subjective Colors

So far, the color phenomena we have discussed have all involved colored stimuli. In contrast, *subjective colors* are color impressions produced by black-and-white stimuli. Try Demonstration 7.7 to see how uncolored figures can produce subjective colors. This pattern is often known as Benham's top, in honor of its 19th-century in-

ventor, C. E. Benham. When this disc rotates at a rate of about 10 revolutions/second, desaturated colors appear along the curved lines (Wyszecki, 1986).

How can we be sure that the colors are really produced within our visual systems? Could it be that the whirling somehow causes white light to break down into its components, much as a prism separates the colors of the spectrum? The question can be answered by taking a color photograph of a spinning Benham's top. If the color can really be traced to different wavelengths in the stimulus, then the color film should register the same color as our visual system. However, the

FIGURE 7.12 Example of op art, illustrating subjective colors. In some lights the middle wavy regions appear yellow. (*Current* by Bridget Riley)

photograph of the spinning top looks gray, rather than colored (Fineman, 1981). The answer lies within the observer, not within the stimulus.

Researchers have discovered that the color pathways vary in their speed of response. For instance, the M-cone pathway apparently processes stimuli faster than the L-cone pathway (Hamer & Tyler, 1992). Such temporal differences might be the basis for the subjective colors observed in Benham's top (Courtney & Buchsbaum, 1991).

Another example of subjective colors occurs in ***op art***, an artistic movement that developed in

---

Demonstration 7.8

Purkinje Shift   Under brightly lit conditions, select an example of a red object and a blue object that look equally bright to you. Now go into a darkened room and wait about 10 minutes until you are mostly dark adapted. Now compare the two objects to see which is lighter.

---

the United States and Europe in the 1960s. Op art tried to produce a strictly optical art, so it emphasized perceptual experiences. Many op art pictures have thin black lines in geometric designs on a white background, and they tend to vibrate and produce visions of pastel (Birren, 1976). Figure 7.12 shows an example. In some lights you will see that the wavy regions in the middle appear yellow.

Purkinje Shift

The color phenomena discussed so far have all concerned the hue dimension of color. The Purkinje shift concerns lightness of various hues. Try Demonstration 7.8 to illustrate the Purkinje shift.

Johann Purkinje, a Czechoslovakian physiologist, was the first to describe this phenomenon in 1825, so it is appropriately named after him. According to the *Purkinje shift,* our sensitivity to various wavelengths *shifts* toward the shorter wavelengths as we change from photopic (cone) to scotopic (rod) conditions. *Mesopic* conditions exist when the light is sufficiently bright that cones are still functional, but sufficiently dim that rods can also function. The prefix *meso-* means "in the middle," and *mesopic* is in the middle between photopic and scotopic conditions.

Figure 7.13 will help you clarify the Purkinje shift. When you tried Demonstration 7.8, you initially selected a blue and a red that were approximately equal in lightness in photopic conditions. In other words, your visual system was about equally sensitive to both samples. Notice that the dotted lines in Figure 7.13 corresponding to the red and blue wavelengths intersect the photopic-condition curve at about the same sensitivity. Now

contrast the sensitivity as you approach scotopic conditions. As you can see, the sensitivity of rods is substantially higher for wavelengths in the blue range compared to the red range. Under mesopic conditions, the shorter wavelengths appear to be lighter because both the rods and cones are active for those wavelengths (Brigner, 1991). The longer

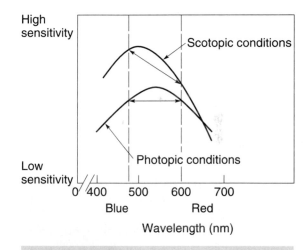

FIGURE 7.13   Purkinje shift. Under photopic conditions (cones only), blue and red are equally light. Under scotopic conditions (rods only), blue is perceived as lighter than red. However, because only rods are involved, both blue and red would appear as grays. Mesopic conditions occur between these two curves. (Imagine the lower curve lifting up to form the upper curve.) Under mesopic conditions, both the cones and the rods are functional. Thus, under mesopic conditions, the combined input of cones and rods would cause a blue flower to appear lighter than a red flower.

wavelengths are producing activity only among the cones.

Color Stereopsis

Color stereopsis refers to the effect of perceived depth differences due to viewing color stimuli binocularly through some lenses (such as magnifying glasses). With color stereopsis, long-wavelength stimuli are normally perceived as nearer than short-wavelength stimuli (Dengler & Nitschke, 1993). Although some people can perceive colors at different depths without looking through lenses, the chromatic aberration of the lens serves to enhance the effect. Shorter wavelengths are refracted more than longer wavelengths, causing the shorter wavelengths to be displaced toward the nose. The normal color stereopsis effects can be reversed if the background is white (Dengler & Nitschke, 1993).

You can easily experience color stereopsis by purchasing Crayola's Jumping Colors. Using the (UC3D) lenses enclosed in each box of markers, you will see powerful depth differences among the colors.

Memory Color

The color phenomena we have been discussing can all be traced to some mechanism in the visual system, although the specific details of those mechanisms may not be clear. In contrast, another color phenomenon can be traced to our expectations and cognitive processes. This phenomenon is called memory color. In *memory color,* an object's usual color influences our perception of that object's actual color.

In a typical experiment, Delk and Fillenbaum (1965) cut shapes out of one piece of orangish red cardboard. Two of the figures, an apple and a valentine heart, are typically orangish red, whereas two other figures, a bell and a mushroom, are typically not that color. Observers were asked to adjust a background field until it contained the same amount of red as each of the figures. The observers tended to se-

lect a redder background when they were trying to match the apple and the heart than when matching the bell and the mushroom. Our knowledge and expectation can often shape our perceptions. Consistent with Theme 4 of this book (see page 12), top-down processing may influence what we perceive.

Categorization of Colors

Human beings have amazing abilities when it comes to color discrimination. That is, when presented with two color patches side by side, observers can correctly report "same" or "different" for up to roughly 1 million colors (Boynton et al., 1989). When colors are presented not simultaneously but sequentially, the observer must have some means of storing the color in memory. To do so might well require that the observer categorize the color by attaching a name to it. Although wavelength (the physical stimulus giving rise to hue) is continuous, color names are discrete and categorical.

Central Colors versus Borderline Colors

First, let's consider the concept of *categorization:* When we categorize, we treat objects as similar or equivalent (Bornstein, 1984a). For example, when you categorize food into meats, vegetables, desserts, and so forth, you are treating all the items within one category as similar, despite their variations in appearance. Thus, green beans, okra, potatoes, and eggplant are all classified as vegetables, despite their obvious differences. Similarly, we can discriminate the differences in wavelength between many different colors in the short-wavelength end of the spectrum, yet all these colors are classified as blue.

However, some items are better examples of the category than others. Thus, you might know that okra is a vegetable, but you are unlikely to say "okra" as the first example that comes to mind when you want to describe the category *vegetable.* Similarly, although we might give the same name to stimuli along a range of wavelengths, some of the wavelengths are more typical of the name. In particular, the colors that fall near the center of color categories are somehow special, in comparison to colors that fall near the boundaries between color categories.

When people were asked to categorize the wavelengths between 485 nm and 500 nm as either blue or green, Bornstein and Monroe (1980) found that observers quickly and reliably called wavelengths below 487 nm "blue" and wavelengths above 497 nm "green." When presented with a borderline color (e.g., 491 nm), people took much longer to name the color. Some colors seem to be simply "better" than others, and they are identified more quickly.

Other research has established that babies prefer to look at colors in the center of categories rather than at borderline colors (Bornstein, 1975). Furthermore, both Americans and people from an isolated tribe in New Guinea perform better on memory tasks involving central colors than borderline colors (Heider & Oliver, 1972; Rosch, 1978). As Bornstein (1985b) concludes, not all stimuli in a category hold the same psychological status.

Can you guess why researchers might be interested in color perception in infants and people from other cultures? In part, researchers want to examine the perceptual experiences of people with no words for colors (infants) and people with radically different words for colors. Do color names influence the way we perceive colors? Do people tend to see colors similarly, in spite of a lack of color names or very different color names? The answers to such questions tell us the extent to which our perceptions are influenced by language or are independent of language.

Recent Cross-Cultural Research

Research on cultural differences in color naming is ongoing, with two major surveys recently completed (Abramov & Gordon, 1994). Earlier research suggested that, over a wide range of cultures, 11 basic color categories are found: blue, green, yellow, orange, red, pink, brown, purple, black, white, and gray (Berlin & Kay, 1969). Notice that among these colors are achromatic colors (white, black, and gray), nonspectral colors (pink, brown, and purple), and spectral colors (blue, green, yellow, orange, and red).

Other cultures do not have distinct names for these 11 colors. However, they tend to have particular subsets, suggesting a universal evolutionary trend in the development of color names. For instance, names for white and black emerge first. Next to emerge are names for colors we might call reds, then greens, yellows, and blues. These four categories may develop because people in all cultures share the same underlying mechanisms for color perception. Thus, the four spectral colors that first emerge are those that are basic to the opponent processes found in the human visual system. In fact, it may be that our visual system (and our languages) represent color in a nonarbitrary fashion determined by the need to maintain constancy (Shepard, 1993).

Languages that have only a small number of color terms use those terms to label all of the color space. Thus, a Chacobo-speaker from Alto Ivon, Bolivia, would use only the four color terms *joxo, cheque, shini,* and *niaba* to label all 330 of the color chips presented by the ethnographer. Wavelengths that you and I might label as blue, yellow, green, and purple could all be called *niaba. Cheque* would be used to label black, dark grays, and brown. What we would label as white or very light yellow, a Chacobo-speaker would call *joxo. Shini* would be used to label wavelengths we would call red, orange, or pink.

Data from languages such as Chacobo are causing consternation among some anthropologists (MacLaury, 1992). On the basis of opponent-process theory, these anthropologists argue that a perceiver should use different terms for yellow, green, and blue. They would contend that the common underlying physiology leads to a common evolution of terms across cultures. Thus, color names that appear to be at odds with opponent-process theory are problematic. However, recent research has uncovered several languages (such as Chacobo) with a single term for yellow-green-blue.

An opposing camp of anthropologists, who consider themselves relativists, are delighted by the new data (MacLaury, 1992). The relativists would argue that color names are more arbitrary and not driven by the underlying physiology. It's still too early to tell how this issue will be re-solved. However, the initial basis for the evolution of color categories may be lightness, not hue. In other words, the universalists might be right, but for the wrong reason.

SECTION SUMMARY

Color Phenomena

1. In simultaneous color contrast, the appearance of a color is changed because of another color present at the same time. For example, a gray looks slightly blue against a yellow background. The double-opponent-process cells may be at least partly responsible for simultaneous color contrast phenomena.

2. In successive color contrast, the appearance of a color is changed because of another color presented earlier. For example, white looks slightly blue if you previously looked at yellow. The explanation may involve depletion of photopigments and/or adaptation at the opponent-process level.

3. An object appears to be the same color under a wide range of illuminations. This phenomenon—color constancy—is an example of the set of constancies that produce stability in our perception of the world.

4. Subjective colors are pastel colors resulting from black-and-white stimuli, such as Benham's top and op art pictures.

5. Color stereopsis occurs when colors are looked at through some lenses. The colors will appear to be at different depths, depending on their wavelengths and the color of the background.

6. In memory color, our expectations about an object's typical color influence our perception of that object's actual color.

7. In the Purkinje shift, the sensitivity of the visual system shifts toward the shorter wavelengths under mesopic conditions.

8. In categorization, we treat objects as similar or equivalent. For example, certain colors are all classified as blue, even though they are discriminable.

9. Colors at the centers of their categories (blue, green, yellow, and red) are named faster, are preferred by infants, and are remembered better. In contrast, colors at the boundaries between color categories do not have this special prominence.

10. Because the names for colors appear to have evolved in a consistent fashion, some anthropologists argue that common underlying mechanisms for color perception are responsible. Other anthropologists argue that the development of color names is more arbitrary.

REVIEW QUESTIONS

1. The next time you are in a supermarket, notice the hue, saturation, and lightness of packages and commercially produced items, such as the colors of laundry detergent packages, wrapping papers, baby cards for boys, and baby cards for girls. Do these items tend to occupy different portions of the color solid? How do they differ from naturally occurring products (vegetables, fruits, etc.)?

2. Each of the following is an example of a color mixture; specify whether it represents a subtractive or an additive mixture: (a) you wind strands of purple and blue yarn together to knit a sweater; (b) you paint a layer of light green paint over a wall painted dark blue; (c) you mix red food coloring into yellow egg yolks; (d) you cover one flashlight with green cellophane and another with red cellophane and then shine them both on a white sheet of paper. Predict the color of the mixtures in as many of the combinations as possible.

3. What are complementary hues? What happens when you make an additive mixture of complementary hues? Why does this make sense, now that you know about opponent-process theory?

4. Summarize the trichromatic theory, as developed by Young and Helmholtz, and the original form of the opponent-process theory, as developed by Hering. Why were the two incompatible, and what modifications in the opponent-process theory made them compatible?

5. Try to explain the model proposed by DeValois and DeValois. Trace the route through which color information is processed—beginning in the retina and ending in V4. At each step (cones, bipolar cells, ganglion cells, LGN, V1, V2, V4) indicate the way the cells respond to chromatic and achromatic stimuli.

6. How does a normal trichromat differ from the three types of dichromats in color perception and in acuity? What everyday color discriminations would each type of dichromat find difficult?

7. Suppose that someone who didn't know much about color vision asked the following questions about phenomena he or she had noticed. What explanations would you provide? (a) Why does a blue bird look gray when it's far away? (b) Why does a white shirt look a little green when worn with a red vest? (c) Why does the world look slightly yellow after you take off blue-tinted dark glasses? (d) Why does a red stop sign look uncolored if you look at it out of the side of your eye? (e) Why do some features on a map appear to be at different depths when viewed through a magnifying glass?

8. Try to think of some evolutionary advantages that color vision afforded our early ancestors. For example, what advantages might come to a predator who could see colors? To be sure that you understand color constancy, first describe what it is and summarize theories about how it might function. Then think of some adaptive advantages that might have been gained by ancestors with color constancy.

9. What is memory color? Describe the research studies discussed in the chapter, and point out why they provide support for the top-down view of perceptual processing. Finally, think about examples in which your expectations about an object's typical color influenced your perceptions of that color.

10. What evidence might you provide to indicate that we process colors from the center of a category differently from the colors at category boundaries? How is this research related to the idea of opponent processes? What do cross-cultural studies tell us about the interaction of language and color perception? Regarding color terms, would you consider yourself a universalist or a relativist? Why?

NEW TERMS

brightness (214)
hue (214)
color wheel (215)
nonspectral hues (216)
monochromatic colors (216)
lightness (216)
color solid (216)
color spindle (216)
achromatic colors (216)

purity (216)
saturation (217)
subtractive mixture (218)
additive mixture (218)
synthetic sense (218)
analytic sense (218)
complementary hues (220)
pointillism (223)
divisionism (223)

metamers (224)
metameric matching (224)
trichromatic theory (225)
microspectrophotometry (226)
spectral sensitivity (226)
opponent-process theory (227)
achromatopsia (231)
color vision deficiencies (233)
normal trichromat (233)

anomalous trichromat (234)
dichromat (234)
protanopes (234)
deuteranopes (234)
tritanopes (235)
monochromat (236)
Ishihara test (236)

simultaneous color contrast (237)
successive color contrast (238)
negative afterimage (238)
achromatic afterimage (238)
chromatic adaptation (238)
color constancy (238)
retinex theory (240)

subjective colors (241)
op art (242)
Purkinje shift (243)
mesopic (243)
color stereopsis (244)
memory color (244)
categorization (244)

RECOMMENDED READINGS

Abramov, I., & Gordon, J. (1994). Color appearance: On seeing red—or yellow, or green, or blue. *Annual Review of Psychology*, *45*, 451–485. If you are interested in a brief review of the state of color perception theory, this article will give you an overview. The authors summarize many of the topics addressed in this chapter, including the model proposed by DeValois and DeValois, the role of achromatopsia, and color categorization.

Jameson, D., & Hurvich, L. M. (1989). Essay concerning color constancy. *Annual Review of Psychology*, *40*, 1–22. Given the complexity of the topic, this essay is quite readable, and it provides insights into some of the more recent theorizing about color constancy.

Ratliff, F. (1992). *Paul Signac and color in Neo-Impressionism*. New York: Rockefeller University Press. You are in for a real treat if you read this richly illustrated book. It is written by an expert in color perception about an apparent love—art. Ratliff does an excellent job of introducing the reader to color perception theory and then showing how it can explain the artist's use of colors. Even if you have only a passing interest in color perception, art, or neo-impressionism, we encourage you to read this book.

Zeki, S. (1993). *A vision of the brain*. Oxford: Blackwell. As we mentioned in Chapter 3, this book is extraordinarily readable and interesting. Zeki argues for the modularity of function within the brain, with color perception centered in Area V4. Not all researchers agree with Zeki, but his book provides an excellent summary of his thinking.

8 Motion

As you are sitting here reading your book, probably little is moving except your eyes. After all, you likely chose a place to study with minimal activity. However, think of the constant activity you find in other situations. In the classroom, the professor may walk around the room, people wiggle, and your pen moves across the notebook. In social situations, speaking people approach us, move their mouths and bodies, and depart. On the road, we are in motion as we gauge the movement of vehicles around us, pulling over when we see and hear a fire truck or ambulance approaching us. Most entertainment involves motion—television, movies, sports, games, dancing, and so on.

As we discussed in Chapter 6, the visual system uses an array of monocular and binocular cues to determine the spatial location of an object. However, objects never remain in the same relative spatial location—either they move or you move. In this chapter we address the processes by which we perceive the motion of objects through the space around us.

We will focus our attention on the visual perception of movement. As you will soon see, researchers distinguish between real and apparent movement. However, the physiological processing of motion perception may be identical for real movement and some forms of apparent movement. We will discuss the physiological bases of visual motion perception, and then we will discuss various theories of visual motion perception.

VISUAL PERCEPTION OF REAL MOVEMENT

We have often used the term *retinal image* in discussing vision. However, many psychologists believe that *flow is a better term* (e.g., Johansson et al., 1980; Lee, 1980). They believe that the kind of static perception implied by the term *retinal image* is artificial. Some psychologists argue that motion is so prominent that our mental representations are dynamic—including those created by static stimuli (Freyd, 1993). Thus, even static

handwritten text may be viewed as the tracks of a dynamic process.

As we saw in Chapter 4, motion on the retina is crucial for vision (Humphreys, 1989). If an image is stabilized on our retina, it will fade away. Moreover, motion is sufficient to give rise to a number of perceptual properties discussed in earlier chapters, such as depth and shape (Proffitt, 1991).

Given the importance of motion for perception, we are fortunate that our eyes are constantly changing their position in space when we walk, drive, ride, and change posture. Probably the only time our heads could remain in a fixed position for any length of time is when they are artificially restrained (Gibson, 1950). Outside of psychology laboratories and torture chambers, most of us don't spend much time wearing head vises—and even then our eyes are in motion!

Because motion is so common, the perception of motion is a fundamental aspect of vision. As Sekuler (1975) notes, "During evolution, motion perception was probably shaped by selective pressures that were stronger and more direct than those shaping other aspects of vision" (p. 387). Even in your relatively civilized life, you have probably found that responding quickly to a moving object is more important than recognizing precisely what has moved. For example, if an object is rapidly approaching your head, you detect the motion and you duck (King et al., 1992). You don't stop to contemplate whether the object is a brick, a book, or a box—you just duck! Even one-week-old infants move their heads to avoid an approaching object. Sekuler suggests that our visual systems contain nerve mechanisms specialized for analyzing motion because of selective evolutionary pressure to detect motion.

Motion perception is so basic that it can be found in organisms that lack other visual skills. For example, babies can follow a moving object with their eyes as soon as they are born (Morton & Johnson, 1991). A more amazing phenomenon—called blindsight—also illustrates the extent to which motion perception is basic. **Blindsight** occurs when a person has some visual experience in spite of damage to the visual cortex (Weiskrantz, 1986). People with damage to their visual cortex are unable to see objects presented in the area of the visual field represented in the damaged area. Thus, they are partially blind. However, if an object is moving in the "blind" portion of their visual field, these people can point to the object in motion (Weiskrantz, 1986, 1992; Zeki, 1993). They typically cannot identify the object, and they feel that they are only guessing about its location. However, they are actually quite capable of tracking the motion of the object. Blindsight may be traceable to parts of the visual pathway through the thalamus (Cowey & Stoerig, 1995; Kaas, 1995). A small number of the LGN cells do not continue to the primary visual cortex, so they might be responsible for blindsight (Zeki, 1993). Another possible explanation for blindsight is that small portions of the visual cortex may remain intact (Gazzaniga et al., 1994). So we are able to detect motion—even with limited neural processing!

Motion perception is not only basic but also surprisingly accurate. When we walk, we typically do not bump into objects or fall into holes. We can accurately determine the openings through which we can and cannot fit (Warren & Whang, 1987). We can judge the trajectory of a rapidly moving ball with sufficient accuracy to hit it (Bootsma & Van Wieringen, 1990; Regan, 1992). When runners or swimmers compete, they usually do not collide. Cutting (1986) estimates that to walk without bumping into stationary objects, we need to be able to judge our direction of locomotion within 5° to 10° of visual angle. (Demonstration 5.1 can refresh your memory regarding visual angle.) Because of the speed at which they are moving, runners and automobile drivers require even greater judgmental accuracy, often within 1°.

If you were asked to design a human visual system, how would you account for motion perception? One answer you might suggest is that we notice motion whenever the image of an object moves around on the retina. This answer is appealing, but it is incorrect. After all, the images of the words on this page are sliding all over your retina as you read, yet the page does not seem to wiggle. In this case, images move, yet we do not perceive motion. Furthermore, as your eyes follow the flight of a bird in smooth pursuit movement, the image of the bird remains on approximately the same part of your retina. In this case, an image does not move on the retina, yet we perceive motion. We must conclude that motion perception involves more than just the movement of images on the retina.

This part of the chapter is concerned with real movement, which involves either movement of the observer or movement of the objects and people being watched by the observer. We first need to discuss the limits of human skill in judging movement, that is, the thresholds for motion perception. Next, we will examine a type of motion that we seem to be particularly adept at perceiving—biological motion. Finally, we will discuss the challenges for motion perception posed by the fact that we are constantly moving.

Threshold for Motion Perception

How good is the human eye in detecting motion? You cannot watch grass grow, or hour hands on clocks move, or bread rise. These movements are all too slow; the eye is impressive, but it isn't *that* good!

The ***velocity detection threshold*** is the minimum velocity that can be detected. We typically measure the velocity in minutes of arc per second, or the number of minutes of angular velocity that an object moves in 1 second of time. Researchers have used an array of methods for measuring velocity thresholds of a wide variety of targets (Bonnet, 1982). Furthermore, observers have different thresholds when they are asked merely to detect motion rather than to report its direction (Bonnet, 1982; Sekuler et al., 1982a). In general, however, humans' velocity detection thresholds range between 10 and 20 minutes of angular velocity per second (Hochberg, 1971). Figure 8.1a shows a concrete example of this threshold.

Several factors influence velocity detection thresholds. For example, detecting motion is more difficult if your eyes are moving in the same

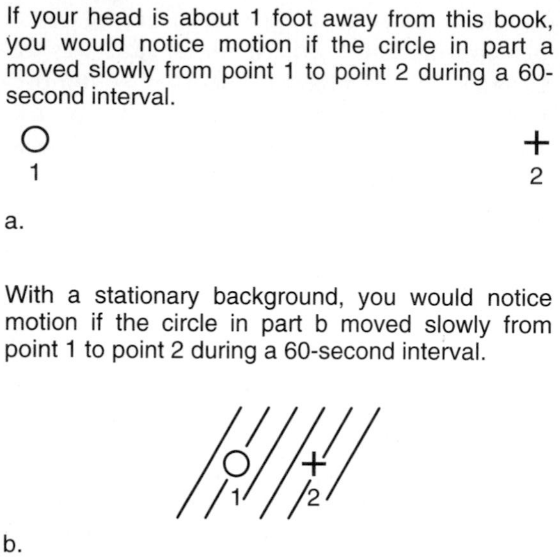

If your head is about 1 foot away from this book, you would notice motion if the circle in part a moved slowly from point 1 to point 2 during a 60-second interval.

O   +

1   2

a.

With a stationary background, you would notice motion if the circle in part b moved slowly from point 1 to point 2 during a 60-second interval.

b.

FIGURE 8.1 Illustration of velocity detection thresholds. Notice that the detection of motion is enhanced by the presence of the background lines.

direction as the object in motion (Wertheim, 1994). Furthermore, velocity detection thresholds are lower if the object moves in front of a stationary background. When some parts of the visual field stay still, the velocity detection threshold for a moving object decreases to about 1 to 2 minutes of angular velocity per second. In other words, a background allows us to detect motion that is 10 times slower than can be detected with no background. Figure 8.1b illustrates this velocity detection threshold.

Furthermore, detecting motion in the center of the visual field is easier when there is no movement at the periphery (Mundt, 1988). People are less able to detect motion of the target stimulus when other objects move to the left and right or above and below the target. People are also much better at detecting motion that occurs in an expected direction (Sekuler, 1995).

Another variable that influences velocity detection thresholds is the region of the retina on which the movement is registered. You'll recall that acuity is much better at the fovea than at the periphery of the retina; this relationship was illustrated in Figure 4.10. You can tell the difference between the letter O and the letter C much better if the letter is registered on your fovea than on the edge of the retina. Usually, we are also more sensitive to motion in the fovea than in the periphery (e.g., Bonnet, 1982; Finlay, 1982).

The fact that the fovea is typically more sensitive to motion than the periphery should not suggest to you that the periphery is *in*sensitive to motion. For example, if an object in the periphery is moving, we can see it more easily than if it is stationary (e.g., Finlay, 1982). Try Demonstration 8.1 to illustrate this point. Notice how often you tend to pay attention to objects that move in your peripheral vision. For example, when you are driving, you can see a car approaching on the left or a pedestrian moving on your right. You also use your peripheral vision for moving objects in social situations and in sports. In summary, then, velocity detection thresholds are not spectacular in the periphery, but people are much better at detecting moving objects than stationary objects in that region.

Demonstration 8.1

Motion Detection in the Periphery of the Retina

Stare at a point straight ahead. Hold the forefinger of your right hand directly in front of your eyes. Move it slowly toward your right, keeping the height at eye level, until you can no longer see it. Keep it stationary and make sure that you cannot see it at this location. Then wiggle your finger rapidly. You probably *will* see it when it is moving.

Perception of Biological Motion

In this section, we will discuss *biological motion,* or the pattern of movement of living things. We will show you that observers can use subtle motion cues to determine what organisms are being depicted, what they are doing, and even subtle differences among members of the same species. These judgments are based on minimal information and very brief exposures, so our performance is particularly impressive.

DETERMINING BIOLOGICAL MOTION IN POINT–LIGHT DISPLAYS

The first research on biological motion perception was conducted by Gunnar Johansson (1973,

1975), who attached small light bulbs to the main joints of a male co-worker. Thus, the man wore lights on his shoulders, elbows, wrists, hips, knees, and ankles. The movie Johansson made of this man as he moved around in a darkened room may be referred to as a *point–light display.* Keep in mind that in a point–light display, the viewer can see nothing but the lights moving around in darkness. Several variants of this procedure have been developed over the years (e.g., Berry et al., 1991), but all the displays provide the observer with extremely limited information about the motion of the actor.

We cannot provide an adequate sense of a point–light display in the static figures of this book. However, you might get some impression of these displays by working through Demonstration 8.2.

Demonstration 8.2

"Frozen" Point–Light Displays

These pictures were created by photographing the light tracks made by a person in a point–light display over time. The person was performing several different activities. Can you figure out what the person was doing? Suppose that you knew that the displays showed a person walking, hopping, curling a medium weight, and throwing an object a far distance? Could you now determine the activity represented in each static display? (From Rosenblue et al., 1993) [See page 274 for answers to these questions.]

a.

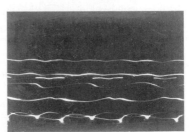

b.

c.

d.

Observers are unable to make any sense of a point–light display when the lights are motionless. (This situation differs from that illustrated in Demonstration 8.2, in which the static display is created by showing a single exposure of the movement of the lights over time.) However, once the lights begin to move, the observer's task is much easier. Johansson (1975) reports that as soon as the person stood up and started to move, observers instantly perceived that the lights were attached to a human being, who was invisible except for the lights. The observers could easily tell the difference between walking and jogging movements. Furthermore, they could recognize subtle peculiarities in the person's movement. For example, when he limped, they could detect it. Remember that observers can detect all this information from very few cues—just 12 tiny lights!

In another study, Johansson (1975) placed 12 lights on each of two dancers and filmed them performing a lively folk dance. Observers who watched the film immediately recognized that the 24 swirling dots represented a dancing couple! We do not need extra cues such as the contours of body parts or the continuous lines of the body to recognize complex movement. Mere spots, representing the body's joints, are sufficient.

People are quite good at assessing the amount of effort expended by a person in a point–light display, even the "frozen" point–light displays seen in Demonstration 8.2 (Rosenblum et al., 1993). In a dynamic point–light display, effort is easily detected. For example, Johansson (1985) used a point–light display of 10 lights attached to a man doing push-ups. With just 10 lights in the display, viewers can clearly detect the elegant, forceful lifting of the body in the beginning of the sequence. As the push-ups continue, viewers note that the push-ups become increasingly shaky, slow, and irregular.

Observers can even determine the distance people are trying to throw a sandbag based on a dynamic point–light display. Runeson and Frykholm (1983) created a point–light display of people throwing a sandbag to targets varying from 1.75 to 8.0 m (5.7 to 26.2 feet) away. We should emphasize that the display did not record the sandbag or its motion through the air. Observers watched the display and tried to guess how far the people had been trying to throw the sandbag.

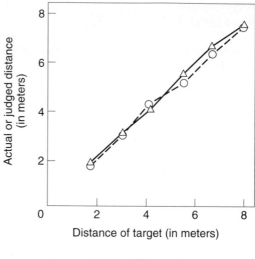

— Actual distance thrown

○ – – – ○ Observers' judgments about distance intended

FIGURE 8.2 Figure showing the accuracy with which people can judge the distance a sand-filled bag was being thrown based only on illuminated-joint information. Results are averaged for male and female throwers. Observers were able to estimate the distance the bag was thrown with great accuracy, even though the bag itself was not visible to the observers. (Based on Runeson & Frykholm, 1983)

Figure 8.2 shows the results of this study. As you can see, observers are extraordinarily accurate in their judgments. The observers' guesses almost precisely match the actual distance that the people in the display threw the sandbag. People are equally good at estimating the weight of bowling balls caught by actors in a point–light display—even when the bowling ball was not visible to the people estimating the weight (Henderson et al., 1993). This research demonstrates that observers can process a rich variety of subtle information from the motion of a small number of points of light (Bingham, 1993b).

From the evidence presented so far, you should be impressed by people's ability to extract a large amount of meaning from the minimal information present in point–light displays. Because of these abilities, we are better able to detect pedestrians at night when they wear reflectors similar to those worn in point–light displays (Owens et al., 1994).

Not only can people detect the biological motion of other humans, but we can also perceive the biological motion of nonhuman animals. In fact, people are very accurate in determining the type of animal (baboon, camel, cat, horse, pig, etc.) moving in a dynamic point–light display (Mather & West, 1993).

Do you think that animals are able to detect biological motion? As Johansson (1985) and Ullman (1983) note, biological motion is ecologically important for the survival of other species, not just for humans. Animals need to recognize the motion of other animals to know which animal is a potential mate, which a potential *dinner,* and which a potential *diner.* Therefore, animals should be quite good at deciphering point–light displays of biological motion. For example, cats can reliably discriminate a dynamic point–light display of a cat walking from a dynamic display that doesn't depict biological motion (Blake, 1993).

DETERMINING GENDER IN POINT–LIGHT DISPLAYS

Okay, so we can detect a range of biological motions from point–light displays. What about more subtle distinctions? For instance, do you think that you could determine a person's gender simply by observing a point–light display of this person walking? Barclay and her colleagues (1978) tested this question with dynamic point–light displays of men and women walking. To insure that no other factors were operating, they selected females and males of about the same height and weight. The movies of the walkers were then shown to a group of viewers. Viewers, who saw each person for only 4.4 seconds, were able to determine whether the walker was male or female!

Barclay and her colleagues also demonstrated that viewers identified gender accurately even when the display was so out of focus that all the lights blurred together. Blurring the lights produced an image that was similar to the one used by Dianne Berry and her colleagues (Berry et al.,

1991), who also found that people were able to make accurate gender judgments.

We can also determine people's gender by dynamic point–light displays of their faces alone (Berry, 1991). In fact, from simple point–light displays of people's faces, we can determine many characteristics, such as emotion, identity, and age-related qualities (Berry, 1990; Berry & Misovich, 1994; Bruce & Valentine, 1988).

THE DIFFICULTY OF MASKING BIOLOGICAL MOTION

So far, we've seen that people are able to discriminate a wide range of actions and even people's gender from point–light displays. The studies we've described have used a limited number of lights, but in most cases the display showed lights attached to a single organism. In reality, of course, biological motion takes place in a motion-filled context—some of which might be biological motion from other organisms (as in the point–light display of people dancing). How well can people discriminate biological motion in a point–light display if other motion is present in the display? Such a question motivated a series of studies by James Cutting, of Cornell University.

Cutting, Johansson, and other researchers have demonstrated that people are extremely good at extracting extensive amounts of information from small numbers of lights strategically placed on people. What would happen if additional irrelevant lights were placed on the display to mask the biological motion?

Cutting and his colleagues (1988) found that it is difficult to mask biological motion. They presented a computer-generated "walker" composed of 11 lights, such as the middle frame of Figure 8.3a. (The outline shown in the figure was not visible on the display screen.) The walker could be shown for a single frame (i.e., no movement for 0.07 second duration), or from 3 (0.2 second) to 12 (0.8 second) frames of motion. Figure 8.3b shows an example of a sequence of frames. Distractor lights, such as those shown in the first and third frames of Figure 8.3a, were superimposed on the walker. The distractor lights could be stationary or could move, independently of the walker, from frame to frame. Detecting the presence of the walker among the masks was too simple a task, so

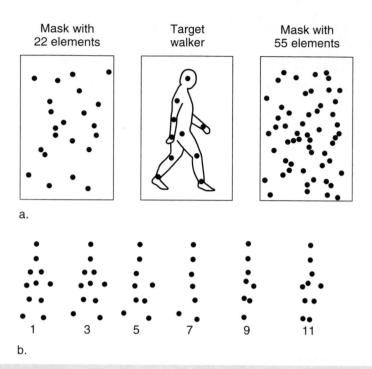

Mask with 22 elements   Target walker   Mask with 55 elements

a.

1   3   5   7   9   11

b.

FIGURE 8.3 Illustration of the stimuli used in Cutting et al.'s (1988) experiment. People were asked to determine whether the dots composing the target walker (a) were moving to the right or to the left when imbedded in masks of irrelevant dots. The outline of the walker, seen in the middle panel of part a, was not actually presented to the observers. Part b illustrates movement of dots that would be consistent with a person moving to the right.

people were also asked to determine whether the walker was facing left or right.

Several interesting results emerged from this study. First, masks were generally more effective in disrupting accuracy when the displays were shorter. Second, viewers were less accurate with 55 elements in the mask than with 22 elements. Finally, the most effective masks were those that resembled the motion of some of the lights in the walker. For instance, in one condition, triads of lights—such as those found on the arms or legs—were placed in motion around the display screen. When 55 masking elements were present on the screen, this scrambled-walker mask was effective for even longer durations.

Thus, when the mask behaves in a uniform fashion (all dots stationary or else all dots moving in the same direction), people can easily deter-

mine the direction of biological motion. When the mask is composed of several different groupings of elements (triads of lights) that can each be seen as an independent unit of movement, people make errors in analyzing biological motion (Cutting et al., 1988).

Bertenthal and Pinto (1994) showed that increasing the number of masking dots to 66 did not affect people's ability to detect biological motion. Like Cutting and his colleagues, Bertenthal and Pinto found that using randomly moving triads of masking dots hindered an observer's ability to detect biological motion. However, the observer still performed at an above-chance level—even in this very confusing display! What *did* affect a person's ability to detect biological motion was to turn the display upside down. Just as inverted faces are more difficult to perceive, people also have a much more difficult time detecting biological motion in upside-down point–light displays (Bertenthal & Pinto, 1994; Dittrich, 1993).

WHAT DOES BIOLOGICAL MOTION TELL US ABOUT PERCEPTION?

The research we have reviewed is quite telling. Humans and other animals seem capable of making extremely fine discriminations about biological motion based on minimal information. Although we are able to determine the nature of some types of motions better than others (Dittrich, 1993), the range of actions that we can discriminate on the basis of point–light displays is truly amazing. Further, we can perceive biological motion even in the context of a fair amount of visual noise.

The studies we have reviewed testify to humans' accuracy in judging biological motion. Johansson (1975, 1985) has suggested that visual systems from the earliest stages of evolution are neurally organized to decode optic flow patterns in an efficient and accurate manner. But are humans born with the ability to appreciate biological motion? Is our visual system prewired to pick up subtle information about the way living organisms move? Although perception of biological motion may not be prewired, the appreciation of biological motion seems to develop during the first year of life. At some time between 6 and 9 months, babies can look at a display of moving lights and interpret the pattern as the motion of a person (Bertenthal, 1993; Bertenthal et al., 1985, 1987).

Johansson (1985) points out the irony that in spite of the mathematical complexity of biological motion, our visual system can process the motion with great ease. In contrast, motion that can be described with mathematically simple equations seems to be more difficult for our visual system. Clearly, our ability to perceive biological motion is especially impressive. ◆

Movement of the Observer

So far, we have discussed the movement of objects and the impressive ability of the human visual system to detect this movement. However, people are rarely stationary, so the perception of motion in the environment is even more complicated. To appreciate the complexity, think of a volleyball player who is in motion at the same time as she is using pursuit eye movements to follow the path of the moving ball. Not only must she move her body, head, and eyes to keep the rapidly moving ball focused, but she must also keep track of the positions of the net and her nearby teammates, who are also in motion!

Several questions emerge when you consider a person moving and looking out at the world. Why does the world seem to be stationary when we move, even though our movement is producing change on the retina? What information allows people to detect their direction of movement through the environment? Can we always tell when we are stationary, or can we become confused about our own motion? Are we better at detecting motion when we are not moving? In this section, we try to answer these questions.

Perceiving a Stable World Despite Motion

First, let's consider the fact that the world remains stable in spite of your movement through the world. When we move our heads, the retinal changes could just as easily have been produced by movement in the environment (Wallach, 1987). Nonetheless, we reliably see the world as stable and attribute the retinal changes to our own movements.

How do we do so? Wallach (1985b, 1987) suggests that several compensation processes evaluate the visual input in comparison with information about body movements. Much information about body movements comes from the vestibular and kinesthetic senses, which we will discuss in Chapter 12. Consistent with Theme 4 of the text, such compensation appears to be the result of higher-level processes that result from experience. As Wallach points out, the environment *does* appear to move when we turn our heads while wearing lenses that invert the incoming visual information. With inverting lenses, the environment appears to move in the same direction as head movements, instead of in the opposite direction. After a couple of days of adaptation to the lenses, however, the environment again becomes stable when the head moves. Keep these observations in mind when we discuss the corollary discharge theory later in this chapter.

Perceiving the Direction of Observer Motion

Think of the complex pattern of movement on your retinas as you drive along a crowded highway. If you are looking at the car directly ahead of you, it remains fairly stable on your retina. Stationary objects—such as signs or bridges—or slowly moving cars in your periphery seem to be a blur as you go past them. Researchers refer to this complex pattern of motion on our retinas as an *optic flow field.* Direct perception theorists argue that the optic flow field is essential for determining many aspects of self-motion, including the direction of movement.

Observer motion, combined with the motion of objects in the field of view, creates complex patterns of optical flow on our retinas (Andersen, 1986). Even though these optic flow patterns are complex, the human visual system can usually determine what is moving—the observer, the object, or both. In fact, even though our eyes are moving as we are in motion, the optic flow patterns provide us with sufficient information to determine our direction of movement accurately (Warren et al., 1988).

Warren and Hannon (1988, 1990) found that people were quite good at determining the direction of movement from optic flow patterns—even when the patterns were complicated—by fixating on a point different from the direction of movement. Their results are consistent with J. J. Gibson's notion that the optic flow field is sufficient to give rise to an accurate sense of self-motion. Other theorists had suggested that observers make use of additional sources of information in determining their self-motion, but Warren and Hannon's results are consistent with the more parsimonious explanation that optical flow is sufficient.

The Self-Motion Illusion

We said that humans can usually determine from optic flow patterns whether they are moving or whether other objects are moving. However, this kind of distinction is sometimes difficult, and we can make mistakes. Perhaps this has happened to you. You may have stopped your car at a traffic light and then sensed that you were moving. You step on the brake firmly, yet you still appear to be moving. Then you look around and discover that other cars are moving, and your car is in fact stationary. You may have had a similar experience looking out an airplane's window, especially if you were expecting your plane to depart. The perception that you are moving when you are really stationary—and other objects are moving—is sometimes called the *self-motion illusion* or visually induced self-motion. The illusion was initially described by pioneering researchers with whom you are already quite familiar—Mach (of the Mach bands and book) and Helmholtz (Andersen, 1986).

In general, the self-motion illusion is more likely when other objects move in your peripheral vision than in your foveal vision (Dichgans & Brandt, 1978). This description may match your own experience with this illusion. When you are stopped at an intersection, your foveal vision may be directed toward the stoplight. The optic flow pattern that convinces you that you are moving comes from the periphery of your retina.

Perception of the Speed of Movement

Some interesting research on observers' movements has examined people's perceptions of their movement speeds (e.g., when they are driving) as well as their judgments about the speeds of other moving objects. For example, a study contrasted motion perception for people driving on highways (and therefore moving) with motion perception for people in a laboratory (Probst et al., 1984). The people in the laboratory were not really moving. However, they had some of the visual information that had been available to the highway drivers. When people ride in a vehicle, their thresholds for perceiving the motion of other vehicles are substantially raised, as are their reaction times to detect motion. These effects are due to perceived self-motion rather than to the motion in the environment per se (Probst et al., 1987).

Fully 50% of automobile accidents involving rear-end collisions occur when the difference in velocity between the two vehicles is less than 12 miles per hour. Thus, when people themselves are in motion, they may not be as sensitive to subtleties in the motion of other vehicles. Drivers should therefore pay particular attention to brake lights. To help drivers do so, manufacturers are now required to mount the additional single brake light seen on the rear of most cars. This innovation illustrates an important real-life application of perceptual research.

If judging the motion of other vehicles when you are in a moving car is difficult, imagine how difficult judging the speed of vehicles in outer space must be! Astronauts who perform visually guided docking maneuvers in space (called proximity operations) must judge distance and speed under very difficult conditions. Obviously, many of the monocular cues are absent in space. Furthermore, lighting conditions vary widely, and the background is continually changing (Haines, 1989). Under these conditions, a crucial cue to speed is the rate of looming, or expansion, of the approaching space vehicle. Haines (1989) found that minimizing the competing visual detail in the astronaut's field of view is important. Even with ideal viewing conditions, however, velocity judgments are poor until the space vehicle is relatively near the observing astronaut.

So far, we have been discussing the perception of real movement. However, in their investigations, many researchers have used movement simulations. Haines (1989) used a computer simulation to study perceived velocity of space vehicles, and Warren and Hannon (1988, 1990) used computer-generated dot displays to study optical flow. Furthermore, Cutting and his colleagues (1988) used computer-generated dots to study biological motion. In other words, many researchers choose to simulate motion to give themselves greater control over the stimulus.

We will now discuss several types of illusory or apparent movement. You should already have the sense that the distinction between real and apparent movement is fuzzy at best (Anstis, 1986).

SECTION SUMMARY

Visual Perception of Real Movement

1. In the real world, static perception is rare. Motion perception is an important aspect of vision; it is both basic and accurate.
2. Velocity detection thresholds are influenced by several factors, including uncertainty about the direction of movement, the presence of a stationary background, and the region of the retina on which the movement occurs.
3. Organisms have evolved to be especially adept at perceiving biological motion. Simply on the basis of the movement of lights attached to a stimulus person's main joints, an observer can identify that person's actions and gender, as well as other information.
4. Not only are we quite accurate in our perception of biological motion, but we are also quite adept at perceiving biological motion in the midst of noise. However, when biological motion is inverted, we cannot determine the nature of the movements.
5. Although we are typically in motion, creating movement on our retinas, we perceive the world as stable. When we are in motion, it is more difficult to judge motion around us.
6. As we move, the optic flow field provides us with a great deal of information about movement, including the direction in which we are moving.
7. Judging the speed of a moving object becomes much more difficult when the observer is also in motion.

ILLUSORY MOVEMENT

We began our discussion of motion perception by focusing on the perception of real movement in the world around us. Now we will discuss apparent or illusory movement, just as we have discussed illusory experiences in earlier chapters. In *illusory movement*, observers misperceive an object's motion. Some illusions lead us to misperceive the trajectories of objects that are in motion. For instance, baseball players speak of rising fastballs. However, such motion is physically impossible because the ball cannot really rise as it approaches the batter. Instead, the illusion appears to be caused by a misperception of the speed of the pitch (Bahill & Karnavas, 1993). In this section, we will focus our attention on the factors that lead stationary objects to appear to be moving.

As we have mentioned, the distinction between real and illusory movement might seem somewhat arbitrary. As you watch television or a movie, you are completely aware that people do not really exist inside the screen, yet you would probably argue that the movements you see are not illusory. Even when watching cartoons or playing video games, especially those in which the animation is well executed, you probably have a sense of motion that is compelling. The fact that you are actually seeing a series of rapidly presented still pictures is completely lost on your visual system!

Needless to say, theories of motion perception must deal with both real and apparent motion. After a brief overview of some types of illusory motion, we will turn our attention to theories that might account for our perception of motion—both real and apparent.

Stroboscopic Movement

Stroboscopic movement is the illusion of movement produced by a rapid pattern of stimulation on different parts of the retina. In a typical demonstration of stroboscopic movement, a light flashes briefly at one location. Less than a tenth of a second later, another light flashes briefly at a different location. Observers usually report that the light seems to move from the first location to the second. Although the path between successive presentations is ambiguous (the path could be a curve, or a curlicue), people tend to perceive the simplest possible path (a straight line) between pairs of presentations. The first serious investigation of this phenomenon was initiated by Max

Wertheimer, the Gestalt psychologist you read about in Chapter 5.

If the spatial separation and the timing of the two stimuli are just right, stroboscopic movement can be a powerful movement illusion. However, the illusion does not work if the situation is not ideal (Burt & Sperling, 1981). The timing of the two light flashes must be precise. With some stimulus conditions, for example, an interval of about 60 milliseconds is ideal to produce the perception of an object moving through space. Intriguingly, an interval of about 100 milliseconds in those same conditions may result in the sensation of *phi movement,* in which observers report that they see movement, yet they cannot perceive an actual object moving across the gap. If the interval is longer than about 200 milliseconds, no apparent movement is perceived—two lights just appear to go on and off.

Motion pictures use stroboscopic movement to give the impression of movement. Movie film is like a series of snapshots pasted together as in Figure 8.4. Have you ever wondered how a series of isolated snapshots can give the impression of movement? Observers perceive movement because the movie projector exposes each frame in the series very quickly, so that the dog's paw in Figure 8.4 exhibits stroboscopic movement from Position 1 to Position 2. You perceive movement from one place to the next, rather than a succession of static views (Hochberg & Brooks, 1978).

Factors other than space and time can affect stroboscopic movement. Some researchers have found that stroboscopic movement works for objects that differ in shape, color, or lightness. Suppose that you were first shown a black square, followed by the simultaneous presentation of a black circle and a white square with a black outline. Would you perceive the black square as moving to the white square or to the black circle? People usually perceive movement between the dissimilar shapes that are similar in lightness (Prazdny, 1986). In other words, the black square appears to move and change its shape into a black circle. Other researchers have found that such apparent movement works best for objects that are similar in both shape and color (Berbaum et al., 1981;

Caelli et al., 1993). Further, with identical shapes that change in size but not in space, people will perceive that the stimulus is expanding and shrinking or that it is moving back and forth in depth (Hershenson, 1992).

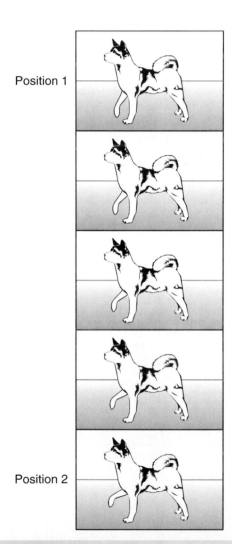

Position 1

Position 2

FIGURE 8.4 Separate still frames of a motion picture. If each successive picture from Position 1 to Position 2 is presented at the proper rate of speed, the dog's right paw will appear to move. Because the dog is not really in motion, this is an illustration of a form of illusory movement referred to as stroboscopic movement.

Ramachandran and Anstis (1986) even found illusions within illusory motion. Figure 8.5a shows how a square and a triangle were first presented on the left, followed by a single square displaced to the right. People reported that both the square and the triangle had moved to the right, with the square covering the triangle.

The effects of apparent occlusion were also seen in another study (Ramachandran & Anstis, 1986). When people observed a display such as Figure 8.5b, they reported seeing two dots move to the same location at the upper right. However, when a dark patch was placed to the right of the lower dot (Figure 8.5c), people reported horizontal movement of both dots! That is, the lower dot appeared to go behind the dark patch. Keep in mind that the only difference between the two displays was the addition of the dark patch in the second display. Nonetheless, the change in apparent movement was dramatic.

Most studies of stroboscopic movement use simple stimuli (points of light, squares, etc.). However, we could just as easily use successive frames showing a human in two different positions. As we saw in the In-Depth section, people seem to be especially sensitive to patterns of motion in other humans. What would happen if people saw two successive frames depicting a human in positions for which the simplest path between the two positions would be impossible?

Figure 8.6 illustrates one such example of biological motion. The picture on the left would be the first frame shown, and the picture on the right would be the second frame shown. Going between the two frames, the simplest path for the woman's right hand would be directly through her head. Of course, the actual path for her hand would be outward *around* her head. If you saw these two pictures presented rapidly, to produce stroboscopic movement, what would you see the woman's hand doing?

What you perceive depends on the speed with which the two pictures are presented (Shiffrar, 1994; Shiffrar & Freyd, 1990, 1993). When the presentation times are very rapid, you would perceive the impossible—the woman's hand would appear to move directly *through* her

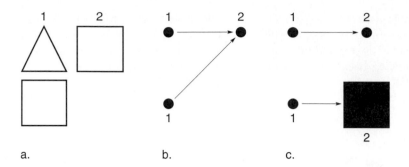

FIGURE 8.5 Illusions in illusory movement produced by apparent occlusion. In each part of the figure, time is indicated by the numbers above the displays. First the figures under 1 were presented, then removed, and the figures under 2 were presented. In part a, people perceive the square and triangle moving to the right, with the square covering the triangle. In part b, people perceive the two dots as moving to the right, with the paths indicated by the arrows. In part c, a simple dark patch is added to the display in part b, and the apparent movement of the two dots changes drastically; now the lower dot appears to move horizontally. (From Ramachandran & Anstis, 1986)

FIGURE 8.6 Two frames of biological motion. The simplest path between the left and right frame is directly through the woman's body. At rapid presentation rates, people will perceive such biologically impossible action. When presentation rates are slowed, people will perceive a more realistic path, with the woman's hand moving around the outside of her body. (From Shiffrar, 1994)

head! However, at an appropriately longer presentation time, you would perceive the biologically correct pathway (around her head).

When Shiffrar and Freyd used inanimate objects, rather than humans, an object always appeared to take the straight path between two positions (Shiffrar, 1994), regardless of the presentation time. However, other researchers have found that inanimate objects will stray from the simplest path. For example, when a real object is placed in the path of apparent movement, the path of apparent movement may curve around the real object rather than going through it (Berbaum & Lenel, 1983).

Autokinesis

Autokinesis occurs when a stationary object, with no clear background, appears to move. Presumably, the spontaneous tiny movements of the eyes produce autokinesis, although some researchers disagree (Mack, 1986). For example, Pola and Matin (1977) placed a contact lens on the eye and recorded eye movements. They found a systematic relationship between the direction of the target's apparent movement and the eye movements they recorded. When you tried Demonstration 4.2 (page 96), you experienced the autokinetic effect.

As you might expect, the autokinetic effect is reduced if another, similar stimulus is nearby. For instance, when a second stimulus is added 1 degree from the fixated stimulus, autokinesis is reduced by about 50% (Post et al., 1982).

Cognitive factors influence the autokinetic effect, because when observers are told to expect movement in a certain direction, the stimuli do tend to move in that direction (Leibowitz et al., 1983). Early researchers noted that with proper instructions and reinforcement, a few people would even report that autokinetic movement produces words (Rechschaffen & Mednick, 1955). However, Lovelace (1988) was unable to replicate this effect. Even when he praised them for reporting that the movement produced words, most people reported only random movement.

Induced Movement

Induced movement occurs when a visual frame of reference moves in one direction and produces the illusion that a stationary target is moving in the opposite direction. In a typical study of induced movement, an observer in a dark room views a luminous dot that is surrounded by a luminous rectangular frame (Wallach, 1959). When the rectangular frame moves to the right, the observer perceives the frame as stationary and the dot as moving to the left. The next time the moon is bright and the sky is cloudy, see whether you notice any induced movement. The moon is essentially stationary, yet the clouds are moving in front of it. Consequently, the moon may appear to move in a direction opposite to the clouds' motion.

Psychologists have investigated induced movement with a wide array of response measures, frames, and speed and type of frame movement, to name just a handful of the variables examined. A number of explanations have emerged from these investigations (Reinhardt-Rutland, 1988). One of the earliest explanations might be called a frame-of-reference theory, which argues that our visual system is predisposed to view smaller and more centrally located areas as moving. Such perceptions might arise due to an inference based on our experience with the world (Rock, 1983). Because of the complexity of perceptual experience, where a single frame of reference might be difficult to identify, this approach may not be adequate.

Others have suggested that induced movement occurs because of eye movements, but such illusory motion is not due to errors in tracking the target (Gogel & Sharkey, 1989). Still others have proposed purely physiological explanations of induced movement. These theorists argue that the movement-sensitive neurons that cause movement aftereffects also cause induced movement.

As Reinhardt-Rutland (1988) argues, the variety of stimuli that produce induced movement is so great as to suggest that a single explanation of induced movement is unlikely. On the other hand, the fact that even complex induced motions have the same quality as real motions argues that

---

Demonstration 8.3

*Movement
Aftereffects*

Make a clear, dark photocopy of the spiral shape below. Glue it to firm cardboard and cut out the spiral. Poke a hole in the center and place the figure on a stereo turntable. Turn the turntable to a speed of $33\frac{1}{3}$. Stand directly over the rotating figure and fixate it for 1 to 2 minutes. Then turn off the turntable and hold the platter stationary. The spiral should seem to be moving in a direction opposite to its previous motion, even though nothing is really moving.

---

we can learn a great deal about movement perception by studying induced movement (O'Leary et al., 1988).

Movement Aftereffects

Movement aftereffects occur when you have been looking at a continuous movement and then look at a different surface. The new surface will seem to move in the opposite direction. Interestingly, movement aftereffects can occur after viewing real movement or after viewing apparent movement (van Kruysbergen & de Weert, 1993).

You might try to demonstrate movement aftereffects if you can visit a waterfall. Stare for several minutes at the waterfall, then turn your gaze toward clouds in the sky. The clouds will seem to flow in a direction opposite to that of the waterfall. The longer you look at the inducing stimulus (the waterfall), the more powerful the aftereffect (Hershenson, 1993). Try Demonstration 8.3 to see another example of movement aftereffects.

Movement aftereffects resemble the successive color contrast and achromatic afterimages discussed in Chapter 7. One explanation for those phenomena involves some kind of adaptation or fatigue of cells involved in visual processing. A similar kind of adaptation may be involved in movement aftereffects. The response rate of motion-sensitive cells may be depressed after they have been stimulated for a long time (Sekuler, 1975). Young children seem to be almost as susceptible to this illusion as adults, suggesting that experience does not play a major role (Hershenson & Bader, 1990). However, movement aftereffects cannot be entirely explained by simple, low-level mechanisms. In some cases, a higher-level process must be involved (Weisstein et al., 1982).

SECTION SUMMARY

Illusory Movement

1. Stroboscopic movement is produced by sequential presentation of stimuli at different locations on the retina. The distance and timing between the stimuli are crucial, but the stimuli can have somewhat different shapes.

2. People tend to perceive apparent movement along the most direct path. With sufficiently brief presentations, this tendency leads people to perceive impossible biological movements.

3. Autokinesis, or spontaneous apparent movement of a stationary object, can be influenced by nearby stimuli and by instructions.

4. Induced movement occurs when a visual frame of reference moves.

5. Movement aftereffects occur after watching continuous movement. Stationary objects will appear to move in a direction opposite to the previously viewed movement.

PHYSIOLOGICAL BASIS OF MOTION PERCEPTION

At this point, we have discussed enough examples of motion perception that you should marvel at our abilities. Whether people are perceiving real or apparent movement, their neural apparatus certainly plays an important role. We will now focus on the role of the cortical areas that are crucial for the processing of motion information.

As we saw in Chapter 3, the magno system appears to be primarily responsible for processing movement information (Livingstone & Hubel, 1988). You should briefly review that chapter, paying particular attention to the magno system—from the parasol ganglion cells of the retina through the LGN and the visual cortex. In this section, our discussion will concentrate on the cortical portion of the magno system.

However, information processed by the parvo system may also be essential for motion perception (Stoner & Albright, 1993). For example, the magno system is largely insensitive to chromatic information. However, we can perceive motion in displays that vary only in hue (Dobkins & Albright, 1993; Tyler & Cavanagh, 1991). The color-sensitive parvo system is probably responsible for this phenomenon. Although we will focus on the magno system to explain motion perception, the complexities of both motion perception and cortical organization make it clear that this focus oversimplifies the situation (DeYoe & van Essen, 1988).

The magno pathway begins at the retinal level with the parasol ganglion cells, which seem to be attuned to motion and lightness differences. The information from the parasol cells passes through the two magno layers of the LGN and on to particular cortical layers of area V1 (striate cortex). As a result of the input from these cells, area V1 has a high proportion of cells sensitive to local motion (Sereno, 1993). From V1, one pathway leads to V2 and then on to the middle temporal (MT) area, which is also called V5. Another pathway leads directly from V1 to MT (Dawson, 1991; Sereno, 1993). These two pathways appear to have functional significance (Grossberg & Rudd, 1992). You can see the locations of V2 and V5 (MT) in Figure 7.10, on page 232.

The middle temporal area is probably central in motion perception because of the convergence of motion information on MT and because of the high proportion of motion- and direction-sensitive cells in this part of the cortex (Sereno, 1993; Zeki, 1990, 1993). As we discussed in Chapter 7, the evidence about the centrality of V4 for color perception is somewhat mixed. However, the evidence that MT is necessary and sufficient for normal motion perception seems much clearer (Movshon & Newsome, 1992; Schiller, 1994). Although MT is probably not the only source of motion information, this region certainly seems central.

As we have mentioned in earlier chapters, unfortunate incidents in which people sustain neural damage may lead to important theoretical knowledge. For example, in Chapter 7 we learned that damage to V4 leads to achromatopsia. Thus, achromatopsia serves as important evidence for the centrality of V4 to color perception. Similarly, damage to MT can lead to *akinetopsia*—the inability to perceive movement (Zeki, 1993).

The best-known case study of akinetopsia describes a woman with lesions to both sides of her occipital cortex (Zihl et al., 1983). She had normal acuity and color vision, and could detect some linear movement when it occurred near her foveas. However, she had lost the ability to detect peripheral movement and could not perceive three-dimensional motion. Driving through an intersection was dangerous for this woman, because oncoming cars appeared first to be far away and then to jump very near. Even the simple act of pouring a cup of tea becomes difficult if one cannot perceive motion in depth! Apparently, her visual experience was like a series of still photographs, with little sense of transition between the snapshots. Clearly, MT must be instrumental in the perception of motion.

From MT, the pathway continues on to the medial superior temporal (MST) area. MST has several parts that appear to have different roles in processing motion information. Cells in parts of MST have large receptive fields, suggesting that they encode motion information over large areas of the visual field (Andersen et al., 1993; Sereno, 1993). In general, MST seems to be involved in the smooth pursuit eye movements we discussed in Chapter 4 (Sereno, 1993; Wurtz et al., 1993). From MST, the pathway continues on to other levels of the extrastriate cortex (Dawson, 1991).

In addition to the primary pathway for motion perception, the superior colliculus may also be concerned with movement detection and the control of eye movements (Schiller, 1986). (The superior colliculus is shown in Figure 3.15, on page 71.) Cells in the superior colliculus respond to visual motion when the eye is stationary but not when it is moving. These cells may help to distinguish between situations in which the observer is moving and those in which the stimuli are moving. This distinction is crucial for corollary discharge theory, one of the theories we will discuss in the next section.

SECTION SUMMARY

Physiological Basis of Motion Perception

1. The magno pathway is primarily responsible for motion perception, although the parvo system may also be capable of processing motion information.
2. Two different parts of the magno system both lead to the middle temporal (MT) area, which is crucial for motion perception.
3. Because MT is central to motion perception, damage to this area can lead to akinetopsia—an inability to perceive movement.
4. The superior colliculus is also involved with perception of some types of motion and the control of eye movements.

THEORETICAL EXPLANATIONS FOR MOTION PERCEPTION

We have seen that motion perception is both a basic and an accurate perceptual process. Furthermore, motion perception is a complex process, allowing us to perceive our own movement and that of objects around us. Any adequate theory of motion perception must explain how all this occurs, as well as how we perceive apparent movement. To conclude this chapter, we will examine three different theoretical orientations to motion perception. Two of these theoretical approaches for motion perception should seem familiar to you, as you've seen both the direct perception approach and the computational approach in earlier chapters. First, however, let us discuss an approach that should be new to you—corollary discharge theory.

Corollary Discharge Theory

According to **corollary discharge theory,** the visual system compares the movement registered on the retina with any signals the brain might have sent regarding eye movement (Richards, 1975; Von Holst, 1954). Corollary discharge theory specifically tries to explain why we do *not* perceive movement during normal eye movements, as Wallach's (1985b, 1987) work has emphasized. The theory can explain the perception of movement with movement on the retina and with no movement on the retina. It can also explain the perception of no movement with movement on the retina and with no movement on the retina.

Corollary discharge theory argues that when your brain sends a message to your eye muscles, it also sends a copy of this message to a structure in the visual system. This copy is called a corollary discharge; the word *corollary* means "related." The structure in the visual system to which the corollary discharge is sent has not yet been identified by researchers. Researchers simply refer to it as the *comparison structure* illustrated in Figure 8.7, which shows a schematic representation of the process. Gregory (1973) refers to this portion of the corollary discharge model as the eye–head system. This system might simply track the movement of eyes, but it might also track the overall orientation of the observer (Wertheim, 1994).

When the eyes actually move, some images might be caused to shift across the retina. Gregory refers to this portion as the image–retina system. The comparison structure compares the input from the image–retina system with the input expected to be produced as a result of the corollary discharge from the eye–head system. When the sensory input is consistent with the corollary discharge expectation, the information is canceled and no motion is perceived. When the sensory input is inconsistent with the corollary discharge expectation, motion is perceived.

Four Outcomes in Corollary Discharge Theory

Let's examine four simple outcomes of the interaction of sensory input and corollary discharge,

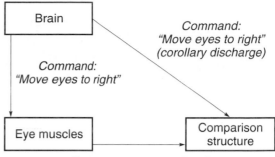

Sensory movement signal
(image has moved on retina)

FIGURE 8.7 A schematic illustration of corollary discharge theory. When the brain sends a signal to move the eyes, a corollary discharge is sent to the comparison structure. Movement on the retina results in a sensory signal, which is also sent to the comparison structure. If the sensory signal is consistent with the expectations produced by the corollary discharge, then no movement is perceived. If the sensory signal is not anticipated by the corollary discharge, then movement is perceived.

beginning with two obvious cases where the eyes are stationary. First, think of the two types of input if you are looking straight ahead at a stationary field of view. No corollary discharge is produced, because the eyes are not being told to move. Likewise, because the eyes are basically stationary, objects in the visual field remain in the same positions on the retina. With no corollary discharge and no sensory input from the retina, no movement is perceived.

Secondly, think of the case when your eyes are stationary and a person moves in front of you. Again, the eye–head system receives no command to move, so no corollary discharge is produced. However, the person moving across your field of view causes movement in your image-retina system. With no corollary discharge—but with sensory input from the retina—movement *is* perceived. In other words, the actual sensory input does not cancel out the corollary discharge expectation. This discrepancy between the actual

1   2   3

a. Stationary woman and moving observer

1   2   3

b. Moving woman and stationary observer

FIGURE 8.8   Two illustrations of motion in the world. In part a, the observer is in motion from right to left and everything else is stationary. Notice that the relation of the woman to the picture remains constant from frame 1 to frame 3. In part b, the woman is moving from right to left and everything else (including the observer) is stationary. Notice that the relation of the woman to the picture changes from frame 1 to frame 3.

sensory input and the corollary discharge is sufficient to give rise to the perception of motion.

In the final two cases, the eyes are moving. Imagine you are in a museum looking at a stationary woman, guard, and picture (Figure 8.8a). When you scan the scene by moving your eyes from right to left, you produce a corollary discharge associated with the command to move your eyes. As you scan from right to left, the woman, for instance, goes from the left to the right of your visual field. The movement of the woman, the guard, and the picture are all consistent with the expectations produced by the corollary discharge. Therefore, the sensory input is canceled out and no movement is perceived.

The final example involves moving eyes as well as a moving object. Suppose that the woman now moves from your right to your left, and you track her movement with your eyes (Figure 8.8b). In this case, a corollary discharge will be produced as you send the message to your eye muscles to track the woman. Any sensory input from your retina that is consistent with the corollary discharge will be canceled out, resulting in the perception of stationary objects (the guard and the picture). The woman you are tracking, however, continues to fall on the same area of the retina, which is *inconsistent* with the corollary discharge. Thus, she is perceived as moving from right to left.

Disrupting the Normal Corollary Discharge

Corollary discharge theory suggests that you will perceive movement whenever the information from the eye–head system is inconsistent with input from the image–retina system. Sometimes the discrepancy can result in the perception of movement that has not occurred. You can demonstrate this motion perception by placing your finger on the side of your upper eyelid and pressing *gently*. Because your eye is moved passively, by your finger, rather than through your brain's normal commands to the eye muscles, no corollary discharge is produced. A sensory signal *is* sent from the retina, however. As Bridgeman and Delgado (1984) explain, the mismatch between the moving retinal image and the lack of corollary discharge results in the perception of movement. The movement of the world perceived by people wearing inverting lenses (Wallach, 1987) might also be explained by the fact that the corollary discharge expectation is so different from the sensory input—at least until people adapt to the lenses.

What would happen if you sent a message to move your eyes, but your eyes were paralyzed? Stevens and his colleagues (Stevens et al., 1976) actually did such research, as we discussed in Chapter 4. Stevens found that if he told his paralyzed eye muscles to move, the whole room appeared to move! In terms of corollary discharge theory, Stevens had created a corollary discharge expectation of movement that was accompanied by *no* sensory input from the retina. The discrepancy between the two pieces of information led to the perception of the movement of the room.

Look again at the explanation of Figure 8.8b. If you tell your eyes to move from right to left, the only objects that should remain stationary on the retina are those that are also moving from the right to the left. Similarly, Stevens told his eyes to move, so the only objects that should have remained stationary on the retina were those that are also moving. However, because his eye muscles were paralyzed, the whole room remained stationary on his retina. The discrepancy between the sensory input (no change) and the corollary discharge (expect change) led to the perception that the room had moved.

In the section on autokinesis, we discussed how involuntary eye movements may at least partially explain this phenomenon. Post and Leibowitz (1985) have developed a theory to explain autokinesis, induced movement, and other phenomena, which involves the smooth pursuit movements discussed in Chapter 4. They cite research to indicate that the pursuit system is activated during autokinesis and induced movement. A neural signal, essentially the corollary discharge, is produced when this pursuit system is activated. As with real movement, the presence of this neural signal—in combination with the stationary image of the stimulus on a particular part of the retina—tells you that the stimulus is in motion. Subsequent research continues to support this theory, providing evidence for the generality of corollary discharge theory (Heckmann & Post, 1988; Koga & Groner, 1990).

Direct Perception Approach

Gibson and others who favor the direct perception approach have argued that the stimulus is rich with information about movement, a claim consistent with Theme 2 of this textbook. In contrast, corollary discharge theory praises the visual processing system. (This praise is, of course, consistent with Theme 3 of this book, on page 10.) Although many theorists have taken positions that differ from the direct perception approach, Gibson's contributions to the study of motion perception were substantial (Blake, 1994). Thus,

Gibson's early work anticipated much of the subsequent research on motion perception. In this current section, we will examine six sources of information available from the stimulus. Gibson would argue that such sources are crucial for the perception of motion.

1. *Relative movement.* We can tell whether we are moving or whether an object is moving by noticing the object's movement relative to its background. Notice in Figure 8.8a that the woman is always in front of the painting. Because the woman does not move in relation to the painting, you conclude that she is stationary and you—the observer—are moving. The patterns of movement shown in the tracking-shot illustration (Figure 6.13) are also consistent with movement of the observer and no movement of the people in the scene. In Figure 8.8b the woman is moving in relation to the background: In the first picture she is to the right of the painting, then she moves in front of the museum guard, and finally she moves in front of the doorway. As the observer, you would conclude that she is moving and you are stationary.

2. *Occlusion and disocclusion.* Furthermore, moving objects show a systematic covering and uncovering of the background. Pick up your textbook and move it to the left in front of your eyes. Your book systematically covers up the background on the left; this process is called **occlusion.** At the same time it systematically uncovers the background on the right; this process is called **disocclusion.** Occlusion and disocclusion tell us the direction of objects' movement (Gibson, 1979).

Objects that move toward us also show a systematic occlusion and disocclusion pattern. Pick up your textbook again and move it toward you so that it is about to hit your face. Notice how the occlusion occurs to the same extent on both the right and the left side of the book. When the occlusion is equal, we perceive that an object is coming directly toward us. At other times the occlusion is not equal—for instance, when you move your book toward your left ear. In this case, the left side of the background becomes occluded at the same time as the right side becomes disoccluded. You perceive that the object will miss you. If the occlusion is extremely unequal, then the object will miss you by a large distance.

The next time you are playing a game such as volleyball, notice how this occlusion/disocclusion process works. You hold your hands in front of your face and move your body so that the occlusion pattern is equal on the right and the left. The ball appears to be coming directly at you. On the other hand, if someone is throwing a snowball at you, you move your head so that the occlusion patterns are unequal, and the snowball will miss you. Notice, then, that you—the perceiver—control what you perceive by adjusting your body.

3. *Image size.* The size of the image also increases as you approach objects and they approach you (Regan et al., 1979). Notice that image size is a monocular cue. Regan proposes that the strength of monocular cues such as image size explains how some pilots and ballplayers can continue to perform effectively after they have lost their vision in one eye. Their professions depend upon successful motion perception, yet they have enough information about motion from monocular cues. Also, have you ever noticed how motion is shown in cartoons? Someone falls off a cliff, and the features on the ground below expand suddenly until we see the final "splat!" from a side view. Thus, cartoonists successfully exploit the image-size cue for motion.

4. *Motion parallax.* Remember that motion parallax, discussed in Chapter 6, occurs when you move your head, and objects at different distances from your head appear to move in different directions. Goodson et al. (1980) have demonstrated that motion parallax is a very important cue to motion.

5. *Motion perspective.* Motion perspective, also discussed in Chapter 6, is a more general term that includes motion parallax. As you drive down a road, motion perspective occurs as images of objects flow across your retina at different rates. If you look straight ahead, for example, nearby objects on either side of you flow by quickly; objects farther away flow slowly. Parts of the world expand and contract as you move around. The next time you are in a car, look straight ahead at a point on the horizon and no-

tice how everything seems to expand outward from that point.

Motion perspective is clearly a useful source of information about motion. Even when we move so fast that the visual flow looks more like a visual blur, motion perspective is still useful (Harrington et al., 1980). A further problem that requires explanation is that we sometimes gaze in a different direction from the one toward which we are moving (Priest & Cutting, 1985; Regan, 1985; Regan & Beverley, 1982). The work of Warren and Hannon (1988, 1990) provides evidence that we are capable of accurate motion perception even under these complex conditions.

6. *Binocular cues.* We have been discussing monocular cues so far. Corollary discharge theory can apply to one eye; background information, the occlusion/disocclusion process, image size, motion parallax, and motion perspective can also work with one-eyed vision. However, binocular cues are also helpful in motion perception (Regan et al., 1979). As a ball moves toward you, for example, the image moves at the same speed on both your right and left retinas. However, if the left retinal image is moving more slowly than the right retinal image, then you perceive that the ball will pass toward your right side. Thus, comparing the speeds of the left and the right retinal images gives you information about the direction of movement.

Computational Approach

Like the direct perception approach we have just examined, the computational approach acknowledges the richness of the visual stimulus. However, unlike the direct perception approach, the computational approach also holds that perception requires problem solving (e.g., Wandell, 1995). Unlike more cognitive approaches, though, the computational approach attempts to solve perceptual problems with general physical knowledge rather than with specific knowledge about objects in the visual field.

In the perception of motion, one problem that a computational theorist attempts to address

is the correspondence problem. Look back at Figure 8.3b and try to imagine how your visual system would "connect" a dot presented in one frame with a dot in the next frame. This is the ***correspondence problem*** faced by the visual system—how are elements of the visual field connected over time (Dawson, 1991; Sekuler et al., 1990)?

Several solutions to the correspondence problem have been proposed (Bruce & Green, 1990), but no solution is generally accepted. Correspondence does appear to depend more on lightness than on shape. For instance, Ramachandran and Anstis (1986) presented the white square seen in the middle of Figure 8.9. Then the white square disappeared and the square outline and the white circle were shown simultaneously. Observers report seeing the white square move and transform itself into a white circle rather than into a dark square. Such results suggest that lightness is more important to correspondence than shape is (Prazdny, 1986; Ramachandran & Anstis, 1986).

All motion perception might well be due to a single process (e.g., Cavanagh & Mather, 1989; Wandell, 1995). However, most researchers assume that at least two different processes underlie motion perception (Anstis, 1986; Grossberg & Rudd, 1992). The ***short-range process*** apparently analyzes movement that is discrete or takes place over short distances or times (Hildreth & Ullman, 1989). The ***long-range process*** analyzes movement over larger distances or times and is probably crucial for the perception of apparent movement (Hildreth & Ullman, 1989). The short-range process might well involve only peripheral processing, but the long-range process probably involves higher-level processing and is therefore more flexible (Petersik, 1989). Although the two processes are somewhat independent, the short-range process is thought to feed information into the long-range process. Physiologically, the short-range process might take place in V1 and MT, whereas the long-range process might take place in parts of MST (Sereno, 1993; Wurtz et al., 1993).

Because less is known about the central processes involved in motion perception, compu-

FIGURE 8.9 An illustration of the importance of lightness for the correspondence problem. First the white square was presented, then removed with the presentation of the square outline and the white circle. People observe the square moving to the right rather than to the left, indicating that lightness is more important to correspondence than shape is. (From Ramachandran & Anstis, 1986)

tational theorists have focused on the short-range process (Juola & Breitmeyer, 1989). For instance, Marr (1982) illustrates how perceivers can sense direction from the same sort of information used to detect edges (discussed in Chapter 5).

Remember that the Mexican-hat filter (Figure 5.13) is capable of detecting intensity changes as zero-crossings. In other words, edge detection can be accomplished by means of a filter that has characteristics much like the receptive fields that are actually found in ganglion cells. Using calculus, Marr (1982) shows that taking the time derivative at zero-crossings will indicate motion in a particular direction. When the time derivative is positive, the edge is moving to the right. When the time derivative is negative, the edge is moving to the left. Further, Marr argues that the human visual system has the neurophysiological mechanisms to perform these computations. The midget ganglion cells serve primarily to encode shape information, whereas the parasol cells could serve to take the time derivative of zero-crossings. We have already seen that the magno system, with input from the parasol cells, is crucial for movement perception. Marr's theory articulates the mechanism by which the parasol cells might operate. More recent computational models (e.g., Grossberg, 1992; Grossberg &

Rudd, 1992) better predict the actual perception of a wide range of complex motions.

In this discussion of theoretical explanations of motion perception, we have mentioned corollary discharge theory, the direct perception approach, and the computational approach. These explanations for motion perception have stressed the richness of the stimulus (Theme 2) and the spectacular construction of the human visual processing system (Theme 3). Experience and higher-level processes (Theme 4) seem to be crucial to corollary discharge theory and to perceiving a stable environment when we move. However, cognitive processes might play a relatively minor role in motion perception. For instance, Johansson (1982) asks us to consider the housefly, an organism not known for its impressive cognitive ability. Johansson describes how the male and female fly perform the mating procedure. The female partner circles around in a random path while the male partner follows the same pattern several inches above her. Johansson remarks that the male housefly's amazing accuracy in motion perception is far more perfect than that of airplane pilots. Certainly our cognitive processes are important in the interpretation of motion, but many aspects of motion perception clearly can be accomplished with little thought or memory.

SECTION SUMMARY

Theoretical Explanations for Motion Perception

1. Corollary discharge theory proposes that the visual system compares the movement registered on the retina (image–retina system) with any signals the brain may have sent about eye movement (eye–head system).
2. The direct perception approach argues that the stimulus provides information that includes background information, occlusion/disocclusion information, image size, motion parallax, motion perspective, and binocular cues.
3. The computational approach provides mathematical models for the computation of movement. To perceive motion, the visual system must solve several problems, including the correspondence problem.

REVIEW QUESTIONS

1. William Shakespeare wrote, "Things in motion sooner catch the eye than what stirs not." How is this comment relevant to your peripheral vision? Compare your peripheral vision and vision in your fovea with respect to velocity detection thresholds.
2. Imagine that an industrial employee has been instructed to report whether a dial on a piece of equipment moves the slightest amount. Describe how uncertainty and the background behind the dial might be important, and mention why apparent movement might be a problem.
3. Summarize the studies on biological motion discussed in the In-Depth section. What kinds of information about motion can we pick up readily without seeing an entire organism? Obviously, we most often see a complete organism. Why, then, is research on biological motion so important for theories of perception?
4. Suppose you are playing baseball and you are up at bat. How would Gibson's theory explain your perception of motion as the ball is being pitched toward you? Suppose you are pitching and you quickly move your head to determine whether the person on second base is trying to steal third. How might corollary discharge theory account for the stability, despite the motion of images across your retina?
5. Name the kind of apparent movement represented in each of the following situations.
   a. On a dark night, you see a single small light in a neighbor's house, and you know that the neighbor is on vacation. The light appears to move, and you suspect a burglar.
   b. A billboard has a line of light bulbs that turn on and off in rapid succession. The light appears to travel across the billboard.
   c. In a planetarium, the star show ends with the stars whirling swiftly about in a clockwise direction for several minutes. Out in the darkened lobby a minute later, the room around you seems to be whirling in the opposite direction.
   d. On a dark night, you watch a plane fly over a radio tower. For a brief moment the plane seems to be stationary and the tower light seems to move.
6. Compare the perception of real movement with illusory movement—particularly stroboscopic movement. To answer this question, think about the movement seen on a movie screen as compared to movement in the real world. Why might you think that the same movement perception system gives rise to the perception of both types of movement?
7. In this chapter, we discussed two different demonstrations of apparent movement from research by Ramachandran and Anstis (Figures 8.5 and 8.9). What general point do you think is being made by both these demonstrations? Are the effects illustrated in these demonstrations consistent with a direct perception approach?
8. Think of a situation involving complex movement perception, such as playing tennis. Players are moving as they track a mov-

ing opponent and the ball being returned to them over a stationary net. How would each of the approaches to movement perception deal with this situation? Which approach do you find best able to deal with the complexities of the situation, and why?

9. Many perceptual phenomena require explanations that are more complicated than you might have anticipated. For example, someone unfamiliar with the topic of motion perception might guess that we simply perceive motion whenever our retinas register a change in an object's position. Why would that explanation be inadequate? What other explanations would you add?

10. In this chapter, we focused on motion perception and argued that it is a basic process. One argument that a person might make for the importance of motion perception is the extent to which it plays a role in other perceptual processes. Using information in previous chapters, show how motion plays a role in other perceptual processes such as shape and distance perception.

NEW TERMS

blindsight (250)
velocity detection threshold (251)
biological motion (253)
point–light display (253)
optic flow field (258)
self-motion illusion (258)
illusory movement (259)

stroboscopic movement (260)
phi movement (260)
autokinesis (263)
induced movement (263)
movement aftereffects (264)
akinetopsia (266)

corollary discharge theory (267)
occlusion (270)
disocclusion (270)
correspondence problem (271)
short-range process (271)
long-range process (271)

RECOMMENDED READINGS

Cutting, J. E. (1986). *Perception with an eye for motion*. Cambridge, MA: MIT Press. This book offers an advanced-level discussion of distance and motion perception, although it does not examine the topic of biological motion, an area to which Cutting has made substantial contributions.

Humphreys, G. W., & Bruce, V. (1989). *Visual cognition: Computational, experimental, and neurophysiological perspectives*. Hove, UK: Erlbaum. This is an excellent advanced undergraduate text that takes a somewhat computational approach to visual perception. Chapter 4, on dynamic visual perception, is particularly relevant to the topic of movement perception. A reader interested in a focused overview of visual perception would find the rest of the text worthwhile reading. David Marr's (1982) book *Vision*, referred to in earlier chapters, also provides a good introduction to a computational approach to motion perception.

Jansson, G., Bergström, S. S., & Epstein, W. (Eds.). (1994). *Perceiving events and objects*. Hillsdale, NJ: Erl-

baum. What a tremendous resource for a person interested in Gunnar Johansson's work! First, this edited book contains reprints of many of Johansson's influential articles. Next, many important researchers contribute original chapters stimulated by Johansson's work. The interested reader will be treated to discussions of event perception, vector analysis, decoding principles, and Johansson's more recent optic sphere theory.

Sereno, M. E. (1993). *Neural computation of pattern motion: Modeling stages of motion analysis in the primate visual cortex*. Cambridge, MA: MIT Press. Sereno has a computational orientation, which leads her to propose a connectionist model of motion perception. Although her model may be too complex to be accessible to the average reader, she first provides an overview of psychophysical and neurophysiological research on motion perception that is quite readable.

[In Demonstration 8.2, part a shows a person curling a medium weight, part b shows a person walking, part c shows a person hopping, and part d shows a person throwing a far distance.]

The Auditory System

Take a minute to appreciate the variety of sounds nearby. You may hear voices and music, rattles, thuds, whines, buzzes, squeaks, roars, and drips. Some sounds are loud and some are soft. Some are high, some low. Each sound also appears to come from a distinct direction.

We assume that vision is our most important perceptual process, assigning hearing to second place. However, consider the variety of ways in which hearing provides us with information about the world. Hearing has provided humans with an evolutionary advantage that was essential in detecting the approach of predatory animals and in locating the flow of streams (Nathan, 1982). Even in the 20th century, hearing can be critically important in informing us of danger. We hear a barking dog, a car horn, and a shout of "Fire!"

Hearing is also vital to human communication because it is central in social interactions and in transmitting knowledge. Evans (1982a) argues that hearing is even more important than vision for humans. As he notes, "It has been said that a blind person is cut off from the world of things, whereas one who is deaf is cut off from the world of people" (p. 239). Furthermore, hearing is a major source of entertainment in music, movies, and plays.

Chapter 3 introduced the visual stimulus—light—and the structure of the visual system. Now we need to examine the equivalent topics for hearing: the auditory stimulus—sound waves—and the structure of the auditory system. In this chapter we also consider hearing impairments.

THE AUDITORY STIMULUS

Auditory stimuli are caused by displacement of an elastic medium. To understand an elastic medium, think of a rubber band. The rubber band can be stretched, but when the pressure is removed, the rubber band returns to its original shape. The molecules of an elastic medium can be displaced, but they have a tendency to return to their original position. Some examples of elastic media include liquids (such as water), the ground, metals, wood, and—most important—air. The vacuum of space cannot transmit sound waves. So, despite any science fiction movies you might have seen, space would always be eerily silent. On earth, elastic media abound. In western movies, you might have seen scouts place an ear to the ground or railroad tracks, enabling them to detect approaching horses or trains. Car mechanics use a trick for learning about the internal functioning of an engine. They listen at the end of a long piece of wood placed against different parts of the engine. Each of these examples illustrates a major advantage of our auditory sense—we can hear things that are out of sight.

Our most common experience of sound comes from the displacement of air molecules. Something vibrates, and the vibration causes molecules of air to change their positions and collide with each other, producing sound waves. Perhaps the easiest way to visualize these sound waves is to consider how air molecules respond to a vibrating diaphragm in a loudspeaker. Try Demonstration 9.1 to appreciate how this diaphragm vibrates impressively by moving forward and backward.

Demonstration 9.1

Vibrations and the Auditory Stimulus

Turn on a stereo to the volume setting you usually use. Now feel around on a speaker to locate where the vibration is the most pronounced. Keep your hand there and notice how it vibrates more intensely when the auditory stimulus sounds loud.

Similarly, the speaker diaphragm influences the surrounding air molecules. When the diaphragm moves forward, it shoves the surrounding air molecules close together. The density of the air molecules next to the diaphragm increases. (Imagine how the density of people standing in a room would increase if one wall were to move inward.) When the diaphragm moves backward, a partial vacuum is created and the surrounding air molecules move apart. As a result, the density of the air molecules decreases. (Imagine how the density of people in a room would decrease if one wall were to move outward.) This change in the density of air molecules produces a corresponding change in atmospheric pressure.

When your stereo plays a typical note, the speaker diaphragm could repeat the cycle of moving forward and backward a total of 500 times in 1 second. In other words, the atmospheric pressure next to the diaphragm could increase and decrease 500 times in the time it takes you to blink your eye. (As we'll see later, it could also vibrate as seldom as 20 times a second or as often as 20,000 times a second.)

Each individual air molecule moves very little during this process. Instead, a wave of pressure moves continuously outward from the vibrating diaphragm. In Figure 9.1, notice the areas of high atmospheric pressure, represented by the high density of air molecules, and the areas of low atmospheric pressure, represented by the low density of air molecules. (Of course, this diagram is schematic, because air molecules are invisible.) This wave of pressure resembles the ripples created when you throw a stone into a pond, with the ripples traveling outward from the source of the disturbance. Each individual water molecule moves very little, but the waves can spread outward for quite a distance. Because the air molecules radiate outward in straight lines—not up and down as the water does—you should think of the peaks and troughs of the water ripples as indicating increases and decreases in air pressure.

Figure 9.2 represents a ***pure tone,*** which is a simple sine wave. In the laboratory, simple sine

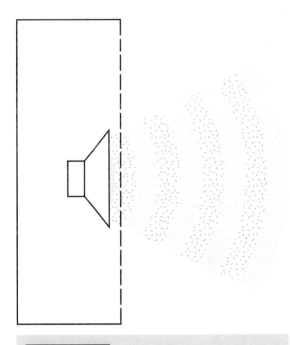

FIGURE 9.1   Areas of high and low atmospheric pressure created by the vibrating speaker diaphragm.

waves are often used as stimuli; in the "real world," pure tones are actually quite rare. Your stereo, for instance, would rarely emit a pure tone. For the sake of simplicity, however, we will focus our discussion on pure tones.

Suppose that your stereo speaker could emit a pure tone. We could measure the atmospheric pressure near the speaker diaphragm, recording the pressure as it increases and decreases before finally returning to its original pressure. The pure sine wave in Figure 9.2 arises from mapping such pressure changes over time. From its resting state, the speaker first pushes out, creating an increase in pressure. The speaker then returns to its resting state, and then goes back behind its original starting point, creating a decrease in pressure. Finally, the speaker returns to the original starting point. The full range of pressure changes from normal, to high, to normal, to low, and back to normal is referred to as a ***cycle.*** You can see that the shape of the sound

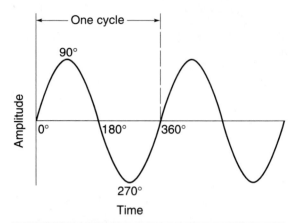

FIGURE 9.2   Characteristics of a sound wave. The change from normal atmospheric pressure to above normal pressure, to below normal pressure, with a return to normal pressure is referred to as one cycle. Within the cycle, the phase angle of the wave changes from 0° to 360°. The frequency of the sound is determined by the number of cycles completed in 1 second. The amplitude of the sound is determined by the height of the wave.

air-pressure changes falling on our ears are called *sounds.*

You hear a sound because of tiny disturbances in air pressure. This seems incredible. How can the motion of invisible air molecules possibly be strong enough to cause your eardrum to move? The sensitivity of the system becomes clearer when you realize that the sounds may need to displace your eardrum by only a minuscule amount—about 0.0000000004 inch (Green, 1976). The distance is difficult to imagine; it is less than 1 billionth of an inch!

In the next sections, we will describe physical properties of sound waves such as frequency, amplitude, and phase angle. Before you begin reading about these properties, try Demonstration 9.2 to give yourself an intuitive feeling for them.

wave resembles the sine-wave functions discussed in Chapters 3 and 7 in connection with light waves.

The wave of pressure traveling outward from your stereo will ultimately reach your eardrum. The rapid increase and decrease in atmospheric pressure will cause your eardrum to move backward and forward. These successive

Frequency

Frequency is the number of cycles a sound wave completes in 1 second. For example, middle C on the piano has a basic frequency of 262 cycles per second, or 262 Hz. (The abbreviation *Hz* is derived from the name of Heinrich Hertz, a German physicist.) Frequency generally corresponds to the psychological experience of pitch, although the correspondence is far from perfect. Thus, middle C on the piano, with a frequency of 262 Hz, sounds higher in pitch than the lowest note on the piano, which has a frequency of about 27 Hz. The sound wave in Figure 9.3a has a higher frequency (the sound source vibrates

Demonstration 9.2

Frequency, Amplitude, and Phase Angle of Sound Waves

Place a rubber band over an open box. By plucking the rubber band gently or vigorously, you can vary the amplitude, or height, of the sound waves. Note the associated changes in sound that accompany the changes in pluck vigor. By adjusting the tension on the rubber band (pulling it more tightly or less tightly against the side of the box), you can vary the frequency of the sound waves. Finally, by pulling up on the rubber band, you can cause the sound wave to start 180° out of phase with a wave initiated by pushing down on the rubber band.

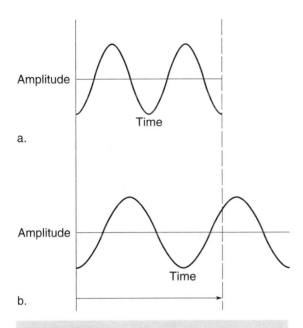

Amplitude

Time

a.

Amplitude

Time

b.

FIGURE 9.3 Two sound waves differing in frequency. The amplitude of the two waves is the same, but in the same period of time the wave in part a goes through two complete cycles, whereas the wave in part b has not completed two cycles.

of the time) for the human auditory range. Research has determined that humans are most sensitive to frequencies from 2000 to 5000 Hz (Gulick et al., 1989; Sivian & White, 1933). Intriguingly, the energy of a baby's cries falls within the range of frequencies to which humans are most sensitive.

The frequency of a tone influences discrimination as well as detection. You will recall from Chapter 2 that psychophysical techniques can be used to measure a difference threshold. A *difference threshold* is the smallest change in a stimulus that can produce a difference that is noticeable 50% of the time. Data on difference thresholds can be expressed in terms of Weber fractions, in which the difference threshold is divided by the frequency of the tone. Compared to the sensitivity of other senses, the Weber fraction is particularly remarkable in the intermediate frequency range. This is the range you are likely to hear in a concert, with basic frequencies between about 500 and 2000 Hz. We are so sensitive to changes in frequency in this range that the Weber fraction can be as small as 0.3% (Evans, 1982c). In other words, we need to change a tone's frequency by only 0.3% to notice a difference. We are less sensitive in judging very low and very high tones. However, Weber fractions for discriminating tones are consistently smaller than for discriminations involving taste (where Weber fractions are usually about 20%) or smell (where Weber fractions are rarely better than about 7%).

So far our discussion of frequency has included only pure tones. Most tones we hear in our everyday lives—including those produced by musical instruments and singers—are complex. *Complex tones* are tones that cannot be represented by one simple sine wave. For example, look at the complex tones illustrated in Figure 9.4, each of which represents the combination of several different pure tones. Notice that the square wave seen in Figure 9.4a is produced by a different combination of pure tones than the sawtooth wave seen in Figure 9.4b. Remember our discussion of Fourier analysis in Chapter 5? No matter how complex the tone, it can be analyzed

more frequently) than the one in Figure 9.3b and will probably sound higher in pitch.

What range of frequencies can humans hear? Young adults can typically hear tones that have frequencies as low as 20 Hz and as high as 20,000 Hz (Gelfand, 1981). Older adults, as we will see in Chapter 14, may have difficulty hearing tones as high as 20,000 Hz. Most of our auditory experience, however, involves only a small fraction of that 20- to 20,000-Hz range. For example, singers at a concert are unlikely to sing a note with a basic frequency below 75 Hz or above 1000 Hz.

Within the range of sounds we can hear, which frequencies do we hear best? Using the methodologies discussed in Chapter 2, we could compute *absolute thresholds* (the smallest amount of a stimulus that can be detected 50%

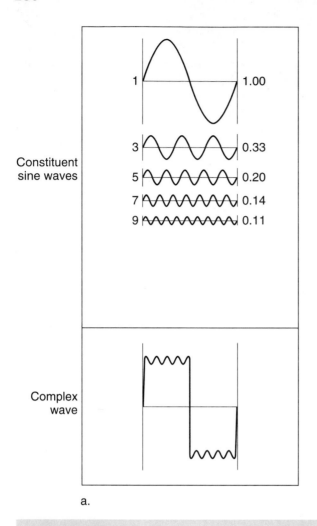

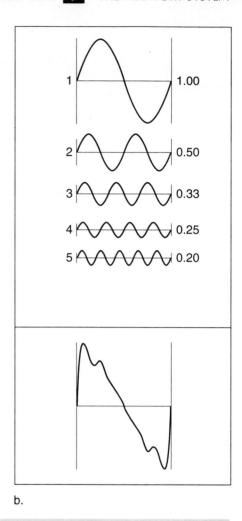

a.   b.

FIGURE 9.4   Two complex waves and their constituent pure sine waves. Both waves can be created by adding together several sine waves in particular phase relationships. For instance, the complex wave shown in part a is created by adding together a pure wave of a particular frequency (arbitrarily 1.0) with a wave having frequencies 3, 5, 7, and 9 times greater. Likewise, by Fourier analysis, such complex waves can be decomposed into their constituent pure sine waves. (Adapted from Gulick et al., 1989)

into component pure tones. We will consider these more complex auditory stimuli in Chapters 10 and 11.

Amplitude

Another aspect of sound waves is their peak *amplitude*—or the maximum pressure change from normal. In general, amplitude corresponds to the psychological experience of loudness. That is, a high-amplitude sound wave moves your eardrum more than a low-amplitude sound wave, and the sound seems louder. Thus, the sound wave in Figure 9.5a has a higher amplitude than the one in Figure 9.5b, and it will usually also sound louder.

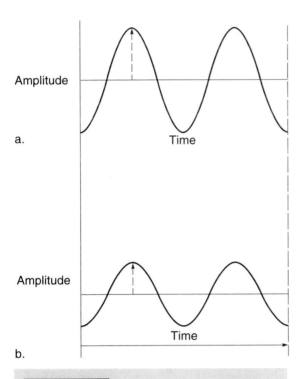

Amplitude

Time

a.

Amplitude

Time

b.

FIGURE 9.5 Two sound waves differing in amplitude. The two waves have identical frequencies, but the maximum and minimum amplitudes are greater in the wave in part a compared to the wave in part b.

$$\text{Number of decibels} = 20 \log \frac{P_1}{P_0}$$

According to this formula for decibels, we multiply 20 times the logarithm of the ratio of P_1 to P_0, where P_1 is the sound-pressure level of the stimulus we want to convert to decibels and P_0 is the reference level of 0.0002 dynes/cm^2. Thus, a sound-pressure level of 2000 dynes/cm^2 would become 140 dB. (Divide 2000 by 0.0002, then take the logarithm of that ratio, and multiply by 20.) At the other extreme, threshold pressure of 0.0002 dynes/cm^2 would translate into 0 dB. So, instead of dealing with numbers between 0.0002 and 2000, researchers can deal with values between 0 and 140.

Don't be confused by the logarithmic scale of decibels. For instance, don't think that an SPL of 140 dB is seven times greater than an SPL of 20 dB. In terms of the actual pressures (2000 and 0.002 dynes/cm^2), the higher pressure is a million times greater than the lower pressure! In fact, with every 6 additional dB of sound-pressure level, the sound pressure doubles. Table 9.1 shows some representative decibel levels for sounds that humans can hear. Notice that decibels are standardized so that 0 dB represents the weakest 1000-Hz tone you can hear. Values near 140 dB are painful and can cause permanent hearing loss.

Sound pressure can be measured in terms of a standard force (called a *dyne*) per square centimeter. A 1000-Hz tone can just barely be detected under ideal conditions when produced with about 0.0002 dynes/cm^2 of pressure. Human beings begin to feel pain if the amplitude is above 2000 dynes/cm^2. So the range of sound pressure—from detection to pain—is greater than about 10 million to 1. Because these numbers are a bit unwieldy for day-to-day use, researchers developed a logarithmic scale of sound pressures relative to the threshold pressure (0.0002 dynes/cm^2). This scale is *sound pressure level (SPL),* measured in units called decibels.

A *decibel (dB)* of SPL is computed by means of the following equation:

TABLE 9.1

Some Typical Amplitudes of Various Noises, Measured by Decibel Scale

Level	dB	Example
	160	Loudest rock band on record
Intolerable	140	Jet airplane taking off
	120	Very loud thunder
Very noisy	100	Heavy automobile traffic
Loud	80	Loud music from radio
Moderate	60	Average conversation
Faint	40	Quiet neighborhood
	20	Soft whisper
Very faint	0	Softest detectable noise

We discussed our impressive ability to discriminate differences in frequency. Humans are also spectacular in their ability to discriminate differences in amplitude. The human auditory system is so remarkable that it can discriminate two complex sounds, each consisting of 21 tones of identical frequencies, in which a single tone in one of the complex sounds is somewhat greater in amplitude. Despite the subtlety of the difference between the two sounds, observers can tell that they are not identical (Green, 1983; Green et al., 1983).

Phase Angle

We can also characterize the sound wave in terms of the position of the pressure change as it moves through one complete cycle. As seen in Figure 9.2, *phase angle* indicates the angle in degrees at each phase, or position, of the cycle. If you think of sounds moving through air, 0° represents normal air pressure just before the air pressure begins to increase. Normal air pressure is a function of altitude, so it would be lower for higher altitudes, and vice versa. The wave returns to normal pressure at 180°, on its way to less-than-normal pressures. Maximum pressure occurs at 90°, and minimum pressure occurs at 270°.

As we will see in Chapter 10, phase angle is particularly useful in comparing two different sound waves, or the same sound wave at two different times. When you hook up your stereo system, your instructions probably cautioned you to be sure that the speaker wires were hooked up identically to both speakers. If you did not do so, the speakers would be out of phase. Thus, when one speaker was pushing out (0° through 90°), the other speaker would be going in (180° through 270°). As a result, the sound coming from your speakers would not be as rich (or as loud) as it would be if the speakers were in phase (with both speakers going out and in at the same time). In fact, if two waves are identical in frequency and amplitude but perfectly out of phase, they would cancel each other out—producing silence. This principle has been useful in the development of headphones that reduce the ampli-

tude of unwanted low-frequency sounds (Klasco & Baum, 1994). Car manufacturers have already developed similar anti-noise systems that will reduce the noise inside cars without the use of headphones.

SECTION SUMMARY

The Auditory Stimulus

1. Sound waves can be described in terms of their frequency and their amplitude. Frequency (measured in Hz) is the number of cycles that a sound wave can complete in 1 second; frequency is an important determinant of pitch. Humans hear pure tones with frequencies between 20 and 20,000 Hz.

2. We detect the presence of tones best in the 2000–5000-Hz range. We can discriminate between two very similar tones in the 500–2000-Hz range, where the Weber fraction can be as small as 0.3%.

3. Pure tones are represented by sine waves. Although pure tones are used frequently in auditory research, complex tones are more common and represent the combination of a number of different pure tones.

4. Amplitude is the maximum pressure created by sound waves, often measured in decibels; amplitude is an important determinant of loudness.

5. The phase angle of a sound wave is measured in degrees; it indicates the position of a wave in its cycle.

THE AUDITORY SYSTEM

Now that we have briefly reviewed the physical stimuli important to audition, we need to look at the transduction process. Once these sound-pressure changes have been transmitted to a human observer, changes must occur in the auditory system to transform (or *transduce*) the physical energy into a kind of energy that can be processed by neurons. What happens to sound waves when they reach the ear, and how do the various parts of the ear contribute to the transformation of sound waves into neural information?

The ear has three anatomical regions. Fortunately, their names are refreshingly straightforward: the outer ear, the middle ear, and the inner ear. All three parts develop in the human embryo out of the surface epithelium, the covering that will later become the skin (Nathan, 1982). We will see that the receptors in the inner ear resemble the receptors in the skin because they detect pressure and movement. As stressed in Theme 1 of this textbook, the perceptual systems share important similarities.

Outer Ear

The most obvious part of the outer ear is what people ordinarily refer to as "the ear." The technical name for this flap of external tissue is the *pinna*. The pinnae are important because they slightly increase the sound amplitude (Scharf & Buus, 1986). They also help somewhat in determining the direction from which a sound is coming, as we will discuss later in the chapter. However, other animals—such as dogs, horses, owls, and bats—have more useful pinnae (Stebbins, 1983; Stokes, 1985). Their pinnae can be moved around to help localize sounds.

Figure 9.6 shows other structures in the outer ear. Notice the tube, called the *external auditory canal*, that runs inward from the pinna. The external auditory canal is about 0.3 inch in diameter and 1 inch long. This structure helps keep insects, small objects, and dirt away from the sensitive eardrum (Scharf & Buus, 1986). Furthermore, this canal behaves somewhat like a resonant tube, such as an organ pipe, and can amplify some frequencies impressively. The maximum amplification is about 10 dB for frequencies of about 3000 Hz (Gulick et al., 1989). (Use

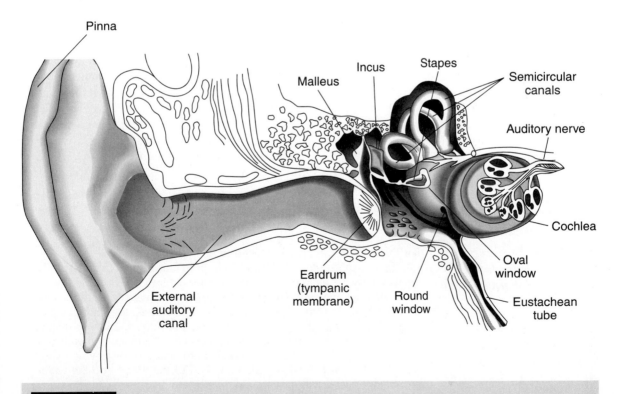

FIGURE 9.6 Anatomy of the ear, showing the major parts of the outer, middle, and inner ear.

the formula for decibels to see for yourself that a 10-dB increase means that the sound-pressure amplitude is roughly tripled.) If you are able to hear the piccolo in a symphony orchestra, partial credit goes to your external auditory canals!

Finally, we come to the *eardrum,* or *tympanic membrane,* the thin piece of membrane that vibrates in response to sound waves. Puncturing the eardrum results in a hearing deficit. Depending on the size and location of the puncture, the deficit can be quite extreme (Gulick et al., 1989). For this reason, you might have been advised never to stick anything smaller than your elbow in your ear. Heed the advice, because it is well founded. The eardrum is the most important structure in the outer ear and marks the boundary between the outer and middle ear.

Middle Ear

The middle ear is the area on the inner side of the eardrum, occupying a volume of only about 2 cm^3 (0.1 cubic inch). The middle ear contains three bones known as the *ossicles,* the smallest bones in the human body. They are individually called the *malleus* (or hammer), the *incus* (or anvil), and the *stapes* (or stirrup), all referring rather poetically to their shapes.

The ossicles are not merely decorative structures but are critical in solving a basic prob-

lem faced by the auditory system. Sound waves travel through the air until they reach the middle ear. Air does not offer much opposition to the flow of sound waves. Within the inner ear, however, sound waves must travel through liquid, a medium that opposes the movement of sound waves. This resistance to the passage of sound waves is known as *impedance* (Yost & Nielsen, 1985). You can demonstrate the differences in impedance for air and water by trying Demonstration 9.3. When the impedances for two media differ, *impedance mismatch* results, and sound waves cannot be readily transmitted from one medium to another. When the sound in air reaches a liquid, the sound-pressure loss is about 30 dB, or about 99.9% of the power. Most of the sound energy is simply reflected back into the air (Warren, 1982).

Two processes help solve the impedance mismatch problem by increasing the efficiency with which sound is transmitted to the inner ear. The first, and more important, process occurs because the tympanic membrane is much larger than the oval window (Pickles, 1988). You can see this relationship in Figure 9.6. In humans the ratio of the effective size of the tympanic membrane to the size of the base of the stapes may be as high as 17 to 1 (Luce, 1993). This difference in area helps minimize the impedance mismatch because moving the larger area (the tympanic membrane) will move the smaller area (the oval

---

Demonstration 9.3

Difference in Impedance for Air and Water

For this demonstration you'll need to be in a swimming pool (or a less satisfactory substitute, a bathtub). First, note that sounds that are easily heard with your head above water are almost impossible to hear with your head below water. The greater impedance of water causes most of the energy in the sound waves to be reflected. Notice, too, that you can overcome the impedance mismatch if you can make the waves directly in the water. To try this, take a long object (e.g., a piece of metal) and bang on it out of the water. It will be hard to hear the sound when your head is below water. Next, place one end of the metal into the water and bang on it. It will now be much easier to hear when your head is under water.

window) more efficiently. In the second process, the three ossicles act like a lever, which offers a small but important mechanical advantage.

When these two factors are combined, the magnitude of the sound waves is increased by a factor of almost 30 dB (Luce, 1993). Thus, much of the loss due to the impedance mismatch is compensated for by the magnification in the middle ear. Still, much of the energy falling on the eardrum is lost in the middle ear due to friction and other factors (Rosowski et al., 1986). However, the middle ear does provide for a much more efficient transfer of sound energy from the external world than would an auditory system in which the sound waves fell directly on the oval window of the inner ear. As stressed in Theme 3 of this book (see page 10), our perceptual systems are impressive structures that are well-suited to accomplish perceptual tasks.

Another example of the elegance of our perceptual systems comes from the middle-ear muscles. The two smallest skeletal muscles in the body are actually attached to the ossicles. The ossicles serve to amplify sounds, but what happens when a very loud sound falls on our ears? If the sound were further amplified by the ossicles, damage might be done to the delicate structures of the inner ear (or to the ossicles themselves). The middle-ear muscles in humans contract in a reflexive fashion shortly after either ear is exposed to sounds about 80 dB over threshold (Luce, 1993). The muscles also contract reflexively just before humans and other animals are about to utter a sound (speaking, whispering, crying, singing, etc.). This occurs, presumably, to "protect the inner ear from fatigue, interference and potential injury caused by one's own loud utterances, which can result in high sound levels in one's head" (Borg & Counter, 1989, p. 74). Most of the effectiveness of these contractions comes from the muscle attached to the stapes; the contraction displaces the stapes slightly. Depending on the amount of the displacement of the stapes, low-frequency sounds can be reduced between 10 and 30 dB, with lesser attenuation for high-frequency sounds (Pang & Peake, 1986).

Each middle ear also contains a *eustachian tube,* which connects the middle ear to the throat. The eustachian tubes help equalize the air pressure in the auditory system. When you swallow, for instance, the eustachian tubes open up and allow air to flow into or out of the middle ear. You've probably heard your ears "pop" when you change altitudes in an airplane or in an elevator in a tall building. The tiny explosion represents the sudden flow of air during a dramatic change in pressure.

Inner Ear

The hardest bone in the human body is found at each side of the head, and within this bone is found a cavity containing the two structures that make up the inner ear. You learned that the pupil in the eye does not really exist as a separate structure, but is simply the area where the iris is retracted. Similarly, the inner ear does not really exist as a freestanding structure, but is just the area where the bone is absent (Gulick et al., 1989). As seen in Figure 9.6, the semicircular canals and the cochlea make up the inner ear. The inner ear "is an evolutionary triumph of miniaturization, a three-dimensional inertial-guidance system and an acoustical amplifier and frequency analyser compacted into the volume of a child's marble" (Hudspeth, 1989, p. 397). We will wait until Chapter 12 to discuss the semicircular canals, because they deal with our sense of orientation (inertial-guidance) and not with audition. The fluid-filled *cochlea,* which contains receptors for auditory stimuli, is crucial for audition. Cochlea means "snail" in Latin, appropriately describing its coiled shape. Because an understanding of the cochlea is crucial to understanding audition, we will now discuss it in some detail.

The stapes is attached directly to the *oval window,* a membrane that covers an opening in the cochlea. When the stapes vibrates, the oval window vibrates, creating pressure changes in the liquid inside the cochlea. Figure 9.7 shows a schematic diagram of the cochlea, including the relationship between the stapes and the oval

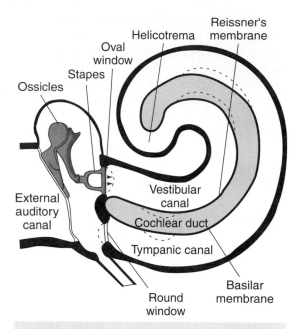

FIGURE 9.7 Schematic depiction of the inner ear, with the cochlea partially uncoiled. The stapes pushes on the oval window (shown pushed in as a dashed line), displacing the fluid of the vestibular canal. The fluid passes through the helicotrema and into the tympanic canal, causing the round window to move (dashed line) in opposition to the movement of the stapes. The cochlear duct is suspended between the two canals, separated from the vestibular canal by Reissner's membrane and from the tympanic canal by the basilar membrane. The movement of the stapes causes the traveling wave to move along the basilar membrane. The dashed lines along the basilar membrane and Reissner's membrane illustrate the motion.

cochlea were stretched out, whereas Figure 9.8 clarifies the fact that the cochlea is really wrapped around and around itself, like the shell of the snail for which it is named.

The canal into which the stapes pushes is called the *vestibular canal*. At the far end of the vestibular canal is a tiny opening called the *helicotrema*. Here the fluid can flow through to the second canal, the *tympanic canal*. Notice that the tympanic canal has its own membrane-covered

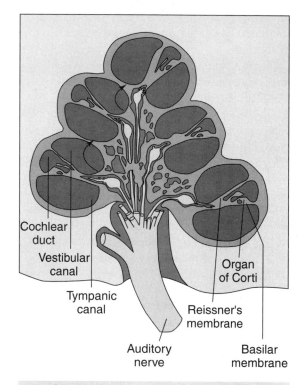

FIGURE 9.8 Cross section of the cochlea. See how the canals wrap around the cochlea. Pay particular attention to the basilar membrane and the organ of Corti as they wind through the cochlea. Note the auditory nerve fibers, and how they reach into the hair cells of the organ of Corti. The actual orientation of the cochlea in the upright head is quite different from that displayed here (see Figure 9.6).

window. If the cochlea were uncoiled, it would be about 1.4 inches long.

Figure 9.7 also shows that the cochlea has three canals running through its entire length. To keep you from being misled by the schematic nature of Figure 9.7, Figure 9.8 shows a cross section of the cochlea. Figure 9.7, then, shows the relationships among the three canals as if the

Stapes end of
basilar membrane ⟶ Helicotrema end of
basilar membrane

Direction of movement

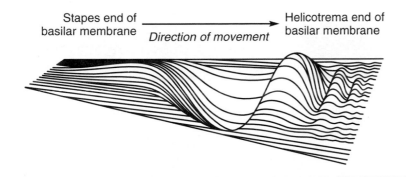

FIGURE 9.9 Traveling wave moving through the basilar membrane. Notice that the end of the basilar membrane nearest the stapes is narrower than the end near the helicotrema. Also notice how the wave dies down rapidly after peaking.

opening, the ***round window.*** The round window must move in opposition to the oval window, because the fluid within the vestibular and tympanic canals (perilymph) is difficult to compress (Gulick et al., 1989). Were it not for the round window, the stapes would have a difficult time pushing into the oval window.

The ***cochlear duct*** is the smallest of the three canals in the cochlea and the one that houses the auditory receptors. The cochlear duct is separated from the vestibular canal by ***Reissner's membrane,*** and from the tympanic canal by the ***basilar membrane*** and the bony shelves to which the basilar membrane is attached. Not only is the cochlear duct separate from the other two canals, but it also contains a completely different type of fluid, called endolymph.

When the stapes causes the oval window to vibrate, the vibration is transmitted to the basilar membrane, on which the auditory receptors rest. This vibration in turn stimulates the receptors. The basilar membrane is relatively narrow and stiff at its base (near the stapes). As it winds through the cochlea it becomes wider (as the bony shelf to which it is attached gets narrower) and also more flexible. The pattern of vibration within the basilar membrane is referred to as a ***traveling wave.*** Have you ever set out with your garden hose to water a distant flower bed and found that the hose is caught on a rock or curb? If, instead of walking back to the obstruction, you've shaken the end of the hose up and down to free it, you are familiar with a traveling wave. As you yank on the hose, a wave travels along the length of the hose, with the wave getting much smaller as it nears the faucet. Figure 9.9 provides a schematic representation of a traveling wave moving along the basilar membrane.

Now let's enter the cochlear duct, which holds several structures crucial to hearing. Figure 9.10 shows an enlargement of the triangular-shaped cochlear duct and the organ of Corti. The ***organ of Corti*** contains the receptors that transduce the pressure energy from a sound wave into the kind of electrical and chemical energy that can be carried through the higher pathways in the auditory system.

The basilar membrane forms the base of the organ of Corti, and the ***tectorial membrane*** rests on top of the organ of Corti. (It may help to remember that *b*asilar is the *b*ottom and *t*ectorial is the *t*op.) The organ of Corti also includes the ***hair cells,*** the actual receptors for hearing. The basilar membrane in the inner ear therefore resembles skin, as mentioned earlier in the chapter, because hairs protrude from its surface.

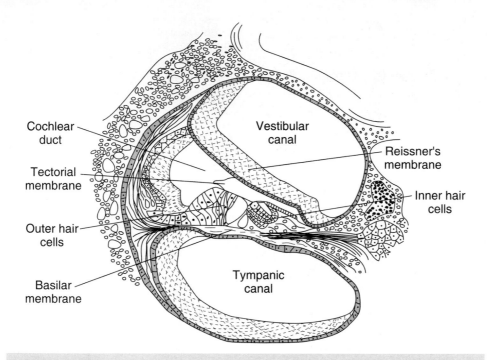

FIGURE 9.10 Detailed cross section of a portion of the cochlea. To orient yourself properly, compare this figure to Figure 9.8. Be sure to note the position of the inner and outer hair cells, the basilar membrane, and the tectorial membrane. (Adapted from Bloom & Fawcett, 1975)

IN-DEPTH   **Inner and Outer Hair Cells**

Just as the retina contains two kinds of vision receptors, the cochlea contains two kinds of hair cells. You'll be pleased to learn that their names are straightforward: inner hair cells and outer hair cells. Figure 9.11 shows an electron micrograph of these structures after the tectorial membrane has been removed. The ***inner hair cells*** are arranged in a single row along the inner side of the organ of Corti, and they are relatively scarce (about 3,500). Three or four rows of ***outer hair cells*** are located on the outer side of the organ of Corti, and they are relatively abundant (about 12,000).

HAIR-CELL STRUCTURE AND TRANSDUCTION

The hairs you see extending from the hair cells in Figure 9.11 are called ***stereocilia.*** In a typical

inner hair cell, about 40 stereocilia are formed in the shape of a shallow U. In a typical outer hair cell, about 150 stereocilia are formed in the shape of a V or a W. As you can see in Figure 9.12, each hair cell contains several rows of stereocilia. The inner-hair-cell stereocilia are free-floating, but the longer stereocilia of the outer hair cells are embedded in the tectorial membrane (Pickles, 1988). As the basilar membrane vibrates, the tectorial membrane stimulates the embedded outer hair cells by pushing back and forth on them in a shearing motion.

The shorter stereocilia of the outer hair cells are not embedded in the tectorial membrane, but the stereocilia are linked to one another by fine strands (tip links and sideways links). To appreciate how thin these connecting strands are, keep in mind that the stereocilia themselves are only about 0.05 micrometers in width (0.00000005 meters).

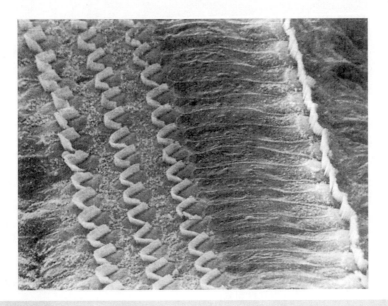

FIGURE 9.11 A picture of the inner and outer hair cells, with the tectorial membrane pulled back. The stereocilia of the inner hair cells (single row on the right) and the outer hair cells (three rows on the left) are visible, as is the basilar membrane. (Photo courtesy of Dr. David Lim)

In Chapter 3, you learned that the photoreceptors produce graded potentials that ultimately produce action potentials in the bipolar cells and connected neurons. Similarly, the hair cells produce graded potentials that cause action potentials (firing) in bipolar cells of the auditory nerve. The **auditory nerve** is the bundle of nerve fibers that carries information from the inner ear to higher centers of the auditory system. What, exactly, is the transduction process? What changes the mechanical wave information of the basilar membrane into changes in hair-cell potential? Although the answer to that question is still an open one, some research has offered a promising theory.

Everyone agrees that the transduction takes place in the hair cells as a result of stimulation of the stereocilia. As you might imagine, from the small displacement of the eardrum sufficient to give rise to the perception of sound, a very small movement of the stereocilia is sufficient to produce a change in the potential of the hair cells.

According to Hudspeth, a displacement of 0.3 nm ($\frac{3}{10}$ of a billionth of a meter) is sufficient to give rise to the perception of sound—the proportional equivalent to the top of the Eiffel Tower moving a thumb's breadth (Gutin, 1993)!

The resting potential for inner and outer hair cells is –45 mV and –70 mV, respectively. When the stereocilia are displaced toward the inner part of the cochlea, the hair cells become hyperpolarized (more negative than their resting potentials). When the stereocilia are displaced toward the outer part of the cochlea, the hair cells become depolarized (less negative than their resting potentials). Hyperpolarization is thought to inhibit the firing of the bipolar cells, and depolarization is thought to excite the bipolar cells.

Hair cells in the inner ear respond to stimuli that change so rapidly that they would not be detectable if they were visual stimuli falling on the retina. How can the hair cells respond so rapidly? The answer lies in the tip links of the short- and middle-length stereocilia, seen in Figure

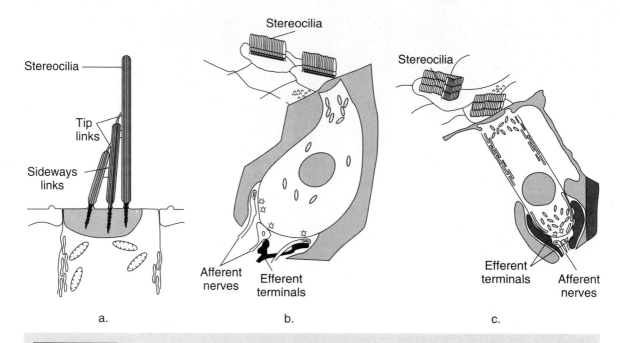

FIGURE 9.12 Detailed schematics for hair cells. Part a shows a cross section of a generalized hair cell, with the tip links and sideways links connecting the stereocilia. Part b shows an inner hair cell; part c shows an outer hair cell. (Adapted from Pickles, 1988)

9.12. The tip links serve as mechanical devices that are responsible for the rapid response of the hair cells to basilar membrane displacement (Hudspeth, 1989; Pickles, 1993a, 1993b). When the stereocilia are displaced toward the outer part of the cochlea, the tip links pull on the stereocilia. This pulling allows a greater number of positive ions from the endolymph into the hair cell, depolarizing it. When the stereocilia are displaced toward the inner part of the cochlea, pressure would be removed from the tip links. As a result, the flow of positive ions into the hair cell is closed off, and the hair cell becomes hyperpolarized (Dallos, 1992; Pickles, 1992).

INNERVATION OF HAIR CELLS

The ascending nerve fibers that carry information from the inner ear to the higher-level brain structures are referred to as **afferent fibers** (from the Latin "to bring toward"). The auditory nerve con-

tains about 32,000 of these afferent fibers, but the inner hair cells and the outer hair cells do not share the auditory nerve fibers equally. As you may recall from the discussion of the visual receptors, the retina has more rods than cones. Thus, many rods have to "share" a ganglion cell, whereas relatively few cones are connected to each ganglion cell. Similarly, in the auditory system, the relatively scarce inner hair cells have the luxury of "owning" about 90–95% of the afferent fibers (Helfert et al., 1991; Luce, 1993; Webster, 1991). In contrast, the relatively abundant outer hair cells must share the remaining 5–10% of the afferent fibers. In the organ of Corti, as in life itself, resources are distributed unequally.

In addition to the afferent fibers, the inner ear also has some efferent fibers (from the Latin "to carry away"). **Efferent fibers** carry information downward from higher-level brain structures to lower-level brain structures involved in audition, as well as to the hair cells (Spangler & Warr,

1991; Webster, 1991). As we will see shortly, these efferent fibers allow neural impulses to manipulate inner-ear functioning, which may improve the encoding of frequency information in the inner ear. Relatively few efferent fibers are found in the inner ear, and their connections to the outer hair cells are thought to be crucial (Pickles, 1988).

Recording the electrical activity of the hair cells and the impact they have on the auditory nerve is a difficult task. Gulick and his coauthors (1989) compare the process to setting up a microphone on a crowded street corner and recording all the auditory activity on a paper record. The squiggles would be closer together when high-frequency sounds were present and farther apart when low-frequency sounds were present. The heights of the squiggles would reflect the amplitude of the sounds. Of course, on a busy street corner, all these sounds often happen simultaneously. Now suppose you gave that paper record to someone—even an expert in audition—and asked him or her to tell you exactly what the waves represent. Even telling you that the waves represent a busy street corner would be an accomplishment. Picking out the pounding jackhammer, the clicking heels, the rumbling bus, and the honking horns on the paper record would be virtually impossible. If this mental image helps you to understand the difficulty of probing the electrical activity within the inner ear, then you'll be sympathetic with the researchers who work to understand cochlear transduction. Many different electrical potentials exist in the cochlea, and we will focus on two related to the outer hair cells.

COCHLEAR MICROPHONIC

In 1930, Wever and Bray were recording from the auditory nerve and playing the output through an amplifier and into a speaker. They found that whatever material they played into the ear was faithfully reproduced in their speaker (Wever & Bray, 1930). In other words, if you sang the national anthem into the ear of the auditory nerve from which they were recording, you heard the national anthem through the speaker! The visual equivalent would be passing the output from a microelectrode imbedded in the optic nerve into

a television set and seeing on the television screen whatever the eye was looking at.

It turns out that the sounds Wever and Bray were hearing were not summated action potentials from the auditory nerve, as they initially thought. Instead they were actually hearing graded potentials primarily produced by the outer hair cells. These graded potentials, which mimic the waveform falling on the ear, are referred to as the *cochlear microphonic.* The cochlear microphonic replicates not only the frequency characteristics of the wave falling on the ear but also its amplitude over a wide range of pressure.

How did researchers learn that the outer hair cells were the primary source of the cochlear microphonic? They could rule out auditory-nerve activity because the cochlear microphonic is unaffected by degeneration of the auditory nerve (Gulick et al., 1989). In a clever experiment, Dallos found that the cochlear microphonic was greatly reduced when outer hair cells were damaged by a drug that has no effect on inner hair cells (Pickles, 1988).

Although researchers have been able to trace the cochlear microphonic to the outer hair cells, no one really knows its function. A process as precise as this must play some role in human audition. As we have noted throughout this textbook, most of the mysteries of human perceptual systems are far from being resolved. Perhaps one of you reading this book will go on to provide us with a better understanding of the cochlear microphonic.

OTOACOUSTIC EMISSIONS

As surprised as Wever and Bray were to uncover the cochlear microphonic, researchers were also surprised and delighted by Kemp's finding that the ear actually emits sounds in response to stimulation (Kemp, 1978). Kemp presented a click to the ear while a miniature microphone was inserted into the external auditory canal. After a short delay (10 msec), a much weaker echo was recorded. These echoes are known as *evoked acoustic emissions* or *Kemp echoes.* The search for the source of these evoked acoustic emissions would have been sufficient to occupy auditory researchers for a while. However, shortly after Kemp reported his findings, researchers began reporting that they could record sounds in the external auditory canal *without* presenting a stimulus (Kemp, 1979; Wier et al., 1984; Zurek, 1981, 1985)! Emissions when no click or tone is presented are called **spontaneous acoustic emissions** and, together with Kemp echoes, are referred to as **otoacoustic emissions** (the prefix *oto-* means "related to the ear"). In some rare cases, these spontaneous emissions are loud enough that—without amplification—they can be heard *outside* a person's ear.

All otoacoustic emissions seem to share similarities, probably because of their common origin (Zwicker & Schloth, 1984). For instance, spontaneous otoacoustic emissions occur in about 40% of people with normal hearing. They are typically around 1000 to 2000 Hz in frequency and are low in amplitude (less than 20 dB SPL). Surprisingly, the people themselves are totally unaware of the emissions (Wier et al., 1984; Zurek, 1981). So the odds are pretty good that at this very moment your ears are emitting a soft sound of which you are totally unaware!

Why might our ears produce these otoacoustic emissions? We will discuss frequency encoding and pitch perception in greater detail in Chapter 10. For now, though, you should realize that human beings can make very fine discriminations among stimuli varying in frequency. (Remember our discussion of the Weber fraction for frequency discrimination at the beginning of this chapter?) For a number of reasons, auditory researchers and theorists have been puzzled by our frequency-discrimination ability, given the nature of the inner ear. The information produced by basilar membrane motion cannot account for the fine discriminations among frequencies that humans can make. All sorts of mechanisms were proposed, including a theory (quickly dismissed by others) that active fibers in the hair cells produced positive feedback (Gold, 1948, 1989; Gold & Pumphrey, 1948). Along with the prediction of active positive feedback in this theory was the notion that the feedback would not always be stable, and that the instabilities would produce emissions!

About 40 years after that original theory was proposed and dismissed, auditory researchers are embracing the notion that our superb frequency-discrimination abilities are due, in part, to activity produced by the efferent fiber innervation of the outer hair cells. Although all the details remain to be determined, some pieces of the puzzle are emerging. For instance, although spontaneous otoacoustic emissions are found in some animals, they are absent in a group of chinchillas raised in an environment protected from extreme sounds (Zurek, 1985). This finding suggests that spontaneous otoacoustic emissions are the result of instability in the positive feedback produced by some minor damage to the hair cells of the inner ear. People (or chinchillas) who have not been exposed to stimuli that harm the hair cells would not produce these emissions because their active filter had not become destabilized.

Theorists currently think that the mechanism for the positive feedback involves the outer hair cells (Pickles, 1988). As we will discuss in the next section, researchers have found that outer hair cells are capable of elongation (Ashmore, 1987; Brownell et al., 1985). Two questions remain. First, what effect might this change in the outer hair cells have on the tectorial membrane? Second, how do these outer hair cell changes affect the inner hair cells (Mountain & Cody, 1989; Teas, 1989)?

OUTER HAIR CELL MOTILITY

Research on the role of the outer hair cells is currently quite active and exciting. The outer hair cells are capable of graded potential changes, just like the inner hair cells. However, unlike the inner hair cells, they have relatively few afferent connections. The presence of efferent connections to the outer hair cells indicates that the information coming from the brain to the outer hair cells is extremely important. What could the brain be "telling" the outer hair cells to do?

One clue to the role of the outer hair cells is their **motility**—the independent elongation and contraction of the cells (Dallos, 1992; Pickles, 1993a). The inner hair cells tend to move passively along with the basilar membrane. In contrast, the outer hair cells seem to bounce "up and down like manic kids on a trampoline" (Gutin, 1993, p. 52). Such motility appears to be due to the presence of musclelike actin filaments in the walls of the outer hair cells (Savage & Slepecky, 1993). This outer-hair-cell motility may well serve to amplify a traveling wave (Pickles, 1993a; J. P. Wilson, 1992). The feedback generated by the outer hair cells appears to selectively enhance the inner hair cell responses (Russell & Kössl, 1992).

In summary, current research on the hair cells suggests that the inner hair cells are responsible for the transmission of auditory information through the afferent fibers of the auditory nerve. The inner hair cells presumably undergo graded potential changes (depolarizing or hyperpolarizing) as a result of displacement of their stereocilia in one direction or the other. The outer hair cells are able to move independently, and thereby influence the movement of the basilar membrane—presumably due to efferent input. Outer-hair-cell motility appears to enhance our ability to make fine frequency discriminations. ◆

Taken as a whole, the auditory system includes an appropriate distribution of bony structures and elastic structures to guarantee that the sound pressure (which the middle ear works so hard to maintain) is ultimately transmitted to the auditory transducers and then to the auditory nerve. Figure 9.13 illustrates the process from the sound wave through the auditory nerve firing. At this point in your reading, jargon shock may have reached an advanced state. Keep in mind, however, that each of these tiny structures has an important function. In Chapter 10 we will explore the ways in which these structures work together to enable us to hear. For now, however, we will trace the path of the auditory information into the auditory cortex.

Higher Levels of Auditory Processing

Just as the optic nerve carries information from the retina to the cortex, the afferent fibers in the auditory nerve carry information from the cochlea to the cortex. Researchers interested in auditory nerve function also use the microelectrode recording techniques we discussed in Chapter 3. Unlike the circular receptive fields found in the optic nerve, neurons in the auditory nerve re-

spond best to particular frequencies of sound played into the ear.

Researchers can record the activity of an individual fiber in the auditory nerve to determine the frequency to which the fiber is most sensitive. You may recall that we discussed single-cell recording from a simple cell in the visual cortex to determine an orientation tuning curve, a graph showing the relationship between the orientation of a line and the cell's response rate. (A representative orientation tuning curve is seen in Figure 3.19, on page 78.) Similarly, a *frequency tuning curve* is a graph showing the relationship between the frequency of an auditory stimulus and an auditory nerve fiber's response rate. This information can be graphed in several ways. Figure 9.14 shows a typical frequency tuning curve, with stimulus frequency along the x-axis and the intensity of sound (in dB) required to produce neural firing along the y-axis. As you can see, lower decibel values are associated with greater sensitivity. The nerve fiber in this diagram is particularly sensitive (has the lowest threshold) to a stimulus around 1000 Hz, a frequency often found in speech. Other auditory nerve fibers have frequency tuning curves with sensitivities in other frequency ranges. Now let's trace the pathway of auditory stimuli, from the inner ear to the auditory cortex, and then we'll see how stimuli are processed within the auditory cortex.

The Pathway from the Inner Ear to the Auditory Cortex

Figure 9.15 provides a simplified illustration of the afferent auditory pathway. Keep in mind that the actual processing of auditory information is much more complex, with several efferent connections among the structures illustrated in Figure 9.15 (Webster, 1991). These descending connections provide feedback loops that influence the processing of auditory information (Spangler & Warr, 1991).

After leaving the inner ear, the auditory nerve travels to the *cochlear nucleus,* which is at the bottom of the back part of the brain. In the cochlear nucleus, the auditory nerve cells transmit their information to new cells (Brugge,

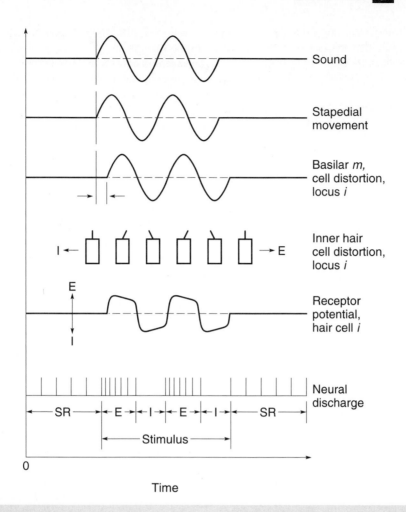

Time

FIGURE 9.13 A summary of the auditory transduction process. Moving from left to right in the figure indicates the passage of time. Moving from top to bottom indicates the processes involved. At the top of the figure, the changes in the physical stimulus are shown. The sound-pressure changes produce movement in the stapes, which produces movement in the basilar membrane. The basilar membrane motion produces movement of the stereocilia, producing a graded potential response in the hair cells. Depolarization of the hair cells causes increased firing in the connected neurons (E), and hyperpolarization of the hair cells causes decreased firing in the connected neurons (I), relative to the standard rate of firing (SR). (Adapted from Gulick et al., 1989)

1992). Because inhibitory connections have not been found within the auditory nerve, the cochlear nucleus provides the first opportunity for inhibitory connections (Sachs & Blackburn, 1991). The lateral inhibition found in the cochlear nucleus probably serves to enhance frequency resolution of pure tones (Pickles, 1988).

You may recall that the visual system has a complex mechanism for ensuring that the information from each eye is distributed to both sides

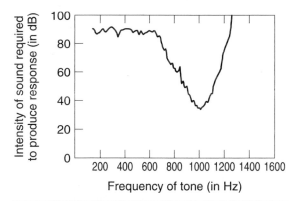

FIGURE 9.14 A typical frequency tuning curve. The neuron from which this curve was obtained is tuned to a frequency of 1000 Hz, since that is the frequency at which the smallest sound pressure is required to produce firing. Note the characteristic sharp rise to the right of the curve (for frequencies higher than the tuned frequency).

of the brain. Similarly, in the auditory system, output from each of the two cochlear nuclei goes to the ***superior olivary nucleus*** on the same side of the brain as that cochlear nucleus, as well as to the superior olivary nucleus on the opposite side of the brain. Because the auditory nerve and the cochlear nucleus on either side of the head only receive input from the cochlea on that side of the head, the auditory information is ***monaural*** (*mono* means "one"). Beyond the cochlear nuclei, however, the auditory information is ***binaural*** (*bi* means "two") because at the superior olivary nucleus and beyond, input from both ears is present. The binaural auditory information at the superior olivary nucleus and beyond allows a comparison of the information from the two ears (Webster, 1991). We will discuss the significance of this comparison in Chapter 10 when we focus on how we determine the direction from which a sound is coming.

Each superior olivary nucleus sends its information to an ***inferior colliculus***, which is just below (or inferior to) the superior colliculus discussed in the anatomy of the visual system. The inferior colliculus is a major way station in the auditory pathway. Virtually all of the afferent and efferent auditory fibers synapse in the inferior colliculus (Oliver & Huerta, 1991).

Most of the cells in the inferior colliculus are sensitive to binaural information, which means that the inferior colliculus plays a major role in processing auditory spatial information (Caird, 1991). Auditory information is also sent to the superior colliculus, allowing integration of auditory and visual spatial information (Irvine, 1992; King et al., 1988; Stein & Meredith, 1993).

The inferior colliculus also illustrates the geographical arrangement of auditory information. Remember that parts of the visual system demonstrate a retinotopic organization. That is, information from adjacent areas of the retina are represented in adjacent areas of the lateral geniculate nucleus and the visual cortex. Similarly, the auditory system is arranged in terms of frequency information. This arrangement is referred to as a ***tonotopic*** organization, meaning that neurons sensitive to similar frequencies are found near one another in the inferior colliculus (Pickles, 1988). As we will discuss further in Chapter 10, higher frequencies cause the greatest displacement along the basilar membrane near the stapes. Lower frequencies cause the greatest displacement along the basilar membrane near the helicotrema. Thus, the correspondence operates as if a map of the basilar membrane were laid out on the inferior colliculus. This similarity between the auditory and visual systems is another illustration of Theme 1 of this text (see pages 9–10).

From the inferior colliculus, information passes on to the ***medial geniculate nucleus*** of the thalamus, a structure near the lateral geniculate nucleus of the visual system. Incidentally, we should mention that the frequency tuning curves discussed earlier are not unique to the auditory nerve. They have also been found in the cochlear nuclei, the superior olivary nuclei, the inferior colliculi, and the medial geniculate nuclei (Moore, 1982). In other words, at all these points between the cochlea and the cortex, each nerve fiber is particularly sensitive to a fairly nar-

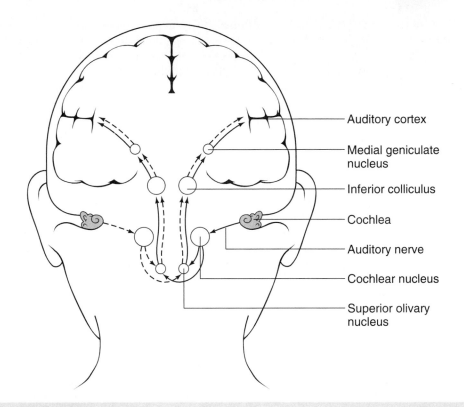

Auditory cortex

Medial geniculate nucleus

Inferior colliculus

Cochlea

Auditory nerve

Cochlear nucleus

Superior olivary nucleus

FIGURE 9.15   Schematic representation of the pathway from the ear to the brain. Only structures on the right side of the head have been labeled; notice corresponding structures on the left side of the head. Notice also that input from both ears is present from the superior olivary nucleus onward.

row frequency range. However, some of the cells within the medial geniculate nucleus are not as sharply tuned to frequency as cells in other parts of the auditory pathway (Clarey et al., 1992).

Processing in the Auditory Cortex

Information from the medial geniculate nucleus next travels to the *primary auditory cortex,* which is in a deep groove on the temporal lobe of the cortex (at the side of the brain). Much of the early research on the human primary auditory cortex was invasive, typically conducted in the process of brain surgery. However, recent technological developments, such as positron emission tomography, allow researchers to study the

functioning of the auditory cortex in people who are awake (Clarey et al., 1992). These new techniques are important because the anesthesia used in surgery affected the functioning of cells in the auditory cortex.

We have pointed out several similarities between auditory processing and visual processing, similarities that provide additional evidence for Theme 1 of this book. The superior colliculus contains both a visual and an auditory spatial map, which are closely interrelated (Oliver & Huerta, 1991; Stein & Meredith, 1993). The tonotopic organization of the auditory system, with nearby places on the basilar membrane connected to neurons near one another along the auditory pathway, is very similar to the retinotopic organization of the visual system, with nearby places on the retina connected to neurons near one another along the visual pathway. The tonotopic organization continues into the auditory cortex (Clarey et al., 1992).

At the cortical level, an additional similarity emerges. Recall that some cells in the visual cortex respond optimally to certain visual features, such as the orientation of a line or its movement pattern. Similarly, some cells in the auditory cortex frequently respond to more complex characteristics of stimuli than simple frequency and intensity (Pickles, 1988). In fact, many cortical neurons do not respond to pure tones that have constant intensity. Many neurons, for example, respond only to complex stimuli such as bursts of noise, clicks, and sounds resembling kissing. Some neurons respond to tones, but only if their frequency is changing—a situation similar to that of the cells in the visual cortex that respond only to a moving line. In the auditory cortex, some cells are most responsive to a sequence of tones that moves from low to high frequency, and others are most responsive to the reverse pattern. The rate of change in frequency may also influence a cell's response rate (Evans, 1982b).

How essential is the auditory cortex? People with disorders in this region have difficulty discriminating changes in the timing within a sequence of sounds. Speech perception is usually a major problem for such people. They also have difficulty localizing sounds in space. Thus, the auditory cortex is essential for more complex kinds of auditory tasks.

We have pointed out several similarities between the auditory and visual systems (in keeping with Theme 1). However, several differences are also observed. For instance, lateral inhibition is absent in the cochlea but is prevalent in the retina. (Lateral inhibition of auditory information does occur beyond the cochlea.) Further, the auditory stimulus appears to be processed more completely peripherally (prior to the brain) than the visual stimulus (Zwislocki, 1981). In part, this difference might be because we know a good deal less about the functioning of the auditory cortex

than we do about the visual cortex. As Pickles (1988) points out, after more than 40 years of research, the role of the auditory cortex in frequency discrimination is still unclear.

SECTION SUMMARY

The Auditory System

1. The outer ear consists of the pinna, the external auditory canal, and—most important for audition—the tympanic membrane.

2. The middle ear contains three bones—the malleus, the incus, and the stapes—important in reducing the effects of the impedance mismatch between air pressure and the fluids of the inner ear.

3. The inner ear contains the cochlea, which houses the organ of Corti, a structure that contains the auditory receptors, or hair cells; the organ of Corti also includes the basilar membrane and the tectorial membrane.

4. Relatively few inner hair cells are found in the inner ear, although they monopolize most of the afferent auditory nerve fibers. On the other hand, relatively many outer hair cells are found; although they share a small number of the afferent auditory nerve fibers, they receive many of the efferent fibers. The efferent fibers going to the outer hair cells are probably responsible for adjusting the motion of the outer hair cell stereocilia, which might well serve to amplify the traveling wave.

5. The actual transduction taking place in the inner ear is due to displacement of the stereocilia of the hair cells. The tip links of the stereocilia appear to be crucial to the rapid response of hair cells to displacement.

6. The graded potentials of the hair cells serve as input to the afferent fibers of the auditory nerve.

7. The auditory nerve has nerve fibers sensitive to particular frequencies; this nerve travels to the cochlear nucleus. The auditory pathway continues to the superior olivary nucleus, then to the inferior colliculus, then to the

medial geniculate nucleus, and finally to the auditory cortex.

8. Parts of the inferior colliculus and the auditory cortex are organized tonotopically; furthermore, some cells in the auditory cortex respond to complex characteristics of sounds. The auditory cortex is essential for sound localization, speech perception, and other complex auditory tasks.

HEARING IMPAIRMENTS

Several kinds of disorders can occur in the auditory system. For example, *tinnitus* is a high-pitched ringing or background noise in the ears (McFadden, 1982; McFadden & Wightman, 1983). The ringing or noise does not seem to be particularly loud to the sufferers, but it is quite annoying. Just as a fever can be a symptom for several different illnesses, tinnitus can have several different causes, including tumors in the auditory nerve, head traumas, and overdoses of drugs—even aspirin. Aspirin, a medication that once seemed so harmless, can also produce a temporary difficulty in hearing low-intensity sounds (McFadden & Plattsmier, 1983). Consequently, aspirin should be used with caution. Given the wide range of causes, you won't be surprised to learn that researchers have not determined treatments for all kinds of tinnitus. In some cases, no treatment seems effective.

Just as the visual system is affected by advancing age (presbyopia), so is the auditory system. *Presbycusis* refers to the loss of hearing (most often high-frequency) that often accompanies the aging process. We will have more to say about presbycusis in Chapter 14.

The most well-known kind of hearing impairment, however, is deafness. In the United States, over 28 million people are hearing impaired (Soli, 1994). However, only about 5 million of these people own hearing aids. Hearing aids are not effective for all hearing impairments, but more people would be likely to use hearing aids if they were satisfied with the results

of wearing the devices (Barnes & Wells, 1994; Soli, 1994).

Deafness can be assessed by a variety of techniques (Jacobson & Northern, 1990; Martin, 1994). However, deafness is most commonly assessed by *audiometry*, the measurement of the sensitivity of audition. One audiometry method presents a series of pure tones, using the method of constant stimuli, generally at frequencies of 250, 500, 1000, 2000, 3000, 4000, 6000, and 8000 Hz. Typically, the audiologist measures the decibel difference between a person's threshold at each frequency and the average threshold of a normal population (Martin, 1994). Other hearing tests measure the perception of speech sounds.

Let's consider how three hypothetical people might respond to a standard audiometry test. Figure 9.16 illustrates the hearing in one ear of a normal person and two hearing-impaired people. Notice that Person A shows a consistent loss of about 35 dB at all the tested frequencies. In contrast, Person B shows little loss at the lower frequencies but substantial loss at the higher frequencies.

Person A and Person B are representative of two different kinds of hearing problems, known as conduction deafness and nerve deafness. *Conduction deafness* involves problems in conducting the sound stimulus; the problem occurs in either the external ear or the middle ear. We have already mentioned one category of conduction deafness, which results from a puncture of the eardrum. *Ear infections* are another common disorder, especially among young children. In an ear infection, the eustachian tube becomes swollen, cutting off the middle ear from the respiratory tract. Bacteria may multiply in the middle ear, resulting in a painful earache and the presence of fluid in the middle ear, which may impair sound conduction. Children who have frequent ear infections may have difficulties developing normal language (Eimas & Kavanagh, 1986). *Otosclerosis* is an inherited bone disease that can lead to immobilization of the stapes, making conduction of the sound stimulus difficult (Gulick et al., 1989). About 7% of the adult population has otosclerosis.

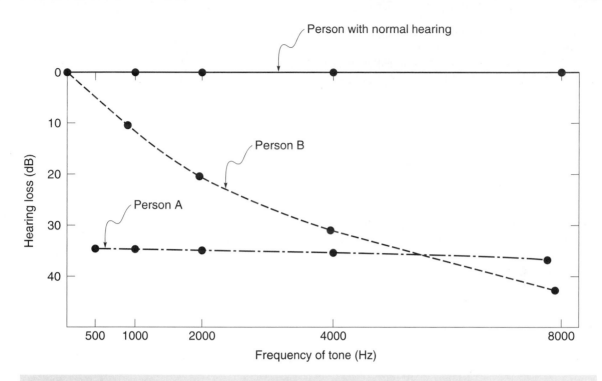

Person with normal hearing

Person B

Person A

FIGURE 9.16 Hearing loss in two hearing-impaired people, in comparison with a person with normal hearing. The *y*-axis represents hearing loss in decibels, so at 1000 Hz, Person A would require about 35 dB additional pressure for the sound to be as loud as for a person with normal hearing. Person B would require about 10 dB additional pressure for the sound to be as loud as for a person with normal hearing.

Person A in Figure 9.16 shows conduction deafness and would be helped by a hearing aid, which would make sounds of all frequencies louder. This person can hear sounds conducted through the bone surrounding the cochlea at normal levels. However, she or he has difficulty hearing sounds through the normal middle ear channel. (Try Demonstration 9.4 to illustrate bone conduction.) A hearing aid would be useful for people with moderate levels of conduction deafness. The hearing aid can overcome outer and middle ear problems by channeling airborne sound waves to

Demonstration 9.4

Sound Waves Traveling Through Bone and Through Air

Tape record your own voice and play it back. This recording captures the sound waves from your voice that travel only through the air. Now talk in a normal voice; you hear both the sound waves that travel through the air and the sound waves that travel through the bony part of your skull. Finally, plug your ears so that no sound waves can travel through the air and pass into your external auditory canal; you hear only the sound waves that travel through the bony part of the skull.

the bony part of the skull around the ear, making it vibrate and stimulate the cochlea.

The other kind of deafness is called nerve deafness. Person B in Figure 9.16 has nerve deafness. In *nerve deafness* the problem occurs either in the cochlea or in the auditory nerve. For example, if the ear is exposed to extremely loud noises, the stereocilia of the hair cells in the organ of Corti may be destroyed. (Figure 9.11 showed intact hair cells.) As we will see in Chapter 10, such hair-cell damage is usually localized to a portion of the organ of Corti. If all the hair cells in an area are damaged, no receptors are in that location to transduce the sound waves. Thus, neither airborne sound nor bone-conducted sound can be transduced; the person is deaf. A simple hearing aid would not help someone with complete nerve deafness, just as a pair of glasses would not help someone who has a detached retina.

What can be done for someone with nerve deafness? If some hair cells are intact, a standard hearing aid can be modified so that it amplifies those frequencies for which the hearing loss is greatest. For example, Person B does not require amplification of the low-frequency tones but does require amplification of the high-frequency tones. However, people with nerve deafness also often show a disorder related to loudness perception, called recruitment. *Recruitment* is a condition in which a partially deaf person perceives very loud sounds normally. This person's perception does not differ from a hearing person's perception if we consider only loud sounds. However, very weak sounds are not heard at all. Thus, the design of a hearing aid for a nerve-deaf person must take care of two problems: a differential sensitivity to the various pitches and a differential sensitivity to the various loudnesses.

Although it might sound like science fiction, great strides are being made in the development of electronic devices to provide hearing to deaf people who have intact auditory nerves. A microphone is placed in the person's ear, which sends the auditory information to a sound processor and then to an electronic device implanted in the cochlea. The implant stimulates the afferent fibers directly (Loeb, 1985). Currently, about 10,000 people worldwide have cochlear implants (Ubell, 1995). Although only about 20% of the operations are completely successful, cochlear implants offer great promise for many deaf people. Some of the deficiencies in cochlear implant use can be offset by a range of supporting devices (Schum & Tye-Murray, 1995). In the very near future, physicians will be able to bypass the auditory nerve and stimulate the brain directly—even restoring hearing to those with damaged auditory nerves (Ubell, 1995; Zimmer, 1993).

Consistent with Theme 1, hearing impairments can have an impact on visual processing. In a recent study, deaf children showed poorer visual attention than hearing children (Quittner et al., 1994). The children were asked to watch a stream of numbers presented on a computer screen. When the number 9 appeared after the number 1, the children were told to press a button. They were not to press the button for any other number, nor were they to press the button if 9 followed any other number. Interestingly, children who had greater experience with cochlear implants also performed better than deaf children.

SECTION SUMMARY

Hearing Impairments

1. Tinnitus is a ringing in the ears or perception of background noise that can result from a range of causes.

2. A person with conduction deafness shows a consistent loss of hearing at all frequencies. Because the sound stimulus is not properly conducted, this person can be helped by a hearing aid. Conduction deafness results from outer or middle ear impairments such as punctured eardrums, ear infections, or otosclerosis.

3. A person with nerve deafness shows a hearing loss at certain frequencies, although hearing

may be normal for other frequencies; this person often shows recruitment. Thus, designing a hearing aid for nerve-deaf people is difficult because of their differential sensitivity to various pitches and loudnesses.

4. Electronic devices, such as cochlear implants, are being developed to restore hearing to deaf people.

REVIEW QUESTIONS

1. Describe the auditory stimulus with respect to frequency, amplitude, phase, and complexity. Then turn back to Chapter 3 and compare the auditory stimulus with the visual stimulus. For instance, how do the perceivable auditory and visual stimuli differ in frequency?

2. Draw a rough sketch of the auditory system, identifying the parts of the outer ear, middle ear, inner ear, and the pathway from the inner ear to the auditory cortex. Point out the similarities between the higher levels of auditory processing and the higher levels of visual processing.

3. The organ of Corti should strike you as quite different from the retina, yet both structures perform similar transduction functions for audition and vision. Describe the similarities and differences between the two structures. To what extent do you think the differences are due to the nature of the differences between the auditory and the visual stimuli? What might be the source of the similarities between the organ of Corti and the retina?

4. You might think of the auditory system as a type of game. The goal of the game is to deliver the auditory stimulus to the receptors so that the dB level is as high as possible. Points are lost because of some events, and points are gained because of other events. Describe this "game" with particular attention to the obstacles (e.g., impedance mismatch) and the means of overcoming them.

5. Discuss the two kinds of hair cells and point out the similarities with each of the two kinds of receptors in the visual system.

6. The efferent connections in the cochlea appear to play an important role in audition. Describe the role they are thought to play, and illustrate how they might give rise to otoacoustic emissions.

7. Inserting a microelectrode into the auditory nerve is a procedure very similar to that used in studying the activity of ganglion cells in the optic nerve. Work through the similarities and differences between the activity in the auditory and optic nerves. Do you think that there is any equivalent of the cochlear microphonic in the visual system?

8. Tinnitus might be confused with otoacoustic emissions. Given the definition of tinnitus and the evidence on otoacoustic emissions, why would you argue that the two are different?

9. Suppose that you know two people who are deaf. One has conduction deafness and the other has nerve deafness. List various ways in which the perceptual experiences of these two people would differ.

10. A cochlear implant operation can cost between $20,000 and $40,000. Costly as it is, the operation is only completely successful 20% of the time. If you had a deaf child, would you want your child to undergo this operation? What arguments might you use to justify this costly procedure for your deaf child? What do your arguments tell you about the importance of our auditory sense?

NEW TERMS

pure tone (277)
cycle (277)
sounds (278)
frequency (278)
Hz (278)
absolute thresholds (279)
difference threshold (279)
complex tones (279)
amplitude (280)
dyne (281)
sound pressure level (SPL) (281)
decibel (dB) (281)
phase angle (282)
pinna (283)
external auditory canal (283)
eardrum (284)
tympanic membrane (284)
ossicles (284)
malleus (284)
incus (284)
stapes (284)
impedance (284)
impedance mismatch (284)

eustachian tube (285)
cochlea (285)
oval window (285)
vestibular canal (286)
helicotrema (286)
tympanic canal (286)
round window (287)
cochlear duct (287)
Reissner's membrane (287)
basilar membrane (287)
traveling wave (287)
organ of Corti (287)
tectorial membrane (287)
hair cells (287)
inner hair cells (288)
outer hair cells (288)
stereocilia (288)
auditory nerve (289)
afferent fibers (290)
efferent fibers (290)
cochlear microphonic (291)
evoked acoustic emissions (291)

Kemp echoes (291)
spontaneous acoustic
    emissions (292)
otoacoustic emissions (292)
motility (292)
frequency tuning curve (293)
cochlear nucleus (293)
superior olivary nucleus (295)
monaural (295)
binaural (295)
inferior colliculus (295)
tonotopic (295)
medial geniculate nucleus (295)
primary auditory cortex (296)
tinnitus (298)
presbycusis (299)
audiometry (299)
conduction deafness (299)
ear infections (299)
otosclerosis (299)
nerve deafness (300)
recruitment (300)

RECOMMENDED READINGS

Gulick, W. L., Gescheider, G. A., & Frisina, R. D. (1989). *Hearing: Physiological acoustics, neural coding, and psychoacoustics*. New York: Oxford. This text provides a good overview of the processing of auditory stimuli, from physical properties, through transduction, to neural processing. The level of the text seems appropriate for advanced undergraduates and graduate students, with balanced coverage of sensory and perceptual aspects of hearing.

Luce, R. D. (1993). *Sound & hearing: A conceptual introduction*. Hillsdale, NJ: Erlbaum. Luce's text and the accompanying CD, filled with auditory demonstrations, are a nice addition to the upper-level introductions to audition. Luce's focus is on basic processes, concentrating on the physics of sound waves, properties of the auditory system, and auditory psychophysics.

Martin, F. N. (1994). *Introduction to audiology* (5th ed.). Englewood Cliffs, NJ: Prentice Hall. This textbook provides a good introduction to the assessment and treatment of hearing impairments. Martin provides a clear introduction to both pure tone and speech audiometry. In addition, he provides a good overview of the auditory system, showing the problems that can afflict each part of the system.

Pickles, J. O. (1988). *An introduction to the physiology of hearing* (2nd ed.). London: Academic. As indicated by its title, this text provides great detail about the sensory functioning of the auditory system. Given the complexity of some of the material, the text is a model of clarity, with many figures and a clear writing style.

Rossing, T. D. (1990). *The science of sound*. Reading, MA: Addison-Wesley. If you want to learn more about sound waves and how they are produced by musical instruments, the human voice, and stereos, this is the book for you. It's very interesting reading and provides coverage of a wealth of interesting topics.

CHAPTER 10

Basic Auditory Functions

Listen to a sound right now and think about the perceptual qualities you notice. The sound is high or low (pitch) and loud or soft (loudness). You can also distinguish the quality of the sound (timbre); for example, the tone of a flute is different from that of a clarinet. In addition, the sound appears to be coming from a particular direction. All these qualities are subjective, or psychological, qualities of sound, as opposed to the physical qualities such as frequency and amplitude discussed in Chapter 9.

If you recall our discussion of color mixing in Chapter 7, you'll remember that we described vision as a synthetic sense and hearing as an analytic sense. So when several sounds are presented simultaneously, our auditory system is capable of distinguishing the composite sounds. After reading Chapter 9, you should now think of the analytic properties of audition as a minor miracle. A tiny, thin, hairy piece of tissue on each side of your head is bouncing wildly up and down in a complex fashion, and from that you can hear distinct instruments in the background music and conversations going on around you. Perhaps you can even recognize distinctive voices and tell roughly where all the sounds come from.

In this chapter, we will first analyze several basic auditory perceptual experiences such as pitch, timbre, and loudness. Next, we will focus on auditory localization. Our discussion of localization will allow us an opportunity to discuss the relationship between audition and vision. Thus, we have an opportunity to address an important theme of this text—our senses work together to analyze the world around us (Perrott, 1993; Stein & Meredith, 1993). Although we may think of vision as much more effective for analyzing space, our ability to localize sounds is equally good under many circumstances (Perrott et al., 1993). Taken together, visual and auditory input enable us to locate an individual voice in a choir with reasonable accuracy.

In the final part of the chapter, we will examine simultaneously occurring sounds. For all the phenomena in this chapter, we examine the linkage from the physical stimulus to the perceptual experience, as well as the factors that influence our perceptual experiences. We begin by studying the perceptual experience of pitch.

PITCH PERCEPTION AND RELATED PHENOMENA

The frequency of a sound is the primary determinant of our perceptual experience of *pitch*. Generally, high-frequency sounds have a high pitch and low-frequency sounds have a low pitch. Because we can learn a lot about our perception of pitch by examining the way in which frequency information is encoded in the inner ear, that is where we will begin. Keep in mind, however, that the relationship between frequency and pitch is not a simple one. After we look at the encoding of frequency information, we shift our attention to the complexities of that relationship.

In Chapter 9, we examined how sound waves are transmitted into the inner ear. But how does the inner ear register frequency? When middle C is played on the piano, you hear a different pitch than if, say, the note A is played. How can the excitation of various stereocilia in the organ of Corti possibly account for the subtle kinds of distinctions we make with respect to sound? This question has puzzled researchers for centuries. Although we now understand quite a bit of the underlying process, much remains to be determined. Let's first consider the two broad approaches to frequency encoding that emerged—place theory and frequency theory.

Background: Early Theories of Pitch Perception

The *place theory* proposes that particular frequencies are encoded at specific locations on the basilar membrane (see Figure 9.7). This theory has existed since the 1600s, but its modern versions can be traced to Hermann von Helmholtz (1863), the 19th-century researcher whose work is discussed throughout the book. Helmholtz knew that the width of the basilar membrane increases from the area near the stapes toward the area near the helicotrema. He proposed that the basilar membrane consists of a series of transverse fibers under tension, with each segment resonating to a tone of a particular frequency (Gulick et al., 1989). Just as particular strings of a harp or a piano vibrate in response to sound waves falling on them, so Helmholtz thought that the fibers in the basilar membrane vibrated in response to sound stimuli.

Helmholtz's theory presented several problems, not the least of which is that the basilar membrane is not under tension. Further, even if the basilar membrane fibers were under tension, the range of basilar membrane widths could not give rise to the wide range of frequencies to which humans are sensitive (Gulick et al., 1989). Given the problems with early place theory, you shouldn't be surprised that a competing theory developed.

William Rutherford (1886) argued that the rate of vibration of the basilar membrane was crucial for pitch perception. He was very much influenced by advances in the communication technology of his era—specifically, the telephone. Even very complex auditory stimuli such as speech could be encoded by vibrations of the diaphragm in the telephone, producing electrical changes. Rutherford needed only a short conceptual leap to infer that the vibrations of the basilar membrane produced electrical changes in the neurons of the auditory nerve.

According to *frequency theory*, the basilar membrane vibrates at a frequency that matches the frequency of a tone. This part of the original theory is essentially correct. For example, the membrane vibrates 25 times each second for a 25-Hz tone and 1,600 times each second for a 1600-Hz tone. The vibration rate in turn causes nerve fibers in the auditory nerve to fire at a matching rate, for example, 25 times each second. Neurons can easily keep pace with a 25-Hz tone. But what about the 1600-Hz tone? As we mentioned when discussing the visual system, neurons take a rest after firing, called the *refractory period*. This refractory period restricts the maximum number of responses to 1,000 each second, still an impressive rate. If a neuron is limited to 1,000 responses a second, how can we hear frequencies of 1600 Hz,

let alone 20,000 cycles per second? Thus, early frequency theory also presented some problems. As we will see, modern proponents of both place and frequency theories have addressed these early problems.

Developments in Place Theory

The details of Helmholtz's theory are not accurate, but the spirit of his theory was further developed by Georg von Békésy, whose research earned him the Nobel Prize in 1961. Using evidence from mechanical models and cadavers, Békésy (1960) proposed that vibration of the stapes produces a traveling wave along the basilar membrane. As you might recall, a *traveling wave* describes the physical motion of the basilar membrane, as illustrated in Figure 9.9. The traveling wave would reach a peak of maximum displacement at some point, which would then create the greatest displacement of the stereocilia in that area.

The location of this maximum-displacement point has been shown to depend on the frequency of the auditory stimulus. For example, a low-frequency tone of 25 Hz produces the greatest displacement in a region near the helicotrema, about 1.4 inches from the stapes. In contrast, a higher-frequency tone of 1600 Hz produces the greatest displacement in the middle of the basilar membrane, about 0.7 inch from the stapes. In other words, if someone nearby is playing a scale on a piano, running from low to high notes, the displacement is initially greatest at the inner tip of the cochlea; by the end of the scale, the area closest to the stapes shows the greatest displacement.

Let's relate Békésy's observations to the auditory receptors. Suppose that a 1600-Hz tone is sounded, producing maximum displacement 0.7 inch from the stapes. At this location, the stereocilia in the hair cells of the organ of Corti will be bent the most. These particular stereocilia will therefore produce the greatest change in electrical potential in the hair cells, which will ultimately be picked up by the auditory nerve.

The frequency of the sound determines not only the location of the peak along the basilar

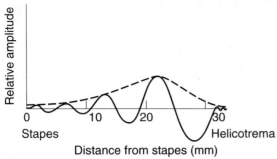

a. Map of the traveling wave envelope for a typical auditory stimulus

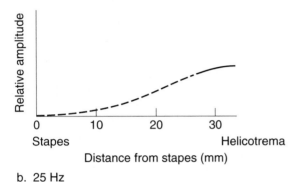

b. 25 Hz

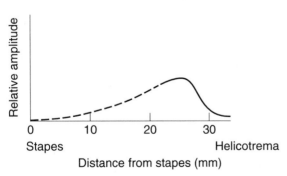

c. 400 Hz

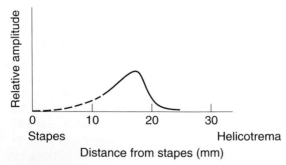

d. 1600 Hz

membrane but also the sharpness of that peak. To simplify the picture, researchers often just display the *envelope* of the traveling wave—a line connecting the peaks of the wave as it progresses. Figure 10.1a shows a side view "snapshot" of a typical traveling wave moving along the basilar membrane, with the peaks of the waves connected to form the envelope. The traveling-wave envelopes shown in Figures 10.1b through 10.1d illustrate that low-frequency stimuli reach their peaks toward the helicotrema and have relatively wide peaks. In contrast, high-frequency stimuli reach their peaks near the stapes and have relatively sharp, narrow peaks. Békésy determined that the basilar membrane is stiffer near the stapes than at the helicotrema, which causes the traveling wave to die out more rapidly near the stapes (Zwislocki, 1981).

The peak of the traveling wave is also apparent in studies of stimulation deafness. In a *stimulation deafness experiment,* animals are exposed to an extremely high-amplitude tone of a particular frequency. Although this technique is crude, it illustrates the differential effects of frequency on the basilar membrane. The delicate stereocilia—remember how small they are—are damaged by the loud tone. A loud low-frequency tone damages the stereocilia nearer the helicotrema, and the damage extends over a fairly wide area. A loud high-frequency tone damages the stereocilia nearer the stapes, and the range of damage is fairly narrow. Note that the nature of the damage to the stereocilia is consistent with

FIGURE 10.1 Traveling wave envelopes. Part a shows how the envelope is determined, by connecting the high points of the traveling wave. Parts b through d show the traveling wave envelopes for increasingly high-frequency sounds. Note that the peaks of the envelopes are wider and nearer the helicotrema for low-frequency sounds and narrower and nearer the stapes for high-frequency sounds. Note, also, that the relative amplitude of the waves reaches a maximum, then decreases rapidly. (From Békésy, 1960)

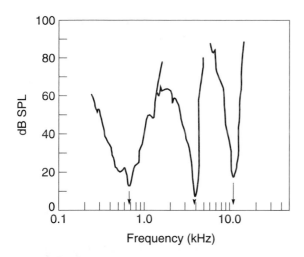

FIGURE 10.2 Representative tuning curves for neurons in the auditory nerve. The low points for each of the curves is the frequency (*x*-axis) for which the smallest sound pressure (*y*-axis) can cause firing in the neuron. Note that this point is sharper for the high-frequency sounds. The curves are also steeper to the right than to the left of the low point in all cases. The steepness is due to two factors. First, the traveling wave of higher-frequency sounds dies out rapidly. Thus, increasing the amplitude of higher-frequency sounds is not sufficient to affect points further along the basilar membrane. Second, the axis is logarithmic, which places higher frequencies closer together. (From Kiang, 1975)

the traveling-wave envelopes shown in Figure 10.1. (Keep stimulation deafness experiments in mind the next time you're tempted to crank up the volume on your Walkman!)

Conducting stimulation deafness experiments on humans would be unethical, but naturalistic studies have produced similar data. People who work in environments with very loud noises often experience hearing losses for particular frequencies. Some terminally ill patients with such hearing losses allowed their inner ears to be examined postmortem. Hair-cell damage has been found along exactly the portions of the basilar membrane that one would have predicted from the hearing losses observed in the patients before death.

Auditory tuning curves, such as the one you saw in Figure 9.14, also confirm the importance of place information. Figure 10.2 illustrates the differential sensitivity of three auditory neurons. Remember that the auditory tuning curve represents the activity of an auditory neuron when tones of particular frequencies and amplitudes are played. The *x*-axis represents the frequency of the tone presented, and the *y*-axis represents the amplitude of the tone necessary to produce firing in the neuron. So the low point on the curve is the frequency to which the neuron is "tuned," because the neuron requires the least stimulation to fire at that frequency. Higher and lower frequencies might cause the neuron to fire, but these stimuli would require a greater amplitude. The neuron from which the recording is being made is connected to hair cells at a particular location along the basilar membrane, so the place to which the neuron is connected is most sensitive to a particular frequency.

In spite of all the evidence for place theory, some problems have lingered. One problem is that the peak of the traveling wave shifts location with changes in the amplitude of the sound (Zwislocki, 1991). Another problem, which we mentioned in Chapter 9, is that human frequency-discrimination abilities seem to be much more precise than one would expect, given the wide peak of the traveling wave. This paradox led researchers to search for a "second filter" that would sharpen the perceptual response to frequency information. The search turned out to be unnecessary. One source of the problem was Békésy's dependence on observing basilar membrane motion in the cochleas of nonliving subjects. However, with technological developments, researchers are now able to observe the traveling wave in living organisms (J. P. Wilson, 1992).

For instance, in one technique (the Mössbauer technique) a small radioactive source is placed on the basilar membrane. By measuring shifts in radiation frequency, a researcher can determine the velocity of the basilar membrane at the location of the radioactive source. In another technique, a laser beam is directed at a tiny gold mirror that has been placed on the basilar membrane. Using these techniques, researchers determined that the peak of the traveling wave is much sharper than Békésy had thought (Johnstone & Boyle, 1967; Khanna & Leonard, 1982). Why were the traveling waves less sharp in the "postmortem" cochleas? Probably because the outer hair cells no longer receive efferent input, so they cannot function to tune the basilar membrane response (Robles et al., 1986). Current research, therefore, suggests that the traveling-wave envelope in a living human is sufficient to give rise to the auditory tuning curves typically obtained (such as those in Figure 10.2). Because the traveling wave is sharper for the higher-frequency sounds, the auditory tuning curves are also sharper for higher-frequency sounds.

Complex Waves and Timbre

Basilar membrane information may be sufficient to account for observed neural tuning curves, but that does not mean that basilar membrane information is sufficient to explain our *perception* of pitch. The problem becomes apparent when we consider complex sound waves. Remember that in our everyday experience, complex waves are far more common auditory phenomena than the pure sine waves used in much auditory research. A complex wave is composed of several sine waves and is characteristic of speech and musical instruments, for example.

The component of a complex tone that has the lowest frequency is called the **fundamental frequency.** Thus, 100 Hz is the fundamental frequency in a complex tone representing 100 Hz, 200 Hz, and 300 Hz. The other components of a complex tone are called **harmonics** (or **overtones**). Therefore, harmonics have higher frequencies than the fundamental. In this example, 200 Hz and 300 Hz are harmonics. Using another example, if you play the A above middle C on the piano, the fundamental frequency of 440 Hz is produced. In addition, the vibrations of the multiple piano strings produce overtones of 880 Hz (2×440) and 1320 Hz (3×440), as well as higher-frequency overtones.

The fundamental frequency typically contributes the greatest amplitude to the tone, but the harmonics also contribute substantially. Suppose that you play the A above middle C on a variety of instruments. The fundamental frequency of 440 Hz will be produced in each case, so the pitch will be identical for all instruments. One instrument, however, may emphasize the overtone of 880 Hz; this overtone may have a greater amplitude than other overtones. In contrast, a different instrument may emphasize the overtone of 1320 Hz. Other instruments, such as the flute and piccolo, produce very few overtones—as we'll see in Chapter 11.

Our ears can analyze complex tones and detect which overtones are emphasized. Thus, we can distinguish among the sounds made by different instruments. Some instruments, such as the flute, have very few overtones, and any overtones that do exist have relatively low amplitude. As a consequence, the tones produced by the flute sound pure. In contrast, other instruments, such as the guitar, have many high-amplitude overtones. As a consequence, the tones produced by the guitar sound thick and rich.

Figure 10.3 shows how complex sound waves can be analyzed into their component sine waves by Fourier analysis. In our discussion of shape perception in Chapter 5 we considered Fourier analysis in some detail. You may wish to review that portion of the theory of spatial frequency analysis. Our auditory system is designed to perform a Fourier analysis for complex tones. Thus, the system can isolate several simple sound waves when we hear a complex tone. Auditory perception involves more than a simple Fourier analysis, however, because tone combinations produce complex perceptions, as we will see shortly.

The psychological quality **timbre** (pronounced "tamber"), corresponds to the physical quality of complexity. Timbre is a tone's sound quality. Two sounds may have the same pitch and the same loudness yet differ in quality. A piece of chalk squeaking across a blackboard seems different in quality from the sound produced by a valuable violin, and they both seem different from the voice of a soprano—even though the three may be

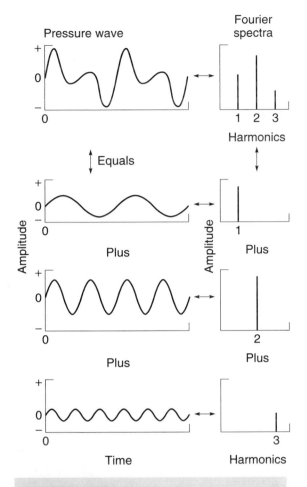

FIGURE 10.3 Fourier analysis of a complex wave. The complex wave is shown at the top of the figure, with a typical representation of a Fourier analysis shown to the right of the complex wave. The Fourier analysis indicates that the complex wave is composed of a fundamental frequency (1) with moderate amplitude, an overtone of twice the fundamental frequency (2) and high amplitude, and an overtone of three times the fundamental frequency (3) and very low amplitude. Each of these three waves is shown separately in the lower part of the figure. If you were to take each discrete point in time along the x-axis and add up the amplitudes of the three waves in the lower part of the figure, you would arrive at the complex wave seen at the top of the figure (Fourier synthesis). (From Handel, 1989)

nearly identical in pitch and loudness. Furthermore, think about two males you know whose voices are similar in pitch and loudness but quite different in timbre. Timbre involves qualities such as richness, mellowness, brightness, and so on (Evans, 1982c).

Scharf and Houtsma (1986) point out that the advance of computer music and electronic musical instruments makes it important to understand timbre, yet we have little knowledge or theory in this area. As they complain, "Hardly more than a handful of studies on timbre exists" (pp. 15–31). Nonetheless, timbre is clearly an important attribute of sound. Consider how you use timbre to identify a friend's voice on the telephone; pitch and loudness would not be sufficient clues. Timbre is the quality that makes each musical instrument and human voice distinctive. Unfortunately, the dimensions of timbre that underlie this identification process have not really been studied.

Complex Waves and the Problem of the Missing Fundamental

A phenomenon known as the missing fundamental poses a major problem for place theory, because that theory holds that each pitch is encoded at a particular place on the basilar membrane. The *missing fundamental* refers to a complex sound in which the harmonics are present but the fundamental frequency is absent. Let's now consider an example of a missing fundamental. Suppose that an experimenter presents a complex tone that contains 200-Hz, 300-Hz, 400-Hz, and 500-Hz tones. In other words, this complex tone is missing the 100-Hz fundamental for which these four tones represent harmonics. Even though this fundamental is missing, listeners still report that they hear a pitch similar to the pitch produced by a 100-Hz tone.

You've actually experienced the missing fundamental when listening to a male friend speak on the telephone. The range of frequencies reproduced in a telephone is approximately 300–3000 Hz. However, the fundamental frequency for most men is around 150 Hz. Because you fill in the missing fundamental, you don't hear your male friends speaking in a falsetto (Luce, 1993).

Demonstration 10.1

The Missing Fundamental

Good demonstrations of the missing fundamental are actually available, even on compact disc. In all likelihood, however, you have already experienced the missing fundamental without thinking much about it. To perform this demonstration, you need a car and source of music (e.g., car stereo). A fancy car stereo system is actually somewhat detrimental to this demonstration—cheap speakers will make the demonstration more powerful. All you have to do is drive and listen to the music. Now the road and tire noise will be creating a cheap source of low-frequency noise for you, which will wipe out most of the low frequencies in the music. Keep the volume at a low to moderate level and notice that you can still perceive low pitches (deep voices, bass guitars, etc.). The fundamental frequencies of the complex musical and vocal sounds are being obscured by the road noise, yet you still hear the music as essentially the same as when the car is not moving. Our ability to hear these frequencies is an example of the way in which the harmonics of complex sounds can give rise to a perception of their fundamental—even when it's missing!

Demonstration 10.1 provides another illustration of the functioning of the missing fundamental.

In a way, the case of the missing fundamental is similar to visual illusions (van den Brink, 1982). Just as the visual system can see an illusory contour that is not physically there, the auditory system can detect a tone that is not physically there. Consistent with Theme 4 (page 12), because musicians have more experience with pitch perception, they are better able to determine the pitch of the missing fundamental (Preisler, 1993).

Recent research (Pantev et al., 1989) suggests that the tonotopic organization in the auditory cortex is in terms of perceived pitch rather than in terms of the actual frequencies presented. Thus, a 100-Hz pure tone and a complex sound composed of the overtones of a 100-Hz tone (with the 100-Hz fundamental missing) both give rise to activity in the same part of the auditory cortex. At some point between the cochlea and the auditory cortex, then, neurons are activated by *perceived* pitch rather than the frequency information present at the cochlea.

Can you see why the missing fundamental is a problem for place theory? With no 100-Hz component to the complex sound, no activity should exist at the 100-Hz location on the basilar membrane. However, people typically report hearing a 100-Hz tone. Licklider provided a compelling demonstration of the missing fundamental at the 1954 meetings of the Acoustical Society of America (Green, 1988a). He presented a scale of pure tones in alternation with the same scale made up of complex tones. Then he turned on noise that wiped out the pure tones and the fundamentals of the complex tones. The audience could no longer hear the scale produced by the pure tones, but they could still hear the scale produced by the complex tones. So the *place* on the basilar membrane where the scale information is presumably encoded could not be the source for the scale heard by the audience, because the noise was overriding any activity in that part of the basilar membrane.

Developments in Frequency Theory

Place theory, therefore, seems to have a major problem. Can the alternative—frequency theory—provide an adequate explanation of pitch perception? Remember that the problem with

Rutherford's frequency theory was that neurons could not fire at a rate fast enough to encode the high frequencies that humans can clearly hear. Wever has been the primary advocate of frequency theory in this century. He proposed a *volley principle*, whereby groups of neurons share in producing the required firing rate (Wever, 1949). Consider an analogy. Suppose that for some obscure reason you wanted to produce one scream each second for about a minute. This task would be impossible for you alone, but with the appropriate community effort you and four friends could organize your screams so that you would take turns. Each of you would need to produce only one scream every 5 seconds—a manageable task. The net result, however, would be the required one scream per second. Similarly, a 1000-Hz tone could be registered if each of five neurons fired 200 times each second—again, a manageable task.

Research has demonstrated that nerve fibers in the auditory nerve can indeed fire at a rate to match some tones (e.g., Rose et al., 1967). When the stimulus frequency is not too high, fibers in a group tend to fire irregularly rather than neatly taking turns, but they do consistently fire when the pressure of the sound wave is at or near its maximum. Thus, a group of nerve fibers could represent a particular frequency by "cooperating" to produce a given firing rate. For the volley principle to work, the cooperating neurons would each have to fire at a consistent point in the curve, such as the maximum, and different fibers would have to respond to different peaks in the waveform.

The frequency of neuronal firing probably plays an important role in pitch perception, but only for very low frequencies. The volley principle might allow neurons to encode frequencies somewhat higher than 1000 Hz. However, frequency theory clearly has major limitations, especially for the higher frequencies.

Conclusions about Registration of Frequency

We have seen that frequency theory has difficulty explaining how we hear high-frequency tones. As it happens, place theory has difficulty explaining how we hear the very lowest frequency tones. We can make discriminations between two tones that are more precise than could be predicted by minor differences in maximum displacement of the basilar membrane by a 100-Hz tone and a 105-Hz tone, for example. (Remember, at the lowest frequencies the envelope of the traveling wave has a very wide peak.)

Frequency theory seems to work well only for explaining how very low-frequency tones are registered, and place theory explains how the remaining tones are registered. The most common approaches to pitch perception today tend to be modified place theories (Green, 1988a). The theories have been developed to account for the problem posed by the missing fundamental, and they also describe how central processing contributes to pitch perception.

Most of the early theories of pitch perception proposed that the inner ear provided sufficient frequency analysis. However, the results of an experiment by Houtsma and Goldstein (1972) changed all that. Houtsma and Goldstein modified the typical missing fundamental experiment by presenting one overtone to the left ear and another overtone to the right ear. Subjects reported hearing the fundamental frequency for which the two tones were overtones. Because neither ear alone had sufficient information to determine the missing fundamental, our perception of pitch must be due not only to inner ear activity but also to higher-level processing in which inputs from both ears are present. Clearly, much more research is required before we can understand the complex process of transforming frequency information into pitch perception.

Relationship between Frequency and Pitch

As we mentioned earlier, the relationship between sound frequency and pitch is not a simple one. Some of the reasons are general psychophysical ones. For instance, some auditory frequencies are too high or low to be audible, so no sense of pitch will be created. Further, two different frequencies might not be discriminable, and so they might give rise to the same pitch (Gulick et al., 1989). Several other examples suggest that the relationship between frequency and pitch is complex.

For example, pitch perception can depend upon the amplitude of the sound. In experiments using pure tones, the pitch of low-frequency tones (e.g., 200 Hz) typically seems slightly lower as the amplitude of the tone is increased. In contrast, the pitch of high-frequency tones (e.g., 6000 Hz) typically seems slightly higher as the amplitude of the tone is increased (Rossing, 1990). When the duration of the sound is short (40 msec), however, increased amplitude leads to a decrease in pitch for most pure-tone frequencies (Rossing & Houtsma, 1986). On the other hand, the pitch of complex tones is relatively *unchanged* by variations in amplitude. In other words, when a conductor instructs a band to play louder, the pitch of the piccolo and the tuba will not be substantially distorted, because musical instruments produce complex tones.

The relationship between frequency and pitch can also be disrupted for very brief tones. With extremely short-duration tones, the abrupt onset and offset of the tone produces a broad distribution of frequency components that will cause it to be heard as a click.

Furthermore, the pitch of a tone can also be influenced by a previous tone (Scharf & Houtsma, 1986). This effect can be observed when the previous tone is similar in frequency (within 5%) to the test tone and is presented for at least a minute. The pitch of the test tone shifts away from the pitch of the previous tone. In other words, if the test tone is higher in frequency, its pitch is perceived as still higher; if the test tone is lower in frequency, the pitch is perceived as still lower. The magnitude of the effect of the previous tone is not large, but the effect does suggest that the auditory system features a process that may be similar to adaptation.

One further reason that the correlation between frequency and pitch is not perfect is that characteristics of the observer can influence

pitch. For example, arousal can influence pitch perception (Thurlow, 1971). If you are sleepy, a tone will sound lower in pitch than it would if you were alert.

Is pitch related to the frequency of a tone? Yes, definitely! As we have seen, however, pitch perception can be influenced by several factors, including amplitude, duration, the effects of the previous tone, and characteristics of the observer. In Chapter 2, we stressed that physical stimuli are often related in complex ways to psychological responses. Similarly, we saw in Chapter 7 that wavelength and hue are related to each other in a complex fashion. The information on the less-than-perfect relationship between frequency (a physical quality) and pitch (a psychological quality) adds further evidence about the complexity of perceptual processes.

Measuring Pitch

We talked about the units of measurement used to scale the physical attribute, frequency. We can determine the frequency of a sound with an accuracy of better than 0.1% by using modern laboratory equipment (Wightman, 1981). Unfortunately, an equally accurate pitch meter cannot be constructed. Because pitch is a psychological phenomenon, we cannot measure it directly. Pitch exists only in a listener's head.

Musicians and psychologists have both tackled the problem of a scale for pitch. Musicians use the term ***octave,*** which represents a doubling of frequency. From one C to the next higher C or the next lower C on the piano is an octave difference. For instance, middle C has a frequency of about 262 Hz, the next higher C has a frequency of about 523 Hz, and the next lower C has a frequency of about 131 Hz.

In describing pure tones, psychologists often use the mel scale, which was suggested by S. S. Stevens and his colleagues (1937). You may recall Stevens's name from the discussion of Stevens's power law and magnitude estimation in Chapter 2. In the ***mel scale,*** a 1000-Hz pure tone is arbitrarily assigned a pitch of 1000 mels. Then lis-

Demonstration 10.2

Informal Construction of a Mel Scale

You'll need a piano for this demonstration, because this instrument has the widest range in frequency among the standard musical instruments. (A true mel scale is created with pure tones; however, the piano produces complex tones.) Also locate a volunteer who can either play appropriate notes on the piano while you create a scale or who can provide the scaling judgments while you play.

First play the C two octaves above middle C. (Its frequency of 1046 Hz is reasonably close to the 1000-Hz tone used in formal experiments.) Assign this tone the value of 1000 mels. Now play other Cs on the keyboard in the following order: C#3, C#8, C#2, C#7, C#5, C#1, C#4, C#7, C#3, C #5, C#8, C#2, C#4, C#1. Note that each C is presented twice. (Each C is recorded in terms of its position on the keyboard. The lowest C, three notes from the bottom, is 1, the standard C is 6, and the highest C is 8. You may want to place these numbers, written on masking tape, on the keys before you begin so that they can be located quickly and accurately.)

Ask the listener to supply a judgment for each note. Just before each judgment, play the standard C so that this reference tone can be kept in mind. After running through the sequence, take the average response for each note. Record the average value on the graph below. The value of C#6 was set at 1000, so this point is already recorded on the graph. What is the relationship between notes on the scale, as represented by octaves, and the way these notes are judged in mels? Keep in mind that an increase of one octave represents a doubling of the actual frequency.

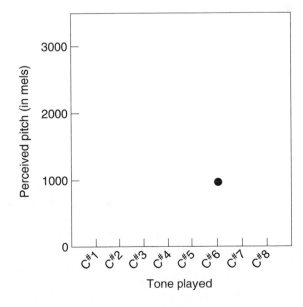

teners are asked to adjust a comparison tone until it seems to be half as high as this 1000-Hz tone; this tone is assigned a value of 500 mels. Other points in the scale are filled in by asking listeners to locate comparison tones that represent other fractions and multiples of the standard 1000-Hz tone. Try Demonstration 10.2 to illustrate an informal construction of a mel scale.

SECTION SUMMARY

Pitch Perception and Related Phenomena

1. Two major theories explain how the ear registers frequency information: (a) The place theory proposes that each sound-wave frequency causes a traveling wave, which makes a particular place on the basilar membrane vibrate to a greater extent than other places. (b) The frequency theory proposes that sound-wave frequency is matched by the vibration rate on the basilar membrane, which then causes nerve fibers in the auditory nerve to fire at a matching rate; the volley principle is added to explain higher frequencies.

2. Timbre, a tone's sound quality, corresponds to complexity, which involves the combination of sound waves. The auditory system performs a crude Fourier analysis to analyze a complex sound wave into its components. The nature of the overtones is one determinant of the timbre of musical instruments and the timbre of human voices.

3. Modified place theories are currently the most popular explanations for how we hear pitch. At lower frequencies, we seem to rely primarily on frequency information, but much of pitch perception is dependent on place information.

4. Pitch depends mainly upon frequency, but it also depends on duration, amplitude, previous tones, and the arousal of the perceiver.

5. Pitch can be measured by octaves, a measurement system used by musicians, and by the mel scale, a system developed by psychophysicists.

LOUDNESS PERCEPTION

Registration of Amplitude

How does the auditory system code a near-painful 130-dB rock band, in contrast to the faint, 25-dB sounds that occur when a CD by that same band plays at the other end of a long hallway? Researchers in auditory perception assume that the neural correlate of amplitude is the number of neuronal impulses generated each second (Hellman & Hellman, 1986, 1990).

This explanation makes sense because the basilar membrane is displaced a greater amount for high-amplitude sounds. Thus, as stimulus amplitude increases, a greater number of neural fibers all along the basilar membrane are firing more often than they would with a less vigorous wave (Scharf & Houtsma, 1986). Higher amplitude sounds would create greater up-and-down movement along the basilar membrane, which would cause greater activity among the hair cells over the active regions of the organ of Corti.

This theory of loudness perception has much to recommend it. On the other hand, loudness perception is too complex a process to arise from simply summing the neural firing in the auditory nerve (Clarey et al., 1992; Irvine, 1992). For instance, researchers have not yet determined how auditory neurons are capable of encoding the 100-dB loudness range people can perceive. As in the case of pitch perception, so many factors influence loudness perception that a complete explanation requires a fairly complex theory.

Relationship between Amplitude and Loudness

As noted earlier, *loudness* is roughly determined by a tone's amplitude. Just as was the case for pitch and frequency, we find that the correlation between loudness and amplitude is not perfect. One factor that affects loudness perception is the duration of a tone. Tones briefer than 150–300 milliseconds are perceived as less loud than

---

Demonstration 10.3

Influence of Previous Noises on Loudness

Find a watch that ticks and place it where you can clearly hear it; the ticking should definitely be above threshold. Then turn on a stereo or a radio so that it is loud but not painfully loud. Leave it on for 10 minutes, then turn it off. Return to the location from which you originally heard the ticking watch. Judge its loudness relative to your original judgment.

---

longer tones of equal frequency, amplitude, and so on (Gulick et al., 1989).

A second factor that affects loudness is the context in which the sound occurs. One influential type of context is background noise, a topic to which we will return at the end of this chapter. Another type of context is produced by the other sounds that occur in proximity to the target sound. For example, observers listened to a sequence of low-frequency tones of low amplitude alternating with high-frequency tones of high amplitude. These observers judged that the low-frequency tones sounded louder due to the context in which they occur (Marks, 1992, 1993, 1994). In contrast, listening to low-frequency tones of high amplitude alternating with high-frequency tones of low amplitude leads observers to hear the low-frequency tones as less loud.

A third factor that complicates the relationship between amplitude and loudness is the state of the observers themselves. As Scharf (1978) notes, the loudness of a sound depends on whether we pay attention to it or merely hear it as background noise. Perceived loudness also depends on whether our ears are "fresh" or recently exposed to sound. We adapt to auditory stimuli just as we adapt to different aspects of visual stimuli. Thus, when we listen to a continuous tone, it seems to decrease in loudness over time (Miskiewicz et al., 1993; Scharf et al., 1992). Try Demonstration 10.3 to illustrate the influence of previous sounds upon loudness perception.

A fourth factor may be the most important of all: Perceived loudness depends on the frequency of a tone. We noted earlier that pitch perception depends on the amplitude of a tone. Similarly,

loudness perception depends on the frequency of a tone. The exact same amplitude of a sound (e.g., 40 dB) sounds louder if it is presented at 1000 Hz than if it is presented at 100 Hz.

The relationship between stimulus frequency and loudness perception is most often explored in equal loudness contours (also called Fletcher–Munson curves). The basic procedure for determining an equal loudness contour is simple: One tone (e.g., a 1000-Hz tone) is presented at a particular intensity level (e.g., 40 dB). This tone serves as a reference tone throughout the experiment. A comparison tone of a different frequency is then varied in amplitude until the listener judges its loudness to be equal to that of the reference tone; this amplitude is recorded. Then the procedure is repeated with tones of other frequencies. The relationship between tone frequency and the number of decibels required to produce a tone of equal loudness is called an *equal loudness contour*. As the name suggests, all the points along an equal loudness contour sound equally loud.

Figure 10.4 shows a set of seven different equal loudness contours in which the reference tone is presented at amplitudes up to 120 dB SPL. Let's first concentrate on the lowest curve, marked "hearing threshold." This curve represents the absolute threshold of audition for varying frequencies. For instance, the reference tone of 1000 Hz is just barely audible at about 5 dB. Suppose that observers are asked to match the reference tone with an equally loud (i.e., just detectable) tone of 5000 Hz. As you can see, they adjust the amplitude to about 0 dB. Likewise, if asked to match the reference tone with a tone of

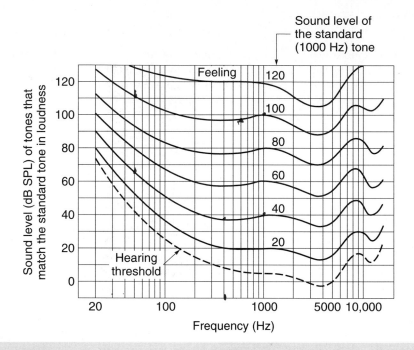

Sound level of
the standard
(1000 Hz) tone

FIGURE 10.4 Equal loudness contours. Each of the lines is an equal loudness contour, so any point along the line will sound equally loud. The figure illustrates the relationship between sound pressure and frequency in determining our perception of loudness. The low points on each curve indicate that for certain frequencies (roughly 1000–5000 Hz) less sound pressure is necessary for the sound to appear as loud as other frequencies outside that range. The dashed curve (labeled "Hearing threshold") represents the minimal pressure necessary to hear a pure tone at each frequency level. Pressure-frequency combinations that fall below the dashed curve would not be audible. The area above the highest curve (labeled "Feeling") represents pressure-frequency combinations that are perceived as pressure or pain as much as sound. (Adapted from Fletcher & Munson, 1933)

20 Hz, they set the 20-Hz tone to about 75 dB. The rest of that "hearing threshold" line seen in the figure is obtained by presenting the range of frequencies to the observers, who match the loudness of each frequency to the reference loudness. The lowest line on the figure represents the absolute thresholds for the typical audible range of frequencies.

Before moving on, let's be sure that you are clear on the lowest equal loudness contour (for absolute thresholds). Because all of the points on that line are equally detectable, and just barely de-

tectable, what would happen if you presented a frequency at an amplitude that would be below the line? For instance, suppose you presented a 20-Hz tone at 40 dB. What would an observer report? If you said "Nothing!" you're absolutely correct. A 20-Hz tone requires more sound pressure than 40 dB to be audible. To add more evidence to the points we've been making about distinctions between physical and perceptual dimensions, notice that an equal level of sound pressure (40 dB) for other frequencies (e.g., 1000 Hz) would be clearly audible (i.e., above the lowest curve).

Let's make two more points about equal loudness contours. First of all, notice that for each curve the smallest amplitude required to match the reference tone is at 3000–5000 Hz. This finding is entirely consistent with the sensitivity information presented in Chapter 9—we are most sensitive to frequencies in this range. Second, notice that the higher curves are also flatter. That is, the range of amplitudes on the contour becomes attenuated. For the lowest curve, the smallest amplitude needed to match the reference tone is below 0 dB, and the highest amplitude is above 70 dB. The 100-dB reference contour is the highest curve that shows the full range of frequencies. Here, the smallest and largest amplitudes are about 90 and 130 dB, respectively. Therefore, at higher amplitudes, audible frequencies are perceived to be more similar in loudness than is the case at lower amplitudes.

If you have understood all this, you can now appreciate the function of the loudness button found on many stereos. If you never play your stereo at a low amplitude, you'll never need to touch your loudness button. The loudness button functions to boost the amplitude of low-frequency sounds while leaving higher-frequency sounds untouched. As we mentioned earlier, the difference between the low-frequency sounds and the higher-frequency sounds is more pronounced at lower amplitudes. Pushing in a loudness button selectively raises the amplitude of these lower frequencies, without affecting the other frequencies—essentially flattening the equal loudness contour. At low amplitudes, the bass guitar might be difficult to hear. With the loudness button engaged, the bass guitar would now be appropriately loud.

Now shift your attention to the curve in Figure 10.4 representing the points obtained in matching the 1000-Hz reference tone at 80 dB. Suppose you present a 1000-Hz tone, as well as a 20-Hz tone, both at an amplitude of 80 dB. Which would an observer say was louder? The observer should report that the 1000-Hz tone is much louder (even though it has equal amplitude). How much sound energy would you have to put into the 20-Hz tone for the observer to say

that it seemed as loud as the 1000-Hz tone? Roughly 110 dB. Suppose that you left your loudness button engaged but turned up your stereo so that it was pumping out 80 dB of sound pressure. Now the bass guitar will be far too loud!

Intensity Discrimination

Researchers are interested not only in the relationship between amplitude and loudness perception (and factors that might influence that relationship) but also in listeners' abilities to discriminate intensities. In terms of the discussion in Chapter 2, psychologists are also interested in discrimination of intensity differences, or just noticeable differences (jnd's). The Weber fraction for intensity discrimination (intensity jnd as a function of the original intensity) is about 0.3. This fraction is little influenced by the frequency of the pure tones judged (Gulick et al., 1989). Therefore, a 30% change in sound intensity is sufficient to produce the perception of a change in loudness. Notice, then, that we are not superbly skilled in noticing changes in sound intensity.

Auditory researchers are increasingly using complex sounds as stimuli, in contrast to the pure tones often used in the past (Yost, 1992). Studies of auditory intensity discrimination increasingly tend to use complex sounds. David Green (1983, 1988b) has argued that people can detect changes in complex sounds by comparing the activity taking place all along the basilar membrane at one instant in time, a process he calls **profile analysis.** Intensity discrimination of complex sounds is much more difficult when the two sounds have substantially different component frequencies. In the visual realm, judging the relative brightness of two hues is more difficult when the hues have very different wavelengths. Conversely, when the profiles created by complex sounds are more similar, then observers can detect very small changes in the intensity of just one of the component frequencies. So the Weber fraction cannot be easily determined with complex stimuli, because the component frequencies of the complex sound have a strong influence on discriminability.

Measuring Loudness

In the discussion of pitch, we saw that musicians and psychologists have both developed methods for measuring pitch. Likewise, musicians and psychologists have developed methods for measuring loudness. Musicians, for example, scale loudness in terms of an eight-level marking system that ranges from *ppp* for the very softest sound (about 30 dB) through *fff* for the very loudest sound (about 90 dB) (Pierce, 1983).

Psychologists measure loudness in a number of different ways. One of the most widely used systems is the sone scale (S. S. Stevens, 1955). The *sone scale* is a scale of loudness obtained by the magnitude estimation technique. In the sone scale, a 40-dB pure tone at 1000 Hz is arbitrarily assigned a loudness of 1 sone. Researchers asked listeners to judge the loudness of other tones in relationship to this standard tone. Thus, a tone that appears to be twice as loud would be judged as 2 sones, and a tone that appears to be half as loud would be judged as 0.5 sone.

In general, Stevens found that the sound pressure of a tone had to be increased by 10 dB for listeners to judge it to be twice as loud. Thus, a 50-dB tone appeared to be twice as loud as a 40-dB tone; the 50-dB tone would therefore equal 2 sones. We noted earlier that about 6 dB of sound pressure represents a doubling of physical intensity, so a doubling of physical intensity does not produce a doubling of *perceived* loudness.

An advantage of the sone scale is that the measures correspond to our everyday perceptions of sound in a more meaningful fashion than do the measures of the decibel system. For example, suppose that you are working in a quiet office where the general noise level is measured at 40 dB, or 1 sone. The company may wish to bring in a new kind of equipment that will raise the general noise level to 50 dB. This 10-dB increase would not strike most people as substantial, and they would not be alarmed at the prospect of such a change. You now know, however, that this increase represents an increase from 1 sone to 2 sones. The new noise level would really sound *twice* as loud, which represents a major increase in perceived loudness.

Despite its advantages, the sone scale has been criticized because people's judgments are heavily influenced by the order in which stimuli are presented, the range of stimuli, and other biasing factors (Moore, 1982). Nevertheless, many researchers support the use of this sone scale. For example, Algom and Marks (1984) discovered that individual differences are remarkably small when a single method of judgment is used in a magnitude estimation study. As these authors conclude their article, "To be sure, magnitude estimation scales of loudness show diversity, individuality, and idiosyncrasy; but beneath lies a common core of uniformity in sensory–perceptual processing of sound intensity and, at one stage of processing at least, in the underlying scale for loudness" (p. 591).

SECTION SUMMARY

Loudness Perception

1. Loudness depends mainly on amplitude, but it also depends on duration, background noises, characteristics of the perceiver, and frequency.
2. All the points along equal loudness contours are perceived as equally loud. In general, as seen in Figure 10.4, tones in the 1000- to 5000-Hz range sound louder to us than equal-amplitude tones outside that range.
3. The Weber fraction for intensity discrimination of pure tones is about 0.3. Current research—for example, profile analysis—is exploring the use of complex tones in such experiments.
4. Loudness can be measured by an eight-level musical system devised by musicians and by the sone scale, a measurement system based on magnitude estimation.

AUDITORY LOCALIZATION

You reach out in the darkness of early morning to turn off the ringing alarm clock, and your hand locates the source of that unpleasant noise. A button pops off your coat and rolls away, but you can trace it from its sound effects. You accurately determine the arrival time of an oncoming car based solely on auditory cues (Rosenblum et al., 1994).

The human auditory system allows us to identify with some accuracy where a sound is coming from. In other words, we show ***auditory localization***—the ability to locate objects in space solely on the basis of sounds they make. The formation of the auditory image that enables us to localize sounds in space may be the very reason that auditory systems evolved (Yost, 1991).

Researchers have long been intrigued by the auditory localization ability of humans and other animals. One reason that sound localization is so mysterious is that auditory space is not represented directly on the basilar membrane (Oldfield & Parker, 1984). Frequency, amplitude, and complexity are all represented, but the basilar membrane cannot indicate, for example, that a dog is barking directly behind your head. The auditory system must encode this information in another fashion.

In our discussion of vision, we saw that binocular vision offers a distinct advantage in trying to determine the location of an object. Remember, however, that the monocular cues are sufficient to give rise to a rich sense of depth. Monocular depth cues probably work, in part, because a two-dimensional map of space is present on the retina. In discussing auditory localization, binaural cues are even more important than in vision. Having two ears is extremely useful when we try to localize sounds (Yost & Dye, 1991). (In contrast, pitch, loudness, and timbre can all be appreciated with monaural hearing.) In fact, the major portion of our ability to localize sounds can be traced to the fact that our ears are some distance away from each other, so they receive somewhat different stimuli from the same sound source (Phillips & Brugge, 1985).

In this section we look at the auditory localization abilities of humans and other creatures, the neural underpinnings of localization, and interrelationships between spatial perception using vision and audition.

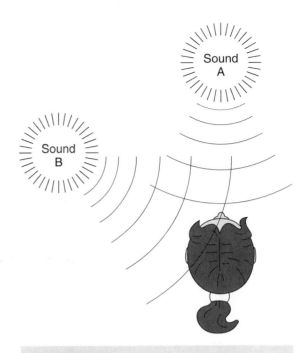

FIGURE 10.5 Diagram of interaural time difference. Sound A would appear to come from directly ahead of the observer, because it reaches the two ears at the same time. Sound B would appear to come from the left of the observer, because it reaches the listener's left ear before the right ear.

Sources of Information for Sound Localization

For purposes of sound localization, why are our ears located about 6 inches apart? As Figure 10.5 illustrates, a sound coming from the left will have to travel different distances to the two ears. This difference in distance has two consequences with respect to temporal effects: (1) the sound will arrive at one ear before the other, producing an ***onset difference;*** and (2) the sound will be at different phases within a cycle when it arrives at the two ears—perhaps at the maximum point in its cycle for the right ear and at the minimum point for the left ear, producing the ***phase difference*** illustrated in Figure 10.6. These are the two

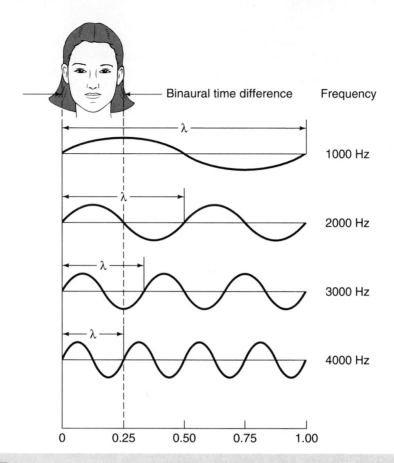

FIGURE 10.6 Diagram of interaural phase difference. Given the width of the observer's head, a 1000-Hz sound directly to the right of the observer would reach the left ear 90° out of phase with the right ear. A 2000-Hz sound would be 180° out of phase, a 3000-Hz sound would be 270° out of phase, and a 4000-Hz sound would be in phase at both ears. Note that the localization information in the 4000-Hz sound is ambiguous, since a 4000-Hz tone directly ahead of the observer would also be in phase at both ears. (Adapted from Gulick et al., 1989)

components of the interaural time difference. The ***interaural time difference,*** therefore, is a cue to sound localization that is produced by the different arrival times at the two ears.

The onset difference is a useful source of information for sounds throughout the entire frequency range. Figure 10.7 shows typical findings on the relationship between the direction from which the sound is coming and the size of the onset difference. As you can see, when the sound comes directly from the side (e.g., straight out

from the right ear), the sound reaches one ear about 0.6 milliseconds before reaching the other ear. Obviously, this is not an enormous discrepancy, but the auditory system can use this minuscule time difference to figure out the location of sounds.

The phase difference of pure tones is not useful throughout the entire frequency range. Phase differences are much easier to detect for low-frequency sounds. The human auditory system cannot discriminate phase discrepancies when the

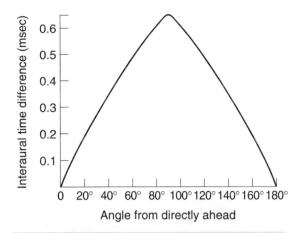

FIGURE 10.7 Interaural time differences as a function of sound location. The greatest disparity (about 0.6 msec) would occur for a sound directly to one side of the observer (90°). There would be no timing disparity for sounds directly ahead of the observer (0°) or directly behind the observer (180°).

peaks of the waves come close together at the higher frequencies in pure tones. In everyday life, however, this inability is not a major disadvantage because most sounds are complex, and we can detect phase differences in complex high-frequency sounds (Hafter et al., 1990). This is yet another instance in which the trend toward using more complex tones has caused psychologists to reevaluate the earlier theories based on research involving pure tones.

The interaural time difference—with its two components of onset difference and phase difference—is only one of the two major binaural factors that provide information for sound localization. The second factor is called *interaural intensity difference,* because in general the sound reaches the two ears at different intensities. For example, the left ear is closer than the right ear to Sound B in Figure 10.5, so the sound is slightly more intense in the left ear. More important, however, is the fact that the head produces a sound shadow, or a barrier that reduces the intensity of the sound. We are accustomed to a reduction in

intensity when something large—such as a bedroom door—separates us from a sound source. Surprisingly, your head blocks some of the sound coming from sources on the opposite side.

This shadow effect is particularly strong for high-frequency sound waves, which have difficulty bending around the head. What is crucial to creating the intensity difference is the frequency of the sound waves *relative* to the size of the head. To give you an idea of the relationship between head size and frequency, think about ocean waves falling on rocks. Waves hitting against a large rock formation jutting out of the water create spray on the ocean side, as the rock breaks up the waves. Just behind the large rock, on the shore side, the water is typically calm. In this example, the frequency of the waves is high relative to the size of the rock.

With smaller rocks protruding out of the water, you've probably noticed little or no spray, and the waves just roll right around the rock. In this example, the frequency of the waves is low relative to the size of the rock. In these two examples, the frequency of the ocean waves is roughly constant and the obstruction varies in size. The same principles operate with sound waves and the head. What is different is that for auditory localization, the obstruction (your head) is the same size, and the sound waves vary in frequency. The important fact is that your head is large relative to high-frequency sounds and small relative to low-frequency sounds.

Thus, the interaural intensity difference is especially strong for high-frequency tones. (As you'll recall, the interaural time difference was a particularly useful cue for low-frequency tones.) For example, for high-frequency tones above about 4000 Hz, the difference in intensity may be close to 30 dB (Phillips & Brugge, 1985). That is a substantial difference!

Resolving Ambiguities in Sound Localization

Although people are fairly good at localizing sounds, some factors inhibit our ability to locate sound sources. On the basis of our discussion of the sources of information about localization, you might be able to infer one factor that influences localization—frequency. We are better at locating low-frequency sounds through timing differences, whereas we are better at localizing high-frequency sounds through intensity differences. What about sounds in the mid-range (around 2000 Hz)? Interestingly, we have a difficult time localizing pure tones in the mid-range (Luce, 1993). Note that these are the very frequencies that we can detect readily!

As an aside, you might be interested to know that we also cannot easily localize very low-frequency sounds. Satellite speaker systems that incorporate a subwoofer are effective due to this fact. Because the subwoofer reproduces only very low-frequency sounds, the speaker can be placed virtually anywhere within the listening room. If you have the opportunity to listen to such a system, you will note the difficulty of localizing the sounds coming from the subwoofer.

Sound frequency is not the only factor that influences localization. We also have difficulty determining whether a sound is coming from ahead or behind (Middlebrooks & Green, 1991). (You may have discovered this if you were driving and trying to figure out the location of an ambulance siren.) Sounds directly ahead of you, above your head, or directly behind you reach both ears simultaneously and also at the same phase within the sound wave. Furthermore, the tone reaches both ears with the same intensity. For other locations even a small distance away from this midline, however, both interaural time differences and interaural intensity differences will be present.

Figure 10.8 illustrates another source of ambiguity in an example referred to as the ***cone of confusion***. Every location on a circular slice through the cone is an equal distance from the near ear (e.g., 2 feet) and an equal distance from the far ear (e.g., 2 feet plus head width). Therefore, sound sources at any locations on that slice should theoretically send the same set of information about the source of the sound to each ear. That is, the interaural time differences and the interaural intensity differences for sounds coming from these locations will be similar. For ex-

FIGURE 10.8 The cone of confusion. Sounds located on any circular slice through the cone of confusion would appear to come from the same location.

ample, a sound from every point on that surface might reach the left ear 0.4 milliseconds faster than the right ear.

Obviously, we manage to surmount these problems because we can localize sounds fairly accurately, even within potentially ambiguous regions. Three factors contribute solutions to these problems:

1. Most sounds are complex tones rather than pure tones. The localization of complex tones is much easier than localization of pure sounds. Thus, even though localization is often a difficult task, we perform much better when the stimuli are complex sounds (Middlebrooks & Green, 1991).

2. The discussion so far does not take the pinnae into account. Those generally useless flaps of external ear help to resolve the confusion. Take a look in the mirror to inspect the structure of your pinnae; they have ridges and valleys and interesting twists. These features force the sound waves to bounce around slightly before entering the ear. The pattern of delay depends upon the original location of the sound (Batteau, 1967; B. C. J. Moore, 1982). Thus, the pinnae contribute to the encoding of sound location and help resolve ambiguities.

TABLE 10.1　Mechanisms for Auditory Localization

Physical Bases for Auditory Localization	Factors That Improve Auditory Localization
Interaural Time Difference (Low Frequencies)	Complex Tones
Onset difference	Effect of Pinnae on Incoming Sounds
Phase difference	Head and Body Movement
Interaural Intensity Difference (High Frequencies)	

3. We move our heads and our bodies. For example, suppose that a sound reaches your two ears at the same time and the same intensity, so that you don't know whether its source is ahead of or behind you. Simply rotate your head a few inches, and you create interaural time differences and interaural intensity differences. This process is fairly automatic. We don't pause, contemplate the ambiguity, and reason that we could create interaural differences by head rotation! We solve ambiguities, however, by moving our bodies and exploring. This point is stressed by theorists who encourage psychologists to apply Gibson's ecological approach to audition. As Noble (1983) observed, "An ecologically oriented form of study of [localization] replaces the model of a static and passive receiver of stimuli with one of an active, exploring agent, a listener with powers to discover the whereabouts of sources of sound" (p. 331).

Consistent with Theme 3 of this text, we have evolved to make great use of auditory information in localizing sound-emitting objects in the world. We are particularly good at localizing the complex sounds that are commonly emitted. When ambiguities in auditory localization emerge, we can overcome the ambiguity. Table 10.1 illustrates the various factors that influence our ability to locate a sound source.

Measuring Localization Accuracy

One measure developed to assess our localizing abilities is the minimum audible angle. The ***minimum audible angle (MAA)*** is the smallest angle between two sound sources that a person can detect. To determine the MAA, researchers first present one tone, followed by a second tone. The observer reports whether the tones came from the same location or not. For instance, if the MAA is 10°, then the directions of the two sound sources separated by less than 10° could not be reliably discriminated. However, sound sources separated by more than 10° would appear to come from different locations.

A classic study was conducted on the roof of a building at Harvard University. Stevens and Newman (1936) put a speaker at the end of a boom that could be rotated around the observer. By using the roof, Stevens and Newman did not have to worry about reflected sounds. Furthermore, by using the boom they could rotate the sound source to many different locations in a horizontal plane (the elevation of the sound source was constant). This study and similar studies (Mills, 1958) indicate that humans are quite accurate in localizing sounds when the stimuli are in front of the observer. Here the MAA can be as small as 1° (Phillips & Brugge, 1985). We are not as good at localizing sounds that are off to the side. Then, again, we can overcome this deficit by moving our heads.

In the vertical dimension, we are not quite as accurate as in the horizontal dimension, with an MAA of about 4° for sounds coming from straight ahead (Perrott & Saberi, 1990). Vertical localization is actually a bit better off to the side than it is directly ahead (Makous & Middlebrooks, 1990). Given the similarity of information reaching our two ears from sources that differ in the vertical dimension, however, such discrimination is quite impressive.

Demonstration 10.4

Monaural Sound Localization

Ask a friend to help you with this demonstration. Choose a location where the light is equally bright in all directions. Close your eyes and turn around several times. Then ask your friend to make a noise of a very brief duration. Point to your friend's location and then open your eyes to determine your accuracy. Now place your index finger in one ear, or use an earplug. (Caution: Do not insert other foreign bodies into the auditory canal.) Repeat the demonstration, and try it several other times in both binaural and monaural conditions. Were you more accurate with information from two ears?

When the stimuli are pure tones, we can better localize those that are low in frequency or high in frequency. As we mentioned earlier, tones from the middle range (1000–5000 Hz) are more difficult to localize—that is, they have larger MAAs.

For several reasons, much research has been done with headphones rather than speakers. For instance, headphones allow researchers to exercise greater control over the stimuli presented to the two ears. When headphones are used, the stimuli typically give rise to the experience that the sound is inside the observer's head rather than outside, as is the case when speakers are used. Only with great care can one achieve a sense of the sound being outside the head when using headphones (Wightman et al., 1987). When the typical localization cues are manipulated over headphones, the sound seems to shift to the right or to the left *inside* the head. Thus, these studies using headphones are called **lateralization** studies instead of localization studies (Yost & Hafter, 1987). If you haven't already noticed this phenomenon, you can easily try it out for yourself if your stereo system has both speakers and headphones.

What effects does the position of the sound source have on localization accuracy, under normal conditions in which people can move their heads and use visual cues? According to Oldfield and Parker (1984), people are relatively accurate in identifying locations in front of them, as opposed to locations in back of the head.

How accurate are people in monaural conditions, when they have information from only one ear? Oldfield and Parker (1986) replicated earlier research by demonstrating that listeners were substantially less accurate when they lacked information from two ears. Try Demonstration 10.4 to illustrate the accuracy of monaural sound localization. Oldfield and Parker's observers, however, still had the ability to make rough judgments about sound localization. To some extent, the cues provided by the pinna may be helpful in these monaural judgments (Musicant & Butler, 1984; Phillips & Brugge, 1985).

Physiological Basis of Auditory Localization

As mentioned earlier, the basilar membrane does not record information about the direction of a sound source. How is sound localization processed? As you may recall from Chapter 9, information from the two ears remains segregated until it reaches the superior olivary nucleus. This structure seems to be critical in sound localization (Brugge, 1992). The superior olivary nucleus is a structure composed of several smaller cell groups, two of which are important in sound localization. One of these cell groups, the **medial superior olivary nucleus,** is specialized for processing low-frequency information. Research has demonstrated that cells in this area are excited by input from each ear and are sensitive to interaural time differences, which—as mentioned earlier—is a more effective cue for low-frequency information. Another cell group, the **lateral superior olivary** *nucleus,* is specialized for processing high-frequency information. Research has also demonstrated that—because most cells in this structure are excited by input from one ear and inhibited by input from the other ear—the cells are sensitive to interaural intensity differences (Brugge, 1992; Pickles, 1988).

Researchers cannot easily record neural activity in the superior olivary nucleus. Thus, most of the physiological research is conducted on the higher levels in auditory processing. For example, the superior olivary nucleus sends its information on to the inferior colliculus. In a classic study, researchers discovered a group of neurons within the inferior colliculus that were sensitive to a specific interaural time difference (Rose et al., 1966). This work has been replicated in research demonstrating that interaural time differences of less than 0.25 millisecond produced optimal responses (Yin & Kuwada, 1983).

Thus, the auditory system can take advantage of information from the two ears, in terms of both the timing of the two sounds and their intensity. The inferior colliculus appears to have both a tonotopic *and* a spatial organization. That is, within layers of the inferior colliculus, the neurons are arranged tonotopically (i.e., according to pitch). However, the layers themselves are related to spatial position (Pickles, 1988).

The medial geniculate nuclei and the auditory cortex contain cells sensitive to intensity and phase differences between the two ears, so they also play important roles in localization (Clarey et al., 1992). So far, we have emphasized how we humans localize sound. How do other animals accomplish this task?

IN-DEPTH Nonhuman Localizing Abilities

"Asking" an owl about the location of a sound source should strike you as a difficult task. Fortunately, researchers have devised ingenious solutions to such methodological problems for various species, including the owl. For instance, an important methodological advance for studying an animal's head position is to use a coil (nick-named "Herb's hoop" after its inventor) mounted on the animal's head. The animal is placed in horizontal and vertical magnetic fields, and any movement of the animal's head can be reliably recorded by the researcher's instruments. This methodology has been used with success in several species.

The results of several different types of experiments suggest that humans have much better localization abilities than do many other animals. For instance, most birds, fish, and rodents have larger minimum audible angles than humans (Brown & May, 1990). These cross-species differences in localization abilities are partly due to the size of the animals' heads, although some animals with larger heads do seem to rely on timing rather than intensity differences (Heffner & Masterson, 1990). As good as humans are at localizing sounds, the real champs of auditory localization are barn owls and bats. We now focus on the amazing localization abilities of these creatures.

BARN OWLS

Because barn owls hunt small rodents and other prey at night, they don't have much competition. But hunting at night requires them to pursue their prey without being able to see them. How can they accomplish this task? Auditory cues seem to be rich enough to allow owls to hunt their prey, and their auditory systems have evolved to localize sounds in the 3000- to 9000-Hz range.

The possibility remains that these owls may be aided in their predation by being able to smell their prey or detect their body heat. Either could aid the owl in its nocturnal hunting. These possibilities were ruled out in a clever demonstration (Konishi, 1973). An owl was waiting in a dark room that was outfitted with a foam rubber pad on the floor to cut down on noises. A mouse was released into the room, and a ball of paper was tied to the mouse's tail by a short piece of string. Dinner time, right? In fact, the owl attacked the ball of paper that was rustling behind the quietly running mouse—even though the mouse was only a few inches away! So the barn owl seems to be totally dependent on auditory cues for locating prey in the dark.

Actually, because mice are not clever enough to think of the old ball-of-paper trick, the barn owl is fairly adept at catching them in the wild. The owl's skill can be traced to several features that enhance localization. The barn owl is able to localize sounds in the vertical direction better than any other animal. This ability is due to an asymmetrical ear structure—the right ear is oriented upward and the left ear is oriented downward. In addition, the feathers on the owl's face serve as a parabolic reflector to enhance the perception of high-frequency sounds (6000–12,000 Hz). These two features are illustrated in Figure 10.9.

Researchers demonstrated the importance of the ear asymmetry in owls by systematically plugging one ear or the other, and noting that the owl made both horizontal and vertical errors in localization (Konishi, 1973). The importance of the facial feathers was clarified by shaving the owl's face, with resulting vertical, but not horizontal, localization errors (Knudsen, 1981). The barn owl must be using the same sorts of cues used by humans for localization—intensity and

timing differences. However, the owl seems to use intensity for vertical localization and timing for horizontal localization (Konishi, 1993; D. Moore, 1989).

The sounds made by the barn owl's typical victim fall right within the owl's localization range. In addition, the sounds are complex—and owls are much more adept at localizing complex sounds than they are at localizing pure tones. The sounds do not have to be continuous for the owl to capture its prey. In fact, with a sound source that changed locations midway through the owl's flight and was on for only about 20% of its flight, the owl made few localization errors (Konishi, 1973). This accuracy is especially interesting because the wind over the barn owl's wings makes a fair amount of noise in flight—but the frequencies are much lower (below 1000 Hz) than the frequencies used for localization (Knudsen, 1981). (If you've ever flown in a glider, you know that the absence of engine noise doesn't mean that the flight is quiet.)

Given the barn owl's superior localizing abilities, you shouldn't be surprised to learn that the physiology of the owl's auditory system has been of great interest to researchers (D. Moore, 1989). The importance of auditory localization for the barn owl is reflected in a spatial arrangement of neurons in the owl's equivalent of the inferior colliculus. These auditory neurons have spatial receptive fields, and they are arranged so that neurons near one another are excited by sounds near one another in space. The fact that this information is absent at the ears means that it must be constructed from binaural inputs, as we suggested earlier. Timing and intensity information is separate before this information reaches the inferior colliculus (Konishi, 1993). However, researchers have located a spatial map in the inferior colliculus combined from both sources of localization information (Takahashi, 1989).

As you saw in Chapter 9, the human superior colliculus contains spatial maps of both visual and auditory information that are in alignment with one another. The same is true of the barn owl. Furthermore, the alignment of the visual and auditory maps in the barn owl's brain is determined by visual experience (Knudsen, 1983; Knudsen & Brainard, 1991). As we stated in Theme 1, the senses share similarities and inter-

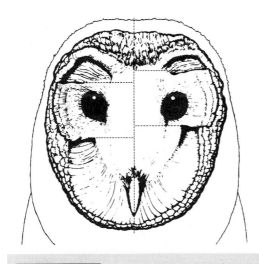

FIGURE 10.9 Facial structure of the barn owl. The barn owl is able to localize vertically because of its facial feathers. The left ear is more sensitive to sounds coming from below, because the opening for the left ear is tilted downward. The right ear is more sensitive to sounds coming from above, because the opening for the right ear is tilted upward. (From Knudsen, 1981)

act with one another. The impact of visual experience on the alignment of the auditory map in the owl's superior colliculus is an exciting example of Theme 1. After discussing auditory localization in bats, we will explore similar interactions between vision and audition in humans.

BATS

Most species of bats rely heavily on auditory information for survival. Bats are nocturnal creatures, evolving in a niche of lessened competition. Few flying carnivores are about at night, so bats can concentrate on being predators without worrying about becoming prey themselves. Most bats hunt insects, although some eat fruit and others eat fish or small amphibians. Despite our aversion to bats, they represent little potential for harm to humans, and in fact some species of bats consume huge numbers of that dreaded predator of humans—the mosquito. The aversion to bats probably comes from several sources, such as the fact that bats are not especially cute creatures.

In the late 1700s, Spallanzani became one of the first people to conduct research on bats. By blinding the bats and observing that they were still able to fly without hitting obstacles, he determined that bats do not need visual information to navigate through the environment. Spallanzani was not able to proceed any further in determining the means of bat spatial perception. In fact, only with the development of extremely sensitive sound-recording instruments have researchers begun to unravel the complexities of bat spatial perception.

As we now know, bats are able to navigate in the dark because of their ability to use **echolocation,** sending out an auditory signal and gathering information about the environment from the returning echoes. No wonder Spallanzani could not figure out how the bats were navigating after being blinded—he couldn't hear them make any noise! Most of the sounds used by bats are far above the range of frequencies of tones detected by humans. The actual frequencies emitted, and the patterns of emission over time, are characteristic of particular species of bats.

As Suga (1990) points out, echolocation is an amazingly sensitive navigational instrument. For instance, some bats can detect and avoid wires just a bit larger than 0.5 millimeter—about the width of a cotton thread (Gustafson & Schnitzler, 1979). Bats are also amazingly good at distinguishing mealworms (which they actually *like* to eat) from similarly sized plastic and metal pieces that they encounter as they fly. (The experiment is actually done by launching the edible and inedible targets into the flight path of the bat.) The basis of such a discrimination is likely an analysis of the fine details of the echoes returning from the edible and inedible objects (Simmons & Chen, 1989).

The relations between predators and prey are interesting. For instance, many insects have developed evasive tactics when they perceive the bat's signals (May, 1991). Bats also appear to have had an impact on the development of various prey. Tropical bats that hunt frogs do so by listening for the frog's mating call. Bats are capable of discriminating among frog calls, preferring smaller frogs and avoiding a species of poisonous frog. Tuttle and Ryan (1981) found that bats were far less successful in catching the frogs when the frogs were quiet. Also, the frogs seemed to be shortening their mating calls over time to enhance their chances at procreation without becoming a bat's meal.

Although they rely heavily on echolocation, the saying "Blind as a bat" is not at all accurate. In fact, bats' visual abilities are equivalent to those of many nocturnal creatures (Ellins & Masterson, 1974). Even when auditory cues are available, bats do depend on their eyes. To illustrate this fact, researchers placed normal bats in a lighted room with glass windows and a glass door. The bats would often crash into the windows and door, indicating that they were ignoring any echolocation cues (Masterson & Ellins, 1974). Blinded bats were much less likely to crash into the glass.

Bats also use their sense of smell. Thousands of bats line the walls of the caves in which bats rest, with all the young pups often together in one area. How does a returning mother find her young? Apparently, she first goes back to the general location where she last left her young. Then she calls and listens for the voices of her young, and finally she sniffs them to be sure they are really hers before nursing them—using input from three senses (Sullivan, 1984).

Just as the auditory system of the owl has evolved to provide for auditory localization, so the bat's auditory system is exquisitely adapted to the needs of the organism. Keep in mind that the bat is typically flying along as it emits sounds. Thus, any returning echoes will be compressed, or Doppler-shifted, just as a train's whistle changes pitch as it comes toward you. So the bat has to emit one frequency, but it must be especially sensitive to a different returning frequency. The bat is more sensitive to the returning frequency (61.2 kHz, for kiloHertz, or 61,200 Hz) than to the emitted frequency (below 60 kHz) because of a differential stiffness in the basilar membrane. The bat's brain, typically the size of a large pearl, has an amazingly complex auditory system, with parts of the auditory cortex specializing in different tasks (Pollak, 1989; Suga, 1990).

Although human beings are quite effective in localizing sounds in the environment, humans are far less effective than most owls and bats. The processes of adaptation have enabled these creatures to make extraordinary use of sound information. ◆

Visual Effects on Auditory Localization

We perceive the world around us as three-dimensional, with great correspondence between the auditory and visual spatial information we receive. The superior colliculus, because of its closely related auditory and visual spatial maps, must play a role in our unitary perception of space (Stein & Meredith, 1993). One frequently asked question is, Which of these two senses is dominant? We have already seen that the auditory spatial map of barn owls is affected by their visual experience. Jay and Sparks (1984) have determined that the auditory spatial map in monkeys actually shifts around in the superior colliculus as a result of where the monkey is looking! Researchers have not yet established that humans also exhibit this shifting auditory spatial map.

Much of the evidence does suggest that in humans, as in owls and monkeys, visual information can influence activity in the auditory modality (Bohlander, 1984). You may have noticed how

vision can bias auditory localization while watching a movie in a theater. The sound is really coming from speakers on both sides of the screen, yet it appears to be coming from the actors' lips. The same principle enables a ventriloquist to fool us (Stein & Meredith, 1993).

Researchers have developed experimental analogs of ventriloquism. For instance, Bertelson and Radeau (1981) found that visual cues can dominate auditory cues. The researchers asked people on some trials to point to the source of a sound and on other trials to the source of a light. The trick was that on several trials, the light and sound would be presented simultaneously—and at different locations. For example, when people were asked to point to a sound, the light was an irrelevant cue. The interesting question concerned where the people would point when the irrelevant cue was in a different location from the relevant cue. When asked to point to a sound source, people would often point to a sound location that was biased toward the irrelevant light (Bertelson & Radeau, 1981). Such a bias was not evident when the task was to point to the light, and sound was the irrelevant cue.

Using a different paradigm, Perrott (1993) found little evidence for the "ventriloquism effect." When people were presented with conflicting visual and auditory information, the visual stimulus had little influence on auditory localization. Further research will be required to determine the nature of the relationship between visual and auditory localization information. To date, most evidence supports the notion that visual localization cues are more likely to influence auditory localization than the reverse.

Of course, in the real world the auditory and visual localization cues are entirely consistent. When people are presented with consistent visual and auditory information, they are able to localize the stimuli better than when either visual or auditory information is presented alone. Thus, two senses are better than one in "normal" circumstances, in which an object is visible and emits a sound. Visual input can improve auditory localization, and auditory input can improve visual localization (Perrott et al., 1993).

In spite of a good deal of evidence that our visual system is masterful at localizing objects in space, we are even more accurate when auditory information is added to visual information. This advantage becomes even more apparent in complex stimulus situations, such as piloting a modern aircraft (Perrott et al., 1991). You should expect to see increasing use of auditory localization information in the design of remote-control devices (Durlach, 1991). Certainly, operators would benefit from the addition of binaural auditory input to displays that have been purely visual or displays that have only monaural sound capabilities.

Of course, we often localize sound sources that we can both see and hear. In those circumstances, the combination of auditory and visual information leads to better localization. However, suppose that you were trying to localize a sound source that you could *not* see. Would you be better able to locate the invisible sound source if you could see? Some researchers have argued that you can better localize these purely auditory stimuli if you have your eyes open (Salter, 1988; Shelton et al., 1982).

Do these findings fit with your own experience? What do you do when you are trying to localize a sound that is produced by something you cannot see (e.g., a mouse scratching within a wall)? Do you close your eyes to help localize the sound?

Lovelace and Anderson (1993) found that having one's eyes open had no effect when localizing an invisible sound source. Lovelace and Anderson used complex sounds (2-sec bursts of speech) that came from hidden speakers. People responded by pointing their fingers or eyes at the sound source. Visual input *was* useful in helping people adjust the direction in which their hands were pointing, but not for actually localizing the sound source.

In this section on sound localization, we have examined the sources of information that help identify the location of a sound source. The two ears receive different information about the sound's timing and the sound's intensity, and other cues are also available if that information is ambiguous. We also looked at accuracy on sound-localization tasks, as well as the physiological basis for sound localization. In addition, we considered how bats and owls localize sound and how vision may influence sound localization in humans.

Sound localization occurs almost effortlessly. The richness of information about sound that is available in the stimulus (Theme 2) and the impressive capacity of auditory systems to make use of this information (Theme 3) combine to accomplish this task of identifying the direction of a sound. In addition, because visual and auditory information about the location of a sound is typically consistent, the interaction of the senses (Theme 1) enhances our ability to localize sounds in space.

SECTION SUMMARY

Auditory Localization

1. Sound localization involves identifying the direction and the distance of a sound. One cue to the direction of a sound comes from the fact that a sound has to travel different distances to the two ears, creating an interaural time difference with two components, an onset difference and a phase difference. The interaural time difference is particularly useful for low-frequency sounds.

2. A second cue to the direction of a sound comes from the fact that a sound reaches the two ears at different intensities, creating an interaural intensity difference. The interaural intensity difference is particularly useful for high-frequency sounds.

3. When the auditory system has information only about interaural time difference and interaural intensity difference, some ambiguities might emerge; information based on pinnae contours and head or body movements helps to resolve these ambiguities.

4. Localization accuracy is influenced by head movement, the position of the sound source, and monaural conditions. We are able to localize complex sounds far better than pure tones (sine waves).

5. The superior olivary nucleus is an important structure in sound localization. Within that

structure, the medial superior olivary nucleus processes low-frequency information and is sensitive to interaural time differences. The lateral superior olivary nucleus processes high-frequency information and is sensitive to interaural intensity differences.

6. Barn owls and bats both have amazingly effective auditory localization abilities. Barn owls are particularly effective in vertical localization. Bats rely on echolocation (listening to the echoes of their own extremely high-frequency emissions) for maneuvering in the dark.

7. Our "map" of space is a unified one, with strong interrelations between auditory and visual information. However, humans seem to be more dependent on visual than on auditory information for localizing sound-emitting objects.

PERCEPTION OF SIMULTANEOUS SOUNDS

Typically, we do not hear a single sound in isolation. The computer's disk drive and fan purr along, birds chirp in the background, neighbors converse—and we hear it all at once. Researchers have been particularly interested in certain types of simultaneously occurring sounds. We will take a look at three such instances.

Perception of Tone Combinations

So far, we have discussed how a single complex tone can consist of several component tones. Now let's consider a related question. What happens when we add together several different pure tones? In Chapter 7 we considered the perception of color mixtures. A combination of a yellow light and a blue light, as we saw, produces a gray light rather than the separate components of yellow and blue. What happens when we combine two tones? The answer depends on the similarity of the two tones.

When two tones that are similar in frequency are sounded, we do not hear two distinct components. Instead, we hear a single strange tone whose quality depends on the difference in frequency between the two notes. We can distinguish three kinds of combination tones (Nordmark, 1978; R. M. Warren, 1982):

1. When the tones differ by less than 6 Hz (e.g., 400 Hz and 404 Hz), we hear a single tone that surges up and down in loudness at a frequency equal to the difference between the two tones (in this example, 4 Hz).
2. When the tones differ by 6 Hz to 24 Hz, we hear a single tone that appears to be a series of distinct impulses; the number of impulses per second equals the difference in frequency. Thus, a 400-Hz tone and a 412-Hz tone would produce 12 impulses per second.
3. When the tones differ by 25 Hz to about 10% of the frequency, we hear an unpleasant roughness rather than distinct impulses. For example, a 400-Hz tone would produce roughness when presented with any tone between 425 Hz and 440 Hz.

The changes in loudness found in the first and second categories—either the tone that surges up and down or the distinct impulses—are called *beats*. These beats occur by combining the two sounds outside the head and can be heard with one ear (monaural beats). Interestingly, beats can also occur if one low-frequency sound is played to the left ear, and another sound to the right ear (B. C. J. Moore, 1982). That is, we hear beats that arise from some neural combination of the information from both ears (Yost & Dye, 1991). Such beats are called binaural beats, to distinguish them from monaural beats.

What happens when we present a monaural combination of two tones that differ substantially? When two tones differ in frequency by more than 10%, we can hear two distinct tones. A *consonance* is a combination of two or more tones, played at the same time, judged to be pleasant. In general, tone combinations are consonant if the ratios of the frequencies of the two tones are simple fractions. For example, if you strike the A above middle C (440 Hz) and the A one octave higher (880 Hz), the combination is very pleasant.

Notice that the ratio of their frequencies is 2/1, a simple fraction. Other frequency ratios such as 3/2 and 4/3 also sound consonant.

In contrast, a ***dissonance*** is a combination of two or more tones, played at the same time, judged to be unpleasant. In general, when the ratio of two tones is not a simple fraction, the combination sounds dissonant. Dissonance occurs when the tone combinations produce a roughness or beating (Krumhansl, 1991). Consonance and dissonance are thought to be the result of matches and mismatches among the notes' overtones.

Masking

We discussed visual masking in Chapter 5. As we saw, in some conditions the presence of one visual stimulus prevents the perception of another. Similar masking phenomena occur in audition. Once again, then, we see a resemblance between vision and audition, an observation consistent with Theme 1 of the book.

Masking occurs when one tone becomes harder to hear because of the presence of another tone (Yost & Nielsen, 1985). The ability of one tone to mask another depends almost as much on the frequencies of the tones as on their intensities. The range of frequencies that can be masked by a particular tone is referred to as the ***critical band*** of that tone (Luce, 1993). In general, a tone masks other tones higher in frequency than itself. A tone is less successful in masking other tones lower in frequency than itself (Evans, 1982c). The width of the critical band is larger for higher-frequency tones and smaller for lower-frequency tones (Handel, 1989). Such masking effects are quite complex, and more recent research is causing people to revise their notions of critical bands and masking. However, researchers do believe that masking effects are due to the peripheral neural encoding of the stimuli (Luce, 1993).

We mentioned in connection with shape perception that backward masking was easier to demonstrate than forward masking. In other words, a mask presented after the test stimulus was more effective in blocking perception than a mask presented before the test stimulus. In audition, both forward and backward masking can also be demonstrated. However, forward masking tends to be more effective than backward masking (Jesteadt et al., 1982; Kallman & Massaro, 1979; Kallman & Morris, 1984). Thus, a tone can block you from hearing another tone presented either earlier or later. Auditory perception takes place over time, and the effects of a stimulus outlast its presentation; audition does not occur instantaneously.

Noise

Think about the noise you customarily experience in your daily life. *Noise* is irrelevant, excessive, or unwanted sound (Kryter, 1985). Of course, people differ with respect to their judgments about noise. A sound that is irrelevant, excessive, and unwanted to you may be sweet music to a friend.

In recent years, psychologists, engineers, and audiologists have become increasingly concerned about noise at home, entertainment places, and work. For example, people whose homes are near airports may experience a 120-dB sound every time a nearby jet takes off or lands. Rock groups can produce 110- to 120-dB music, nonstop, for several hours. Virshup (1985) measured the noise at various exclusive restaurants in New York City. It ranged from 66 dB at the classic Four Seasons to 94 dB at a trendy new restaurant.

Consider the noise that can be produced in work settings. A jackhammer produces sounds of 120 dB, for example. In some cases, noise at work has produced deafness. For example, weavers in a mill were exposed to a sound level of about 100 dB for an 8-hour day. This level was so intolerable that the weavers were partially deaf—even on weekends—after several years of employment (Taylor et al., 1965). As another example, our government pays millions of dollars monthly to compensate military veterans for hearing loss (Martin, 1994).

Effects of Noise

For ethical reasons, psychologists cannot study noise by presenting extremely loud noises to humans. A common approach is therefore to present loud, but safe, tones to humans for short periods and to observe the temporary changes that occur in hearing ability.

To discuss these changes in hearing ability, we need to examine the difference among three terms: masking, auditory adaptation, and auditory fatigue. Masking, a term discussed in the previous section, occurs when a stimulus cannot be heard because another stimulus is presented simultaneously or shortly before or after. In contrast, auditory adaptation and auditory fatigue concern the inability to hear a tone because a previous tone was presented for a long time. Specifically, *auditory adaptation* occurs when one tone is presented continuously; the perceived loudness of that tone decreases as time passes. In normal ears, a 1-minute exposure to a continuous tone produces loudness adaptation of 15 to 20 dB (Evans, 1982c; B. C. J. Moore, 1982). The auditory system therefore shows an adaptation similar to the adaptation in other perceptual systems, consistent with the first theme of the book.

Auditory adaptation involves the continuous presentation of the same tones. In contrast, *auditory fatigue* can be demonstrated when a stimulus is presented and then turned off, causing a change in threshold for *other* stimuli. For example, when people are exposed to a complex noise having an intensity of 120 dB for 5 minutes, their threshold for a 4000-Hz test tone presented 2 minutes later may shift by 40 dB (J. D. Miller, 1978). In other words, before exposure to the loud noise, they might have been able to hear the tone if it were presented at 0 dB. After the loud noise, the tone would have to be presented at 40 dB (the loudness of a quiet neighborhood) to be heard at all. Keep this in mind if you are planning on hearing a 120-dB band this weekend!

Auditory fatigue can lead to two kinds of changes in hearing threshold. *Temporary threshold shift* is a temporary increase in a hearing threshold as a result of exposure to noise. The threshold may not return to normal for several hours or days (Evans, 1982c). In the laboratory, temporary threshold shifts in humans are often studied because of the insights they may provide regarding permanent threshold shifts.

A *permanent threshold shift* is a permanent increase in a hearing threshold as a result of exposure to noise. Sometimes a permanent threshold shift is produced by a single loud noise, such as an extremely loud firecracker explosion. This shift has also been produced when a ringing cordless telephone is placed near the ear (Orchik et al., 1985). More often, permanent threshold shifts are a result of repeated exposures to noise on a regular basis, as in the case of the weavers mentioned earlier, or in the case of people who are regularly exposed to loud music. Hartman (1982) tested college students who regularly visited two dance clubs where the decibel level ranged between 123 and 129. He found that 32% of these students showed substantial permanent hearing loss in the high-frequency range.

Reducing Noise Pollution

In order to protect the hearing of workers, we must first identify those environments that place workers at risk (Lipscomb, 1992). Current government regulations prohibit industries from exposing their workers to more than an 85-dB sound level for an 8-hour day (Martin, 1994). Even though this sound level may produce some hearing loss, special-interest groups continually pressure the government to increase or eliminate this limit. Thus, factory workers still need to be concerned about the possibility of hearing loss. As you might imagine, the government guidelines call for very low levels of noise in some settings, such as hospitals (Grumet, 1993).

One approach to the problem is to provide earplugs or earmuffs to workers exposed to loud noises. Some types are inadequate, especially if they are being worn in vigorous working conditions (Casali & Park, 1990). However, with experience, people do become more adept at using the protectors properly (Merry et al., 1992).

Unfortunately, these protective devices are often uncomfortable and interfere with work. Thus, people may not wear hearing protectors if they perceive the devices as barriers to their ability to hear what is going on around them. People are more likely to wear protective devices if they are aware of the benefits (Lusk et al., 1995). Educating workers to the benefits of wearing such protective devices seems crucial.

Some efforts have been made to modify noise at its source. For example, the design of some jet airplanes has been changed to reduce their noise at takeoff and landing. Furthermore, some companies have included sound absorbers, either on machines or in walls. These absorbers, however, are much more effective for high-pitched sounds than for low rumbles. Ultimately, as Bershader (1981) says, "Quiet is a commodity that costs money" (p. 74). Individuals and industries will have to decide how much must be paid to reduce the noise in our environment.

SECTION SUMMARY

Perception of Simultaneous Sounds

1. When two tones are combined, the resulting sound depends on the difference in frequency between the two tones; we can hear beats, roughness, or two distinct tones.

2. The combination of two distinct tones can sound consonant if the ratios of the frequencies of the two tones form a simple fraction; otherwise, the combination sounds dissonant.

3. One tone can mask another in a tone combination, depending on the relative amplitude and frequency of the two tones.

4. Auditory adaptation produces a decreased perceived loudness for a tone that is presented continuously. Auditory fatigue occurs when a loud noise is presented and then turned off, making other tones difficult to hear.

5. Auditory fatigue can lead to a temporary threshold shift or a permanent threshold shift. Psychologists study temporary threshold shifts to gain insight about permanent threshold shifts.

6. Noise, or unwanted sound, is an increasing problem in modern society.

7. Noise pollution effects can be reduced by limiting workers' exposure to loud noises, providing earplugs or earmuffs, and modifying noise at its source.

REVIEW QUESTIONS

1. Discuss the place and frequency theories of pitch perception, going over the evidence in support of each theory. Point out the problems with both theories, and illustrate ways in which they might both be correct.

2. In the auditory tuning curves shown in Figure 10.2, notice that the curves are sharper for high-frequency tones, and that the curves are steeper to the right than they are to the left. Can you use what you know (especially Figure 10.1) to explain these phenomena?

3. Discuss why pitch is not perfectly correlated with frequency. Consider the factors that influence pitch and describe the conditions that would make the pitch abnormally high and the conditions that would make it abnormally low. Repeat this same process with

the relationship between frequency and loudness.

4. Using the equal loudness contours shown in Figure 10.4, answer the following questions (answers are given below):

   a. For a 1000-Hz tone at 40 dB, what sound pressure will be equally loud for a 300-Hz tone? A 50-Hz tone?

   b. For a 1000-Hz tone at 100 dB, what sound pressure will be equally loud for a 150-Hz tone? A 50-Hz tone?

5. Discuss the ways in which sound intensity and sound frequency might be measured, and contrast this with the ways in which pitch and loudness are measured.

6. Notice a sound in your present environment and list the cues that help you judge the di-

rection of the sound source. What are the factors that could help you resolve potential ambiguities about the location of that sound? Using only intensity differences, what frequency range would best be localized by a mouse, a human, and an elephant? (Hint: Think of the size of the head.)

7. Our perception of space is unitary—auditory and visual information provides us with consistent detail about the world. Compare the information we discussed in Chapter 6 on visual space perception with what you have learned in this chapter. How do you think the information might be integrated?

8. The kangaroo rat is able to avoid owls better than other prey of owls. Further, the kangaroo rat is particularly sensitive to sounds around 1000 Hz. How might that help the kangaroo rat avoid owls, and how have some prey of bats adapted behaviors to avoid being eaten?

9. Discuss the difference between monaural and binaural beats, and illustrate what binaural beats tell us about audition by discussing Houtsma and Goldstein's work on the missing fundamental.

10. Point out the differences among masking, auditory adaptation, auditory fatigue, temporary threshold shift, and permanent threshold shift. Which of these terms is relevant for the study of noise?

[For Question 4 on page 333, the answers are:
a. a 300-Hz tone at *40 dB* would be as loud as a 1000-Hz tone at 40 dB; a 50-Hz tone at *65 dB* would be as loud as a 1000-Hz tone at 40 dB;
b. a 150-Hz tone at *100 dB* would be as loud as a 1000-Hz tone at 100 dB; a 50-Hz tone at *110 dB* would be as loud as a 1000-Hz tone at 100 dB.]

NEW TERMS

pitch (304)
place theory (304)
frequency theory (305)
refractory period (305)
traveling wave (305)
envelope (306)
stimulation deafness
    experiment (306)
fundamental frequency (308)
harmonics (308)
overtones (308)
timbre (308)
missing fundamental (309)
volley principle (310)
octave (312)

mel scale (312)
loudness (314)
equal loudness contour (315)
profile analysis (317)
sone scale (318)
auditory localization (318)
onset difference (319)
phase difference (319)
interaural time difference (319)
interaural intensity
    difference (321)
cone of confusion (322)
minimum audible angle
    (MAA) (323)
lateralization (324)

medial superior olivary
    nucleus (324)
lateral superior olivary
    nucleus (324)
echolocation (327)
beats (330)
consonance (330)
dissonance (331)
masking (331)
critical band (331)
noise (331)
auditory adaptation (332)
auditory fatigue (332)
temporary threshold shift (332)
permanent threshold shift (332)

RECOMMENDED READINGS

Green, D. M. (1988a). Audition: Psychophysics and perception. In R. C. Atkinson, R. J. Herrnstein, G. Lindzey, & R. D. Luce (Eds.), *Stevens' handbook of experimental psychology* (2nd ed.) (pp. 327–376). New York: Wiley. Green's chapter provides a good overview of the material covered in this chapter of your textbook. Green has made major contributions to our understanding of the perception of loudness of complex sounds, so you might also want to read his article on profile analysis that appeared in *American Psychologist* (1983), 133–142. If you're really ambitious, you could try his book (1988b) *Profile analysis: Auditory intensity discrimination.* New York: Oxford University Press.

Handel, S. (1989). *Listening: An introduction to the perception of auditory events.* Cambridge, MA: MIT Press. This book is similar to the text by Rossing mentioned in the previous chapter. The organization of the text is a bit idiosyncratic, which is a large part of its charm. The writing style is clear, and each chapter is quite readable (even the chapters on the physics of sound and the physiology of sound perception), but the chapters on stream segregation and identification of sounds are particularly good.

Kryter, K. D. (1994). *The handbook of hearing and the effects of noise: Physiology, psychology, and public health.* San Diego: Academic. This book contains a wealth of recent information about the effects of environmental noise. If you are interested in practical applications of the auditory principles that we have been discussing, you will enjoy this book.

Middlebrooks, J. C., & Green, D. M. (1991). Sound localization by human listeners. *Annual Review of Psychology, 42,* 135–159. This review article provides a fairly comprehensive and very readable overview of research on auditory localization.

Stein, B. E., & Meredith, M. A. (1993). *The merging of the senses.* Cambridge, MA: MIT Press. This book is particularly appropriate for this chapter because of its coverage of the integration of visual and auditory information in the superior colliculus. If you enjoy discussions of the neural underpinnings of the senses, you will take particular delight in this book.

11 Auditory Pattern Perception

By this point in the text, you are certainly aware that our perceptual world is an extremely complex one. Objects around us vary in many ways, including size, shape, wavelength of reflected light, and distance—which our visual system has evolved to represent. Those objects also give rise to extremely complex sound waves—which our auditory system has evolved to represent.

In Chapters 9 and 10 we examined the structure and function of the auditory system, particularly for processing simple auditory stimuli. Because our auditory world is not so simple, this chapter addresses the perception of complex auditory stimuli. Stop for a minute and listen carefully to the sounds around you. You are unlikely to hear anything remotely resembling the pure tones often used in the laboratory. Instead, in spite of your best efforts to find a quiet place to read, you might hear music playing, people talking, and the welter of sounds produced by machinery.

All of these sound waves reach our ears, producing an extremely complex set of vibrations along our basilar membranes. As you might imagine, the task of analyzing the complex waveform in our inner ears into the various streams of information is not easy. Right now you might be listening to the cars passing by outside the window, the music playing gently in the next room, the wind rustling through the trees, and the whirring of the computer fan. The auditory stimuli provide no signposts to the auditory system saying that one ripple in the wave is due to voices, another due to a guitar, and others due to the wind or a fan. Nonetheless, most often our auditory experience is effortlessly analytical. We do not hear a complex waveform, we simply hear voices, guitars, and fans. The puzzle of how we do so is endlessly intriguing to most people.

As we indicated in Chapter 10, researchers are using complex tones more frequently in the laboratory. The peripheral auditory apparatus (the inner ear) may be sufficient for analyzing simple tones. However, tones of greater complexity begin to tax the analytical ability of the inner ear. Consistent with Theme 4 of this text (see page 12), central processes (knowledge and expectations) become crucial for the perception of complex sounds.

The sound waves discussed in this chapter are extremely complex in that the multiplicity of frequencies is varied, or modulated, over time. After discussing some research on perceiving patterns in such complex auditory stimuli, we will turn our attention to two specific examples of complex auditory stimuli—music and speech.

PERCEPTION OF COMPLEX AUDITORY PATTERNS

Why has it taken so long for psychologists to begin studying complex sounds? Perhaps you've heard the joke about the stranger who comes upon a drunk searching for his keys under a streetlight. The stranger joins in the unsuccessful search for a while, and then asks the drunk where he lost his keys. The drunk points further up the road, prompting the stranger to ask, "Then why are you searching here?" The drunk replies, "Because the light is better here."

The necessity for precise control in the laboratory often leads researchers to address questions that are limited by available technology— searching where the "lighting" is good even when more crucial problems lie elsewhere. As we have seen in previous chapters, technological advances typically pave the way for important empirical advances.

Similarly, interest in the perception of complex auditory patterns grew out of technological advances that allowed researchers to control several parameters of the sound stimulus simultaneously. These technological advances were coupled with a growing trend toward a view that hearing takes place "in the brain rather than in the ear . . . [and] . . . depends on skill, experience, learning, memory, and other variables generally called 'central factors' in perception" (Espinoza-Varas & Watson, 1989, p. 68). You should recognize this position as identical to Theme 4 of this text.

These higher-level processes become crucial to a discussion of complex auditory stimuli, just as they are crucial for a discussion of complex visual stimuli. As a result, our discussion will overlap substantially with the earlier discussion of visual pattern perception. As you will recall, our discussion focused on the central processes used by the visual system to make sense of complex visual stimuli—contributions of the Gestalt and cognitive psychologists. After first describing the nature of the problem facing our auditory system, we will revisit the Gestalt approach and the cognitive approach from the perspective of audition.

Analyzing Simultaneous Complex Sounds

As Theme 2 of this text suggests, our perceptual world is rich with information. At times, though, the world seems overpowering in its richness. Our ears are assaulted by a welter of simultaneous auditory stimuli. The nature of the problem is illustrated by the following visual example from Bregman (1990):

```
AI CSAITT STIOTOS
```

What could this possibly mean?

The problem emerges because two different messages are mixed together. Such a mixture of information along our basilar membranes is quite typical. Our auditory system has evolved to enable us to segregate the various streams of information. To make the visual example easier to segregate, we can highlight some of the letters and offset them slightly:

```
A CSAITT SIOTS
 I    I T  I O
```

Now the meaning becomes clear! How do we segregate the various auditory streams of information falling on our ears? What factors allow us to segregate one auditory message ("A cat sits") from another ("I sit too")?

Our auditory system appears to latch onto salient features of the sound stimuli in organizing the incoming information. One important feature is frequency (Bregman, 1990, 1993). That is, we tend to organize (and group together) incoming auditory information that is similar in frequency.

For example, Barsz (1988) showed that people were better able to segregate alternating tones when they differed substantially in frequency.

We find examples of auditory stream segregation based on frequency in both music and speech. As we will discuss in more detail later, you can more easily identify two streams of musical information if they differ in frequency range (W. J. Dowling, 1973). Have you ever had difficulty following the threads of conversations that swirl around you at a crowded party? If so, then you've experienced the "cocktail party" problem. Any line of conversation is harder to follow when the competing voices are similar in pitch. You can more easily separate two messages delivered simultaneously by someone with a high-pitched voice and someone with a low-pitched voice.

Timbre may also be used to organize auditory information, with sounds of more similar timbre grouped together (Bregman, 1993; Hartmann & Johnson, 1991). This principle enables us to distinguish instruments and voices that might be similar in frequency. Spatial location and timing may also be useful cues for segregating auditory information (Bregman, 1990, 1993). Furthermore, amplitude may be used by the auditory system to organize incoming sounds. Louder sounds tend to be organized together, and softer sounds tend to be organized together. However, most research suggests that amplitude is not as useful as other cues (Bregman, 1990).

Bregman (e.g., 1990, 1993) refers to the auditory system's ability to analyze simultaneous complex sounds as auditory scene analysis. He argues that the complexities of such analysis suggest that several processes are probably involved (Bregman, 1993). One way to think about how we organize the overlapping auditory information into separate streams is to invoke some of the Gestalt principles discussed earlier. We'll do so now, then proceed to explore a more cognitive approach.

Gestalt Principles

Just as the Gestalt psychologists had a profound influence on the study of visual pattern perception, they have also had an impact on the study of auditory pattern perception. In fact, many of the Gestalt principles we discussed earlier may be applied to auditory stimuli (Bartlett, 1993; Deutsch, 1986a). Because of the differences between auditory and visual stimuli, some of the details of the Gestalt principles are slightly modified, but the underlying concepts remain intact.

In the preceding section, we discussed the features of complex auditory stimuli that allow us to segregate the complex input into various streams. For example, researchers have found evidence for the operation of two Gestalt principles, good continuation and closure. An example of "homophonic continuity" is found when a continuous stimulus of constant frequency is very briefly increased in amplitude and then returned to its original amplitude. When this variation in amplitude happens repeatedly, people perceive a tone of constant amplitude, with an occasional briefly added tone of equal frequency swelling the overall amplitude (R. M. Warren, 1982). The principle of closure is at work in producing the phonemic restoration effect discussed later in the chapter. When a small portion of a spoken word, for instance, is obliterated by a cough, people report hearing the word as complete.

In Gestalt terms, Pragnänz might emerge because of similarity in frequency or proximity in time, linking the similar sounds into a stream (Bregman, 1990). With segregation into streams, we can selectively attend to one stream while disregarding the other streams (Matlin, 1994). This process should strike you as the auditory equivalent of the separation of figure and ground.

In summary, the Gestalt laws of grouping and the figure–ground relationship are not limited to the visual system. Auditory processing also shows the tendency for a distinct figure to be seen against a less prominent background and the tendency to find patterns on the basis of qualities such as similarity. We will also discuss these organizing principles in the section on music perception.

Cognitive Principles

In this chapter, you have already seen several illustrations of the necessity to invoke higher-order processes to explain how we process complex auditory stimuli. One reason that cognitive processes play an important role is that complex auditory stimuli, such as music and speech, occur over fairly long periods of time. Thus, memory is vital for the integration of music and speech over time (McAdams & Bigand, 1993a).

Our ability to recognize music and speech clearly indicates the operation of auditory memory (Crowder, 1993; McAdams, 1993). We certainly have the melodies of numerous songs floating around in our memories (Dowling, 1994; Hubbard & Stoekig, 1992). Think of a song that you know very well. Can you "hear" the song playing in your mind? Can you recognize the timbre of the singer's voice and the instruments? Do the words and the music seem to go together? Research indicates that we do store many aspects of the auditory stimulus—such as pitch, timbre, and rhythm—in memory. Furthermore, we seem to construct an integrated memory of the particular words *and* melody of the song (Crowder, 1993).

Memory is also apparent when we find evidence of learning—improvement in performance of a task over time. If auditory research used only simple sine waves, researchers would find little evidence of learning. For instance, people are just as adept at discriminating details of pure tones at the beginning of testing as they are after prolonged training (Espinoza-Varas & Watson, 1989). In contrast, people are much better at discriminating *complex* sequences of tones after substantial training than they are at the beginning of testing (Leek & Watson, 1984; Neisser & Hirst, 1974). Thus, the study of complex auditory stimuli indicates that experience aids perception in a way that the study of simple auditory stimuli would never have supported.

Charles Watson's laboratory at Indiana University has been the source of a number of interesting experiments illustrating the importance of cognitive factors in auditory perception (e.g., Kelly & Watson, 1986; Leek & Watson, 1984; Watson & Foyle, 1985). To illustrate one area of Watson's research, let's examine a prototypical experiment (Espinoza-Varas & Watson, 1989). People were asked to listen to many thousands

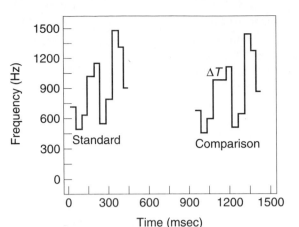

FIGURE 11.1 Typical complex stimuli used in studies by Watson and his colleagues. The 10-tone sequence is identical for both the standard and the comparison stimulus except for one change. In this case, the fourth tone in the sequence is slightly longer in the comparison sequence. On some trials the standard stimulus is repeated twice, and on other trials the standard is followed by the comparison sequence. People listen to a series of trials and indicate whether they think the two sequences are the same (standard–standard) or different (standard–comparison). With practice, people improve their ability to discriminate between tone sequences, illustrating the importance of experience for perception of complex stimuli. (From Espinoza-Varas & Watson, 1989)

of pairs of 10-tone sequences, with each pair separated by a brief interval. The listener then judged whether the tone sequences were the same or different. On half the trials, the pairs were in fact identical. When the pairs were different, a single tone in the sequence might differ in frequency, intensity, or duration. Figure 11.1 illustrates a pair of sequences in which the fourth tone differs in duration.

Watson and his colleagues have found that people are far better at making such discriminations (compared to discriminating simple tones in isolation) when they have had some experience

and when they have an idea where in the segment the difference might occur. Such improvements in performance due to practice or knowledge suggest the operation of central processes. When listeners know nothing about the sequence, they appear to switch to a more global listening strategy that allows them to detect only major differences (Espinoza-Varas & Watson, 1989). The various listening strategies adopted under different conditions provide further evidence that higher-order processes are operating.

The effects of learning and memory found in Watson's laboratory parallel those found in David Green's work in profile analysis. As we discussed in Chapter 10, profile analysis requires people to discriminate complex auditory stimuli that are presented simultaneously. Identifying small changes in a single component of the multitone complex is a very difficult task. However, research on profile analysis also reveals that people become much more adept at such tasks when they have had a great deal of experience (Green, 1988b; Kidd et al., 1986).

In summary, cognitive processes contribute to many aspects of auditory functioning. Auditory memory certainly plays an important role in the processing of complex stimuli. Furthermore, improvements with practice argue for the operation of central processing of complex auditory information, whether the complex stimuli are created by presenting sequences of tones over time or by simultaneously presenting a complex of tones. We now turn our attention to two extremely complex types of auditory stimuli—music and speech.

SECTION SUMMARY

Perception of Complex Auditory Patterns

1. The growing trend toward the study of complex auditory patterns stems from technological advances and a belief in the importance of central processes in auditory perception.

2. Although complex sounds often occur simultaneously, we are able to separate the many different streams of information. We segre-

gate the streams on the basis of many properties of the sound stimuli, such as frequency, timbre, location, timing, and amplitude.

3. Gestalt principles of organization (proximity, similarity, closure, good continuation, etc.) and the figure–ground relationship can be readily applied to the perception of complex auditory patterns.

4. The importance of central processes is illustrated by research showing that auditory memory, practice, and advance knowledge are crucial when we perceive complex auditory patterns.

MUSIC PERCEPTION

We have already presented evidence that music is a complex auditory phenomenon. Each sound that the instruments emit is a complex wave. At any given time in the musical piece, several different instruments are likely to be playing simultaneously. However, the sounds are rarely salient as isolated notes. Instead, they are woven into a melodic contour of pitch and rhythm (Dowling, 1994; Krumhansl, 1985, 1991). Furthermore, the listener is not a passive perceiver, but is actively engaged in processing the music—bringing acoustic memories, aesthetic judgments, and expectations to bear on the piece (Bartlett, 1993; Bharucha, 1994; Hubbard, 1993). The experience of music is not purely cognitive or aesthetic, because music is also capable of arousing an emotional response (Meyer, 1994; Storr, 1992).

Given this complexity, the organizing principles we have just been discussing certainly apply to music perception. Moreover, the patterns that are present in music share commonalities with several nonauditory areas, as illustrated by Douglas Hofstadter (1979) in his thought-provoking book *Gödel, Escher, Bach: An Eternal Golden Braid.* The close ties among mathematics, computer science, visual art, and music illustrated by Hofstadter serve to make the study of music perception a remarkably rich area of research. In this section of the chapter, we will first review some

of the perceptual qualities discussed in Chapter 10—pitch, tone combinations, timbre, and loudness. However, this time we will emphasize how these qualities are important in music. Then we will consider music as complex auditory patterns.

Perceptual Qualities and Music

In this chapter, we are primarily concerned with music as auditory pattern. To provide some background and to relate music perception to the auditory principles discussed in previous chapters, we will start with an overview of some basic auditory features such as pitch, timbre, and loudness. As you will soon see, patterns become apparent even within such basic features.

Pitch

At this point in the textbook, you probably would not be the least surprised to learn that an early theory of musical pitch perception was proposed by Hermann von Helmholtz (1863). Helmholtz's range of perceptual interests is truly amazing, even if modern theorists have criticized him as reductionistic (Butler, 1992).

In Chapter 10 we saw that humans can hear frequencies in the range of 20 to about 20,000 Hz. Music represents a substantially narrower range of pitches, particularly at the upper end. Figure 11.2 shows that the fundamental frequencies on the piano range from 27.5 to 4186 Hz. As you can also see, all the instruments in an orchestra—and also the human voice—have even more limited ranges. Their ranges are typically less than half the range of the piano. Given the narrow range of fundamental frequencies important to music, you might well wonder why stereo systems tout their ability to reproduce sounds over a wider range (often the full 20- to 20,000-Hz range). The answer is that the overtones produced by musical instruments are multiples of their fundamental frequencies, and these overtones can easily reach into the upper range of our auditory capabilities. The rich timbre of musical instruments can be reproduced only with the faithful rendition of the fundamental frequency *and* the overtones.

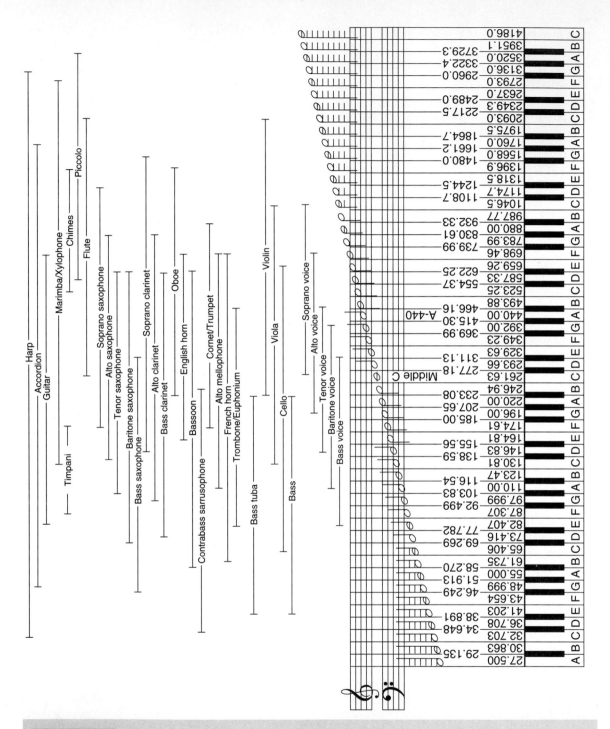

FIGURE 11.2 Pitch of musical instruments, with the piano keyboard as a reference. The white keys are referred to as naturals, and the black keys are sharps or flats. As you go up the keyboard from one key to the next key of the same name, the frequency produced by the key is doubled. The successive doublings of frequency are referred to as octaves. Notice that other instruments have an even narrower range of fundamental frequencies than the piano. (From Pierce, 1983)

Figure 11.2 shows a piano keyboard with tones progressing from low to high, an arrangement that suggests that pitch is one-dimensional. Nothing could be further from the truth! Organizing principles operate even for such basic qualities as pitch. These principles are evident on the keyboard in the repetitive arrangement of the keys. After every 12 keys, the pattern repeats itself. As you can see, the white keys are labeled C, D, E, F, G, A, and B. The tones produced by the intervening black keys are called sharps (or flats)—$C^\#$, $D^\#$, $F^\#$, $G^\#$, and $A^\#$ (or, alternatively, D^b, E^b, G^b, A^b, and B^b).

People—at least in Western cultures—tend to organize tones on the basis of the doubling or halving of their frequencies, forming the octave discussed in Chapter 10. If one tone is twice the frequency of another tone, the two tones are an *octave* apart, and these tones are given the same name. We tend to perceive tones in this two-to-one relationship as more similar than tones in any other relationship (Deutsch, 1992a). *Tone chroma* refers to the similarity shared by all musical tones that have the same name (Butler, 1992). For example, all C's on the piano sound similar, even though they differ in frequency and are separated by many other tones.

Tone height refers to the increase in pitch that accompanies an increase in frequency (Krumhansl, 1991). The highest C on the piano has greater tone height than all the other C's. Following the musical convention of using subscripts to represent a tone's position on the piano, C_1 is the lowest C, C_2 is the next higher C, and so forth, up to C_8. Because C_1 has a frequency of 32.7 Hz, C_2 has a frequency of 32.7 × 2, or 65.4 Hz. Conceptually, then, you should probably think of pitch organized as in Figure 11.3, rather than in the linear keyboard fashion shown in Figure 11.2. Figure 11.3 highlights the repetitive organization of pitch, with each tone chroma appearing at increasing tone heights.

Other evidence against the one-dimensional view of pitch comes from research on tonality. *Tonality* is the organization of pitches around one particular tone. This tone, known as the *tonic,* is one of the 12 pitches within an octave,

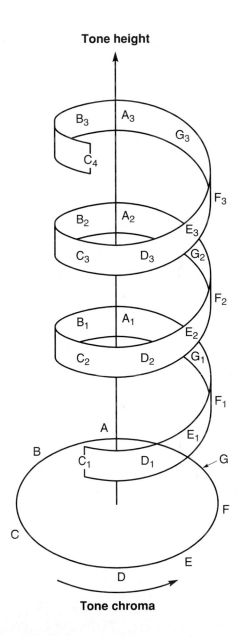

FIGURE 11.3 Schematic diagram of pitch, showing tone chroma and tone height. This spiraling representation captures the nature of perceived pitch better than the linear representation of the piano keyboard because it illustrates the basic similarity of tone chromas.

represented on the piano by the 7 white keys plus the 5 black keys within an octave. In Western music, the tonic is the same as the key of a piece of music (Krumhansl, 1985).

Carol Krumhansl used a method called the probe-tone technique to examine tonality in music (Krumhansl, 1983, 1985; Krumhansl & Kessler, 1982). In the **probe-tone technique,** listeners first hear a musical chord or a scale, either of which provides sufficient information to establish a key. Then a single pitch, or probe tone, is presented; this tone is one of the 12 tones found within the octave of the key being examined. The listeners are instructed to rate how well that tone fits within the scale or chord presented earlier. For example, in a typical trial, listeners might first hear a scale in the key of C major. Then they might hear the probe tone of F and be asked to judge how well that F fits within the framework of the C-major scale. Incidentally, the listeners who were tested in this research had each studied a musical instrument for at least 5 years, although they had received little instruction in musical theory.

The results showed, as expected, that some tones were judged to fit much better than others within a given key. For example, in the key of C major the tone that received the highest rating was C, which is the tonic for this key. The next "best" tone for this key was G, followed in order by E, F, A, D, and B. All the five tones with sharps (C#, D#, F#, G#, and A#, represented by the black keys on the piano) were judged equally unsuitable for the key of C. A C# might be right next to a C on the piano, but *psychologically* it does not belong within the key of C.

Krumhansl was curious to see whether these ratings of probe tones were correlated with the use of these tones in classical music. Luckily, statistical analyses have been conducted on several pieces by composers such as Mozart, Schubert, and Strauss. These analyses list the total duration of each tone in a particular piece of music (because some tones are short and some are long). The relationship between probe-tone ratings and total duration of occurrence in a piece by Schubert is illustrated in Figure 11.4.

Although the Schubert piece is in the key of C, the music is tonally oriented toward G major (Pollino, 1993). Thus, G is the tone that has the longest total duration, and G was also the most highly rated tone. Clearly, people's probe-tone ratings are closely related to Schubert's use of those tones. Tones that received high ratings using the probe-tone technique occur often in Schubert's piece, and tones that received low ratings occurred far less often.

The accumulating evidence strongly supports the importance of tonal structure in determining the tones used in musical compositions (Krumhansl, 1991). People learn tonal hierarchies through the typical tone distributions found in their musical experience. In Western music, the tonal hierarchy—in conjunction with rhythmic changes—serves to mark melodic phrase boundaries (Boltz, 1989, 1992). Thus, not only are particular tones related, given a tonic, but they also serve to direct the listener's attention to transitions in the music. Obviously, knowledge of tonal structure is vitally important for music composition and theory.

Absolute Pitch Perception

Many of us cannot carry a tune, even given a metaphorical bucket. However, some people have amazing pitch perception. People with **absolute pitch** are extremely accurate in identifying an isolated tone or producing a requested tone. When they do make errors in identification, they often name the note accurately, but they are off by an octave (Krumhansl, 1991; Luce, 1993). On the basis of a number of studies, people with absolute pitch can identify tones with about 90% accuracy (Takeuchi & Hulse, 1993).

One factor that influences the ability of people with absolute pitch to identify a tone is its timbre. Another factor that influences identification is the tone chroma. People with absolute pitch are faster and more accurate at identifying the notes that are produced by white keys on the piano than notes produced by black keys. One explanation for this effect derives from the finding that almost all people with absolute pitch began to study music before they were 5 years

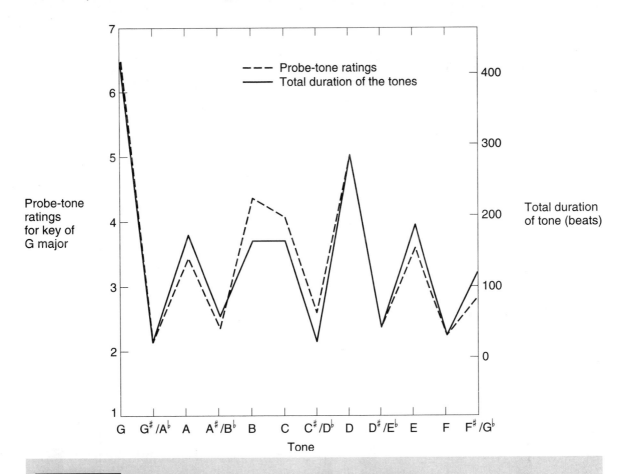

FIGURE 11.4 Relationship between probe-tone ratings and total duration of tones, for Schubert's "Moments Musicaux," op. 94, no. 1. Because the piece is tonally oriented toward G major, G is the most common note (longest duration). The probe-tone technique suggests that D, B, A, and E are musically related to G, and those tones were used frequently by Schubert in constructing this piece. (From Krumhansl, 1985)

old (Krumhansl, 1991; Takeuchi & Hulse, 1993). The white-key pitches form the scale of C major, which is a common scale for teaching beginning students. Assuming that early training focuses on the white keys, children may grow out of the critical period for developing absolute pitch before they have had sufficient exposure to the black keys (Takeuchi & Hulse, 1993).

C major is a very familiar key to musicians. Therefore, it is not surprising that musicians with

absolute pitch are better able to identify the notes of this scale. Obviously, they have had enormous experience with the component notes and their relationships to one another. What would happen to identification scores if people with absolute pitch were given unusual keys? To investigate this question, Miyazaki (1993) asked people to identify intervals in three key contexts: C major, F# major, and a slightly out-of-tune E major. People who did not have absolute pitch performed the

Demonstration 11.1

Consonant and Dissonant Tone Combinations

Locate a piano. You do not have to know how to play it to try this demonstration, but you do need to be able to locate middle C. The figure below illustrates the notes included in this octave. Musicians have provided names for many of the intervals or tone combinations, as listed below. Play each of the first seven tone combinations and judge the pleasantness of each of these pairs. Now try the three dissonant tones whose combinations form complex fractions. You may want to experiment with other possible combinations.

Name of Interval	Notes (in C-major key)	Frequency Ratio
Octave	C–C	2/1
Major third	C–E	5/4
Minor third	E–G	6/5
Fourth	C–F	4/3
Fifth	C–G	3/2
Major sixth	C–A	5/3
Minor sixth	E–C	8/5
(Dissonance)	C–C#	262/277
(Dissonance)	C–D	262/294
(Dissonance)	C–D#	262/311

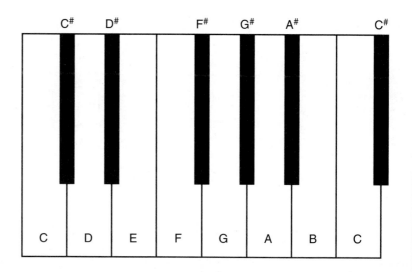

same in all three key contexts. In contrast, people with absolute pitch showed much poorer performance on the unusual keys. On this interval-identification task, at least, people with absolute pitch are thrown off by unusual keys.

Another way to assess absolute pitch perception is to have people produce tones by singing them or adjusting an oscillator. Naming tones that are presented is an easier task than producing tones, just as it would be easier to identify the

Mona Lisa than it would be to produce it. Even people with absolute pitch make minor errors in producing a common tone (A_4). Interestingly, these errors are not random; instead, they tend to vary in a cyclical fashion over time (Wynn, 1993).

Most people think of absolute pitch as a rare ability. However, many more people may have some form of absolute pitch than had been previously thought (Krumhansl, 1991). If theories of the development of absolute pitch are correct, the ability occurs because of experience during a critical period of development. As such, it has important implications for pitch perception and for perceptual development.

Perception of Tone Combinations

Chapter 10 discussed how two tones could be combined to produce either consonant or dissonant combinations. Let us now examine how the frequencies of the tones in a consonant tone combination tend to form a ratio that is a simple fraction. For example, you know that if a tone is combined with another tone exactly one octave lower, the higher tone is twice the frequency of the lower tone; the ratio is a simple 2/1. Try Demonstration 11.1 to illustrate various consonant and dissonant tone combinations. This demonstration also lists the commonly used names for the musical intervals.

Musicians have known about these ratios for thousands of years. For example, a Babylonian tablet from earlier than 1000 B.C. describes the 4/3 ratio in tuning (Pierce, 1983). You'll recall learning the Pythagorean theorem about the sides of triangles in high school. Pythagoras also developed theories in the sixth century B.C. about the ratios of the lengths of vibrating strings (Warren, 1982). These theories provided a basis for contemporary research.

The consonance of tone combinations largely depends on whether the frequency of two tones forms a simple ratio. Furthermore, people are quite good at detecting deviations from simple ratios (Krumhansl, 1991). However, consonance is not determined solely by simple ratios (Shepard, 1982). You might have expected this conclusion, because you know that perceptual ex-

periences do not tend to be related to physical stimuli in a simple fashion. For example, pitch depends on more than frequency, loudness depends on more than amplitude, and timbre depends on more than the nature of the harmonics.

The perception of consonance and dissonance also depends upon individual differences and cultural backgrounds. For example, an American who hears East Indian music for the first time may judge the combination of notes dissonant and unpleasant. Many musical intervals in Indian music do not correspond to simple ratios; however, the combinations do not sound unpleasant to Indians. Instead, the music sounds rich and extremely varied in mood (B. C. J. Moore, 1982). Similarly, cultural preferences change as a function of time. The music of Stravinsky was condemned as unpleasant dissonance 60 years ago, yet it sounds consonant to most of us today.

Timbre

As we have discussed, timbre has received much less attention than pitch. Deutsch (1986a) points out, "Timbre may be described as that perceptual quality of a sound that distinguishes it from other sounds, when simple attributes such as pitch and loudness are held constant" (pp. 32–34). For example, a flute and an oboe may both play the same tone at the same loudness, but you can still distinguish between the nasal quality of the oboe and the pure quality of the flute.

As discussed earlier, an important determinant of timbre is the harmonics or overtones that supplement the fundamental frequency. Figure 11.5a shows the fundamental frequency and harmonics resulting from Fourier analysis of one of the higher tones in the oboe's range. Notice that the harmonics are relatively high amplitude, in comparison to the fundamental frequency, and this particular tone contains eight harmonics. Contrast this distribution of harmonics with that of the flute, in Figure 11.5b, for one of the higher tones in the flute's range. Impressively, this tone has only a single harmonic, and its amplitude is so low that you might miss it on first inspection. An important characteristic of the flute's distribution of energy is that

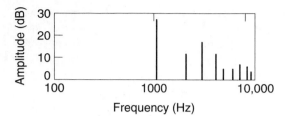

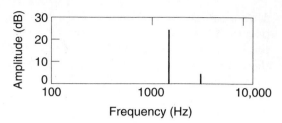

a. Note with frequency of 1046 Hz, played on the oboe

b. Note with frequency of 1568 Hz, played on the flute

FIGURE 11.5 Fourier analysis of notes played on an oboe (a) and a flute (b). Although the fundamental frequencies for the two instruments are similar, the oboe produces several harmonics. As indicated in Chapter 10, the flute creates few harmonics. (From Olson, 1967)

when a tone in the high range is played, the fundamental frequency carries almost all the energy output. The harmonics are practically nonexistent. As a result, the sound in this range is clear and pure (Rossing, 1990).

Helmholtz's classical view of timbre proposed that differences in the sound quality of musical instruments could be traced entirely to the distribution of harmonics (Deutsch, 1986a; Risset & Wessel, 1982). More recent theories, however, stress the importance of an additional factor, the attack. A musical tone has three sections during the time it is played: (1) the *attack,* or the beginning buildup of a tone; (2) the *steady state,* or the middle portion of a tone; and (3) the *decay,* or decrease in amplitude at the end of a tone.

Electronic synthesizers can mimic most instruments and even human voices. To do so, they must control not only the amplitude of various harmonics but also the attack of the harmonics. Certain harmonics appear quickly, perhaps 0.02 second after the initiation of a tone, whereas other harmonics may not appear until 0.04 second after initiation. Most important, each instrument has a distinctive pattern within the attack portion of a tone. This portion is critical when we try to recognize an instrument, because recognition accuracy drops when the attack portion of a tone has been eliminated from a recording or when a tone is played backwards (Deutsch, 1986a;

Risset & Wessel, 1982). Although the attack portion of the complex sound is crucial, changes made in the attack have a smaller impact on sounds played in a musical context than on complex sounds played in isolation (Carterette & Kendall, 1989). Interestingly, the decay segment of a tone does not seem to add much information. Listeners do not attend to the speed with which the harmonics fade (Deutsch, 1984).

Pattern and Organization in Music

As Trehub (1990) states, "Musical patterns are simply complex auditory sequences that are multidimensional and highly structured, and thus are particularly well suited for the study of auditory information processing" (p. 430). Obviously, music is a sequence of tones occurring over time. However, we do not typically hear these tones as disconnected. Instead, we hear an integrated whole. For example, in the tune "Yankee Doodle," the two tones corresponding to "Yankee" seem to belong together.

What are the factors that lead us to organize the individual notes into melodic structures? Given our earlier discussions, you should correctly surmise that the factors that enable us to analyze complex auditory scenes are also applied to music. Thus, the qualities of the notes (pitch, timbre, spatial location, loudness) and how they are spaced in time lead us to organize the notes into melodies (Deutsch, 1986a). You are able to follow the melody played by a flute because the notes played by the flute are similar in quality and occur fairly close together in time.

Because of our focus on the tones involved in music, we are paying scant attention to another important factor in musical organization—rhythm. The proximity that allows us to link notes together into a melodic structure is aided by the rhythmic structure as well as the auditory qualities of the notes (Boltz, 1992; M. R. Jones, 1993; Jones & Yee, 1993).

Not only must the notes occur in reasonable proximity, but the notes must also be played for an appropriate duration. If the notes are too brief (less than 200 msec) or too long (more than 1.5 sec), we cannot identify even common melodies such as "Yankee Doodle" (Warren, 1993). Just like the bears' porridge, the duration must be just right—not too short and not too long.

As we have mentioned earlier, Gestalt laws of grouping and the figure–ground relationship can be applied to music (Bartlett, 1993; Cuddy, 1993; Dowling, 1994). Consider the law of similarity, for example, which states that similar objects tend to be seen as a unit. Deutsch (1982) points out that classical music compositions can exploit this law. Look at the music by Beethoven in Figure 11.6. This is a melody played by a single instrument. As you can see, the tones alternate between two different pitch ranges. In ordinary music, listeners tend to group a tone with immediately preceding or following tones because of the law of

proximity. When the Beethoven passage is played fast enough, however, listeners prefer to group a tone with tones from approximately similar pitch ranges. As a consequence, listeners report hearing two simultaneous melodic streams—one high and one low—rather than a single melody that flutters between high and low pitch. At slower speeds, listeners still tend to group in terms of similarity rather than proximity, although the grouping is not nearly so compelling.

Another important Gestalt principle involves the figure–ground relationship. As Sloboda (1985) points out, in music only one melodic line can be heard as "figure" at any given time. We focus our attention on this line so that we can notice relationships within the melody and recognize it. In contrast, the other melodic line (or lines) forms the background. We are aware of these other lines, but they merely add interest. As with the famous vase–faces illustration in Figure 5.9, we cannot concentrate on both the figure and the ground at the same time. However, we can usually force ground to become figure. You might want to turn on the radio and notice whether you can readily force a guitar melody to become the figure, making the singer's melody retreat into the ground.

In an experiment we mentioned earlier, Dowling (1973) examined listeners' ability to separate two melodies and perceive figure–ground relationships. He presented two familiar tunes, "Mary Had a Little Lamb" and "Three Blind Mice." In this unusual presentation, however, the tones in the two tunes were interwoven, so that "Three Blind Mice" was played for tones 1, 3, 5, and so on, and "Mary Had a Little Lamb" was played for tones 2, 4, 6, and so on. When the two tunes were presented in similar pitch ranges, observers were unable to perceive two different tunes. However, two separate melodies could be recognized if the tunes were spaced about an octave apart, or if the two tunes were made to differ in timbre or loudness (Dowling & Harwood, 1986). Once the melodies were recognized, however, listeners reported an interesting figure–ground relationship. When they attended to "Three Blind Mice," for example, "Mary Had a

FIGURE 11.6 Melody typically heard as two melodic streams on the basis of the law of similarity. (From Beethoven's *Six variations on the duet* "Nel cor piu non mi sento" from Paisiello's *Molinara*)

Little Lamb" became background. The two melodies could not be simultaneously perceived as figures. Similarly, attending to "Mary Had a Little Lamb" forced "Three Blind Mice" into the background.

Because music is one form of complex auditory pattern, central factors such as experience also have an impact on music perception. For example, experience plays a role in developing expectations of tonal structure (Bartlett, 1993; Bharucha, 1994; Dowling, 1993; Hubbard, 1993). Even nonmusicians can recognize when notes to familiar songs are misplayed or when an unfamiliar song has a discordant note. Expectations also help us identify songs (Carterette & Kendall, 1989). For example, in the Dowling experiment, if people are not told the names of the songs being played, they are rarely able to recognize the actual songs.

Experience has as much to do with speech perception as music perception. You have probably had a difficult time understanding the lyrics of a song heard for the first time. However, after you have listened to the song several times, all of the lyrics seem fully comprehensible. Clearly, your experience is aiding your perception of the song. As we have already mentioned, cognitive factors play a major role in the perception of complex auditory stimuli such as musical pieces (Bigand, 1993; Crowder, 1993).

Constancy in Music

If you've seen the classic Bogart film *Casablanca,* you'll surely recall the scene in which Ingrid Bergman says, "Play it, Sam" and sings the melody of the song that Sam used to sing for her and Bogart. Sam launches into the memorable tune "As Time Goes By." Edworthy (1985) points out, however, that Sam does not play the same intervals that Bergman sings. Nevertheless, Sam, Bergman, and the filmgoers are all equally unperturbed by the discrepancy. Both sets of intervals share the same contour, so the correspondence satisfies us all. The fact is that we can readily recognize tunes that are not exact duplicates of each other (Dyson & Watkins, 1984).

In 1890 the early Gestalt psychologist Von Ehrenfels pointed out that melodies can retain their perceptual identities even when they are transposed to different keys, as long as the relationships between adjacent tones in the melody remain constant (Deutsch, 1986a). A good deal of research suggests that people—even young infants—represent familiar melodies in an abstract fashion that preserves the relationships among the tones but not the absolute pitches themselves (Trehub, 1990). Changing the key of a piece of music from C major to F major, for example, would change the pitch of each note while still preserving the relationships among the tones. Such a change is referred to as a *transposition.* Because more people were thought to have relative pitch, rather than absolute pitch, researchers thought that they would be unaware of transpositions. However, people may be much better at recalling the exact key in which a song is typically sung than researchers had previously believed (Halpern, 1989; Levitin, 1994).

Everyone agrees that transpositions have no effect on our ability to recognize the identity of a piece of music. In that sense, music exhibits a type of constancy similar to the shape and size constancies found in the visual system. However, as in the case of size constancy (remember the Ames room), constancy in music is observed only within limits. What happens if we greatly increase the size of the intervals in a melody, for example, making one *octave* between each of the first three tones in "Three Blind Mice"—rather than just one tone? The tune becomes unrecognizable, unless you first tell the listener the name of the tune (Deutsch, 1987).

Illusions in Music

One of the themes of this book is that the perceptual processes share important similarities. We have seen that music perception, like vision, shows organization and constancy. Similarly, a number of musical illusions have been described by psychologists and others interested in research on music; illusions are not limited to visual processes. For instance, Shepard (1964) used a computer to produce a series of complex tones that seem to increase endlessly in pitch. Each tone seems to be distinctly higher in pitch than the previous tone, yet after numerous tones you are back to the tone where you began! By carefully manipulating the harmonics, Shepard created the illusion of increasing pitch. This illusion is worth hearing and is available from several sources (e.g., Houtsma et al., 1987). Variations of the original illusion have also been created (e.g., Burns, 1981; Pollack, 1978). Does this illusion remind you of the twisted-cord illusion in Demonstration 5.4?

Another remarkable illusion created by Deutsch (1983) is called the ***octave illusion.*** (This illusion is also included on the CD from the Acoustical Society of America.) One tone is presented to one ear and another tone an octave away is simultaneously presented to the other ear. For example, the first combination presented to the listener in Figure 11.7 is G_4 (392 Hz) presented to the left ear and G_5 (784 Hz) presented to the right ear. In the next tone combination, however, the tones are shifted between the ears, so that G_4 is presented to the right ear and G_5 is presented to the left ear. Think of these shifts between the ears as equivalent to spatial changes—localizing the tone first to the right and then to the left.

Surprisingly, listeners do not perceive the stimuli accurately. Most listeners perceive a single tone, G_5, in the right ear, followed by a single tone, G_4, in the left ear, and continuous alternation so that the right ear hears only high tones and the left ear hears only low tones. This bias to hear the higher-frequency tone in the right ear appears to be due to an asymmetry between brain hemispheres in processing frequency information (Ivry & Lebby, 1993).

Deutsch (1992a, 1992b, 1992c) has investigated another perplexing auditory experience called the tritone paradox. The ***tritone paradox*** involves a misperception of tone heights, so it is related to the Shepard illusion mentioned earlier. In Figure 11.8, you see the tones of a scale portrayed in circular fashion. If you hear adjacent tones in a clockwise direction, you perceive the second tone to be higher than the first tone.

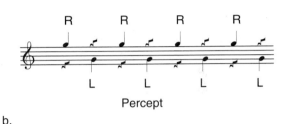

FIGURE 11.7 The octave illusion as studied by Diana Deutsch. As illustrated in part a, the right ear and the left ear are simultaneously presented with tones (alternating H-L-H . . . in the right ear and L-H-L . . . in the left ear). However, as illustrated in part b, people typically hear the high tone only in the right ear and the low tone only in the left ear. This means that people hear the low tone in the right ear when the high tone is actually being presented to that ear! (From Deutsch, 1987)

If you hear adjacent tones in a counterclockwise direction, you perceive the second tone to be lower than the first one. This effect is the basis for the Shepard illusion.

However, what would happen if the tones were not adjacent but far apart, such as D and G#? In the tritone paradox, pairs of complex tones on opposite sides of the pitch class circle are presented to listeners. The listeners judge simply whether the second tone is higher or lower in pitch than the initial tone.

Two interesting results emerge from judgments of these tone pairs. First, some people will

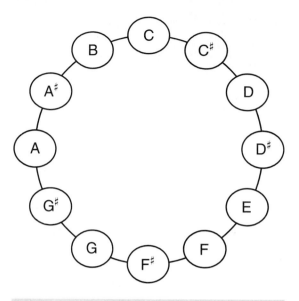

FIGURE 11.8 The pitch class circle. Complex tones that go around this circle in a clockwise fashion appear to rise. Complex tones that go around this circle in a counter-clockwise fashion appear to fall. When pairs of tones that are not near one another (e.g., D and G#) are played one after the other, some people perceive them to rise and other people perceive them to fall. (From Deutsch, 1991)

more likely to hear G# as higher than D, but people from California are more likely to hear D as higher than G#. Deutsch hypothesizes that these differences arise from the pitch range that is typical of the speaking voices experienced in a particular geographical region.

As in the case of visual illusions, you should find these auditory illusions to be very interesting. Again, however, the illusions are important for their implications for perceptual processes. Investigations of these auditory illusions inform us about the role of neurophysiological and cognitive processes in the perception of complex auditory stimuli.

We have covered a lot of ground in our brief overview of music perception. At a very basic level, we can describe a musical passage in physical terms, with the two auditory canals receiving sound waves that vary in frequency, amplitude, and complexity. Our perceptual experience, however, is far richer than the information present in the physical stimuli (Bigand, 1993). Because experience is important, researchers are paying close attention to the development of music perception (Pick & Palmer, 1993; Trehub & Trainor, 1993; Trehub et al., 1993; Zenatti, 1993). Consistent with Theme 4 (see page 12), cognitive processes are crucial to organizing the music, as they are for complex auditory patterns in general. Consistent

hear the second tone as higher in pitch than the first, and other people will hear the second tone as lower in pitch than the first. As illustrated in Figure 11.9, the identical series of tones would be heard one way by one person (a) and in a completely different way by another person (b). Second, for the same person, an identical relative upward shift from one complex tone to another will appear to be upward with one starting tone and downward with a different starting tone!

What might form the basis for the individual differences in perception of the ordering of these complex tone pairs? In a series of studies, Deutsch and her colleagues have accumulated a good deal of evidence that experience plays a major role (Deutsch, 1990, 1991, 1992a, 1992c, 1994). Thus, people from southern England are

a.

b.

FIGURE 11.9 An illustration of differing perceptions possible as a result of special stimuli created by Diana Deutsch. Some people would hear the sequence of tones as illustrated in part a, and other people would hear the same sequence of tones as illustrated in part b. (From Deutsch, 1986b)

with Theme 3 (see page 10), our auditory system (peripheral and central components together) is extremely competent in perceiving complex stimuli. However, the auditory system will occasionally be led astray by particular stimuli—producing illusory experiences.

SECTION SUMMARY

Music Perception

1. Two aspects of pitch are tone chroma and tone height. Chromas at different heights are separated by octaves (doubling of frequency), and they are psychologically similar.

2. In any given key, some tones seem to fit better than others. These tones are also found more often in musical selections in that key. The probe-tone technique was developed to study these principles.

3. Musical instruments differ in their pattern of harmonics, which is an important component of timbre. The initial (attack) component of an instrument's sound wave is also important.

4. The frequency ratios of consonant tone combinations tend to be simple fractions. Perceptions of consonance and dissonance also depend upon individual differences and cultural experience.

5. Music perception shows pattern and organization, based on the principles that seem to govern the organization of complex auditory stimuli. Along with the physical aspects of the stimuli (pitch, loudness, timbre), cognitive processing is crucial for perceiving the patterns in music.

6. The Gestalt laws of grouping are important for organizing music. For example, the law of similarity can be demonstrated when listeners perceive two simultaneous streams of music by grouping together tones that are similar in pitch. The figure–ground relationship can be observed in music; this effect can also be demonstrated when two tunes have been combined.

7. Musical constancy holds in many cases, but not when the transformation is too drastic.

8. Researchers have devised several musical illusions (e.g., the octave illusion), indicating that our auditory system does not always perceive stimuli in a completely accurate fashion.

SPEECH PERCEPTION

Human speech is the most complex of the auditory stimuli we hear on a regular basis. However, we typically underestimate the complexity of speech because we perceive speech so effortlessly. Given that speech is a complex auditory stimulus, you should anticipate that central processes will play a large role in speech perception. To illustrate the complexity of speech and the operation of these central processes, consider the occasions on which you might have overheard a conversation in a foreign language. The speakers seem to talk very rapidly, with no pauses between words. In fact, the boundaries dividing words into the neat little bundles of letters on the printed page are simply not present in any spoken language. Jusczyk (1986) provides us with a neat visual analog of the problem confronting our auditory system. Read the following line:

THEREDONATEAKETTLEOFTENCHIPS.

Without spaces (the visual analog of pauses in speech), and with multiple potential interpretations, you'll struggle to read the line. Did you read the line as "There, Don ate a kettle of ten chips," or as "The red on a tea kettle often chips"? Did you have difficulty simply reading the line?

Even when the speech stimulus lacks any clear, crisp pauses, we are usually able to perceive the boundaries among words in our own spoken language (W. E. Cooper, 1983). Cole and Jakimik (1980) estimate that a physical event, such as a pause, marks a word boundary less than 40% of the time. As Cohen and Grossberg (1986) observe, even an individual word can present several potential groupings; "myself" can be a single word, two words, or extra sounds plus "elf." Interestingly, however, the boundary between words seems to be more distinct for adults who can read than for adults who cannot (Morais et al., 1979). If the segmentation is not typically present in the speech stimulus, where do you think it comes from? Clearly, the patterns (distinct words) must be superimposed on the incoming auditory stimulus through the operation of higher-level processes.

These processes are not foolproof. Bond and Garnes (1980) catalogued several kinds of "slips of the ear," or cases in which we misperceive speech. One common kind of misperception involves word-boundary errors, which take three forms. Sometimes the word boundary is deleted; "Get a pill out" was heard as "Get a pillow." Other times the boundary is shifted; "There's some iced tea made" was heard as "There's a nice teammate." Still other times, a word boundary is inserted; "Oh, he's Snoopy in disguise" was heard as "Oh, he's Snoopy in the skies."

We will discuss several issues in speech perception. First let's begin with the physical stimulus—how speech is produced and what the sound waves look like when they reach our ears. After you have a better idea of the complexities present in the speech stimulus, you will see the difficulties facing the auditory system.

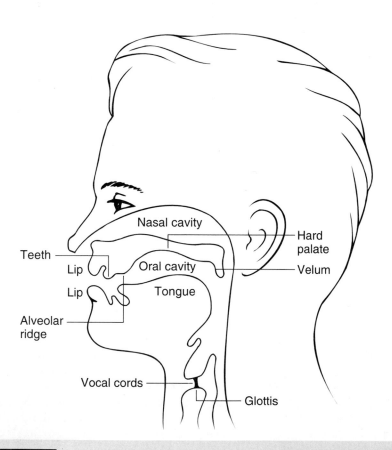

FIGURE 11.10 Major features in vocal tract. Vibration in the vocal cords produces voicing. Various places of articulation are also illustrated.

The Speech Stimulus

If we are concerned about speech *perception*, why should we discuss characteristics of speech *production?* Gelfand (1981) points out that the two subjects are inherently related: "We must be able to speak what we can perceive, and we must have the ability to perceive the sounds that our speech mechanisms produce" (p. 323). As you will see later, some theorists think that speech production is crucial to speech perception.

Producing Speech

People interested in research on speech characteristically begin with the phoneme. A ***phoneme*** is the basic unit of speech, that is, the smallest unit that makes an important difference between speech sounds. Thus, /h/ and /r/ are both phonemes in English because it makes a difference whether you say you want to wear a "hat" or a "rat." (Notice, incidentally, that a phoneme is written with slashes on either side.) A phoneme can also be viewed as a group of sounds classified as the same by people who are native speakers of a language (Gelfand, 1981). For example, try pronouncing the words "pie" and "top," attending to the pronunciation of the phoneme /p/. When you pronounce the /p/ in "pie," you release a small puff of air; no air puff is released for the /p/ in "top." The two sounds are actually slightly different, and this difference may be important in other languages. Native speakers of English, however, classify both of these sounds as belonging to the same /p/ phoneme category (Gelfand, 1981).

Let us examine how the basic phonemes in English are produced. Figure 11.10 shows the major features in the ***vocal tract,*** the anatomical structures involved in speaking that are above the vocal cords. We speak by allowing air to pass through the vocal tract in a fashion that uniquely specifies the various phonemes. Thus, the vocal tract serves as a filter for the sounds emerging from the lungs (Rosen & Howell, 1991). Table 11.1 shows how the tongue is important in producing vowels. For example, notice that when the front part of your tongue is raised high in

TABLE 11.1
Producing Vowel Sounds

Part of Tongue Used	Height of Raised Portion of Tongue		
	High	**Medium**	**Low**
Front	tr*ee*	l*a*te	f*a*t
	h*i*d	l*e*t	
Middle	carr*y*	sof*a*	n*u*t
Back	r*oo*t	c*oa*t	t*o*p
	n*u*t	s*ough*t	

your mouth, you can produce either the *ee* sound in "tree" or the *i* sound in "hid."

The consonant sounds vary along three dimensions, as illustrated in Demonstration 11.2: (1) ***place of articulation,*** which specifies where the airstream is blocked when the consonant is spoken (e.g., blockage by the two lips pressed together); (2) ***manner of articulation,*** which specifies how completely the air is blocked and where it passes (e.g., complete closure or blockage); and (3) ***voicing,*** which specifies whether the vocal cords vibrate. In Demonstration 11.2, the top member of each pair of words is a ***voiceless consonant,*** which means that the vocal cords do not vibrate. Hold the palm of your hand on your throat as you pronounce the phoneme /p/; you should feel no vibration. In contrast, the bottom member of each pair of words in Demonstration 11.2 is a ***voiced consonant,*** and the vocal cords *do* vibrate. With the palm of your hand on your throat, contrast the vibration for the phoneme /b/ as opposed to /p/.

Physical Characteristics of the Speech Stimulus

In the previous section you learned that researchers can classify speech sounds by the way they are produced. If you watch a person speak, however, you will quickly see how difficult it is to determine exactly what the mouth, tongue, and vocal cords are doing at every instant. Thus, researchers developed a second classification method that emphasizes the physical qualities of the sounds themselves. As we have already dis-

Demonstration 11.2

Pronouncing the Consonant Sounds

Refer to Figure 11.10 to help you locate several anatomical structures that are essential in pronouncing consonants. The place of articulation in the table below shows the portion of the vocal tract involved in making a particular sound. The rows in the table show the manner of articulation (e.g., complete closure vs. narrowing of the passageway). Finally, the top member of each pair of words is voiceless, and the bottom member is voiced; this distinction illustrates the third dimension of consonant production, voicing. Pronounce each of these consonants to appreciate the variety of ways in which sounds can be produced.

Manner of Articulation	Place of Articulation						
	Two Lips	Lip + Teeth	Tongue + Teeth	Tongue to Alveolar Ridge	Tongue to Palate	Tongue to Velum	Glottal
Complete closure	_p_in _b_in			_t_oe _d_oe	_ch_ip _j_am	_k_ilt _g_ive	
Narrowing at point of articulation		_f_it _v_igor	_th_ick _th_is	_s_ave _z_ebra	_sh_are a_z_ure		_h_ill —
Mouth closed; nasal cavity open	— _m_ice			— _n_ice		— si_ng_	
Glides and laterals	_wh_ere _w_ere			— _l_ess	— _y_es, _r_im		

cussed, analysis of speech sounds shows that boundaries between words are not typically evident. We now examine visual representations of auditory stimuli, known as speech spectrograms, which allow us to study the speech stimulus. Using such tools for analysis, researchers have identified wide variations in pronunciation of words that our auditory system processes with aplomb.

A *speech spectrogram* or *sound spectrogram* is a diagram that shows the frequency components of speech. Figure 11.11 shows a speech spectrogram produced when a speaker said the word "dough." As you can see, a spectrogram represents the passage of time along the *x*-axis, with the word "dough" requiring somewhat less than half a second to produce. The frequency of the sound waves is shown along the *y*-axis. The amount of energy at each frequency/time combination is indicated by the darkness of the region. White areas of the figure indicate that at a particular time virtually no energy was present at the corresponding frequency.

Notice that Figure 11.11 shows horizontal bands of concentrated sound energy called *formants*. In this figure, a first (lowest frequency) formant is located at about 500 Hz, and a second formant is initially located at about 1500 Hz, but it moves downward a mere $\frac{1}{10}$ of a second later. You can also see a third formant at about 2500 Hz and a fourth formant at about 3800 Hz.

Analyses of speech spectrograms have revealed some interesting characteristics of human speech. For example, we might guess that the phonemes of a spoken word would appear as discrete units in time, rather like beads on a string.

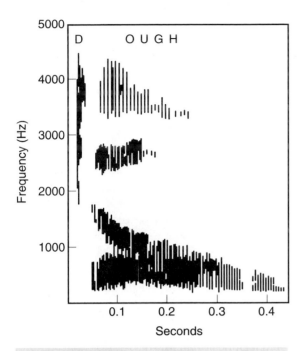

Speech spectrogram of the word "dough." Time is indicated on the *x*-axis and frequency on the *y*-axis. Darker areas of the figure illustrate increased amounts of sound energy at those particular frequency/time combinations. Thus, there is virtually no energy at 2000 Hz after 0.1 second (figure is all white across from 2000 Hz after 0.1 second). The four darkened areas are referred to as formants. The lowest formant (F1) shows a slight upward formant transition, and the second formant (F2) shows a downward formant transition (from 1500 Hz to about 1000 Hz). (Speech spectrogram courtesy of Speech Science Laboratory, Department of Speech Pathology and Audiology, State University of New York at Geneseo)

Thus, you might expect that the word "dog" would have a spectrogram with three segments, with /d/ first, then /o/, and finally /g/. Contrary to expectations, speech spectrograms typically reveal that the phonetic segments overlap considerably (Jusczyk, 1986). Some acoustic energy from the final /g/ sound is present even before the energy from the initial /d/ sound has faded completely. As Hockett (1955) picturesquely described spoken language, the stimulus reaches the listener not in the form of beads on a string but like a row of uncooked colored Easter eggs run through a wringer! This tendency for some of the sounds in a syllable to be transmitted at about the same time—that is, in parallel—rather than one at a time is called *parallel transmission.* Each phoneme is not pronounced in isolation, and its sound is modified by the processes used to generate the surrounding phonemes.

Because of parallel transmission, speech sounds flow together. As a result, a small segment of speech cannot carry all the acoustic information about one phoneme. Instead, that information is distributed across several segments. Furthermore, a phoneme's sound can change, depending on which phonemes precede and follow it. In other words, phonemes often do not have a single, constant pronunciation. The information in Demonstration 11.2 implied that a consonant phoneme always has a consistent pronunciation, for example, that an /s/ always requires the same placement of tongue and lips, restriction of airflow, and vibration of vocal cords, no matter what word uses the /s/ phoneme. However, pay attention to the shape of your mouth for the /s/ sound when you say the words "seat" and "sorry." As you have discovered, phonemes are quite complex. The corners of your mouth are stretched far apart in "seat" but are close together in "sorry." Your mouth anticipates the letters that follow the /s/ sound.

Spectrograms confirm that a single phoneme has varying sounds as a result of the context of other sounds in the word. Furthermore, speech spectrograms indicate that a particular word is *not* consistently pronounced by all speakers on all occasions. The variation is overwhelming! Consider, for example, how speakers differ. Physical differences in the vocal apparatus create variety. When the word "cat" is spoken by a 6-year-old boy, the physical characteristics of the sound waves may be entirely different in amplitude, frequency, and complexity from when that same word is spoken by his 60-year-old grandfather. Even among adults, the vocal tract—which is used to produce speech—is 15% longer in males than in females (Jusczyk, 1986). As a consequence, female speakers have comparatively higher formant frequencies than males.

Variability in Speech Production

Think about the other ways in which speakers differ in their pronunciations. In fact, individual differences are so strong that analyses of speech spectrograms may show that two different words spoken by the same person are more physically similar than the same word spoken by two different people (Levinson & Liberman, 1981). Also, you have little trouble understanding English spoken with southern, British, or Caribbean accents, even though the rhythms and pronunciations of specific sounds vary tremendously.

Although we can understand the speech of a wide range of individuals, we have more difficulty when listening to several different speakers. Recent studies indicate that word recognition and memory for words spoken by different people are worse than the same words spoken by the same person. Our ability to understand several different speakers seems to be at some cost in terms of mental effort (Mullenix & Pisoni, 1989; 1990).

We have seen that the auditory system can handle the variability in words spoken by different people. The auditory system also handles variability in words spoken by the same person. For example, think how the pitch of your voice would change if you wanted to say the sentence "Isn't that just marvelous?" with sarcasm, as opposed to enthusiasm. Clearly, emotions can change the speech stimulus (Huggins, 1981; Scherer, 1986). For example, when people smile, their vocal tracts shorten somewhat, which raises the pitch of their voices. Emotions can also influence speaking rate, pauses, and the amount of pitch variation. Of course, pronunciation can also be influenced by what the speaker is doing while talking. You can interpret a spoken message even when the speaker is eating a cookie, chomping on a pipe, or using a toothbrush.

Still one other source of variability in pronunciation is our own sloppiness. If people are asked to read a list of isolated words, their pronunciation is reasonably precise and standard-ized. However, almost all speech perception involves strings of words. In everyday language, our pronunciation of words is imprecise and variable. Cole and Jakimik (1980) point out how the word "what" can be pronounced numerous ways in the sentence "What are you doing?" They include the variants "Whacha doing?"; "Whadaya doing?"; and "Whaya doing?" You may be able to add other possibilities. Out of context, pronunciation is often so sloppy that you can barely identify a word or phrase. For example, in a classic study Pollack and Pickett (1964) recorded the conversation of people waiting for an experiment to begin. Later, these same people were asked to identify isolated words and phrases from their own conversations. People who heard a single word were only about 50% accurate, and recognition rose to only about 70% when two or three words were presented.

In short, any given word can be pronounced in a wide variety of ways because of differences in the age and gender of the speaker, other sources of individual differences, dialect, emotions, and sloppiness. And yet—miraculously—we generally manage to perceive the stimulus accurately. In this respect, speech perception resembles two visual processes. Recall that our discussion of pattern recognition pointed out how we can identify the letter *M* even when it is written in a variety of sizes and styles. Furthermore, the discussion of constancy pointed out our ability to perceive qualities of an object even though the distance, angle of orientation, and brightness differ from one viewing to the next. An inherent property of perceptual systems is that they can extract important information out of potentially misleading clutter.

The task facing our auditory system is further complicated by the enormous number of patterns it must be prepared to decipher—the average high school graduate's vocabulary is about 50,000 words (Huggins, 1981). The mystery, then, is that we can perceive speech quickly and with a generally high degree of accuracy when so many potential words exist, when those words are pronounced with such variability, and when clear boundaries between individual words are nonexistent. Given the complexity of the problems involved in speech perception, several theorists have proposed that humans must have evolved specialized processors for speech. We now turn our attention to one of the major controversies in theories of speech perception.

Theories of Speech Perception

Theories of speech perception can be divided into two broad camps: the Special Mechanism account and the General Mechanism account of speech perception (Kuhl, 1989). Advocates of the ***Special Mechanism account*** argue that speech perception rests on a special speech (phonetic) module. A ***module*** is a separate, special-purpose neural mechanism designed for a specific task such as object recognition or color perception (Fodor, 1983).

People in favor of the Special Mechanism account feel that we have a separate speech module that confers distinct abilities on the listener, much like sound localization in the barn owl and echolocation in the bat (Liberman, 1982, 1992; Liberman & Mattingly, 1989; Mattingly & Liberman, 1988). The proposed speech module is thought to enable listeners to segment the blurred stream of auditory information exhibited in spectrograms into distinct phonemes and words. Many of these theorists also believe that humans are born with an innate ability to represent speech at a phonetic level. Furthermore, these theorists believe that a more generalized auditory perception module handles other acoustic information. However, they contend that the speech module actually takes precedence over the auditory module (Whalen & Liberman, 1987).

In contrast, proponents of the ***General Mechanism account*** argue for a more parsimonious interpretation—no special speech module exists. These theorists argue that our auditory systems have evolved in such a way that humans are able to process both speech and nonspeech stimuli by means of the same mechanisms. Speech perception is thought to be a learned ability, not an ability that is innate in all humans.

We have spent so much time detailing the difficulties involved in speech perception that you might be inclined to side with the Special Mechanism account theorists. After all, speech perception is so difficult that evolution of a specialized speech module might well be an adaptive response.

In fact, several pieces of evidence argue for the unique status of speech perception. For instance, as Jusczyk (1986) points out, speech sounds are different from other auditory stimuli because the relationship between sounds and meanings is arbitrary and symbolic. No logical or necessary connection exists between the sounds in a word and its meaning. In English, we call a certain kind of pet a *dog*, but it is called *perro* in Spanish, and it could just as easily be called a *murj*. In contrast, most other auditory stimuli have a logical connection with the forces that produce them. When your car collides with a telephone pole, the "crash" sound is not arbitrary. In fact, the same noise would result if your car collided with a telephone pole in Madrid! So speech is different from other sounds because speech symbols must somehow be processed to decode the messages they symbolize.

More compelling evidence comes from studies in which listeners heard synthetic speech. For example, people performed much differently on identification and discrimination tasks if they perceived the stimuli as speech sounds rather than nonspeech sounds (Best et al., 1981). (However, in both cases the stimuli were actually the same.) Once we know that a stimulus is a word, we may switch into a "speech mode" and process it differently.

Alvin Liberman (1982, 1992) is the theorist most closely associated with the Special Mechanism account of speech perception. In his view, humans have specialized modules that allow them to perceive phonemes. Liberman's argument is related to his earlier motor theory of speech perception (e.g., Liberman & Studdert-Kennedy, 1978). According to Liberman's ***motor theory of speech perception,*** humans have a specialized device that allows them to decode speech stimuli and permits them to connect the stimuli they hear with the way these sounds are produced by the speaker. For example, you can hear the phoneme

/t/ in any word and immediately recognize that it was made by pressing the tongue against the alveolar ridge, thereby blocking air passage while not vibrating the vocal cords. We should stress that this recognition occurs automatically and without cognitive analysis. This explanation is somewhat similar to the explanation we considered in Chapter 8 for our immediate perception of biological motion (Johansson, 1985). Our perceptual systems may be specially designed to process messages from other human beings, whether those messages represent body movement or speech.

Consistent with Theme 3 (see page 10), our perceptual processes are well suited to the tasks they must accomplish. Humans are particularly well suited for the processing of speech, as the preceding examples have illustrated. However, researchers are uncertain whether we need to invoke the presence of a specialized speech module to explain our amazing abilities (Jenkins, 1991). We will now survey two major battlegrounds—categorical speech perception and duplex perception—that have developed in the controversy between the Special and General Mechanism theorists.

Categorical Speech Perception

In Chapter 7 we discussed how the smooth continuum represented by the color spectrum that runs between 400 and 700 nm does not produce a similarly smooth continuum in our perception. Instead, we tend to categorize the colors of the spectrum. For example, an abrupt boundary in the region of 490 nm separates the greens from the blues. On one side of the boundary, we consider the colors green; on the other side, we consider the colors blue.

As Bornstein (1987) has pointed out, the perceptual categories in vision and in audition show remarkable similarities. He compares these two separate areas of study—each providing dozens of studies about categories in perception—and concludes that the similarities are striking. Consistent with Theme 1 of the book, the perceptual systems share important similarities.

In general, *categorical perception* occurs when we have difficulty discriminating between members of the *same* category but we are readily able to discriminate between members of *different* categories (Jusczyk, 1986; B. C. J. Moore, 1982). When we consider speech sounds, for example, listeners can easily discriminate between sounds from two different categories, such as /p/ and /b/. Their discrimination between two different /p/ sounds from the same speaker should be poor.

What is the basis for the discrimination between /p/ and /b/? As we have already mentioned, /b/ is a voiced consonant and /p/ is an unvoiced consonant; otherwise they are similar sounds. Vowels, such as the /a/ in "pad," are voiced. Therefore, when we say "pad," the voicing does not begin until the /a/ phoneme. However, /b/ is a voiced consonant, so voicing begins with the /b/ when we say "bad." The onset of voicing in "bad" comes marginally sooner than the voicing in "pad," and in fact determines whether we will hear "bad" or "pad." The time from the beginning of an utterance until voicing begins is referred to as *voice onset time (VOT)*.

Using artificially created "speech" stimuli, researchers can vary VOT systematically. Varying the onset of voicing before /a/ continuously from 0 to 60 milliseconds does *not* result in continuous perceptual changes. Instead, people report hearing either "ba" or "pa" (see Figure 11.12a). With very brief VOTs, people always report "ba," and with longer VOTs, people always report "pa." (Keep in mind that the basis for these discriminations is a difference of a small fraction of a second.)

At an intermediate voice onset time, around 25 milliseconds, people shift from reporting "ba" to reporting "pa." The point at which people shift from reporting one phoneme to reporting the other phoneme is referred to as the *phonetic boundary.* On either side of the phonetic boundary, people have difficulty discriminating between the sounds. For example, VOTs of 0 or 20 milliseconds would both be heard as "ba."

How did categorical speech perception become a battleground among speech perception theorists? The Special Mechanism theorists argued that categorical perception was due to the specialized speech module. Continuous non-

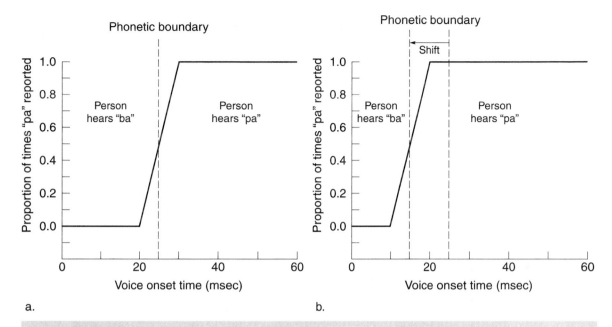

FIGURE 11.12 An illustration of categorical perception. Voice onset time is shown on the *x*-axis, and the proportion of times people report hearing "pa" is indicated on the *y*-axis. Part a illustrates that the phonetic boundary between "ba" and "pa" is at a voice onset time of about 25 milliseconds (msec). When voicing doesn't begin until after 25 msec, people are more likely to report hearing "pa." When voicing begins earlier, people report hearing "ba." Part b illustrates the impact of first adapting the listener to "ba"—a shift in the phonetic boundary that leads to the perception of "pa" with a shorter voice onset time. (From Eimas & Corbit, 1973)

speech auditory phenomena, they argued, were perceived as continua, and not categorized. As further evidence, they presented a particular speech sound (such as "ba") until people showed adaptation. In a fashion similar to that observed with visual stimuli, adaptation was thought to "fatigue" the speech module, leading to a shift in the phonetic boundary seen in Figure 11.12b. After people listened to "ba" for a long time, the phonetic boundary shifted so that a much shorter VOT was sufficient for them to report hearing "pa."

The evidence compiled by the Special Mechanism camp seems quite strong. However, the General Mechanism theorists have been able to provide even stronger counterevidence. Because nonhuman species do not have the speech abilities of humans, they should not have a speech module. Therefore, one would not expect nonhu-

man species to exhibit categorical perception. However, using methods adapted to the various species involved, researchers have demonstrated categorical perception among a veritable zoo-full of animals, including chinchillas, Japanese quail, and macaques (Kuhl, 1989; J. L. Miller, 1990; Moody et al., 1990).

The General Mechanism theorists have marshalled further evidence against the Special Mechanism account (Jusczyk, 1986). They found not only that species lacking speech capabilities exhibit categorical perception but also that humans exhibit categorical perception for complex *nonspeech* sounds (Pastore et al., 1990). This finding argues that categorical perception in humans is most likely a product of a more general auditory processor. Furthermore, researchers have found that—with extensive practice—people are able to make discriminations among speech sounds on the *same* side of the phonetic boundary.

The Special Mechanism account supporters were not about to give up their position, however, even though categorical perception does not appear to be produced by a specialized speech module. The proponents of the Special Mechanism account felt that they had another strong piece of evidence in support of their position, and we address that issue now.

Duplex Perception

Another effect that could reflect the operation of a special speech module is referred to as duplex perception. **Duplex perception** arises when the same sound can have both speech and nonspeech qualities (Liberman, 1982; Liberman & Mattingly, 1989; Mattingly & Liberman, 1988). Ordinarily, as seen in Figure 11.13a, speech sounds are heard as a complex sound present at both ears (binaural). Duplex stimuli are created by excising a small portion of a speech sound—a formant transition—as illustrated in Figure 11.13c. When presented in isolation, this sound is heard as a chirp. In a typical experiment, the formant transition is presented to one ear and the remaining speech sound segment (base) that would typically be heard as "da" is presented to the other ear (see Figure 11.13b). Interestingly, what people typically report hearing when these two sound stimuli are presented together is a chirp in one ear and "da" or "ga" in the other ear (depending on which of the nine formant transitions is presented). Similar results are obtained with 3- and 4-month-old infants (Eimas & Miller, 1992).

Thus, the same sound (the formant transition) is heard as a simple nonspeech sound *and* as part of a speech sound. In fact, the formant transition can combine with the base to form either "da" or "ga." This result appears to support the Special Mechanism account, because the same acoustical information is processed as both general auditory information and as a part of a speech sound. Furthermore, Liberman and his colleagues found that when people directed attention to the ear in which the base sounds were being presented, they were better able to discriminate between two composite

sounds near the phonetic boundary. When people directed attention to the ear in which the formant transitions were being presented, they were better able to discriminate between two sounds located far from the phonetic boundary. These additional findings also support the notion that speech is processed by some special mechanism.

As in the case for categorical perception, however, proponents of the General Mechanism account were able to offer evidence that argues against these interpretations of duplex perception (Mattingly & Studdert-Kennedy, 1991). For example, Ciocca and Bregman (1989) varied the duplex perception procedure very slightly. They presented repetitive sequences of formant transitions (chirps) to one ear and then presented the typical base to the other ear simultaneously with one of the formant transitions. Earlier duplex perception studies presented only a single formant transition (chirp) in one ear, while simultaneously presenting the base to the other ear.

In the Ciocca and Bregman study, when the base was presented in one ear simultaneously with the formant transition in the other ear, their stimuli were *identical* with those used in previous research. Their research differed from earlier work because prior to presenting the base coupled with the formant transition, a series of formant transitions were presented. With this slight contextual change, people were much less likely to integrate the formant transition with the base.

Consistent with the Gestalt principle of similarity, the series of formant transitions (chirps) form an integrated stream. When the base is eventually presented simultaneously with one of the chirps, the auditory system does not integrate the base with the formant transition. Instead, after the first hearing of the series of chirps, the chirp seems to go with the other chirps and not with the base. A special module for speech should *always* hear a speech sound (base plus formant transition) when it occurs. Because the base plus formant transition was not heard as a speech sound, Ciocca and Bregman interpret their results as arguing against a special speech module. Similar arguments have been made by a number of other researchers (Bailey

a.

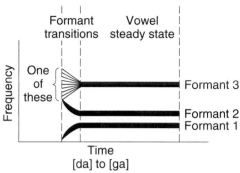

Normal (binaural) presentation

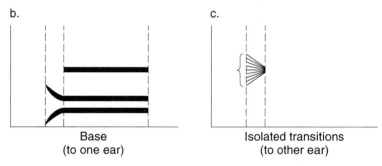

Duplex-producing (dichotic) presentation

FIGURE 11.13 A schematic figure of speech spectrograms to illustrate a typical duplex perception experiment. As in Figure 11.11, the *x*-axis indicates time and the *y*-axis indicates frequency, but the spectrogram is simplified to show the formants and formant transitions more clearly. The top of the figure shows the base sound and the nine possible formant transitions of the third formant (Formant 3) leading to the perception of sounds from "da" to "ga." When the formant transitions are presented to one ear alone, a person reports hearing an upward or downward chirp. When presented with the base sound alone, a person would typically report hearing "da." When the formant transition is presented in one ear simultaneously with the base in the other ear, a person hears a chirp in the ear to which the formant transition was presented and a speech sound that combines the formant transition and the base sound in the ear to which the base sound was presented. The fact that the same auditory information (formant transition) can take on both speech and nonspeech characteristics was seen as evidence that humans have both a general acoustic module and a specialized speech module. (From Liberman, 1982)

& Herrmann, 1993; Fowler & Rosenblum, 1990; Hall & Pastore, 1992).

Clearly, the Special Mechanism account of speech perception will continue to draw adher-

ents. Currently, however, the two strongest pieces of evidence for the existence and primacy of a specialized speech module have been seriously weakened by subsequent research. Although the proponents of the General Mechanism account appear to be winning most of the battles, the controversy is far from settled. As Liberman (1992) admits, however, the Special Mechanism account is currently the unconventional view. Even if a special mechanism exists, it is unlikely to be totally independent of the mechanisms that process other auditory phenomena (Darwin, 1991).

Top-Down Processing in Speech Perception

Our discussion of auditory perception in Chapter 10 and in this chapter has focused primarily on physical characteristics of sound stimuli and how these stimuli can be transformed by the auditory system. According to Theme 4 of this book, our prior knowledge, context, and expectations are critical in shaping our perceptions. Given that speech is a complex auditory phenomenon, these higher mental processes would certainly be expected to influence speech perception. Our perception of speech, for example, will be aided by top-down processing as well as bottom-up processing. That is, we perceive speech because of the combination of our cognitive processes and the information available in the auditory stimulus. Let's discuss the variety of ways in which top-down processing aids speech perception, with an emphasis on the phonemic restoration effect.

Phonemic Restoration

Suppose that you join some friends for dinner. You make a screeching sound with your chair as one friend asks you to pass the salt. You still perceive her message as an intact utterance, with no missing phonemes. Every day, in every possible setting, portions of our utterances are concealed by both intentional and unintentional noises of short duration. Nevertheless, we perceive speech accurately, without lamenting the missing sounds. In everyday life—and also in the laboratory—we demonstrate *phonemic restoration,* which occurs when a speech sound is replaced or masked by an irrelevant sound, and the percep-

tual system restores or fills in the gap appropriately. In most cases, phonemic restoration works so well that the listener cannot identify which speech sound was missing.

Richard Warren and Roslyn Warren (1970) reported the classic study on the phonemic restoration effect. They recorded the sentence "The state governors met with their respective legislatures convening in the capital city." Then they carefully cut one phoneme out of the recorded sentence, specifically, the first /s/ in "legislatures." A coughing sound was inserted to fill the gap. (Thus, in the laboratory studies, a phoneme is actually missing rather than concealed.) When listeners heard this revised sentence, they experienced a compelling auditory illusion. They reported that the /s/ sound was just as clear as any of the phonemes that were actually present. Even when they listened to the sentence repeatedly, they judged the sentence to be intact. The cough seemed to supplement the sentence rather than replace any speech sounds (Warren, 1983).

Furthermore, one group of listeners was told that the cough had completely replaced a speech sound, and they were asked to locate the missing phoneme. They were unable to do so. They could not even identify precisely where the cough appeared in the sentence (Warren, 1983).

However, on other trials, a phoneme was simply deleted (replaced by a silent gap). Intriguingly, listeners were highly accurate in locating the gap and noting that a phoneme was missing completely. Relatively short gaps of silence (under 0.1 second) were heard as interruptions of continuous speech (Bashford et al., 1988; Bashford & Warren, 1987). However, when the same speech was interrupted by louder noises of similar pitch, the interruptions could last even longer (from 0.2 to 0.3 second) without the listener noting the interruption of speech. In other words, phonemic restoration is far more pronounced when a phoneme is replaced by a noise.

Why should phonemic restoration operate more powerfully in one condition? As Warren (1983) proposes, listeners may perceive the silent gap as being intrinsic to the actual speech, which is heard as "rough" or "bubbly" when silent gaps are added. In contrast, a cough superimposed upon the sentence is perceived as extrinsic and irrelevant to the flow of speech.

In the study in which the word "legislatures" was interrupted, the phonemes are so highly constrained that "s" is the only possible missing sound that would complete the word in a meaningful way. What happens when phonemes are not so highly constrained? In other research, Warren and Warren (1970) played four sentences that were identical except for a different word spliced on at the end of each sentence. In these sentences, the asterisk symbol, *, represents the loud cough that replaced a phoneme.

1. "It was found that the *eel was on the axle."
2. "It was found that the *eel was on the shoe."
3. "It was found that the *eel was on the orange."
4. "It was found that the *eel was on the table."

What did the listeners report hearing? Warren and Warren found that the interpretation of the ambiguous word "*eel" depended upon which final word they had heard. Listeners reported hearing "wheel" in the first sentence, "heel" in the second, "peel" in the third, and "meal" in the fourth. Context clearly influenced speech perception, and memory must be involved because the people did not hear the contextual cue until late in the sentence.

In a typical phonemic restoration study, noise is placed where a portion of a word had been deleted. However, outside the laboratory, the noise is superimposed over a word. When noises were added to whole words in the laboratory, phonemic restoration still occurred (Samuel, 1981). Interestingly, not only is the noise-altered word perceived as whole, but the noise itself is also perceived differently than it would be perceived in isolation (Warren et al., 1994).

Samuel and Ressler (1986) propose that phonemic restoration occurs because the configurational properties of a word prevent listeners from paying attention to the individual phonemes. Impressively, people who have been trained on the phonemic restoration task still show the restoration effect. Also, Samuel (1987) demonstrated that

phonemic restoration is particularly likely if more than one restoration is possible. (For example, "*egion" could be restored as either "legion" or "region," whereas "*esion" could be restored as only "lesion.") Furthermore, Samuel (1987) found that phonemic restoration occurred more often when the initial syllable of the word was relatively unique. If you hear a word that begins with "veg-," you are likely to complete that word and restore any phoneme missing from remaining portions of the word. If a word begins with a common prefix such as "sub-," however, phonemic restoration is not nearly so compelling.

As a further indication of the operation of top-down processes, phonemic restoration is stronger for high-frequency words and for longer words (Samuel, 1981). In other words, when people are very familiar with the stimuli, or the context is richer, phonemic restoration is especially strong.

Notice that when phonemic restoration studies are conducted in the laboratory, context does not increase the *accuracy* of identifying the physical stimulus. People did not report hearing "cough-eel." As Warren (1984) observed, phonemic restoration is a kind of illusion: "These perceptual reconstructions do not correspond accurately to the sounds at the listeners' ears" (p. 381). Under normal listening conditions, however, phonemic restoration does enhance accuracy. A phoneme really *is* hidden underneath the screech of a chair or the crash of a dropped platter. In ordinary life, we understand speech more accurately if we ignore the interference from the extraneous noise (Warren, 1983). In the laboratory, phonemic restoration is an illusion; in real life, it is a good strategy! You may recall a similar situation with the Ponzo illusion. Turn back to Figure 6.24 and notice that the top figure, constructed in the laboratory, is an illusion. The bottom figure, a real-life cornfield, illustrates the use of a good strategy (in this case, size constancy).

In summary, then, a series of experiments by Warren and by Samuel has illustrated that top-down processes are important in speech perception. When we hear a word in noisy conditions, we are likely to restore a missing phoneme.

Phonemic restoration is more likely to occur in some circumstances than others, however, particularly when factors such as context constrain the possible interpretations. The phonemic restoration effect certainly demonstrates that we do not need to hear every phoneme distinctly to perceive speech. Any theory that attempts to explain the mystery of speech perception must therefore point out that speech perception is clearly facilitated by top-down processing. Consistent with Theme 4 of this book, our expectations have an important influence on perception.

Factors Influencing Speech Perception

Top-down processing facilitates speech perception in a number of ways; these factors involve both global and specific kinds of information.

1. *Listeners perceive better if they know they will be hearing speech.* This principle was best demonstrated in a study by Remez, Rubin, Pisoni, and Carrell (1981). They recorded a spoken sentence, "Where were you a year ago?" and then transformed the sentence by eliminating some of the acoustical information. One group of listeners was told nothing about the nature of the sounds; they were simply asked to report their impressions of the stimuli. Most did not realize that it was speech, and only 2 people out of 18 correctly identified the sentence. Another group of listeners was told that they would hear a sentence produced by a computer; half the people correctly identified the sentence in this condition. If we are oriented toward hearing speech, we are more likely to perceive it.

2. *Listeners perceive better if the phonemes appear in a word.* In an often-cited study, Rubin and his colleagues (1976) demonstrated that listeners could detect a target consonant, /b/, more quickly when it began a word such as "bit" than when it began a nonword such as "bip." The word provides a context that facilitates recognition. If we perceive speech just as a sequence of phonemes in order, with no interrelationships among them, then a word should offer no particular advantage over a nonword—the /b/ should be identified equally quickly in both conditions. However, people took only 593 milliseconds to locate the target phoneme in a word, in contrast to 644 milliseconds to locate that same phoneme in a nonword. As the authors conclude, "Higher order properties of a speech event affect the detection of its constituent parts" (p. 396).

3. *Listeners perceive better if the words appear in a phrase or sentence.* This principle is clearly related to the preceding one; context is important in identifying either phonemes or words. We already discussed one study supporting this principle. Recall that Pollack and Pickett (1964) found that people listening to fragments of their own previous conversations were much better at identifying words if two or three words were presented, rather than an isolated word.

Furthermore, contextual information is helpful, even when words are carefully pronounced (Cole & Jakimik, 1980). For example, people quickly identified a phoneme when it occurred in a word that was highly likely in a sentence. They responded slowly when a word was highly unlikely (Morton & Long, 1976). For instance, you would identify the /b/ more rapidly in the sentence "The sparrow sat on the branch" than in the sentence "The sparrow sat on the bed."

In fact, context is so powerful that people will "hear" words when no words are present. When people are presented with backwards speech or music—without any special instructions—they rarely hear any messages, Satanic or otherwise. However, when first presented with a suggestion about the content of the passage, people are much more likely to hear the suggested message (Vokey & Read, 1985).

4. *Listeners perceive better if they know the topic of conversation.* Reddy (1976) presented sentences that had unusual word orders, and he asked listeners to repeat the sentences. The sentence "In mud eels are; in clay none are" was read without substantial intonation. The typical listener heard "In model sar; in claynanar." The sentence "In pine tar is; in oak none is" was heard as "In pyntar es; in oak nonus." If the listeners had been told that the first sentence concerned the habitats of amphibians and that the second sentence concerned the properties of trees, accuracy would have been higher. Again,

context helps in perceiving speech, whether that perception involves the detection of phonemes or location of word boundaries.

5. *Listeners perceive speech better if they can see lip movements.* Consistent with a revised motor theory of speech perception, people perceive speech better when they can see the face of the person speaking (Dodd, 1977; Summerfield, 1991). For instance, Massaro and Cohen (1983) observed that vision can bias auditory perception when we watch a ventriloquist: "Ventriloquists do not throw their voices; rather a listener's percept is thrown by the visual input of the apparent speaker" (p. 753). In their own research, Massaro and Cohen specifically instructed listeners to report what they heard rather than what they saw. Nevertheless, the listeners relied heavily on lip movement.

We may not realize the helpfulness of this visual information until we listen to a man with less-than-perfect articulation whose lips are partly concealed by a mustache. The mustache may be an even larger impediment to a hearing-impaired person, for whom lip movements are vitally important to speech perception (Kent, 1995). In the final section of this chapter, we will review research that investigates the relationship between auditory and visual information.

SECTION SUMMARY

Speech Perception

1. Speech perception is a complex process because our vocabularies are large, the speech stimulus varies in several ways (such as pitch, speaking rate, and pronunciation—both between and within speakers), and true segmentation between words is rarely observed. Nonetheless, people can recognize words and identify the boundaries between them.

2. A phoneme, the smallest unit that makes a difference between speech sounds, is produced by a unique combination of characteristics such as place of articulation, manner of articulation, and voicing.

3. A speech spectrogram illustrates the frequency components of speech. Speech spectrograms reveal that sounds in a syllable show parallel transmission. In addition, a phoneme's sound can change, depending on the surrounding sounds.

4. The auditory system appears to treat speech sounds differently from other auditory stimuli. Speech sounds, unlike many other sounds, are arbitrary and symbolic. Furthermore, people perform differently on perception tasks when they know that the material consists of speech sounds.

5. Speech perception theorists typically hold one of two basic orientations: Special Mechanism or General Mechanism. The Special Mechanism theorists argue that humans have a specialized module for speech perception. The General Mechanism theorists argue that speech is processed by the same mechanisms that process all auditory stimuli.

6. Two pieces of evidence for the Special Mechanism account of speech perception are categorical speech perception and duplex perception. However, proponents of the General Mechanism account have provided more compelling evidence that neither categorical speech perception nor duplex perception requires the existence of a special speech module. As a consequence, the General Mechanism account is currently more widely held.

7. Phonemic restoration occurs when the perceptual system fills in a missing phoneme that has been replaced by an irrelevant sound. Listeners are unable to locate the position of the missing phoneme, and phonemic restoration is influenced by the nature of the sentence. Silence is not as effective as noise in producing phonemic restoration.

8. Factors that influence phonemic restoration are word frequency, word length, and phoneme category. Furthermore, it is more likely to occur with multiple possible restorations and when the initial syllable is unique.

9. Top-down processing facilitates speech perception because listeners perceive better if

they know they will be hearing speech; if the phonemes appear in a word; if the words appear in a phrase or sentence; if they know the topic of conversation; and if they can see lip movements.

Interactions between Auditory and Visual Stimuli

In the last section, we saw that speech perception can be influenced by lip movements. As we saw in Chapter 10, in our everyday experience, sounds and the objects that produce them tend to go together. When they do coincide, auditory information seems to enhance visual localization, and visual information seems to enhance auditory localization. As Theme 1 suggests, such interactions among the senses are quite important. In this section, we will review a number of studies that investigate the interactions between vision and audition.

INTERACTIONS BETWEEN MOVIE SCENES AND BACKGROUND MUSIC

First, let's consider the background music in movies. We've already discussed the possibility that music can arouse emotional responses (Meyer, 1994). How aware are you of the background music when watching a movie? Does the background music serve to heighten the suspense or excitement you feel in certain scenes? To investigate the role of background music, Marilyn Boltz and her colleagues (1991) presented short clips from films. Half of the clips portrayed positive emotions (a happy ending) and half portrayed negative emotions (a tragic ending). Music was also extracted from the films, half of which was judged to be positive and half to be negative in emotional content.

In one experiment, people watched 16 film clips. Half of the clips were paired with "appropriate" (mood congruent) music and half with "inappropriate" (mood incongruent) music. Thus, half the clips with happy endings were accompanied by appropriately upbeat music and half by inappropriate somber music. Half the clips with tragic endings were accompanied by appropriately somber music and half by inappropriate upbeat music. People were first asked to recall as much detail as possible about the clips. Memory was better for the scenes from the film clips with appropriate background music.

Next, people were asked to pick out the 16 background melodies from a series of 32 melodies (16 old and 16 new). Although the people had previously heard the background music, they could not readily recognize it when tested on memory for the music by itself. Thus, memory for the background music by itself was poor.

After testing the memory for music by itself, Boltz and her colleagues tested the extent to which people could match music with scenes from the film clips. People were reasonably good at matching the background music with the appropriate clip—even for film clips they had not recalled on the initial test. Thus, background music can enhance memory for visual scenes. The intertwining of music and visual scenes might be similar to the integration of lyrics and melody we discussed earlier (Crowder, 1993).

INTERACTIONS BETWEEN FACIAL INFORMATION AND AUDITORY INFORMATION

Auditory stimuli can influence visual stimuli, but what about the impact of visual stimuli on perception of complex auditory stimuli? Given that vision is often the dominant sense, as in the ventriloquism effect, you should expect that visual stimuli can affect auditory perception. Moreover, as we have discussed in earlier chapters, a particularly salient visual stimulus is the face. What happens when facial information disagrees with auditory information? Have you ever been to a foreign film in which the English dialogue was dubbed? Or have you ever seen a movie in which the soundtrack was out of synch, so that the actors' lip movements did not match the dialogue? If so, then you know how disturbing such disparity between lip movements and dialogue can be. Even infants find the disparity disturbing (Summerfield, 1992).

To investigate a particular disparity between vision and audition, McGurk and McDonald

Acoustic signal

Perception

"Ba-ba"

Da-da

Lips Ga-ga

FIGURE 11.14 An illustration of the McGurk effect. The observer sees a speaker repeating "ga" over and over, but the voice the observer hears is repeating "ba" over and over. Surprisingly, the observer typically hears neither "ga" nor "ba" but hears "da" being repeated. The McGurk effect illustrates the interaction of auditory and visual information in the perception of speech.

(1976) used a video of a woman speaking sounds, and they then superimposed different audio information over the video. As illustrated in Figure 11.14, people see the lips of a speaker form one sound, such as "ga," while they hear a different sound, such as "ba." The **McGurk effect** arises because of the disparity between the speech sounds heard and visual information of the speaker's lips.

In this example, what do you think people hear? If vision dominates, they should hear "ga." If audition dominates, they should hear "ba." Instead, they hear neither "ba" nor "ga" but a completely different sound produced by fusing the auditory and visual input—in this case "da." These effects are quite powerful and have been replicated by a number of different researchers

(Rosenblum & Saldaña, 1992; Saldaña & Rosenblum, 1994; Summerfield, 1987). For example, Dominic Massaro (1987; Massaro & Cohen, 1990) used computer-generated faces to manipulate the McGurk effect more precisely. Using the more advanced technology at his disposal, Massaro produced "ba" and "da" sounds and three intermediate sounds. He also produced a face saying "ba" and "da" and three intermediate lip movements. Massaro found that when people heard "ba" and saw the face mouth "ba," they were very likely to report hearing "ba." However, when the facial movements changed only slightly from "ba" toward "da," people were extremely unlikely to report hearing "ba," even though that was the sound reaching their ears.

We do not typically realize how important it is to be able to see people's lips as they speak. We can easily hear people speaking over a radio or telephone, so we know that seeing a person's lips is not crucial for hearing what they say. Nonetheless, sighted people are all lip readers to a certain degree, and they can use the visual information to help make speech less ambiguous (Campbell, 1992b, 1992c; Summerfield, 1992). Lip reading becomes particularly important in noisy situations, or for people who have hearing impairments (Kent, 1995).

The McGurk effect occurs even under unusual circumstances that you might think would bias the observer toward either audition or vision. For example, the McGurk effect still occurs when a person is watching a female face but hearing a male voice (Green et al., 1991). The effect is less powerful than that obtained with faces, but researchers have found a similar effect with cellos! Saldaña and Rosenblum (1993) showed people a video of a cellist either plucking the strings of a cello or running a bow over the strings. Although people were told to judge only the sounds they heard, their judgments were affected when an inconsistent sound accompanied the video (e.g., plucking sound with cellist using a bow). Thus, when they saw a cellist using the bow, listeners were more likely to rate the sound they heard as being produced by the bow moving on the strings—even when the strings were being plucked. Similarly, seeing the cellist plucking the strings led the listeners to hear the cello being plucked, even when the sound was actually produced by a bow.

The McGurk effect is interesting because it highlights the interaction between vision and audition, supporting Theme 1 of this text. In later chapters, we will return to this important theme when discussing other senses. ◆

SECTION SUMMARY

Interactions Between Auditory and Visual Stimuli

1. Background music influences people's processing of visual images in movies, enhancing their ability to recall the scenes.

2. With the McGurk effect, there is a disparity between the lip movements and the sound being heard. People report hearing a sound that is intermediate between the sound that ordinarily accompanies the lip movements and the sound actually heard.

3. The McGurk effect highlights the importance of lip reading for ordinary speech perception. Lip reading becomes even more important in noisy environments.

4. The McGurk effect can occur even when the gender of the voice doesn't match the gender of the face and when the sound of a musical instrument doesn't match the action producing it.

REVIEW QUESTIONS

1. Contrast complex auditory stimuli with the simple auditory stimuli discussed in Chapters 9 and 10. Why is pitch more complicated than a simple arrangement of notes from low to high? Be certain to mention the concepts of the octave and tonality. Then discuss how notes with similar tone chromas from different octaves are similar to each other.

2. Perception of complex auditory stimuli shares many similarities with perception of complex visual stimuli. Illustrate as many similarities between auditory and visual pattern perception as you can. Pay particular attention to cognitive factors. Why do you think these similarities might have emerged?

3. Imagine yourself at a concert of your choice. Discuss how the material in the music perception portion of the chapter might make you more aware of perceptual qualities of the music. Be certain to mention pitch, tonality, loudness, timbre, and tone combinations.

4. Speech perception seems so easy and effortless. Nonetheless, theories of speech perception are complex. Why? In your discussion, be sure to describe the competing evidence for the Special Mechanism and the General Mechanism accounts of speech perception.

5. Cognitive psychologists propose that people often operate according to a small number of heuristics, or rules of thumb, that typically work well in solving problems in everyday life. However, these heuristics often lead us to incorrect answers when we face special kinds of situations in the laboratory. Use information from this chapter, particularly the phonemic restoration material, to illustrate differences between some laboratory experiments and everyday life experiences.

6. Describe the role that experience seems to play in the perception of auditory patterns. Does experience also seem to affect more basic auditory perception? Where does its role seem more important? What does your discussion lead you to believe about the relative importance of nature versus nurture in auditory pattern perception?

7. Imagine that you have just heard a sentence on television that was part of a news report. You heard all of it distinctly except for one blurred phoneme in one word. Discuss how

each of the five factors mentioned in the top-down processing section could help you identify the phoneme. How might you relate this process of disambiguation to the phonemic restoration effect?

8. In earlier chapters, we often commented on the importance of context for visual perception. In this chapter, you have seen a number of examples in which context influences auditory perception. Use several examples from this chapter to clarify the role of context in perception. Does the role of context seem to differ when dealing with auditory stimuli?

9. Top-down (or conceptually driven) processing becomes especially important in the perception of complex stimuli. Describe the operation of top-down processes in the perception of complex auditory stimuli. How do bottom-up (data-driven) processes function in the perception of complex auditory stimuli? Which class of processes do you think is dominant in the perception of complex stimuli?

10. The McGurk effect is a powerful demonstration of the interaction of vision and audition. Based on the evidence you have seen so far, which sense is dominant? Why? Given your discussion, which sense would the McGurk effect lead you to believe is dominant?

NEW TERMS

octave (343)
tone chroma (343)
tone height (343)
tonality (343)
tonic (343)
probe-tone technique (344)
absolute pitch (344)
attack (348)
steady state (348)
decay (348)
transposition (350)
octave illusion (351)

tritone paradox (351)
phoneme (355)
vocal tract (355)
place of articulation (355)
manner of articulation (355)
voicing (355)
voiceless consonant (355)
voiced consonant (355)
speech spectrogram (356)
sound spectrogram (356)
formants (356)
parallel transmission (357)

Special Mechanism account (359)
module (359)
General Mechanism
    account (359)
motor theory of speech
    perception (359)
categorical perception (360)
voice onset time (VOT) (360)
phonetic boundary (360)
duplex perception (362)
phonemic restoration (364)
McGurk effect (369)

RECOMMENDED READINGS

Aiello, R., & Sloboda, J. A. (Eds.). (1994). *Musical perceptions*. New York: Oxford University Press. This edited text focuses entirely on music perception. Each of the chapters is quite well done, with a helpful introduction to each chapter written by Rita Aiello. She reports that she has used the chapters in courses she teaches at Juilliard and New York University, which makes the reader envious of the students in her courses.

Butler, D. (1992). *The musician's guide to perception and cognition*. New York: Schirmer. This very readable book is made even more useful because of the auditory examples provided on an accompanying compact disc. Butler does a great job of presenting the essentials of auditory perception from the perspective of a musician.

Masters, I. G. (1990–1991). The basics. *Stereo Review*. If you are interested in the relationship between audition and stereo reproduction of music, you would enjoy reading Ian Masters' series that ran in *Stereo Review* through 1990 and 1991. Masters focuses on stereo equipment and terminology, but he does a good job of relating information about reproducing sound to auditory theory.

Mattingly, I. G., & Studdert-Kennedy, M. (Eds.). (1991). *Modularity and the motor theory of speech perception: Proceedings of a conference to honor Alvin M. Liberman.* Hillsdale, NJ: Erlbaum. This book grew out of a conference to honor Liberman, the person most closely associated with the Special Mechanism approach to speech perception. Interestingly, many of the papers in this book are critical of the Special Mechanism approach. If you are interested in the controversy, you will find many of the chapters in this book compelling reading.

McAdams, S., & Bigand, E. (Eds.). (1993b). *Thinking in sound: The cognitive psychology of human audition.* New York: Oxford University Press. All of the chapters in this edited book are quite interesting. Bregman has contributed a chapter that provides an excellent introduction to his approach to complex auditory scene analysis. Crowder has written a chapter on auditory memory, and Bigand reviews some interesting work on music cognition. Each chapter provides an excellent review of one area of complex auditory pattern perception.

The Skin Senses

In elementary school, your teacher might have told you about the five senses: vision, hearing, touch, smell, and taste. Aristotle used this classification system more than 2,300 years ago, and it is probably still the most common one. Aristotle also thought that touch could be further subdivided (J. C. Stevens, 1991), and in this chapter we will discuss several related senses that collectively might be called skin senses.

Your skin represents the largest sensory system you own, with about 2 square yards of receptive surfaces (Sherrick & Cholewiak, 1986). Contrast this size with the relatively minuscule receptive surfaces for vision and hearing. We often ignore the importance of the skin, even though its size is impressive. Vision and hearing seem highly important to us, and we may contemplate how our lives would be changed if we were blind or deaf (Loomis & Lederman, 1986). However, have you ever contemplated what your skin and the skin senses can accomplish? First, consider the protective value of the skin. The skin senses protect you from extremely hot or extremely cold temperatures. Further, the skin senses also protect you from potential tissue damage when you feel pain. The skin senses inform you that a potentially suffocating object is covering your face. In this chapter we'll explore the operation of these related skin senses: temperature perception, pain perception, and touch. Finally, we'll consider the vestibular and kinesthetic senses, which inform you about whether you are standing upright or tilted and where your body parts are in relation to each other.

THE SKIN

Figure 12.1 shows a diagram of **hairy skin,** the kind that covers most of your body and contains either noticeable or almost invisible hairs. Another kind of skin, called **glabrous skin,** is found on the soles of your feet, the palms of your hands, and on the smooth surfaces of your toes and fingers. Glabrous skin is similar to hairy skin except that its outer layer is thicker and it has a more complex mixture of receptors. This complexity is probably related to the fact that these areas are sensitive to stimulation and that we use these areas of skin (especially our hands) to actively explore the physical qualities of objects (Carlson, 1991; Vallbo, 1981).

Notice that the skin in Figure 12.1 can be divided into three layers. The **epidermis,** or outer layer, has many layers of dead skin cells. The **dermis** is the layer that makes new cells. These new cells move to the surface and replace the epidermis cells as they are rubbed off. Underneath the dermis is the **subcutaneous tissue,** which contains connective tissue and fat globules. Also notice that the skin contains an impressive array of veins, arteries, sweat glands, hairs, and receptors. The skin varies greatly in thickness, with facial skin being about 0.5 mm thick (about as thick as five pages of this book pressed tightly together) and skin on the sole of your foot being about 10 times as thick (Sherrick & Cholewiak, 1986).

Scattered throughout the skin are many kinds of receptors, distinguished by structural and, presumably, functional differences. In spite of the variety, all skin receptors are the endings of neurons that carry information from the skin to the higher processing levels.

Some skin receptors have **free nerve endings;** as Figure 12.1 shows, these receptors do not have any small bulbs or capsules on the end nearest the epidermis. In contrast, skin receptors with **encapsulated endings** have small capsules on the end nearest the epidermis. These endings differ in their size, shape, and degree of organization.

The combination of two pieces of information should strike you as suggestive. First, people experience a range of sensations through their skin (temperature, touch, pain, etc.). Second, the receptors might have different sizes and shapes to enable them to perform different functions—so each receptor might be tailor-made to perform a particular function. Unfortunately, the relationship between skin-receptor type and function is not quite so straightforward. Let's examine several theories that have been proposed to explain the relationship between receptors and skin sensations.

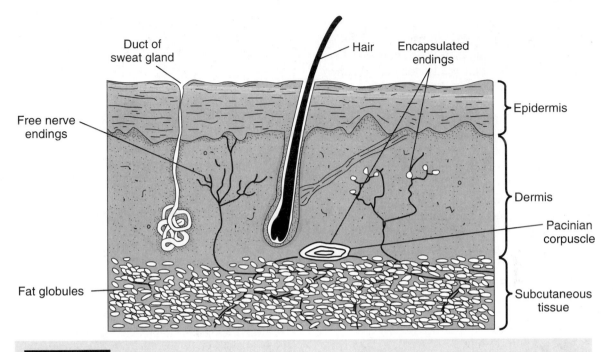

FIGURE 12.1 A schematic cross section of a segment of hairy skin. Notice the three layers of skin and the distribution of the receptors throughout the skin.

Theories about the Skin Senses

The first theory we'll address—specificity theory—is based on the logical thinking we've just been pursuing. Specificity theory was based upon the **doctrine of specific nerve energies**, an idea proposed by an early 19th-century physiologist, Johannes Müller, that different sensory nerves have their own characteristic type of activity and therefore produce different sensations. A later researcher named von Frey extended the doctrine of specific nerve energies by suggesting different types of receptor structure for touch, warmth, cold, and pain. Thus, **specificity theory** states that each of the different kinds of receptors responds exclusively to only one kind of physical stimulus (for example, pain), and each kind of receptor is therefore responsible for only one kind of sensation.

Painfully accumulated evidence (pun intended) argues against von Frey's specificity theory. In a typical study, a researcher might take a sharp needle and poke around on his or her own skin until a tiny region of skin was found that was particularly sensitive to the pain. Then the researcher would snip out that small region of skin and use a microscope to determine what kind of receptor was located beneath the surface. The procedure was repeated to locate receptors that might be associated with either touch or temperature. Eventually these mutilated researchers concluded that the type of receptor was not related to the type of sensation.

A second theory, **pattern theory**, suggests that the *pattern* of nerve impulses determines sensation. According to pattern theory, each kind of receptor responds to many different kinds of stimulation, but it responds more to some than to others. Thus, a particular receptor might respond vigorously to a cold stimulus, less vigorously to a touch stimulus, even less to a pain stimulus, and very little to a hot stimulus. The brain can eventually interpret a code in terms of the relative strengths of the receptors' responses. Melzack and Wall (1962) incorporated some aspects of each theory into their proposal. Their paper is now regarded as a landmark in the theory of skin sensitivity, and the basic assumptions of the theory still appear correct (Sherrick & Cholewiak, 1986). These authors rejected the idea that each different receptor is specifically matched to a particular sensation, but they accepted the idea that the receptors differ. Specifically, each kind of receptor is specialized so that it can convert a particular kind of stimulus into a particular pattern of impulses. We feel pain if the impulses in one kind of nerve fiber are dominant. If the impulses in another kind of nerve fiber are dominant, however, we feel other sensations such as warmth, cold, or pressure. Melzack and Wall developed their theory in more detail for painful stimuli, so we will discuss this issue further in the section on pain.

From the Skin to the Brain

The chapters on vision and hearing discussed the pathways from the visual receptors and the auditory receptors to the brain. In each case the receptors occupied a relatively small, compact space. In contrast, the skin receptors are distributed over the entire body, so the task is more challenging and complicated.

One important aspect of neuronal transmission is that information travels from the skin receptors to the brain by means of two systems: the spinothalamic system and the lemniscal system. The **spinothalamic system** has smaller nerve fibers and slower transmission. (In fact, it may be helpful to recall that the s̲pinothalamic system is s̲mall and s̲low, whereas the l̲emniscal system is l̲arge.) Although the spinothalamic system carries some crude information about touch, this system is primarily involved in the perception of temperature and pain (Pinel, 1993). In contrast, the **lemniscal system** is composed of larger fibers and is the major pathway for conveying touch information. Both the lemniscal and the spinothalamic systems eventually pass on their information to the somatosensory cortex, shown in Figure 12.2.

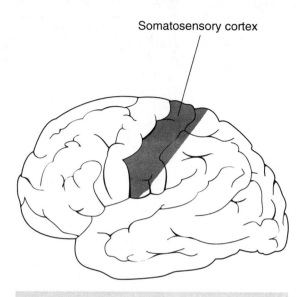

Somatosensory cortex

FIGURE 12.2 Location of the somatosensory cortex, the ultimate destination of information from the skin receptors through the spinothalamic and lemniscal systems.

SECTION SUMMARY

The Skin

1. Skin is the largest sensory system; many kinds of receptors are found in the skin, with either free nerve endings or encapsulated endings. No perfectly clear-cut relationship between the type of skin receptor and its function has been determined.

2. Specificity theory is based on the doctrine of specific nerve energies; specificity theory states that each of the different kinds of receptors responds to only one kind of physical stimulus.

3. Pattern theory proposes that the pattern of nerve impulses determines sensation.

4. Melzack and Wall's theory combines specificity and pattern theory; the basic assumptions of this theory are widely accepted.

5. Two systems convey information from receptors to the brain: the spinothalamic system

and the lemniscal system. The spinothalamic system primarily conveys information about temperature and pain. The lemniscal system primarily conveys information about touch.

6. Both the lemniscal system and the spinothalamic system pass their information on to the somatosensory cortex.

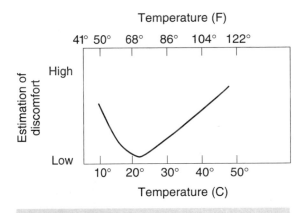

FIGURE 12.3 Estimated amount of discomfort as a function of temperature.

TEMPERATURE

This section discusses the perception of warmth and cold. In particular, we will examine four topics: body temperature regulation, warm and cold spots, temperature thresholds, and adaptation.

Body Temperature Regulation

How hot or cold do you feel right now? Probably you feel reasonably comfortable. Your body has an impressive ability to regulate its own temperature and keep it at about 37° C (98.6° F). If you are in a snowstorm and your body temperature starts to drop, you shiver, a useful process for making more heat. Also, the blood vessels near the surface of the skin shrink in diameter so that less of the warmth from your blood will be lost on the surface. If you are playing a fierce tennis game in the hot August sun, you sweat, and that cools your skin. Also, the blood vessels expand in diameter, so that more of the blood's warmth can be released. Poulton (1970) notes that we may lose consciousness if our body temperature falls below 33° C or rises above 41° C. Thus, the skin's role in temperature regulation is not merely a pleasant luxury; it is absolutely necessary.

Generally, we find that a surrounding temperature of about 22° C (72° F) is most comfortable. Figure 12.3 shows ratings of discomfort associated with various temperatures. Hancock (1986) reviewed a number of studies on the relationship between surrounding temperature and performance. He concluded that people's performance generally decreases at temperatures greater than 29° C (85° F). This decrement is particularly strong for people who are not very

skilled at a task. Thus, the temperature of your surroundings can influence both how comfortable you feel and how well you perform.

Warm and Cold Spots

The section you are reading is labeled "temperature," so you might be tempted to think that we have just one kind of temperature sense. However, we really have separate systems for a warmth sense and for a cold sense. Researchers concluded that two separate systems must exist because they were able to identify separate warm and cold spots on the skin. For example, Dallenbach (1927) took a stimulus the size of a pinhead, cooled it, and touched it to various precise locations in a 2-cm² (0.3 square inches) patch of skin. The same procedure was repeated for the same patch of skin using a heated stimulus. He found no correspondence between areas that responded to the cool stimulus and areas that responded to the warm stimulus. (Also, as you might have guessed from our earlier discussion, he found no correspondence between the type of sensation and the type of receptor underlying the skin at the stimulation point.) Thus, we should not speak of a "temperature sense" as if it were a single sense; the warmth sense and the cold sense are really separate. Subsequent research has established that these warm and cold spots are about 1 mm (0.04 inches) in diameter (Hensel, 1982).

Perhaps you have had the following experience. You put your hand out to test the temperature of the shower water before entering. A few drops convince you that the water temperature is chillingly cold; however, a moment later you realize that the water is really scaldingly hot. If so, you have experienced paradoxical cold. A paradox is something with seemingly contradictory qualities, and *paradoxical cold* occurs when a hot stimulus produces the sensation of cold when it stimulates a cold spot. The ideal temperature to produce paradoxical cold is about 45° C (113° F) (Sherrick & Cholewiak, 1986). It may be that cold spots are active in that temperature range as well as in colder temperatures.

We can also experience paradoxical heat, but not in exactly the same way as we experience paradoxical cold. Many people experience painful heat when they place their hands on a grating of alternating warm and cool surfaces. Sherrick and Cholewiak (1986) refer to this demonstration as a "quaint museum piece" and point out that it is not always successful—suggesting a wide range of individual differences. This demonstration can be found in museums such as the Ontario Science Center, and the experience can be a very powerful one! Placing your hand on one set of tubes leads to a perception of cold, and placing your hand on the alternating set of tubes leads to a perception of

warmth. However, touching both sets of tubes simultaneously leads to a sense of burning heat. If you are one of the people who feel the paradoxical heat, the experience is powerful even though you know that the tubes cannot possibly be hot.

Thresholds for Temperature

Try Demonstration 12.1 to illustrate how temperature sensitivity varies greatly for different parts of your body. According to Stevens et al. (1974), the forehead is particularly sensitive to heat. The chest, stomach, shoulder, and arm are less sensitive, and the calf is the least sensitive. Perhaps you have noticed the difference in temperature sensitivity if you have sat at a camp fire trying to warm your hands. Your forehead probably felt much hotter than your hands, even though it was farther away from the fire.

Sensitivity to cold also varies with differences in body region. J. C. Stevens (1979) found that the trunk was most sensitive, an observation you can appreciate when your doctor places a cold stethoscope on your chest. Arms and legs are somewhat less sensitive to cold, followed by the cheeks, and finally the forehead.

We can often detect small changes in temperature, as minute as 0.003° C (0.006° F) (Kenshalo, 1978). No single value can be supplied as the absolute threshold for warm and cold sensations because the threshold depends on several factors. For example, the larger the portion of

---

Demonstration 12.1

Temperature Thresholds for Various Body Parts

Find a metal fork or spoon. Touch the bottom of the handle to your forehead, chest, stomach, shoulder, arm, foot, and calf. Notice that the handle feels cold when you touch some parts of your body, but its temperature is not noticeable on other body parts. Now run hot water on the utensil handle, wipe it off quickly, and touch it to your forehead. Repeat the heating, drying, and touching process for your other body parts. Where is the heat most noticeable? To test for temperature thresholds with cold stimuli, place a bunch of pennies in a freezer for a couple of hours. Touch the pennies to the same body parts you tested earlier. Where is the cold most noticeable?

skin exposed to the warm or cold stimulus, the smaller the threshold. It makes sense that we can detect a tiny change more readily on an entire arm than on a pinpoint-sized dot of skin. Also, if the temperature changes quickly, we are more likely to notice it than if the change is gradual (Kenshalo et al., 1968). Other important factors that influence threshold include current skin temperature, phase of the menstrual cycle in women, time of day, and stress (Kenshalo, 1978).

People are remarkably poor at localizing temperature sensations for above-threshold stimuli. In one study, they were asked to judge whether a stimulus was presented below or above a particular reference point on their arm (Taus et al., 1975). Even with the warmest stimulus, accuracy for this simple judgment ranged between 80% and 95%. In fact, if the thermal stimulus does not touch our skin, we often have a difficult time determining if the warm stimulus was presented to our chest or to our back (Cain, 1973)!

Adaptation to Temperature

When you first sit down in a hot bath, the temperature may seem unpleasantly hot. After a few minutes the temperature seems comfortable. If you then slide down further into the water so that your back is submerged, the temperature of the water surrounding your back is—once again—unpleasantly hot. The rest of your body had adapted to the hot temperature, but the newly immersed skin had not.

As you know, adaptation occurs when a stimulus is presented continuously; the perceived intensity of the stimulus decreases over time. ***Thermal adaptation*** is therefore a decrease in the perceived intensity of a hot or cold temperature as time passes. Thermal adaptation is usually studied by placing warm or cold stimuli on the skin and asking the subject to report when the temperature sensation disappears. For example, Kenshalo (1971) reports that people seem to be able to adapt completely to temperatures on the skin in the range of about 29° C to 37° C (84° F to 99° F), starting from a normal skin temperature of approximately 33° C (92° F). Outside this

range, the temperature will seem persistently cold or warm, no matter how long the stimulus is left on the skin.

Try Demonstration 12.2 to illustrate an adaptation effect that John Locke reported in the 17th century. Notice that your left hand, which has adapted to the hot water, feels cold in the neutral-temperature water. In contrast, your right hand, which has adapted to the cold water, feels warm in the same neutral-temperature water. Our skin is not an accurate thermometer; we perceive relative, rather than absolute, temperature. A particular temperature can feel cold or hot, depending on the temperature to which we have become accustomed.

People seem to be able to adapt fairly well to cold stimuli. Hensel (1981) describes research on people who are repeatedly subjected to cold conditions. For example, if you were to place your hand in ice water, your blood pressure and heart rate would increase. If you repeated this process several times with room-temperature intervals in between, you would respond less dramatically. Some people are repeatedly exposed to cold conditions, either because of the region they live in or their profession (e.g., fishing). Research shows that they feel little or no pain when their hands are exposed to cold (Hensel, 1981).

SECTION SUMMARY

Temperature

1. The body has several mechanisms for regulating its temperature.
2. Separate warm and cold spots are found on the skin.
3. Paradoxical cold occurs when a hot stimulus produces the sensation of cold. Paradoxical heat may occur when warm and cold spots are stimulated simultaneously.
4. Thresholds for temperature are influenced by factors such as body part, amount of skin exposed, and speed of temperature change. People are poor at localizing temperature.
5. Thermal adaptation is a decrease in the perceived intensity of a hot or a cold tempera-

Demonstration 12.2

Temperature Adaptation

Locate three bowls. Fill one with very hot tap water (but not so hot that it is painful). Fill the second bowl with very cold tap water. Fill the third with a mixture from the other two bowls. Arrange the three bowls as illustrated below. Place your left hand in the hot water and your right hand in the cold water. Leave your hands in these bowls for approximately 3 minutes and then quickly transfer both your hands to the middle (lukewarm) bowl. Notice the apparent temperature of each hand.

Right hand   Left hand

Cold water   Lukewarm water   Hot water

---

ture as a function of repeated exposure. People can adapt fairly well to cold stimuli, for example, if their living conditions or occupations require repeated contact with cold.

PAIN

We've all experienced pain, yet our language seems unable to convey the fullness of the experience. Pain researchers who are members of the International Association for the Study of Pain define *pain* as "an unpleasant sensory and emotional experience associated with actual or potential tissue damage . . ." (Merskey, 1986). Note the tight linkage of the sensory and emotional components of pain, which has not been the case in

our discussion of other senses. Although the sensory and emotional components may not be entirely independent of one another, both are clearly crucial to our perception of pain (Fernandez & Turk, 1992).

Like all perceptual experience, pain is subjective. However, seeing and hearing are stimulated by external events, whereas pain seems to be stimulated by internal events (Wall, 1979). If you and your friend view a beautiful sunset, you are both likely to feel comfortable discussing the shared visual experience. Notice, however, that even if you see your friend suffer an injury, it's very difficult to know how much pain she is experiencing. The pain seems uniquely *her* pain.

We all realize that blindness and deafness create major life problems. In contrast, most of us—especially if we have an excruciating headache or have just hit our thumb with a hammer—would gladly give up the experience of pain. That would be a rash decision, however. People who have pain-perception disorders and cannot feel pain often die prematurely. Pain protects your body from further damage, so it has important survival value.

For example, children who are born with pain insensitivity have completely picked away their nostrils and bitten off their tongues and fingers by mistake (Sternbach, 1978). One such person felt only a mild headache when an axe was buried in his skull (Dearborn, 1932). In a well-documented case, a woman died because of infections resulting from damage done to her spine when she did not make the usual kinds of posture adjustments that we routinely make when our muscles and joints begin to ache (Melzack & Wall, 1982). Yes, pain is uncomfortable, but consider the dangers we would encounter without its warning capacity!

This section on pain has four parts. The first section considers the mechanisms that produce pain. The next two sections discuss how we measure pain and pain adaptation. The last section examines a variety of methods of relieving pain.

Mechanisms of Pain Perception

How, exactly, are painful stimuli processed to give rise to the perception of pain? As we mentioned previously, the spinothalamic system is the pathway for much of pain perception (as well as for temperature perception). Thus, painful stimuli activate fibers that carry information through the spinal cord and the thalamus to the somatosensory cortex (Pinel, 1993). The spinothalamic system is not the only system involved in pain perception. Another system carries pain information to a part of the limbic system. The *limbic system* is composed of a number of subcortical parts of the brain thought to be involved in motivation. One part of the limbic system is thought to regulate emotions, and the pain signal is sent to this area (Talbot et al., 1991). If you stimulate the skin, but not painfully, no signal is

sent to this system. Therefore, the emotional content of pain perception may be due to the signal sent to the limbic system.

Researchers do not completely understand the process by which a stimulus becomes painful. Two of the proposed theories—specificity theory and pattern theory—have been abandoned for a theory that combines specificity theory and pattern theory. Let's first review the shortcomings of the two earlier theories so that we can better appreciate the contributions of a theory that combines them.

Specificity Theory

The *specificity theory of pain perception* states that pain is produced by the stimulation of free nerve endings, which transmit information directly to a pain center in the brain. Thus, when these receptors are stimulated, we must *always* feel pain, and we must *only* feel pain—rather than any other sensation. One problem with the specificity theory is that researchers have had difficulty identifying a particular pain receptor. Furthermore, the free nerve endings definitely are not specific to pain perception; they register other sensations as well.

Although researchers have not identified receptors that are specific to pain perception, they have identified three types of nerve fibers that *transmit* pain information. Two of these types of fibers are smaller (*A-delta fibers* and *C-fibers*) and one (*A-beta fibers*) is larger. Of course, we're talking relative size—none of these fibers is large! The smaller fibers have diameters of 0.3 to 5 microns (one-thousandth of a millimeter) and the larger fibers have diameters of 5 to 20 microns. Similarly, the fibers differ in the speed with which they conduct information. The A-delta fibers conduct information more rapidly than the C-fibers, with the A-beta fibers in between. Because of the speed difference between A-delta and C-fibers, when injured we may feel first a sharp pain followed by dull pain, known as *double pain* (Rollman, 1991).

Many psychological variables influence the amount of pain that people report (Rollman, 1992), which also poses problems for the specificity theory of pain perception. Soldiers and police officers who have been seriously injured in the middle of a crisis often report feeling little pain until after the event is past (Melzack & Wall, 1982; Melzack et al., 1982). Thus, stress can reduce the perception of pain (Mogil et al., 1993b).

Specificity theory also cannot account for **phantom limb pain,** which is perceived pain in an amputated arm or leg. How could someone feel pain in a missing arm when the specific pain receptors in the skin no longer exist? Clearly, in addition to pain receptors on the skin, higher-level processes must either reduce or increase the perception of pain. Later in this section we will return to the fascinating topic of phantom limbs for an in-depth discussion.

Pattern Theory

The **pattern theory of pain perception** states that pain is produced by particular patterns of stimulation. Although no specific pain receptor is involved, we perceive pain when the combined stimulation of different receptors reaches a critical level. Research has found "specialization of receptor activity in response to particular dimensions of energy impinging on the skin, and this activity results in the production of neural patterns" (Sherrick & Cholewiak, 1986, p. 12.49).

Gate Control Theory

A third theory emphasizes the importance of psychological factors and combines the specificity theory and the pattern theory (Weisenberg, 1984). Ronald Melzack and his colleagues have argued that specificity theory ignores psychological factors and pattern theory ignores physiological evidence (Melzack & Casey, 1968; Melzack & Wall, 1965, 1982). Their **gate-control theory** proposes that pain perception is a complex process in which the neural fibers interact and that the brain also has an important influence on pain perception.

To understand the gate-control theory, consult Figure 12.4. Admittedly, this diagram may look only slightly less complicated than a map of the New York City subway system; pain perception is not a simple process. Let's begin with

input from the two kinds of neural fibers on the left. These are the large-diameter (A-beta fibers) and small-diameter (A-delta and C-fibers) fibers we mentioned earlier. They ultimately have different influences on the gate-control system. Notice first that both of these have a direct effect on the transmission cells, located in the spinal cord. Pain information is sent to the brain via the **transmission cells.** Both the large fibers and the small fibers directly excite (+) the transmission cells, leading to the perception of pain.

The neural fibers also influence another part of the spinal cord, called the **substantia gelatinosa.** Both inhibitory and excitatory fibers are located within the substantia gelatinosa. When stimulated, the inhibitory fibers send a message to decrease the firing of the transmission cells. On the other hand, stimulating the excitatory fibers sends a message to increase the firing of the transmission cells. Thus, the substantia gelatinosa serves as a gate for pain information. When the inhibitory fibers are stimulated, the gate is closed and pain is decreased. When the excitatory fibers are stimulated, the gate is open and pain is increased.

Input from the small fibers stimulates (+) the excitatory fibers of the substantia gelatinosa, increasing the perception of pain. Input from the large fibers stimulates (+) the inhibitory fibers of the substantia gelatinosa, closing the gate and decreasing the perception of pain. In summary, the basic operation of the gate-control system shows that when substantial large-fiber activity is present, the perception of pain is decreased. When substantial small-fiber activity is present, the perception of pain is increased.

Notice, also, that the brain can influence pain perception. We have repeatedly emphasized the importance of cognitive processes in perception (Theme 4), and cognitive control is an important part of the gate-control theory. Signals from the brain excite the inhibitory cells in the substantia gelatinosa, just like the large fibers. Thus the brain can inhibit the firing of the transmission cells, reducing the perception of pain. As we will note later in the chapter, treatments for pain often involve cognitive processes. By now

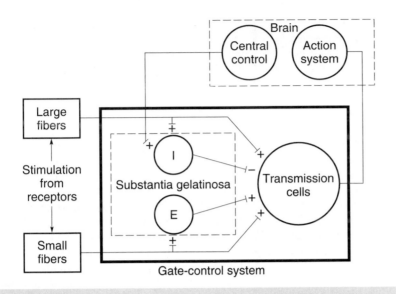

Schematic depiction of the gate-control theory of pain. The painful stimulus causes the receptors to fire, sending signals along both the large and small fibers. Input from these fibers directly excites (+) the transmission cells to send along a message of pain to the brain. The action system then attempts to avoid the pain. In addition to affecting the transmission cells, the small fibers also stimulate excitatory (E) fibers within the substantia gelatinosa of the spinal cord. The large fibers also stimulate inhibitory (I) fibers within the substantia gelatinosa, leading to an inhibition (–) of the transmission cells. Note also that the brain can send a descending inhibitory signal to reduce the perception of pain by stimulating the inhibitory fibers of the substantia gelatinosa.

you should readily agree that pain perception involves much more than simple stimulation of the free nerve endings!

IN-DEPTH Phantom Limb Pain

As we mentioned previously, when people have a limb amputated, virtually all of them continue to feel that the limb is present. They may even feel pain in the nonexistent limb. How can a person experience a limb when no receptors exist to send information from that limb? The exact cause of phantom limbs remains somewhat elusive, but a number of researchers have begun to unravel this most mysterious experience. In fact, in the process they have helped to change our notions of the rigidity of neural connections in adult

brains. The very perplexing experience of phantom limbs has a great deal to tell us about kinesthesia, pain, and touch—indeed, about perception in general.

Although experience plays a major role in perception, we must emphasize that phantom limb experience is not due to learning to use a limb or to processing input from a limb. The evidence for this is quite strong—people who were born without limbs experience phantom limbs (Melzack, 1992b; Scatena, 1990). This evidence suggests a strong genetic component to our sense of our bodies (Melzack, 1992b).

What is the kinesthetic experience of the phantom limb? Typically it appears to be attached to the stump in a "normal" position (L. A. Jones, 1988). The amputee will even perceive the limb to move in synchrony with the stump, as a normal limb would. Thus, a woman missing both arms still continues to "use" them to stress the points she makes in a heated discussion (Shreeve, 1993).

In some cases, however, the phantom limb seems to be located in an unusual position. In fact, one stroke victim actually experienced a third phantom arm extending from the middle of his chest (Halligan et al., 1993)! Ronald Melzack (1992b) reports that one man felt that his phantom arm was stuck behind his back, so he was uncomfortable sleeping on his back. Another man felt that his phantom arm was stuck out perpendicular to his side. He even walked through doors sideways, to be able to fit this phantom arm through the doorway. We might surmise that should this man walk through a door in a normal fashion, he would feel his phantom arm pass through the door frame. That is the common experience of people with phantom limbs. If the man were to move his arm toward a wall, he would first feel his fingers enter the wall. Once his stump hit the wall, however, he might feel his fingers retract until they were directly attached to his stump (L. A. Jones, 1988).

Early clues about what might be producing phantom limbs emerged in research conducted by Michael Merzenich and his colleagues (Merzenich et al., 1984). After amputating a monkey's finger, they found that the areas of the somatosensory cortex that had previously been stimulated by that finger were now affected by the adjacent fingers. Thus, stimulating an adjacent finger would make it feel as though the missing finger were being stimulated! Researchers initially thought that such reorganization would occur only over adjacent areas of the cortex. More recent research, however, indicates that over longer periods of time much more widespread reorganization is possible (Pons et al., 1991).

Vilayanur Ramachandran of the University of California at San Diego has observed such reorganization in human amputees. In one case, Ramachandran worked with a young man who had recently lost his left arm in an accident. After blindfolding the young man, Ramachandran rubbed a cotton swab against parts of the man's face. Although he felt the pressure on his face, he also felt it on his missing hand! Ramachandran dribbled warm water down the face of another amputee, who reported that he felt the water moving down his arm (Shreeve, 1993). So an amputee feeling an itching sensation on a missing arm might actually need to scratch his or her face.

As we will explain later in this chapter, the portion of the somatosensory cortex that receives input from the arm and hand is actually near the area receiving input from the face. Because of the speed with which the remapping of inputs takes place, Ramachandran believes that it cannot be due to the growth of neurons, as Pons and others believe (Ramachandran, 1993). Instead, he believes that the "phantom connections" in the somatosensory cortex between the intact arm and the face areas are already present prior to amputation, but the stronger input determines our perception. That is, when we brush something against our face, we are also stimulating the area of the cortex that receives input from our arm. However, the actual input from the arm is so strong that we only perceive the stimulation of our face. After the arm is amputated, it no longer sends the stronger signal, so brushing against the face is also perceived as stimulating the arm.

So the research of Ramachandran and others suggests that the absence of sensory input to the cortex can lead to a reorganization of brain structure. The motto "Use it or lose it" seems to apply not only to developing organisms but to adults as well (Shreeve, 1993). Thus, blind people who read braille actually have larger areas of their cortex devoted to input from their index fingers (Blakeslee, 1992a).

Given that massive reorganization is taking place after amputation, one still must wonder about the source of *pain* from the phantom limb. Unfortunately, phantom limb pain is quite common, with roughly 70% of amputees experiencing pain in their phantom limbs (Dernham, 1986; Rasmussen & Jensen, 1992). This pain is so perplexing to some amputees that they don't even ask for pain medication—knowing that it is arising from a nonexistent part of their bodies (P. G. Wilson, 1994). The phantom pain typically begins within four days of amputation and is described as knifelike or sticking, but two years later it is more likely to be described as burning, squeezing, or crushing (Rasmussen & Jensen, 1992).

One theory about the source of phantom limb pain can be discarded. When a limb is amputated, the severed nerves that used to carry information from the limb remain in the stump. At first, researchers thought that these nerves continued to send signals to the somatosensory cortex, so they tried various means of stopping the input from these nerves. Although such treatments were often temporarily effective, the pain typically returned. It now appears quite clear that the source of phantom limb pain is in the brain itself (Melzack, 1992b; Ramachandran, 1993).

To explain such pain, Ronald Melzack of McGill University proposes that each person's brain has a unique configuration of neurons called the **neuromatrix.** This neuromatrix "continuously generates a characteristic pattern of impulses indicating that the body is intact and unequivocally one's own" (Melzack, 1992b, p. 123). He proposes that three systems are components of the neuromatrix. One is the sensory system for the skin senses that we've been discussing (thalamus and somatosensory cortex). The second system is the limbic system, which we discussed earlier because of its important role in the emotional component of pain. The third system is crucial for a sense of self and is located primarily in the parietal lobe of the brain. One man with damage to this portion of his brain kept throwing his own leg out of bed, thinking that it was someone else's leg (Sacks, 1985)! Given the presence of phantom limbs in people with congenitally absent limbs, Melzack believes that the essence of the neuromatrix is "hardwired," or built into us all (Melzack, 1992b).

One source of the sense of burning pain often reported in the phantom limb could be the lack of sensory input from the amputated limb to the neuromatrix. It might be that in the absence of inhibitory input from the limb, portions of the neuromatrix begin to fire wildly; the person experiences these sensations as burning pain. Another possibility is that the neuromatrix may try harder and harder to generate movement in absent limbs. These increasingly strong but ineffective motor commands might also be interpreted as burning (Melzack, 1992b). Although the exact source of phantom limb pain remains unclear, the recent evidence provides hope that we will soon know the source and remedy for the perceived pain.

What does the phantom limb experience tell us about perception? As Melzack writes, "The brain does more than detect and analyze inputs; it generates perceptual experience even when no external inputs occur. . . . Sensory inputs merely modulate that experience; they do not directly cause it. . . . We do not need a body to feel a body (Melzack, 1992b, p. 126)." These are, indeed, important lessons to learn. ◆

Measurement of Pain

How might you describe the pain you are experiencing? The task is made difficult by the lack of vocabulary for describing the pain experience. We do provide involuntary cues to the pain we are experiencing, through body reactions and facial expressions (Prkachin, 1992a; Prkachin et al., 1994). People are reasonably good at decoding facial expressions of pain, to the point of being able to distinguish between facial responses to genuine pain and facial expressions that feign pain (Prkachin, 1992b). Although such involuntary responses to pain are useful, researchers have devoted a great deal of effort to providing people with means of reporting their perceived pain.

As you might well imagine, researchers have applied the entire range of methods discussed in Chapter 2 to measure pain. Some researchers have used the method of limits to determine the point at which a hot stimulus or a needle pressed into the skin becomes painful (Rollman, 1992). Other researchers have used signal detection methods to separate sensory abilities from criteria used to judge pain (Fernandez & Turk, 1992; Irwin & Whitehead, 1991; Rollman, 1992). Still other researchers have used magnitude estimation methods to judge the severity of pain (Algom & Lubel, 1994; Price & Harkins, 1992). Clearly, the range of methods used to study pain is extremely wide.

The range of stimuli used to *produce* pain is equally wide. As Sherrick and Cholewiak (1986) note:

The full array of devices and bodily loci employed in the study of pain would bring a smile to the lips of the Marquis de Sade [from whose name the word "sadism" is derived]. . . . Mechanical, thermal (conductive and radiant), chemical, and electrocutaneous stimuli have been applied to or injected into the limbs, torso, genitalia, face, cornea, palate, scalp, and tooth pulp of humans and animals in an unremitting search for either the conditions of stable production of pain or of reliable relief from it (pp. 12–39).

Researchers have employed the classical psychophysical methods to determine the pain threshold. The ***pain threshold*** is the intensity of stimulation at which an observer says, "It's painful" half the time and, "It's not painful" half the time. Notice, however, that in some ways the pain threshold is more like a difference threshold than an absolute threshold. When we measure pain thresholds, a perceivable stimulus is always present, and we ask people to tell us when the quality of the stimulus changes. For example, we might use a heat stimulus that would be perceived to be warm and then hot as the temperature was increased to a painful level (Lautenbacher et al., 1992).

Pain thresholds depend upon many different factors. For instance, different parts of the body have different sensitivities to pain. The cornea, the back of the knee, and the neck region are particularly sensitive, whereas the sole of the foot, the tip of the nose, and the inside lining of the cheek are particularly *in*sensitive. You have probably already discovered that parts of the body differ in their sensitivity if you have ever compared the pain of a tiny paper cut under a fingernail with the pain of a large gash on the sole of your foot.

A term related to pain thresholds is ***pain tolerance,*** the maximum pain level at which people voluntarily accept pain. Although research in pain perception is extremely important, this research is even more difficult to conduct because of ethical considerations (American Psychological Association, 1992; Sternbach, 1983).

Both pain threshold and pain tolerance show enormous variation from one individual to another. For instance, using electric shock to produce pain, Rollman and Harris (1987) found an eightfold ratio from largest to smallest pain threshold

and tolerance for the 40 participants in their study. A particular stimulus may be perceived by one person as being below his or her pain threshold, whereas the same stimulus may be perceived as above another person's pain tolerance.

In Chapter 2 we stressed that an advantage of signal detection theory is that it allows us to measure both the observer's sensitivity and his or her decision-making strategy. If we only use classical psychophysical techniques to explore pain, we cannot know whether a person's pain tolerance is due to low sensitivity or a high criterion, requiring intense pain before she or he complains (Irwin & Whitehead, 1991). Given the strong role of cognitive factors in pain perception, any measurement device must take into consideration such cognitive factors (Rollman, 1992). Although the use of signal detection theory in the assessment of pain has great intuitive appeal, the results of such experiments may be difficult to interpret (Rollman, 1977, 1980).

Given the emotional component of pain, several pain measurement instruments have been developed that attempt to separate the sensory and emotional components of pain (Fernandez & Turk, 1992; Rollman, 1992). One instrument, the McGill Pain Questionnaire, asks the respondent to choose descriptive terms that are thought to tap into either the sensory (e.g., sharp, hot, dull) or the affective (e.g., sickening, terrifying, punishing) components of pain (Melzack & Katz, 1992). Such distinctions might seem arbitrary to you—is *punishing* a purely affective term? If so, then you are sensitive to the difficulty of developing any instrument to measure the many dimensions of pain.

Adaptation to Pain

Think about the last time you had a severe pain, such as a headache or a burn. If you took no medication, did the intensity of the pain seem to decrease over time? Most people report that the pain seems just as excruciating after half an hour as it did initially. In other words, pain adaptation does not seem to occur for intense pains (Price et al., 1992).

Demonstration 12.3

Adaptation to Pain   Take a glass of cold water and add several ice cubes. Place your index finger in the water. Notice that you feel mild pain in your finger initially. Leave your finger in the water for several minutes. Do you still notice the pain?

Adaptation *does* occur for mild pains. Try Demonstration 12.3 to illustrate how you can adapt to a mildly painful cold stimulus, particularly when only a small area of skin experiences pain. As Kenshalo (1971) points out, the physiological reason why we can adapt to painful cold stimuli is that the chilling of nerve tissue blocks receptor activity and the conduction of impulses.

Adaptation also occurs for other mild pains, such as a pinprick and mildly painful hot stimuli. For example, we show adaptation for hot water temperatures up to about 45° C (113° F). On the other hand, we show little or no adaptation for hot water temperatures above 45° C (Price et al., 1992). If your doctor advises you to soak an infected finger in water as hot as you can tolerate, keep the temperature below 45° C.

Pain Control

Although pain is an important signal about potential damage to our bodies, its survival value decreases once we've become aware of the problem. Because we don't adapt to severe pain, persistent pain can have a serious negative effect on our lives. In fact, persistent pain might be life-threatening. John Liebeskind and his colleagues at UCLA have found that natural defenses against tumor-producing cells become less effective when the organism is experiencing pain (Touchette, 1993). The medical community had been reluctant to use measures such as drugs to combat pain. However, the accumulation of recent evidence should lead to a greater use of a range of methods to control pain (Cailliet, 1993). In this section we will briefly review some phar-macological, physical, and psychological interventions in the treatment of pain.

Pharmacological Interventions

When you have a headache, you may take an aspirin. Aspirin is an ***analgesic medication,*** a drug specifically designed to relieve pain. Analgesics also include Novocain (which your dentist may inject before filling a cavity in your tooth), codeine (an opium derivative that is stronger than aspirin and classified as a weak narcotic agent), and morphine (another opium derivative, but stronger than codeine). Because of its effectiveness as an analgesic, morphine is of great interest to pain researchers and physicians. Morphine is used less often than it might be because of a concern about its addictive properties. One way in which addiction becomes apparent is through increasing tolerance levels. Research indicates that increased morphine tolerance levels might have less to do with its pharmacological properties than the contexts in which this drug is administered (Feinberg & Riccio, 1990). That is, when morphine is administered in hospital contexts, it is less likely to become addictive.

As a further indication of the powerful influence of context, morphine may be addictive when taken primarily for its euphoric effects, but it is rarely addictive when taken to relieve pain (Melzack, 1990). In fact, when morphine is used as an analgesic, tolerance typically increases slightly and then levels off. Morphine and other opium derivatives appear to be effective means of preventing pain with few side effects and little chance of addiction for psychologically healthy people (Melzack, 1992a).

Opium-based drugs such as codeine and morphine are effective because certain parts of the brain are particularly sensitive to such opiates (Cailliet, 1993; Solomon, 1994). These **opiate receptors** are specific locations on the surfaces of brain cells that respond to opiate drugs in a fashion similar to a lock and a key (Feuerstein et al., 1986). Why should our brains be so cleverly designed to match the structure of opiates? Researchers realized that such substances must occur naturally inside our bodies; in other words, these are *endogenous* substances. Indeed, such endogenous substances were discovered soon afterward, and they were called **endorphins,** as a shortened name for endogenous morphinelike substances. These substances have analgesic effects that resemble morphine's impressive ability to reduce pain (Cailliet, 1993).

Additional evidence indicates that these endorphins are similar to the opiate drugs. A drug named naloxone negates the pain-killing effects of opiate drugs such as morphine. (In fact, naloxone is sometimes given to people who have taken overdoses of morphine.) Intriguingly, naloxone also blocks the pain relief normally produced by other mechanisms, such as stress. Thus, these pain-control procedures must cause the release of endorphins.

We've already mentioned that stress can lead to a reduction in pain. Studies in **stress-induced analgesia** have demonstrated that lower levels of stress lead to the release of endorphins. Mogil and his colleagues conducted research on mice, indicating that higher levels of stress appear to involve a nonopioid mechanism for pain inhibition that may be sex specific (Mogil et al., 1993a; Mogil et al., 1993b). Can you figure out how these researchers determined that the pathway involved a nonopioid mechanism? As you may well have reasoned, they found that some stress-induced analgesia was not blocked by naloxone, which meant that this particular analgesia was not produced by endorphins.

Physical Interventions
You may have discovered that the intensity of pain from a wound can be reduced by scratching the surrounding skin. Several methods of pain control involve **counterirritants,** which stimulate or irritate one area to diminish pain in another.

One kind of counterirritant is the classical Chinese technique called acupuncture. **Acupuncture** involves the insertion of thin needles into various locations on the body. Acupuncturists use many different techniques, including twirling the needles, or passing electrical current through the needles (Thompson & Filshie, 1993).

Many charts and models are available to illustrate the different acupuncture points. Stimulation of a particular location on the body relieves a particular symptom. Surprisingly, the stimulated location is often far away from the painful area. For example, dental and facial pain can be reduced by stimulating the fingers (Melzack, 1994). Surgery for removal of the stomach is accomplished with four acupuncture needles in the pinna of each ear (Melzack, 1973). In fact, in traditional Chinese acupuncture, the ear is thought to be a pathway to the internal organs (Thompson & Filshie, 1993).

Physicians in the United States have been reluctant to accept acupuncture as a method of controlling pain. In fact, most Americans were not interested in acupuncture until an American columnist, James Reston, had his appendix removed with the aid of acupuncture in an operation in China (Hassett, 1980). Melzack (1973) reports that a large proportion of patients in China—perhaps as high as 90%—undergo surgery with the acupuncture method. Patients who experience surgery with acupuncture are reported to be fully conscious during the operation. They chat pleasantly with the doctors, eat pieces of orange, and are keenly interested in the procedures of the operation. In China, acupuncture is part of an entire approach to medicine that involves rapport, explanations, and expectations (Liebeskind & Paul, 1977).

Naturally, it is difficult to duplicate these conditions in Western medical practice. Although acupuncture has been used effectively even in the United States, the number of people currently making use of this therapy is quite small (Eisenberg et al., 1993). This number might well grow in the future, especially given the fact that an acupuncture treatment can relieve pain for weeks (Thompson & Filshie, 1993).

Another kind of counterirritant method is called stimulation-produced analgesia. **Stimulation-produced analgesia** involves the electrical stimulation of certain regions of the brain, which leads to analgesia, or a loss of sensitivity to pain. To provide the neural stimulation, stimulators have been implanted in people's brains and spinal cords (North, 1994). Another effective stimulation technique for reducing pain, called **transcutaneous electrical nerve stimulation (TENS),** is produced by a stimulator placed on the surface of the skin (Cailliet, 1993). In fact, TENS seems very much like acupuncture with electrical stimulation of the needles (Melzack, 1994). TENS has been found to be particularly effective in relieving back pain.

The mechanisms underlying all the counterirritant methods are likely to be similar. The gate-control theory seems useful for understanding the processes involved. Some of the analgesic effect is likely due to the stimulation of the large fibers, which inhibit the pain signal. An additional analgesic effect is likely to be due to more central control processes, such as the release of endorphins or the nonopioid pathway (Mogil et al., 1993b; Thompson & Filshie, 1993).

Psychological Interventions

So far we have seen that pain can be controlled by analgesics, by the release of endorphins, and by being prodded with sharp needles and electrical stimulation. Now let's look at some procedures based on psychological principles: placebo effects, hypnosis, and cognitive–behavioral therapy.

A **placebo** is an inactive treatment or substance, such as a sugar pill, that the patient believes is an effective therapy. If a doctor gives a patient a placebo and announces that it is a sugar pill, the pill will not have any effect. If the placebo is believed to be an analgesic, however, it may reduce pain significantly (Wall, 1993). In fact, the history of medicine up to the 1600s may really have been the history of the placebo effect, because none of the treatments was inherently helpful (Critelli & Neumann, 1984).

Why are placebos effective? Placebos may prompt the release of endorphins—although this explanation is controversial—or they may serve to decrease anxiety (Turner et al., 1994). Interestingly, placebos often appear to function as normal medication, producing side effects such as drowsiness or headaches and a decrease in effectiveness after initial administration.

Another approach that relies on the power of the mind is hypnosis. **Hypnosis** is an altered state of consciousness in which a person is susceptible to suggestions made by the hypnotist (Barber, 1986). It has been used to help people suffering from chronic pain and to prevent pain in patients undergoing surgery. Hypnosis can provide dramatic relief in some cases. For example, Bellisimo and Tunks (1984) cite the case of a man suffering from painful cancer of the throat. Under hypnosis he was told that he would feel a pleasant tingling sensation, similar to a weak electric current, whenever he started to sense pain in his throat. The patient successfully substituted the pleasant tingling for the pain. In patients suffering from severe burns, hypnotic suggestion that the patient feels cool and comfortable can substantially reduce the pain and also the number of times patients request narcotic medications (Ewin, 1986; Kihlstrom, 1985; Patterson et al., 1992a).

We should stress that some researchers are skeptical about hypnosis. Typically, they acknowledge that hypnosis may indeed relieve pain, but they argue that people generally show as much pain reduction when provided with pain-reduction suggestions under waking conditions as they do when hypnotized (Spanos et al., 1994). The results suggest that hypnosis produces effective pain relief compared to no treatment at all, but it may not be any more successful than the less mysterious techniques such as those used in cognitive–behavioral techniques.

Cognitive–behavioral approaches focus on helping the patient to become actively involved in developing more adaptive cognitive and behavioral reactions to pain (Turk, 1994; Turk & Rudy, 1994). They include a wide variety of techniques. Some techniques that emphasize the cognitive aspect include teaching the patient to identify negative thoughts related to pain, substitute more adaptive thoughts, and use coping strategies such as distraction to minimize suffering. Cognitive–behavioral approaches also borrow from behaviorism. Patients are frequently taught operant conditioning principles, in which behavior not related to pain—such as increased physical activity—is reinforced.

These approaches have been found to be effective in treating many different types of pain (Turk & Meichenbaum, 1994). For instance, cognitive–behavioral techniques are prominently featured in prepared childbirth. For example, ***prepared childbirth methods*** (e.g., the Lamaze method) focus on educating women about the anatomy and physiology of childbirth and controlled muscular relaxation; prepared childbirth also teaches them to pay attention to something other than pain (Wideman & Singer, 1984). The studies using this technique have demonstrated that women who have received prepared childbirth training are more tolerant of pain and require less medication during childbirth.

SECTION SUMMARY

Pain

1. Pain involves the perception of tissue damage and the personal experience of unpleasantness. It often has survival value, protecting us from further damage.
2. The specificity theory of pain perception states that pain is transmitted directly from pain receptors to a pain center in the brain. This theory cannot account for the fact that psychological variables influence the amount of pain that people report.
3. The pattern theory of pain perception states that pain is produced by a particular pattern of stimulation from the receptors. This theory cannot account for the physiological evidence that free nerve endings do seem to be responsible for pain perception.
4. Melzack and his colleagues proposed a gate-control theory in which pain perception is hypothesized to be the result of complex interactions of large fibers and small fibers

with the transmission cells and the substantia gelatinosa. In addition, cognitive control from the brain has an important influence on pain perception.
5. Phantom limbs and phantom limb pain are due to central processes, including the reorganization or neural connections after amputation. Phantom limb pain poses particular problems for some theories of pain perception.
6. The pain threshold is the lowest intensity of stimulation at which we perceive pain. Pain tolerance is the maximum pain level at which people accept pain, and pain tolerance is found to vary across individuals.
7. Humans adapt to mild pains but not to severe ones.
8. Pain can be controlled by analgesics, such as aspirin, codeine, and morphine. Naturally produced endorphins have analgesic properties and appear to be released by stressful experiences.
9. Counterirritants, which diminish pain in one area by stimulating or irritating another area, include acupuncture, stimulation-produced analgesia, and transcutaneous electrical nerve stimulation.
10. Psychological techniques for controlling pain include placebo effects, hypnosis, and cognitive–behavioral approaches.

TOUCH

Touch involves the sensations produced by deformation of the skin. That is, your skin becomes slightly distorted when you touch an object or an object touches you. The sensations arising from pressure on your skin are important in several different areas. For instance, touch is important to both infants and their parents in the development of infant–parent attachment (C. C. Brown, 1984). The effects of even a subtle touch can be substantial. For example, students rated a library's staff and facilities more positively if the clerk touched their hands just briefly while returning their library cards (Fisher et al., 1976).

Consider, too, how a pat or a handshake carries a different message from a hostile punch in the nose. Finally, the importance of touch in sexual interactions is obvious.

Sensory Aspects of Touch

As we discussed earlier, pressure on the skin excites the various nerve endings embedded in the skin. Researchers now categorize these nerve endings into four different classes based on the speed of adaptation of the receptor and the size of the receptive field associated with the receptor (Bolanowski, 1989; Cholewiak & Collins, 1991). We have already discussed adaptation in reference to vision and audition, and the principles are similar for touch stimuli. Some receptors respond best to changes in pressure but adapt rapidly to the stimulus. These *rapidly adapting (RA) receptors* are particularly good at picking up vibrations on the skin. Other receptors don't adapt as rapidly to the stimulus, continuing to respond to steady pressure on the skin. These *slowly adapting (SA) receptors* are particularly good at picking up constant pressure on the skin.

The skin's receptors are distinguished not only by the speed of adaptation but also by the size of their receptive fields. If you recall our discussion of receptive fields in the visual system, you might guess correctly that the receptive field is the area on the skin where pressure will cause a fiber to increase its firing rate. Those receptors with smaller receptive fields are better able to detect edges and detail in stimuli.

The combination of speed of adaptation and size of receptive field determines the four types of receptors. Thus there are RA receptors with a small receptive field and RA receptors with a large receptive field. Likewise, there are SA receptors with a small receptive field and SA receptors with a large receptive field. In fact, the SA receptors with small receptive fields are up to three times better at detecting spatial detail than the RA receptors with large receptive fields (Johnson & Hsiao, 1992). For example, the ability to detect spatial detail in the braille alphabet is due to the SA receptors with small receptive fields.

Pacinian Corpuscles

The best understood of the encapsulated nerve endings are Pacinian corpuscles. The *Pacinian corpuscles* are the largest sensory end organs in the body (about 0.5 mm wide and 1.0 mm long), and they are rapidly adapting receptors with a large receptive field. Each Pacinian corpuscle consists of about 70 layers assembled in an onionlike fashion on the end of an axon. The unusual layered structure apparently permits the successive layers to slip over each other so that this receptor is more sensitive to a change in touch than to sustained touch. Thus, a Pacinian corpuscle in the sole of your foot would not continue to send out signals after you have been standing at a party for 3 hours, deforming the structure continuously. The structure of this receptor would, however, be sensitive to a *change* in stimulation, so that it could readily detect the vibrations of a subway rumbling under the apartment in which you have been standing (Carlson, 1991; Cholewiak & Collins, 1991).

These impressive receptors seem to be strategically located, with about 1,000 to 1,500 Pacinian corpuscles on the palm side of each hand (Sherrick & Cholewiak, 1986). Even though the Pacinian corpuscles have relatively large receptive fields, their very density in some areas of the skin enables them to effectively signal the location of a stimulus (Sherrick et al., 1990). Nonetheless, the Pacinian corpuscles are primarily responsible for detecting rapid vibration on the skin, which also allows them to detect the roughness of surfaces rubbed against the skin (Cholewiak & Collins, 1991; Johnson & Hsiao, 1992).

The Correspondence between Skin and Cortical Locations

Stimulation of skin receptors produces firing in the afferent nerves leading to the somatosensory cortex. For many years, researchers have tried to discover the relationship between points on the body and points on the cortex. For example, Penfield and Rasmussen (1950) obtained information on patients whose skulls were opened up for tumor removal. Penfield and Rasmussen electrically stimulated various points on the somatosen-

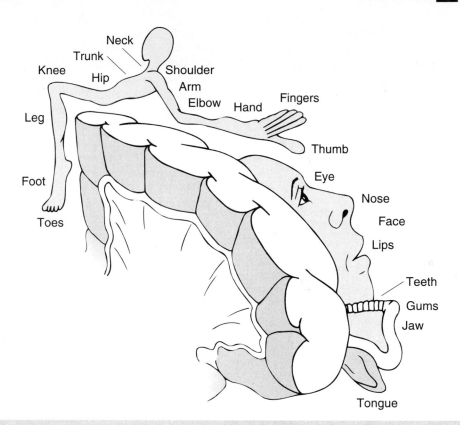

Neck
Trunk
Knee
Hip
Shoulder
Arm
Elbow
Hand
Fingers
Leg
Thumb
Eye
Nose
Foot
Face
Lips
Toes
Teeth
Gums
Jaw
Tongue

FIGURE 12.5 Correspondence between parts of the somatosensory cortex and body parts, as viewed from the front. The greater the size of the body part depicted, the larger the area of the cortex devoted to input from that part. (Based on Penfield & Rasmussen, 1950)

sory cortex. Then they asked the patients, who were alert because they had only local anesthetics, to identify the part of their body that tingled.

Figure 12.5 shows the correspondence they found. Notice that this distorted creature has its body parts scattered along the edge of the cortex in a pattern that bears little resemblance to your own body. As we mentioned earlier, in the context of phantom limbs, the area for the hand is located near the area for the face. Furthermore, some large body parts, such as the leg, receive much less cortex space than some much smaller body parts, such as the lip.

In the next section we will see that the amount of space occupied on the cortex is related to

thresholds of the various body parts. More recent research has revealed further details about the organization of the somatosensory cortex. You will recall that the visual cortex is organized in columns. Similarly, a columnar arrangement was discovered in the somatosensory cortex even before it was discovered in the visual system (Carlson, 1991; Mountcastle, 1957). Furthermore, the somatosensory cortex appears to be divided into between five and ten different maps of the body surface. Within each of these maps, cells respond to stimulation of a particular kind of receptor. For example, one such map might correspond exclusively to the Pacinian corpuscles (Carlson, 1991; Dykes, 1983).

Demonstration 12.4

Touch Thresholds for Various Body Parts

Take a small piece of cotton (or fragment of a tissue) and lightly touch it to the following parts of your body: the thick part of the sole of your foot, your cheek, your back, your nose, and your thumb. Notice that the parts of your body are not uniformly sensitive to touch.

Passive Touch

Somatosensory activity can be produced by stimulating skin receptors in either of two general ways. In ***passive touch***, an object is placed on a person's skin. ***Active touch*** involves a person's actively seeking interactions with the environment by exploring objects and touching them. We need to explore both types of stimulation because several pieces of research suggest that they lead to differing perceptions. Active touch will be examined later; let's first explore passive touch.

Absolute Thresholds for Touch

In classic studies on passive touch, researchers measure thresholds for the detection of a single skin indentation. Try Demonstration 12.4 to illustrate how parts of your body differ in their sensitivity. The cotton was probably particularly noticeable when it touched your cheek, yet its impact on the sole of your foot was so minimal that you probably had to check visually to be certain that you were really touching it. As you may recall, an ***absolute threshold*** is the boundary point at which something is reported half the time. The most extensive research on thresholds was conducted by Weinstein (1968). He examined both men and women, touching them on 20 different body parts with a nylon hairlike strand for which the force could be precisely measured. Figure 12.6 shows the sensitivity for females and males. Notice three features of this diagram: (1) Women are more sensitive to touch than men for several parts of the body (that is, their

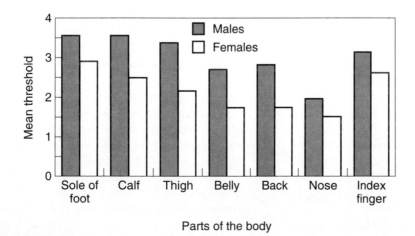

FIGURE 12.6 A comparison of detection thresholds for males and females. Females are typically more sensitive than males. Some body parts are more sensitive than others in both males and females. (Adapted from Weinstein, 1968)

thresholds are lower); (2) the parts of the body vary in sensitivity—for example, people are more sensitive in the facial area than around the feet; and (3) women and men differ in their specific patterns of sensitivity—for example, women's bellies and backs are nearly as sensitive as parts of their faces, but these body parts are relatively insensitive for men. Although women are more sensitive at several bodily locations, at other locations, such as the tongue, women and men appear to be equally sensitive (Fucci et al., 1990; Petrosino et al., 1988).

Two-Point Thresholds for Touch

We have been discussing absolute thresholds. Another kind of threshold is a *two-point discrimination threshold,* which measures the ability to notice that the stimulus is touching two points on your skin, rather than a single point. Typically, two-point discrimination thresholds are assessed by selecting two blunt but narrow-diameter prongs and placing them perhaps 2 cm (0.8 inch) apart. The observer is asked to report whether he or she feels one or two stimuli. On descending trials, the distance between the two stimuli is decreased until the observer consistently reports one stimulus. On ascending trials, the distance between the two stimuli is systematically increased, as you might expect from the methodology described in Chapter 2.

The two points are often presented simultaneously. As we saw in the previous chapter, however, timing can have a tremendous influence on perception. Timing also plays a role in tactile perception. For example, Geldard and Sherrick (1986) found that the perceived location of a stimulus is strongly influenced by the presentation of a second stimulus. As the duration between the presentation of the first and second stimulus increases, so does the perceived spatial displacement of the two stimuli.

Try Demonstration 12.5 to illustrate two-point discrimination thresholds. We should mention that if you ever visit a neurologist for an extensive neurological examination, you are unlikely to escape without a test similar to this demonstration. We should also mention that peo-

ple's performance on this task can be substantially improved by practice, evidence consistent with Theme 4 of this text (Sherrick & Cholewiak, 1986). Demonstration 12.5 points out how two-point discrimination thresholds vary as a function of body location. When two toothpicks touch your calf, you feel one single touch rather than two. On your nose, however, you experience two distinctly separate touch sensations.

Weinstein (1968) measured two-point discrimination thresholds as well as the absolute thresholds discussed earlier. Again, the face was generally more sensitive than other regions. Weinstein also found that the fingers and toes are extremely sensitive in detecting two separate touch sensations. As we age, our senses become less acute, and this loss of sensitivity is found in touch as well (Verrillo, 1993).

Figure 12.5 illustrated that certain body parts correspond to large areas on the cortex, whereas other body parts correspond to smaller cortical areas. Weinstein discovered a consistent relationship between measures of cortical area and the size of the two-point thresholds. For example, a large space on the cortex is devoted to the lip, and the lip is also very sensitive in its two-point discrimination threshold. In contrast, relatively little space on the cortex is devoted to the leg, and our discrimination is also poor in this area.

You may recall a similar relationship from Chapter 3. The largest space on the visual cortex is devoted to the fovea, which also happens to be the area in which discrimination is best. Thus, the pattern is uniform; when a large region of the cortex is devoted to information from a particular area of skin surface, we are usually able to make precise discriminations when that area of skin is touched. This similarity between touch and vision, another illustration of Theme 1 of this textbook, can also be found in other phenomena. For example, Craig (1989) found that the presence of irrelevant tactile stimuli made it more difficult to locate target tactile stimuli. This result is similar to several visual phenomena we've discussed, such as the difficulty of judging motion when irrelevant peripheral stimuli are also moving. Touch also demonstrates certain

---

Demonstration 12.5

Two-Point Discrimination Thresholds

Find two toothpicks and hold them so that their points can both touch your skin at the same time. Separate the toothpicks by about 1 cm (0.5 inch). Touch your cheek with the toothpicks and describe the sensation. Now touch your calf with the toothpicks and notice whether the sensation is different. Move the toothpicks closer together and touch your cheek once more. How close can they be moved toward each other before you perceive only a single touch? Now move the toothpicks farther apart and touch your calf once more. How far apart can they be moved before you perceive two separate touches?

---

principles discussed in connection with visual perception, such as illusory movement, masking, and figure–ground relationships (Berlá, 1982; Craig & Sherrick, 1982; Loomis & Lederman, 1986; Sherrick & Cholewiak, 1986).

Adaptation to Touch

We discussed adaptation in the vision and hearing sections of this book. In *touch adaptation,* the perceived intensity of a repeated tactile stimulus decreases over time. This morning when you first put on your clothes, you might have noticed the pressure of your waistband, your socks, and your watch. Very quickly, however, the sensations disappeared. You probably were not even aware of pressure from your clothes until you read this paragraph.

We seem to notice a stimulus as long as its weight moves our skin downward. When the skin

movement stops, however, we no longer notice it. Once the stimulus is removed, though, our skin moves upward, and we notice pressure sensations once more. As you could infer from our discussion of Pacinian corpuscles, skin movement is an important factor in touch perception.

Try Demonstration 12.6 to illustrate touch adaptation. This powerful phenomenon has not been extensively studied. The most elaborate series of studies was conducted by Nafe and Wagoner (1941), who examined the hairy skin on the thigh next to the knee. As Carlson (1991) points out, however, adaptation to touch cannot be explained by "fatigue" in the receptor processes. Instead, adaptation can probably be traced to the mechanical construction of the receptors. For example, the Pacinian corpuscles mentioned earlier respond best when the receptor is bent under pressure or when it is released. Under constant

Demonstration 12.6

Touch Adaptation

Place a square piece of paper the size of a pea on the hairy-skin side of your hand and notice how long it takes until you can no longer feel the paper. Repeat this exercise with the glabrous-skin side of your hand. Continue these comparisons in touch adaptation by trying stimuli of different sizes and weights and on different regions of both sides of your hand. Compare touch adaptation in both locations and—more important—notice the general phenomenon of touch adaptation.

---

pressure, however, the nerve ending simply floats within all the protective onionlike layers, and it does not continue to produce signals following the initial stimulation.

Perception of Complex Passive Touch

In general, studies of passive touch assess thresholds either for a single touch or for vibrations. One area involving more complicated perception concerns people's ability to read letters and numbers traced on their skin. A neurologist's examination, for example, might include a test in which the examiner traces a series of letters on your fingers or foot, asking you to identify them one at a time.

People who are blind may soon be helped by a device that is based on complex passive touch. The **Optacon II** translates written letters and numbers into a vibratory display (Sherrick, 1991). The user points a camera at a written passage and the information is typically translated into a 20×5 vibrotactile array for the left index finger. Essentially, blunt pins in the array vibrate where the camera detects darkness, creating a tactile image of the symbol being viewed by the camera. Although reading rates using the Optacon are slower than those for reading braille text, the Optacon allows a person who is blind to read text that has not been translated into braille.

One limitation on the speed of reading with the Optacon is the number of sequentially presented tactile letters that can be remembered. We can assess the limitations of this memory through a digit-span task (memory for a randomly presented list of numbers). Heller (1987b) found that people can remember about 7 numbers when the stimuli are slowly "drawn" on the skin. Such performance is roughly equivalent to that found with number sequences presented to other senses. When the stimuli are presented rapidly at the same location on the skin, digit span is much lower (Heller, 1980, 1987b). People who are blind also remember tactually presented numbers more accurately at slower presentation rates, but their performance is not quite as good as the performance of sighted people (Heller, 1989b).

Heller's results are consistent with studies reporting that identification of letters becomes worse as the delay between successively presented stimuli is decreased, due to backward masking (Horner & Craig, 1989). Tactile backward masking works in a fashion similar to backward masking in vision and audition—a subsequently presented stimulus makes perception of an earlier stimulus more difficult (Mahar & Mackenzie, 1993). Also consistent with research in the other senses, discrimination tasks are easier than identification tasks. In other words, even when people can't tell which letters are being presented on their skin, they can tell whether they are the same or different. You might think that although identification becomes more difficult when stimuli follow one another after short durations, discrimination would be easier when the stimuli are presented closely together. Horner and Craig (1989) found that masking effects were so powerful that even a simple discrimination task became difficult when the second letter rapidly followed the first letter.

Active Touch

So far we have discussed situations in which a person sits patiently, waiting to be prodded, poked, and drawn upon. Many touch experiences in the world are much more active. The perception of objects by touch is called ***haptic perception.***

Identifying Objects

Roberta Klatzky, Susan Lederman, and their coworkers have had a tremendous impact on haptic perception research. Recently they've identified a number of different procedures people use when exploring different dimensions of objects (Klatzky & Lederman, 1993). Touch is particularly helpful in determining hardness and texture, but our hands move in different ways as we try to determine these two qualities. Try Demonstration 12.7 to illustrate haptic perception and the various ways we explore objects by touch.

What would happen if you were to present people with 100 common objects (e.g., comb, compact disc, paper clip, hammer, fork) and ask them to identify the objects on the basis of active touch alone? As you might well imagine, people can identify the objects with almost perfect accuracy after only brief tactile exploration (Klatzky et al., 1985). Of course, one explanation for these results is that people have a good deal of experience handling such common objects.

Active touch is typically more precise and useful than passive touch (Appelle, 1991). For example, when a tiny raised dot is pressed against the skin, people can detect a dot about 10 micrometers high. (A micrometer is one-*thousandth* of a millimeter.) This perceptual ability is fairly impressive until it is compared with the threshold for active touch, which can be even less than 1 micrometer (Johansson & LaMotte, 1983). When people are allowed to stroke their fingers across a surface, they are much more sensitive to a tiny irregularity in that surface.

James Gibson (1966) had an important influence on theories of vision, and he also was central in pointing out the importance of active touch. Consistent with his general approach to perception, Gibson proposed that the study of active touch would provide more information about people's daily activities, whereas information about passive touch would be far less useful. Gibson (1962) compared active and passive perception for six small metal cookie cutters shaped like a teardrop, a star, a triangle, and so forth. When a cookie cutter was pressed against the palm of the hand (passive perception), accuracy was only 29%; however, when people were encouraged to feel each cookie cutter (active perception), accuracy soared to 95%.

Morton Heller of Winston-Salem State University extended Gibson's findings. For passive

---

Demonstration 12.7

Haptic Perception

First assemble 10 miscellaneous objects of similar sizes that you find in your room. Place them on your desk and close your eyes. Identify an object by exploring it with active touch. Pay attention to how you move your fingers around an object to determine its identity. Next determine the hardness of your desktop and other nearby objects. Do you use your hands differently than you did when identifying objects? Finally, use your fingers to determine the texture of your shirt and other objects. You should again notice that your fingers move in a different fashion to perform this task.

FIGURE 12.7 Raised-line drawings explored tactually by congenitally blind, late-blind, and sighted people. The items are a battery, key, rubber stamp, face, watch, telephone, bottle, person, hanger, cane, umbrella, and sewing scissors. When confusions arose, they often made sense, such as calling the hanger a Hershey's kiss. (From Heller, 1989a)

touch, in addition to simply pressing the cookie cutters onto the skin, Heller also rotated the cookie cutter over a passive fingertip of some participants. He found that active touch produced much higher identification accuracy than passive touch, regardless of the means of passive presentation (Heller, 1984). In fact, people with only 5 seconds of active touch exposure were more accurate than people in the passive groups who had a full 30 seconds of exposure. We can certainly conclude that active touch provides useful information about objects, even when the exposure is brief.

Object Identification by Blind Individuals
Morton Heller has also investigated active touch in sighted, congenitally blind, and late-blind people (Heller, 1989a). These individuals were presented with raised-line drawings of the stimuli seen in Figure 12.7. All judgments were made on the basis of tactile information alone. You might find it difficult to name a couple of these objects using your eyes—so you can easily imagine the difficulty faced by the participants in Heller's study. After one attempt at identifying the stimuli, people were given a list of the objects' names in a random order and asked to try one more time.

None of the people had prior experience with raised-line drawing kits such as those used in this experiment. Can you guess which group performed best? Obviously, the blind people were more experienced at using only touch to learn about the world. Would you expect both the late-blind and the congenitally blind people to outperform the sighted people?

Heller found that the late-blind group outperformed the other two groups, as seen in Figure 12.8. Their performance was presumably en-

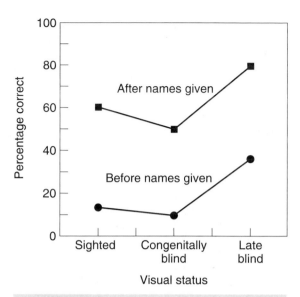

FIGURE 12.8 Results of Experiment 2 from Heller (1989). Notice that all groups perform better after being told the names of the objects depicted in the raised-line drawings (Figure 12.7). Pay particular attention to the performance of the late-blind group, compared to the other two groups. (Adapted from Heller, 1989a)

hanced because they combined some visual experience of pictures prior to losing their sight with practice on perceiving the world through touch since losing their sight. The experience of blind people led them to explore many of the stimuli more rapidly than the sighted people, and to make use of both hands—a tactic that typically leads to superior performance (Craig, 1985). Because the performance of the sighted people did not differ from that of the congenitally blind people, it is clear that neither haptic nor visual experience alone is sufficient for perceiving raised-line drawings. Accurate perception of these raised-line drawings with active touch appears to depend on a combination of prior visual *and* tactile experience.

For simpler discriminations, however, active touch offers little advantage over passive touch. Both blind and sighted people were equally good at determining the smoother of two surfaces, re-

gardless of whether they felt the abrasive stimuli with active or passive touch (Heller, 1989c). Interestingly, sighted people were better at discriminating smoothness of fine sandpapers on the basis of touch rather than vision. As we will see in the next section, a far more typical finding is that visual information takes precedence over touch.

Interactions between Touch and Vision

We have emphasized the relationships among the senses in Theme 1 and have already explored the interaction of vision and audition. The auditory system shares capabilities with the visual system (e.g., spatial perception) but also provides independent information (e.g., our ability to hear the approach of a train that we cannot see). Likewise, our sense of touch is capable of performing tasks that our visual system can also perform (e.g., raised-letter perception) but also provides independent information (e.g., perception of hardness of objects or smoothness of fine-grained surfaces). In this section we will continue to highlight relations among the senses by comparing touch and vision.

Suppose that your eyes saw one object, but simultaneously your hands felt a somewhat different object. Which sense would you trust more? Reviews of a large number of studies have noted that when a discrepancy is found between vision and touch, people generally trust their vision (Warren & Rossano, 1991). Studies of this sort typically involve looking at stimuli through distorting lenses that make an object look smaller than it is, or curved when it is straight. Even if what we see is a distortion of reality, vision wins. Tactile perception is recalibrated so that it matches what we see!

Tasks involving the perception of simple contours also provide evidence for the dominance of vision over touch (Klatzky et al., 1987). Observers typically judge stimuli that could be easily perceived visually (e.g., raised-line drawings or the cookie cutters discussed earlier) but are impoverished from a tactile perspective. Given the imbalance in stimulus information, it is not surprising that people are more inclined to trust their visual input. We should keep in mind that vision and touch have evolved to solve different problems, so we should expect the capabilities of the senses to differ.

One reason that we see contours better than we feel them might well be that vision allows us to integrate contour information over a fairly large "window." When we are forced to describe the contour of a stimulus that is so large that it cannot fit into our field of view at one time, we are far less effective. Try to draw an accurate picture of a mountain that you've climbed but not seen from afar! The window for touch may not be much larger than a fingertip in size, which makes it much harder to gain an accurate sense of contour for larger stimuli. When our visual window is artificially reduced in the laboratory, touch and vision become much more similar (Loomis et al., 1991).

Morton Heller has also provided us with an interesting situation in which we actually rely upon touch more than vision (Heller, 1992b). In our discussion of visual perception, we indicated that visual stimuli in unusual orientations are difficult to process—especially when the stimuli are upside down. Suppose that you were asked to discriminate between pairs of raised-line letters (*p* and *q*, *b* and *d*, and *W* and *M*) that you could only see upside down in a mirror. Not surprisingly, you would think that a *p* was a *b*, and so on. (Get a mirror and try this.) Heller found that if you could also touch these raised-line letters, seen along with your hand in the mirror, you would often base your decision on how the letter *felt* rather than on what you *saw*.

The results of these and other studies are consistent with the notion that, although our senses might overlap in some capabilities, one sense will often be particularly well-suited to perform a specific task. Our visual system seems to be very good at judging shape and size, and it will typically dominate the other senses in making such discriminations. In contrast, touch is particularly good at judging texture and hardness, and vision will not dominate touch in making such discriminations (Klatzky et al., 1987). Touch is only inferior to vision when asked to compete on

turf where vision is the acknowledged champion. The combination of independence and interdependence of sensory systems seems a particularly effective means of dealing with the perception of a range of stimulus dimensions in the world.

Applications of Active Touch

An important application of active touch is the development of material for people who are blind. The best-known system was developed by Louis Braille, a blind Frenchman who lived in the 19th century. He was discouraged by the difficult task of trying to read the limited number of books specially prepared with raised versions of standard letters. After all, our visual system can readily distinguish a *P* from an *R*, but the task is much more challenging for our tactile system.

Figure 12.9 illustrates the letters in the ***braille*** alphabet. Each black dot represents the raised portion of a 3×2 grid less than $\frac{1}{4}$ inch high. As you might imagine after looking at the figure, reading braille is a difficult skill to master. In fact, most people who are blind never learn braille. However, highly skilled braille readers can read at a rate of better than 200 words per minute (Foulke,

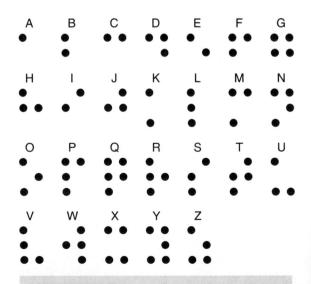

FIGURE 12.9 The braille alphabet.

1991). Although rate depends on the nature of the material being read, a person who is blind often reads braille at about the pace of a sighted person reading aloud.

We have already seen that our tactile system is less able to perceive structures and patterns, such as braille print, than is our visual system. People typically perform better when visual and tactile inputs are combined (Heller, 1993; Warren & Rossano, 1991). Nonetheless, in the absence of visual input, touch can be used for pattern recognition tasks, such as braille reading. The task of braille reading by touch alone is made much more difficult, however, if the orientation of the braille letters is nonstandard (Heller, 1987a, 1989b, 1992a).

Other tactile aids for people who are blind have been developed. For example, several systems have been developed to enable people who are blind to explore raised-line pictures, such as those described in Heller's research (Heller, 1989a; Kennedy, 1982). Mobility maps have also been designed to represent the physical layout of streets in a town, pedestrian subways, and shopping centers (G. A. James, 1982).

Touch can be useful for people who are deaf as well as people who are blind. For example, using the ***Tadoma method,*** a person who is deaf or deaf-blind places his or her hand on the lips and jaw of the speaker to pick up tactile sensations of speech such as airflow, lip and jaw movement, and vibration (Loomis & Lederman, 1986). Several systems have also been developed to present tactile displays of speech patterns (Carney, 1988; Kirman, 1982).

A final but extremely important application of active touch occurs in medicine. A physician must palpate a patient's skin to determine the location, size, and shape of a fetus inside a pregnant woman's uterus or a swollen appendix (Loomis & Lederman, 1986). Consider, also, the usefulness of active touch in detecting breast cancer. In 1993, approximately 182,000 women developed breast cancer and an estimated 46,000 died from this disease (Boring et al., 1993). Because early detection of cancer makes survival more likely, breast self-examination is a crucial tool in com-

bating death from breast cancer. Breast self-examination is a risk-free procedure, so it is routinely recommended for all women over the age of 20. Statistics suggest that a woman who examines her breasts once a month for possible lumps will reduce her chances of dying from breast cancer by about 15% (Foster et al., 1985).

Touch may not be so central to our lives as vision or hearing. On the other hand, it is useful in many phases of daily life. It also has important applications for helping people who are blind or deaf, as well as for medical diagnosis.

SECTION SUMMARY

Touch

1. Studies of passive touch show that thresholds are different for females and males and for various body parts.

2. Two-point discrimination thresholds are also different for various body parts; these correspond to the amount of space occupied by that body part on the cortex.

3. Humans show touch adaptation, or a gradual decrease in touch sensation as a result of prolonged stimulation.

4. Active touch is important when we explore objects and try to discover their properties; this is also called haptic perception. We use different haptic procedures depending on the quality of the object we are interested in investigating. Active touch is more precise and useful than passive touch.

5. The senses are particularly dominant in their areas of specialization, and vision functions better than touch for the perception of structural features of stimuli, such as shape or size. Touch functions better than vision for the perception of hardness or roughness. Touch also provides more reliable information when the stimuli are in an unusual orientation for our visual systems (e.g., upside down).

6. Applications of touch include braille, designed to help people who are blind, and the Tadoma method, designed to help people who are deaf. Active touch is also important in medical diagnosis.

VESTIBULAR AND KINESTHETIC SENSES

Are you sitting down? Okay, try this. Close your eyes, grab your knees with your hands, and then rock forward and backward. Notice that even with your eyes closed you can tell when you're upright and when you're leaning forward. You can also feel your elbows bending and flexing as you rock back and forth. Your fingers are tightly (or loosely) grasping your knees. Most of the perceptual information about our bodily orientation, movement, and position comes through our vestibular and kinesthetic senses.

Although these two senses provide us with information about our bodies, as the skin senses do, they have little else in common with the skin senses. For example, the mechanisms underlying the vestibular sense have more in common with our auditory system than with the skin senses. So

first, as promised in Chapter 8, we will return to a discussion of the semicircular canals of the inner ear. These are the organs of our vestibular sense. We will see how motion of the fluid in these canals gives rise to our sense of bodily orientation and movement. Next we will examine the kinesthetic sense, which gives us our sense of how our various body parts are positioned.

Vestibular Sense

Our *vestibular sense* provides us with information about our body's orientation and whether or not we are in motion. We call it the vestibular sense because the semicircular canals are located at the entrance (the vestibule) to the inner ear.

Mechanisms of the Vestibular Sense

The three semicircular canals seen in Figure 12.10 are filled with fluids and lined with hair

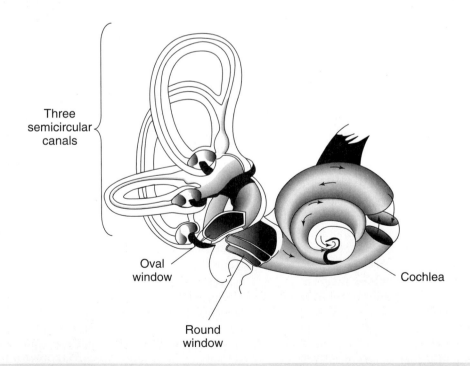

Three semicircular canals

Oval window

Round window

Cochlea

FIGURE 12.10 The inner ear, showing the cochlea and the semicircular canals. The semicircular canals are the organs of the vestibular sense.

Demonstration 12.8

Importance of the Vestibular Sense

Stand up and lift one leg. Notice how your body automatically adjusts to retain your balance in this somewhat precarious position. Now repeat this exercise with your eyes closed. You should find the task to be much more difficult. Vision clearly aids the vestibular sense in maintaining body balance. As one final illustration, first spin around rapidly and then try to stand on one leg. The unusual stimulation of your vestibular sense caused by spinning around will make the task very difficult—even with your eyes open. Thus, the vestibular sense must be very important for maintaining our balance.

---

cells. Because the semicircular canals are part of the inner ear, the fluids and the hair cells within them are similar to those found in the cochlea. Therefore, much of what you learned regarding the receptors of the inner ear will apply to the vestibular sense as well.

It may be hard to tell from the two-dimensional figure, but the canals are arranged much like the *x*-, *y*-, and *z*-axes in a three-dimensional graph. As a result, the semicircular canals are remarkably well adapted to detect motion that is forward or backward, left or right, and up or down. When our bodies move, we cause the fluid in the semicircular canals to move. The fluid then deflects the stereocilia of the hair cells (see Figure 9.12), whose firing tells us about the speed and direction of the movement (Hudspeth, 1983). Try Demonstration 12.8 to appreciate the vestibular sense more thoroughly.

Vestibular Perception

Although we are typically unaware of the operation of our vestibular sense, this perceptual system is quite important. For instance, if you move your head from side to side, notice how your eyes tend to rotate in the direction opposite to the direction of your head movement. This coordination of the vestibular information and eye muscle function occurs because of the ***vestibuloocular reflex (VOR),*** which serves to stabilize our view of the world (Miles & Busettini, 1992; Soechting & Flanders, 1992; Tan et al., 1992).

We become consciously aware of input from the vestibular sense only under unusual circumstances. For example, you may experience an illusion of continued movement if you have been spinning around for an extended time—perhaps on a ride in an amusement park—and come to a sudden halt (Benson, 1982). People who have Ménière's disease of the inner ear, or even simple inner ear infections, may experience vertigo or a loss of balance (Guedry, 1992).

If you've ever experienced motion sickness, for instance, after taking a boat ride, your vestibular sense is responsible (Watt et al., 1992). However, unusual stimulation of your vestibular sense is not sufficient to produce motion sickness. Instead, the most common theory attributes motion sickness to a conflict between actual sensory inputs, or between anticipated input and actual input (Oman, 1991). Control over the motion of a vehicle may play an important role in reducing motion sickness, which is why drivers of cars rarely get motion sickness (Rolnick & Lubow, 1991).

One extremely unusual situation for our vestibular sense occurs when people become weightless. The lack of gravity experienced by astronauts causes the fluids in the semicircular canals to float, which leads to atypical vestibular information to say the least! Given the irregular input from the vestibular system, it's not surprising that astronauts under conditions of weightlessness tend to rely much more on their visual sense for determining "up" and "down" (Lackner, 1993). With their eyes closed, these astronauts cannot reliably determine their orientation relative to their surroundings (Lackner, 1992). When they return to earth, the astronauts often have to avoid unnecessary movement for several days because they have trouble walking due to a loss of balance (Guedry, 1992; Paloski et al., 1992).

A number of studies have been conducted on the perception of being upright (Howard, 1986). In some experiments people sit in a chair that can be tilted from side to side, and the chair is centered in a small room that can also be tilted from side to side. If you were a participant in the tilted-room experiment, you would be asked to adjust your chair until it is perfectly upright. Suppose that the surrounding room had been tilted so that it was at a 20 degree angle. Would you adjust your chair to match the up-down orientation of the walls of this room or to line up straight with the force of gravity?

People resolve this discrepancy between visual cues and vestibular cues in different ways. People who rely on the orientation of the room (visual cues) are called *field dependent,* whereas people who rely on the orientation of their bodies (vestibular cues) are called *field independent.* In view of the significant individual differences in this area, it's surprising that individual differences have not been examined in the way people resolve conflicts between the other skin senses and vision. For example, it would be interesting to know whether some people consistently pay attention to touch, whereas others consistently pay attention to vision in the kinds of experiments discussed earlier in the chapter.

The widespread influence of J. J. Gibson is also seen in research on orientation. For instance, Thomas Stoffregen and Gary Riccio (Riccio & Stoffregen, 1990; Stoffregen & Riccio, 1988) have used Gibson's ecological approach in the study of orientation and the vestibular system. They argue that the vestibular system is not of primary importance for the perception of gravitational force and orientation, as others have claimed. Instead, they believe that our sense of orientation derives from several sources of input—visual, kinesthetic, and vestibular—none of which is primary. Their arguments have met with criticism from researchers who argue that the vestibular system is crucial for detection of gravity and motion (Curthoys & Wade, 1990), making this a fruitful area for future research.

Kinesthetic Sense

Kinesthesia is derived from a Greek word meaning "perception of movement." As it is usually employed today, the term **kinesthesia** refers to the sensation of movement or the sensation of static limb position (Clark & Horch, 1986). In its broadest sense, kinesthesia includes sensations that come from the position and movement of body parts; this movement can be active or passive. A similar term typically used interchangeably with kinesthesia is **proprioception.** To help increase your appreciation for kinesthesia, try Demonstration 12.9.

Mechanisms for Kinesthesia

The central nervous system has two methods for obtaining information about the position and the movement of body parts: (1) It can monitor the commands it sends to the muscles, on the assumption that the muscles carry them out, and (2) it can receive information from appropriate sensory receptors. Just as the visual system uses more than one source of information to determine the distance of an object, as you learned in Chapter 6, the kinesthetic system uses more than one source to determine the position of the body parts. If you stretch your arm out to the right in the direction of a pen, your central nervous system knows where your arm is because it sent that arm on this particular errand and because feedback from the arm tells your central nervous system where the arm is. These two kinds of kinesthetic information are supplemented by other senses. For example, your vision informs the central nervous system about the location of your arm, your touch senses let you know when your finger makes contact with the pen, and even your hearing may contribute information about the slight scrape that the pen

---

Demonstration 12.9

Importance of Kinesthesia

Close your eyes and extend your arms out at your sides. Point your index fingers, folding your thumb and remaining fingers into a fist. Now bring your index fingers quickly toward each other in front of your body. See whether you can make them touch—without looking. Try this several times and assess your success. Then close your eyes and use an index finger to touch each of your toes. Repeat this exercise several times and assess your success. You might also be interested in seeing whether you are equally successful touching your index fingers together *behind* your back; most people are somewhat less accurate.

---

makes on the desk surface as your hand reaches its destination (Clark & Horch, 1986).

Most of the time we are actively moving our bodies, as in reaching for a pen, when we make a kinesthetic judgment. Occasionally, however, we make a decision about limb position when we are stationary or when our limbs are being moved for us. In both cases it appears that receptors within our muscles play a major role in our sense of limb position. One kind of receptor that has been extensively researched is the Golgi tendon organ. The tendon is the tough, fibrous material that attaches the muscle to the bone. ***Golgi tendon organs,*** located in these tendons, respond when the muscle exerts tension on the tendon (Carlson, 1991). As a result, the Golgi tendon organs are effective in signaling the position of our limbs when we are actively moving.

For determining limb position with passive movement, it appears that muscle spindles are important. ***Muscle spindles*** are receptors that are located within the muscle itself, rather than in the tendon. Unlike the Golgi tendon organs, the muscle spindles don't respond to tension but instead respond to muscle length (Pinel, 1993). An interesting piece of evidence that muscle spindles are involved in detection of passive limb position is the effect of vibration on perceived limb position (Gandevia et al., 1992). If the muscles are vibrated at a rate that causes the muscle spindles to fire, people will experience an illusory sense of limb position. In some cases, people even report

the limb to be in an anatomically impossible position, such as the hand bent back to the forearm (L. A. Jones, 1988).

Kinesthetic Perception

Researchers have explored a number of topics within kinesthetic perception. For example, people can make accurate judgments of linear distance, based on the distance traced by their fingers (Loomis & Lederman, 1986). Kinesthetic perception also allows them to make accurate judgments about the width of wood blocks (Baker & Weisz, 1984) and accurate discriminations about an object's weight (Brodie & Ross, 1984).

In Chapter 10 we examined auditory localization, which involves judgments about the direction of a sound source. As you may recall, researchers find that visual input often biases auditory input. Vision also tends to dominate kinesthetic input when the discrepancy is created by using prism lenses (Welch & Warren, 1980). If you looked through lenses that showed your hand several inches away from its true location, your vision would strongly bias your sense of where your hand was. Vision cannot *completely* influence kinesthesia, however, because kinesthetic information has a modest influence on judgments of the location of body parts when visual and kinesthetic information conflict. What happens when kinesthetic information and auditory information are discrepant? Welch and Warren (1980) conclude that kinesthetic information biases audition more strongly than audition biases kinesthesia. You'll therefore trust proprioception, rather than your ears.

The importance of kinesthetic feedback is stressed by the case of Ian Waterman (Cole, 1991). Due to illness, he lost the input from the nerves in his skin and muscles. Because he was unable to control his body, he simply collapsed. People thought that he would have to live the rest of his life in a wheelchair. Ultimately, however, he was able to walk and write by relying on visual input—in the total absence of touch or kinesthetic input!

SECTION SUMMARY

Vestibular and Kinesthetic Senses

1. The vestibular senses are concerned with orientation, movement, and acceleration. The vestibular receptors are the semicircular canals of the inner ear.
2. Although we are rarely aware of the functioning of our vestibular sense, it is crucial for the coordination of eye and head movement through the vestibuloocular reflex. We do become aware of the vestibular sense under unusual conditions such as inner ear infections, motion sickness, and weightlessness.
3. When vestibular information and visual information conflict, individual differences in response occur; some rely more on vestibular information (field independent), whereas others rely more on visual information (field dependent).
4. Kinesthesia refers to the sensation of movement and the sensation of static limb position. Sources of information about kinesthesia include monitoring of commands sent to muscles and information from sensory receptors, supplemented by visual, auditory, and tactile information.
5. Kinesthetic receptors include Golgi tendon organs and muscle spindles.
6. One topic studied in kinesthesia is the response to discrepancies between kinesthetic information and visual information; people rely more on vision than on kinesthesia. When kinesthetic information and auditory information conflict, people rely more on kinesthesia than on audition.

REVIEW QUESTIONS

1. Refer to material in the chapter to explain each of the following observations about temperature perception:
   a. You stand too close to a kettle full of boiling spaghetti sauce, and a drop splatters on your wrist; surprisingly, it seems cold.
   b. Maria has been sitting in front of the fire, and the kitchen seems cold to her; Pat has been outside in the snow, and the kitchen seems warm to her.
   c. Your internal temperature remains at about 37° C, whether you spend your winter in Vermont blizzards or the Caribbean sunshine.
   d. You know a man who works for hours at a time with frozen foods, without gloves, and he claims that the cold doesn't bother his hands.

2. In this chapter we discussed thresholds for temperature (both warmth and cold), pain, and touch. We saw that each of these thresholds varied from one part of the body to another. Summarize the findings on these various kinds of thresholds and note the similarities and differences.

3. Adaptation was also a recurring theme in this chapter, and throughout the text. Discuss adaptation to temperature, pain, and touch. Think of an example of each of these kinds of adaptation from your own recent experience. Can you think of an occasion when adaptation did not occur? Try to relate the experience of adaptation in these senses to adaptation in other senses.

4. What is pain, why does it differ from other perceptual experiences, and why are its thresholds different? What function does pain serve? What is phantom limb pain and what does it tell us about theories of pain perception in particular and perception in general?

5. Discuss specificity theory and pattern theory, both in their application to the general skin senses and in their application to pain perception. Then discuss the gate-control theory in as much detail as possible.

6. Throughout the text, we've emphasized the importance of central processes in perception. Explain why each of the following topics documents the importance of central psychological processes in pain perception: (a) phantom limb pain, (b) placebo action, (c) acupuncture, (d) cognitive–behavioral approaches, and (e) hypnosis. Then discuss other aspects of touch perception that indicate the operation of central processes.

7. Refer to material in the chapter to explain each of the following observations about touch:
   a. Something touches your leg, and you have no idea what shape it is; then it touches your face, and its shape seems clear.
   b. The fabric on a chair seems rough against your arm when you first sit down, but you do not notice it after 5 minutes.
   c. You've placed your sleeping bag on a surface without noticing that a twig is underneath. In reality, the twig has two prominent points, yet when some parts of your body rest on the twig, it seems like a single point.

8. Heller's research suggests several advantages in touch perception for people who are not blind from birth. If you are now sighted, imagine that you found out that you were going blind. Describe specific things you could do to take advantage of the advance notice that you're going blind. Once you were completely blind, how would your perceptual experience differ from that of sighted people (concentrate on touch and audition)?

9. Compare the senses discussed in this chapter with vision and hearing. Mention, for example, (a) the size of the receptive system, (b) the kind of receptors, (c) the ability to discriminate, (d) sensitivity, and (e) the nature of the stimuli. Think of yourself as an organism designed to interact with the environment. How do the senses work together to provide a "picture" of the world? What happens when the senses provide conflicting information?

10. Suppose you know a student taking introductory psychology. The chapter on perception in that student's textbook does not mention the kinesthetic and vestibular senses. Briefly summarize the nature of these senses and how they are important in daily life.

NEW TERMS

hairy skin (374)
glabrous skin (374)
epidermis (374)
dermis (374)
subcutaneous tissue (374)
free nerve endings (374)
encapsulated endings (374)
doctrine of specific nerve
   energies (375)
specificity theory (375)

pattern theory (375)
spinothalamic system (376)
lemniscal system (376)
paradoxical cold (378)
thermal adaptation (379)
pain (380)
limbic system (381)
specificity theory of pain
   perception (381)
A-delta fibers (381)

C-fibers (381)
A-beta fibers (381)
double pain (381)
phantom limb pain (382)
pattern theory of pain
   perception (382)
gate-control theory (382)
transmission cells (382)
substantia gelatinosa (382)
neuromatrix (385)

RECOMMENDED READINGS

Brannon, L., & Feist, J. (1992). *Health psychology: An introduction to behavior and health*. Belmont, CA: Wadsworth. This excellent textbook in the emerging discipline of health psychology includes a useful chapter on coping with pain.

Cailliet, R. (1993). *Pain: Mechanisms and management*. Philadelphia: Davis. This useful book is written and illustrated by a physician who has authored several books about pain. It provides a current and thorough review of the causes of and treatment for pain. Because of the range of topics covered in under 300 pages, some of the information is densely packed. Nonetheless, most of the information in the text is quite accessible to an interested layperson.

Cole, J. (1991). *Pride and a daily marathon*. Cambridge, MA: MIT Press. This fascinating book describes the case of Ian Waterman, whose neuropathy deprived him of his sense of touch and proprioception. Although people thought that he would live the rest of his life in a wheelchair, Mr. Waterman overcame his affliction with the aid of his physician (the author).

Heller, M. A., & Schiff, W. (Eds.). (1991). *The psychology of touch*. Hillsdale, NJ: Erlbaum. The editors of this volume have done a superb job of collecting, organizing, and integrating a wide range of chapters written by experts on the skin senses. It includes chapters on more basic phenomena such as sensory processes and temperature perception, chapters on more complex phenomena such as tactile pattern perception, and a chapter on the relationship between touch and vision.

Wall, P. D., & Melzack, R. (Eds.). (1994). *Textbook of pain* (3rd ed.) Edinburgh: Churchill Livingstone. This book contains over 80 chapters covering a range of topics in pain mechanisms and treatments. Some of the chapters are likely to be too specific for the general reader, but many chapters about pain mechanisms and treatments are quite accessible.

13 The Chemical Senses: Smell and Taste

Think of the best meal that you've ever eaten. If you can't identify a "best" meal, try to call to mind a particularly memorable meal. Now ask yourself what made that meal so memorable. One influential aspect of the meal was probably the flavor of the food. The word *flavor* is used to refer to the wide variety of perceptions we experience when we eat. **Flavor** includes both smell and taste, as well as touch, pressure, pain, and so on (McBurney, 1978). (You are certainly familiar with the possibility of pain as a part of flavor if you've tasted the right recipe for chili.)

In this chapter we'll discuss smell and taste, which are frequently grouped together under the name **chemical senses** because the receptor cells for smell and taste are both sensitive to chemical stimulation. These two sensations are very closely related to one another. For instance, when people say that something tastes good, they are really reporting on stimulation to their nose as much as to their palate. We've already discussed relationships between vision and audition as support for Theme 1 of this textbook, but smell and taste are even more closely interrelated.

Recall that memorable meal, and try to describe exactly what made the meal memorable. We're willing to bet that your description will have two aspects that are common to most other readers of this text. First, the context in which the meal took place was probably special. Was it a special occasion? Were you particularly hungry? Was it eaten in a restaurant with a tremendous reputation, where great care was taken in the presentation of the meal?

Do you see our point? Consistent with the themes we've been addressing throughout the text, your perception of that meal was influenced by several factors beyond the flavors involved. Your expectations certainly had a tremendous impact (consistent with Theme 4). As rich as the information present in the food itself, the context in which the meal was consumed had an influence (Theme 2). Also, smell and taste were probably intertwined with vision, touch, and possibly audition (consistent with Theme 1).

Did you experience any difficulties in describing the tastes or aromas? If so, then you'll agree with our second point. What, *exactly*, made the meal so tasty? Humans have developed a rich language for describing visual and auditory experience, but our common language for describing smells and tastes is relatively impoverished (Richardson & Zucco, 1989). You can immediately see the difficulty in communicating the concept of "redness" to a person born blind, because the person who is blind lacks the visual experience that you would like to draw on to illustrate the concept. But try to tell a friend with a normal sense of smell and taste about broccoli sautéed in butter and garlic without using the words "butter," "garlic," or "broccoli." The odors and tastes are certainly distinctive. However, we do not seem to have a sufficiently rich language for describing the experiences. Soon you will see that the lack of an extensive vocabulary for describing smells and tastes has had an impact on the research conducted in these areas.

As we have already done for vision and audition, in this chapter we will discuss the stimuli involved in smell and taste, along with the systems through which these stimuli are processed. We will also discuss some aspects of each sense separately, as well as interactions between these two senses and other senses.

SMELL

Patrick Süskind, in his novel *Perfume* (1987), illustrates the importance of smell:

> . . . people could close their eyes to greatness, to horrors, to beauty, and their ears to melodies or deceiving words. But they could not escape scent. For scent was a brother of breath. Together with breath it entered human beings, who could not defend themselves against it, not if they wanted to live. And scent entered into their very core, went directly to their hearts, and decided for good and all between affection and contempt, disgust and lust, love and hate. He who ruled scent ruled the hearts of men (p. 189).

Süskind's points should be amply illustrated in your everyday experience. For example, you meet someone at a party and dislike him instantly because his after-shave lotion reminds you of someone you loathe. You smell a piece of fish and decide to throw it out because of the spoiled odor. You pause in the doorway of a new Chinese restaurant and decide to enter because the aroma contains the appropriate mix of garlic, ginger, and sesame oil. You visit a friend's house, and one whiff immediately makes you think of your grandmother's attic, which you have not visited in 10 years.

Despite its importance, we know less about smell than vision or hearing. Martha Teghtsoonian (1983) claims that vision and hearing are like the two pampered daughters, whereas smell is the Cinderella of perception. Although researchers can publish their work in a journal devoted to the chemical senses, much more research funding and journal space is lavished on vision and hearing.

Why should smell, also known as *olfaction,* suffer such neglect? As Teghtsoonian notes, classifying the stimuli for smell is difficult, whereas specifying the dimensions of visual and auditory stimuli is easy. In addition, the field of perception currently emphasizes cognition and thought. Vision and hearing are clearly important in our thought processes, but the relationship between smell and thought is more remote. As Trygg Engen (1982) points out, smell may be more closely linked with emotion. If the discipline of psychology in general—and perception in particular—were to place more emphasis on emotion than on cognition, we would probably see a blossoming of research on the topic of odor.

Sensory Aspects of Smell

Let's begin our discussion with an examination of the sensory aspects of smell. First we will discuss the smell stimulus, or *odorant*. Next, we will discuss the structure of the sensory receptors and the system that processes olfactory stimuli.

The Smell Stimulus

As we discussed previously, the basic stimulus for vision is electromagnetic radiation and the stimulus for hearing is sound pressure changes. For smell, the stimulus is a molecule of a volatile substance that moves through the air to our receptors. The range of these molecules is so extensive that human beings are able to discriminate (i.e., tell if two odors are the same or different) roughly 500,000 odors (Cain, 1988).

Throughout the ages, people have attempted to classify these odorants into a smaller number of categories. For instance, Aristotle considered four basic categories: pungent, succulent, acid, and astringent (Doty, 1991). Since Aristotle's early attempt, many other systems have been proposed. For the most part, these have been based on people's perception of the odorant.

One commonly discussed system of classifications was proposed by Henning (1916). Figure 13.1 illustrates the prism-shaped figure he constructed to show how smells can be defined in terms of six basic odors.

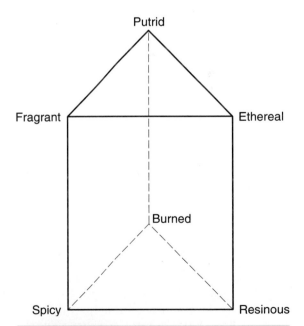

FIGURE 13.1 Smell prism devised by Henning. According to Henning, simple odors must be located on the surfaces of the prism, not inside the prism.

TABLE 13.1
Primary Odors Suggested by Amoore (1970)

Odor	Example
Camphoraceous	Mothballs
Pungent	Vinegar
Floral	Roses
Ethereal	Dry-cleaning fluid
Minty	Peppermint stick
Musty	Musk perfume
Putrid	Rotten egg

Amoore (1970) proposed a different classification system. Most systems emphasized perceivers' reactions to odors, whereas Amoore's system focuses on the chemical structure of odors. According to Amoore's **stereochemical theory,** odorous molecules have definite shapes that determine the kind of odor we smell. Amoore initially suggested 7 primary odors. Table 13.1 shows one version of the list of primaries, together with examples. In a later version, Amoore (1977) expanded the total number of human primary odors to 32.

Because people have identified problems with every classification system that has been proposed, interest in classifying odorants has waned in the past 20 years (Doty, 1991). Although such classification systems still have some value in applied settings, recent attempts to understand the olfactory system have focused on the interaction between the chemical properties of the odorant and the receptor site. Let's turn our attention to the olfactory system, including some interesting developments in the study of olfactory receptor function.

Olfactory System

Figure 13.2 illustrates the anatomy of the nasal (or nose) area. First, look at the region called the **nasal cavity,** the hollow space behind each nostril. Air containing odors reaches the nasal cavity through two routes. Most obviously, we sniff and inhale to bring in the outside air. Air can also come up from the back of the throat when we

breathe through our mouth and when we chew or drink. Astronauts often report losing their sense of smell in space, perhaps because of the effects of zero gravity on odorant molecules (Ackerman, 1990).

Using Figure 13.2, trace the pathway from the mouth, up the throat, to the nasal cavity. Notice the importance of this throat passage the next time you are eating food with a strong odor. Plug your nostrils and notice its blandness. Suddenly release your fingers. A current of air will quickly flow from your mouth, carrying odor molecules up the throat and into the nasal cavity. Instantly, you will experience a burst of flavor.

Notice the three bones neatly lined up in the nasal cavity, called the **turbinate bones.** (Think about how these bones would cause *turbulence* in the airstream, similar to rocks in a river.) Because of their position, these bones force most of the air you breathe in to go down your throat. Thus, only a little of the air will make its way up to the smell receptors at the top of the cavity.

The hidden location of the smell receptors makes them difficult to study. Also, as we will discuss shortly, their hidden location guarantees that only a small portion of the inhaled molecules will reach this surface. As a side benefit, the air that does travel up to the top of the cavity has most of the dust cleaned away by the time it arrives.

At the top of the nasal cavity is the olfactory epithelium. The word *epithelium* refers to skin, so **olfactory epithelium** is the kind of skin you smell with! The size of the olfactory epithelium is about 2 cm^2 for each nostril, and it contains approximately 6 million receptors (Getchell & Getchell, 1991). These are illustrated in Figure 13.3, which is an enlargement of a portion of Figure 13.2.

Unlike receptors in other sensory systems, your olfactory receptors are continually renewed throughout your life (Farbman, 1992). Each receptor functions for less than 8 weeks and is then replaced (Gesteland, 1982). An important feature of each mature receptor is the tiny *cilia*, or hairlike fringes, protruding out of each cell. Immature receptors lack the cilia (Farbman, 1992). The cilia serve the important role of catching the odorant molecules that enter the olfactory

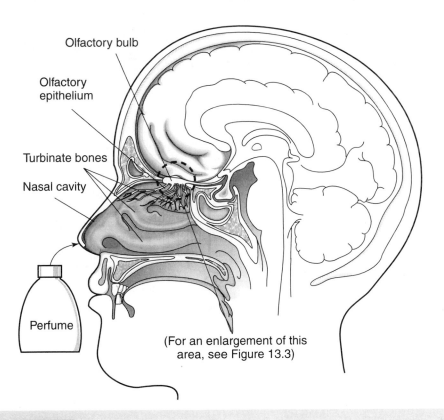

Olfactory bulb

Olfactory
epithelium

Turbinate bones

Nasal cavity

Perfume

(For an enlargement of this
area, see Figure 13.3)

FIGURE 13.2 Anatomy of the olfactory system. Odors can enter the olfactory epithelium through the nose and through the mouth. The frontal cortex (near the eyes) is the location to which much of the neural olfactory information is transmitted.

epithelium (Getchell & Getchell, 1991). The interaction of a molecule with the cilium begins the process of olfaction.

All of the olfactory receptors appear to be identical, so how are the receptors capable of responding to millions of different chemicals (Lancet et al., 1993)? Recent research has begun

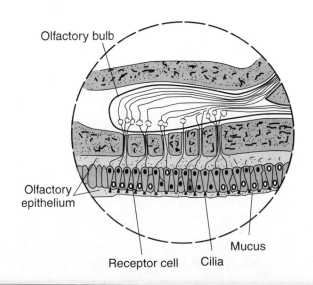

Olfactory bulb

Olfactory
epithelium

Receptor cell   Cilia

Mucus

FIGURE 13.3 An enlargement of part of the olfactory system. The olfactory bulb contains several layers of cells involved in the processing of olfactory information. Some efferent nerves have their endings in the olfactory bulb as well.

to shed light on this mystery. The first step was the identification of a family of about a thousand GTP-binding proteins, or, for short, **G-proteins** (Getchell & Getchell, 1991). Many different G-proteins are located at the base of each olfactory receptor. When the odorant molecules come in contact with the cilia, the G-proteins are released into the cell. This begins a series of chemical reactions that actually amplifies the odorant signal (Bartoshuk & Beauchamp, 1994; Lancet et al., 1993).

These G-proteins seem to function like proteins in the immune system that bind to specific molecules (Bartoshuk & Beauchamp, 1994). In fact, Linda Buck, who had previously worked with the immune system, was the first to clone the genes for these receptors (Barinaga, 1991a; Buck & Axel, 1991). Buck (1993) has further shown that different G-proteins are distributed in "zones" throughout the olfactory epithelium. This finding presumably accounts for the fact that different parts of the epithelium respond better to some odorants than to others. Interestingly, although we need only 3 of our 100,000 genes to code color vision, we need about 1,000 to produce the G-proteins necessary for olfaction (Freedman, 1993).

The entire population may have 1,000 different olfactory receptor genes in all. However, each individual may have far fewer genes, which could account for individual differences in olfactory abilities (Lancet et al., 1993). For instance, most of us find the smell of skunk unpleasant (to say the least), but some people like the odor so much that, given the opportunity, they roll down their car windows to enjoy it (Freedman, 1993)!

In spite of the exciting developments in our understanding of the molecular basis of olfaction, much remains to be discovered. As mentioned, our olfactory receptors seem to respond to millions of different chemicals, and we can identify (i.e., tell what the odor is) around 10,000 different odors. A single individual probably does not have more than a few hundred distinct G-proteins. Therefore, researchers still need to determine how we can perceive so many unique odors with far fewer types of receptors (Lancet et al., 1993).

The chapter on color vision showed how the combinations of firing patterns from three types of cone receptors allow us to see a wide range of colors. Similarly, our perception of different odors probably arises from various combinations of firing patterns from the olfactory receptors.

The smell receptors are clearly the most important receptors in the olfactory epithelium. However, these patches of skin also store a second kind of receptor, which is not illustrated in Figure 13.3. The **trigeminal nerve** has free nerve endings that extend into the olfactory epithelium, and these endings register sensations important in both smell and taste. These receptors serve to register such sensations as the "bite" of a chili pepper or the "burn" of ammonia (Cain, 1981). Humans apparently react to such stimulants with a reflexive response, leading to changes in the epithelium that serve to protect it from damage (Holley, 1991).

Let's return to Figure 13.3. Notice that a structure located above the receptor cells is labeled the olfactory bulb. The **olfactory bulb** performs the first processing on the signals from the smell receptors (Holley, 1991). Figure 13.3 illustrates that the endings of the receptor cells synapse with new neurons in the olfactory bulb. The olfactory bulb is actually the enlarged ending of the olfactory lobes at the front of the brain (Engen, 1982). Research suggests that the perception of particular odors is due to the pattern of firing of all the neurons in the bulb, rather than a specific subset of neurons (Freeman, 1991). If you recall our discussion of the skin senses, you should conclude that this research supports a pattern theory rather than a specificity theory of olfactory bulb function.

Neurons leave the olfactory bulb and olfactory cortex through two pathways (Freeman, 1991). One pathway is through the thalamus, an area of the brain rich in synapses from all the senses. This pathway seems to be involved in the olfactory discrimination and odor memory (Mair et al., 1995). The other pathway is through the limbic system, which is involved in regulating behaviors such as fleeing, fighting, feeding, and sexual behavior (Pinel, 1993). Thus, this pathway is likely involved in the olfactory aspects of eating. The strong emotional component of olfaction may also be due to the limbic pathway. Both pathways ultimately terminate in the frontal lobe of the cortex (Cain, 1988).

Olfactory Processes

Now that we have discussed the stimuli that give rise to our sense of smell—and the sensory apparatus that processes those stimuli—we will turn our attention to various olfactory processes. What are the perceptual abilities that arise from the stimulation of our sensory apparatus?

Absolute Thresholds

As you'll recall from Chapter 2, several methods can be used to measure an ***absolute threshold*** (the boundary point at which something is reported half the time). Using these methods, the absolute threshold would be the concentration of a chemical for which a person says, "Yes, I smell it" half the time and "No, I don't smell it" half the time. For example, a person may be able to detect a chemical that has a concentration of 3.08 mg of the chemical per liter of air. Sensitivity can also be assessed with signal-detection techniques, although the number of trials required for this procedure makes it a bit difficult to use in olfaction.

Olfactory absolute thresholds are not easily measured. Part of the problem stems from the fact that controlling the concentration of olfacto-

ry stimulus reaching the nose is quite difficult (Doty, 1991). The situation is even more complicated because many molecules that enter the nose will be absorbed by the nose lining before they reach the receptors (Mozell, 1971).

In spite of measurement difficulties, humans are impressively sensitive to some odors. For example, when *National Geographic* was preparing its "smell survey" (Gibbons, 1986), it distributed several scratch-and-sniff panels to readers. Humans are so sensitive to one of these unidentified odorants that the publishers required less than 1 ounce of the substance to encapsulate it on the approximately 11 million copies of the survey!

Several thresholds for different odorants appear in Table 13.2. To place some of these impressive thresholds in perspective, let's translate the threshold for the musky odorant into more concrete terms. A peanut weighs about 1 gram. Imagine dividing that peanut into 10 billion parts and dispersing one of those parts through 1 liter of air. This invisible fragment of a peanut still weighs more than the amount of that musky chemical that you can detect in a liter of air!

Do not confuse absolute thresholds with identification. An absolute threshold task only requires a person to determine whether an odor is present, but not necessarily to say what the odor is. In a subsequent section, we will discuss people's abilities to identify odors. For now, it's enough that you realize that the same odorant doesn't produce the same reaction in all people. One of

TABLE 13.2 Some Representative Thresholds for Odorants

Odorant	Smell	Concentration at Threshold (in mg/L air)
Carbon tetrachloride	Sweet	4.533
Amyl acetate	Banana oil	0.039
Hydrogen sulfide	Rotten eggs	0.00018
Citral	Lemonlike	0.000003
Ethyl mercaptan	Decayed cabbage	0.00000066
Camphor	Mothballs	0.000000113
Trinitro-tertiary-butyl xylene	Musk	0.000000075

Source: Based on Engen, 1982; Wenger et al., 1956.

the odorants in the *National Geographic* survey was androstenone. About a third of the people in the survey reported that they couldn't smell it at all (although that might be because they couldn't attach a label to it). Another third reported that it had a floral smell like that of sandalwood, and the rest had very different reactions. As Morley Kare, director of the Monell Chemical Senses Center, says, "A woman can put it on thinking she smells like sandalwood. A man may think she smells like a stale urinal" (Steiman, 1988).

Humans demonstrate individual differences in sensitivity to different odors such as androstenone, presumably due to genetic differences (Wysocki et al., 1992). Individuals also show a wide range of sensitivity *across* smells. For example, we need more than 4 mg of carbon tetrachloride per liter of air to detect that odorant. We are also remarkably insensitive to the smell of some dangerous gases, such as carbon monoxide. Furthermore, humans are less sensitive to odors than some animals. For instance, dogs are used for tracking because they are about 100 times more sensitive than humans to some smells (Gibbons, 1986; R. W. Wright, 1982). Still, the average human is better at detecting odors than is a physical sensor such as a smoke detector (Engen, 1982).

Many factors influence thresholds. From our discussions of other senses, you probably already expect that people differ in smell sensitivity. These individual differences may be in the range of 20 to 1 (Rabin & Cain, 1986). Thus, in a group of people, the "best smeller" might detect 0.05 mg of a substance per liter of air, whereas the "worst smeller" might require 20 times as much, or 1.0 mg, to detect the same substance. However, the range of individual differences may be exaggerated by using a single test of a person's threshold. This range would be smaller if we calculated an average threshold (Stevens & Dadarwala, 1993). Interestingly, people appear to have lower thresholds for stimuli presented to the right nostril than to the left nostril (Cain & Gent, 1991; Zatorre & Jones-Gotman, 1990).

Smokers or people regularly exposed to tobacco smoke typically have elevated odor thresholds, as do older people (C. Murphy, 1995; Richardson & Zucco, 1989; Schiffman, 1992). By "older people" we mean middle-aged adults! For example, Cain and Gent (1991) found that people in their twenties had lower thresholds than those in their forties. Comparing "sniffers" over 65 years of age with those under 30, Stevens and Dadarwala (1993) found a definite increase in olfactory threshold with age. Even when researchers use a variety of tests, older people typically require increasing amounts of odorants to detect them (de Wijk & Cain, 1994). Not only does odor detection decrease with increasing age, but so does identification of 80 common odors (C. Murphy, 1995).

Several studies have demonstrated that females are more sensitive to odorants than males (Doty, 1991). Furthermore, the gender differences are larger for odorants that might be considered biologically meaningful. Women's sensitivity to all odors, biologically significant or not, has been found to vary with the menstrual cycle (Richardson & Zucco, 1989). We will discuss gender differences further in the section on the recognition of odors.

Will people report smelling an odor when no odor is present? At the end of a television show about the chemical senses, viewers were told that smell could be transmitted via sound. Viewers were specifically told that when a particular sound was presented, they would smell a pleasant country fragrance. Out of 179 viewers who responded, 155 reported smelling hay, grass, flowers, trees, and fruits! We have discussed visual illusions in several chapters. This study shows that expectations will have an influence on odor perceptions—producing a smell illusion (O'Mahony, 1978).

In summary, absolute sensitivity to odorants depends on several factors, including the substance studied and the species. People differ substantially in their smell sensitivities, and women appear to be more sensitive than men. Finally, as we discussed in Chapter 2, researchers can produce the equivalent of a false alarm—reporting the presence of an illusory odor that is not really present—by affecting people's expectations.

Theme 4 stresses the importance of cognitive factors in perception, and smell illusions clearly arise from cognitive processes. When no stimulus is present—so the sensory receptors cannot be stimulated—the suggestions about smell give rise to expectations. These expectations can lead us to report odors that have not even been presented!

Smelling More Intense Stimuli

In the section on absolute thresholds we saw that the nose can detect impressively tiny concentrations of certain substances. Our difference thresholds are generally much less impressive. As you will recall from Chapter 2, the **difference threshold** is the difference between two stimuli that a person can just barely tell apart. For example, one study discussed by Mozell (1971) examined acetic acid, which has a vinegar odor. Two samples of acetic acid must differ by about 26% to be detected. Thus, you should be able to tell the difference in intensity between 100 g of vinegar and 126 g of vinegar.

The ability to detect a difference of 26% might sound reasonably sensitive until you compare the difference thresholds for smell with similar thresholds for other senses. For example, people can tell the difference between two sounds if they differ by as little as 0.3%, a difference threshold roughly 100 times as sensitive.

Why are the difference thresholds relatively large for olfaction? As R. W. Wright (1982) points out, difference judgments are generally not important for biological survival. It's difficult to imagine a situation in which a person is more likely to survive because of the ability to tell that one odorant is stronger than another. Although difference thresholds are not crucial to survival, they do have their application in cooking and eating and other tasks of civilized life.

Does the intensity of an odor always increase as the concentration of the odorant increases in the nose? Not always, if the increased concentration is due to taking more vigorous sniffs (Teghtsoonian et al., 1978). Participants breathed odors at two different "sniff vigors," one twice as strong as the other. Then the participants sniffed various odors using either strong or weak sniff vigors.

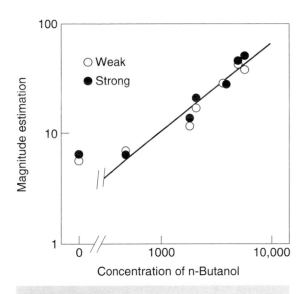

FIGURE 13.4 Magnitude estimation as a function of odor concentration and sniff vigor. Regardless of the amount of odorant inhaled, judgments were reasonably consistent—suggesting odor constancy. (From Teghtsoonian et al., 1978)

Figure 13.4 shows the magnitude estimations for different concentrations of one odor. People supply larger numbers for greater concentrations, showing that they can detect differences. A more interesting finding, however, is that at each concentration the estimates are almost identical for the weak and the strong sniff vigors. The two dots are actually touching each other at six of the seven concentrations. People therefore supply equivalent judgments for a weak sniff and a sniff that is twice as strong, even though the stronger sniff presumably brings in twice as many molecules.

These researchers propose that the results can be explained by odor constancy. **Odor constancy** means that the perceived strength of an odor remains the same despite variations in sniff vigor. Odor constancy is therefore similar to the visual constancies. For example, in size constancy, the size of the object remains the same despite variations in distance. Teghtsoonian and his colleagues suggest that information about the num-

---

Demonstration 13.1

Odor Constancy

For this demonstration you will need paper, tweezers, perfume or shaving lotion, and four containers. Cut a strip about 1 cm wide from the piece of paper. Cut this strip into pieces so that you have tiny pieces 2 cm, 3 cm, and 4 cm long. Take one container, fill it with water, and add one drop of perfume or shaving lotion. With the tweezers, dip each of the tiny pieces in the scented water, swirl it around, and place it in one of the three remaining (empty) containers.

Now take a sniff of the 2-cm container, so that you estimate you are taking in about twice as much air as normal. Now take a normal sniff of each of the three containers. Try to identify which of the three has the same intensity as your first large sniff. If you have odor constancy, the 2-cm container should smell constant in its intensity, despite changes in sniff vigor. If you have no odor constancy, the 4-cm container may be your choice. If you have partial constancy, you may choose the 3-cm container.

---

ber of odor molecules is combined with information about sniff vigor so that the resulting perception of odor strength remains constant. Try Demonstration 13.1 to see whether you can find evidence for odor constancy.

Adaptation

You have probably had this experience. You walk into a room in which onions have been frying, and the odor is overpowering. If you stay in the room for several minutes, however, the smell seems fainter and fainter. After a while, you notice only the faintest odor. You have experienced *adaptation*, the temporary loss of sensitivity as a result of continued stimulation (Köster & de Wijk, 1991). Adaptation may occur when a single

odorant is presented repeatedly, or when one repeated odorant is followed by a similar stimulus.

Self-Adaptation

When the same odorant leads to a loss of sensitivity to itself, the process is called *self-adaptation*. The power of adaptation is particularly impressive if you leave the room in which you have become adapted to an odor and then return to it. The odor is once again overwhelming. Try Demonstration 13.2 to illustrate the adaptation process.

Adaptation has both advantages and disadvantages in everyday life. If you are sitting in a room crowded with sweaty bodies, be thankful for adaptation! Adaptation will also reduce the odor from a neighboring chemical plant. On the other hand, perfumes seem to fade after a few

---

Demonstration 13.2

Adaptation

Find a substance with a strong odor, such as an onion, perfume, or shaving lotion. Place it near your nose as you read your book for the next 10 minutes. Notice how much fainter the odor seems after that time. Remove the substance for the next 5 minutes, then bring it back for a final whiff. At this point the odor should seem just about as strong as it did when you first smelled it.

minutes, and this property may be due to our noses as well as to the perfumes. A burning smell from an automobile may be unnoticeable after a short period of driving, when it may be a warning sign for electrical problems. More dangerously, we may not notice a poisonous gas if we have adapted to the odor.

Cain (1978) points out that self-adaptation reduces our sensitivity to an odor, but it does not eliminate the sensitivity completely. We still smell something. On the average, the perceived magnitude of an odor decays at the initial rate of about 2.5% each second. After less than a minute, self-adaptation is essentially complete. At this point, the perceived magnitude of an odor is about 30% of the initial magnitude. Thus, the perceived magnitude certainly does not decrease to zero. Nonetheless, a 70% reduction is impressive.

What physiological explanations can account for this enormous reduction in sensitivity? The answer is not completely clear. One nice, intuitive answer might be that the receptors simply become tired after high levels of stimulation. Olfactory receptors probably do play a role in adaptation (Köster & de Wijk, 1991; P. A. Moore, 1994). However, differences in the time it takes an organism to adapt to an odorant and the time it takes a receptor to reduce its firing rate suggest that adaptation does not occur solely at the receptor level. Adaptation also seems to occur at higher processing levels. Some evidence also suggests an important role for the olfactory bulb in adaptation, particularly with respect to the connections involving the neurotransmitter noradrenaline (Gervais et al., 1988). One pathway in the olfactory system passes through the limbic system. This system is closely associated with memory, and so it may be partially responsible for adaptation processes.

Try repeating Demonstration 13.2, but plug your left nostril as completely as possible. After 2 minutes, quickly plug the right nostril and unplug the left one. You will find that the sensitivity in the left nostril is somewhat lowered, even though the smell receptors in that nostril received only minimal stimulation when it was plugged. Some mechanism must have reduced your sensitivity at a level more advanced than the receptors.

Cross-Adaptation

We have been discussing self-adaptation, the temporary loss of sensitivity to an odor when that odor is presented for several minutes. Another process, called *cross-adaptation,* means that exposure to one odor reduces sensitivity to other odors. Because cross-adaptation leads to a smaller reduction in sensitivity compared to self-adaptation, you might be less aware of its presence (Berglund & Engen, 1993; Köster & de Wijk, 1991). Nonetheless, you might have experienced this phenomenon. When someone has been frying onions, are you less sensitive to the odor of frying garlic? When you have been smelling one perfume at a cosmetics counter, does another perfume seem less fragrant?

Would you guess that cross-adaptation is due to the perceptual similarity of the odorants? Although this is a reasonable perspective, it has received only mixed support over the past several decades. To test this hypothesis further, Cain and Polak (1992) used two compounds that both smelled like bitter chocolate but differed chemically and structurally. Let's refer to these two compounds as TMP and PMF. Cain and Polak found substantial self-adaptation with both these odorants. That is, people smelled an increasingly weak chocolate odor as TMP was presented over time. The same was true for PMF.

What happened when people first smelled TMP and then were presented with PMF? Although cross-adaptation did occur (i.e., the chocolate odor of the PMF was judged to be weaker), the effects were not as powerful as those found with self-adaptation. Similar results were found when people first smelled PMF and then were asked to judge the strength of TMP. As we noted earlier, cross-adaptation is often found to be weaker than self-adaptation. In fact, some researchers even think that the mechanisms underlying the two processes might differ.

From the discussion of light and dark adaptation in Chapter 3, you should see that adaptation to odors is more like light adaptation (where we become less sensitive to light) than dark adaptation (where we become more sensitive to light). Making such comparisons with other senses that you've learned about will make the material more memorable and will serve to illustrate one of our themes—that the senses have many commonalities.

Recognition of Odors

How accurate are humans at recognizing odors? If you were presented with a common odorant, such as vinegar or an orange, could you unfailingly supply its name? If several odorants were presented at the beginning of an experimental session, could you reliably indicate 10 minutes later which ones you had smelled earlier and which were new? Finally, how accurate would you be in identifying other people based only on their odors? Let's first examine the identification of familiar odors and then move on to the recognition of humans on the basis of their odors.

Identification of Familiar Odors
Try Demonstration 13.3 to illustrate an informal variation of experiments that assess the identification of familiar odors. Notice that the task is much more difficult than simply determining that two odors are different (a discrimination task). Although humans are thought to be able to discriminate roughly 500,000 odors, identification abilities are much more limited.

A typical identification study was conducted by Desor and Beauchamp (1974), who presented people with common, everyday odors such as fried liver, popcorn, and motor oil. People were fairly accurate for odors such as coffee, paint, banana, and chocolate. Fewer than 20% of the participants could correctly identify smells such as cigar, cat feces, ham, and sawdust. Furthermore, people were less accurate on items they rated as unfamiliar. People seemed to make mistakes because they could not give the correct label, not because they confused the odors with other odors. In other words, errors can be traced to an inadequate vocabulary rather than an inadequate olfactory system.

Desor and Beauchamp also tested the effects of practice. In the second part of the study, people were trained extensively until they could identify 32 different odors on two successive trials. When they returned to the laboratory 5 days later, their performance was nearly perfect. Furthermore, these same people later learned to correctly identify 64 different odors. As is often the case, practice at a task such as the recognition of odors leads to enhanced performance (R. S. Smith et al., 1993).

We mentioned earlier that females are somewhat more sensitive than males to various odors; they have lower thresholds. Similarly, females are more accurate on odor identification tasks (de Wijk et al., 1995). For example, Cain (1982) discovered that females are better at identifying the name of stereotypically feminine substances such as baby powder and nail-polish remover. Furthermore, they are better at identifying virtually all foods, which are presumably neutral with respect to gender associations. Finally—and most

---

Demonstration 13.3

Recognizing Odors

For this demonstration you will need about a dozen odorous substances. Use your imagination to find them. Some suggestions are pencil shavings, a green leaf, mud, partly chewed gum, carbon paper, cinnamon, ground coffee, cheese, onion, and mustard. Take each of the substances and cover it with a sheet of paper. (If you can find opaque containers, they would be even better.) Invite several friends to see if they can identify the odors. See which odors are easiest and which are most difficult. Also notice whether your friends differ in their overall accuracy.

surprising—females are also better at identifying stereotypically masculine substances such as cigar butts and machine oil. Females' superiority in odor identification might be due to superior discrimination abilities, or possibly to deliberate attempts to learn about odors (e.g., in food preparation), or to some other factor (Cain, 1980). Some evidence does suggest that female olfactory abilities may exceed male abilities as early as 2 days after birth (Balogh & Porter, 1986).

People who are blind may be better than sighted people at odor identification. For example, in one study blind people were better at identifying 80 different everyday odors (Murphy & Cain, 1986). This accuracy probably cannot be explained by a difference in sensitivity, because absolute thresholds for detecting alcohol were *higher* for people who are blind compared to those of sighted people. These results may be somewhat dependent on the methodology used. Using a different procedure, other researchers found no advantage in odor identification for blind people (R. S. Smith et al., 1993).

The kinds of tasks discussed so far require the participant to supply a name for an odorant. In contrast, another kind of task asks people to recognize whether an odor had been presented previously; no labels are required. Let's consider a study by Engen and Ross (1973), who presented an odorant to participants, then several seconds later presented a pair of odorants. You should recognize this as the two-alternative forced choice method, in which participants were instructed to indicate which of the two odorants was "old" and which was "new." When they were first tested, the participants' accuracy was only about 70%. With the passage of time, olfactory recognition declined only slightly (Engen & Ross, 1973). Even after a year, recognition dropped only an additional 5%. A full 12 months later, people were still better than the 50% chance level in selecting which member of the pair they had smelled before.

In another study, Michael Rabin and William Cain (1984) presented 20 familiar odorants such as chocolate, leather, popcorn, and soy sauce. Participants in this study first rated the familiarity of these odorants and tried to supply labels for them. For over 50% of the odors, the people were able to supply the correct label or a nearly correct label. Then, after delays of 10 minutes, 1 day, or 7 days, the participants were given a recognition task in which they tried to pick the 20 original odors from a group of 40 familiar odors. Accuracy decreased with longer delays and for substances that had been rated low in familiarity. Furthermore, people were less accurate when they had been unable to attach a correct label to the originally presented odor. Thus, language exerts a powerful influence on olfactory identification and memory (Schab, 1991). Studies such as these suggest that much of the difficulty in identifying odors arises from the difficulty of attaching a name to the odor (de Wijk et al., 1995).

Recognition of Humans

Among the odor-producing stimuli in our environment are other people (Labows & Preti, 1992; Stoddart, 1990). The American obsession with masking body odors is indicated by the enormous amounts of money we spend each year on perfumes, deodorants, and mouthwashes. People spend $3.5 billion on women's perfumes alone (Kanner, 1993). Are these personal odors stable over time? Are they distinctive enough to allow us to identify people? Several researchers have been studying human odors, and they have reached some startling conclusions.

In a prototypical study, people are asked not to wash or use deodorants for a day and then to wear a T-shirt for 24 hours. At the end of the day, researchers collect the T-shirts, which serve as stimuli in the experiments. People are very accurate, for instance, at identifying their own odors by picking out the T-shirt they had worn from a set of 3 T-shirts (Russell, 1976). Children are very good at distinguishing their sibling's odor from a stranger's odor, and parents are able to distinguish among their children solely on the basis of odor (Porter & Moore, 1981).

Mothers are highly accurate at identifying the odor of their newborn children, even if they had experienced only minimal contact with the children (Porter et al., 1983). In fact, women who are not mothers are quite good at identifying infants by their odor (Kaitz & Eidelman, 1992). Cernoch and Porter (1985) found that breast-feeding infants were quite good at discriminating their mother's odor from that of other women. These infants were unable to discriminate their father's odor, and bottle-feeding infants were unable to discriminate their mother's odor. Odor is an important component of the mother-infant bond, but infants don't necessarily learn their mothers' natural body odor. They might learn to orient to a distinctive perfume and may feed better if their mothers have recently consumed garlic (Bartoshuk & Beauchamp, 1994).

The more genetically related people are, the more likely they are to have similar body odors (Porter, 1991). Recent research has identified a particular set of genes that appears to be responsible for the individuality of body odor (Bartoshuk & Beauchamp, 1994). Thus, strangers are fairly good at matching the odors of genetically related people, such as mothers and their children. However, they are unable to match the odors of people who may share many life experiences but who are not genetically related, such as husbands and wives (Porter et al., 1985). Identical twins, who share genetic material, smell so similar that even bloodhounds find it difficult to discriminate between them (Engen, 1991).

The source of the scent by which we recognize other humans is probably the odorous steroids secreted by sweat glands (Gower et al., 1988). These steroids have been isolated in several species, and some research suggests that they might even have an impact on behavior—a topic to which we will now direct our attention.

Behavioral Influences of Odors

The research indicates that humans and other animals are relatively adept at perceiving odors, but do these odors have an influence on their behaviors? Smell does have an important role in communication among members of a species (Doty & Müller-Schwarze, 1992). Researchers are especially intrigued by substances called **pheromones,** which act like chemical signals in

communicating with other members of the same species. The name *pheromone* looks like *hormone*, which is a chemical used to send communications from one part of the body to another. Hormones are internal, though, and pheromones are external. Pheromones are excreted through the urine and various sweat glands.

These chemical signals are processed in the **vomeronasal organs,** olfactory sense organs located on either side of the septum, which separates the two nostrils (Farbman, 1992). These organs are found in many mammals, but they had been thought to be vestigial in humans. Thus, although the importance of chemical signals to lower animals is well established, researchers thought that such signals were less effective for humans. Recently, however, research has suggested that humans might have vomeronasal organs, which would enable chemical communication in humans (Bartoshuk & Beauchamp, 1994; Schleidt, 1992). We'll now briefly review some evidence for the functioning of chemical signals in lower animals and in humans.

Odor Effects on Behavior in Lower Animals
A female dog, horse, or cow releases pheromones when she is in heat. These odors attract the sexual interest of the males of the species. Pheromones also have an important role in pregnancy in some species. Research on mice has shown that if an unfamiliar male mouse is placed near the cage of a newly pregnant female, she is likely to abort the fetuses (Parkes & Bruce, 1961; Rogel, 1978).

Pheromones are also crucial in insect communication. This has important applications, for example, in controlling the destructive gypsy moth. Beroza and Knipling (1972) describe how a sex-attractant pheromone, called disparlure, can be used to lure male gypsy moths inside special traps. With the males captured, they cannot breed with the females, and the population of moths declines (P. Nathan, 1982).

Many animals mark their territories with chemical signals. Both wolves and dogs use urine to mark their territories. Deer also use urine to mark territories, but they also have odor-producing glands in their foreheads. Dominant male deer often mark trees by rubbing against them with their antlers and foreheads (Fudge et al., 1992).

In the previous chapter, we discussed stress-induced analgesia, the finding that stress could lead to a lessening of pain. Researchers have also found that such analgesia can be produced by exposing an animal to a natural predator. For instance, when a mouse is exposed to a cat, the mouse activates the endogenous analgesic mechanisms we discussed (Lester & Fanselow, 1985). Interestingly, the natural predator's odor alone is sufficient to induce analgesia. Thus, deer mice and meadow voles activate endorphins in response to the odor of a weasel (Kavaliers et al., 1992).

Odor Effects on Behavior in Humans

One of the most striking illustrations of the possibility of pheromone activity in humans was demonstrated by a college student. Martha McClintock was a senior at Wellesley College when she examined the folk belief that if women live together, their menstrual cycles become similar (McClintock, 1971). She found at the beginning of the school year that close friends and roommates differed by 8 to 9 days in the date of menstrual cycle onset. Over the school year, the difference decreased to an average of 5 days apart.

The similarity in menstrual cycles might have been due to the fact that the women were undergoing similarly timed stresses, but McClintock hinted that pheromones might be involved. To test this hypothesis, other researchers took gauze pads that women with regular menstrual cycles had worn under their arms and at regular intervals rubbed them on the upper lips of women volunteers. After several months, the menstrual cycles of these volunteers shifted significantly toward the cycles of the "donor" women (Russell et al., 1980).

Not everyone agrees with the concept of menstrual synchrony (H. Wilson, 1992). However, many researchers believe that chemical signals between women often lead them unconsciously to synchronize their menstrual cycles (Bartoshuk & Beauchamp, 1994; Engen, 1991; Weller & Weller, 1993). Exposure to male body odors may also affect the female menstrual cycle (Freedman, 1993).

Although pheromones might affect menstrual cycles, they probably do not influence sexual behaviors or serve as a sexual attractant (Engen, 1982; Filsinger & Fabes, 1985; Rogel, 1978). Nevertheless, a number of companies suspect that profit may be found in human pheromones. The Monell Chemical Senses Center has filed applications for four pheromone patents (Leo, 1986). Furthermore, the perfume industry—as you might expect—has entered the competition. Such perfumes are already entering the market, though they are not true pheromones (Krantz, 1994). So you shouldn't be surprised to see someone hawking such wares on a cable channel in the near future.

The effects of various scents on human behavior may not be as direct as those found in lower animals, but research suggests that scents *can* have an impact on people (Lawless, 1991; Stoddart, 1990). For instance, in mock interviews, males rate "applicants" lower on a number of dimensions if they wear scents than if they do not, but females rate the applicants higher if they wear scents (Baron, 1988). Pleasant fragrances can also improve performance on worklike tasks, such as a word construction task (Baron & Bronfen, 1994). Other researchers have found effects of odors on physiological measures, such as blood pressure and heart rate (Lawless, 1991).

Olfaction is also tightly linked to memory. For example, although you may not have smelled Play-Doh in a long time, you might be able to recall its distinctive odor right now. Such effects have even been demonstrated in the laboratory (Goldman & Seamon, 1992). In addition to dredging up the memory for such childhood odors, the odors themselves may help you to retrieve childhood memories. Odor is capable of evoking memories of quite old events that are laden with emotion (Herz & Cupchik, 1992).

According to the principle of encoding specificity, the context in which events are experienced is important for the later recall of those events. As a student, you should therefore learn material under conditions similar to those under which you are likely to be tested. In a classic example of encoding specificity, the author Marcel Proust's memory of his youth was enhanced by the aroma of a French pastry. You may also find that particular odors evoke memories of events from your past. Some research indicates that words learned in the presence of a particular odor are better recalled when that odor is also present at recall (Schab, 1990). So although humans may be less controlled by odorants than other species, we may be more influenced by them than we realize.

Deficits in Olfaction

If you were forced to lose one of your senses, you'd probably be quick to offer smell as a possibility. People with no sense of smell are said to suffer from *anosmia,* and they would tell you that the loss of one's olfactory abilities is not trivial. Anosmia typically results from a head trauma or a viral infection (Doty et al., 1991). As we mentioned at the beginning of this chapter, food flavors are vitally dependent on olfactory information, so food becomes virtually tasteless without smell. In some cases, the ability to smell returns periodically for brief periods. One anosmiac describes the change as comparable to "the moment in *The Wizard of Oz* when the world is transformed from black and white to Technicolor" (Birnberg, 1988).

Although we tend to minimize the importance of smell, you can now appreciate that we are very much dependent on olfaction. Our sensory system has evolved to allow us to discriminate a wide range of olfactory stimuli, and many of these stimuli might well have behavioral consequences. As is often the case, we tend to take abilities for granted. Anosmia helps to clarify the importance of our sense of smell. At the end of the chapter, we will make some further comments on the sense of smell when we see how it interacts with the sense of taste.

SECTION SUMMARY

Smell

1. Smell and taste are called the chemical senses. Far less research has been conducted on the chemical senses than on vision or audition.

2. People have proposed many different classification systems for odorants. Henning's classification system defines smells in terms of six basic odors. Amoore proposed a classification system in which the shape of the odor molecule determines the odor. For several reasons, neither Henning's nor Amoore's system appears perfectly satisfactory.

3. The nasal cavity is the hollow space inside the nose, and the olfactory epithelium—located at the top of the nasal cavity—contains the smell receptor cells. The cilia of the receptor cells make contact with the odorants. G-proteins located at the base of the receptor determine the odorants to which that receptor is most sensitive.

4. The olfactory bulb processes information from the smell receptors, and information is then transmitted to the frontal cortex.

5. Factors influencing absolute thresholds—which can be extremely low for some odors—include kind of odorant, species, individual differences, and gender. Under certain conditions, smell illusions can be demonstrated in which people report smells that were never presented.

6. Difference thresholds are relatively large in everyday life. People seem to show odor constancy; the perceived strength of an odor remains the same despite variations in sniff vigor.

7. Self-adaptation typically involves a 70% reduction in sensitivity. The explanation involves higher neural levels in addition to the receptors. In cross-adaptation, exposure to one odor influences the threshold for other, similar odors. Cross-adaptation is typically less powerful than self-adaptation.

8. Some odors can be readily recognized, whereas others cannot. People are more accurate in recognizing an odor if they have supplied an accurate label and if the odor seems familiar. People seem to be fairly accurate in identifying their relatives on the basis of body odors. Women are more accurate than men in odor identification.

9. Pheromones are chemical signals, excreted in the urine and by the sweat glands, that are

important determinants of the behavior of nonhuman animals. The possibility of pheromone effects in humans remains controversial.

10. Anosmia is a disorder in which a person is unable to smell; it can be brought on by a blow to the head or a virus.

TASTE

As we mentioned earlier, food flavor is a combination of several perceptual experiences, including smell and taste. Humans are *omnivores*—animals that will eat just about anything. Thus, humans experience an amazing range of foods and flavors. As Diane Ackerman (1990) points out,

> The Masai enjoy drinking cow's blood . . . Germans eat rancid cabbage (sauerkraut), Americans eat decaying cucumbers (pickles), Italians eat whole deep-fried songbirds, Vietnamese eat fermented fish dosed with chili peppers, Japanese and others eat fungus (mushrooms), French eat garlic-soaked snails . . . Chinese of the Chou dynasty liked rats, which they called "household deer," and many people still do eat rodents as well as grasshoppers, snakes, flightless birds, kangaroos, lobsters, snails, and bats (pp. 132–133).

The flavors that arise from the wide variety of foods consumed by humans are only partially determined by smell and taste. As we masticate our food, we process surface texture properties such as the smooth surface of noodles, the slippery surface of butter, and the hard crust of pumpernickel bread, which was named because it was thought to be so difficult to digest that even the devil *(Nickel)* would become flatulent *(pumpern)* if he were to eat it (Ackerman, 1990). When we chew, we can register a substance's consistency. We note the thickness of a substance; it may be thin broth or the thick, rubbery texture of the 3-day-old gelatin dessert served in the cafeteria. The consistency may also be elastic, soft, hard, or brittle. These different textural factors are part of the experience of flavor.

People often use the term "taste" inappropriately to describe the flavor of a food. Strictly speaking, however, *taste* refers only to the perceptions that result from the contact of substances with the special receptors in the mouth (Bartoshuk, 1971). When psychologists speak about taste, they mean only a very limited portion of the perceptions involved in the everyday usage of the word *taste*—only perceptions such as sweet and bitter.

Our approach to the sense of taste will parallel our approach to smell. We will first address the taste stimulus, then the sensory apparatus for processing taste information, and then various taste processes that are similar to those discussed for smell.

Sensory Aspects of Taste

Our sensory experience of taste arises from taste stimuli falling on our taste receptors, which process the information and relay it to the brain areas responsible for taste. In this section we will discuss each aspect of the route along which taste information is encoded.

Stimulus

Although the stimuli we smell seem to resist neat categories or measurement systems, the stimuli we taste are somewhat more cooperative. The search for the basic categories for taste dates back to Greek history. For example, Aristotle proposed this list of basic categories: sweet, bitter, salty, sour, astringent, pungent, and harsh. Hans Henning (1927) is generally credited with promoting the idea of four basic tastes. Remember that Henning proposed a six-sided prism to represent the six basic odors. Similarly, Henning proposed a *taste tetrahedron,* a four-sided figure with one of the basic tastes at each of the four corners. Some controversy exists, but most psychologists tend to agree that we taste four basic kinds of stimuli: sweet, bitter, salty, and sour (Bartoshuk & Beauchamp, 1994).

Even though the classification based on four primary tastes is currently dominant, some researchers argue that more than four primaries exist (Shallenberger, 1993). For example, these researchers have argued that studies are likely to confirm the four-primaries theory because they use stimuli from only these four categories and because experimenters bias participants by using the words *sweet, bitter, salty,* and *sour* in the instructions (O'Mahony & Thompson, 1977). Interestingly, Japanese tasters add a fifth label, corresponding to the taste of Ac'cent, which is used frequently in their cooking (O'Mahony & Ishii, 1986). Still other researchers argue that more than four primary tastes are possible because mixtures (e.g., sweet and salty) tend to taste different from their components (Erickson, 1982; Schiffman & Erickson, 1980). Supporters of the traditional, four-primary classification system interpret those results differently. For example, Bartoshuk (1980) maintains that the components of taste mixtures can be individually recognized; mixtures do not create new taste sensations.

Although we may have more than four tastes, a good deal of evidence argues for the primacy of the four tastes. Each of the four basic tastes serves an important ecological function: "ensuring energy reserves (sweet), maintaining electrolyte balance (salt), guarding pH (sour, bitter), and avoiding toxins (bitter)" (Scott & Plata-Salaman, 1991, p. 350). We will focus our attention on perception of these four basic tastes.

Taste Receptors

The basic receptor for taste stimuli is called the *taste bud.* Taste buds are visible only with a microscope. They are located throughout your mouth, not just on the surface of your tongue. For example, taste buds are present inside your cheeks, on the roof of your mouth, and in your throat (Farbman, 1988; Smith & Frank, 1993). Most of the research and discussion, however, examines the taste buds on the upper surface of the tongue.

The taste buds are on little bumps on the tongue known as *papillae.* Each papilla is small, but it can be seen with the unaided eye, as Demonstration 13.4 shows.

Researchers have identified at least six kinds of papillae (Miller & Bartoshuk, 1991). They seem to have somewhat different functions, although these functions are far from clear-cut. The number and type of papillae in different regions of the tongue, as well as the number of taste buds per papilla, vary across individuals (Miller & Bartoshuk, 1991). Figure 13.5 shows an enlarged picture of a papilla. Note that taste buds are lined up in the pits on either side of the papilla. Thus, the taste buds are not on the actual tongue surface.

Figure 13.6 shows an enlargement of a taste bud from Figure 13.5. This pear-shaped taste bud contains several taste cells arranged like the segments of an orange. The tips of the taste cells reach out into the opening and can touch any taste molecules in the saliva that flows into the pit. At the tips of the taste cells are *microvilli,* which fill the opening of the taste bud, called the *taste pore.*

Because of the individual variation found in humans, most of us probably have between 2,000 and 5,000 taste buds on our tongues (Miller & Bartoshuk, 1991). Other species differ widely. For example, chickens have only about 24 taste buds (Kare & Ficken, 1963), so a fine wine would be wasted on them. On the other hand, consider the catfish, which has more than 175,000 taste buds (Pfaffmann, 1978). Most of these taste buds

---

Demonstration 13.4

Looking at the Papillae on Your Tongue

Take a small glass of milk or a spoonful of ice cream and stand in front of a mirror. Coat your tongue with the milk or the ice cream and immediately look at your tongue in the mirror. You will notice rounded bumps that rise above the milky surface of your tongue. These are the papillae that contain taste buds. The smaller bumps do not contain taste buds.

Papilla   Pit   Papilla

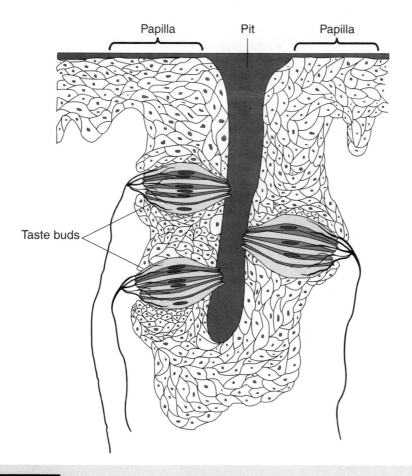

Taste buds

FIGURE 13.5 Enlargement of the papilla on the surface of the tongue, containing many taste buds.

are on the external body surface, so the catfish can "taste" the water it is swimming in without even opening its mouth.

Our mouths are not particularly hospitable environments. Very hot and cold liquids pass over the taste buds, and the teeth and interior of the mouth wear down the taste buds. As a result, the cells within your taste buds are dying rapidly. In fact, the life span of the average taste cell is only about 10 days (McLaughlin & Margolskee, 1994). The fairly rapid turnover of cells within taste buds has important implications for taste, as was true for olfactory receptors. That is, at any

given point, some of your taste cells will be immature and not function well. Furthermore, the developing taste cells must make synaptic connections with the existing taste neurons (Farbman, 1988). Because of the turnover of cells within taste buds, we can expect that loss of taste due to trauma will eventually be restored as the cells regenerate.

Earlier, we discussed the free nerve endings of the trigeminal nerve. Stimulation of these free nerve endings by substances such as ammonia produces a sensation of pungency. Similarly, free nerve endings of the trigeminal nerve are located

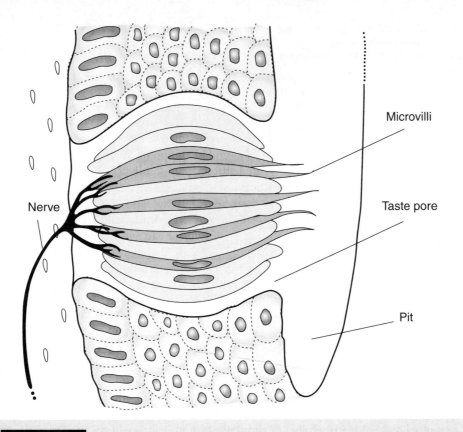

Microvilli

Nerve

Taste pore

Pit

FIGURE 13.6   Enlargement of a taste bud. The taste stimuli in the saliva are thought to interact with molecules in the membranes of the microvilli.

in the mouth. For example, one kind of papilla has even more free nerve endings than it has taste buds (Lawless, 1984). These free nerve endings register spiciness when you eat chili peppers. The irritation produced by eating chili peppers may actually encourage the brain to release endorphins. This could explain the enthusiasm with which some of us pursue spicy foods (Naj, 1986). We also become desensitized due to continued stimulation by the chemical that makes chili peppers spicy, leading to greater tolerance for the irritation (Karrer & Bartoshuk, 1991).

Relationship between Taste and Tongue Regions

You can probably remember learning that different regions of the tongue are sensitive to differ-

ent taste qualities. In fact, McBurney (1978) speculates that this concept is probably the most generally known "fact" about taste. Unfortunately, the basis for this belief was a misinterpretation of a 1901 thesis by Hänig (Miller & Bartoshuk, 1991). In fact, as Hänig had found, all four qualities can be perceived on all the tongue regions that contain receptors (Bartoshuk & Beauchamp, 1994). However, these regions are not uniformly sensitive to the different taste qualities (Shallenberger, 1993).

Taste receptors are located in different regions of the tongue and the *soft palate*, a region on the upper part of the mouth, just above the back of the tongue. The middle of the tongue lacks taste buds, so it could be called a "blind spot." Like the blind spot on your retina, this location has no receptors. Sour tastes are most noticeable on the sides of the tongue. Salty and sweet tastes are most noticeable on the front of the tongue. Bitter tastes are most noticeable on the soft palate (Shallenberger, 1993). Within the regions of the tongue alone, however, bitter tastes are most noticeable on the front, not on the back, as is commonly believed (Collings, 1974).

Problem of Taste Coding

Even if you choose to use the most extensive classification scheme for tastes, the number of categories is limited compared to the number of smells we can distinguish. Because of the widespread acceptance of the four-part classification scheme, researchers have focused on the receptors that encode those four tastes.

Recently, researchers have come to believe that G-proteins—discussed earlier in connection with olfaction—are responsible for our perception of sweet and bitter (McLaughlin & Margolskee, 1994). The taste cells for sweet and bitter apparently work in a fashion similar to that of olfactory receptors. The G-proteins are located at the base of the taste cells. When an appropriate molecule reaches the taste cell, the interaction of the molecule with the G-proteins leads to a cascade of chemical changes that results in a neural impulse (Freedman, 1993; Shallenberger, 1993).

The mechanism for the perception of salty and sour tastes appears to be different. An increase in the concentration of sodium or hydrogen ions in saliva is thought to give rise to our perception of salty and sour tastes, respectively (Scott & Plata-Salaman, 1991). These ions seem to flow directly through special channels in the cells (Freedman, 1993). In addition to the special channels, some of the effects of saltiness are due to ions flowing around the taste cells. Table salt, sodium chloride, tastes particularly salty because both the sodium and the chloride ions flow easily through tight junctions around the cell (Barinaga, 1991b).

We still need some explanation for the fact that the regions of the tongue respond somewhat differently to the taste qualities. For example, why should the taste buds at the tip of the tongue

be particularly responsive to sweet stimuli? Currently, most researchers believe that each taste bud responds most vigorously to only one taste, although it may respond to more than one taste (Shallenberger, 1993). For instance, Figure 13.7 shows the relative thresholds for a hypothetical taste bud that is particularly sensitive to a bitter taste. It could be called a "bitter-best" taste bud. Notice that this taste bud is most sensitive to bitter tastes, least sensitive to sweet tastes, and moderately sensitive to salty and sour tastes. Some other taste buds may have little or no sensitivity to a particular taste. For example, a "sweet-best" taste bud might be floating in vinegar and refuse to respond.

In summary, most taste buds do not restrict their responses to a single stimulus, although they probably respond better to one kind of stimulus than to any other. The higher levels of stimulus processing, beyond the receptor level, must somehow take into account these relative response rates when they code the range of tastes we experience (Logue, 1991).

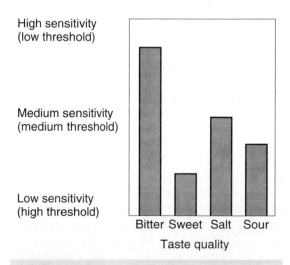

FIGURE 13.7 Sensitivities for a hypothetical taste bud sensitive to bitter. Although this taste bud is maximally sensitive to bitter, it still responds to the other three taste qualities.

Pathway from Receptors to Brain

Figure 13.6 on page 428 showed a nerve receiving information from the taste cell. The nerves in the mouth and throat gather into three bundles, one from the front of the tongue, one from the back of the tongue, and one from the throat. These three nerves travel from the mouth area to the thalamus. From there, information travels to several regions in the cortex, primarily the *somatosensory cortex,* the part discussed in connection with touch.

The four basic tastes seem to be represented neurally throughout the taste pathways. That is, one can find neurons that are particularly sensitive to each of the four tastes (Scott & Plata-Salaman, 1991). For example, although most cortical taste cells respond to three or four of the four basic taste stimuli, they respond most vigorously to only one or two of these stimuli (Yamamoto et al., 1981). However, the notion that taste qualities are encoded through the functioning of specific types of neurons remains controversial (Smith & Frank, 1993).

Other research has suggested that the cortex may not be essential to the most primitive kinds of taste reactions. For example, some infants are born with birth defects so severe that they lack a cortex. Still, they manage to make the same kind of negative facial expressions that normal babies make when they taste sour and bitter solutions (Keverne, 1982; Steiner, 1979). Interestingly, these facial reactions to unpleasant tastes are also found in adults, but they may be exaggerated in the presence of other people (Jäncke & Kaufmann, 1994).

Taste Processes

Now that we have explored the sensory mechanisms for taste, we will direct our attention to the perceptual processes that arise in taste perception. As you will notice, many of the topics are similar to those discussed for the other senses, including absolute and difference thresholds, adaptation, and problems in taste perception.

Thresholds

We have already discussed one aspect of absolute thresholds—the fact that they vary across the regions of the tongue. Thus, a particular concentration of a solution may be just at your threshold on the side of your tongue, and way above threshold on the tip of your tongue. As you might expect, thresholds vary from one substance to another. Bitter quinine sulphate is easy to detect in small quantities. In contrast, relatively large quantities of sweet glucose are necessary for detection. You can test your thresholds for table sugar (sucrose) by trying the demonstrations in Chapter 2.

Absolute thresholds are also influenced by the volume of stimulus used in the study. Brosvic and McLaughlin (1989) increased the volume of stimulus presented from 0.05 to 0.90 ml. The threshold for salt decreased by over 30%, and the threshold for sucrose decreased by over 60%. Thus, lower concentrations of salt and sucrose could be detected if the volume of the stimulus was increased. Presumably, the lower thresholds are due to the fact that more of the stimulus molecules are coming in contact with wider areas of the mouth. In fact, Linschoten and Kroeze (1994) found that doubling the area of stimulation lowered thresholds for perception of salt— whether the two locations were on the same side or different sides of the tongue!

As we noted in our discussion of olfaction, detecting the presence of some stimulus is very different from identifying what that stimulus is. For taste, the *recognition threshold* is the concentration of a solution that can be identified by quality (McBurney, 1978). In other words, the recognition threshold specifies the amount of a substance that must be added to distilled water for tasters to recognize whether the taste is salty, bitter, sweet, or sour. Thus, recognition thresholds are generally higher than absolute thresholds because tasters require a relatively strong concentration of a substance to identify it as, for example, salty.

As discussed before, the difference threshold is the difference between two stimuli that a person can just barely tell apart. Difference thresholds have not been thoroughly studied in the area of taste (McBurney, 1978). Psychologists have shown little interest in this area, perhaps because we do not seem to make much use of intensity information during tasting.

The research conducted, however, indicates that our difference thresholds are not impressive. In general, the concentration of a substance must be increased by 15% to 25% for us to notice a difference in its taste. Thus, if a sauce contains 5 teaspoons of lemon juice, you need to add about 1 more teaspoon to make it noticeably more sour. You may recall that our difference thresholds for smell are similarly unimpressive, about 20% to 30%.

One interesting finding about taste thresholds concerns the amount of time required for judgments. As Kelling and Halpern (1983) point out, we can see a remarkable amount during one lightning flash, and we can also hear an identifiable sound in the fraction of a second during which a twig snaps or a person gasps. These researchers decided to discover what people could identify in a "taste flash," a taste presented for a fraction of a second. Even when a salty or sweet taste was presented for as short a period as one tenth of a second, people could reliably discriminate these tastes from water. Thus, we do not seem to need an extended period of contact between a taste stimulus and the receptors in order to judge its quality.

Adaptation

Remember that when a smell is presented continuously, sensitivity to that smell decreases. Self-adaptation, or a decrease in sensitivity following the continuous presentation of a stimulus, also occurs for taste (Shallenberger, 1993). In other words, when a specific substance is placed on your tongue, your threshold for that substance increases—you require a stronger concentration of the substance to taste it. The threshold reaches its maximum in about 1 minute. This relationship is illustrated in Figure 13.8. Notice that when the substance is removed, the threshold rapidly recovers to normal.

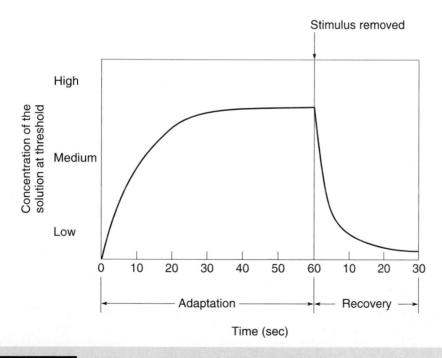

FIGURE 13.8 Adaptation to a specific taste. As the stimulant remains in contact with the receptors, the threshold increases up to a maximum at about 30 seconds. When the stimulant is removed, the threshold begins to drop rapidly, so that about 30 seconds after removal of the stimulus the threshold has returned to its original position.

Demonstration 13.5

Adaptation to Salt in Saliva

Take a quart jar, fill it with water, and add 1/2 teaspoon of salt. Stir the solution until the salt dissolves. Take four small glasses and fill the first glass with the solution. Fill the second glass three-fourths full, the third glass one-half full, and the fourth one-fourth full. Add water to these last three glasses until they are full, and then mix the solutions thoroughly.

Take a sip of the solution in the fourth glass, swish it around in your mouth, and see whether you detect any trace of saltiness. If you do, mix up several glasses of increasingly diluted salty water; wait several minutes before proceeding.

If you do not taste saltiness in the fourth glass, test the third glass to see if you detect salt. Continue with the second and first glasses until you can just barely notice the salt. Record the number of the glass that contains a barely noticeable amount of salt.

Now rinse your mouth thoroughly with water. Use distilled water if possible because tap water may be somewhat salty. Keep rinsing for about a minute. Repeat the threshold-measurement process. Your threshold should now be lower, so that you detect lower concentrations of salt.

Try Demonstration 13.5 to see one example of how self-adaptation works. When your tongue is adapted to the salt in your own saliva, your threshold for salt is relatively high. When you rinse your mouth out with distilled water or tap water, however, your tongue becomes adapted to a salt-free environment. Your receptors are now more sensitive to salt; in other words, your threshold is relatively low (Bartoshuk, 1980; O'Mahony, 1984).

Self-adaptation works for spicy substances as well as for the four standard taste qualities. Lawless (1984) found that spicy peppers and ginger were judged less intense when they followed a strong substance than when they followed a weak one.

These laboratory studies on self-adaptation may not accurately describe your everyday encounters with substances. For example, tastes last longer when people sip a solution than when it is poured on their tongues, which is the more common practice in the laboratory (Lawless & Skinner, 1979). The tongue movement involved in sipping may actually prolong the taste. Also, in the laboratory, the taste stimulus is placed on a small area of the tongue. Outside the laboratory, when you eat a salty cracker, your chewing movements and your tongue movements shift the salty substance around so that it comes into contact with many different receptors. Thus, a single receptor is unlikely to have prolonged, constant stimulation.

Halpern and Meiselman (1980) point out another difference between the laboratory and everyday eating experiences. When you are drinking your lemonade, you sip the liquid and swallow at least once. Then you may pause before sipping again. In other words, the receptors experience noncontinuous stimulation. Halpern and Meiselman tried duplicating more closely the natural alternation between taste stimulus and no stimulus by presenting alternate spurts of salt water and "artificial saliva." (This substance—probably less commercially profitable than cola drinks—contains the important chemicals of real saliva.) People who tasted alternating spurts of salt water and saliva experienced no decrease in the intensity of the salt, whereas people who tasted only spurts of salt water reported a sizable decrease in intensity. For a variety of reasons, then, we show less self-adaptation in everyday life than in typical laboratory studies.

In this section, we have seen that self-adaptation affects both thresholds and judgments of intensity, both for the four traditional taste qualities and for spicy substances. Self-adaptation is less likely in everyday experiences because when we normally eat or drink, we sip, move our tongues, and pause to swallow.

Cross-Adaptation and Cross-Enhancement

Cross-adaptation and cross-enhancement both refer to the fact that adaptation to one substance can influence the taste of another substance. As we discussed in the section on smell, cross-adaptation means that adaptation to one substance *raises* the threshold for another substance; we will be less sensitive to the second substance. **Cross-enhancement,** which is just the opposite, means that adaptation to one substance *lowers* the threshold for another substance; we will be more sensitive to the second substance. (You can recall which is which by remembering that adaptation is a decrease in sensitivity, whereas enhancement means an increase in sensitivity.)

Think of situations in which you have experienced cross-adaptation and cross-enhancement. For example, if you have been drinking tea with lemon, the vinegar in the salad dressing will not taste so sour; you have experienced cross-adaptation. In contrast, if you have been eating a sweet roll at breakfast, the orange juice tastes unpleasantly bitter; you have experienced cross-enhancement.

In general, cross-adaptation is specific to a particular taste quality (Shallenberger, 1993). For example, if you are adapted to a sour taste, you will be less sensitive to other sour tastes. Adaptation to a sour taste will not decrease your sensitivity to salty, sweet, and bitter tastes, because these tastes represent different taste qualities. In fact, your sensitivity to these other substances may be increased through cross-enhancement.

McBurney and Gent (1979) point out how the results on cross-adaptation support the theory of four basic taste qualities. Because little cross-adaptation is found across qualities, it seems likely that separate receptor mechanisms exist for each taste quality. In a representative study on cross-adaptation, Lawless and Stevens (1983) found that the sweet taste of sucrose induced cross-adaptation for other sweeteners such as saccharin and aspartame.

Now let's turn to cross-enhancement. Kuznicki and McCutcheon (1979), for example, focused on the influence of sweet tastes on later sour tastes. These authors asked the participants to stick out their tongues. Then they placed a tiny drop of a substance on an individual papilla that was sensitive to both sweet and sour. These careful techniques minimized the spread of the substance. First a drop of a sweet liquid was presented, followed 15 seconds later by a drop of a sour liquid. In the control condition a drop of water, rather than sweet liquid, was presented prior to the sour liquid. In each case, people used magnitude estimation, supplying a number to indicate the intensity of the sour liquid. People judged the intensity of the sour solution to be greater when it had been preceded by a sweet taste than when it had been preceded by water. Kuznicki and McCutcheon favor an explanation for cross-enhancement that involves chemical interactions on the surface of the receptors.

Cross-adaptation and cross-enhancement are involved in several other taste processes. Two of these are the taste of water and taste modifiers.

Water taste. What could be as tasteless as water? Actually, water can have a distinct taste when your tongue has been adapted to another taste; this phenomenon is called **water taste.** Try Demonstration 13.6 to show how water can acquire a specific taste that depends upon what you have previously eaten. In general, sour and bitter substances produce a sweet water taste, and sweet or salty substances produce a sour or bitter water taste. Incidentally, urea (a component of human urine) is one of the few substances that produce a salty water taste.

McBurney and Shick (1971) examined the water tastes of 26 compounds. They wanted to determine if the relationship between the taste of a compound and its water taste was as clear-cut as

---

Demonstration 13.6

Water Taste

Here are three ways to produce a sweet water taste with an adaptation procedure. Try as many of these ways as possible.

1. Take a mouthful of diluted vinegar and swirl it around in your mouth for 30 to 40 seconds. Spit it out and then take a drink of plain water.
2. Repeat this procedure with strong coffee that contains caffeine. (A teaspoon of instant coffee dissolved in a small amount of water works well.)
3. Eat some artichokes (canned ones work well), making sure that they are thoroughly spread throughout your mouth. After swallowing them, sip some plain water.

Here are two ways to produce a sour or bitter water taste:

1. Dissolve a teaspoon of salt in a small amount of water. Swirl it around in your mouth for 30 to 40 seconds, spit it out, and sip some plain water.
2. Repeat this procedure with sugar.

You may find it difficult to decide whether the water tastes produced by salt and sugar are sour or bitter, but the taste is definitely *not* salty, sweet, or neutral.

---

the opponent-process relationship we saw for color vision in Chapter 7. For instance, do sweet substances give water a sour taste, and vice versa? Unfortunately, their data did not support an opponent-process view; many relationships were not complementary. Try to notice the nature of various water tastes by drinking water with your meals. This amazing low-calorie beverage can assume many disguises!

Taste modifiers. Several special substances change the flavor of other food by modifying the receptors on the tongue; these are called *taste modifiers.* The one you are most likely to have tasted is monosodium glutamate *(MSG),* which is frequently sold with spices in grocery stores under the trade name Ac'cent. MSG is used extensively in Asian cooking. By itself, MSG has an unusual taste that seems to combine the four taste qualities; when added to other foods, however, the thresholds for sour and bitter tastes are reduced (Moskowitz, 1978a). In other words, if a Chinese hot-and-sour soup contains MSG, the chef will not

need to add as much vinegar for the sour taste to be detected.

Another taste modifier is *gymnema sylvestre,* a climbing plant found in India and Africa. A British officer stationed in India first reported its effects in the Western literature after noticing that after chewing the leaves of the plant, he could not taste the sugar in his tea. In fact, gymnema sylvestre reduces the perceived sweetness of a range of sweeteners such as aspartame and saccharin (Frank et al., 1992). Bartoshuk (1974) notes that after one tastes gymnema sylvestre, sugar crystals are indeed tasteless and feel like sand on the tongue.

A third substance, popularly called *miracle fruit,* changes the taste of sour substances eaten afterward. Africans have used miracle fruit to sweeten sour wines and beers (Bartoshuk, 1974, 1980). Linda Bartoshuk lectured on taste modifiers several years ago and distributed samples of miracle fruit. This amazing substance had the potential to transform the pure lemon juice that we drank afterward into the most delicious sweetened lemonade. The name "miracle fruit" is appropriate because a taste of this substance imparts a sweet taste to sour substances eaten in the next hour (Henning et al., 1969).

Bartoshuk (1974) discussed some practical applications of these taste modifiers. Foods made from yeast and algae are extremely nutritious, but their taste is reported to be loathsome. Special diets designed for patients with particular diseases are similarly unappealing. In these cases, using conventional flavorings is often impossible or undesirable. However, the taste of food can be controlled by temporarily altering the taste receptors. Furthermore, substances such as miracle fruit could be explored as alternatives to nonnutritive sweeteners such as cyclamates and saccharin, chemicals that may have undesirable side effects.

Hedonics of Foods

Hedonic preferences, or **hedonics,** involve judgments of pleasantness and unpleasantness, which are central in our perceptual responses to food. For example, suppose you have just lifted your spoon to your mouth to consume the first bite of maple-pecan-fudge-ripple ice cream. The issue of thresholds might be important if you contemplate whether you can detect the maple, which may be partly masked by the fudge sauce. Adaptation may be important because subsequent spoonfuls might be perceived as less sweet. Cross-adaptation should be considered because if your prior cup of coffee contained aspartame, the ice cream may taste less sweet than if the coffee contained saccharin. For most people, however, the perceptual reaction that really matters most is, "Does this taste good?"

Given the wide range of foods that people in one culture think are delicious, but people in another culture would find unpalatable, hedonic preferences must be largely learned (Zellner, 1991). For instance, the research suggests that repeated exposure to a particular stimulus can lead people to like that stimulus more than they did prior to exposure. Repeated exposure may also enhance liking for some foods, but the social context in which the exposure takes place is also important (Zellner, 1991). If your parents don't

like fish, for example, you would be unlikely to enjoy fish. Your distaste for fish could be due to your infrequent exposure to the taste of fish and also to not seeing your parents eating fish with regularity.

Even within cultures, however, substantial individual differences are found. For example, people on a low-sodium diet for several months came to prefer much less salty food than before (Bertino et al., 1982). A control group on a normal moderate-sodium diet showed no such shift in hedonic judgments. You probably know people who have been advised by their doctors to reduce their salt intake so that their blood pressure can be lowered. Ask them whether they have noticed any change in their preferences for salty food. They are likely to tell you that potato chips or ham now taste unpleasantly salty.

People differ not only in the foods they like but also in the foods they can't stand. These food aversions are often learned, in the sense that they develop as a result of a person becoming nauseated or ill after consuming a particular food (Bernstein, 1991). Eleanor Midkiff and Ilene Bernstein (1985) of the University of Washington distributed questionnaires to introductory psychology students asking whether they had any learned food aversions. Midkiff and Bernstein found that 57% of the respondents reported at least one aversion. Intriguingly, most of the food aversions involved foods that are sources of protein. People often reported learned aversions to chicken or meat. However, they were unlikely to report learned aversions to orange juice or chocolate chip cookies.

The authors point out an important consequence of their study. When people undergo chemotherapy to treat cancer, they often develop food aversions to foods eaten around the time of their chemotherapy. If these food aversions involve protein foods—and this research indicates it is likely—cancer patients may develop nutritionally deficient diets. A strategy for avoiding the development of such aversions is to give the cancer patient a "scapegoat" flavor, such as a strongly flavored candy. The patient is then more likely to develop an aversion to the scapegoat flavor than to the nutritious foods the patient is consuming (Bernstein, 1991).

Learned food aversions might also be involved in the development of eating disorders (Bernstein & Borson, 1986). People who suffer from anorexia nervosa often have aversions to sugarless solutions, compared to people who do not suffer from the disorder (Sunday & Halmi, 1991). These aversions were found at both the beginning and end of treatment. Interestingly, the anorexics, bulimics, and control tasters did not differ in their sensitivity to solutions varying in sweetness and percentage of fat. So, although the thresholds were similar for the three groups, they showed definite differences in taste hedonics.

Deficits in Taste Perception

Damage to a taste nerve can lead to the perception of a taste that isn't present—a disorder known as *dysgeusia*. People with dysgeusia may experience salty, metallic, or bitter tastes in their mouths even though no stimuli are present (Bartoshuk & Beauchamp, 1994; Doty et al., 1991). Dysgeusia is also the side effect of certain drugs.

Ageusia means that a person has lost the ability to taste a substance. Total ageusia is the loss of the ability to taste anything. This condition is very rare, but it can occur following radiation therapy or head trauma (Bartoshuk, 1988). Total ageusia can also occur through a very rare inherited condition in which people have no taste buds or papillae and have fewer than normal neurons in their tongues (Doty et al., 1991). Obviously, such people are insensitive to stimuli in their mouths, including the shape or feel of such foods.

Much more common are partial losses of tasting abilities, including the inability to taste one specific quality (such as bitter). These losses can be caused by tumors or lesions of the taste pathways, or by drug use (Doty et al., 1991; Schiffman, 1991).

Finally, some people have inherited taste disorders (partial ageusia). We have seen that some individuals respond abnormally to some stimuli in every sensory system. For instance, we saw in Chapter 7 that most people with color deficiencies are not really color-blind because they can see some colors but not others. Similarly, people with inherited partial ageusia really can taste most substances. However, because they are far less sensitive to particular tastes, they are called *nontasters*. This inherited disorder provides additional evidence for Theme 1, the similarity among the perceptual systems.

Researchers have found nontasters for two specific substances—phenylthiocarbamide *(PTC)* and 6-n-propylthiouracil *(PROP)*. The ability to taste these bitter substances is genetically acquired, just like eye color or height. We noted the role of G-proteins in taste for sweet and bitter substances and discussed how the genetic material is responsible for the G-proteins. Therefore, it makes sense that such taste disorders could be genetically acquired.

However, even PTC-nontasters can taste PTC if the concentration is about 300 times the normal concentration (Hall et al., 1975). Furthermore, PTC-nontasters are also much less sensitive to the bitter taste of caffeine than PTC-tasters. Also, PROP-nontasters are less sensitive to the sweet tastes of sucrose and saccharin than people who can taste PROP (Marks et al., 1992). Because nontasters can taste these substances in sufficiently high concentrations, they may have a smaller number of receptors for both bitter and sweet substances.

IN-DEPTH | **Interaction of Taste with Smell and Other Senses**

Consistent with Theme 1 of this text, we have been stressing the interrelationships among the senses. In this final part of the chapter, we will explore this theme in detail with the senses of smell and taste. How do they interact with one another, and how are they influenced by other senses?

INTERACTION OF SMELL AND TASTE

This chapter includes separate sections on smell and taste, and this separation of topics might lead you to conclude that these perceptual systems are

---

Demonstration 13.7

Importance of Smell for Taste Experiences

Take a piece of an apple, an onion, and a potato. Close your eyes, plug your nose, and in turn take a bite out of each of them. Notice how the tastes for all three are remarkably similar. They all have crisp textures, so that if you are deprived of odor cues, you cannot distinguish among them.

---

largely independent. Don't be misled by the separation of the two systems. We rarely encounter "pure" taste stimuli—independent of their odors—outside the laboratory (Burdach et al., 1984). When you sit down to consume a pizza, the odors of the crust, the oregano, and the mozzarella combine with the salty taste to produce the familiar flavor. Often, as in the case of pizza, smell is even more important than taste in determining flavor. Demonstration 13.7 illustrates the contribution of smell to flavor.

The importance of smell in flavor thresholds has been experimentally tested. In one study, some participants were allowed to taste and to smell solutions of orange juice, vinegar, and chocolate syrup. Other people wore swimmers' nose clips to block the smell of the stimuli. This experiment used the two-alternative forced choice method; one cup contained the stimulus, and the other cup (presented either before or after the stimulus) contained only water. Participants were instructed to tell which cup contained the stimulus (detection) and what it was (identification).

The results of this study showed that the participants were much more accurate in judging orange juice and chocolate syrup when they were also allowed to smell these stimuli (Hyman et al., 1979). For vinegar, however, the "taste plus smell" group performed no better than the "taste only" group. In other words, smell is often—but not always—helpful.

Stevens and Cain (1986) found similar results for estimates of the magnitude of solutions containing varying concentrations of salt and ethyl butyrate (which resembles fruit-flavored chewing gum). When younger subjects tasted the stimuli with their noses pinched, the taste intensity was minimized. Older subjects, however,

showed less difference in intensity between judgments made with the nose pinched or unpinched. Apparently, as we age, we lose the ability to combine smell and taste information.

Smell and taste are major components of our perception of flavor, but how do they interact to give rise to flavor? The research to date supports the notion that the intensity of perceived flavor is due to both taste and odor intensity (Enns & Hornung, 1988). However, judgments of the total intensity are typically less than the sum of the individual judgments of smell intensity and taste intensity (Enns & Hornung, 1985; Hornung & Enns, 1989; Murphy & Cain, 1980; Murphy et al., 1977). For example, Enns and Hornung (1985) worked with almond extract, which participants smelled, tasted, or simultaneously smelled and tasted. In each case they supplied magnitude estimations of the substance's intensity. On the average, the estimates of overall intensity (both smell and taste) were 33% less than the sum of the separate estimates for smell and taste.

David Hornung and Melvin Enns (1986) have suggested a model that accurately predicts total intensity judgments from the addition of smell and taste intensity. Consistent with Theme 4 of this text, Hornung and Enns attribute the disparity between total intensity judgments and the component smell and taste intensity judgments to a cognitive component (Enns & Hornung, 1988; Hornung & Enns, 1986). Hornung and Enns's model of flavor intensity involves only the simple addition of smell and taste intensity. However, mounting evidence suggests that smell and taste interact with one another to a great extent (Hornung & Enns, 1989). As mentioned earlier, outside of controlled laboratory conditions, we probably never taste anything that has not influenced our olfactory system. Odorants also influence the taste system, but to a lesser extent (Hornung & Enns, 1989).

EFFECTS OF VISION ON SMELL AND TASTE

As we noted in earlier chapters, vision has an impact on audition and the skin senses. You should not be at all surprised to find that visual input can also influence smell perception. For instance, Engen (1972) found that with odor stimuli near threshold, people were more likely to falsely report the presence of the odor if an odorless stimulus was colored. However, Debra Zellner and Mary Kautz (1990) used stimuli well above threshold. Their observers were unlikely to report the presence of an odor just because the stimulus was colored. Still, the perceived *intensity* of a

consistently colored odorant (e.g., green with a mint odor, yellow with a lemon odor) was increased, when compared to the same odorant with no color. Surprisingly, even inappropriately colored odorants (e.g., yellow with a mint odor, red with a lemon odor) were perceived to be more intense than colorless odors or odors judged blindfolded. This last finding is of great interest because it suggests a more general impact of color on odor perception. In fact, subsequent research replicated the effect; the use of an appropriate color cue improved odor identification (Zellner et al., 1991).

The color of a substance can also influence taste. For example, Johnson and Clydesdale (1982) found that red-colored sugar solutions were judged to be sweeter than uncolored solutions. Another study showed that cherry-flavored drink is more often misidentified as orange-flavored when it is orange-colored (DuBose et al.,

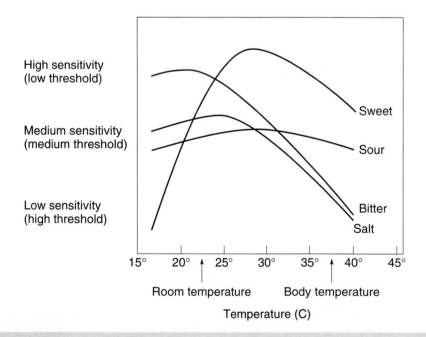

FIGURE 13.9   Relationship between temperature and taste. Sour tastes show relatively little impact of temperature (the curve is relatively flat), whereas the other three taste qualities show a substantial effect of temperature. For instance, sweet tastes become much more difficult to detect at lower temperatures (e.g., 15° C) and easier to detect at higher temperatures (e.g., 30° C).

Demonstration 13.8

Temperature and Taste

Take four small (4-oz) glasses and place two pinches of sugar in each. Fill the first two with cold water from the tap. Stir until the sugar is dissolved and then add an ice cube to glass 1. Add lukewarm water to glass 3 and very hot water to glass 4. Now taste each of the four solutions. Do glass 2 and glass 3 contain the sweetest-tasting solutions?

1980). Furthermore, red birch beer (which has a flavor similar to that of root beer) is thought to be cherry soda (Hyman, 1983). If you'd like your lemon pudding to have a recognizable flavor, then it's best not to add green food coloring!

Food color can also influence hedonic taste preferences. Moskowitz (1978b) reports on a study conducted by Moir (1936), who prepared a buffet of foods in which many of the foods were inappropriately colored. Some of the diners complained about the off-flavor of many of the foods, and several even reported feeling ill at the end of the meal.

EFFECTS OF TEMPERATURE ON TASTE

Although most researchers agree that temperature does influence taste, they often disagree about the exact nature of this relationship. McBurney (1978) states that the majority of studies show that people are most sensitive to tastes when the substance is served at about room temperature or body temperature. Typical results are shown in Figure 13.9. Notice that sour substances are less affected by temperature than salty, sweet, or bitter substances. All the curves do show a maximum sensitivity (that is, a lowest threshold) at a point between 22° and 32° C. Now try Demonstration 13.8 to see if you notice the same effect.

If you look at the sweetness curve of Figure 13.9, you will see that sweetness is more difficult to detect at lower temperatures. It turns out that saccharin remains equally sweet across a range of temperatures, unlike other sweeteners (glucose, fructose, and aspartame). These data suggest that our perception of sweetness is not a unitary phenomenon (Green & Frankmann, 1988).

Think about the practical applications of the relationship between taste and temperature. Cookbooks frequently mention that the final sea-

soning of a dish must be performed when the food has reached the temperature at which it will be served. Suppose that you salted a soup when its temperature was about 25° C and then you heated it to 40° C. According to Figure 13.9, you would now be less sensitive to its saltiness—it might not taste salty enough. On the other hand, suppose you were preparing a lemon pudding. If you adjusted the amount of sugar and lemon so that it tasted just right when it was very hot, it would taste too sweet and too sour when it cooled down.

Temperature also influences hedonics, although the suggested ideal temperatures may vary from individual to individual. For example, Americans vacationing in Greece often notice that the food they eat occasionally tastes less than ideal because it is served close to room temperature, rather than steaming hot. To a Greek the moussaka might be best at 25° C, but an American might prefer it at 45° C. Americans prefer their beer cold, but other cultures prefer beer at room temperature.

These cultural differences suggest that the effect of temperature on taste hedonics is learned. For example, people prefer tea and chocolate milk to be either cold or hot, but not room temperature (Zellner et al., 1988). For most other beverages (e.g., water, cola, white wine), people like cold temperatures better than room temperatures, which are preferred to hot. Coffee and chicken bouillon, however, were enjoyed more when hot. When people are given unfamiliar beverages (guanabana or tamarind juice), they also prefer the juices to be cold rather than room temperature. However, if they are first told that these unfamiliar juices are normally consumed at room temperature, people like the juices just as much served at room temperature as they do when the juices are cold. ◆

As you can now tell, the separate discussions of smell and taste were somewhat misleading because they treated the two senses as completely independent of one another. In the laboratory, we can separate the two senses, but in real life they are greatly intertwined—providing vivid support for Theme 1 of the text. The other senses also have an impact on smell and taste, providing further support for our theme.

As functioning organisms, humans are surrounded by a wealth of sensory information—all of which is processed more or less simultaneously by our sensory systems. At any particular time, we might choose to emphasize one sense over another, and the evidence suggests a strong reliance on visual input, but the input from *all* our sensory systems is continually being processed. We do not live in a visual world, or an auditory world, or a tactual world, but in a world rich with information of all kinds. To think of smell or taste information as somehow second-rate is to ignore the unitary experience we have of a vibrant, complex world filled with a wealth of information.

SECTION SUMMARY

Taste

1. Taste refers only to perceptions resulting from substances in contact with special receptors in the mouth. Although some controversy exists, most psychologists believe that humans can taste four basic kinds of stimuli: sweet, bitter, salty, and sour.

2. The taste receptors, called taste buds, are located on the sides of some of the papillae of the tongue. Typical taste cells within a taste bud have a life span of about 10 days. Each taste bud may respond to stimuli with different tastes, but it responds most vigorously to only one.

3. All tastes can be experienced wherever taste buds are found, but each taste is most noticeable in a particular location. Sour tastes are most noticeable on the sides of the tongue, bitter on the soft palate, and salty and sweet on the front of the tongue. The

middle of the tongue is relatively insensitive to all tastes.

4. The nerves from the mouth and throat travel to the thalamus, and taste information is then transmitted from the thalamus to the somatosensory cortex. The cortex may not be essential for the most basic kinds of taste reactions.

5. Self-adaptation is a decrease in sensitivity when the same stimulus is presented continuously. Laboratory demonstrations of self-adaptation may not accurately describe our everyday experiences, in which we seem less likely to show taste adaptation.

6. Cross-adaptation occurs when adaptation to one substance raises the threshold of another substance. Cross-enhancement occurs when adaptation to one substance lowers the threshold of another substance.

7. Various substances can modify the taste of water. For example, after vinegar, water tastes sweet.

8. Three taste modifiers are MSG (which lowers the threshold for sour and bitter tastes), gymnema sylvestre (which makes sugar tasteless), and miracle fruit (which makes sour substances taste sweet).

9. Hedonic taste judgments, or what people find pleasant, vary widely from culture to culture. Within a culture people vary considerably, with learned taste aversions found in some people who dislike the taste of foods that others in the culture enjoy.

10. Total ageusia, the total loss of taste, is very uncommon. Partial ageusia, the loss of taste for particular substances, is more common. Nontasters are insensitive to certain substances, such as PTC and PROP.

11. Smell and taste contribute significantly to flavor perception. The intensity of a smell–taste combination is about 33% less than the sum of the separate estimates for smell and taste. Smell and taste interact with one another; they are probably never separate outside of laboratory conditions.

12. Visual input, particularly color, has an impact on both smell and taste. Color can lead

people to perceive smells that are not there, can increase the intensity of smells that are present, and can lead to misperception of flavors. Inappropriate food colors can change food preferences.

13. Temperature has an effect on taste thresholds and taste preferences, but temperature preferences for foods and beverages are learned.

REVIEW QUESTIONS

1. What are the important characteristics of stimuli that determine whether they are odorous? Suppose you sniff an orange and a lemon, and they smell similar. How would Henning's and Amoore's systems explain the similarities?

2. In a laboratory at your college, a professor measures a student's threshold for a particular odor, and it is high. In a laboratory at another college, a different professor measures a different student's threshold for a second odor, and it is low. Identify as many factors as possible that might explain the different results.

3. Compare smell with vision on the following dimensions: amount of research performed; nature of the stimulus; nature of the receptors; memory for the stimuli. Also suggest any other characteristics that you think provide a useful comparison.

4. Point out aspects of the following topics that might be relevant for a perfumer: absolute thresholds, difference thresholds, adaptation, cross-adaptation, odor recognition, and odor constancy.

5. Two portions of this chapter discussed humans smelling other humans—the section on smell recognition and the section on pheromones. Summarize the results of these two sections. Point out how gender differences are important in these areas.

6. Distinguish between taste and flavor. What are some of the components of flavor, and how does odor contribute to flavor?

7. Describe the four basic taste qualities that humans perceive. Where is each of these qualities most noticeable in the mouth? Why does the information on taste coding indicate a less-than-perfect relationship between taste receptors and these four basic taste qualities?

8. Suppose that you have put too much sugar in a salad dressing. Speculate how your dinner guests' ability to detect the sugar could be influenced by each of these factors:
   a. You serve the salad after the main course—a somewhat sweet vegetable casserole—rather than before the meal.
   b. You add yellow food coloring to the dressing.
   c. You chill the salad thoroughly.

9. Discuss the three kinds of taste modifiers mentioned in this chapter and note whether each one causes cross-adaptation or cross-enhancement.

10. Describe how smell and taste are influenced by input from other senses. Use examples from your own life to illustrate these principles where you can.

NEW TERMS

flavor (410)	nasal cavity (412)	trigeminal nerve (414)
chemical senses (410)	turbinate bones (412)	olfactory bulb (414)
olfaction (411)	olfactory epithelium (412)	absolute threshold (415)
odorant (411)	cilia (412)	difference threshold (417)
stereochemical theory (412)	G-proteins (414)	odor constancy (417)

RECOMMENDED READINGS

Bartoshuk, L. M., & Beauchamp, G. K. (1994). Chemical senses. *Annual Review of Psychology, 45,* 419–449. In the *Annual Review* series, you find excellent summaries of recent advances in the field, and this chapter is no exception. The authors provide a tightly written review of research on the chemical senses. They also provide you with a wealth of references to important advances in the field.

Engen, T. (1991). *Odor sensation and memory.* New York: Praeger. Engen's book provides a very interesting summary of olfaction, with a much stronger emphasis on perception and odor memory than on sensory aspects of olfaction. Although it doesn't have the "page-turning" aspects of a good novel, this is an engaging book that most readers will be tempted to finish in one sitting.

Getchell, T. V., Doty, R. L., Bartoshuk, L. M., & Snow, J. B. (Eds.). (1991). *Smell and taste in health and disease.* New York: Raven. This is an excellent compendium of 55 chapters by specialists in their fields. There are 19 chapters that provide detailed coverage of basic topics in taste and smell. Five chapters cover the impact of the chemical senses on behavior. In addition, you will find 18 chapters covering disorders and another 13 chapters discussing factors that have an adverse effect on taste and smell.

Logue, A. W. (1991). *The psychology of eating and drinking: An introduction* (2nd ed.). New York: Freeman. Logue's book expands beyond the topics in this chapter to include topics such as anorexia, obesity, and alcohol abuse. Her style is clear and interesting, so the book can be read by those with little background in perception.

Schab, F. R., & Crowder, R. G. (Eds.). (1995). *Memory for odors.* Mahwah, NJ: Erlbaum. The nine chapters in this edited volume provide a current perspective on much of the research on recognition and identification of odorants. If you are interested in olfaction, this book is essential reading.

Van Toller, S., & Dodd, G. H. (Eds.). (1988). *Perfumery: The psychology and biology of fragrance.* London: Chapman and Hall. This book has a very applied orientation, with 13 chapters devoted to a range of issues from biological bases of olfaction to fragrance therapies and perfume selection.

14 Perceptual Development

The previous 13 chapters have provided information about how people perceive the world. In the final chapter we will look at the development of perceptual abilities. This chapter will also allow you to review a variety of important concepts from earlier chapters.

A central controversy in human development is called *the nature–nurture question:* Are abilities due to inborn factors (nature), or are they the result of learning and experience (nurture)? As you can imagine, psychologists have concluded that the nature–nurture question has no simple answer. Instead, development is determined by both nature and nurture, just as the area of a rectangle is determined not simply by its width or its length, but by the combination of both factors (Maccoby, 1990). Incidentally, Theme 3 of this textbook emphasizes the natural abilities of the senses, whereas Theme 4 emphasizes the importance of learning.

In this chapter we will focus on the development of vision and audition in both the early and the later years of a person's life. We will see that infants come into the world with remarkably competent perceptual systems, which continue to develop and mature. We will also emphasize that many aspects of perception remain strong throughout old age, although other aspects show some deterioration and loss as we grow older. Let's begin by examining some important issues related to infant perception, and then we will consider infant vision, infant audition, and perception during late adulthood.

STUDYING PERCEPTUAL DEVELOPMENT IN INFANCY

William James, the 19th-century American psychologist, proclaimed that the newborn's world is a "blooming, buzzing confusion" (James, 1890, p. 488). According to this perspective, newborn infants open their eyes and see an unstructured, random chaos. In the last 100 years, however, psychologists have drastically revised their ideas about infant perception. We now know that the newborn has remarkable perceptual abilities— much better than the early researchers had imagined. Even very young infants impose a structure on the world, unlike the chaos suggested by William James (E. J. Gibson, 1987).

One reason that early researchers underestimated infants' perceptual skills is that infants' motor and verbal skills are very limited. After all, an infant cannot say to the researcher, "The left-hand figure is farther away." Therefore, psychologists have been forced to invent clever methods for discovering infants' perceptual capacities. The results obtained with these methods are the major reason for the newer, more optimistic assessment of infant perception.

This chapter will examine variations of three basic methods: preference, habituation, and conditioning. If we simply watch an infant, we will underestimate his or her perceptual skills. However, the chapter will illustrate how these three more sensitive techniques allow us to overcome the communication barrier and discover what infants can see and hear.

The communication problem is not the only problem confronting the developing infant. We have seen examples of Theme 1 throughout this book; the perceptual abilities are interrelated. For example, we saw in Chapter 6 that distance perception depends on binocular perception, and size perception depends on distance perception. Chapters 5 and 8 pointed out that shape perception is influenced by the motion of objects. However, each of these perceptual systems develops at a different rate, causing additional difficulties and limitations for the developing organism.

Eleanor Gibson (1987) summarizes the research on infant perception and illustrates the interconnections among the perceptual systems. We have already pointed out the misconceptions that might arise if you think of the senses as separable, as they might appear to be when pigeonholed into separate chapters in a textbook. Gibson provides evidence for the unity of the senses in infancy by noting that even newborns will turn toward a sound and open their eyes to look at it. We will see additional evidence of this impressive coordination of the senses in the "in-depth" section on intermodal perception later in the chapter.

FIGURE 14.1 Two kittens, previously reared in the dark, being exposed to an environment of vertical stripes. The kitten on the right is active in its exploration of the environment. The kitten on the left is passively carried via the actions of the other kitten, although it has identical visual experience. The passive kitten has poorly developed perceptual abilities as a result of its diminished experience. (After Held & Hein, 1963)

Gibson also emphasizes the active nature of perception, consistent with an emphasis of this textbook. As she writes,

> Perception is active, exploratory, and motivated even in the neonate. Rather than being passive recipients of energy that falls willy-nilly on some receptor surface, very young infants can and do actively obtain information. (Gibson, 1987, p. 515)

An early experiment by Held and Hein (1963) provides strong evidence for the importance of an active involvement with the environment. These researchers raised kittens in total darkness until they were several weeks old. After that time, the kittens were divided into two groups. Some of the kittens were allowed to actively explore the visual environment you see in Figure 14.1. These kittens could walk around freely. In contrast, the remaining kittens were passively engaged with their environment, because they were simply carried around in a little cart—propelled by the movement of the active kittens.

When the kittens were later tested, the active kittens showed normal depth perception, but the passive kittens did not. For instance, if you take a normal kitten and place it near a flat surface such as a table, it will extend its paws to meet the surface. The active kittens in Held and Hein's study extended their paws appropriately, but the passive kittens did not. Keep in mind that all kittens had identical visual experiences—they differed only in their degree of active engagement with the environment. This research therefore emphasizes that active exploration is crucial for normal perceptual development.

Studying Perceptual Development in Infancy

1. William James proposed that the newborn's perceptual world is unstructured and random. More recent research is more optimistic, primarily because of the newer research methods—including preference, habituation, and conditioning—that allow us to overcome the communication barrier.

2. In infants, as in adults, the perceptual systems are interconnected. However, these systems develop at different rates, causing limitations for the developing infant.

3. According to Eleanor Gibson, infant perception is active and exploratory, rather than a passive process.

4. According to research on kittens, active engagement with the environment is crucial for perceptual development.

VISION IN INFANCY

Our discussion of infant vision will include several topics: visual abilities, shape perception, distance perception, motion perception, and color perception.

Visual Abilities

When we compare the visual systems of newborns and adults, we see that newborns have some disadvantages—though not in all areas. The optical quality of the young infant's eye appears to be remarkably good (Banks & Salapatek, 1983; Movshon & Van Sluyters, 1981). That is, the cornea and the lens have the capability to focus an image on the retina. However, the retina itself is still not fully developed. As it happens, the rods and the cones in the periphery of the retina are nearly adultlike. Unfortunately, though, the fovea in the newborn is fairly immature, and the visual receptors are literally few and far between (Dobson, 1993; Teller & Lindsey, 1993). As we will discover, this immaturity has important implications for acuity.

As we move to higher levels in the visual system, we see that the lateral geniculate nucleus (LGN) is already distinctly layered in the newborn infant (Banks & Salapatek, 1983). However, the neural pathways between the LGN and the cortex—as well as the visual cortex itself—are not fully developed at birth. Nevertheless, these regions develop rapidly, and they are fairly mature by 4 months of age (M. H. Johnson, 1990). During these early months, the newborn also makes rapid progress with respect to acuity and many other perceptual skills.

Acuity

Consider the difficulty of measuring an infant's acuity. When ophthalmologists measure your acuity, they may ask you to name the letters in each row of the Snellen eye chart. Researchers interested in infant perception face a daunting obstacle: How can they coax these young infants to "tell" us what they see?

The breakthrough came when Robert Fantz (1961) developed the preference method to measure acuity. The ***preference method*** is based on the idea that if the infant spends consistently longer looking at one figure in preference to another figure, then the infant must be able to discriminate between the two figures (Spelke, 1985). Researchers using the preference method try to discover the smallest width of a striped pattern that a baby will prefer to a uniform gray pattern of equivalent brightness.

Fantz (1961) placed the infants in a small crib inside a special "looking chamber." He attached pairs of test objects—slightly separated from each other—onto the ceiling of the chamber. The researcher could look through a peephole to see the infants' eyes. Mirrored in the center of the eye, just over the pupil, would be the tiny image of the test object that the infant was looking at (e.g., a striped patch or a gray patch). The amount of time the infant spent looking at the striped patch and the amount of time spent looking at the gray patch were both recorded. For example, a particular infant might look at the striped patch 65% of the time and the gray patch 35% of the time. The testing sessions were carefully controlled so that the striped patch would appear on the left side half the time and on the right side half the time to ensure that any effects of position preference did not confound the study.

What does the information about looking times tell us? Well, if the infants were *unable* to tell the difference between the two objects, then the two looking times should be roughly equivalent. For example, the baby might look at one figure 48% of the time and at the other figure 52% of the time. However, if the baby looks at one figure for a consistently longer time (such as 65% for a striped patch and 35% for a gray patch), then we can conclude that the baby can tell the difference between the two figures. That is, the baby's acuity is good enough to distinguish the narrow stripes from the gray patch.

Studies using Fantz's preference method show that 1-month-olds can distinguish between a gray patch and stripes $\frac{1}{16}$ inch (1.6 mm) wide, when both patches are placed 10 inches (25 cm) from the infants' eyes (Atkinson & Braddick, 1981). This acuity—in Snellen notation—would be 20/400, or about 5% of adult acuity. Although this acuity is not very impressive, it is still sufficient to provide infants with a basic impression of their immediate environment (Hainline & Abramov, 1992).

Acuity improves rapidly, particularly as the receptors in the fovea develop. Babies 6 months old can discriminate stripes $\frac{1}{64}$ inch (0.4 mm) wide, which is equivalent to 20/100 vision (Bornstein, 1984a). By 1 year of age, acuity is approximately 20/60 (Gwiazda et al., 1980). Now try Demonstration 14.1 to illustrate the preference method for measuring infant acuity.

Demonstration 14.1

Preference Method for Measuring Acuity

Prop up your textbook and walk backward until the narrow-striped patch on the right is indistinguishable from the uniform gray patch in the middle. If 1-month-old babies saw these two patches at a distance of 10 inches, they would look at them equally; the patches would appear to be the same. However, if the striped patch on the left looked as different from the uniform gray patch as it does to you now, babies might look at the striped patch more than at the uniform gray patch; the patches would appear to be different. Incidentally, when all stimuli are presented at a distance of 10 inches from babies, 1-month-olds can distinguish the left-hand striped patch (1/16″ wide) from the uniform gray patch; 6-month-olds can distinguish the right-hand striped patch (1/64″ wide) from the uniform gray patch.

Using a variation of the preference method, Stephens and Banks (1987) found that infants less than 3 months old required much greater contrast than adults to perceive the spatial frequency gratings discussed in Chapter 5. Stephens and Banks used a grating of 6 cycles per degree, a visual stimulus that adults see especially well (as shown in Figure 5.4). These researchers varied the contrast between the alternating stripes. They found that young infants required about 10 times more contrast than adults viewing the same stimuli.

Researchers have also found that infants' accommodation abilities are limited; objects nearer or farther than $7\frac{1}{2}$ inches are relatively blurry (Aslin, 1988). We have seen, then, that the visual abilities of an infant are not precise. However, infants do not need the extremely precise acuity required to hunt distant prey or to read the figure captions in a textbook. Fortunately, their vision is good enough to allow them to see nearby objects and to interact with people in their environments (Hainline & Abramov, 1992).

Eye Movements

If you have had the opportunity to watch a newborn baby, you may have noticed something unusual about the baby's eye movements. In particular, the eyes occasionally move in different directions from each other (Bornstein, 1984b). In Chapter 4, we discussed several different types of eye movements. You may recall that *vergence movements* are necessary to align the foveas of both eyes with an object. Infants' imprecise vergence movements are apparently due to the fact that young infants do not yet have the ability to make use of disparity information from the two eyes (Aslin, 1988). Until the infant can use this disparity information, accurate vergence movements yield little advantage.

You may also recall that *saccadic movements* are the rapid shifts of fixation that move the eye from one position to the next. Adults can perform a single saccade to align the fovea with an interesting object. Infants can also direct their attention toward nearby interesting objects. However, infants younger than 4 months of age perform a series of short saccades, rather than one single, highly efficient saccade (Aslin, 1988). By the time the infant is 6 months old, both vergence movements and saccadic movements are much more accurate.

Shape Perception

Researchers have examined many components of shape perception during infancy. In this section, we'll concentrate on two aspects, face perception and Gestalt principles.

Face Perception

One of the most persistent questions in this area is whether infants have some inborn preference for the spatial arrangement inherent in the human face. In one of the early studies, Fantz (1961) used the preference method we described earlier. He demonstrated that 2- and 3-month-olds preferred to look at a cartoonlike face rather than other patterns or bright solid colors.

However, it's not clear whether infants have an inborn preference for faces. Some researchers argued that newborn infants like to look at faces simply because faces have a high degree of contour and because they move. They pointed out that other objects with the same amount of contour and movement capture babies' attention just as much as faces (Flavell, 1985). The controversy seemed to be settled.

In 1991, however, Morton and Johnson rekindled the argument. They studied normal, healthy newborns and tested them within the first *hour* after birth. Each of three figures, as shown in Figure 14.2, was presented to the newborn and was slowly moved from side to side. The infants moved their eyes an average of 48 degrees for the facelike stimulus, in contrast to 40 degrees for the scrambled stimulus and 21 degrees for the blank stimulus (Morton & Johnson, 1991). These differences were statistically significant. So, to be honest, we cannot yet draw conclusions about whether the preference for faces is part of the "nature" of a newborn.

Other research on infants' perception of faces asks a different question: How old must an

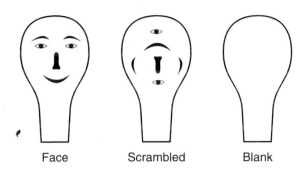

Face   Scrambled   Blank

FIGURE 14.2 In Morton and Johnson's (1991) study, newborns moved their eyes further to track an intact, schematic face, in contrast to a scrambled face or a blank face.

infant be to recognize a parent's face? Psychologists had previously been pessimistic about infants' ability to recognize faces. In fact, they argued that infants could not form emotional attachments to their parents until at least 6 months of age because they could not distinguish parents from strangers. However, more recent studies—with more sensitive research methods—have demonstrated that we had underestimated infants' abilities. Research in the 1980s concluded that infants can make these visual discriminations somewhere between 1 and 3 months of age (Barrera & Maurer, 1981; Bushnell, 1982; Ruff, 1982). However, even younger infants may be able to recognize their mothers. Walton and her coauthors (1992) found that newborns around 24 hours old produced significantly more sucking responses to a video of their mother than to a video of a female stranger. In summary, infants can distinguish between Mother and a stranger at an early age. However, we do not know whether this ability is present in the first hours after birth . . . or the first months.

Gestalt Principles
You will recall some of the Gestalt laws of grouping from Chapter 5, such as the laws of proximity, similarity, and closure. For example, if you

place your arm across this page of your textbook, the law of closure guarantees that you still see your textbook as a single, complete figure. As an adult, you do not see two separate, isolated segments on either side of your arm. As it happens, this same law of closure operates during infancy, at least in some situations.

In order to describe this research, we need to introduce a second important method for assessing perception in infants, called habituation. The **habituation method** is based on a phenomenon known as habituation, which is a decrease in attending to a repeated stimulus. We have discussed adaptation throughout this book, and initially habituation may sound like adaptation. However, adaptation involves a decrease in responsiveness from the sensory receptors. In contrast, habituation is a cognitive process, which involves mental representations and memory (Bornstein, 1985a). When a baby pays less attention to an object that has been presented several times, the baby is demonstrating that he or she remembers seeing the object.

In perception research, a stimulus is presented repeatedly until the baby shows habituation. Now if we present a *different* stimulus, the baby may show **dishabituation**, or an increase in looking time. We can use the habituation technique to encourage infants to tell us, "Yes, I can tell the difference between this new stimulus and that tired old stimulus you kept showing me before." However, if the baby ignores this new stimulus, we conclude that the baby is basically saying, "Ho-hum, this is the same stimulus you've shown me on the previous 20 trials."

Let's see how Kellman and Spelke (1983) used the habituation method to test whether infants appreciate the law of closure. In this study, 4-month-olds were shown a rod moving back and forth behind a wooden block (see Figure 14.3a). Then the infants kept watching the stimulus until their looking time had decreased by 50%, which was the operational definition of habituation in this study.

Next, Kellman and Spelke showed the infants the two kinds of test stimuli that you see at the bottom of Figure 14.3. One stimulus showed

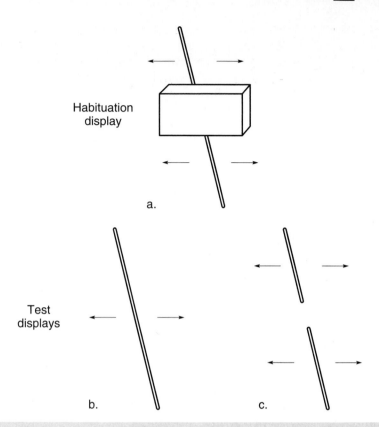

Habituation display

a.

Test displays

b.　　　c.

FIGURE 14.3 In Kellman and Spelke's (1983) study, 4-month-olds habituated to a rod that moved back and forth behind a block. Later, they did not look long at Test Display b, but they spent a long time looking at Test Display c. We can infer that they believe that a solid, continuous rod is hidden behind the block.

a single, intact rod moving back and forth. The other stimulus showed two rod-fragments, moving back and forth. Basically, then, these researchers found a clever way to ask babies what they thought was behind the wooden block, a single rod or two unattached fragments.

The results showed that the infants were indeed governed by the law of closure. Their responses suggested that they thought a single, intact rod was behind the wooden block; they looked at this rod (Figure 14.3b) for the same amount of time as the original stimulus (Figure 14.3a). In contrast, however, they showed dishabituation for the two rod-fragments (Figure 14.3c). They had spent an average of only 10 seconds looking at the single rod, whereas they spent an average of 40 seconds looking at this unexpected stimulus. By the age of 4 months, then, infants solve the mystery "What's behind the wooden block?" in the same way you and I do, by obeying the law of closure.

Distance Perception

A 10-month-old infant crawls down the hallway and pauses at the top of the stairs, looking back and forth between the floor and the first step down. Can infants see depth? Are they aware

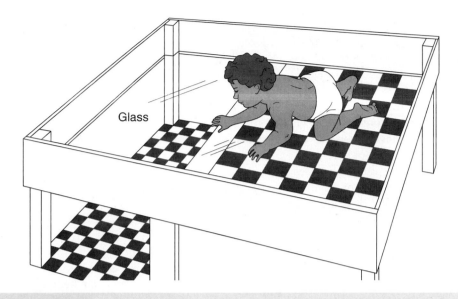

Glass

FIGURE 14.4 A crawling infant experiencing a visual cliff, such as that found in the study by Gibson and Walk. (1960)

which surfaces are farther away from them? These questions were investigated by Gibson and Walk (1960), who measured depth perception with a visual cliff.

As Figure 14.4 shows, a ***visual cliff*** is a kind of apparatus in which infants must choose between a side that looks shallow and a side that looks deep. Babies are placed on a central board with a sheet of strong glass extending outward on both sides. On one side, a checkerboard pattern is placed directly under the glass. On the other side, the same checkerboard pattern is placed some distance beneath the glass. The apparatus is called a visual cliff because of the apparent drop-off on the "deep side" of the central board. To an adult, the pattern on the upper side of Figure 14.4 looks farther away because the elements in the pattern are smaller. Gibson and Walk wondered whether infants' perceptions would be similar.

In one experiment, Gibson and Walk tested 36 babies between 6 and 14 months of age. They placed a baby on the central board and asked the baby's mother to call to the baby from both the shallow and the deep side. Gibson and Walk found

that 27 babies moved off the central board at some time during the experiment, and all 27 crawled at least once onto the shallow side. In contrast, only 3 babies crawled onto the deep side. Thus, babies old enough to crawl are able to discriminate between deep and shallow. Their depth perception is well enough developed that they could avoid the potentially dangerous deep side.

More recent research has used more sensitive techniques. We now know that babies can use binocular depth information by the age of 3 months (Yonas & Owsley, 1987). Several months later, babies begin to make use of the kind of monocular information found in pictures. They appreciate factors such as interposition, familiar size, and shading (Yonas & Owsley, 1987). By the time babies reach the ripe old age of 6 months, they are reasonably expert in knowing that their toes are farther away than their knees and that the mobile above their crib is closer than the ceiling.

In several earlier chapters, we talked about the nightmare that would result if we did not have perceptual constancies. Objects would grow and shrink, transform their shapes, and change from light to dark. Objects would also change their color, speed, location, and even their existence from moment to moment. We saw in the earlier chapters that adults have perceptual constancy. Fortunately, infants seem to develop constancies fairly early, especially for moving stimuli (E. J. Gibson, 1987). Specifically, size constancy is well developed by the age of 6 months (Dodwell et al., 1987; Yonas & Owsley, 1987). Undoubtedly, the rapid development of depth perception during the first six months of life facilitates the appreciation for size constancy. The related skill of shape constancy develops even earlier—probably by 3 months of age (Dodwell et al., 1987).

Motion Perception

Babies respond to movement as soon as they are born. For example, infants consistently turn their heads to follow a facelike stimulus when they are tested in the first *hour* of life (Goren et al., 1975; Morton & Johnson, 1991). By 5 months, babies can make relatively subtle motion discriminations (Freedland & Dannemiller, 1987; Ruff, 1985). For instance, by that age they can tell whether movement on their retinas has been produced by their own movements, rather than by something moving out in the environment (Kellman et al., 1987).

Babies also appreciate biological motion. As you will recall from the discussion in Chapter 8, biological motion is the pattern of movement of living things. At some time between the ages of 3 and 5 months, babies develop the ability to look at a display of moving lights and perceive the pattern as representing the motion of a person (Bertenthal, 1993; Bertenthal et al., 1985, 1987; Fox & McDaniel, 1982). Thus, babies are born with the ability to appreciate primitive motion, and an understanding of more subtle kinds of movement develops before they are 6 months old.

Color Perception

Can babies see color? In general, the evidence suggests that infants under 1 month of age do not have color vision. However, color vision im-

proves dramatically during the following weeks, consistent with the development of receptors in the fovea. By the age of 3 months, the typical infant can discriminate among a variety of colored stimuli (A. M. Brown, 1990; Teller & Bornstein, 1987). In short, young infants rapidly develop the skills to appreciate a visual world that is rich with information about shape, distance, motion, and color.

SECTION SUMMARY

Vision in Infancy

1. The fovea of the newborn is not mature at birth; the visual pathways and the visual cortex are also not fully developed.
2. The preference method can be used to measure acuity by finding the narrowest stripes that will be looked at for a longer time than a uniform gray patch. Acuity develops rapidly during the first year of life.
3. The vergence eye movements of young infants are imprecise. Infants also use several short saccades to accomplish the eye movements that adults can make in a single saccade.
4. Infants prefer to look at facelike stimuli by the time they reach the age of 3 months; some research even suggests that the preference is inborn. Similarly, infants can discriminate between parents and strangers by the time they are 3 months old, but some research suggests that they can discriminate at the age of 1 day.
5. Using the habituation method, Kellman and Spelke showed that 4-month-olds can use the law of closure in perceiving a rod hidden behind a wooden block.
6. Studies suggest that 3-month-old babies use binocular depth information in perceiving distance. By 6 months, they are able to use the kind of monocular cues found in pictures.
7. Size constancy is well developed by 6 months, and shape constancy by 3 months.
8. Newborns appreciate simple motion, and 5-month-olds can perceive biological motion.

9. Color vision is not present in the 1-month-old, but it develops by the age of 3 months.

HEARING IN INFANCY

Auditory Abilities

Even before babies are born, they have many opportunities to hear. Life in the uterus may be dark, but it certainly isn't quiet. For example, the sound level near the fetus's head is about 80 dB, primarily due to the noise from the mother's pulse. This is approximately the intensity of loud music from the radio. Noises from the outside world also reach the fetus; low-frequency sounds may be only 20 dB less intense inside the uterus (Morse & Cowan, 1982). A pregnant woman should think twice before buying tickets for a heavy-metal rock concert, because the fetus can't wear earplugs!

We discussed the difficulty of determining what a newborn can *see*. It is even trickier to determine what a newborn can *hear*. In visual research we can measure an infant's eye movements or fixation patterns; however, we cannot directly measure the ear's "fixation patterns" (Aslin et al., 1983). Therefore, the methods we discussed in connection with infant vision must be modified to accommodate the additional challenges of measuring infant audition.

Infants' auditory skills are substantially more advanced than their visual skills (Fernald, 1990). The auditory system develops early in the prenatal period. For example, the eustachian tube is largely formed at 10 weeks after conception, and the ossicles (the bony structures in the middle ear) have reached their adult size and general shape by about 15 weeks after conception (Bredberg, 1985). However, the neural pathways between the ear and the cortex—and the auditory cortex itself—are not fully mature until the child is between 1 and 2 years of age (Kuhl, 1987; Morse & Cowan, 1982).

Research on 3-month-olds shows that their auditory thresholds are about 25 decibels higher than those of adults (Olsho et al., 1988). By the time infants reach the age of 1 year, their thresholds are only about 10 dB higher than those of adults (Bargones, 1994). So, infant hearing is not quite as acute as adult hearing, but it is still quite impressive. Perhaps the more astonishing skills involve infants' perception of music and of speech, as well as their ability to coordinate vision and audition—a topic we will explore in the in-depth section of this chapter.

Music Perception

Infants are remarkably skilled in their ability to discriminate between two highly similar musical selections. For example, researchers have discovered that infants can listen to melodies consisting of five notes and detect the difference from an almost identical melody when just one note is changed by just one half-step (Cohen et al., 1987). Impressively, these infants are only 7 to 11 months old. In some cases, infants are even more accurate than adults (Trainor & Trehub, 1992).

This research on melody discrimination also shows that 6-month-old North American infants are just as skilled at detecting mistunings in melodies from non-Western music—specifically music from Java—as they are for Western melodies. However, North American adults are typically better on Western than on non-Western melodies (Lynch et al., 1990). This research argues for the "nurture" side of the nature–nurture controversy; our experience with a musical culture enhances our ability to make relevant discriminations.

Perceptual competence requires us to be skilled in appreciating similarities as well as differences. For example, we mentioned earlier that infants show size constancy by 6 months of age. That is, they realize that an object has the same size even when its distance is changed. In the same fashion, they can recognize short tunes, even when the tunes are transposed into a slightly higher or lower key. Using the habituation method, Trehub (1985) showed that infants as young as 2 months of age paid more attention to a melody that was a rearrangement of a familiar six-note tune, in contrast to the same familiar tune at a slightly higher or lower pitch. The constancy in music discussed in Chapter 10 therefore begins to develop very early in infancy. Even 2-month-olds appreciate that the general contour stays the same in the two tunes, even though the physical stimulus involves a different actual pitch (Trehub, 1993).

Speech Perception

Language is one of the most remarkable human accomplishments. By the age of 6, children have some mastery of about 14,000 words. To acquire a vocabulary this large, children must learn about eight new words each day from the time they are a year old until their sixth birthday (Clark, 1991). How can children master language so readily? Research in recent decades demonstrates that they have a "head start." Young infants have inborn knowledge and a capacity for language. They can discriminate speech sounds and other characteristics of language before they are old enough to produce any recognizable sounds of their own. They can also appreciate similarities between speech sounds, revealing constancy for the elements of our language.

Phoneme Discrimination
The research shows that infants have a remarkable ability to discriminate between highly similar phonemes, the basic units of speech we discussed in Chapter 11. The classic research on this topic was conducted by Peter Eimas and his colleagues (1971), who tested speech perception in infants between 1 and 4 months of age. Basically, they used the habituation method combined with the high-amplitude sucking procedure (Jusczyk, 1985). In the ***high-amplitude sucking procedure,*** babies suck on a pacifier attached to a recording device. If they suck fast enough, a machine presents a speech sound. For example, babies might suck to produce the sound "bah." At first, the babies would suck vigorously to produce the "bah" sound. However, after about 5 minutes, habituation occurred, and the number of sucking responses decreased. Then the researchers presented a new sound, such as "pah."

Eimas and his colleagues found that babies showed dishabituation when the new speech sound was presented; sucking returned to the previous vigorous level. In other words, babies indicated by their dishabituation that "pah" sounded different from "bah." Other research has shown that infants discriminate between "sah" and "vah," between "rah" and "lah," and between "fah" and "thah" (Eilers & Minifie, 1975; Eimas, 1975). Eimas's research inspired 30 additional published studies during the following decade, and these studies showed that infants could make more than 50 different contrasts between speech sounds (Kuhl, 1987).

One of the most interesting research projects was conducted by Janet Werker and Richard Tees (1984), who wondered about the influence of language environment on infants' ability to discriminate between speech sounds. Would Canadian infants, reared in an English-speaking environment, be able to discriminate between two speech sounds that are considered the same in English—but considered different in another language? For example, in Hindi, the /t/ sound is made sometimes by placing the tongue against the back of the teeth and sometimes by placing the tongue farther back along the roof of the mouth. Try it, and you'll appreciate how these sounds might be perceived as different in another language but not in English. In fact, only 10% of English-speaking adults can make this discrimination (Werker, 1994).

Werker and Tees tested 6- to 12-month-old infants who had been reared in English-speaking homes. The stimuli included a variety of phoneme contrasts in Hindi and in Salish, a North American Indian language. All phonemic contrasts were ones that are not important in English.

As you can see from Figure 14.5, the youngest infants made accurate discriminations. However, this ability declined dramatically until it was negligible at 1 year of age. Furthermore, notice that 1-year-old infants from Hindi and Salish backgrounds have no difficulty making these distinctions. Apparently, infants about 6 months old can make discriminations in languages other than

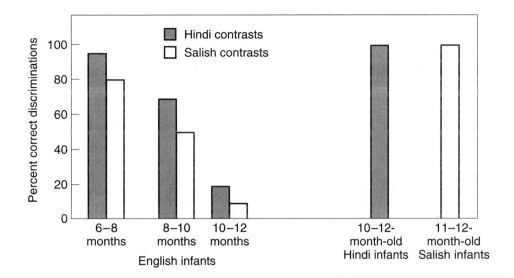

FIGURE 14.5 The ability to perform phonemic contrasts, as a function of age and linguistic experience. (Based on Werker & Tees, 1984)

their own (Werker & Desjardins, 1995). However, this ability fades as children use their own language. In contrast, infants for whom this distinction is important will improve their ability to make these same discriminations.

Other Discriminations Related to Speech

Infants' language skills are not restricted to simple phonemes. Researchers have discovered that infants can discriminate between speakers, between different languages, and even between different passages spoken in the same language.

At what age can babies discriminate between their mother's voice and the voice of a stranger? The research of Anthony DeCasper and William Fifer (1980) of the University of North Carolina at Greensboro suggests that 3-day-olds have this capability. In this study, babies sucked on pacifiers at different rates to produce either the voice of their mother or the voice of a female stranger. Amazingly, these tiny babies produced their mother's voice more frequently than the stranger's voice. The mother's voice seems to be

transmitted to the fetus prior to birth, without substantial distortion in quality. As a recent review of the research concludes, "It is clear that the human fetus hears its mother's voice in the womb, registers some characteristics of her voice, and postnatally prefers her voice" (Burnham, 1993, p. 1135).

We also know that infants can discriminate between different languages. For example, 4-day-old newborns prefer to listen to speech produced in their mother's native language, rather than a foreign language. Specifically, French infants preferred to listen to a stranger speaking French, rather than the same woman speaking Russian (Mehler et al., 1988). Furthermore, American 9-month-olds listened longer to English than to Dutch. In contrast, Dutch 9-month-olds listened longer to Dutch than to English (Jusczyk et al., 1993).

So far, we have seen that infants can distinguish between speakers and between languages. They can also distinguish between specific passages of speech. DeCasper and Spencer (1986) asked pregnant women to recite the Dr. Seuss story *The Cat in the Hat* twice a day for the last 6 weeks of their pregnancies. After the babies were born, they were tested when they were 2 to 3 days old. These newborns preferred to listen to *The Cat in the Hat* rather than to a similar but unfamiliar children's story. This effect has also been replicated in other conceptually similar research (e.g., Cooper & Aslin, 1989).

Speech-Sound Constancy

So far, our examination of speech perception during infancy has emphasized babies' skill in making discriminations, in determining whether two speech sounds are different. However, linguistic skill depends not simply on detecting *differences* but also on appreciating *similarities* (Kuhl, 1992). An infant needs to appreciate that when the sound /a/ is spoken by her 3-year-old sister, it matches the sound /a/ that is spoken by her uncle with a deep, bass voice. As an adult, you have speech-sound constancy, because you can appreciate that when the phoneme /a/ is spoken with a high-pitched child's voice, perhaps with a falling intonation, it matches the phoneme /a/ spoken in a low-pitched adult's voice, perhaps with a rising intonation. Language mastery depends on learning not only which differences you must pay attention to, but also which differences you must *ignore*.

Let's consider a recent study by G. Cameron Marean and his colleagues (1992), which used a clever adaptation of a conditioning method to test infants' speech-sound constancy. So far, we have discussed two methods for conducting research with infants, the preference method (testing whether the baby systematically prefers one stimulus rather than another) and the habituation method (which tests whether a habituated baby shows renewed interest in a new stimulus). In the third major technique, the **conditioning method,** the experimenter selects a response that the baby can make and delivers a reward when the baby makes that particular response.

Marean and his colleagues used the conditioning method to reinforce the infant for identifying a change in a vowel sound. In more detail, let's imagine that 2-month-old Jason is sitting on his mother's lap. Both his mother and the lab experimenter are wearing headphones, and they cannot hear the vowel sounds that Jason is hearing. The experimenter sits directly in front of Jason, jiggling some intriguing toys so that the infant will face straight forward. Then a stream of sounds is presented. On the no-change trials, a series of five /a/ sounds is presented (like the vowel sound in pop). On the vowel-change trials, Jason hears one /a/ sound, then one /i/ sound (like the vowel sound in *peep*), then three more /a/ sounds. During the training portion of this study, Jason must learn that if he turns his head to the side during one of the vowel-change trials, he will be rewarded by the activation of a truly fascinating mechanical toy. However, if Jason turns his head to the side on a no-change trial, nothing happens. Training continues until Jason has mastered the task. During this training portion, all the vowels are spoken by a male voice.

Next, Jason progresses to the categorization phase of the study. The critical question here is how Jason responds to the stimulus in which he hears a male voice saying /a/ on the first, third, fourth, and fifth position, but a *female* voice saying /a/ in the second position in the five-vowel sequence. This is a critical condition because we want to know whether Jason indeed turns his head to the side, thus informing us that he regards the /a/—spoken by a female voice—to be a change. However, if Jason keeps looking straight ahead, he is "telling" us that he considers the five /a/ sounds to be the same, whether they are spoken by a male or a female.

Marean and his colleagues found that when only the voice changed—and not the vowel—infants continued to look straight ahead. Apparently the infants are telling the researchers, "You can't fool me—it doesn't matter whether /a/ is spoken by a male or a female, because I have speech-sound constancy." The infants made the correct response 80% of the time, whether they were 2, 3, or 6 months old. In contrast, in another condition, the second vowel in the five-vowel sequence was switched in both the sex of the speaker (from male to female) and in the vowel sound (from /a/ to /i/). Now the infants *should* turn their heads in this condition; after all, we have changed the vowel on them! And indeed they do turn their heads, 70% of the time for 2- and 3-month olds, and 100% of the time for 6-month-olds. In short, then, infants as young as 2 months of age have speech-sound constancy. They appreciate that an /a/ sound remains an /a/, even when it is spoken by a female rather than a male voice.

IN-DEPTH Coordinating Vision and Audition

As we have stressed throughout this textbook, the senses interact with one another. For example, vision and audition do not live separate lives. In our everyday experience, we know that when our visual senses inform us that a book is falling to the floor, our auditory senses will also inform us, with a distinctive thud. Furthermore, we know that something looking like a book makes a different kind of thud from something looking like a pillow. As it happens, babies also appreciate the correspondence between vision and audition. Some studies do not show this kind of intermodal correspondence (e.g., Lewkowicz, 1992). However, let's consider some examples from four areas of intermodal perception.

INANIMATE OBJECTS

Many studies examine the noises made by inanimate objects when they hit other objects (e.g., Spelke, 1987). In one of the earliest experiments on this topic, Elizabeth Spelke of Cornell University used a modification of the preference method. She showed two films, presented side by side, to 4-month-old infants. Each film showed an unfamiliar stuffed animal, which was lifted into the air by a string and then dropped to the ground repeatedly. The two films were out of sequence, so that one toy hit the ground before the other. Infants heard a percussion sound coming from a speaker placed between the two films. This sound was timed so that it matched the impact of the toy in one film but didn't match the rhythm of the other film. Spelke found that infants preferred to look at the film of the one that matched, in which the sight and the sound were coordinated.

Infants appreciate not only appropriate timing but also appropriate noises that match the objects. Soft and squishy objects should make one kind of noise when they collide with each other; rigid-looking objects should make a very different kind of noise. Bahrick (1983) showed infants a film of two soggy sponges colliding with each other. Babies' responses indicated that they knew this event should produce a squishy sound. Bahrick also showed a film in which two wooden blocks collided. Again, babies' responses indicated their awareness that these objects should produce a harsher, clacking sound. In other words, babies appreciate a cohesiveness and unity for inanimate objects in their environment.

MOUTH CONFIGURATIONS DURING SPEECH

Babies also appreciate intermodal relationships when they interact with people. In Chapter 11, we discussed how your speech perception can be influenced by watching a speaker's lips as well as by hearing the auditory stimulus. As it happens, babies also integrate the speech they hear with the visual information from the speaker's lips.

Patricia Kuhl and Andrew Meltzoff (1982) tested babies who were 4 to 5 months old, using a setup like the one with the stuffed animals. Specifically, the babies watched two films, placed side by side. Each film showed a woman's face. However, one film showed her making the /a/ sound from "pop," and the other film showed her making the /i/ sound from "peep." Meanwhile, they heard a tape recording of either the vowel sound from "pop" or the vowel sound from "peep."

The results showed that infants looked consistently longer at the film in which the lip configuration matched the sound. Similar results have been reported by Burnham and Dodd (1994). In other words, if babies hear an "ee" sound, they want to see the corners of the speaker's mouth drawn apart in a configuration appropriate to that vowel. This phenomenon has an important implication. Babies are significantly more likely to imitate a sound if the mouth configuration is paired with the appropriate vowel than if it is mismatched. Thus, intermodal perception may encourage language development (Legerstee, 1990).

MATCHING VOICES WITH INDIVIDUALS

As you might guess, babies know that certain voices should be paired with certain people. For example, in one study, 3- to 7-month-olds faced their mother and father (Spelke, 1985). One parent's tape-recorded voice was then presented from a location in between the two parents. Even the 3-month-olds tended to turn toward the appropriate parent. They realize, then, that Mother's voice should come from Mother's face, and Father's voice should come from his face. Furthermore, by the time they reach 6 months of age, infants acquire more general knowledge; they realize that male faces go with male voices (Walker-Andrews et al., 1991).

MATCHING VOICE TONE WITH FACIAL EXPRESSION

So far, you have learned that infants can coordinate sight with sound, whether they are perceiving inanimate objects, mouth configurations, or individual people. By now, you may be so habituated that you will not be impressed by this final skill in intermodal perception: Babies appreciate that the expressions on people's faces must match the emotional tone of their voices. Arlene Walker-Andrews (1986) used a method similar to others we discussed to examine 7-month-olds. Babies heard a recording of either a happy or an angry voice while they watched a pair of films. A happy face appeared on one side, and an angry face appeared on the other side. A voice that was either happy or angry came from a speaker in between the two faces. Now if babies were allowed to see the speaker's entire face, they might be able to guess which face went with which speech pattern—using just the cues from the lips. Consequently, Walker-Andrews covered the lower one-third of each face. Of course, her solution also eliminated much of the most critical facial information; a smile or a scowl is crucial in conveying emotion.

Nevertheless, the results showed that the babies who heard the happy voice tended to watch the happy face, and babies who heard the angry voice tended to watch the angry face (Figure 14.6). Soken and Pick (1992) have also replicated this experiment. In short, then, the results on

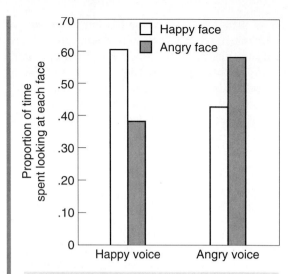

FIGURE 14.6 Proportion of time spent looking at happy and angry faces, as a function of the type of voice heard. Notice that the infants spend more time looking at a face when the voice matches the facial expression. (Based on Walker-Andrews, 1986)

intermodal perception during infancy provide strong support for the first theme of this book. Even during the first months of life, infants are able to appreciate the coordination between the sights they see and the sounds they hear. ◆

SECTION SUMMARY

Hearing in Infancy

1. The auditory system develops early in the prenatal period, but higher levels of auditory processing are not mature at birth. Audition is usually more advanced than vision.
2. Infants have somewhat higher auditory thresholds than adults.
3. Infants can discriminate between two very similar musical melodies. They also show constancy for the contour of melodies when they are presented at different pitches.

4. Young infants can discriminate between highly similar phonemes, though this ability declines for phonemic contrasts not found in their language environment.

5. Infants can also discriminate between a mother's voice and a stranger's voice, between their native language and a foreign language, and between a familiar passage of language and an unfamiliar one.

6. By 2 months of age, infants show speech-sound constancy.

7. Young infants appreciate that the visual properties of inanimate objects must match their auditory properties, that speakers' utterances must match their mouth configurations, that individuals' voices should match their visual appearances, and that voice tone should match facial expression.

VISION AND HEARING IN LATE ADULTHOOD AND OLD AGE

Before we examine perceptual changes during aging, let's discuss some potential methodological problems in studies using elderly people. One problem is the difficulty of locating a group of young people identical to the elderly group in all important characteristics except age. Imagine, for example, that you want to determine whether hearing sensitivity declines during aging. You test a group of college students whose average age is 19 and a group of residents of a nursing home whose average age is 78. Suppose that you find that the college students have more sensitive hearing.

The problem is that the two groups differ not only with respect to age but also with respect to a number of confounding variables. A *confounding variable* is a factor—other than the factor being studied—that is present to different extents in the two groups. For example, the college students are probably much healthier than the nursing home residents.

An additional confounding variable is that the college students almost certainly have had more education than a general population of people in a nursing home. Many studies fail to equate the education level or intelligence of the young and elderly people. For example, Basowitz and Korchin (1957) used young doctors and nurses for their young group and a general nursing-home population for their elderly group in a study on figure–ground relationships. Storandt (1982) points out another confounding variable. Elderly people, particularly those living in nursing homes, are more likely than younger people to be taking medications that interfere with perceptual processes.

Here is the dilemma. Suppose that researchers make no attempt to control for confounding variables such as health, education level, and medication intake. It is entirely possible that any differences between the young and the elderly people could be due to these variables rather than the critical factor, the changes in the perceptual processes that occur with aging. Thus, we must be cautious about interpreting age-comparison studies, particularly when other factors might be responsible for any differences in performance.

An additional problem arises if researchers decide to use response latency to measure perceptual processes. Studies consistently show that elderly people experience *cognitive slowing,* or a slower rate of responding on a variety of tasks (e.g., Plude, 1990; Salthouse, 1991). The young and elderly people might have highly similar perceptual skills, but the elderly people may simply *respond* more slowly.

Even when we avoid the potential research problems, however, some sensory processes clearly change during aging. As you read the rest of this chapter, try to imagine what daily life would be like with these alterations in your perceptual experiences. How would you try to compensate for these changes?

Vision in Late Adulthood and Old Age

Let us first examine some changes that occur in vision during aging. We will begin with the more basic visual abilities; then we will consider visual perception.

Visual Abilities

Some major changes occur in the structure and functioning of the visual system as humans grow older. For example, pupil size decreases (Whitbourne & Powers, 1996). Aging also has implications for the lens, acuity, and glaucoma.

The lens. Over the course of the life span, the lens grows something like an onion, adding layer after layer (Bornstein, 1984b). As a result, the lens becomes substantially thicker and cloudier (Dalziel & Egan, 1982; Spector, 1982). Severely cloudy lenses are called **cataracts.** About one-third of people over the age of 75 show visual loss traceable to cataracts (Heller, 1991). This thickening of the lens, the decrease in pupil size, and other age-related changes in the eye decrease the amount of light that can reach the retina. In fact, the retina of a 60-year-old receives only about one-third as much light as the retina of a 20-year-old (Ordy et al., 1982). Many elderly people complain that the instrument panels on their automobiles are too dimly lit—an obvious result of diminished light reaching the retina (Kline et al., 1992). As you may have read, dark glasses that reduce the exposure to ultraviolet light are helpful in minimizing this problem.

The thickening of the lens also has an important influence on color vision. Specifically, the layers of the lens are pigmented. As these layers accumulate, the pigments absorb light primarily in the blue portion of the spectrum. As a result, elderly people have difficulty making discriminations in the green–blue–violet and in the yellow portions of the spectrum. For example, elderly people have difficulty distinguishing between blue and green pills, as well as between yellow and white pills (Hurd & Blevins, 1984; Whitbourne & Powers, 1996). Obviously, special precautions need to be taken to make certain that elderly people do not take the wrong medication by mistake.

As we discussed in Chapter 3, the thickening of the lens has yet another implication for vision. As the lens thickens, it also becomes less elastic (Elworth et al., 1986; Whitbourne & Powers, 1996). As a result, the eye muscles have difficulty changing the shape of the lens so that nearby objects can be seen, resulting in **presbyopia** (Koretz & Handelman, 1988). (The word stem *presby* means old, and *opia* refers to eyes, so presbyopia literally means "old eyes.") A person who previously was nearsighted—seeing nearby but not distant objects—may now require bifocals. **Bifocals** are special eyeglasses that have two types of lenses, an upper lens for improving eyesight for distant objects and a lower lens to be used for reading and other close work. Older people who have presbyopia and do not use glasses find that they can see an object more clearly if they hold it some distance from their eyes.

We have seen that changes in the lens of the eye can create problems in the amount of light that reaches the retina, in color vision, and in accommodation. In addition, changes in the lens are primarily responsible for the difficulty that older people have with glare (Bailey, 1986; Carter, 1982; Whitbourne, 1985). Because the lens becomes thicker, more opaque, and more pigmented, the lens scatters the light. Thus, on a bright, sunny day, elderly people may have trouble locating a friend on a beach or noticing a stop sign when they are driving. Inside the home, elderly people need more illumination than younger people, and a too-bright lamp might make it difficult to read the slick surface of some magazines. Facilities designed for elderly people should be carefully planned to reduce the problem of glare.

Acuity. Another problem as people grow older is decreased acuity. (Owsley et al., 1983; Weale, 1982; Whitbourne, 1985). This decrease is especially noticeable for moving objects and for objects seen in peripheral vision (Hartley & McKenzie, 1991; Scialfa et al., 1992). To some extent, this decrease can be traced to a loss of visual pigments in the photoreceptors for elderly people (Kilbride et al., 1986). However, elderly people sometimes receive poor scores on acuity tests like the Snellen test (Figure 4.9) because they are less willing than young people to make guesses about letters on the eye chart (Sekuler et al., 1982b).

The standard kind of acuity tests may not predict how well an older driver can see at night.

FIGURE 14.7 Scene as it would look to a young adult (left) and an older adult (right). (Photos courtesy of L. A. Pastalan)

For example, in one study, elderly and young people were matched in terms of static acuity with a well-lit target (Sivak et al., 1981). Then they drove in an automobile at night while watching for a small reflecting sign that had been placed along the side of the road. The sign showed the letter E, which faced either right or left. The results showed that young observers identified the sign at a distance of about 660 feet, much sooner than the elderly observers (460 feet). Consider the important implications of this study for night driving. In contrast to younger drivers, older drivers have much less time to act on the information in highway signs.

What does the world look like for an elderly person? Leon Pastalan (1982) of the University of Michigan designed a special pair of spectacles to simulate the visual experiences of elderly people. The lenses let in less light, reduced acuity, and mimicked the thickened lenses of the eye. The left-hand photo in Figure 14.7 shows a typical scene without the lenses; the right-hand photo shows how the same scene might look to

an elderly person. Notice, for example, that contrasts are blurred and that some objects (such as the arrows on the glass doors) seem to fade drastically. The comparison between the two photos is indeed impressive. However, notice that many important contours and details are still retained in the photo that simulates vision in the elderly.

Many visual abilities decrease as people grow older, and we need to be aware of this problem (Kline et al., 1992). However, the majority of elderly people find that vision still remains adequate for most purposes.

Glaucoma. Unfortunately, an estimated 2,000,000 Americans have glaucoma, and nearly 80,000 are blind from it (Vaughn & Riordan-Eva, 1992). You may recall the discussion of glaucoma in Chapter 3. In **glaucoma,** extra fluid inside the eyeball causes too much pressure, which may damage the optic nerve. The type of glaucoma associated with old age develops gradually rather than suddenly. Also, it is not related to the kinds of problems for which people typically consult an eye specialist, such as needing a new pair of glasses. Regular physical examinations of older people should include an assessment of fluid pressure in the eyeball, just as physical exams include blood pressure assessment. With regular examinations for glaucoma, abnormal eyeball-pressure problems could be detected before they cause damage.

Visual Perception

We have discussed structural changes within the eye as people grow older, and these changes can influence basic visual abilities. Does aging also influence the higher levels of visual processing, the aspects of vision typically associated with perception rather than sensation? Unfortunately, far fewer studies have been conducted on perception in the elderly than on perception in infancy. As a result, our knowledge about visual perception in the elderly is often incomplete.

Some evidence suggests that depth perception is diminished in elderly people (Corso, 1981; Whitbourne & Powers, 1996). For example, binocular disparity seems to be less useful for people over the age of 50. This topic deserves much more research. Elderly people are likely to suffer from broken bones when they fall. If depth perception is really a problem for elderly people, this deficit could contribute to accidental injuries.

Hoyer and Plude (1982) argue that elderly people may be able to compensate in some areas of visual perception. They agree that the visual stimulus reaching the receptors may be somewhat limited because of age-related changes. People who emphasize bottom-up or data-driven approaches to perception might therefore stress the limitations of vision in the elderly. However, Hoyer and Plude point out that we must examine top-down or conceptually driven processes for elderly people. In particular, as Theme 4 of this book emphasizes, our knowledge and expectations can guide perception—even when the "data" are less than ideal.

A study by Cohen and Faulkner (1983), which provides support for Hoyer and Plude's argument, examined how sentence context facilitated the recognition of individual words. In Chapter 5 we discussed the word-superiority ef-

fect; a letter can be recognized more readily within the context of a word. Similarly, in Chapter 10 we saw that auditory perception is influenced by sentence context. If people read the sentence "The dentist advised the children to brush their ____," it should be easy to recognize the last word as *teeth*.

Cohen and Faulkner tested both young (19- to 34-year-old) and old (63- to 80-year-old) people and found that both groups recognized words faster when sentence context was supplied. When the sentence context strongly predicted the final word (as in the dentist sentence), the young and old participants showed similar contextual facilitation. However, when the sentence context suggested several possibilities, the older participants showed significantly greater contextual facilitation than the younger participants. For example, consider the sentence "When they traveled abroad they visited lots of ruins"; many words other than *ruins* could have been used in the sentence. The older people benefited more than the younger ones from these sentence contexts. It seems that older people have learned to take advantage of the hints provided by context, even when the hints are rather subtle. Cohen and Faulkner conclude that elderly people make increased use of context to compensate for decreased sensory processing.

Hearing in Late Adulthood and Old Age

The most common auditory problem associated with aging is presbycusis. (Just as presbyopia means "old eyes," presbycusis means "old hearing.") Technically, **presbycusis** means a progressive loss of hearing in both ears for high-frequency tones. The term actually encompasses a variety of specific auditory disorders. Somewhere between one-tenth and one-third of people over the age of 65 have substantial hearing impairments due to presbycusis (Whitbourne, 1985). Thus, a substantial number of elderly people—though not a majority—suffer from presbycusis.

Interestingly, the incidence of presbycusis is different in cultures that are less noisy. Specifically, elderly people in Africa are less likely than elderly North Americans to experience presbycusis (Bornstein, 1984b). Of course, confounding variables create problems in cross-cultural studies (Corso, 1981). However, the studies do suggest that presbycusis is largely caused by a noisy environment. Presbycusis is not inevitable as people grow old, and its incidence could be decreased by reducing or avoiding loud noises.

Presbycusis and Speech Perception

Elderly people who have nearly normal perception for simple tones are likely to have difficulty with speech perception (Cranford & Stream, 1991; Neils et al., 1991). Thus, the problem does not simply involve sensory loss; some deficits in more central processing must also lead to impaired speech perception.

Because presbycusis involves high-frequency tones, the English phonemes that are most affected by presbycusis are those with high-frequency components. These include the underlined sounds in the following words: plu*s*, *z*ebra, *sh*ip, a*z*ure, wren*ch*, and dru*dge* (Whitbourne & Powers, 1996). A person with presbycusis will often confuse two acoustically similar words, such as *fifty* and *sixty*. Think of the implications of this confusion when discussing the cost of an item, a friend's address, or someone's age. Also, because the /s/ phoneme is especially difficult, English-speaking people with presbycusis will inevitably have trouble distinguishing between the singular and plural forms of a word.

A large-scale study demonstrated how the age-related differences in speech perception are magnified in certain settings (Bergman et al., 1976). The participants in this study were 282 adults between the ages of 20 and 89. Some test sentences were presented normally, without any distortions or other competing noises. As Figure 14.8 shows, people of all ages performed reasonably well on these normal sentences. For example, people in the oldest age group (80 to 89) made only about 15% more errors than people in the youngest age group (20 to 29).

However, the pattern was different when the speech was distorted in several different ways. For example, when the sentences were presented in a reverberation pattern—which resembled listening to echoing speech in a hall with poor acoustics—the elderly group made close to 60% more errors than the youngest age group. In many of these speech-distorted conditions, even people in the 40 to 49 age group made substantially more errors than people in the youngest age group. In other research, Bergman (1980) demonstrated that elderly people are especially likely to have difficulty hearing speech in the context of loud noises or when they are trying to listen to the telephone while people around them are talking. In summary, most elderly people can understand speech well

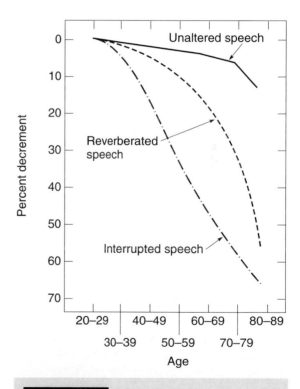

FIGURE 14.8 Age-related differences in intelligibility for speech in a cross-sectional study. Notice that there are few age differences for unaltered speech. With altered speech, however, the performance of older people decreases. (From Bergman et al., 1976)

in an ideal, quiet environment. However, in a noisy environment or when speech is distorted, older people have more difficulty than young people understanding speech.

Practical Implications of Presbycusis

Some people have argued that hearing loss in later life causes emotional problems such as social isolation and depression. However, Whitbourne and Powers (1996) conclude from their examination of the literature that older people with hearing loss are not typically maladjusted or disturbed. Nonetheless, interpersonal relationships may be strained because people may fail to communicate appropriately with hearing-impaired people.

Furthermore, elderly people with hearing impairments may be isolated from the cognitive stimulation of radio, television, and general conversation. Consequently, they may feel that they have little to contribute to a discussion. Clearly, people with normal hearing should help arrange the auditory environment so that a person with hearing impairments can hear as well as possible, and they also need to include the hearing-impaired in conversations and other social interactions.

In this section on older adults, we have seen that sensory and perceptual changes accompany aging. However, these changes are often small, and some areas are not substantially affected by age. Also, individual differences are enormous; only a small proportion of elderly people experience disabling visual or hearing problems. Finally, we should remember Hoyer and Plude's (1982) important point that elderly people may compensate for sensory deficits by taking advantage of top-down processes. Their knowledge and prior learning can guide and clarify their perceptual experiences.

SECTION SUMMARY

Vision and Hearing in Late Adulthood and Old Age

1. Frequently, studies compare elderly people with college students, who differ from them not only in age but probably also in education level, intelligence, health, and medication status. Cognitive slowing may also create larger age differences.
2. The lens of the eye thickens during old age. This thickening has several implications: reduced light to the retina, changes in color perception, presbyopia, and difficulty seeing under glare conditions.
3. Acuity decreases with old age, especially for moving objects, for objects in the periphery, and for nighttime driving.
4. Glaucoma is also a problem for the elderly; depth perception may also be reduced.
5. Older adults may compensate for perceptual deficits by using top-down processing. For example, older people are more likely than younger people to benefit from subtle contextual information.
6. Between one-tenth and one-third of elderly people suffer from presbycusis, although its incidence is lower in less noisy cultures.
7. An important consequence of presbycusis is difficulty in speech perception, which is magnified when speech is distorted or when speech occurs in the presence of loud noises.
8. Although some sensory and perceptual changes occur as people grow older, these are seldom disabling. Individual differences are large, and top-down processing can help to compensate.

REVIEW QUESTIONS

1. To what extent does the infant's visual world resemble the "blooming, buzzing confusion" that William James described? In what areas do infants have more perceptual ability than

you might have imagined before reading this chapter?
2. The section on infancy introduced you to three experimental methods. Name them,

describe how each was used to test perceptual skills, and discuss how you might use each to discover something about infants' capacities for smell.

3. Imagine that you have been asked to design toys that will be interesting for infants under the age of 6 months. What kinds of characteristics should these toys have?

4. As we mentioned, a frequent issue in developmental psychology is the nature–nurture question. What would you conclude about the components of speech perception? What implications does your conclusion suggest for the development of language?

5. In what ways do young infants appreciate the relationship between sights and sounds? Spend a few minutes moving around your room, moving objects and making noises with them. What other aspect of intermodal perception would be interesting to test with infants? Be specific about which of the three experimental methods you would use, and provide details about the study you would design to test your hypothesis.

6. Develop a time line of perceptual development (i.e., what ability has developed by a given month). Be sure to include both vision and hearing. Given that various processes

are interrelated and that they develop at different rates, what implications can you derive from differences in development of various perceptual abilities?

7. Studying perception in the very young and the very old presents particular challenges to a researcher. Describe the problems these researchers face and the methodological solutions they have adopted.

8. How do the visual and auditory abilities of infants differ from those of elderly people? What similarities and differences do you notice? How well do infants and elderly people see objects closer than 6 inches, or objects that are very far away? How readily do infants and elderly people hear speech sounds?

9. Suppose that an elderly relative will be visiting you for the weekend. What kinds of information from this chapter would be helpful in making the visit as successful as possible? Be sure to discuss both vision and hearing.

10. Throughout the text, you have seen instances of the importance of context for perception (Theme 2). Compare examples of the role of context found in this chapter with examples from earlier chapters.

NEW TERMS

the nature–nurture question (444)
preference method (446)
vergence movements (448)
saccadic movements (448)
habituation method (449)
dishabituation (449)

visual cliff (451)
high-amplitude sucking procedure (454)
conditioning method (456)
confounding variable (459)
cognitive slowing (459)

cataracts (460)
presbyopia (460)
bifocals (460)
glaucoma (461)
presbycusis (462)

RECOMMENDED READINGS

Gibson, E. J. (1987). Introductory essay: What does infant perception tell us about theories of perception? *Journal of Experimental Psychology: Human Perception and Performance, 13,* 515–523. Eleanor Gibson is one of the pioneers in the area of infant perception. Her clearly written overview of the discipline is superb!

Goodman, J. C., & Nusbaum, H. C. (Eds.). (1994). *The development of speech perception: The transition from speech sounds to spoken words.* Cambridge, MA: MIT Press. This recent volume provides an excellent introduction to the discipline; the chapters by Jusczyk and by Werker are especially interesting.

Granrud, C. E. (Ed.). (1993). *Visual perception and cognition in infancy*. Hillsdale, NJ: Erlbaum. This useful book contains chapters on many aspects of infant vision, including color vision, motion perception, and theoretical issues.

Trehub, S. E. (1993). The music listening skills of infants and young children. In T. J. Tighe & W. J. Dowling (Eds.), *Psychology and music: The understanding of melody and rhythm* (pp. 161–176). Hillsdale, NJ: Erlbaum. In addition to discussing melody perception, Trehub's review also examines infants' appreciation of rhythm and children's understanding of emotional aspects of music.

Whitbourne, S. K. (1985). *The aging body: Physiological changes and psychological consequences*. New York: Springer-Verlag. Every public and college library should own this clearly written and comprehensive book, which contains chapters on age changes in touch, taste, and smell, as well as vision and audition.

Glossary

A guide has been provided for words whose pronunciation may be ambiguous; the accented syllable is indicated by italics.

A-beta fibers One of the three types of nerve fibers that transmit pain. The A-beta fibers are relatively large and moderately fast.

A-delta fibers One of the three types of nerve fibers that transmit pain. The A-delta fibers are relatively small and fast. Their speed likely makes them responsible for the initial sharp pain felt in double pain. (*See also* Double pain.)

Absolute pitch People with absolute pitch are extremely accurate in identifying the pitch of an isolated tone or producing a requested tone.

Absolute threshold The smallest intensity required for a stimulus to be reported 50% of the time.

Accommodation Change in the shape of the lens of the eye, necessary to keep an image in proper focus on the retina; it occurs as the observer focuses on objects at different distances.

Achromatic (a-crow-*maa*-tick) Without color.

Achromatic afterimage Image that appears after the presentation of a stimulus; both the stimulus and the afterimage are uncolored, and one is the opposite of the other.

Achromatic colors Colors found along the middle axis of the color spindle—white, shades of gray, and black.

Achromatopsia A disorder of the visual cortex leading to an inability to see color.

Action potentials Short bursts of electrical activity such as those generated by the ganglion cells.

Active touch Touch perception in which a person actively explores objects and touches them.

Acuity Degree of precision with which fine details can be seen.

Acupuncture A procedure to relieve pain that involves inserting thin needles into various locations on the body.

Adaptation Change in sensitivity. (*See also* Dark adaptation and Light adaptation.)

Adaptation stimulus In dark adaptation studies, the intense light to which observers are exposed prior to the darkness.

Additive mixture In color mixing, the addition of beams of light from different parts of the spectrum.

Afferent fibers Nerve fibers carrying information from the receptors to the brain.

Affordances Actions one could perform with objects—a concept introduced by James J. Gibson.

Ageusia The inability to perceive taste.

Akinetopsia The inability to perceive motion, caused by damage to the cortex.

Albedo Proportion of light reflected by an object; the albedo remains constant despite changes in the amount of light falling on the object.

Albinos Individuals who are born without pigmentation. The lack of pigmentation in the iris leads to visual problems.

Amacrine cells (*am*-ah-krihn) Cells in the retina that allow the ganglion cells to communicate with each other. They also allow the bipolar cells to communicate with each other.

Ambiguous figure–ground relationships   Situations in which the figure and the ground reverse from time to time, with the figure becoming the ground and then becoming the figure again.

Ames room   Room specially designed to produce distance and size illusions (see Figure 6.28).

Amplitude   In vision, the height of the light wave; amplitude is related to the brightness or lightness of a visual stimulus. In audition, the change in pressure created by sound waves; amplitude is related to the loudness of an auditory stimulus.

Analgesic medication   Class of drugs specifically designed to relieve pain.

Analytic sense   Sense in which the observer can detect the separate parts. For example, in hearing, an observer can typically separate two notes played together.

Analytical orientation   In contrast to a holistic orientation, an analytical orientation emphasizes the importance of the components that combine to form our perceptual experiences.

Anomalous trichromat   The most common form of color deficiency. An anomalous trichromat has all three cone systems, but one of the systems has an abnormal absorption spectrum.

Anosmia   Inability to perceive smells.

Antagonistic surrounds   The surrounding or outer region of a receptive field that responds in an opposite manner to the inner region. For example, if the inner region is excited by a light stimulus, the outer or antagonistic surround will be inhibited by it.

Anterior chamber   The area directly behind the cornea and in front of the iris—contains the aqueous humor.

Aperture   The part of a camera analogous to the pupil.

Apparent-distance theory   Theory of the moon illusion in which the moon seems to be farther from the viewer when it is on the horizon than when it is at the zenith.

Aqueous humor (*a*-kwee-us)   Watery liquid found between the cornea and the lens.

Area 17   Area of the visual cortex where the neurons from the lateral geniculate nucleus terminate. Also called the striate cortex or the primary visual cortex.

Ascending series   Series of trials in the method of limits in which the stimulus is systematically increased.

Astigmatism   Visual disorder in which the cornea is not perfectly round. Therefore, if the eye is focused for some parts of the cornea, it is out of focus for others.

Atmospheric perspective   Distance cue provided by the fact that distant objects often look blurry and bluish in contrast to nearby objects.

Attack   In music perception, the beginning buildup of a tone.

Attention   Focusing or concentration of mental activity.

Audiometry   Measurement of the sensitivity of audition, typically by measuring thresholds for tones of differing frequency.

Auditory adaptation   Decrease in the perceived loudness of a tone after it has been presented continuously.

Auditory fatigue   Change in thresholds for other tones that occurs after a loud tone is presented and then turned off.

Auditory localization   Ability to identify the location of sound sources in the environment.

Auditory nerve   Bundle of nerve fibers that carries information from the inner ear to the auditory cortex.

Autokinesis (ah-toe-kin-*nee*-siss)   Illusion of movement in which a stationary object, with no clear background, appears to move.

Autostereogram   Developed by Tyler, an autostereogram is a single image that contains binocular depth information when viewed appropriately.

β (beta) (*bay*-tuh)   Symbol for criterion, which in signal detection theory is the measure that assesses the observer's willingness to say, "I detect the stimulus."

Backward masking   Phenomenon in which accuracy is reduced for reporting a stimulus because it was followed rapidly by a second stimulus. Backward masking is found in both vision and audition.

Basilar membrane   Membrane on the base of the organ of Corti, in the inner ear.

Beats   Changes in loudness produced by combinations of pure tones with similar frequencies.

Behaviorism Approach to psychology that stresses the objective description of an organism's behavior.

Bifocals Special eyeglasses that have two types of lenses, one for viewing distant objects and one for viewing close objects.

Binaural (buy-*nohr*-ul) Pertaining to both ears.

Binocular disparity Source of distance information provided by the fact that the two eyes have slightly different views of the world.

Binocular rivalry Occurs when the images falling on each eye are too different to be fused into one unified percept.

Biological motion Pattern of movement of living things.

Bipolar cells (*buy*-pole-ur) Cells in the retina that receive information from the rods and cones and pass it on to ganglion cells.

Blind spot Region of the eye in which there is no vision because the optic disk contains no light receptors.

Blindsight Blindsight occurs when a person has some visual experience in spite of damage to the visual cortex that would typically preclude such experience.

Blobs "Blob"-shaped cells distributed throughout the column structure in the primary cortex; these cells are responsive to color.

Bottom-up processing Approach that emphasizes how the sensory receptors register the stimuli, with information flowing from this low level upward to the higher (more cognitive) levels.

Boundary extension A tendency to report seeing more of a scene than was actually visible.

Braille Representation of letters in the alphabet by a system of raised dots, used in books for the blind.

Brightness Psychological reaction corresponding to the intensity of light waves; the apparent intensity of a light source.

C-fibers One of the three types of nerve fibers that transmit pain. The C-fibers are relatively small and slow. Their speed likely makes them responsible for the terminal dull pain felt in double pain. (*See also* Double pain.)

Cataract Clouding of the lens of the eye, caused by injury or disease.

Categorical perception Grouping perceptions into categories. People have difficulty discriminating between members of the same category, even though discriminations can be readily made between members of different categories.

Categorization Process of treating objects as similar or equivalent, as in categorical perception.

Cerebral cortex (suh-*ree*-brul) Outer part of the brain.

Chemical senses Smell and taste.

Choroid (*kore*-oid) Layer on the back of the eye just inside the sclera. The choroid provides nutrients for the retina and absorbs extra light.

Chromatic adaptation Decrease in response to a color after it is viewed continuously for a long time.

Cilia (*sill*-ee-uh) Tiny hairlike protrusions from the receptor cells in the auditory and olfactory systems.

Ciliary muscle (*sill*-ee-air-ee) Muscle that controls the shape of the lens.

Cochlea (*cock*-lee-ah) Bony, fluid-filled structure containing the receptors for auditory stimuli.

Cochlear duct (*cock*-lee-er) One of the canals in the cochlea.

Cochlear microphonic Phenomenon in which a waveform falling on the ear is replicated by graded potentials from the outer hair cells.

Cochlear nucleus A structure in auditory processing to which the auditory nerve travels after leaving the inner ear.

Cognition Acquisition, storage, retrieval, and use of knowledge.

Cognitive–behavioral approaches In the treatment of pain, methods that help the patient develop more adaptive cognitive and behavioral reactions to a physical problem.

Color constancy Tendency to see the hue of an object as staying the same despite changes in the color of the light falling on it.

Color solid Three-dimensional figure, resembling two cones joined together, that represents the hue, saturation, and lightness of all colors; also called a color spindle.

Color spindle A color solid.

Color stereopsis Depth differences due to viewing color stimuli binocularly through some lenses (such as magnifying glasses).

Color vision deficiencies Disorders or difficulties in discriminating different colors, commonly called color-blindness.

Color wheel Circle with the different wavelengths arranged around the edge; used to represent the colors of the spectrum.

Column In the visual cortex, a vertical series of cells that have the highest response rate to a line of one particular orientation.

Common region An area determined by edges or shading, within which we tend to group stimuli together (see Figure 5.10).

Comparison stimulus The stimulus in discrimination studies that varies throughout the experiment.

Complementary hues Hues whose additive mixture makes gray, such as blue and yellow.

Complex cells Cells in the primary visual cortex that respond most vigorously to moving stimuli.

Complex tones Tones that cannot be represented by a simple sound wave and are more likely to be encountered in everyday life.

Computational approach Approach to perception suggesting that although the stimuli themselves are rich in information, higher-level processes involving general physical principles are also necessary for perception to occur.

Conceptually driven processing Approach that emphasizes the importance of the observers' concepts and cognitive processes in shaping perception.

Conditioning method In testing infant perception, a method in which the experimenter selects a response that the baby can make and delivers a reward when the baby makes that particular response. Later, the experimenter tests for generalization to new stimuli.

Conduction deafness Type of deafness that involves problems in conducting the sound stimulus, occurring in either the external ear or the middle ear.

Cone of confusion Cone-shaped area around each ear in which the auditory system receives the same set of information about the location of the source of the sound.

Cones Photoreceptors used for color vision under well-lit conditions.

Confounding variable Factor in an experiment—other than the factor being studied—that may be responsible for the effects being observed.

Consonance Combination of two or more tones, played at the same time, that is judged pleasant.

Constancy Tendency for qualities of objects to seem to stay the same, despite changes in the way people view the objects.

Constrict Refers to the action of the iris that makes the pupil become smaller.

Constructivist theory Theory that proposes that the perceiver has an internal constructive (or problem-solving) process that transforms the incoming stimulus into the perception.

Contour Location at which lightness, brightness, or color changes suddenly; also called an edge.

Contrast sensitivity function Diagram that shows the relationship between spatial frequency and sensitivity.

Converge When viewing nearby objects, each eye rotates in its socket, bringing the pupil toward the nose. (*See also* Diverge.)

Convergence (of eyes) Type of vergence movement used when looking at nearby objects. (*See also* Converge.)

Convergence (of photoreceptors) Refers to the number of photoreceptors that synapse onto each ganglion cell. For the rods, a great deal of convergence occurs (perhaps 100 rods per ganglion cell). For the cones, much less convergence occurs (a few cones per ganglion cell).

Cornea (*kore*-nee-uh) Clear membrane just in front of the iris.

Corollary discharge theory Theory of motion perception in which the visual system compares the movement registered on the retina with signals that the brain sends regarding eye movements.

Correct rejection In signal detection theory, a correct rejection occurs when a signal is not presented and the observer does not report it.

Correspondence problem The correspondence problem is the difficulty our visual system can face in linking the input from the two retinas. The difficulty occurs in both distance and motion perception when input at similar areas of the two retinas differs.

Cortical magnification Overrepresentation of information from the fovea with respect to the cortex.

Counterirritants Methods of pain control that stimulate or irritate one area so that pain is diminished in another.

Criterion The measure in signal detection theory that assesses the observer's willingness to say, "I detect the stimulus."

Critical band The range of frequencies that can be masked by a particular tone is referred to as the critical band of that tone.

Cross-adaptation In odor perception, the change in threshold for one odor that occurs after exposure to another.

Cross-enhancement Lowering a threshold for one substance after adaptation to another.

Cross-modality matching Technique in which observers are asked to judge stimuli in one mode of perception (such as hearing) by providing responses from another mode (such as sight).

Crossed disparity Objects nearer to the viewer than to the focal point create crossed disparity, with the image falling outside of the focal point on each retina.

Cue Any factor that lets an observer make a decision automatically, such as a distance cue; cues do not require elaborate thought.

Cycle For sound stimuli, a cycle is the full range of pressure changes from normal, to high, to normal, to low, and back to normal.

d′ (dee prime) In signal detection theory, an index of sensitivity; *d′* depends upon the intensity of the stimulus and the sensitivity of the observer.

Dark adaptation Increase in sensitivity that occurs as the eyes remain in the dark.

Dark adaptation curve Graph showing the relationship between the time in the dark and the threshold for the test stimulus.

Dark focus An intermediate resting state of the lens due to relaxation of the ciliary muscles—thought to be caused by a balance of input from the sympathetic and parasympathetic systems.

Data-driven processing Approach that emphasizes how sensory receptors register stimuli, with information flowing from this low level upward to the higher, more cognitive levels.

Decay In music perception, the decrease in amplitude at the end of a tone.

Decibel (dB) One measure of the amount of pressure created by a stimulus such as a sound wave.

Depolarization Process in which a neuron changes from its resting potential to a less negative potential.

Depth of field Refers to the range over which we can see objects clearly. When the pupil is smaller, we are able to see objects over a wider range more clearly than when the pupil is larger—we have a greater depth of field.

Depth perception Perception of objects as three-dimensional, having depth in addition to height and width.

Dermis Middle layer of skin, which makes new skin cells.

Descending series Series of trials in the method of limits in which the stimulus is systematically decreased.

Detection In acuity measures, a task that requires the observer to judge whether a target is present or absent.

Deuteranopes (*doo*-tur-uh-nopes) People who are dichromats and are insensitive to red and green.

Dichromat (*die*-krow-mat) Person who requires only two primary colors to match his or her perception of all other colors due to a missing cone system.

Difference threshold The smallest change in a stimulus that is required to produce a difference noticeable 50% of the time.

Diffuse bipolar cells Diffuse bipolar cells make several connections with different photoreceptors, typically rods, initiating the convergence process. (*See also* Midget bipolar cells.)

Dilate Refers to the action of the iris that makes the pupil become larger.

Direct perception approach Approach to perception proposed by J. J. Gibson. It suggests that the stimuli themselves contain all the necessary information for perception to occur—learning and cognition are not needed.

Discrimination In psychophysics, the smallest amount that a stimulus must be changed to be perceived as just noticeably different.

Disc shedding Process of shedding old discs in the photoreceptors.

Dishabituation Increase in looking time that occurs when a new stimulus is presented following repeated presentation of another stimulus.

Disocclusion (dis-uh-*clue*-zyun) Process in which a moving object systematically uncovers the background.

Disparity-selective cells Disparity-selective cells are important for depth perception because they have high rates of electrical discharge when stimuli are registered on different (disparate) areas of the two retinas.

Dissonance Combination of two or more tones, played at the same time, that is judged unpleasant.

Distal stimulus Stimulus or object as it exists in the world, as opposed to the proximal stimulus.

Distance perception Distance perception refers to your ability to perceive the distance relationships within the visual scene. (*See also* Depth perception.)

Diverge Rotation of the eyes to bring the pupils to the center, for viewing distant objects. (*See also* Converge.)

Divergence Type of vergence movement of the eyes in which the eyes rotate away from each other. (*See also* Diverge.)

Divisionism A painting technique that is based on the interactive effects of larger patches of colors than pointillism. (*See also* Pointillism.)

Doctrine of specific nerve energies Theory proposed by Müller that each different sensory nerve has its own characteristic type of activity and therefore produces different sensations.

Double pain Experience of sharp pain followed by dull pain, presumably caused by A-delta and C-fibers.

Duplex perception Kind of auditory perception in which the listener perceives both a speech and a nonspeech sound from the same auditory information—originally thought to provide support for a distinct speech module.

Duplicity theory Approach to vision that proposes two separate kinds of photoreceptors: rods and cones.

Dyne Unit for measuring energy.

Dysgeusia Damage to a taste nerve can lead to the perception of a taste that is not present.

Eardrum Thin piece of membrane that vibrates in response to sound waves.

Ear infection Condition in which the eustachian tube becomes swollen, cutting off the middle ear from the respiratory tract.

Echolocation Sensory technique used by bats, in which the emission of a high-frequency sound is translated into a measure of distance based on the time elapsed before the sound returns.

Edge Place where there is a sudden change in brightness, lightness, or color; an edge is necessary for vision.

Efferent fibers Nerve fibers carrying information from the brain to the receptors.

Egocentric distance Distance between the observer and an object, as used in depth perception.

Electromagnetic radiation All forms of waves produced by electrically charged particles.

Emmert's law Principle that an afterimage appears larger if it is projected on a more distant surface.

Empiricism Approach to perception that states that basic sensory experiences are combined, through learning, to produce perception.

Encapsulated endings Small capsules or bulbs on the end of some kinds of skin receptors.

Endorphins Morphine-like substances that occur naturally within the body.

End-stopped cells Some simple and complex cortical cells are referred to as end-stopped cells because they respond most vigorously if the stimulus ends within the cell's receptive field.

Envelope The shape of a traveling wave determined by connecting the maximum and minimum points of the wave.

Epidermis Outer layer of skin, which has many layers of dead skin cells.

Epistemology Branch of philosophy that concerns how we acquire knowledge.

Equal loudness contour Graph showing the relationship between tone frequency and the number of decibels required to produce a tone of equal loudness.

Errors of anticipation Errors in psychophysics testing in which observers provide a different answer from the one they provided on the last trial; they "jump the gun."

Errors of habituation Errors in psychophysics testing in which observers keep giving the same answer as on the last trial.

Eustachian tube (you-*stay*-she-un) Structure in the middle ear that connects the ear to the throat.

Evoked acoustic emissions Phenomenon in which a sound presented to the ear is echoed back.

Excitation Stimulation of neurons sufficient to generate an action potential.

External auditory canal Tube that runs inward from the pinna to the eardrum.

Extrastriate cortex (*ex*-tra-*strie*-ate) Region of the visual cortex that receives information already processed by the primary visual (or striate) cortex as well as from the superior colliculus.

Eye-movement explanation Explanation of illusions in terms of eye-movement patterns.

False alarm In signal detection theory, a false alarm occurs when the signal is not presented yet the observer reports it nevertheless.

Familiar size An object's customary or standardized size, used as a source of information in distance perception.

Far point The farthest point that the viewer can see clearly.

Farsighted Referring to people who cannot see nearby objects.

Feature-integration approach Approach suggesting that we use different levels of processing for different kinds of shape perception.

Fechner's law (feck-nurz) ($R = k \log I$) Fechner's law says that the magnitude of the psychological reaction (R) is equal to a constant (k) multiplied by the logarithm of the intensity (I) of the physical stimulus.

Field dependent Reliant on the orientation of the room to determine an upright position.

Field independent Reliant on the orientation of one's own body to determine an upright position.

Figure In shape perception, a distinct shape with clearly defined edges.

Fixation pause The pause between two saccadic eye movements.

Flavor Experience of taste, smell, touch, pressure, and pain associated with substances in the mouth.

Floaters Solid matter suspended in the vitreous humor that will become visible under appropriate conditions.

Focused attention In Treisman's feature-integration theory, the identification of objects in the second stage of processing.

Form An area set off from the surrounding space by its edges.

Formants Horizontal bands of concentrated sound in a speech spectrogram.

Fourier analysis (foo-*ryay*) Process in which a stimulus is analyzed into its component sine waves.

Fourier synthesis Process of adding together a series of sine waves; the reverse of Fourier analysis.

Fovea (*foe*-vee-ah) Central region of the retina in which vision is sharpest.

Free nerve endings Skin receptors that do not have bulbs or capsules on the end nearest the epidermis.

Frequency Number of cycles a sound wave completes in 1 second.

Frequency theory Theory of auditory processing that proposes that the entire basilar membrane vibrates at a frequency that matches the frequency of a tone.

Frequency tuning curve Graph showing the relationship between the frequency of an auditory stimulus and an auditory nerve fiber's response rate.

f-stop The setting on a camera that controls the aperture size; analogous to the human iris.

Fundamental frequency The component of a complex sound wave that has the lowest frequency.

G-proteins Short for GTP-binding proteins, this family of about 1,000 proteins is important in vision and the chemical senses.

Ganglion cells (*gang*-glee-un) Cells that run from the bipolar cells of the retina toward the brain.

Ganzfeld (*gahnz*-feldt) A visual field that has no contours, based on the German word for "whole field."

Gate-control theory Theory that proposes that pain perception is a complex process in which the neural fibers interact and the brain also has an influence.

General Mechanism account Theory of speech perception positing that speech and other kinds of auditory information are processed by the same mechanisms (no special speech module).

Geons (geometric icons) Basic shapes from which objects may be constructed.

Gestalt (geh-*shstahlt*) Configuration or pattern.

Gestalt approach Approach to perception that emphasizes that we perceive objects as well-organized, whole structures rather than as separated, isolated parts.

Gibsonian approach (gibb-*sone*-ee-un) Approach to perception that emphasizes that perceptions are rich and elaborate because the stimuli in the environment are rich with information rather than because thought processes provide that richness; the Gibsonian approach is named after psychologist J. J. Gibson. (*See also* Direct perception approach.)

Glabrous skin Kind of skin on the soles of the feet and the palms of the hands; does not contain hairs.

Glaucoma (glaw-*koe*-mah) Visual disorder in which excessive fluid inside the eye causes too much pressure, ultimately producing damage to the ganglion cells in the retina and to the optic nerve.

Golgi tendon organs (*goal*-jee) Receptors in tendons that respond when the muscle exerts tension on the tendon.

Ground In shape perception, the background that appears to be behind the figure.

Ground theory Theory proposed by J. J. Gibson, in which distance perception depends upon information provided by surfaces in the environment.

Gymnema sylvestre A taste modifier that reduces the intensity of sweet substances.

Habituation method In testing infant perception, a method based on a decrease in attention to repeated stimulation.

Hair cells Receptors for auditory stimuli, located in the organ of Corti.

Hairy skin Type of skin that covers most of the human body and contains hairs.

Haptic perception Perception of objects by touch.

Harmonics Those multiples of the fundamental frequency that are present in a complex sound; also called overtones.

Hedonics (hih-*donn*-icks) Area of perception that involves judgments of pleasantness and unpleasantness.

Height cues Distance information provided by the fact that objects near the horizon are farther away than those far from the horizon.

Helicotrema (*hell*-ih-koe-*treh*-ma) Tiny opening at the end of the vestibular canal in the inner ear.

High-amplitude sucking procedure Technique used to assess infant perception, in which babies suck on a pacifier attached to a recording device; a sufficiently fast sucking rate produces a stimulus such as a speech sound.

Hit In signal detection theory, a hit occurs when the signal is presented and the observer reports it.

Holistic orientation Characterized by the Gestalt approach, a holistic orientation argues that the final percept that we experience is not simply the sum of its parts. (*See also* Analytical orientation.)

Horizontal cells Cells in the retina that allow the photoreceptors to communicate with each other.

Horizontal–vertical illusion An illusion shaped like an inverted T, in which the vertical line looks longer than the horizontal line (see Demonstration 6.8).

Horopter An imaginary curved line that can be drawn to represent all the points that are the same distance from the observer as the focal object.

Hue Psychological reaction of color that corresponds to the length of light waves.

Hypercolumn A sequence of 18 to 20 adjacent columns in the visual cortex. A hypercolumn includes enough columns to complete a full cycle of stimulus-orientation preferences.

Hypermetropic Refers to people who are farsighted and cannot see nearby objects.

Hyperpolarization Process in which a neuron changes from its resting potential to a more negative potential.

Hypnosis Altered state of consciousness in which a person is susceptible to suggestions from the hypnotist. Hypnosis is sometimes used to help people suffering from chronic pain.

Hz (hurtz) Abbreviation for the name of Heinrich Hertz; Hz represents the number of cycles a sound wave completes in 1 second.

Illusion An incorrect perception.

Illusory conjunction In Treisman's feature-integration theory, an inappropriate combination of features from two stimuli.

Illusory contour Phenomenon in which contours are seen even though they are not physically present.

Illusory movement Perception that an object is moving even though it is really stationary.

Impedance Resistance to the passage of sound waves.

Impedance mismatch Condition in which the impedances for two media differ; sound waves cannot be readily transmitted when an impedance mismatch exists.

Incorrect comparison explanation An explanation of illusions that states that observers base their judgments on the incorrect parts of the figure.

Incus A small anvil-shaped bone in the middle ear.

Indirect perception approaches Approaches that assume that the information received by the senses is insufficient by itself to arrive at an accurate description of the world.

Induced movement Illusion of movement that occurs when a visual frame of reference moves in one direction and produces the illusion that a stationary target is moving in the opposite direction.

Inducing areas Regions of an illusory contour figure in which true contours exist.

Inducing lines Lines in an illusory contour figure that encourage the perception of illusory contours.

Inferior colliculus (kole-*lick*-you-luss) Structure in auditory processing between the superior olivary nucleus and the medial geniculate nucleus.

Inferior temporal cortex The inferior temporal cortex is located on the lower part of the side of the cortex and is important for object perception.

Information-processing approach The approach that identifies psychological processes and connects them by specific patterns of information flow. (*See also* Cognition.)

Inhibition Stimulation of a neuron that results in a reduced rate of action potentials.

Inner hair cells Auditory receptors on the inner side of the organ of Corti, most likely sensitive to a tone's frequency.

Interaural intensity difference Cue to auditory localization based on small sound intensity differences between the two ears.

Interaural time difference Cue to auditory localization based on small differences between the time a sound arrives in each ear.

Interblobs Cells between blobs that are sensitive to orientation and not wavelength.

Interposition Distance cue in which one object partly covers another.

Intraocular lens Substitute lens inserted into the eye after surgical removal of a defective lens.

Invariants In the theory of J. J. Gibson, the aspects of perception that persist over time and space and are left unchanged by certain kinds of transformations.

Involuntary eye movements Unavoidable small eye movements that occur during fixation.

Iris Ring of muscles in the eye surrounding the pupil; the colored part of the visible eye.

Ishihara test (ih-she-*hah*-rah) Test for color deficiencies, in which the observer tries to detect a number hidden in a pattern of different-colored circles. (See Color Plate 5.)

Just noticeable difference (jnd) Smallest difference in sensation that can be noticed.

Kemp echoes Phenomenon in which a sound presented to the ear is echoed back.

Kinesthesia Sensation of movement or static limb position.

Kinesthetic information Nonvisual information (such as muscular information) that can be used to judge distance.

Kinetic depth effect Phenomenon in which a figure looks flat when it is stable but appears to have depth once it moves.

Lateral geniculate nucleus (LGN) (jen-*ick*-you-late) Part of the thalamus where most of the ganglion cells transfer their information to new neurons.

Lateral inhibition Inhibition of neural activity for points near the part of the retina that is stimulated by light.

Lateralization The perception that sounds move from side to side inside the listener's head, because the sounds are delivered through headphones. (*See also* Auditory localization.)

Lateral superior olivary nucleus Part of the superior olivary nucleus that is specialized for processing high-frequency auditory information.

Law of closure Gestalt law that says that a figure is perceived as closed and complete rather than containing a blank portion.

Law of common fate Gestalt law that says that items perceived as moving in the same direction are seen as belonging together.

Law of good continuation Gestalt law that says that a line is perceived as continuing in the same direction it was going prior to intersection.

Law of Prägnanz (*Prahg*-nahntz) Gestalt law that says that when faced with several alternate perceptions, the one that will actually occur is the one with the best, simplest, and most stable shape.

Law of proximity Gestalt law that says that objects near each other are grouped as one unit.

Law of similarity Gestalt law that says that items that are similar are grouped together.

Laws of grouping Ideas that explain the way we organize or group information.

Left visual field Portion of the visual world on the left-hand side.

Lemniscal system (lemm-*niss*-kull) One of the two neuronal systems responsible for the skin senses. It has larger nerve fibers and faster transmission than the spinothalamic system.

Lens Structure inside the eye whose shape changes to bring objects into focus.

Light Portion of the electromagnetic radiation spectrum made up of waves that range in length from about 400 nm to about 700 nm.

Light adaptation Decline in sensitivity that occurs as the eyes remain in the light.

Lightness Psychological reaction corresponding to the amount of light reflected by an object.

Lightness constancy Phenomenon in which an object seems to stay the same lightness despite changes in the amount of light falling on it.

Limbic system A portion of the brain that is involved in regulating behaviors such as fleeing, fighting, feeding, and sexual behavior.

Linear perspective Distance cue provided by the fact that parallel lines appear to meet in the distance.

Logarithm Type of numerical transformation; the logarithm of a number equals the exponent to which 10 must be raised to equal that number.

Long-range process Analysis of the kind of movement that occurs over a long distance or time.

Loudness Psychological reaction that corresponds roughly to a tone's amplitude.

Mach band (mock) Phenomenon in which bright and dark regions are perceived within a single stripe, although there is no corresponding variation in the physical distribution of light.

Magnitude estimation Technique in which the observer is told that one particular stimulus is to be assigned a certain value, and this value is used as a "yardstick" to estimate the magnitude of all future stimuli.

Magno pathway The magno (short for magnocellular) pathway is involved in the perception of illumination differences and moderate or rapid movement. The pathway begins with information passing from the photoreceptors through diffuse bipolar cells and parasol ganglion cells.

Maintained activity In the absence of a visual stimulus, a ganglion cell fires at a relatively low rate, referred to as spontaneous or maintained activity.

Malleus (*mal*-lee-uss) A small hammer-shaped bone in the middle ear.

Manner of articulation One of the three dimensions in pronouncing consonants; it specifies how completely the air is blocked and where it passes.

Margin illusion We usually perceive the margins of a page as taking up little room, but in fact they can take up over a third of the page.

Masking A phenomenon in which one stimulus makes another stimulus difficult to perceive. The masking stimulus can precede the obscured stimulus (forward masking) or it can follow the obscured stimulus (backward masking).

McGurk effect Occurs when listeners are exposed to one phoneme and simultaneously observe a speaker saying a different one. Listeners report hearing a completely different phoneme that is actually a combination of the two.

Medial geniculate nucleus (jen-*ick*-you-late) Structure involved in auditory processing that lies between the inferior colliculus and the auditory cortex.

Medial superior olivary nucleus Part of the superior olivary nucleus specialized for processing low-frequency information.

Mel scale In audition, a scale produced by magnitude estimation, in which a 1000-Hz tone with an intensity of 60 dB is assigned a pitch of 1000 mels, and comparison tones are assigned other, relative mel values.

Memory color Phenomenon in which an object's typical color influences the observer's perception of the object's actual color.

Mesopic Mesopic conditions exist when the light is sufficiently bright that cones are still functional, but sufficiently dim that rods can also function.

Metameric matching Process in which a subject can match any hue of a single wavelength by combining various amounts of three different colored lights (usually red, green, and blue).

Metamers Pairs of lights that look exactly the same but are composed of physically different stimuli.

Method of adjustment Psychophysical technique in which observers adjust the intensity of the stimulus until it is just barely detectable.

Method of adjustment for measuring discrimination Psychophysical technique in which observers themselves adjust the comparison stimulus until it seems to match the standard stimulus.

Method of constant stimuli Psychophysical technique in which the stimuli are presented in random order.

Method of constant stimuli for measuring discrimination Psychophysical technique in which the experimenter presents the comparison stimuli in random order and asks observers to judge whether each comparison stimulus is greater than or less than the standard stimulus.

Method of limits Psychophysical technique in which the researcher begins with a stimulus that is clearly noticeable and then presents increasingly weaker stimuli until observers are unable to detect the stimulus; these trials alternate with trials in which increasingly stronger stimuli are presented.

Method of limits for measuring discrimination Psychophysical technique in which the standard stimulus remains the same, and the comparison stimulus varies from low to high on some series and from high to low on other series.

Mexican-hat filter A filter with characteristics similar to the receptive fields found in the visual system (see Figures 5.13 and 5.14b). Computational theorists have demonstrated that this filter is capable of extracting edges from visual input.

Microelectrode Very small electrode used in single cell recording.

Microspectrophotometry Procedure in which an extremely small beam of light from one part of the color spectrum is passed through individual receptors in dissected retinal tissue. The amount of light absorbed at each wavelength is then measured.

Microvilli (*my*-crow-*vill*-lie) Tips of the taste receptors.

Midget bipolar cells Cells that connect to a single cone or a small number of cones, initiating the parvo pathway. (*See also* Diffuse bipolar cells.)

Midget ganglion cells Cells that carry information away from the midget bipolar cells, continuing the parvo pathway. (*See also* Parasol ganglion cells.)

Minimum audible angle (MAA) The smallest difference (measured in degrees) between two sound sources such that a listener can perceive them as coming from two different sources.

Miracle fruit A taste modifier that sweetens the taste of sour substances.

Misapplied constancy explanation According to the misapplied constancy explanation, an illusion occurs because observers interpret portions of the illusion as cues for maintaining size constancy.

Miss In signal detection theory, a miss occurs when a signal is presented and the observer does not report it.

Missing fundamental An auditory illusion in which only the harmonics but not the fundamental frequency of a complex sound are present. Nonetheless, listeners do not perceive its absence.

Module A special-purpose neural mechanism used to process one kind of information.

Monaural (monn-*ahr*-ul) Pertaining to only one ear.

Monochromat (*mah*-noe-crow-mat) Person who requires only one color to match his or her perception of all other colors; every hue looks the same to this person.

Monochromatic colors Colors produced by a single wavelength.

Monocular factors Factors seen with one eye that can provide information about distance.

Moon illusion Illusion in which the moon at the horizon looks bigger than the moon at its highest position.

Motility The independent elongation and contraction of the outer hair cells that enhances our ability to make fine frequency discriminations.

Motion parallax Distance cue provided by the fact that as the observer moves the head sideways, objects at different distances appear to move in different directions and at different speeds.

Motion perspective Continuous change in the way objects look as the observer moves about in the world.

Motor theory of speech perception   Theory in which humans possess a specialized device that allows them to decode speech stimuli and permits them to connect the stimuli they hear with the way these sounds are produced by the speaker.

Movement aftereffects   Illusion of movement that occurs after looking at continuous movement. When looking at another surface, it will seem to move in a direction opposite that of the original movement.

MSG   Monosodium glutamate; a substance used in cooking that reduces the thresholds for sour and bitter tastes.

Müller–Lyer illusion (*mew*-lur *lie*-ur)   Famous illusion in which two lines of the same length appear to be different in length because of wings pointing outward on one line and inward on the other line (see Figure 6.20).

Muscle spindles   Muscle spindles are receptors that are located within the muscle itself, which are important for kinesthesia. (*See also* Kinesthesia.)

Myopic   Refers to people who are nearsighted and cannot see faraway objects.

Nanometer (nm)   One-billionth of a meter; measure used for wavelength.

Nasal cavity   Hollow space behind each nostril.

Nature–nurture question   Are abilities—such as perceptual abilities—due to inborn factors (nature), or are they the result of learning and experience (nurture)?

Near point   The nearest point that the viewer can see clearly.

Nearsighted   Refers to people who cannot see faraway objects.

Negative afterimage   Image that appears after the presentation of a stimulus. The afterimage is the opposite of the original stimulus. (*See also* Successive color contrast.)

Nerve deafness   Type of deafness that involves problems either in the cochlea or in the auditory nerve.

Neuromatrix   Proposed by Ronald Melzack, the neuromatrix receives input from three brain systems to generate a unique pattern of impulses that serves to identify the self.

Neurons (*new*-rons)   Nerve cells.

Noise   In signal detection theory, the situation in which no signal occurs. In audition, irrelevant, excessive, or unwanted sound.

Nonspectral hues   Hues that cannot be described in terms of a single wavelength from a part of the spectrum.

Nontasters   In taste perception, people who are insensitive to some particular tastes.

Normal trichromat (*try*-krow-mat)   Person who requires three primary colors to match all other colors.

Occlusion (uh-*clue*-zyun)   Process in which a moving object systematically covers up the background.

Octave   A doubling of frequency; used by musicians to represent the distance between two notes that have the same name, such as two successive C notes on the piano.

Octave illusion   Musical illusion in which one tone is presented to one ear and another tone an octave away is simultaneously presented to the other ear. The tones shift from ear to ear, yet the listener reports one ear hearing only high notes and the other hearing only low notes.

Ocular dominance   Tendency for cells in the visual cortex to have a higher response rate for one of the two eyes.

Odorant   Smell stimulus.

Odor constancy   Odor constancy means that the perceived strength of an odor remains the same despite variations in sniff vigor.

Olfaction   Smell.

Olfactory bulb   Structure that receives the signals from the smell receptors.

Olfactory epithelium   Region at the top of the nasal cavity that contains the smell receptor cells.

Omnivore   Plant-and-animal-eating organism.

Onset difference   An important cue in auditory localization, because a sound originating from one side will arrive at the ear on that side prior to arriving at the ear on the other side. (*See also* Interaural time difference.)

Op art   Artistic movement that developed in the 1960s that attempted to produce a strictly optical art.

Ophthalmologists   Doctors specializing in eye diseases.

Ophthalmoscope   Special tool used to look inside the eye.

Opiate receptors   Specific locations on the surface of brain cells that respond to opiate drugs in a lock-and-key fashion.

Opponent-process theory   Theory of color vision that states that there are cells in the visual system that respond to stimulation by an increase in activity when one color is present and by a decrease in activity when another color is present.

Optacon II   The Optacon II translates written letters and numbers into a vibratory display, to allow people who are blind to read.

Optic chiasm (*kie*-as-em)   Area in which the two optic nerves come together and cross over.

Optic disc   Region of the retina in which the optic nerve leaves the eye.

Optic flow field   The complex pattern on our retinas where peripheral objects move more rapidly than central objects. The optic flow field is important for motion perception.

Optic nerve   Bundle of ends from the ganglion cells that passes out of the eye toward the optic chiasm.

Optic tract   Bundle of nerve fibers in the visual system that runs between the optic chiasm and the superior colliculus or the lateral geniculate nucleus.

Organ of Corti (*court*-eye)   Part of the cochlea that contains the auditory receptors.

Orientation tuning curve   Graph illustrating the relationship between the angular orientation of a line and a cell's response rate.

Ossicles   Three small bones in the middle ear: malleus, incus, and stapes.

Otoacoustic emissions   All emissions produced by the ear, whether in response to a stimulus or not.

Otosclerosis   A bone disease that causes immobility of the stapes, ultimately making conduction of sound stimuli difficult.

Outer hair cells   Auditory receptors on the outer side of the organ of Corti, most likely responsible for tuning the traveling wave on the basilar membrane to allow fine frequency discrimination. (*See also* Motility.)

Oval window   Membrane that covers an opening in the cochlea.

Overtones   Harmonics, or the other components of a complex tone, excluding the fundamental frequency, that are multiples of that fundamental frequency.

Pacinian corpuscles   One variety of skin receptors with encapsulated endings; they are very sensitive to the indentation of the skin.

Pain   Perception of actual or threatened tissue damage and the private experience of unpleasantness.

Pain threshold   Intensity of stimulation in which pain is reported on half the trials.

Pain tolerance   Maximum pain level at which people voluntarily accept pain.

Panum's area   An area on and near the horopter in which the images of the object on the two retinas can be fused. (*See also* Horopter.)

Papillae (paa-*pill*-ee)   Small bumps on the tongue that contain the taste buds.

Paradoxical cold   Phenomenon in which a very hot stimulus produces the sensation of cold by stimulating a cold spot.

Parallel process   Process that allows several targets or tasks to be handled simultaneously, typically by different modules. (*See also* Module.)

Parallel transmission   Tendency for some sounds in a syllable to be transmitted at about the same time rather than one at a time.

Parasol ganglion cells   Ganglion cells with widely spread dendrites, which are primarily connected to rods. These cells receive input from diffuse bipolar cells, continuing the magno pathway. (*See also* Diffuse bipolar cells.)

Parvo pathway   The parvo (short for parvocellular) pathway is predominantly responsible for carrying information about the color and detail of stimuli, as well as slowly moving stimuli. The pathway begins with input from photoreceptors passing to midget bipolar and midget ganglion cells.

Passive touch   Touch perception in which an object is placed on a person's skin.

Pattern theory   Theory about the skin senses that proposes that the pattern of nerve impulses determines sensation.

Pattern theory of pain perception   States that pain is perceived when the sum of all the individual receptor cells' levels of stimulation surpasses a critical point.

Payoff   In signal detection theory, the rewards and punishments associated with a particular response.

Perception   Interpretation of sensations, involving meaning and organization.

Permanent threshold shift   Permanent increase in a hearing threshold as a result of exposure to noise.

Phantom limb pain   Perceived pain in an amputated arm or leg.

Phase angle   Phase angle is the position of the wave in degrees over one complete cycle (0 degrees, 90 degrees, etc.). It helps to describe the wave's pressure at each position. For example, at 90 degrees, pressure is at a maximum, and at 270 degrees a minimum.

Phase difference   The difference in phase angle of a sound at the two ears, which serves as a cue to the location of the sound source (see Figure 10.6).

Phenomenological observation   Approach in which observers look at their immediate experience and attempt to describe it completely.

Pheromones (*fear*-uh-moans)   Substances that act like chemical signals in communicating with other members of the same species.

Phi movement   Illusion of movement in which observers report that they see movement, yet they cannot perceive an actual object moving across a gap; phi movement can be produced by two light flashes about 100 milliseconds apart.

Phoneme   Basic unit of speech, such as an /h/ or an /r/ sound.

Phonemic restoration   Phenomenon that occurs when a speech sound is replaced or masked by an irrelevant sound and the perceptual system restores or fills in the gap appropriately.

Phonetic boundary   Refers to auditory perception; the point on a continuum where our perception of phonemes changes—to the left of the boundary we perceive one phoneme, and to the right we hear a different one.

Photopic vision (foe-*top*-ick)   Vision that uses cones.

Photopigments   Chemical substances that accomplish the transduction of light.

Photoreceptors   Light receptors; the rods and cones.

Pictorial cues   Cues used to convey depth in a picture.

Pinna   Flap of external tissue that aids in auditory localization, typically referred to as "the ear."

Pitch   Psychological reaction that corresponds to the frequency of a tone.

Placebo (pluh-*see*-bow)   Inactive substance such as a sugar pill that the patient believes is a medication.

Place of articulation   One of the three dimensions for consonants; specifies where the airstream is blocked when the consonant is spoken.

Place theory   Theory of auditory processing that proposes that frequency information is encoded at different places along the basilar membrane.

Pointillism   Artistic technique in which discrete dots of pigment are applied to a canvas; the dots blend into solid colors when viewed from a distance.

Point–light display   A display that shows only points of light at the joints of an organism. Such a minimal display is useful in studying biological motion.

Ponzo illusion   Illusion in which two parallel lines the same length appear to be different lengths because of the presence of depth cues.

Preattentive processing   In Treisman's feature-integration theory, the automatic registration of stimulus features.

Preference method   In testing infant perception, a method based on the idea that if the infant spends consistently longer looking at one figure in preference to another figure, the infant must be able to discriminate between the two figures.

Prepared childbirth methods   Methods that educate women and men about the anatomy of childbirth, controlled muscular relaxation, and focusing attention on something other than pain (e.g., the Lamaze method).

Presbycusis (prez-bee-*koo*-siss)   Progressive loss of hearing in both ears for high-frequency tones, occurring with aging.

Presbyopia (prez-bee-*owe*-pee-ah)   Type of far-sightedness that occurs with aging, caused by inelasticity of the lens.

Primal sketch   A kind of map for shape perception produced by the visual system, which yields edges and intensity differences.

Primary auditory cortex   Located in the temporal lobe, it receives information from the medial geniculate nucleus.

Primary visual cortex Area of the visual cortex where the neurons from the lateral geniculate nucleus terminate.

Probe-tone technique Technique in which the listener hears either a musical chord or a scale in order to establish a key; then a probe tone is presented and the listener is asked to rate how well that tone fits within the octave of the key being examined.

Profile analysis Process in which subjects are able to detect differences in intensities of complex tones by comparing the activity that each produces on the basilar membrane.

PROP Bitter substance, 6-n-propylthiouracil, which some people cannot taste.

Proprioception Sensation of movement or static limb position; synonym for kinesthesia.

Prosopagnosia A disorder in which a person cannot organize facial features to recognize a face.

Protanopes (*proe*-tuh-nopes) People who are dichromats and insensitive to deep red.

Prototype Ideal figure proposed to serve as a basis of comparison in the prototype-matching approach to pattern recognition.

Prototype-matching approach Approach to shape perception suggesting that we have information regarding various abstract shapes and patterns stored in memory (the prototype) and recognition occurs when we match a newly presented stimulus to a prototype.

Proximal stimulus Representation of objects in contact with a sense organ, such as the representation on the retina, as opposed to the distal stimulus.

Psychophysics Study of the relationship between physical stimuli and psychological reactions to those stimuli.

PTC Bitter substance, phenylthiocarbamide, which some people cannot taste.

Pupil Opening in the center of the iris.

Pure tone Tone that can be represented by a simple sine wave.

Purity In the description of color, the lack of white light. Colors low in purity have large amounts of white light added to the monochromatic light.

Purkinje shift (purr-*kin*-gee) Phenomenon in which an observer's sensitivity to various wavelengths shifts toward the shorter wavelengths as he or she shifts from cone to rod conditions.

Pursuit movements Slow, smooth eye movements used in tracking an object moving against a stationary background.

Rapidly adapting (RA) fibers Kind of touch receptors that respond to a change in stimulation.

Ratio principle According to the ratio principle, the important factor that determines how light an object appears is the stimulus intensity of that object in comparison to other objects in the scene.

Receiver operating characteristic (ROC) curve In signal detection theory, a curve showing the relationship between the probability of a hit and the probability of a false alarm.

Receptive field For a given cell, the portion of the retina that, when stimulated, produces a change in the activity of that cell.

Recognition-by-components approach The approach suggesting that recognition of complex shapes occurs by analyzing the basic components from which they are constructed.

Recognition threshold In taste perception, the concentration of a solution that can be recognized by quality.

Recruitment Condition in which a person who is deaf perceives very loud sounds normally but does not hear weak sounds at all.

Reference theory Theory of the moon illusion in which both the sky and the ground are important referents when observers judge the size of the moon.

Refractory period Time immediately following an action potential, during which a nerve cell returns to its resting potential.

Reissner's membrane Membrane separating the cochlear duct from the vestibular canal.

Relative distance Distance between two objects, as used in depth perception.

Relative size Object's size relative to other objects, used as a cue in distance perception.

Relative-size explanation Theory of size constancy in which people notice the size of an object compared to other objects, thereby retaining constancy.

Retina (*reh*-tin-nuh) Portion of the eye that absorbs light rays; contains the photoreceptors.

Retinex theory Retinex theory seeks to explain color perception and color constancy based primarily on perception of the pattern of reflectances from the stimuli.

Retinotopic Arrangement in which the spatial distribution is similar to that found on the retina. For example, in the lateral geniculate nucleus (LGN), ganglion cells that originated on neighboring parts of the retina also terminate on neighboring parts of the LGN.

Rhodopsin (roe-*dopp*-sin) Photopigment found in rods.

Right visual field Portion of the visual world on the right-hand side.

Rods Photoreceptors used for black-and-white vision under poorly lit conditions.

Round window Membrane that covers an opening in the tympanic canal.

Saccade (suh-*kaad*) A single rapid eye movement in which the eye is moved from one location to the next.

Saccadic movement (suh-*kaad*-dick) Very rapid eye movements in which the eye is moved from one fixation point to the next.

Sander parallelogram Line-length illusion involving the diagonal lines in a parallelogram (see Figure 6.22).

Saturation Psychological reaction to the purity of a light; a highly saturated light appears to have very little white light added to it.

Sclera Shiny white part of the external eye.

Scotoma (skuh-*toe*-muh) Blind area caused by damage to the visual cortex; plural is scotomata (skuh-*toe*-muh-tuh).

Scotopic vision (skoe-*top*-ick) Vision that uses rods.

Secondary visual cortex Region of the visual cortex that receives information that has already been processed by the primary visual cortex as well as from the superior colliculus.

Selective adaptation procedure Technique in which a particular stimulus is continuously exposed in order to produce "fatigue" in neurons sensitive to certain spatial frequencies.

Self-adaptation When a particular odorant leads to a loss of sensitivity to that odorant, the process is called self-adaptation.

Self-motion illusion Perception that you are moving, although you are really stationary.

Sensation Immediate and basic experiences generated by isolated, simple stimuli.

Sensitivity Ability to detect a change in the stimulus; sensitivity is inversely related to threshold level.

Serial process Processing information that requires the targets or tasks to be handled one at a time.

Shading Distance cue provided by the pattern of light and shadows.

Shape Area set off from the rest of a visual stimulus because it has a contour.

Shape constancy Phenomenon in which an object seems to stay the same shape despite changes in its orientation.

Shape from highlights Cue to the three-dimensionality of a shape arising from light reflected from the surface of the object.

Shape from motion Cue to the three-dimensionality of a shape arising from the motion of the object. (*See also* Kinetic depth effect.)

Shape from shading Cue to the three-dimensionality of a shape from the shadows attached to the object.

Shape-slant invariance hypothesis Theory of shape constancy in which the viewer calculates objective shape by combining information about an object's retinal shape and its slant.

Short-range process Analysis of the kind of movement that occurs over a short distance or time.

Signal Stimulus used in psychophysics studies, most often in signal detection theory.

Signal detection theory (SDT) Psychophysical approach that assesses both the observer's sensitivity and his or her decision-making strategy (or criterion).

Signal + noise In signal detection theory, the situations in which the appropriate signal occurs, in addition to the irrelevant "noise."

Simple cells Cells in layer IVb of the primary visual cortex that respond most vigorously to lines.

Simultaneous color contrast The changing of an object's perceived color, or hue, due to the surrounding color.

Sine wave Smooth wave pattern resembling the pattern of light waves or pure tones.

Single cell recording Research technique in which small electrodes are placed in a precise location to record action potentials, such as those generated by a single ganglion cell.

Sinusoidal grating (sine-you-*soid*-ul) Set of blurry stripes that alternate between dark and light.

Size constancy Phenomenon in which an object seems to stay the same size despite changes in its distance.

Size cues Distance information conveyed by relative size.

Size-distance invariance hypothesis Theory of constancy in which the viewer calculates an object's perceived size by combining the object's retinal size and its perceived distance.

Slowly adapting (SA) receptors Kind of touch receptor that responds to steady continuous stimulation (pressure on skin).

Soft palate Region in the upper part of the mouth above the back of the tongue.

Somatosensory cortex Region of the cortex that processes information about touch and taste.

Sone scale Scale of loudness obtained by the magnitude-estimation technique, in which a 40-dB tone at 1000 Hz is assigned a loudness of 1 sone.

Sound pressure level (SPL) A logarithmic scale of sound pressure relative to threshold pressure. It is used to measure amplitude in decibels.

Sounds Successive changes in atmospheric pressure.

Sound spectrogram Diagram that shows the frequency components of speech.

Spacing illusion An illusion in which lines whose ends are separated by a constant amount will seem to be closer together when the lines are tilted (see Figure 6.25).

Spatial frequency analysis approach Approach to shape perception suggesting that to process visual information, the visual system breaks the stimulus down into a series of light and dark stripes. (*See also* Fourier analysis.)

Spatial frequency channels Channels in the visual system that are sensitive to a narrow range of spatial frequencies.

Special Mechanism account Theory of speech perception positing that speech is processed by a distinct unit separate from that used for other auditory information. (*See also* Module.)

Specificity theory Theory based on the doctrine of specific nerve energies stating that each kind of skin receptor responds exclusively to only one kind of physical stimulus, and each kind of receptor is responsible for only one kind of sensation.

Specificity theory of pain perception Theory stating that pain is produced by the stimulation of specific pain receptors.

Spectral sensitivity Region of the spectrum in which light is absorbed, such as the region in which a particular kind of cone absorbs light.

Speech spectrogram Diagram that shows the frequency components of speech.

Spinothalamic system (spy-know-thuh-*laa*-mick) One of the two neuronal systems responsible for the skin senses. It has smaller nerve fibers and slower transmission than the lemniscal system.

Spontaneous acoustic emissions Emissions produced by the ear when no stimulus has been presented.

Stabilized retinal image An image that is kept on the same part of the retina through various means. A stabilized retinal image will ultimately disappear, showing the importance of change for perception.

Standard stimulus The stimulus in discrimination studies that remains constant throughout the experiment.

Stapes (*stay*-peas) Small stirrup-shaped bone in the middle ear.

Steady state In music perception, the middle portion of a tone.

Stereochemical theory Theory proposed by Amoore that odorous molecules have definite shapes that determine the kind of odor we smell.

Stereocilia Tiny hairs attached to the ends of the inner and outer hair cells. Displacement of the stereocilia causes action potentials to be produced, the first step in auditory perception.

Stereopsis Ability to judge depth with two eyes, as provided by binocular disparity.

Stereoscope Piece of equipment that presents two photographs of a scene taken from slightly different viewpoints; one picture is presented to each eye, creating the impression of depth.

Stereoscopic picture Two pictures, one presented to the right eye and one presented to the left eye, creating the impression of depth.

Stevens's power law ($R = kI^n$) Stevens's power law says that the magnitude of the psychological reaction (R) is equal to a constant (k) multiplied by the intensity (I) of the stimulus, which has been raised to the nth power.

Stimulation deafness experiment An experiment in which an animal is exposed to an extremely high-amplitude tone, which causes damage to the stereocilia. The location of the damage depends on the frequency used.

Stimulation-produced analgesia Procedure in which certain regions of the brain are electrically stimulated, leading to a loss of sensitivity to pain.

Stress-induced analgesia A reduction in pain perception caused by stress.

Striate cortex (*strie*-ate) Area of the visual cortex where the neurons from the lateral geniculate nucleus terminate, called striate because of its microscopically visible stripes. This area is also called the primary visual cortex and Area 17.

Stroboscopic movement (stroe-buh-*skope*-ick) Illusion of movement produced by a rapid pattern of stimulation on different parts of the retina.

Subcutaneous tissue Inner layer of skin, which contains connective tissue and fat globules.

Subjective colors Impressions of color that are produced by a black-and-white stimulus (like Benham's top).

Subjective contour Phenomenon in which contours are seen even though they are not physically present; also known as illusory contour.

Substantia gelatinosa Proposed part of the gate-control theory, which produces stimulation with input from the large fibers and inhibition with input from the small fibers.

Subtractive mixture In color mixing, combining dyes or pigments, or placing two or more colored filters together.

Successive color contrast Situation in which the appearance of a color is changed because of another color presented beforehand. (*See also* Negative afterimage.)

Superior colliculus (kole-*lick*-you-luss) Portion of the brain important for locating objects and their movement.

Superior olivary nucleus A structure in auditory processing between the cochlear nucleus and the inferior colliculus.

Synapse The gap between neurons across which chemical messages are sent.

Synthetic sense One of the senses in which an observer cannot detect the separate parts; for example, in vision an observer cannot detect the components of a color mixture.

Tadoma method Method of communication in which a person who is deaf places his or her hands on the lips and jaw of the speaker to pick up tactile information about speech.

Tapetum The equivalent of the human choroid in nocturnal animals. Unlike the choroid, though, the tapetum reflects light rather than absorbing it.

Taste Perceptions that result from the contact of substances with special receptors in the mouth.

Taste bud Receptor for taste stimuli.

Taste modifiers Special substances that change the flavor of other food by modifying the receptors on the tongue.

Taste pore The opening in the taste bud.

Taste tetrahedron Four-sided figure representing one of the four basic tastes (sweet, salty, bitter, and sour) at each of the four corners.

Tectorial membrane Membrane that rests at the top of the organ of Corti in the inner ear.

Template-matching approach Approach to shape perception suggesting that we store specific patterns of information in memory and that recognition occurs when we match a newly presented stimulus to a template.

Temporary threshold shift Temporary increase in a hearing threshold as a result of exposure to noise.

Test stimulus In dark adaptation studies, the small spot of light for which the threshold is measured after the lights have been turned off.

Texture gradient Distance cue provided by the fact that the texture of surfaces becomes denser as the distance increases.

Thermal adaptation Decrease in the perceived intensity of a hot or cold temperature as time passes.

3-D sketch Relating to Marr's theory of space perception, the third step in achieving a 3-D percept. Here the percept changes from viewer- to object-centered, providing a more accurate representation of depth than the 2.5-D sketch.

Timbre (*tam*-burr) A tone's sound quality.

Tinnitus High-pitched ringing in the ears, caused by a high fever, ear infection, or large doses of aspirin.

Tonality Organization of pitches around one particular tone.

Tone chroma (*crow*-mah)   Similarity shared by all musical tones that have the same name.

Tone height   Increase in pitch of a tone that accompanies an increase in frequency.

Tonic   One of the 12 pitches within an octave; serves as the tone around which all others in the octave are organized.

Tonometry   Technique in which a special instrument is used to measure the pressure inside the eye.

Tonotopic   Arrangement in which neurons sensitive to similar frequencies are near one another in the inferior colliculus.

Top-down processing   Approach that emphasizes the importance of the observers' concepts and cognitive processes in shaping perception.

Touch adaptation   Decrease in the perceived intensity of a repeated tactile stimulus.

Transcutaneous electrical nerve stimulation (TENS)   An effective technique for reducing pain produced by stimulating the surface of the skin.

Transduction   Process of converting a physical stimulus into a form that can be transmitted through the perceptual system.

Transmission cells   Cells proposed by the gate-control theory that are in the spinal cord and receive input from two kinds of neural fibers.

Transposition   In a piece of music, changing the pitch of each note while retaining the same spatial relationships.

Traveling wave   Pressure wave in auditory processing that travels from the base to the apex of the cochlea.

Trichromatic theory   Theory of color vision stating that there are three kinds of color receptors, each sensitive to light from a different part of the spectrum.

Trigeminal nerve   A nerve important in olfaction and taste; it has free nerve endings extending into the olfactory epithelium and also registers the spiciness of food such as chili peppers.

Tritanopes (*try*-tuh-nopes)   People who are dichromats and have difficulty with blue shades.

Tritone paradox   The tritone paradox involves a misperception of tone heights.

Trompe l'oeil (tromp *ley*-yeh)   Technique in painting that "fools the eye" by creating an impression of depth when the surface is really just two-dimensional.

Turbinate bones   Three bones located in the nasal cavity.

Two-alternative forced choice procedure (2AFC)   Psychophysical procedure with several variants. In one variant, a person is presented with a stimulus and then must decide which of two subsequent stimuli is identical to the original stimulus. This procedure eliminates consideration of a criterion, because the stimulus is always one of the two subsequently presented stimuli.

Two-point discrimination threshold   Point at which the perceiver can determine that two distinct stimuli—rather than one—are being presented. For touch perception, this is done by pricking the skin with two pinpoints.

2.5-D sketch   Relating to Marr's theory of space perception, the next step in achieving a 3-D percept after the primal sketch is achieved. It is viewer-centered and contains information about motion and the primal sketch.

Tympanic canal   Canal in the cochlea.

Tympanic membrane   Thin piece of membrane that vibrates in response to sound waves.

Unconscious inference   Proposed explanation for constancy in which the observer arrives at a perception via a reasoning-like process without conscious awareness.

Uncrossed disparity   Objects behind the horopter create uncrossed disparity, which is a cue that objects are far from us. (*See also* Horopter.)

Uniform connectedness   According to the principle of uniform connectedness, we organize input as a single unit when we perceive a connected region of uniform visual properties, such as lightness, color, and so on.

Velocity detection threshold   The minimum velocity that can be detected in motion perception.

Vergence movement   Eye movements in which the angle between the lines of sight changes and the eyes move toward or away from each other.

Version movement   Eye movement in which the angle between the lines of sight remains constant and the eyes move in the same direction.

Vestibular canal (ves-*tib*-bue-lur)   Canal in the cochlea on which the stapes rests.

Vestibular sense   System that provides information about orientation, movement, and acceleration.

Vestibuloocular reflex (VOR)   The vestibuloocular reflex (VOR) coordinates vestibular information with eye muscle function, which serves to stabilize our view of the world.

Virtual lines   Lines that are not actually present in a display, but are "created" by our perceptual system to organize the display into "objects." (*See also* Illusory contours.)

Visual acuity   Ability to see fine details in a scene.

Visual agnosia   Caused by temporal lobe damage, a person with visual agnosia has intact basic visual abilities but cannot identify a picture of an object.

Visual angle   Size of the angle formed by extending two lines from the observer's eye to the outside edges of the target.

Visual cliff   Kind of apparatus in which infants must choose between a side that looks shallow and a side that looks deep.

Visual cortex   Portion of the cerebral cortex that is concerned with vision.

Vitreous humor (*vit*-ree-us)   Thick, jellylike substance found within the eye, behind the lens.

Vocal tract   Anatomical structures involved in speaking, located above the vocal cords.

Voiced consonant   Consonant that is spoken with vibration of the vocal cords.

Voiceless consonant   Consonant that is spoken without vibration of the vocal cords.

Voice onset time (VOT)   In speaking, the VOT is the time before the voiced part of the vowel begins.

Voicing   One of the three dimensions for consonants; voicing specifies whether the vocal cords vibrate.

Volley principle   Proposal that was added to the frequency theory of auditory processing, which stated that clusters of neurons could "share" in producing a required firing rate.

Vomeronasal organs   Olfactory sense organs located on either side of the septum, which separates the two nostrils.

Water taste   Distinct taste for water following adaptation to another taste; for example, water tastes sweet after adaptation to a sour substance.

Wavelength   The distance light travels during one cycle.

Weber's fraction (k)   Number obtained in discrimination studies that represents the change in stimulus intensity divided by the original intensity.

Weber's law (vay-burz) ($\Delta I/I = k$)   Weber's law says that if we take the change in intensity (ΔI) and divide it by the original intensity (I), we obtain a constant number (k).

Word-apprehension effect   Word-superiority effect.

Word-superiority effect   Phenomenon in which letters are perceived better when they appear in words than in strings of unrelated letters.

Zero-crossing   Related to edge perception; the point of a change in intensity within the visual field.

Zonules   Tiny fibers that connect the lens and the ciliary muscle.

References

Abramov, I., & Gordon, J. (1994). Color appearance: On seeing red—or yellow, or green, or blue. *Annual Review of Psychology, 45*, 451–485.

Abrams, R. A. (1992). Planning and programming saccadic eye movements. In K. Rayner (Ed.), *Eye movements and visual cognition: Scene perception and reading* (pp. 66–88). New York: Springer-Verlag.

Ackerman, D. (1990). *A natural history of the senses.* New York: Random House.

Agostini, T., & Proffitt, D. R. (1993). Perceptual organization evokes simultaneous lightness contrast. *Perception, 22*, 263–272.

Aiello, R., & Sloboda, J. A. (Eds.). (1994). *Musical perceptions.* New York: Oxford University Press.

Albert, M. K., & Hoffman, D. D. (1995). Genericity in spatial vision. In R. D. Luce, M. D'Zmura, D. Hoffman, G. J. Iverson, & A. K. Romney (Eds.), *Geometric representations of perceptual phenomena: Papers in honor of Tarow Indow on his 70th birthday* (pp. 95–112). Mahwah, NJ: Erlbaum.

Albright, T. D. (1992). Form-cue invariant motion processing in primate visual cortex. *Science, 255*, 1141–1143.

Algom, D., & Lubel, S. (1994). Psychophysics in the field: Perception and memory for labor pain. *Perception & Psychophysics, 55*, 133–141.

Algom, D., & Marks, L. E. (1984). Individual differences in loudness processing and loudness scales. *Journal of Experimental Psychology: General, 113*, 571–593.

Allman, J., & Brothers, L. (1994). Faces, fear and the amygdala. *Nature, 372*, 613–614.

American Psychological Association. (1992). Ethical principles of psychologists and code of conduct. *American Psychologist, 47*, 1597–1611.

Ames, A. (1952). *The Ames demonstrations in perception.* New York: Hafner.

Amoore, J. E. (1970). *Molecular basis of odor.* Springfield, IL: Thomas.

Amoore, J. E. (1977). Specific anosmia and the concept of primary odors. *Chemical Senses and Flavor, 2*, 267–281.

Anastasi, A. (1936). The estimation of areas. *Journal of General Psychology, 14*, 201–225.

Andersen, G. J. (1986). Perception of self-motion: Psychophysical and computational approaches. *Psychological Bulletin, 99*, 52–65.

Andersen, R. A., Treue, S., Graziano, M., Snowden, R. J., & Qian, N. (1993). From direction of motion to patterns of motion: Hierarchies of motion analysis in the visual cortex. In T. Ono, L. R. Squire, M. E. Raichle, D. I. Perrett, & M. Fukuda (Eds.), *Brain mechanisms of perception and memory* (pp. 183–199). New York: Oxford University Press.

Anderson, B. L., & Nakayama, K. (1994). Toward a general theory of stereopsis: Binocular matching, occluding contours, and fusion. *Psychological Review, 101*, 414–445.

Anderson, J. R. (1995). *Cognitive psychology and its implications* (4th ed.). New York: Freeman.

Angier, N. (1992, November 17). New clue to vision: People whose glasses must be rose-colored. *The New York Times*, p. C3.

Anstis, S. (1992). Visual adaptation to a negative brightness-reversed world: Some preliminary observations. In G. A. Carpenter & S. Grossberg (Eds.), *Neural networks for vision and image processing* (pp. 1–14). Cambridge, MA: MIT Press.

Anstis, S. M. (1986). Motion perception in the frontal plane. In K. R. Boff, L. Kaufman, & J. P. Thomas

(Eds.), *Handbook of perception and human performance* (pp. 16.1–16.27). New York: Wiley.

Appelle, S. (1991). Haptic perception of form: Activity and stimulus attributes. In M. A. Heller & W. Schiff (Eds.), *The psychology of touch* (pp. 169–188). Hillsdale, NJ: Erlbaum.

Arditi, A. (1986). Binocular vision. In K. R. Boff, L. Kaufman, & J. P. Thomas (Eds.), *Handbook of perception and human performance* (pp. 23.1–23.41). New York: Wiley.

Arend, L. (1994). Surface colors, illumination, and surface geometry: Intrinsic-image models of human color perception. In A. Gilchrist (Ed.), *Lightness, brightness, and transparency* (pp. 159–213). Hillsdale, NJ: Erlbaum.

Arend, L. E. (1993). Mesopic lightness, brightness, and brightness contrast. *Perception & Psychophysics, 54,* 469–476.

Arend, L. E., & Spehar, B. (1993). Lightness, brightness, and brightness contrast: 1. Illuminance variation. *Perception & Psychophysics, 54,* 446–456.

Arnheim, R. (1986). The two faces of Gestalt psychology. *American Psychologist, 41,* 820–824.

Asbury, T., & Sanitato, J. J. (1992). Trauma. In D. Vaughn, T. Asbury, & P. Riordan-Eva (Eds.), *General ophthalmology* (pp. 363–370). Norwalk, CT: Appleton & Lange.

Ashmore, J. F. (1987). A fast motile response in guinea-pig outer hair cells: The cellular basis of the cochlear amplifier. *Journal of Physiology, 388,* 323–347.

Aslin, R. N. (1988). Perceptual development. *Annual Review of Psychology, 39,* 435–473.

Aslin, R. N., Pisoni, D. B., & Jusczyk, P. W. (1983). Auditory development and speech perception in infancy. In P. H. Mussen (Ed.), *Handbook of child psychology* (pp. 574–687). New York: Wiley.

Associated Press. (1990, February 18). Clothes glow? Only the animals know. *Times-Union,* Albany, NY, p. C11.

Atkinson, J., & Braddick, O. (1981). Acuity, contrast sensitivity and accommodation in infancy. In R. N. Aslin, J. R. Alberts, & M. R. Petersen (Eds.), *Development of perception* (pp. 245–277). New York: Academic Press.

Atkinson, R. C., & Schiffrin, R. M. (1968). Human memory: A proposed system and its control processes. In K. W. Spence & J. T. Spence (Eds.), *The psychology of learning and motivation: Advances in research and theory* (Vol. 2, pp. 89–195). New York: Academic Press.

Attneave, F. (1982). Pragnanz and soap bubbles systems: A theoretical exploration. In J. Beck (Ed.), *Organization and representation in perception* (pp. 11–29). Hillsdale, NJ: Erlbaum.

Bahill, A. T., & Karnavas, W. J. (1993). The perceptual illusion of baseball's rising fastball and breaking curveball. *Journal of Experimental Psychology: Human Perception and Performance, 19,* 3–14.

Bahrick, L. E. (1983). Infants' perception of substance and temporal synchrony in multimodal events. *Infant Behavior and Development, 6,* 429–451.

Bailey, I. L. (1986). The optometric examination of the elderly patient. In A. A. Rosenbloom & M. W. Morgan (Eds.), *Vision and aging* (pp. 189–209). New York: Professional Press Books.

Bailey, P. J., & Herrmann, P. (1993). A reexamination of duplex perception evoked by intensity differences. *Perception & Psychophysics, 54,* 20–32.

Baird, J. C. (1982). The moon illusion: II. A reference theory. *Journal of Experimental Psychology: General, 111,* 304–315.

Baird, J. C., & Noma, E. (1978). *Fundamentals of scaling and psychophysics.* New York: Wiley.

Baird, J. C., & Wagner, M. (1982). The moon illusion: I. How high is the sky? *Journal of Experimental Psychology: General, 111,* 296–303.

Baird, J. C., Wagner, M., & Fuld, K. (1990). A simple but powerful theory of the moon illusion. *Journal of Experimental Psychology: Human Perception and Performance, 16,* 675–677.

Baker, A. H., & Weisz, G. (1984). Misinterpretation of instructions in an aftereffect task. *Perceptual and Motor Skills, 59,* 159–162.

Ballesteros, S. (Ed.). (1994). *Cognitive approaches to human perception.* Hillsdale, NJ: Erlbaum.

Balogh, R. D., & Porter, R. H. (1986). Olfactory preferences resulting from mere exposure in human neonates. *Infant Behavior and Development, 9,* 395–401.

Banks, M. S., & Salapatek, P. (1983). Infant visual perception. In P. H. Mussen (Ed.), *Handbook of Child Psychology* (pp. 435–571). New York: Wiley.

Barber, J. (1986). Hypnotic analgesia. In A. D. Holzman & D. C. Turk (Eds.), *Pain management: A handbook of psychological treatment approaches* (pp. 151–167). New York: Pergamon.

Barclay, C. D., Cutting, J. E., & Kozlowski, L. T. (1978). Temporal and spatial factors in gait perception that influence gender recognition. *Perception & Psychophysics, 23,* 145–152.

Bargones, J. Y. (1994). Adults listen selectively; infants do not. *Psychological Science, 5,* 170–174.

Barinaga, M. (1991a). How the nose knows: Olfactory receptor cloned. *Science, 252,* 209–210.

Barinaga, M. (1991b). The secret of saltiness. *Science, 254,* 654–655.

Barinaga, M. (1992). The brain remaps its own contours. *Science, 258,* 216–218.

Barlow, R. B., Jr. (1990). What the brain tells the eye. *Scientific American, 262*(4), 90–95.

Barlow, R. B., Jr., & Kaplan, E. (1993). Intensity coding and circadian rhythms in the *Limulus* lateral eye.

In R. T. Verrillo (Ed.), *Sensory research: Multimodal perspectives* (pp. 55–73). Hillsdale, NJ: Erlbaum.

Barnes, M. E., & Wells, W. (1994, April). If hearing aids work, why don't people use them? *Ergonomics in Design*, pp. 19–24.

Baron, R. A. (1988). Perfume as a tactic of impression management in social and organizational settings. In S. Van Toller & G. H. Dodd (Eds.), *Perfumery: The psychology and biology of fragrance* (pp. 91–104). London: Chapman and Hall.

Baron, R. A., & Bronfen, M. I. (1994). A whiff of reality: Empirical evidence concerning the effects of pleasant fragrances on work-related behavior. *Journal of Applied Social Psychology, 24*, 1179–1203.

Barrera, M., & Maurer, D. (1981). Recognition of mother's photographed face by the three-month-old infant. *Child Development, 52*, 714–716.

Barrow, H. G., & Tenenbaum, J. M. (1986). Computational approaches to vision. In K. R. Boff, L. Kaufman, & J. P. Thomas (Eds.), *Handbook of perception and human performance* (pp. 38.1–38.70). New York: Wiley.

Barsalou, L. W. (1990). On the indistinguishability of exemplar memory and abstraction in category representation. In T. K. Srull & R. S. Wyer (Eds.), *Advances in social cognition* (pp. 61–88). Hillsdale, NJ: Erlbaum.

Barsz, K. (1988). Auditory pattern perception: The effect of tonal frequency range on the perception of temporal order. *Perception & Psychophysics, 43*, 293–303.

Bartlett, J. C. (1993). Tonal structure of melodies. In T. J. Tighe & W. J. Dowling (Eds.), *Psychology and music: The understanding of melody and rhythm* (pp. 39–61). Hillsdale, NJ: Erlbaum.

Bartoshuk, L. M. (1971). The chemical senses I: Taste. In J. W. Kling & L. A. Riggs (Eds.), *Woodworth & Schlosberg's experimental psychology* (pp. 169–191). New York: Holt, Rinehart & Winston.

Bartoshuk, L. M. (1974). Taste illusions: Some demonstrations. *Annals of the New York Academy of Sciences, 237*, 279–285.

Bartoshuk, L. M. (1980, September). Separate worlds of taste. *Psychology Today*, pp. 48–56.

Bartoshuk, L. M. (1988). Taste. In R. C. Atkinson, R. J. Herrnstein, G. Lindzey, & R. D. Luce (Eds.), *Stevens' handbook of experimental psychology* (2nd ed., Vol. 1, pp. 461–499). New York: Wiley.

Bartoshuk, L. M., & Beauchamp, G. K. (1994). Chemical senses. *Annual Review of Psychology, 45*, 419–449.

Bashford, J. A., Jr., Meyers, M. D., Brubaker, B. S., & Warren, R. M. (1988). Illusory continuity of interrupted speech: Speech rate determines durational limits. *Journal of the Acoustical Society of America, 84*, 1635–1638.

Bashford, J. A., Jr., & Warren, R. M. (1987). Multiple phonemic restorations follow the rules for auditory induction. *Perception & Psychophysics, 42*, 114–121.

Basowitz, H., & Korchin, S. J. (1957). Age differences in the perception of closure. *Journal of Abnormal and Social Psychology, 54*, 93–97.

Batteau, D. W. (1967). The role of the pinna in human localization. *Proceedings of the Royal Society of London Series B, 168*, 158–180.

Beagley, W. K. (1985). Interaction of Müller–Lyer with filled-unfilled space illusion: An explanation of Müller–Lyer asymmetry. *Perception & Psychophysics, 37*, 45–49.

Beard, J. (1991, March 16). . . . and a plastic implant provides a cure. *New Scientist*, p. 27.

Beatty, J. (1995). *Principles of behavioral neuroscience.* Dubuque, IA: Brown & Benchmark.

Beck, J. (1974). Dimensions of an achromatic surface color. In R. B. MacLeod & H. L. Pick, Jr. (Eds.), *Perception: Essays in honor of James J. Gibson* (pp. 166–184). Ithaca, NY: Cornell University Press.

Békésy, G. von. (1960). *Experiments in hearing.* New York: McGraw-Hill.

Bellisimo, A., & Tunks, E. (1984). *Chronic pain.* New York: Praeger.

Benson, A. J. (1982). The vestibular sensory system. In H. B. Barlow & J. D. Mollon (Eds.), *The senses* (pp. 333–368). Cambridge: Cambridge University Press.

Benzschawel, T., & Cohn, T. E. (1985). Detection and recognition of visual targets. *Journal of the Optical Society of America, Series A, 2*, 1543–1550.

Berbaum, K., Bever, T., & Chung, C. S. (1983a). Light source position in the perception of object shape. *Perception, 12*, 411–416.

Berbaum, K., Bever, T., & Chung, C. S. (1984). Extending the perception of shape from known to unknown shading. *Perception, 13*, 479–488.

Berbaum, K., & Lenel, J. C. (1983). Objects in the path of apparent motion. *American Journal of Psychology, 96*, 491–501.

Berbaum, K., Lenel, J. C., & Rosenbaum, M. (1981). Dimensions of figural identity and apparent motion. *Journal of Experimental Psychology: Human Perception and Performance, 7*, 1312–1317.

Berbaum, K., Tharp, D., & Mroczek, K. (1983b). Depth perception of surfaces in pictures: Looking for conventions of depiction in Pandora's box. *Perception, 12*, 5–20.

Berglund, B., & Engen, T. (1993). A comparison of self-adaptation and cross-adaptation to odorants presented singly and in mixtures. *Perception, 22*, 103–111.

Bergman, M. (1980). *Aging and the perception of speech.* Baltimore: University Park Press.

Bergman, M., Blumenfeld, V. G., Cascardo, D., Dash, B., Levitt, H., & Margulies, M. K. (1976). Age-related decrement in hearing for speech: Sampling and longitudinal studies. *Journal of Gerontology, 31*, 533–538.

Bergström, S. S. (1994). Color constancy: Arguments for a vector model for the perception of illumination, color, and depth. In A. Gilchrist (Ed.), *Lightness, brightness, and transparency* (pp. 257–286). Hillsdale, NJ: Erlbaum.

Berkeley, G. (1709/1957). *An essay towards a new theory of vision*. London: Dent.

Berlá, E. P. (1982). Haptic perception of tangible graphic displays. In W. Schiff & E. Foulke (Eds.), *Tactual perception: A sourcebook* (pp. 364–386). Cambridge: Cambridge University Press.

Berlin, B., & Kay, P. (1969). *Basic color terms*. Berkeley, CA: University of California Press.

Bernstein, I. L. (1991). Flavor aversion. In T. V. Getchell, R. L. Doty, L. M. Bartoshuk, & J. B. Snow, Jr. (Eds.), *Smell and taste in health and disease* (pp. 417–428). New York: Raven.

Bernstein, I. L., & Borson, S. (1986). Learned food aversion: A component of anorexia syndromes. *Psychological Review*, *93*, 462–472.

Beroza, M., & Knipling, E. F. (1972). Gypsy moth control with the sex attractant pheromone. *Science*, *177*, 19–27.

Berry, D. S. (1990). What can a moving face tell us? *Journal of Personality and Social Psychology*, *58*, 1004–1014.

Berry, D. S. (1991). Child and adult sensitivity to gender information in patterns of facial motion. *Ecological Psychology*, *3*, 349–366.

Berry, D. S., Kean, K. J., Misovich, S. J., & Baron, R. M. (1991). Quantized displays of human movement: A methodological alternative to the point-light display. *Journal of Nonverbal Behavior*, *15*, 81–97.

Berry, D. S., & Misovich, S. J. (1994). Methodological approaches to the study of social event perception. *Personality and Social Psychology Bulletin*, *20*, 139–152.

Bershader, D. (1981). I can't hear you when the water's running. *The Stanford Magazine*, pp. 14–21.

Bertelson, P., & Radeau, M. (1981). Cross-modal bias and perceptual fusion with auditory-visual spatial discordance. *Perception & Psychophysics*, *29*, 578–584.

Bertenthal, B., Proffitt, D. R., & Kramer, S. J. (1987). Perception of biomechanical motion by infants: Implementation of various processing constraints. *Journal of Experimental Psychology: Human Perception and Performance*, *13*, 577–585.

Bertenthal, B. I. (1993). Perception of biomechanical motions by infants: Intrinsic image and knowledge-based constraints. In C. Granrud (Ed.), *Visual perception and cognition in infancy* (pp. 175–214). Hillsdale, NJ: Erlbaum.

Bertenthal, B. I., & Pinto, J. (1994). Global processing of biological motions. *Psychological Science*, *5*, 221–225.

Bertenthal, B. I., Proffitt, D. R., Spetner, N. B., & Thomas, M. A. (1985). The development of infant sensitivity to biomechanical motions. *Child Development*, *56*, 531–543.

Bertino, M., Beauchamp, G. K., & Engelman, K. (1982). Long-term reduction in dietary sodium alters the taste of salt. *American Journal of Clinical Nutrition*, *36*, 1134–1144.

Best, C. T., Morrongiello, B., & Robson, R. (1981). Perceptual equivalence of acoustic cues in speech and nonspeech perception. *Perception & Psychophysics*, *29*, 191–211.

Bharucha, J. J. (1994). Tonality and expectation. In R. Aiello & J. A. Sloboda (Eds.), *Musical perceptions* (pp. 213–239). New York: Oxford University Press.

Biancolli, A. (1995, February 12). 3-D thrills. *Times-Union*, Albany, NY, pp. G1–G7.

Biederman, I. (1987). Recognition-by-components: A theory of human image understanding. *Psychological Review*, *94*, 115–147.

Bigand, E. (1993). Contributions of music to research on human auditory cognition. In S. McAdams & E. Bigand (Eds.), *Thinking in sound: The cognitive psychology of human audition* (pp. 231–277). New York: Oxford University Press.

Bingham, G. P. (1993a). Perceiving the size of trees: Form as information about scale. *Journal of Experimental Psychology: Human Perception and Performance*, *19*, 1139–1161.

Bingham, G. P. (1993b). Scaling judgments of lifted weight: Lifter size and the role of the standard. *Ecological Psychology*, *5*(1), 31–64.

Birch, J. (1993). *Diagnosis of defective colour vision*. Oxford: Oxford University Press.

Birch, J., & McKeever, L. M. (1993). Survey of the accuracy of new pseudoisochromatic plates. *Ophthalmology and Physiological Optics*, *13*, 35–40.

Birnberg, J. R. (1988, March 21). My turn. *Newsweek*, p. 10.

Birren, F. (1976). *Color perception in art*. New York: Van Nostrand Reinhold.

Biswell, R. (1992). Cornea. In D. Vaughn, T. Asbury, & P. Riordan-Eva (Eds.), *General ophthalmology* (pp. 125–149). Norwalk, CT: Appleton & Lange.

Blake, A., & Bülthoff, H. (1990). Does the brain know the physics of specular reflection? *Nature*, *343*, 165–168.

Blake, R. (1988). A neural theory of binocular rivalry. *Psychological Review*, *96*, 145–167.

Blake, R. (1993). Cats perceive biological motion. *Psychological Science*, *4*, 54–57.

Blake, R. (1994). Gibson's inspired but latent prelude to visual motion perception. *Psychological Review*, *101*, 324–348.

Blake, R., Yang, Y., & Wilson, H. R. (1991). On the coexistence of stereopsis and binocular rivalry. *Vision Research*, *14*, 585–586.

Blakemore, C., & Campbell, F. W. (1969). On the existence of neurones in the human visual system selectively sensitive to the orientation and size of retinal images. *Journal of Physiology*, *203*, 237–260.

Blakeslee, S. (1992a, November 10). Missing limbs, still atingle, are clues to changes in the brain. *The New York Times*, p. B5.

Blakeslee, S. (1992b, October 27). Nerve cell rhythm may be key to consciousness. *The New York Times*, pp. C1, C10.

Bloom, W., & Fawcett, D. W. (1975). *A textbook of histology*. Philadelphia: W.B. Saunders.

Boff, K. R., Kaufman, L., & Thomas, J. P. (Eds.). (1986). *Handbook of perception and human performance*. New York: Wiley.

Bohlander, R. W. (1984). Eye position and visual attention influence perceived auditory direction. *Perceptual and Motor Skills, 59*, 483–510.

Bolanowski, S. J., Jr. (1989). Four channels mediate vibrotaction: Facts, models, and implications. *Journal of the Acoustical Society of America, 85*, S62.

Boltz, M. (1989). Perceiving the end: Effects of tonal relationships on melodic completion. *Journal of Experimental Psychology: Human Perception and Performance, 15*, 749–761.

Boltz, M. (1992). Temporal accent structure and the remembering of filmed narratives. *Journal of Experimental Psychology: Human Perception and Performance, 18*, 90–105.

Boltz, M., Schulkind, M., & Kantra, S. (1991). Effects of background music on the remembering of filmed events. *Memory & Cognition, 19*, 593–606.

Bonaiuto, P., Giannini, A. M., & Bonaiuto, M. (1991). Visual illusory productions with or without amodal completion. *Perception, 20*, 243–257.

Bond, Z. S., & Garnes, S. (1980). Misperception and production of fluent speech. In R. A. Cole (Ed.), *Perception and production of fluent speech* (pp. 115–132). Hillsdale, NJ: Erlbaum.

Bonnet, C. (1982). Thresholds of motion perception. In A. H. Wertheim, W. A. Wagenaar, & H. W. Leibowitz (Eds.), *Tutorials on motion perception* (pp. 41–79). New York: Plenum.

Bootsma, R. J., & Peper, C. E. (1992). Predictive visual information sources for the regulation of action with special emphasis on catching and hitting. In L. Proteau & D. Elliot (Eds.), *Vision and motor control* (pp. 285–314). Amsterdam: Elsevier.

Bootsma, R. J., & Van Wieringen, P. C. W. (1990). Timing an attacking forehand drive in table tennis. *Journal of Experimental Psychology: Human Perception and Performance, 16*, 21–29.

Borg, E., & Counter, S. A. (1989). The middle-ear muscles. *Scientific American, 261*(2), 74–80.

Boring, C. S., Squires, T. S., & Tong, T. (1993). Cancer statistics, 1993. *CA-A Cancer Journal for Clinicians, 43*, 7–8.

Boring, E. G. (1942). *Sensation and perception in the history of experimental psychology*. New York: Appleton-Century-Crofts.

Boring, E. G. (1961). Fechner: Inadvertent founder of psychophysics. *Psychometrika, 26*, 3–8.

Bornstein, M. H. (1975). Qualities of color vision in infancy. *Journal of Experimental Child Psychology, 19*, 401–419.

Bornstein, M. H. (1984a). A descriptive taxonomy of psychological categories used by infants. In C. Sophian (Ed.), *Origins of cognitive skills* (pp. 313–338). Hillsdale, NJ: Erlbaum.

Bornstein, M. H. (1985). Perceptual development. In M. H. Bornstein & M. E. Lamb (Eds.), *Developmental psychology: An advanced textbook* (pp. 81–132). Hillsdale, NJ: Erlbaum.

Bornstein, M. H. (1985a). Habituation of attention as a measure of visual information processing in human infants: Summary, systematization and synthesis. In G. Gottlieb & N. A. Krasnegor (Eds.), *Measurement of audition and vision in the first year of postnatal life* (pp. 253–300). Norwood, NJ: Ablex.

Bornstein, M. H. (1985b). Infant to adult: Unity to diversity in the development of visual categorization. In J. Mehler & R. Fox (Eds.), *Neonate cognition: Beyond the blooming, buzzing confusion* (pp. 115–138). Hillsdale, NJ: Erlbaum.

Bornstein, M. H. (1987). Perceptual categories in vision and audition. In S. Harnad (Ed.), *Categorical perception: The groundwork of cognition* (pp. 287–300). Cambridge: Cambridge University Press.

Bornstein, M. H., & Monroe, M. D. (1980). Chromatic information processing: Rate depends on stimulus location in category and psychological complexity. *Psychological Research, 42*, 213–225.

Bowmaker, J. K., & Dartnall, H. M. A. (1980). Visual pigments of rods and cones in a human retina. *Journal of Physiology, 298*, 501–511.

Boyce, S. J., & Pollatsek, A. (1992a). An exploration of the effects of scene context on object identification. In K. Rayner (Ed.), *Eye movements and visual cognition: Scene perception and reading* (pp. 227–242). New York: Springer-Verlag.

Boyce, S. J., & Pollatsek, A. (1992b). The identification of objects in scenes: The role of scene background in object naming. *Journal of Experimental Psychology: Learning, Memory, and Cognition, 18*, 531–543.

Boyce, S. J., Pollatsek, A., & Rayner, K. (1989). Effect of background information on object identification. *Journal of Experimental Psychology: Human Perception and Performance, 15*, 556–566.

Boynton, R. M. (1971). Color vision. In J. W. Kling & L. A. Riggs (Eds.), *Woodworth & Schlosberg's experimental psychology* (pp. 315–368). New York: Holt, Rinehart & Winston.

Boynton, R. M. (1979). *Human color vision*. New York: Holt, Rinehart & Winston.

Boynton, R. M. (1983). Mechanisms of chromatic discrimination. In J. D. Mollon & L. T. Sharpe (Eds.),

Colour vision (pp. 409–423). London: Academic Press.

Boynton, R. M. (1986). A system of photometry and colorimetry based on cone excitations. *Color Research and Application, 11*, 244–252.

Boynton, R. M. (1988). Color vision. *Annual Review of Psychology, 39*, 69–100.

Boynton, R. M. (1990). Human color perception. In K. N. Leibovic (Ed.), *Science of vision* (pp. 211–253). New York: Springer-Verlag.

Boynton, R. M., Fargo, L., Olson, C. X., & Smallman, H. S. (1989). Category effects in color memory. *Color Research and Application, 14*, 229–234.

Boynton, R. M., & Olson, C. X. (1987). Locating basic colors in the OSA space. *Color Research and Application, 12*, 94–105.

Brainard, D. H., & Wandell, B. A. (1992). Asymmetric color matching: How color appearance depends on the illuminant. *Journal of the Optical Society of America A, 9*, 1433–1448.

Brainard, D. H., Wandell, B. A., & Chichilnisky, E.-J. (1993). Color constancy: From physics to appearance. *Current Directions in Psychological Science, 2*, 165–170.

Brannon, L., & Feist, J. (1992). *Health psychology: An introduction to behavior and health.* Belmont, CA: Wadsworth.

Braunstein, M. L., & Andersen, G. J. (1981). Velocity gradients and relative depth perception. *Perception & Psychophysics, 29*, 145–155.

Braunstein, M. L., & Andersen, G. J. (1984). Shape and depth perception from parallel projections of three-dimensional motion. *Journal of Experimental Psychology: Human Perception and Performance, 10*, 749–760.

Bredberg, G. (1985). The anatomy of the developing ear. In S. E. Trehub & B. A. Schneider (Eds.), *The anatomy of the developing ear* (pp. 3–20). New York: Plenum.

Bregman, A. S. (1990). *Auditory scene analysis: The perceptual organization of sound.* Cambridge, MA: MIT Press.

Bregman, A. S. (1993). Auditory scene analysis: Hearing in complex environments. In S. McAdams & E. Bigand (Eds.), *Thinking in sound: The cognitive psychology of human audition* (pp. 10–36). New York: Oxford University Press.

Breitmeyer, B. G. (1992). Parallel processing in human vision: History, review, and critique. In J. R. Brannan (Ed.), *Applications of parallel processing in vision* (pp. 37–78). Amsterdam: North-Holland.

Bridgeman, B., & Delgado, D. (1984). Sensory effects of eye press are due to efference. *Perception & Psychophysics, 36*, 482–484.

Brigner, W. L. (1991). Contributions to the history of psychology: LXXXII. Authors, perceived color, and light intensity. *Perceptual and Motor Skills, 73*, 485–486.

Brill, M. H., & West, G. (1986). Chromatic adaptation and color constancy: A possible dichotomy. *Color Research and Application, 11*, 196–204.

Brodie, E. E., & Ross, H. E. (1984). Sensorimotor mechanisms in weight discrimination. *Perception & Psychophysics, 36*, 477–481.

Brody, J. E. (1993, March 23). Brain yields clues to its visual maps. *The New York Times*, pp. C1, C10.

Broerse, J., Ashton, R., & Shaw, C. (1992). The apparent shape of afterimages in the Ames room. *Perception, 21*, 261–268.

Brosvic, G. M., & Cohen, B. D. (1988). The horizontal–vertical illusion and knowledge of results. *Perceptual and Motor Skills, 67*, 463–469.

Brosvic, G. M., & McLaughlin, W. W. (1989). Quality specific differences in human taste detection thresholds as a function of stimulus volume. *Physiology & Behavior, 45*, 15–20.

Brou, P., Sciascia, T. R., Linden, L., & Lettvin, J. Y. (1986). The colors of things. *Scientific American, 255*(3), 84–91.

Brown, A. M. (1990). Development of visual sensitivity to light and color vision in human infants: A critical review. *Vision Research, 30*, 1159–1188.

Brown, C. C. (1984). *The many facets of touch.* Skillman, NJ: Johnson & Johnson.

Brown, C. H., & May, B. J. (1990). Sound localization and binaural processes. In M. A. Berkley & W. C. Stebbins (Eds.), *Comparative Perception* (pp. 247–283). New York: Wiley.

Brown, P. (1990, July 21). Cardboard, pencil and paper: New tools to spot glaucoma. *New Scientist*, p. 31.

Brown, P. (1991, March 16). Desktop test catches glaucoma early . . . *New Scientist*, p. 27.

Brown, R. J., & Thurmond, J. B. (1993). Preattentive and cognitive effects on perceptual completion at the blind spot. *Perception & Psychophysics, 53*, 200–209.

Brownell, W. E., Bader, C. E., Bertrand, D., & Ribaupierre, Y. de (1985). Evoked mechanical responses of isolated cochlear outer hair cells. *Science, 227*, 194–196.

Bruce, V., & Green, P. (1990). *Visual perception: Physiology, psychology, and ecology* (2nd ed.). Hove, UK: Erlbaum.

Bruce, V., & Valentine, T. (1988). When a nod's as good as a wink: The role of dynamic information in facial recognition. In M. M. Gruneberg, P. E. Morris, & R. N. Sykes (Eds.), *Practical aspects of memory: Current research and issues* (pp. 169–174). Chichester, UK: Wiley.

Brugge, J. F. (1992). An overview of central auditory processing. In A. N. Popper & R. R. Fay (Eds.), *The mammalian auditory pathway: Neurophysiology* (pp. 1–33). New York: Springer-Verlag.

Buck, L., & Axel, R. (1991). A novel multigene family may encode odorant receptors: A molecular basis for odor recognition. *Cell, 65,* 175–187.

Buck, L. B. (1993). Receptor diversity and spatial patterning in the mammalian olfactory system. In D. Chadwick, J. Marsh, & J. Goode (Eds.), *The molecular basis of smell and taste transduction* (pp. 51–67). New York: Wiley.

Buckalew, L. W., & Coffield, K. E. (1982). An investigation of drug expectancy as a function of capsule color and size and preparation form. *Journal of Clinical Psychopharmacology, 2,* 245–248.

Bülthoff, H., Little, J., & Poggio, T. (1989). A parallel algorithm for real-time computation of optical flow. *Nature, 337,* 549–553.

Bülthoff, H. H. (1991). Shape from X: Psychophysics and computation. In M. S. Landy & J. A. Movshon (Eds.), *Computational models of visual processing* (pp. 305–330). Cambridge, MA: MIT Press.

Bülthoff, H. H., & Mallot, H. A. (1988). Integration of depth modules: Stereo and shading. *Journal of the Optical Society of America A, 5,* 1749–1758.

Burdach, K. J., Kroeze, J. H. A., & Köster, E. P. (1984). Nasal, retronasal, and gustatory perception: An experimental comparison. *Perception & Psychophysics, 36,* 205–208.

Burnham, D. (1993). Visual recognition of mother by young infants: Facilitation by speech. *Perception, 22,* 1133–1153.

Burnham, D. K., & Dodd, B. (1994). Infants' auditory–visual perception of speech in familiar and foreign languages. (Unpublished manuscript)

Burns, E. M. (1981). Circularity in relative pitch judgments for inharmonic complex tones: The Shepard demonstrations revisited, again. *Perception & Psychophysics, 30,* 467–472.

Burt, P., & Sperling, G. (1981). Time, distance, and feature trade-offs in visual apparent motion. *Psychological Review, 88,* 171–195.

Bushnell, I. W. R. (1982). Discrimination of faces by young infants. *Journal of Experimental Psychology, 33,* 298–308.

Butler, D. (1992). *The musician's guide to perception and cognition.* New York: Schirmer.

Caelli, T., Manning, M., & Finlay, D. (1993). A general correspondence approach to apparent motion. *Perception, 22,* 185–192.

Cailliet, R. (1993). *Pain: Mechanisms and management.* Philadelphia: Davis.

Cain, W. S. (1973). Spatial discrimination of cutaneous warmth. *American Journal of Psychology, 86,* 169–181.

Cain, W. S. (1977). Differential sensitivity for smell: Noise at the nose. *Science, 195,* 796–798.

Cain, W. S. (1978). The odoriferous environment and the application of olfactory research. In E. C. Carterette & M. P. Friedman (Eds.), *Handbook of Perception* (pp. 277–304). New York: Academic Press.

Cain, W. S. (1980). Chemosensation and cognition. In H. van der Starre (Ed.), *Olfaction and taste VII* (pp. 347–358). London: IRL.

Cain, W. S. (1981). Olfaction and the common chemical sense: Similarities, differences, and interactions. In H. R. Moskowitz & C. Warren (Eds.), *Odor quality and intensity as a function of chemical structure* (pp. 109–121). Washington, DC: American Chemical Society.

Cain, W. S. (1982). Odor identification by males and females: Predictions vs. performance. *Chemical Senses, 7,* 129–142.

Cain, W. S. (1988). Olfaction. In R. C. Atkinson, R. J. Herrnstein, G. Lindzey, & R. D. Luce (Eds.), *Stevens' handbook of experimental psychology* (2nd ed., Vol. 1, pp. 409–459). New York: Wiley.

Cain, W. S., & Gent, J. F. (1991). Olfactory sensitivity: Reliability, generality, and association with aging. *Journal of Experimental Psychology: Human Perception and Performance, 17,* 382–391.

Cain, W. S., & Polak, E. H. (1992). Olfactory adaptation as an aspect of odor similarity. *Chemical Senses, 17,* 481–491.

Caird, D. (1991). Processing in the colliculi. In R. A. Altschuler, R. P. Bobbin, B. M. Clopton, & D. W. Hoffman (Eds.), *Neurobiology of hearing: The central auditory system* (pp. 253–292). New York: Raven.

Campbell, F. W., & Robson, J. G. (1964). Application of Fourier analysis of the modulation response of the eye. *Journal of the Optical Society of America, 54,* 518A.

Campbell, F. W., & Robson, J. G. (1968). Application of Fourier analysis to the visibility of gratings. *Journal of Physiology, 197,* 551–566.

Campbell, R. (1992a). Face to face: Interpreting a case of developmental prosopagnosia. In R. Campbell (Ed.), *Mental lives: Case studies in cognition* (pp. 216–236). Oxford: Blackwell.

Campbell, R. (1992b). Lip-reading and the modularity of cognitive function: Neuropsychological glimpses of fractionation for speech and for faces. In J. Alegria, D. Holender, J. Junça de Morais, & M. Radeau (Eds.), *Analytic approaches to human cognition* (pp. 275–289). Amsterdam: North-Holland.

Campbell, R. (1992c). The neuropsychology of lipreading. In V. Bruce, A. Cowey, A. W. Ellis, & D. I. Perrett (Eds.), *Processing the facial image* (pp. 39–45). Oxford: Clarendon.

Capaldi, E. J., & Proctor, R. W. (1994). Contextualism: Is the act in context the adequate metaphor for scientific psychology? *Psychonomic Bulletin & Review, 1(2),* 239–249.

Carlson, N. R. (1991). *Physiology of behavior* (4th ed.). Newton, MA: Allyn & Bacon.

Carney, A. E. (1988). Vibrotactile perception of segmental features of speech: A comparison of single-channel and multichannel instruments. *Journal of Speech and Hearing Research, 31,* 438–448.

Carrasco, M., & Sekuler, E. B. (1993). An unreported size illusion. *Perception, 22,* 313–322.

Carter, J. H. (1982). The effects of aging upon selected visual functions: Color vision, glare sensitivity, field of vision, and accommodation. In R. Sekuler, D. Kline, & K. Dismukes (Eds.), *Aging and human visual function* (pp. 121–130). New York: Alan R. Liss.

Carterette, E. C., & Kendall, R. A. (1989). Human music perception. In R. J. Dooling & S. H. Hulse (Eds.), *The comparative psychology of audition: Perceiving complex sounds* (pp. 131–172). Hillsdale, NJ: Erlbaum.

Casali, J. G., & Park, M.-Y. (1990). Attenuation performance of four hearing protectors under dynamic movement and different user fitting conditions. *Human Factors, 32,* 9–25.

Cattell, J. M. (1886). The time it takes to see and name objects. *Mind, 11,* 63–65.

Cavanagh, P., & Mather, G. (1989). Motion: The long and short of it. *Spatial Vision, 4,* 103–129.

Cernoch, J. M., & Porter, R. H. (1985). Recognition of maternal axillary odors by infants. *Child Development, 56,* 1593–1598.

Chang, D. F. (1992). Ophthalmologic examination. In D. Vaughn, T. Asbury, & P. Riordan-Eva (Eds.), *General ophthalmology* (pp. 30–62). Norwalk, CT: Appleton & Lange.

Chapanis, A. (1949). How we see: A summary of basic principles. In *Human factors in undersea warfare.* Washington, DC: National Research Council.

Chaparro, A., Stromeyer, C. F., III, Huang, E. P., Kronauer, R. E., & Eskew, R. T., Jr. (1993). Colour is what the eye sees best. *Nature, 361,* 348–350.

Cholewiak, R. W., & Collins, A. A. (1991). Sensory and physiological bases of touch. In M. A. Heller & W. Schiff (Eds.), *The psychology of touch* (pp. 23–60). Hillsdale, NJ: Erlbaum.

Chung, C. S., & Berbaum, K. (1984). Form and depth in global stereopsis. *Journal of Experimental Psychology: Human Perception and Performance, 10,* 258–275.

Churchland, P. S., Ramachandran, V. S., & Sejnowski, T. J. (1994). A critique of pure vision. In C. Koch & J. L. Davis (Eds.), *Large-scale neuronal theories of the brain* (pp. 23–60). Cambridge, MA: MIT Press.

Churchland, P. S., & Sejnowski, T. J. (1992). *The computational brain.* Cambridge, MA: MIT Press.

Ciocca, V., & Bregman, A. S. (1989). The effects of auditory streaming on duplex perception. *Perception & Psychophysics, 46,* 39–48.

Clarey, J. C., Barone, P., & Imig, T. J. (1992). Physiology of thalamus and cortex. In A. N. Popper & R. R. Fay (Eds.), *The mammalian auditory pathway: Neurophysiology* (pp. 232–334). New York: Springer-Verlag.

Clark, H. H. (1991). Words, the world, and their possibilities. In G. R. Lockhead & J. R. Pomerantz (Eds.), *The perception of structure* (pp. 263–277). Washington, DC: American Psychological Association.

Clark, W. C., & Horch, K. W. (1986). Kinesthesia. In K. R. Boff, L. Kaufman, & J. P. Thomas (Eds.), *Handbook of perception and human performance* (pp. 13.1–13.62). New York: Wiley.

Clulow, F. W. (1972). *Color: Its principles and their applications.* New York: Morgan and Morgan.

Cohen, A., & Rafal, R. D. (1991). Attention and feature integration: Illusory conjunctions in a patient with a parietal lobe lesion. *Psychological Science, 2,* 106–110.

Cohen, A. J., Thorpe, L. A., & Trehub, S. E. (1987). Infants' perception of musical relations in short transposed tone sequences. *Canadian Journal of Psychology, 41,* 33–47.

Cohen, D. (1992). *Convexity assumed.* Unpublished manuscript.

Cohen, G., & Faulkner, D. (1983). Word recognition: Age differences in contextual facilitation effects. *British Journal of Psychology, 74,* 231–251.

Cohen, M., & Grossberg, S. (1986). Neural dynamics of speech and language coding: Developmental programs, perceptual grouping, and competition for short-term memory. *Human Neurobiology, 5,* 1–22.

Cohn, T. E., & Lasley, D. J. (1986). Visual sensitivity. *Annual Review of Psychology, 37,* 495–521.

Cole, J. (1991). *Pride and a daily marathon.* Cambridge, MA: MIT Press.

Cole, R. A., & Jakimik, J. (1980). A model of speech perception. In R. A. Cole (Ed.), *Perception and production of fluent speech* (pp. 133–163). Hillsdale, NJ: Erlbaum.

Coletta, N. J., & Adams, A. J. (1986). Spatial extent of rod–cone and cone–cone interactions for flicker detection. *Vision Research, 26,* 917–925.

Collings, V. B. (1974). Human taste response as a function of locus of stimulation on the tongue and soft palate. *Perception & Psychophysics, 16,* 169–174.

Cooper, L. A. (1994). Probing the nature of the mental representation of visual objects: Evidence from cognitive dissociations. In S. Ballesteros (Ed.), *Cognitive approaches to human perception* (pp. 199–221). Hillsdale, NJ: Erlbaum.

Cooper, L. A., & Schacter, D. L. (1992). Dissociations between structural and episodic representations of visual objects. *Current Directions in Psychological Science, 1*, 141–146.

Cooper, L. A., & Shepard, R. N. (1984). Turning something over in the mind. *Scientific American, 251*(6), 106–114.

Cooper, R. P., & Aslin, R. N. (1989). The language environment of the young infant: Implications for early perceptual development. *Canadian Journal of Psychology, 43*, 247–265.

Cooper, W. E. (1983). The perception of fluid speech. *Annals of the New York Academy of Sciences, 405*, 48–63.

Corballis, M. C. (1988). Recognition of disoriented shapes. *Psychological Review, 95*, 115–123.

Coren, S. (1972). Subjective contours and apparent depth. *Psychological Review, 79*, 359–367.

Coren, S. (1986). An efferent component in the visual perception of direction and extent. *Psychological Review, 93*, 391–410.

Coren, S. (1991). Retinal mechanisms in the perception of subjective contours: The contribution of lateral inhibition. *Perception, 20*, 181–191.

Coren, S., & Girgus, J. S. (1972). Illusion decrement in intersecting line figures. *Psychonomic Science, 26*, 108–110.

Coren, S., & Girgus, J. S. (1978). *Seeing is deceiving: The psychology of visual illusions.* Hillsdale, NJ: Erlbaum.

Coren, S., & Porac, C. (1983). Subjective contours and apparent depth: A direct test. *Perception & Psychophysics, 33*, 197–200.

Coren, S., Ward, L. M., & Enns, J. T. (1994). *Sensation and Perception* (4th ed.). Fort Worth, TX: Academic Press.

Corso, J. F. (1981). *Aging sensory systems and perception.* New York: Praeger.

Courtney, S. M., & Buchsbaum, G. (1991). Temporal differences between color pathways within the retina as a possible origin of subjective colors. *Vision Research, 31*, 1541–1548.

Cowey, A. (1994). Cortical visual areas and the neurobiology of higher visual processes. In M. J. Farah & G. Ratcliff (Eds.), *The neuropsychology of high-level vision: Collected tutorial essays* (pp. 3–31). Hillsdale, NJ: Erlbaum.

Cowey, A., & Stoerig, P. (1995). Blindsight in monkeys. *Nature, 373*, 247–249.

Craig, J. C. (1985). Attending to two fingers: Two hands are better than one. *Perception & Psychophysics, 38*, 496–511.

Craig, J. C. (1989). Interference in localizing tactile stimuli. *Perception & Psychophysics, 45*, 343–355.

Craig, J. C., & Sherrick, C. E. (1982). Dynamic tactile displays. In W. Schiff & E. Foulke (Eds.), *Tactual perception: A sourcebook* (pp. 209–233). Cambridge: Cambridge University Press.

Cranford, J. L., & Stream, R. W. (1991). Discrimination of short duration tones by elderly subjects. *Journal of Gerontology: Psychological Sciences, 46*, 37–41.

Critelli, J. W., & Neumann, K. F. (1984). The placebo: Conceptual analysis of a concept in transition. *American Psychologist, 39*, 32–39.

Cross, D. V., Tursky, B., & Lodge, M. (1975). The role of regression and range effects in determination of the power function for electric shock. *Perception & Psychophysics, 18*, 9–14.

Crowder, R. G. (1993). Auditory memory. In S. McAdams & E. Bigand (Eds.), *Thinking in sound: The cognitive psychology of human audition* (pp. 113–145). New York: Oxford University Press.

Cuddy, L. L. (1993). Melody comprehension and tonal structure. In T. J. Tighe & W. J. Dowling (Eds.), *Psychology and music* (pp. 19–38). Hillsdale, NJ: Erlbaum.

Curthoys, I. S., & Wade, N. J. (1990). A balanced view of otolithic function: Comment on Stoffregen and Riccio (1988). *Psychological Review, 97*, 132–134.

Cutting, J. E. (1986). *Perception with an eye for motion.* Cambridge, MA: MIT Press.

Cutting, J. E. (1987). Perception and information. *Annual Review of Psychology, 38*, 61–90.

Cutting, J. E. (1993). Perceptual artifacts and phenomena: Gibson's role in the 20th century. In S. C. Masin (Ed.), *Foundations of perceptual theory* (pp. 231–260). New York: Elsevier.

Cutting, J. E., Moore, C., & Morrison, R. (1988). Masking the motions of human gait. *Perception & Psychophysics, 44*, 339–347.

Cutting, J. E., Springer, K., Braren, P. A., & Johnson, S. H. (1992). Wayfinding on foot from information in retinal, not optical, flow. *Journal of Experimental Psychology: General, 121*(1), 41–72.

Dallenbach, K. M. (1927). The temperature spots and end organs. *American Journal of Psychology, 39*, 402–427.

Dallos, P. (1992). Neurobiology of cochlear hair cells. In Y. Cazals, L. Demany, & K. Horner (Eds.), *Auditory physiology and perception* (pp. 3–17). Oxford: Pergamon.

Dalton, J. (1798/1948). Extraordinary facts relating to the vision of colours: With observations. In W. Dennis (Ed.), *Readings in the History of Psychology* (pp. 102–111). New York: Appleton-Century-Crofts.

Dalziel, C. C., & Egan, D. J. (1982). Crystalline lens thickness changes as observed by psychometry. *American Journal of Optometry and Physiological Optics, 59*, 442–447.

Damasio, A. R., Tranel, D., & Damasio, H. (1990). Face agnosia and the neural substrates of memory. *Annual Review of Neuroscience, 13*, 89–109.

Dannemiller, J. L. (1989). Computational approaches to color constancy: Adaptive and ontogenetic considerations. *Psychological Review, 96*, 255–266.

Dannemiller, J. L. (1991). Lightness is not illuminant invariant: Reply to Troost and de Weert (1990). *Psychological Review, 98*, 146–148.

Darwin, C. J. (1991). The relationship between speech perception and the perception of other sounds. In I. G. Mattingly & M. Studdert-Kennedy (Eds.), *Modularity and the motor theory of speech perception* (pp. 239–267). Hillsdale, NJ: Erlbaum.

Davis, P. J., & Hersh, R. (1981). *The mathematical experience*. Boston: Houghton Mifflin.

Dawson, M. R. W. (1991). The how and why of what went where in apparent motion: Modeling solutions to the motion correspondence problem. *Psychological Review, 98*, 569–603.

Dawson, W. E. (1982). On the parallel between direct ratio scaling of social opinion and of sensory magnitude. In B. Wegener (Ed.), *Social attitudes and psychophysical measurement* (pp. 151–176). Hillsdale, NJ: Erlbaum.

Day, R. H. (1989). Natural and artificial cues, perceptual compromise and the basis of veridical and illusory perception. In D. Vickers & P. L. Smith (Eds.), *Human information processing: Measures and mechanisms* (pp. 107–129). New York: Elsevier.

Day, R. H. (1993). The Ames room from another viewpoint. *Perception, 22*, 1007–1011.

Dearborn, G. V. N. (1932). A case of congenital general pure analgesia. *Journal of Nervous and Mental Disorders, 75*, 612–615.

DeCasper, A. J., & Fifer, W. P. (1980). Of human bonding: Newborns prefer their mothers' voices. *Science, 208*, 1174–1176.

DeCasper, A. J., & Spencer, M. J. (1986). Prenatal maternal speech influences newborns' perception of speech sounds. *Infant Behavior and Development, 9*, 133–150.

Degoldi, B. R., & Day, R. H. (1992). The Müller–Lyer illusion Mark II. *Perception, 21*, 269–272.

De Graef, P. (1992). Scene-context effects and models of real-world perception. In K. Rayner (Ed.), *Eye movements and visual cognition: Scene perception and reading* (pp. 243–259). New York: Springer-Verlag.

Delk, J. L., & Fillenbaum, S. (1965). Difference in perceived color as a function of characteristic color. *American Journal of Psychology, 78*, 290–293.

DeLucia, P. R., Longmire, S. P., & Kennish, J. (1994). Diamond-winged variants of the Müller–Lyer figure: A test of Virso's (1971) centroid theory. *Perception & Psychophysics, 55*(3), 287–295.

Dengler, M., & Nitschke, W. (1993). Color stereopsis: A model for depth reversals based on border contrast. *Perception & Psychophysics, 53*, 150–156.

Dennett, D. C. (1978). Where am I? In D. C. Dennett (Ed.), *Brainstorms* (pp. 310–323). Cambridge, MA: MIT Press.

Deregowski, J. B. (1980). *Illusions, patterns and pictures: A cross-cultural perspective*. London: Academic.

Deregowski, J. B. (1984). *Distortion in art: The eye and the mind*. London: Routledge & Kegan Paul.

Deregowski, J. B. (1989). Real space and represented space: Cross-cultural perspectives. *Behavioral and Brain Sciences, 12*, 51–119.

Dernham, P. (1986). Phantom limb pain. *Geriatric Nursing, 7*, 34–37.

Desimone, R. (1991). Face-selective cells in the temporal cortex of monkeys. *Journal of Cognitive Neuroscience, 3*, 1–8.

Desor, J. A., & Beauchamp, G. K. (1974). The human capacity to transmit olfactory information. *Perception & Psychophysics, 16*, 551–556.

Deutsch, D. (1982). Grouping mechanisms in music. In D. Deutsch (Ed.), *The psychology of music* (pp. 99–134). New York: Academic Press.

Deutsch, D. (1983). The octave illusion in relation to handedness and familial handedness background. *Neuropsychologia, 21*, 289–293.

Deutsch, D. (1984). Psychology and music. In M. H. Bornstein (Ed.), *Psychology and its allied disciplines* (pp. 155–194). Hillsdale, NJ: Erlbaum.

Deutsch, D. (1986a). Auditory pattern recognition. In K. R. Boff, L. Kaufman, & J. P. Thomas (Eds.), *Handbook of perception and human performance* (pp. 32.1–32.49). New York: Wiley.

Deutsch, D. (1986b). A musical paradox. *Music Perception, 3*, 275–280.

Deutsch, D. (1987, March). Illusions for stereo headphones. *Audio*, pp. 36–48.

Deutsch, D. (1990). The tritone paradox: Correlate with the listener's vocal range for speech. *Music Perception, 7*, 371–384.

Deutsch, D. (1991). The tritone paradox: An influence of language on music perception. *Music Perception, 8*, 335–347.

Deutsch, D. (1992a). Paradoxes of musical pitch. *Scientific American, 267*(2), 88–95.

Deutsch, D. (1992b). Some new pitch paradoxes and their implications. In R. P. Carlyon, C. J. Darwin, & I. J. Russell (Eds.), *Processing of complex sounds by the auditory system* (pp. 391–397). Oxford: Clarendon.

Deutsch, D. (1992c). The tritone paradox: Implications for the representation and communication of pitch structures. In M. R. Jones & S. Holleran (Eds.), *Cognitive bases of musical communication* (pp. 115–138). Washington, DC: American Psychological Association.

Deutsch, D. (1994). *Some new musical paradoxes*. Paper presented at the meeting of the American Psychological Association, Los Angeles.

DeValois, R. L., & DeValois, K. K. (1975). Neural coding of color. In E. C. Carterette & M. P. Friedman (Eds.), *Handbook of perception* (pp. 117–166). New York: Academic Press.

DeValois, R. L., & DeValois, K. K. (1993). A multistage color model. *Vision Research, 33,* 1053–1065.

de Wijk, R. A., & Cain, W. S. (1994). Odor quality: Discrimination versus free and cued identification. *Perception & Psychophysics, 56,* 12–18.

de Wijk, R. A., Schab, F. R., & Cain, W. S. (1995). Odor identification. In F. R. Schab & R. G. Crowder (Eds.), *Memory for odors* (pp. 21–37). Mahwah, NJ: Erlbaum.

DeYoe, E. A., & van Essen, D. C. (1988). Concurrent processing streams in monkey visual cortex. *Trends in Neurosciences, 11,* 219–226.

Dichgans, J., & Brandt, T. (1978). Visual-vestibular interaction: Effects of self-motion perception and postural control. In R. Held, H. W. Leibowitz, & H. L. Teuber (Eds.), *Handbook of sensory physiology: Vol. 8 Perception* (pp. 755–804). Berlin: Springer-Verlag.

Ditchburn, R. W. (1981). Small involuntary eye movements: Solved and unsolved problems. In D. Fisher, R. A. Monty, & J. W. Senders (Eds.), *Eye movements: Cognition and visual perception* (pp. 227–235). Hillsdale, NJ: Erlbaum.

Dittrich, W. H. (1993). Action categories and the perception of biological motion. *Perception, 22,* 15–22.

Dobkins, K. R., & Albright, T. D. (1993). Color, luminance, and the detection of visual motion. *Current Directions in Psychological Science, 2,* 189–193.

Dobson, V. (1993). Commentary: Extending the ideal observer approach. In C. E. Granrud (Ed.), *Visual perception and cognition in infancy* (pp. 317–332). Hillsdale, NJ: Erlbaum.

Dodd, B. (1977). The role of vision in the perception of speech. *Perception, 6,* 31–40.

Dodwell, P. C., Humphrey, G. K., & Muir, D. W. (1987). Shape and pattern perception. In P. Salapatek & L. Cohen (Eds.), *Handbook of infant perception* (pp. 1–77). Orlando, FL: Academic Press.

Doty, R. L. (1991). Olfactory system. In T. V. Getchell, R. L. Doty, L. M. Bartoshuk, & J. B. Snow, Jr. (Eds.), *Smell and taste in health and disease* (pp. 175–203). New York: Raven.

Doty, R. L., Bartoshuk, L. M., & Snow, J. B., Jr. (1991). Causes of olfactory and gustatory disorders. In T. V. Getchell, R. L. Doty, L. M. Bartoshuk, & J. B. Snow, Jr. (Eds.), *Smell and taste in health and disease* (pp. 449–462). New York: Raven.

Doty, R. L., & Müller-Schwarze, D. (Eds.). (1992). *Chemical senses in vertebrates 6.* New York: Plenum.

Dowling, J. E., & Boycott, B. B. (1966). Organization of the primate retina: Electron microscopy. *Proceedings of the Royal Society of London, Series B, 166,* 80–111.

Dowling, W. J. (1973). The perception of interleaved melodies. *Cognitive Psychology, 5,* 372–377.

Dowling, W. J. (1993). Procedural and declarative knowledge in music cognition and education. In T. J. Tighe & W. J. Dowling (Eds.), *Psychology and music* (pp. 1–18). Hillsdale, NJ: Erlbaum.

Dowling, W. J. (1994). Melodic contour in hearing and remembering melodies. In R. Aiello & J. A. Sloboda (Eds.), *Musical perceptions* (pp. 173–190). New York: Oxford University Press.

Dowling, W. J., & Harwood, D. L. (1986). *Music cognition.* New York: Academic Press.

Dresp, B., & Bonnet, C. (1991). Psychophysical evidence for low-level processing of illusory contours and surfaces in the Kanizsa square. *Vision Research, 31*(10), 1813–1817.

DuBose, C., Cardello, A. V., & Maller, O. (1980). Effects of colorants and flavorants on identification, perceived flavor intensity, and hedonic quality of fruit-flavored beverages and cake. *Journal of Food Science, 45,* 1393–1415.

Durlach, N. (1991). Auditory localization in teleoperator and virtual environment systems: Ideas, issues, and problems. *Perception, 20,* 543–554.

Dykes, R. W. (1983). Parallel processing of somatosensory information: A theory. *Brain Research Reviews, 6,* 47–115.

Dyson, M. C., & Watkins, A. J. (1984). A figural approach to the role of melodic contour in melody recognition. *Perception & Psychophysics, 35,* 477–488.

D'Zmura, M., Iverson, G., & Singer, B. (1995). Probabilistic color constancy. In R. D. Luce, M. D'Zmura, D. Hoffman, G. J. Iverson, & A. K. Romney (Eds.), *Geometric representations of perceptual phenomena: Papers in honor of Tarow Indow on his 70th birthday* (pp. 187–202). Mahwah, NJ: Erlbaum.

Earle, D. C. (1991). Some observations on the perception of Marroquin patterns. *Perception, 20,* 727–731.

Edington, B. (1979). Personal communication.

Edworthy, J. (1985). Melodic contour and musical structure. In P. Howell, I. Cross, & R. West (Eds.), *Musical structure and cognition* (pp. 169–188). London: Academic Press.

Eilers, R. E., & Minifie, F. D. (1975). Fricative discrimination in early infancy. *Journal of Speech and Hearing Research, 18,* 158–167.

Eimas, P. D. (1975). Auditory and phonetic coding of the cues for speech: Discrimination of the [r-l] distinction by young adults. *Perception & Psychophysics, 18,* 341–347.

Eimas, P. D., & Corbit, J. D. (1973). Selective adaptation of linguistic feature detectors. *Cognitive Psychology, 4,* 99–109.

Eimas, P. D., & Kavanagh, J. F. (1986). Otitis media, hearing loss, and child development: A NICHD conference summary. *Public Health Reports, 101,* 289–293.

Eimas, P. D., & Miller, J. L. (1992). Organization in the perception of speech by young infants. *Psychological Science, 3,* 340–345.

Eimas, P. D., Siqueland, E. R., Jusczyk, R., & Vigorito, J. (1971). Speech perception in infants. *Science, 171,* 303–306.

Eisenberg, D. M., Kessler, R. C., Foster, C., Norlock, F. E., Calkins, D. R., & Delbanco, T. L. (1993). Unconventional medicine in the United States: Prevalence, costs, and patterns of use. *The New England Journal of Medicine, 328,* 246–252.

Ellins, S. R., & Masterson, F. A. (1974). Brightness discrimination thresholds in the bat Eptesicus fuscus. *Brain, Behavior, and Evolution, 9,* 248–263.

Elworth, C. L., Larry, C., & Malmstrom, F. V. (1986). Age, degraded viewing environments, and the speed of accommodation. *Aviation, Space, and Environmental Medicine, 57,* 54–58.

Engen, T. (1971). Psychophysics: I. Discrimination and detection. In J. W. Kling & L. A. Riggs (Eds.), *Woodworth & Schlosberg's experimental psychology* (pp. 11–46). New York: Holt, Rinehart & Winston.

Engen, T. (1972). The effect of expectation on judgments of odor. *Acta Psychologica, 36,* 450–458.

Engen, T. (1982). *The perception of odors.* New York: Academic Press.

Engen, T. (1991). *Odor sensation and memory.* New York: Praeger.

Engen, T., & Ross, B. M. (1973). Long-term memory of odors with and without verbal descriptions. *Journal of Experimental Psychology, 100,* 221–227.

Enns, M. P., & Hornung, D. E. (1985). Contributions of smell and taste to overall intensity. *Chemical Senses, 10,* 357–366.

Enns, M. P., & Hornung, D. E. (1988). Comparisons of the estimates of smell, taste and overall intensity in young and elderly people. *Chemical Senses, 13,* 131–139.

Enroth-Cugell, C. (1993). The world of retinal ganglion cells. In R. Shapley & D. M.-K. Lam (Eds.), *Contrast sensitivity: Proceedings of the Retina Research Foundation Symposia* (pp. 149–179). Cambridge, MA: MIT Press.

Epstein, W. (1977). Historical introduction to the constancies. In W. Epstein (Ed.), *Stability and constancy in visual perception* (pp. 1–22). New York: Wiley.

Epstein, W., & Franklin, S. (1965). Some conditions of the effect of relative size on perceived distance. *American Journal of Psychology, 78,* 466–470.

Erickson, R. P. (1982). Studies on the perception of taste: Do primaries exist? *Physiology & Behavior, 28,* 57–62.

Escher, M. C. (1971). *The graphic work of M. C. Escher.* New York: Ballantine.

Espinoza-Varas, B., & Watson, C. S. (1989). Perception of complex auditory patterns by humans. In R. J. Dooling & S. H. Hulse (Eds.), *The comparative psychology of audition: Perceiving complex sounds* (pp. 67–94). Hillsdale, NJ: Erlbaum.

Evans, E. F. (1982a). Basic physics and psychophysics of sound. In H. B. Barlow & J. D. Mollon (Eds.), *The senses* (pp. 239–250). Cambridge: Cambridge University Press.

Evans, E. F. (1982b). Functional anatomy of the auditory system. In H. B. Barlow & J. D. Mollon (Eds.), *The senses* (pp. 251–306). Cambridge: Cambridge University Press.

Evans, E. F. (1982c). Functions of the auditory system. In H. B. Barlow & J. D. Mollon (Eds.), *The senses* (pp. 307–322). Cambridge: Cambridge University Press.

Ewin, D. M. (1986). Hypnosis and pain management. In B. Zilbergelt, M. G. Edelstien, & D. L. Araoz (Eds.), *Hypnosis: Questions and answers* (pp. 282–288). New York: Norton.

Falmagne, J. C. (1985). *Elements of psychophysical theory.* Oxford: Oxford University Press.

Fantz, R. L. (1961). The origin of form perception. *Scientific American, 204*(5), 66–72.

Farah, M. J. (1990). *Visual agnosia: Disorders of object recognition and what they tell us about normal vision.* Cambridge, MA: MIT Press.

Farah, M. J. (1994a). Neuropsychological inference with an interactive brain: A critique of the "locality" assumption. *Behavioral and Brain Sciences, 17,* 43–104.

Farah, M. J. (1994b). Specialization within visual object recognition: Clues from prosopagnosia and alexia. In M. J. Farah & G. Ratcliff (Eds.), *The neuropsychology of high-level vision: Collected tutorial essays* (pp. 133–146). Hillsdale, NJ: Erlbaum.

Farbman, A. I. (1988). Taste bud. In G. Adelman (Ed.), *Readings from the encyclopedia of neuroscience: Sensory systems II, senses other than vision* (pp. 128–129). Boston: Birkhäuser.

Farbman, A. I. (1992). *Cell biology of olfaction.* Cambridge: Cambridge University Press.

Fatt, I., & Weissman, B. A. (1992). *Physiology of the eye: An introduction to the vegetative functions* (2nd ed.). Boston: Butterworth-Heinemann.

Fechner, G. T. (1860). *Element der psychophysik.* Leipzig: Breitkopf & Harterl.

Feinberg, G., & Riccio, D. C. (1990). Changes in memory for stimulus attributes: Implications for tests of morphine tolerance. *Psychological Science, 1,* 265–267.

Fernald, A. (1990). *Emotion in the voice: Meaningful melodies in mother's speech to infants.* Paper presented at the meeting of the American Psychological Association, Boston.

Fernandez, E., & Turk, D. C. (1992). Sensory and affective components of pain: Separation and synthesis. *Psychological Bulletin, 112,* 205–217.

Feuerstein, M., Labbé, E. E., & Kuczmierczyk, A. R. (1986). *Health psychology: A psychobiological perspective.* New York: Plenum.

Filsinger, E. E., & Fabes, R. A. (1985). Odor communication, pheromones, and human families. *Journal of Marriage and the Family, 47,* 349–359.

Findlay, J. M. (1992). Programming of stimulus-elicited saccadic eye movements. In K. Rayner (Ed.), *Eye movements and visual cognition: Scene perception and reading* (pp. 8–30). New York: Springer-Verlag.

Fineman, M. (1981). *The inquisitive eye.* New York: Oxford University Press.

Finlay, D. (1982). Motion perception in the peripheral visual field. *Perception, 11,* 457–462.

Finlay, D., & Wilkinson, J. (1984). The effects of glare on the contrast sensitivity function. *Human Factors, 26,* 283–287.

Fischler, M. A., & Firschein, O. (1987). *Intelligence: The eye, the brain, and the computer.* Reading, MA: Addison-Wesley.

Fisher, J. D., Rytting, M., & Heslin, R. (1976). Hands touching hands: Affective and evaluative effects of an interpersonal touch. *Sociometry, 39,* 416–421.

Flavell, J. H. (1985). *Cognitive development* (2nd ed.). Englewood Cliffs, NJ: Prentice-Hall.

Fletcher, H., & Munson, W. A. (1933). Loudness, its definition, measurement, and calculation. *Journal of the Acoustical Society of America, 5,* 82–108.

Fodor, J. A. (1983). *The modularity of mind.* Cambridge, MA: MIT Press.

Foley, H. J., Cross, D. V., & O'Reilly, J. A. (1990). Pervasiveness and magnitude of context effects: Evidence for the relativity of absolute magnitude estimation. *Perception & Psychophysics, 48*(6), 551–558.

Foley, J. M. (1980). Binocular distance perception. *Psychological Review, 87,* 411–434.

Foley, J. M. (1985). Binocular distance perception: Egocentric distance tasks. *Journal of Experimental Psychology: Human Perception and Performance, 11,* 132–149.

Foley, J. M. (1991). Stereoscopic distance perception. In S. R. Ellis (Ed.), *Pictorial communication in virtual and real environments* (pp. 558–566). London: Taylor & Francis.

Foster, R. S., Costanza, M. C., & Worden, J. K. (1985). The current status of research in breast self-examination. *New York State Journal of Medicine, 85,* 480–482.

Foulke, E. (1991). Braille. In M. A. Heller & W. Schiff (Eds.), *The psychology of touch* (pp. 219–233). Hillsdale, NJ: Erlbaum.

Fowler, C. A., & Rosenblum, L. D. (1990). Duplex perception: A comparison of monosyllables and slamming doors. *Journal of Experimental Psychology: Human Perception and Performance, 16,* 742–754.

Fox, R., & McDaniel, C. (1982). The perception of biological motion by human infants. *Science, 218,* 486–487.

Frank, R. A., Mize, S. J. S., Kennedy, L. M., de los Santos, H. C., & Green, S. J. (1992). The effect of *Gymnema sylvestre* extracts on the sweetness of eight sweeteners. *Chemical Senses, 17,* 461–479.

Freedland, R. L., & Dannemiller, J. L. (1987). Detection of stimulus motion in 5-month-old infants. *Journal of Experimental Psychology: Human Perception and Performance, 13,* 566–576.

Freedman, D. H. (1993). In the realm of the chemical. *Discover, 14,* 68–76.

Freeman, W. J. (1991). The physiology of perception. *Scientific American, 264*(2), 78–85.

Freyd, J. J. (1993). Five hunches about perceptual processes and dynamic representations. In D. E. Meyer & S. Kornblum (Eds.), *Attention and performance XIV: Synergies in experimental psychology, artificial intelligence, and cognitive neuroscience* (pp. 99–119). Cambridge, MA: MIT Press.

Frisby, J. P., & Pollard, S. B. (1991). Computational issues in solving the stereo correspondence problem. In M. S. Landy & J. A. Movshon (Eds.), *Computational models of visual processing* (pp. 331–357). Cambridge, MA: MIT Press.

Frumkes, T. E. (1990). Classical and modern psychophysical studies of dark and light adaptation and their relationship to underlying retinal function. In K. N. Leibovic (Ed.), *Science of vision* (pp. 172–210). New York: Springer-Verlag.

Fucci, D., Petrosino, L., Schuster, S. B., & Wagner, S. (1990). Comparison of lingual vibrotactile suprathreshold numerical responses in men and women: Effects of threshold shift during magnitude-estimation scaling. *Perceptual and Motor Skills, 70,* 483–492.

Fuchs, A., & Binder, M. D. (1983). Fatigue resistance of human extraocular muscles. *Journal of Neurophysiology, 49,* 28–34.

Fudge, J. R., Miller, K. V., Marchinton, R. L., Collins, D. C., & Tice, T. R. (1992). Effects of exogenous testosterone on the scent-marking and agonistic behaviors of white-tailed deer. In R. L. Doty & D. Müller-Schwarze (Eds.), *Chemical signals in vertebrates 6* (pp. 477–484). New York: Plenum.

Fujita, I., Tanaka, K., Ito, M., & Cheng, K. (1992). Columns for visual features of objects in monkey inferotemporal cortex. *Nature, 360,* 343–346.

Galanter, E. (1962). Contemporary psychophysics. In R. Brown, E. Galanter, E. H. Hess, & G. Mandler

(Eds.), *New directions in psychology* (pp. 87–156). New York: Holt, Rinehart & Winston.

Gallant, J. L., Braun, J., & Van Essen, D. C. (1993). Selectivity for polar, hyperbolic, and cartesian gratings in Macaque visual cortex. *Science, 259,* 100–103.

Gandevia, S. C., McCloskey, D. I., & Burke, D. (1992). Kinaesthetic signals and muscle contraction. *Trends in Neurosciences, 15,* 62–65.

Gardner, M. (1988). *Perplexing puzzles and tantalizing teasers.* New York: Dover.

Garner, W. R. (1974). *The processing of information and structure.* Potomac, MD: Erlbaum.

Garner, W. R., & Clement, D. E. (1963). Goodness of pattern and pattern uncertainty. *Journal of Verbal Learning and Verbal Behavior, 2,* 446–452.

Gazzaniga, M. S., Fendrich, R., & Wessinger, C. M. (1994). Blindsight reconsidered. *Current Directions in Psychological Science, 3,* 93–96.

Gelb, A. (1929). Die "Farbenkonstanz" der Sehding. *Handbuch der normalen und pathologischen Physiologie, 12,* 594–678.

Geldard, F. A., & Sherrick, C. E. (1986). Space, time and touch. *Scientific American, 255*(1), 91–95.

Gelfand, S. A. (1981). *Hearing.* New York: Marcel Dekker.

Gervais, R., Holley, A., & Keverne, B. (1988). The importance of central noradrenergic influences on the olfactory bulb in the processing of learned olfactory cues. *Chemical Senses, 13,* 3–12.

Gescheider, G. A. (1985). *Psychophysics: Method, theory, and application* (2nd ed.). Hillsdale, NJ: Erlbaum.

Gesteland, R. C. (1982). The new physiology of odor. *Environmental Progress, 1,* 94–97.

Getchell, T. V., Doty, R. L., Bartoshuk, L. M., & Snow, J. B. (Eds.). (1991). *Smell and taste in health and disease.* New York: Raven.

Getchell, T. V., & Getchell, M. L. (1991). Physiology of olfactory reception and transduction: General principles. In D. G. Laing, R. L. Doty, & W. Breipohl (Eds.), *The human sense of smell* (pp. 61–76). Berlin: Springer-Verlag.

Gibbons, B. (1986, September). The intimate sense of smell. *National Geographic,* pp. 324–361.

Gibson, B. S., & Peterson, M. A. (1994). Does orientation-independent object recognition precede orientation-dependent recognition? Evidence from a cuing paradigm. *Journal of Experimental Psychology: Human Perception and Performance, 20,* 299–316.

Gibson, E. J. (1987). Introductory essay: What does infant perception tell us about theories of perception? *Journal of Experimental Psychology: Human Perception and Performance, 13,* 515–523.

Gibson, E. J., & Walk, R. D. (1960). The "visual cliff". *Scientific American, 202*(4), 64–71.

Gibson, J. J. (1950). *The perception of the visual world.* Boston: Houghton Mifflin.

Gibson, J. J. (1959). Perception as a function of stimulation. In S. Koch (Ed.), *Psychology: A study of a science* (pp. 456–501). New York: McGraw-Hill.

Gibson, J. J. (1962). Observations on active touch. *Psychological Review, 69,* 477–491.

Gibson, J. J. (1966). *The senses considered as perceptual systems.* Boston: Houghton Mifflin.

Gibson, J. J. (1979). *The ecological approach to visual perception.* Boston: Houghton Mifflin.

Gibson, J. J. (1982). Perception and judgment of aerial space and distance as potential factors in pilot selection and training. In E. Reed & R. Jones (Eds.), *Reasons for realism* (pp. 29–43). Hillsdale, NJ: Erlbaum.

Gilbert, C. D., & Wiesel, T. N. (1992). Receptive field dynamics in adult primary visual cortex. *Nature, 356,* 150–152.

Gilchrist, A. (1977). Perceived lightness depends on perceived spatial arrangement. *Science, 195,* 185–187.

Gilchrist, A. (1980). When does perceived lightness depend on perceived spatial arrangement? *Perception & Psychophysics, 28,* 527–538.

Gilchrist, A. (1994a). Introduction: Absolute versus relative theories of lightness perception. In A. Gilchrist (Ed.), *Lightness, brightness, and transparency* (pp. 1–34). Hillsdale, NJ: Erlbaum.

Gilchrist, A. (Ed.). (1994b). *Lightness, brightness, and transparency.* Hillsdale, NJ: Erlbaum.

Gilchrist, A., & Jacobsen, A. (1989). Qualitative relationships are decisive. *Perception & Psychophysics, 45,* 92–94.

Gillam, B. (1977). Geometrical illusions. *Scientific American, 242*(1), 102–111.

Glickstein, M. (1988). The discovery of the visual cortex. *Scientific American, 259*(3), 118–127.

Gogel, W. C. (1977). The metric of visual space. In W. Epstein (Ed.), *Stability and constancy in visual perception: Mechanisms and processes* (pp. 129–182). New York: Wiley.

Gogel, W. C. (1990). A theory of phenomenal geometry and its applications. *Perception & Psychophysics, 48*(2), 105–123.

Gogel, W. C. (1993). The analysis of perceived space. In S. C. Masin (Ed.), *Foundations of Perceptual Theory* (pp. 113–182). New York: Elsevier.

Gogel, W. C., & Sharkey, T. J. (1989). Measuring attention using induced motion. *Perception, 18,* 303–320.

Gold, T. (1948). Hearing II. The physical basis of the action of the cochlea. *Proceedings of the Royal Society of London, Series B, 135,* 492–498.

Gold, T. (1989). Historical background to the proposal, 40 years ago, of an active model for cochlear frequency analysis. In J. P. Wilson & D. T. Kemp

(Eds.), *Cochlear mechanisms: Structure, function, and models* (pp. 299–305). New York: Plenum.

Gold, T., & Pumphrey, R. J. (1948). Hearing I. The cochlea as a frequency analyzer. *Proceedings of the Royal Society of London, Series B, 135,* 462–491.

Goldman, W. P., & Seamon, J. G. (1992). Very long-term memory for odors: Retention of odor-name associations. *American Journal of Psychology, 105,* 549–563.

Goodman, J. C., & Nusbaum, H. C. (Eds.). (1994). *The development of speech perception: The transition from speech sounds to spoken words.* Cambridge, MA: MIT Press.

Goodson, F. E., Snider, T. Q., & Swearingen, J. E. (1980). Motion parallax in the perception of movement by a moving subject. *Bulletin of the Psychonomic Society, 16,* 87–88.

Gordon, I. E., & Earle, D. C. (1992). Visual illusions: A short review. *Australian Journal of Psychology, 44*(3), 153–156.

Goren, C. C., Sarty, M., & Wu, P. Y. K. (1975). Visual following and pattern discrimination of face-like stimuli by newborn infants. *Pediatrics, 56,* 544–549.

Gouras, P. (1991). Precortical physiology of colour vision. In P. Gouras (Eds.), *The perception of colour* (pp. 163–178). Boca Raton, FL: CRC Press.

Gower, D. B., Nixon, A., & Mallet, A. I. (1988). The significance of odorous steroids in axillary odour. In S. Van Toller & G. H. Dodd (Eds.), *Perfumery: The psychology and biology of fragrance* (pp. 47–76). London: Chapman and Hall.

Grady, D. (1993). The vision thing: Mainly in the brain. *Discover, 14,* 56–66.

Graham, C. H., & Hsia, Y. (1958). Color defect and color theory. *Science, 127,* 675–682.

Graham, N. (1981). Psychophysics of spatial-frequency channels. In M. Kubovy & J. R. Pomerantz (Eds.), *Perceptual organization* (pp. 1–25). Hillsdale, NJ: Erlbaum.

Graham, N. (1992). Breaking the visual stimulus into parts. *Current Directions in Psychological Science, 1,* 55–61.

Graham, N. V. S. (1989). *Visual pattern analyzers.* New York: Oxford University Press.

Granrud, C. E. (Ed.). (1993). *Visual perception and cognition in infancy.* Hillsdale, NJ: Erlbaum.

Green, B. G., & Frankmann, S. P. (1988). The effect of cooling on the perception of carbohydrate and intensive sweeteners. *Physiology & Behavior, 43,* 515–519.

Green, D. M. (1976). *An introduction to hearing.* Hillsdale, NJ: Erlbaum.

Green, D. M. (1983). Profile analysis: A different view of auditory intensity discrimination. *American Psychologist, 38,* 133–142.

Green, D. M. (1988a). Audition: Psychophysics and perception. In R. C. Atkinson, R. J. Herrnstein, G. Lindzey, & R. D. Luce (Eds.), *Stevens' handbook of experimental psychology* (2nd ed., Vol. 1, pp. 327–376). New York: Wiley.

Green, D. M. (1988b). *Profile analysis: Auditory intensity discrimination.* New York: Oxford University Press.

Green, D. M., Kidd, G., & Picardi, M. C. (1983). Successive versus simultaneous comparison in auditory intensity discrimination. *Journal of the Acoustical Society of America, 73,* 639–643.

Green, D. M., & Swets, J. A. (1966). *Signal detection theory and psychophysics.* New York: Wiley.

Green, K. P., Kuhl, P. K., Meltzoff, A. M., & Stevens, E. B. (1991). Integrating speech information across talkers, gender, and sensory modality: Female faces and male voices in the McGurk effect. *Perception & Psychophysics, 50,* 524–536.

Greene, E. (1993a). Angular induction is modulated by the orientation of the test segment but not its length. *Perception & Psychophysics, 54*(5), 640–648.

Greene, E. (1993b). Both tilt and misalignment are manifestations of angular induction. *Perceptual and Motor Skills, 76,* 1329–1330.

Greene, E. (1994). Collinearity judgment as a function of induction angle. *Perceptual and Motor Skills, 78,* 655–674.

Greene, E., & Fiser, J. (1994). Classical geometric illusion effects with nonclassical stimuli: Angular induction from decomposing lines into point arrays. *Perception & Psychophysics, 56*(5), 575–589.

Greene, E., & Levinson, D. (1994). Angular induction as a function of the length and position of segments and gaps. *Perception, 23,* 785–801.

Greeno, J. G. (1994). Gibson's affordances. *Psychological Review, 101,* 336–342.

Gregory, R. L. (1973). *Eye and brain* (2nd ed.). New York: World University Library.

Gregory, R. L. (1974a). Choosing a paradigm for perception. In E. C. Carterette & M. P. Friedman (Eds.), *Handbook of perception* (pp. 255–284). New York: Academic Press.

Gregory, R. L. (1974b). *Concepts and mechanisms of perception.* New York: Charles Scribner's Sons.

Gregory, R. L. (1991). Seeing by exploring. In S. R. Ellis (Ed.), *Pictorial communication in virtual and real environments* (pp. 328–337). London: Taylor & Francis.

Grossberg, J. M., & Grant, B. F. (1978). Clinical psychophysics: Applications of ratio scaling and signal detection methods to research on pain, fear, drugs, and medical decision making. *Psychological Bulletin, 85,* 1154–1176.

Grossberg, S. (1992). Neural facades: Visual representations of static and moving form-and-color-and-depth. In G. W. Humphreys (Ed.), *Understanding vision: An interdisciplinary perspective* (pp. 232–271). Oxford: Blackwell.

Grossberg, S. (1994). 3-D vision and figure–ground separation by visual cortex. *Perception & Psychophysics, 55,* 48–121.

Grossberg, S. (1993). A solution of the figure–ground problem for biological vision. *Neural Networks, 6,* 463–483.

Grossberg, S. (1995). The attentive brain. *American Scientist, 83*(5), 438–449.

Grossberg, S., & Mingolla, E. (1985). Neural dynamics of form perception: Boundary completion, illusory figures, and neon color spreading. *Psychological Review, 92,* 173–211.

Grossberg, S., & Mingolla, E. (1987). The role of illusory contours in visual segmentation. In S. Petry & G. E. Meyer (Eds.), *The perception of illusory contours* (pp. 116–125). New York: Springer-Verlag.

Grossberg, S., & Rudd, M. (1992). Cortical dynamics of visual motion perception: Short-range and long-range apparent motion. *Psychological Review, 99,* 78–121.

Grosslight, J. H., Fletcher, H. J., Masterson, R. B., & Hagen, R. (1978). Monocular vision and landing performance in general aviation pilots: Cyclops revisited. *Human Factors, 20,* 27–33.

Grumet, G. W. (1993). Pandemonium in the modern hospital. *The New England Journal of Medicine, 328,* 433–437.

Guedry, F. E. (1992). Perception of motion and position relative to the earth. In B. Cohen, D. L. Tomko, & F. Guedry (Eds.), *Sensing and controlling motion: Vestibular and sensorimotor function* (pp. 315–328). New York: The New York Academy of Sciences.

Gulick, W. L., Gescheider, G. A., & Frisina, R. D. (1989). *Hearing: Physiological acoustics, neural coding, and psychoacoustics.* New York: Oxford University Press.

Gunderson, V. M., Yonas, A., Sargent, P. L., & Grant-Webster, K. S. (1993). Infant macaque monkeys respond to pictorial depth. *Psychological Science, 4*(2), 93–98.

Gur, M. (1991). Perceptual fade-out occurs in the binocularly viewed Ganzfeld. *Perception, 20,* 645–654.

Gustafson, Y., & Schnitzler, H.-U. (1979). Echolocation and obstacle course avoidance in the Hipposiderid bat *Asellia tridens. Journal of Comparative and Physiological Psychology, 131,* 161–167.

Gutin, J. A. C. (1993). Good vibrations. *Discover, 14,* 44–54.

Gwiazda, J., Brill, S., Mohindra, I., & Held, R. (1980). Preferential looking acuity in infants from two to fifty-eight weeks of age. *American Journal of Optometry & Physiological Optics, 57,* 428–432.

Haber, R. N. (1974). Information processing. In E. C. Carterette & M. P. Friedman (Eds.), *Handbook of perception* (pp. 313–333). New York: Academic Press.

Haber, R. N. (1992). Perception: A one-hundred-year perspective. In S. Koch & D. E. Leary (Eds.), *A century of psychology as science* (pp. 250–281). Washington, DC: American Psychological Association.

Haber, R. N., Haber, L. R., Levin, C. A., & Hollyfield, R. (1993). Properties of spatial representations: Data from sighted and blind subjects. *Perception & Psychophysics, 54,* 1–13.

Haber, R. N., & Levin, C. A. (1989). The lunacy of moon watching: Some preconditions on explanations of the moon illusion. In M. Hershenson (Ed.), *The moon illusion* (pp. 299–317). Hillsdale, NJ: Erlbaum.

Hafter, E. R., Dye, R. H., Wenzel, E. M., & Knecht, K. (1990). The combination of interaural time and intensity in the lateralization of high-frequency complex signals. *Journal of the Acoustical Society of America, 87,* 1702–1708.

Hagen, M. A. (1986). *Varieties of realism: Geometries of representational art.* Cambridge: Cambridge University Press.

Haines, R. F. (1989, February). Space vehicle approach velocity judgments under simulated visual space conditions. *Aviation, Space, and Environmental Medicine, 60,* 145–151.

Hainline, L., & Abramov, I. (1992). Assessing visual development: Is infant vision good enough. *Advances in Infancy Research, 7,* 39–102.

Hall, M. D., & Pastore, R. E. (1992). Musical duplex perception: Perception of figurally good chords with subliminal distinguishing notes. *Journal of Experimental Psychology: Human Perception and Performance, 18,* 752–762.

Hall, M. J., Bartoshuk, L. M., Cain, W. S., & Stevens, J. C. (1975). PTC taste blindness and the taste of caffeine. *Nature, 253,* 442–443.

Hallett, P. E. (1986). Eye movements. In K. R. Boff, L. Kaufman, & J. P. Thomas (Eds.), *Handbook of perception and human performance* (pp. 10.1–10.112). New York: Wiley.

Halligan, P. W., Marshall, J. C., & Wade, D. T. (1993). Three arms: A case study of supernumerary phantom limb after right hemisphere stroke. *Journal of Neurology, Neurosurgery, and Psychiatry, 56,* 159–166.

Halpern, A. R. (1989). Memory for the absolute pitch of familiar songs. *Perception & Psychophysics, 17,* 572–581.

Halpern, B. P., & Meiselman, H. L. (1980). Taste psychophysics based on a simulation of human drinking. *Chemical Senses, 5,* 279–294.

Hamer, R. D., & Tyler, C. W. (1992). Analysis of visual modulation sensitivity. V. Faster visual response for G- than for R-cone pathway? *Journal of the Optical Society of America, 9,* 1889–1904.

Hancock, P. A. (1986). The effect of skill on performance under an environmental stressor. *Aviation, Space, and Environmental Medicine, 57,* 59–64.

Handel, S. (1989). *Listening: An introduction to the perception of auditory events.* Cambridge, MA: MIT Press.

Harrad, R. A., McKee, S. P., Blake, R., & Yang, Y. (1994). Binocular rivalry disrupts stereopsis. *Perception, 23,* 15–28.

Harrington, T. L., Harrington, M. K., Wilkins, C. A., & Koh, Y. O. (1980). Visual orientation by motion-produced blur patterns: Detection of divergence. *Perception & Psychophysics, 28,* 293–305.

Hartley, A. A., & McKenzie, C. R. M. (1991). Attentional and perceptual contributions to the identification of extrafoveal stimuli: Adult age comparisons. *Journal of Gerontology: Psychological Sciences, 46,* 202–206.

Hartline, H. K., Wagner, H. G., & Ratliff, F. (1956). Inhibition in the eye of Limulus. *Journal of General Physiology, 39,* 651–673.

Hartman, B. J. (1982). An exploratory study of the effects of disco music on the auditory and vestibular systems. *Journal of Auditory Research, 22,* 271–274.

Hartmann, W. M., & Johnson, D. (1991). Stream segregation and peripheral channeling. *Music Perception, 9,* 155–184.

Hassett, J. (1980, December). Acupuncture is proving its points. *Psychology Today,* pp. 81–89.

Hatfield, G., & Epstein, W. (1985). The status of minimum principle in the theoretical analysis of visual perception. *Psychological Bulletin, 97,* 155–186.

Hayhoe, M., Lachter, J., & Feldman, J. (1991). Integration of form across saccadic eye movements. *Perception, 20,* 393–402.

He, Z. H., & Nakayama, K. (1994). Perceived surface shape not features determines correspondence strength in apparent motion. *Vision Research, 34,* 2125–2135.

Heckmann, T., & Post, R. B. (1988). Induced motion and optokinetic afternystagmus: Parallel response dynamics with prolonged stimulation. *Vision Research, 28,* 681–694.

Heffner, R. S., & Masterson, R. B. (1990). Sound localization in mammals: Brain-stem mechanisms. In M. A. Berkley & W. C. Stebbins (Eds.), *Comparative perception: Basic mechanisms* (pp. 285–314). New York: Wiley.

Heider, E. R., & Oliver, D. C. (1972). The structure of the color space in naming and memory for two languages. *Cognitive Psychology, 3,* 337–354.

Heinemann, E. G. (1989). Brightness contrast, brightness constancy, and the ratio principle. *Perception & Psychophysics, 45,* 89–91.

Held, R. (1965). Plasticity in sensory-motor systems. *Scientific American, 213,* 84–94.

Held, R. (1980). The rediscovery of adaptability in the visual system: Effects of extrinsic and intrinsic chromatic dispersion. In C. S. Harris (Ed.), *Visual coding and adaptability* (pp. 69–94). Hillsdale, NJ: Erlbaum.

Held, R., & Hein, A. (1963). Movement-produced stimulation in the development of visually guided behavior. *Journal of Comparative and Physiological Psychology, 56,* 872–876.

Helfert, R. H., Snead, C. R., & Altschuler, R. A. (1991). The ascending auditory pathways. In R. A. Altschuler, R. P. Bobbin, B. M. Clopton, & D. W. Hoffman (Eds.), *Neurobiology of hearing: The central auditory system* (pp. 1–25). New York: Raven.

Heller, M. A. (1980). Tactile retention: Reading with the skin. *Perception & Psychophysics, 27,* 125–130.

Heller, M. A. (1984). Active and passive touch: The influence of exploration time on form recognition. *Journal of General Psychology, 110,* 243–249.

Heller, M. A. (1987a). The effect of orientation on visual and tactual braille recognition. *Perception, 16,* 291–298.

Heller, M. A. (1987b). Improving the passive tactile digit span. *Bulletin of the Psychonomic Society, 25,* 257–258.

Heller, M. A. (1989a). Picture and pattern perception in the sighted and the blind: The advantage of the late blind. *Perception, 18,* 379–389.

Heller, M. A. (1989b). Tactile memory in sighted and blind observers: The influence of orientation and rate of presentation. *Perception, 18,* 121–133.

Heller, M. A. (1989c). Texture perception in sighted and blind observers. *Perception & Psychophysics, 45,* 49–54.

Heller, M. A. (1991). Haptic perception in blind people. In M. A. Heller & W. Schiff (Eds.), *The psychology of touch* (pp. 239–261). Hillsdale, NJ: Erlbaum.

Heller, M. A. (1992a). The effect of orientation on tactual braille recognition: Optimal touching positions. *Perception & Psychophysics, 51,* 549–556.

Heller, M. A. (1992b). Haptic dominance in form perception: Vision versus proprioception. *Perception, 21,* 655–660.

Heller, M. A. (1993). Influence of visual guidance on braille recognition: Low lighting also helps touch. *Perception & Psychophysics, 54,* 675–681.

Heller, M. A., & Schiff, W. (Eds.). (1991). *The psychology of touch.* Hillsdale, NJ: Erlbaum.

Hellman, R. P., & Hellman, W. S. (1986). Limitation of first-order approximations for calculations using intensity jnd's. *Journal of the Acoustical Society of America, 80,* 1341–1345.

Hellman, W. S., & Hellman, R. P. (1990). Intensity discrimination as the driving force for loudness. Application to pure tones in quiet. *Journal of the Acoustical Society of America, 87,* 1255–1265.

Helmholtz, H. von (1863). *Die Lehre von den Tonempfindungen als physiologische Grundlege für die Theorie der Musik [A. J. Ellis, Trans. (1930). The sensations of tone].* New York: Longmans, Green.

Helmholtz, H. von (1866). *Handbuch der physiolgischen optik.* Hamburg & Leipzig: Voss.

Henderson, C. W., Bush, J., & Stoffregen, T. A. (1993). Visual perception of caught weight. In S. S. Valenti & J. B. Pittenger (Eds.), *Studies in perception and action II* (pp. 40–43). Hillsdale, NJ: Erlbaum.

Henning, G. J., Brouwer, J. N., Van der Wel, H., & Francke, A. (1969). Miraculin, the sweet-inducing principle from miracle fruit. In C. Pfaffmann (Ed.), *Olfaction and taste* (pp. 445–449). New York: Rockefeller University Press.

Henning, H. (1916). Die Qualitätsreibe des Geschmacks. *Zeitschrift für Psychologie, 74,* 203–219.

Henning, H. (1927). Psychologische Studien am Geschmacksinn. In E. Abderhalden (Ed.), *Handbuch der biologischen Arbeitsmethoden* Berlin: Urban & Schwarzenberg.

Hensel, H. (1981). *Thermoreception and temperature regulation.* London: Academic Press.

Hensel, H. (1982). *Thermal sensations and thermoreceptors in man.* Springfield, IL: Thomas.

Hershenson, M. (1982). Moon illusion and spiral aftereffect: Illusions due to the loom-zoom system? *Journal of Experimental Psychology: General, 111,* 423–440.

Hershenson, M. (1989a). *The moon illusion.* Hillsdale, NJ: Erlbaum.

Hershenson, M. (1989b). That most puzzling illusion. In M. Hershenson (Ed.), *The moon illusion* (pp. 1–3). Hillsdale, NJ: Erlbaum.

Hershenson, M. (1992). The perception of shrinking in apparent motion. *Perception & Psychophysics, 52*(6), 671–675.

Hershenson, M. (1993). Linear and rotational motion aftereffects as a function of inspection duration. *Vision Research, 33*(14), 1913–1919.

Hershenson, M., & Bader, P. (1990). Development of the spiral aftereffect. *Bulletin of the Psychonomic Society, 28,* 300–301.

Herz, R. S., & Cupchik, G. C. (1992). An experimental characterization of odor-evoked memories in humans. *Chemical Senses, 17,* 519–528.

Higashiyama, A., & Shimono, K. (1994). How accurate is size and distance perception for very far terrestrial objects? Function and causality. *Perception & Psychophysics, 55,* 429–442.

Hildreth, E. C., & Ullman, S. (1989). The computational study of vision. In M. I. Posner (Ed.), *Foundations of cognitive science* (pp. 581–630). Cambridge, MA: MIT Press.

Hochberg, J. (1971). Perception: II. Space and movement. In J. W. Kling & L. A. Riggs (Eds.), *Wood-worth & Schlosberg's experimental psychology* (pp. 475–550). New York: Holt, Rinehart & Winston.

Hochberg, J. (1979). Sensation and perception. In E. Hearst (Ed.), *The first century of experimental psychology* (pp. 89–142). Hillsdale, NJ: Erlbaum.

Hochberg, J. (1988). Visual perception. In R. C. Atkinson, R. J. Herrnstein, G. Lindzey, & R. D. Luce (Eds.), *Stevens' handbook of experimental psychology* (2nd ed., Vol. 1, pp. 195–276). New York: Wiley.

Hochberg, J. (1994). Perceptual theory and visual cognition. In S. Ballesteros (Ed.), *Cognitive approaches to human perception* (pp. 269–289). Hillsdale, NJ: Erlbaum.

Hochberg, J., & Brooks, V. (1978). The perception of motion pictures. In E. C. Carterette & M. P. Friedman (Eds.), *Handbook of perception* (pp. 259–304). New York: Academic Press.

Hockett, C. F. (1955). A manual of phonology, memoir 11. *International Journal of American Linguistics, 21 (pt 1).*

Hoffman, D. D. (1983). The interpretation of visual illusion. *Scientific American, 249*(6), 154–162.

Hoffman, D. D., & Richards, W. A. (1984). Parts of recognition. *Cognition, 18,* 65–96.

Hofstadter, D. R. (1979). *Gödel, Escher, Bach: An eternal golden braid.* New York: Random House.

Holley, A. (1991). Neural coding of olfactory information. In T. V. Getchell, R. L. Doty, L. M. Bartoshuk, & J. B. Snow, Jr. (Eds.), *Smell and taste in health and disease* (pp. 329–343). New York: Raven.

Holway, A. F., & Boring, E. G. (1941). Determinants of apparent visual size with distance variant. *American Journal of Psychology, 54,* 21–37.

Hood, D. C., & Finkelstein, M. A. (1986). Sensitivity to light. In K. R. Boff, L. Kaufman, & J. P. Thomas (Eds.), *Handbook of perception and human performance* (pp. 5.1–5.66). New York: Wiley.

Horlitz, K. L., & O'Leary, A. (1993). Satiation or availability? Effects of attention, memory, and imagery on the perception of ambiguous figures. *Perception & Psychophysics, 53,* 668–681.

Horner, D. T., & Craig, J. C. (1989). A comparison of discrimination and identification of vibrotactile patterns. *Perception & Psychophysics, 45,* 21–30.

Hornung, D. E., & Enns, M. P. (1986). The contribution of smell and taste to overall intensity: A model. *Perception & Psychophysics, 39,* 385–391.

Hornung, D. E., & Enns, M. P. (1989). Separating the contributions of smells and tastes in flavor perception. In D. G. Laing, W. S. Cain, R. L. McBride, & B. W. Ache (Eds.), *Perception of complex smells and tastes* (pp. 285–296). Sydney, Australia: Academic Press.

Horwitz, B., Grady, C. L., Haxby, J. V., Schapiro, M. B., & Rapoport, S. I. (1992). Functional associations among human posterior extrastriate brain regions during object and spatial vision. *Journal of Cognitive Neuroscience, 4,* 311–321.

Houtsma, A. J. M., & Goldstein, J. L. (1972). The central origin of the pitch of complex tones: Evidence from musical interval recognition. *Journal of the Acoustical Society of America, 51,* 520–529.

Houtsma, A. J. M., Rossing, T. D., & Wagenaars, W. M. (1987). *Auditory demonstrations* [CD]. Eindhoven, The Netherlands: The Acoustical Society of America.

Howard, I. P. (1986). The perception of posture, self motion, and the visual vertical. In K. R. Boff, L. Kaufman, & J. P. Thomas (Eds.), *Handbook of perception and human performance* (pp. 18.1–18.62). New York: Wiley.

Howe, E. S., & Brandau, C. J. (1983). The temporal course of visual pattern encoding: Effects of pattern goodness. *Quarterly Journal of Experimental Psychology, 35A,* 607–633.

Howe, E. S., & Jung, K. (1986). Immediate memory span for two-dimensional spatial arrays: Effects of pattern symmetry and goodness. *Acta Psychologica, 61,* 37–51.

Hoyer, W. J., & Plude, D. J. (1982). Aging and the allocation of attentional resources in visual information-processing. In R. Sekuler, D. Kline, & K. Dismukes (Eds.), *Aging and human visual function* (pp. 245–263). New York: Alan R. Liss.

Hubbard, T. L. (1993). Auditory representational momentum: Musical schemata and modularity. *Bulletin of the Psychonomic Society, 31*(3), 201–204.

Hubbard, T. L., & Baird, J. C. (1988). Overflow, first-sight, and vanishing point distances in visual imagery. *Journal of Experimental Psychology: Learning, Memory, and Cognition, 14,* 641–649.

Hubbard, T. L., Kall, D., & Baird, J. C. (1989). Imagery, memory, and size–distance invariance. *Memory & Cognition, 17,* 87–94.

Hubbard, T. L., & Stoeckig, K. (1992). The representation of pitch in musical images. In D. Reisberg (Ed.), *Auditory imagery* (pp. 199–235). Hillsdale, NJ: Erlbaum.

Hubel, D. H. (1982). Explorations of the primary visual cortex, 1955–1978. *Nature, 299,* 515–524.

Hubel, D. H. (1988). *Eye, brain, and vision.* New York: Scientific American Library.

Hubel, D. H. (1990, February). Interview. *Omni,* pp. 74–110.

Hubel, D. H., & Wiesel, T. N. (1965). Receptive fields of single neurons in two nonstriate visual areas (18 and 19) of the cat. *Journal of Neurophysiology, 28,* 229–289.

Hubel, D. H., & Wiesel, T. N. (1979). Brain mechanisms and vision. *Scientific American, 241*(3), 150–162.

Hudspeth, A. J. (1983). The hair cells of the inner ear. *Scientific American, 248*(1), 54–64.

Hudspeth, A. J. (1989). How the ear's works work. *Nature, 341,* 397–404.

Huggins, A. W. F. (1981). Speech perception and auditory processing. In D. J. Getty & J. H. Howard (Eds.), *Auditory and visual pattern recognition* (pp. 79–91). Hillsdale, NJ: Erlbaum.

Hummel, J. E. (1994). Reference frames and relations in computational models of object recognition. *Current Directions in Psychological Science, 3,* 111–116.

Hummel, J. E., & Biederman, I. (1992). Dynamic binding in a neural network for shape recognition. *Psychological Review, 99*(3), 480–517.

Humphreys, G. W., Riddoch, M. J., Donnelly, N., Freeman, T., Boucart, M., & Muller, H. M. (1994). Intermediate visual processing and visual agnosia. In M. J. Farah & G. Ratcliff (Eds.), *The neuropsychology of high-level vision: Collected tutorial essays* (pp. 63–101). Hillsdale, NJ: Erlbaum.

Humphreys, G. W., & Bruce, V. (1989). *Visual cognition: Computational, experimental, and neuropsychological perspectives.* Hove, UK: Erlbaum.

Hunt, D. M., Dulai, K. S., Bowmaker, J. K., & Mollon, J. D. (1995). The chemistry of John Dalton's color blindness. *Science, 267,* 984–988.

Hurd, P. D., & Blevins, J. (1984). Aging and the color of pills. *New England Journal of Medicine, 310,* 202.

Hurvich, L. M. (1981). *Color vision.* Sunderland, MA: Sinauer.

Hurvich, L. M., & Jameson, D. (1957). An opponent-process theory of color vision. *Psychological Review, 64,* 384–404.

Hyman, A. (1983). The influence of color on the taste perception of carbonated water preparations. *Bulletin of the Psychonomic Society, 21,* 145–148.

Hyman, A., Mentzer, T., & Calderone, L. (1979). The contribution of olfaction to taste discrimination. *Bulletin of the Psychonomic Society, 13,* 359–362.

Ilan, A. B., & Miller, J. (1994). A violation of pure insertion: Mental rotation and choice reaction time. *Journal of Experimental Psychology: Human Perception and Performance, 20*(3), 520–536.

Intraub, H. (1985). Visual dissociation: An illusory conjunction of pictures and forms. *Journal of Experimental Psychology: Human Perception and Performance, 11,* 431–442.

Intraub, H. (1989). Illusory conjunctions of forms, objects, and scenes during rapid serial visual search. *Journal of Experimental Psychology: Learning, Memory, and Cognition, 15,* 98–109.

Intraub, H. (1992). Contextual factors in scene perception. In E. Chekaluk & K. R. Llewellyn (Eds.),

The role of eye movements in perceptual processes (pp. 45–72). New York: Elsevier.

Intraub, H., Bender, R. S., & Mangels, J. A. (1992). Looking at pictures but remembering scenes. *Journal of Experimental Psychology: Learning, Memory, and Cognition, 18*, 180–191.

Intraub, H., & Bodamer, J. L. (1993). Boundary extension: Foundation aspect of pictorial representation or encoding artifact? *Journal of Experimental Psychology: Learning, Memory, and Cognition, 19*, 1387–1397.

Intraub, H., & Richardson, M. (1989). Wide-angle memories of close-up scenes. *Journal of Experimental Psychology: Learning, Memory, and Cognition, 15*(2), 179–187.

Irvine, D. R. F. (1992). Physiology of the auditory brainstem. In A. N. Popper & R. R. Fay (Eds.), *The mammalian auditory pathway: Neurophysiology* (pp. 153–231). New York: Springer-Verlag.

Irwin, D. E. (1992). Visual memory within and across fixations. In K. Rayner (Ed.), *Eye movements and visual cognition: Scene perception and reading* (pp. 146–165). New York: Springer-Verlag.

Irwin, D. E. (1993). Perceiving an integrated visual world. In D. E. Meyer & S. Kornblum (Eds.), *Attention and performance XIV: Synergies in experimental psychology, artificial intelligence, and cognitive neuroscience* (pp. 121–142). Cambridge, MA: MIT Press.

Irwin, R. J., & Whitehead, P. R. (1991). Towards an objective psychophysics of pain. *Psychological Science, 2*, 230–235.

Ittelson, W. H., & Kilpatrick, F. P. (1951). Experiments in perception. *Scientific American, 185*(2), 50–55.

Ittelson, W. H., Mowafy, L., & Magid, D. (1991). The perception of mirror-reflected objects. *Perception, 20*, 567–584.

Iverson, G., & D'Zmura, M. (1995). Color constancy: Spectral recovery using trichromatic bilinear models. In R. D. Luce, M. D'Zmura, D. Hoffman, G. J. Iverson, & A. K. Romney (Eds.), *Geometric representations of perceptual phenomena: Papers in honor of Tarow Indow on his 70th birthday* (pp. 169–185). Mahwah, NJ: Erlbaum.

Ivry, R. B., & Lebby, P. C. (1993). Hemispheric differences in auditory perception are similar to those found in visual perception. *Psychological Science, 4*(1), 41–45.

Izmailov, C. (1995). Spherical model of discrimination of self-luminous and surface colors. In R. D. Luce, M. D'Zmura, D. Hoffman, G. J. Iverson, & A. K. Romney (Eds.), *Geometric representations of perceptual phenomena: Papers in honor of Tarow Indow on his 70th birthday* (pp. 153–167). Mahwah, NJ: Erlbaum.

Izmailov, C. A., & Sokolov, E. N. (1991). Spherical model of color and brightness discrimination. *Psychological Science, 2*, 249–259.

Izmailov, C. A., & Sokolov, E. N. (1992). A semantic space of color names. *Psychological Science, 3*, 105–110.

Jacobsen, A., & Gilchrist, A. (1988a). Hess and Pretori revisited: Resolution of some old contradictions. *Perception & Psychophysics, 43*, 7–14.

Jacobsen, A., & Gilchrist, A. (1988b). The ratio principle holds over a million-to-one range of illumination. *Perception & Psychophysics, 43*, 1–6.

Jacobson, J. T., & Northern, J. L. (Eds.). (1990). *Diagnostic audiology*. Boston: Allyn & Bacon.

Jagadeesh, B., Gray, C. M., & Ferster, D. (1992). Visually evoked oscillations of membrane potential in cells of cat visual cortex. *Science, 257*, 552–554.

James, G. A. (1982). Mobility maps. In W. Schiff & E. Foulke (Eds.), *Tactual perception: A sourcebook* (pp. 334–363). Cambridge: Cambridge University Press.

James, W. (1890). *The principles of psychology*. New York: Henry Holt.

Jameson, D. (1983). Some misunderstanding about color perception, color mixture and color measurement. *Leonardo, 16*, 41–42.

Jameson, D., & Hurvich, L. M. (1961). The complexities of perceived brightness. *Science, 133*, 174–179.

Jameson, D., & Hurvich, L. M. (1978). Dichromatic color language: "Reds" and "greens" don't look alike but their colors do. *Sensory Processes, 2*, 146–155.

Jameson, D., & Hurvich, L. M. (1989). Essay concerning color constancy. *Annual Review of Psychology, 40*, 1–22.

Jäncke, L., & Kaufmann, N. (1994). Facial EMG responses to odors in solitude and with an audience. *Chemical Senses, 19*, 99–111.

Jankowiak, J., Kinsbourne, M., Shalev, R. S., & Bachman, D. L. (1992). Preserved visual imagery and categorization in a case of associative visual agnosia. *Journal of Cognitive Neuroscience, 4*, 119–131.

Jansson, G., Bergström, S. S., & Epstein, W. (Eds.). (1994). *Perceiving events and objects*. Hillsdale, NJ: Erlbaum.

Jay, M. F., & Sparks, D. L. (1984). Auditory receptive fields in primate superior colliculus shift with changes in eye position. *Science, 309*, 345–347.

Jenkins, J. J. (1991). Summary of the conference: Speech is special. In I. G. Mattingly & M. Studdert-Kennedy (Eds.), *Modularity and the motor theory of speech perception* (pp. 431–442). Hillsdale, NJ: Erlbaum.

Jesteadt, W., Bacon, S. P., & Lehman, J. R. (1982). Forward masking as a function of frequency, masker level, and signal delay. *Journal of the Acoustical Society of America, 71*, 950–962.

Johansson, G. (1973). Visual perception of biological motion and a model for its analysis. *Perception & Psychophysics, 14*, 201–211.

Johansson, G. (1974). Projective transformations as determining visual space perception. In R. B. MacLeod & H. H. Pick, Jr. (Eds.), *Perception: Essays in honor of James J. Gibson* (pp. 117–138). Ithaca, NY: Cornell University Press.

Johansson, G. (1975). Visual motion perception. *Scientific American, 232*(6), 76–88.

Johansson, G. (1982). Visual space perception through motion. In A. H. Wertheim, W. A. Wagenaar, & H. W. Leibowitz (Eds.), *Tutorials on motion perception* (pp. 19–39). New York: Plenum.

Johansson, G. (1985). About visual event perception. In W. H. Warren, Jr., & R. W. Shaw (Eds.), *Persistence and change: Proceedings of the First International Conference on Event Perception* (pp. 29–54). Hillsdale, NJ: Erlbaum.

Johansson, G., von Hofsten, C., & Jansson, G. (1980). Event perception. *Annual Review of Psychology, 31,* 27–63.

Johansson, R. S., & LaMotte, R. H. (1983). Tactile detection thresholds for a single asperity on an otherwise smooth surface. *Somatosensory Research, 1,* 21–31.

Johnson, J., & Clydesdale, F. M. (1982). Perceived sweetness and redness in colored sucrose solutions. *Journal of Food Science, 47,* 747–752.

Johnson, K. O., & Hsiao, S. S. (1992). Neural mechanisms of tactual form and texture perception. *Annual Review of Neuroscience, 15,* 227–250.

Johnson, M. H. (1990). Cortical maturation and the development of visual attention in early infancy. *Journal of Cognitive Neuroscience, 2,* 81–95.

Johnson, S. H. (1991). Commentary on Tarr & Pinker. *Psychological Science, 2,* 205–206.

Johnstone, B. M., & Boyle, A. J. F. (1967). Basilar membrane vibrations examined with the Mössbauer technique. *Science, 158,* 390–391.

Jones, L. A. (1988). Motor illusions: What do they reveal about proprioception? *Psychological Bulletin, 103,* 72–86.

Jones, M. R. (1993). Dynamics of musical patterns: How do melody and rhythm fit together? In T. J. Tighe & W. J. Dowling (Eds.), *Psychology and music: The understanding of melody and rhythm* (pp. 67–92). Hillsdale, NJ: Erlbaum.

Jones, M. R., & Yee, W. (1993). Attending to auditory events: The role of temporal organization. In S. McAdams & E. Bigand (Eds.), *Thinking in sound: The cognitive psychology of human audition* (pp. 69–112). New York: Oxford University Press.

Jordan, G., & Mollon, J. D. (1993). The Nagel anomaloscope and seasonal variation of colour vision. *Nature, 363,* 546–549.

Julesz, B. (1971). *Foundations of cyclopean perception.* Chicago: University of Chicago Press.

Julesz, B. (1977). Cooperative phenomena in binocular depth perception. In I. L. Janis (Ed.), *Current trends in psychology: Readings from American Scientist* (pp. 173–184). Los Altos, CA: William Kaufman.

Julesz, B. (1995). *Dialogues on perception.* Cambridge, MA: MIT Press.

Juola, J. F., & Breitmeyer, B. G. (1989). A discussion of models of motion perception. In B. A. G. Elsendoorn & H. Bouma (Eds.), *Working models of human perception* (pp. 251–259). London: Academic Press.

Jusczyk, P. W. (1985). The high-amplitude sucking technique as a methodological tool in speech perception research. In G. Gottlieb & N. A. Krasnegor (Eds.), *Measurement of audition and vision in the first year of postnatal life* (pp. 195–222). Norwood, NJ: Ablex.

Jusczyk, P. W. (1986). Speech perception. In K. R. Boff, L. Kaufman, & J. P. Thomas (Eds.), *Handbook of perception and human performance* (pp. 27.1–27.57). Hillsdale, NJ: Erlbaum.

Jusczyk, P. W., Friederici, A. D., Wessels, J. M. I., Svenkerud, V. Y., & Jusczyk, A. M. (1993). Infants' sensitivity to the sound patterns of native language words. *Journal of Memory and Language, 32,* 402–420.

Kaas, J. H. (1995). Vision without awareness. *Nature, 373,* 195.

Kaitz, M., & Eidelman, A. I. (1992). Smell-recognition of newborns by women who are not mothers. *Chemical Senses, 17,* 225–229.

Kallman, H. J., & Massaro, D. W. (1979). Similarity effects in backward recognition masking. *Journal of Experimental Psychology: Human Perception and Performance, 5,* 110–128.

Kallman, H. J., & Morris, M. D. (1984). Backward recognition masking as a function of mask presentation. *Perception & Psychophysics, 35,* 379–384.

Kaneko, H., & Uchikawa, K. (1993). Apparent relative size and depth of moving objects. *Perception, 22,* 537–547.

Kanizsa, G. (1976). Subjective contours. *Scientific American, 234*(4), 48–52.

Kanner, B. (1993, January 25). Scent of a woman. *New York,* pp. 16–19.

Kaplan, E., Mukherjee, P., & Shapley, R. (1993). Information filtering in the lateral geniculate nucleus. In R. Shapley & D. M.-K. Lam (Eds.), *Contrast sensitivity: Proceedings of the Retina Research Foundation Symposia* (pp. 183–200). Cambridge, MA: MIT Press.

Kare, M. R., & Ficken, M. S. (1963). Comparative studies on the sense of taste. In Y. Zotterman (Ed.), *Olfaction and taste* (pp. 285–297). New York: Macmillan.

Karrer, T., & Bartoshuk, L. (1991). Capsaicin desensitization and recovery on the human tongue. *Physiology & Behavior, 49*(4), 757–764.

Kaufman, L., & Rock, I. (1962). The moon illusion, I. *Science, 136*, 953–961.

Kaufman, L., & Rock, I. (1989). The moon illusion thirty years later. In M. Hershenson (Ed.), *The moon illusion* (pp. 193–234). Hillsdale, NJ: Erlbaum.

Kavaliers, M., Innes, D., & Ossenkopp, K.-P. (1992). Predator-odor analgesia in deer mice: Neuromodulatory mechanisms and sex differences. In R. L. Doty & D. Müller-Schwarze (Eds.), *Chemical signals in vertebrates 6* (pp. 529–535). New York: Plenum.

Kelling, S. T., & Halpern, B. P. (1983). Taste flashes: Reaction times, intensity, and quality. *Science, 219*, 412–414.

Kellman, P. J., Gleitman, H., & Spelke, E. S. (1987). Object and observer motion in the perception of objects by infants. *Journal of Experimental Psychology: Human Perception and Performance, 13*, 586–593.

Kellman, P. J., & Spelke, E. S. (1983). Perception of partly occluded objects in infancy. *Cognitive Psychology, 15*, 483–524.

Kelly, W. J., & Watson, C. S. (1986). Stimulus-based limitations on the discrimination between different temporal orders of tones. *Journal of the Acoustical Society of America, 79*, 1934–1938.

Kemp, D. T. (1978). Stimulated acoustic emissions from within the human auditory system. *Journal of the Acoustical Society of America, 64*, 1386–1391.

Kemp, D. T. (1979). Evidence of mechanical nonlinearity and frequency selective wave amplification in the cochlea. *Archives of Otology, Rhinology, and Laryngology, 224*, 37–45.

Kennedy, J. M. (1974). *The psychology of picture perception*. San Francisco: Jossey-Bass.

Kennedy, J. M. (1982). Haptic pictures. In W. Schiff & E. Foulke (Eds.), *Tactual perception: A sourcebook* (pp. 305–333). Cambridge: Cambridge University Press.

Kenshalo, D. R. (1971). The cutaneous senses. In J. W. Kling & L. A. Riggs (Eds.), *Woodworth & Schlosberg's experimental psychology* (pp. 117–168). New York: Holt, Rinehart & Winston.

Kenshalo, D. R. (1978). Biophysics and psychophysics of feeling. In E. C. Carterette & M. P. Friedman (Eds.), *Handbook of perception* (pp. 29–74). New York: Academic Press.

Kenshalo, D. R., Holmes, C. E., & Wood, P. B. (1968). Warm and cool thresholds as a function of rate of stimulus temperature change. *Perception & Psychophysics, 3*, 81–84.

Kent, D. (1995). Seeing is hearing. *APS Observer, 8*(1), 16–17.

Keverne, E. B. (1982). Chemical senses: Taste. In H. B. Barlow & J. D. Mollon (Eds.), *The senses* (pp. 428–477). Cambridge: Cambridge University Press.

Khanna, S. M., & Leonard, D. G. B. (1982). Basilar membrane tuning in cat cochlea. *Science, 215*, 305–306.

Kiang, N. Y.-S. (1975). Stimulus representation in the discharge patterns of auditory neurons. In E. L. Eagles (Ed.), *The nervous system* (pp. 81–96). New York: Raven.

Kidd, G., Mason, C. R., & Green, D. M. (1986). Auditory profile analysis of irregular sound spectra. *Journal of the Acoustical Society of America, 79*, 1045–1053.

Kihlstrom, J. F. (1985). Hypnosis. *Annual Review of Psychology, 36*, 385–418.

Kilbride, P. E., Huttman, L. P., Fishman, M., & Read, J. S. (1986). Foveal cone pigment density difference in the aging human eye. *Vision Research, 26*, 321–325.

Kimchi, R. (1992). Primacy of wholistic processing and global/local paradigm: A critical review. *Psychological Bulletin, 112*, 24–38.

King, A. J., Hutchings, M. E., Moore, D. R., & Blakemore, C. (1988). Developmental plasticity in the visual and auditory representations in the mammalian superior colliculus. *Science, 332*, 73–76.

King, S. M., Dykeman, C., Redgrave, P., & Dean, P. (1992). Use of a distracting task to obtain defensive head movements to looming visual stimuli by human adults in a laboratory setting. *Perception, 21*, 245–259.

Kirman, J. H. (1982). Current developments in tactile communication of speech. In W. Schiff & E. Foulke (Eds.), *Tactual perception: A sourcebook* (pp. 234–262). Cambridge: Cambridge University Press.

Klasco, M., & Baum, R. (1994, December). The noise killers: A new breed of headphones that lower the boom on background noise. *Stereo Review*, 108–114.

Klatzky, R. L., & Lederman, S. J. (1993). Toward a computational model of constraint-driven exploration and haptic object identification. *Perception, 22*, 597–621.

Klatzky, R. L., Lederman, S. J., & Metzger, V. A. (1985). Identifying objects by touch: An "expert system." *Perception & Psychophysics, 37*, 299–302.

Klatzky, R. L., Lederman, S. J., & Reed, C. (1987). There's more to touch than meets the eye: The salience of object attributes for haptics with and without vision. *Journal of Experimental Psychology: General, 116*, 356–369.

Kline, D. W., Kline, T. J. B., Fozard, J. L., Kosnik, W., Scheiber, F., & Sekuler, R. (1992). Vision, aging, and driving: The problems of older drivers. *Journal of Gerontology: Psychological Sciences, 47*(1), 27–34.

Knudsen, E. I. (1981). The hearing of the barn owl. *Scientific American, 245*(6), 112–125.

Knudsen, E. I. (1983). Early auditory experience aligns the auditory map of space in the optic tectum of the barn owl. *Science, 222*, 939–942.

Knudsen, E. I., & Brainard, M. S. (1991). Visual instruction of the neural map of auditory space in the developing optic tectum. *Science, 253*, 85–87.

Koffka, K. (1935). *Principles of Gestalt psychology*. New York: Harcourt Brace.

Koga, K., & Groner, R. (1990). Pursuit eye movements and the perception of object motion. In R. Groner, G. d'Ydewalle, & R. Parham (Eds.), *From eye to mind: Information acquisition in perception, search, and reading* (pp. 59–68). Amsterdam: North-Holland.

Köhler, W. (1947). *Gestalt psychology: An introduction to new concepts in modern psychology.* New York: Liveright.

Kolb, H. (1991). Anatomical pathways for color vision in the human retina. *Visual Neuroscience, 7,* 61–74.

Konishi, M. (1973). How the owl tracks its prey. *American Scientist, 61,* 414–424.

Konishi, M. (1993). Listening with two ears. *Scientific American, 268*(4), 66–73.

Koretz, J. F., & Handelman, G. H. (1988). How the human eye focuses. *Scientific American, 259*(1), 92–99.

Köster, E. P., & de Wijk, R. (1991). Olfactory adaptation. In D. G. Laing, R. L. Doty, & W. Breipohl (Eds.), *The human sense of smell* (pp. 199–215). Berlin: Springer-Verlag.

Kowal, K. H. (1993). The range effect as a function of stimulus set, presence of a standard, and modulus. *Perception & Psychophysics, 54,* 555–561.

Krantz, M. (1994, January). Sex pheromones hit the market. *Omni,* p. 24.

Krauskopf, J. (1963). Effect of retinal image stabilization on the appearance of heterochromatic targets. *Journal of the Optical Society of America, 53,* 741–743.

Krueger, L. E. (1989). Reconciling Fechner and Stevens: Toward a unified psychophysical law. *Behavioral and Brain Sciences, 12,* 251–320.

Krueger, L. E. (1991). Toward a unified psychophysical law and beyond. In S. J. Bolanowski & G. A. Gescheider (Eds.), *Ratio scaling of psychological magnitude: In honor of the memory of S. S. Stevens* (pp. 101–114). Hillsdale, NJ: Erlbaum.

Krueger, L. E. (1992). The word-superiority effect and phonological recoding. *Memory & Cognition, 20*(6), 685–694.

Krumhansl, C. L. (1983). Perceptual structures for tonal music. *Music Perception, 1,* 28–62.

Krumhansl, C. L. (1985). Perceiving tonal structure in music. *American Scientist, 73,* 371–378.

Krumhansl, C. L. (1991). Music perception: Tonal structures in perception and memory. *Annual Review of Psychology, 42,* 277–303.

Krumhansl, C. L., & Kessler, E. J. (1982). Tracing the dynamic changes in perceived tonal organization in a spatial representation of musical keys. *Psychological Review, 89,* 334–368.

Kryter, K. D. (1985). *The effects of noise on man* (2nd ed.). Orlando, FL: Academic Press.

Kryter, K. D. (1994). *The handbook of hearing and the effects of noise: Physiology, psychology, and public health.* San Diego: Academic Press.

Kubovy, M. (1994). The perceptual organization of dot lattices. *Psychonomic Bulletin & Review, 1*(2), 182–190.

Kubovy, M., & Wagemans, J. (1995). Grouping by proximity and multistability in dot lattices: A quantitative Gestalt theory. *Psychological Science, 6*(4), 225–234.

Kuhl, P. K. (1987). Perception of speech and sound in early infancy. In P. Salapatek & L. Cohen (Eds.), *Handbook of infant perception* (pp. 275–382). Orlando, FL: Academic Press.

Kuhl, P. K. (1989). On babies, birds, modules, and mechanisms: A comparative approach to the acquisition of vocal communication. In R. J. Dooling & S. H. Hulse (Eds.), *The comparative psychology of audition: Perceiving complex sounds* (pp. 379–419). Hillsdale, NJ: Erlbaum.

Kuhl, P. K. (1992). Psychoacoustics and speech perception: Internal standards, perceptual anchors, and prototypes. In L. A. Werner & E. W. Rubel (Eds.), *Developmental psychoacoustics* (pp. 293–332). Washington, DC: American Psychological Association.

Kuhl, P. K., & Meltzoff, A. N. (1982). The bimodal perception of speech in infancy. *Science, 218,* 1138–1141.

Kupchella, C. (1976). *Sights and sounds.* Indianapolis: Bobbs-Merrill.

Kuznicki, J. T., & McCutcheon, N. B. (1979). Cross-enhancement of the sour taste on a single human taste papilla. *Journal of Experimental Psychology: General, 108,* 68–89.

Labows, J. N., & Preti, G. (1992). Human semiochemicals. In S. Van Toller & G. H. Dodd (Eds.), *Fragrance: The psychology and biology of perfume* (pp. 69–90). London: Elsevier.

Lackner, J. R. (1992). Sense of body position in parabolic flight. In B. Cohen, D. L. Tomko, & F. Guedry (Eds.), *Sensing and controlling motion: Vestibular and sensorimotor function* (pp. 329–339). New York: The New York Academy of Sciences.

Lackner, J. R. (1993). Orientation and movement in unusual force environments. *Psychological Science, 4,* 134–142.

Lamb, T. D. (1990). The role of photoreceptors in light-adaptation and dark-adaptation of the visual system. In C. Blakemore (Ed.), *Vision: Coding and efficiency* (pp. 161–168). Cambridge: Cambridge University Press.

Laming, D. (1985). Some principles of sensory analysis. *Psychological Review, 92,* 462–485.

Lancet, D., Ben-Arie, N., Cohen, S., Gat, U., Gross-Isseroff, R., Horn-Saban, S., Khen, M., Lehrach, H., Natochin, M., North, M., Seidemann, E., & Walker, N. (1993). Olfactory receptors: Transduction, diversity, human psychophysics and genome analysis. In D. Chadwick, J. Marsh, & J. Goode

(Eds.), *The molecular basis of smell and taste transduction* (pp. 131–146). New York: Wiley.

Land, E. H. (1977). The retinex theory of color vision. *Scientific American, 237*(6), 108–128.

Land, E. H. (1983). Recent advances in retinex theory and some implications for cortical computations: Color vision and the natural image. *Proceedings of the National Academy of Sciences USA, 80,* 5163–5169.

Land, E. H. (1986). An alternative technique for the computation of the designator in the retinex theory of color vision. *Proceedings of the National Academy of Sciences USA, 83,* 3078–3080.

Lashley, K. S. (1941). Patterns of cerebral integration indicated by the scotomas of migraine. *Archives of Neurology and Psychiatry, 46,* 331–339.

Lautenbacher, S., Möltner, A., & Strian, F. (1992). Psychophysical features of the transition from pure heat perception to heat pain perception. *Perception & Psychophysics, 52,* 685–690.

Lawless, H. (1991). Effects of odors on mood and behavior: Aromatherapy and related effects. In D. G. Laing, R. L. Doty, & W. Breipohl (Eds.), *The human sense of smell* (pp. 361–386). Berlin: Springer-Verlag.

Lawless, H. T. (1984). Oral chemical irritation: Psychophysical properties. *Chemical Senses, 9,* 143–155.

Lawless, H. T., & Skinner, E. F. (1979). The duration and perceived intensity of sucrose taste. *Perception & Psychophysics, 25,* 180–184.

Lawless, H. T., & Stevens, D. A. (1983). Cross adaptation of sucrose and intensive sweeteners. *Chemical Senses, 7,* 309–315.

Lee, D. N. (1980). The optic flow field: The foundation of vision. In The Royal Society (Eds.), *The psychology of vision* (pp. 169–179). Cambridge: Cambridge University Press.

Leek, M. R., & Watson, C. S. (1984). Learning to detect auditory pattern components. *Journal of the Acoustical Society of America, 76,* 1037–1044.

Leeuwenberg, E., & Boselie, F. (1988). Against the likelihood principle in visual form perception. *Psychological Review, 95,* 485–491.

Legerstee, M. (1990). Infants use multimodal information to imitate speech sounds. *Infant Behavior and Development, 13,* 343–354.

Leibowitz, H. W. (1971). Sensory, learned, and cognitive mechanisms of size perception. *Annals of the New York Academy of Sciences, 188,* 47–62.

Leibowitz, H. W., Shiina, K., & Hennessy, R. T. (1972). Oculomotor adjustments and size constancy. *Perception & Psychophysics, 12,* 497–500.

Leibowitz, H. W., Shupert, C. L., Post, R. B., & Dichgans, J. (1983). Expectation and autokinesis. *Perception & Psychophysics, 34,* 131–134.

Lennie, P. (1980). Parallel visual pathways: A review. *Vision Research, 20,* 561–594.

Lennie, P. (1993). Roles of M and P pathways. In R. Shapley & D. M.-K. Lam (Eds.), *Contrast sensitivity: Proceedings of the Retina Research Foundation Symposia* (pp. 201–213). Cambridge, MA: MIT Press.

Leo, J. (1986, December 1). The hidden power of body odors. *Time,* p. 67.

Lesher, G. W. (1995). Illusory contours: Toward a neurally based perceptual theory. *Psychonomic Bulletin & Review, 2*(3), 279–321.

Lesher, G. W., & Mingolla, E. (1993). The role of edges and line-ends in illusory contour formation. *Vision Research, 33,* 2253–2270.

Lester, L. S., & Fanselow, F. S. (1985). Exposure to a cat produces opioid analgesia in rats. *Behavioral Neuroscience, 99,* 756–759.

Levinson, S. E., & Liberman, A. M. (1981). Speech recognition by computer. *Scientific American, 244*(4), 64–76.

Levitin, D. J. (1994). Absolute memory for musical pitch: Evidence from the production of learned melodies. *Perception & Psychophysics, 56,* 414–423.

Lewkowicz, D. J. (1991). Development of intersensory functions in human infancy: Auditory/visual interactions. In M. J. S. Weiss & P. R. Zelazo (Eds.), *Newborn attention: Biological constraints and the influence of experience* (pp. 308–338). Norwood, NJ: Ablex.

Liberman, A. M. (1982). On the finding that speech is special. *American Psychologist, 37,* 148–167.

Liberman, A. M. (1992). Plausibility, parsimony, and theories of speech. In J. Alegria, D. Holender, J. Junça de Morais, & M. Radeau (Eds.), *Analytic approaches to human cognition* (pp. 25–40). Amsterdam: North-Holland.

Liberman, A. M., & Mattingly, I. G. (1989). A specialization for speech perception. *Science, 243,* 489–494.

Liberman, A. M., & Studdert-Kennedy, M. (1978). Phonetic perception. In R. Held, H. W. Leibowitz, & H. L. Teuber (Eds.), *Handbook of sensory physiology: Vol. 8. Perception* (pp. 143–178). New York: Springer-Verlag.

Liebeskind, J. C., & Paul, L. A. (1977). Psychological and physiological mechanisms of pain. *Annual Review of Psychology, 28,* 41–60.

Lindauer, M. S. (1984). Phenomenological method. In R. J. Corsini (Ed.), *Encyclopedia of psychology* (pp. 34–35). New York: Wiley.

Lindsay, P. H., & Norman, D. A. (1977). *Human information processing* (2nd ed.). New York: Academic Press.

Link, S. W. (1992). *The wave theory of difference and similarity.* Hillsdale, NJ: Erlbaum.

Link, S. W. (1994). Rediscovering the past: Gustav Fechner and signal detection theory. *Psychological Science, 5*(6), 335–340.

Linschoten, M. R. I., & Kroeze, J. H. A. (1994). Ipsi- and bilateral interactions in taste. *Perception & Psychophysics, 55,* 387–393.

Lipscomb, D. M. (1992). Fallacies and foibles in hearing conservation. *Audiology Today*, *4*, 29–33.

Liss, P., & Reeves, A. (1983). Interruption of dot processing by a backward mask. *Perception*, *12*, 513–529.

Livingstone, M., & Hubel, D. (1988). Segregation of form, color, movement, and depth: Anatomy, physiology, and perception. *Science*, *240*, 740–749.

Llewellyn-Thomas, E. (1981). Can eye movements save the earth? In D. F. Fisher, R. A. Monty, & J. W. Senders (Eds.), *Eye movements: Cognition and visual perception* (pp. 317–321). Hillsdale, NJ: Erlbaum.

Lockhead, G. R., & Wolbarsht, M. L. (1989). The moon and other toys. In M. Hershenson (Ed.), *The moon illusion* (pp. 259–297). Hillsdale, NJ: Erlbaum.

Loeb, G. E. (1985). The functional replacement of the ear. *Scientific American*, *252*(2), 104–111.

Loftus, E. F., & Ketcham, K. (1991). *Witness for the defense*. New York: St. Martin's Press.

Logue, A. W. (1991). *The psychology of eating and drinking: An introduction* (2nd ed.). New York: Freeman.

Loomis, J. M., Klatzky, R. L., & Lederman, S. J. (1991). Similarity of tactual and visual picture recognition with limited field of view. *Perception*, *20*, 167–177.

Loomis, J. M., & Lederman, S. J. (1986). Tactual perception. In K. R. Boff, L. Kaufman, & J. P. Thomas (Eds.), *Handbook of perception and human performance* (pp. 31.1–31.41). New York: Wiley.

Lovelace, E. (1988). The autokinetic projective test: A cautionary note. *Teaching of Psychology*, *15*, 44–45.

Lovelace, E. A., & Anderson, D. M. (1993). The role of vision in sound localization. *Perceptual and Motor Skills*, *77*, 843–850.

Lown, B. A. (1988). Quantification of the Müller–Lyer illusion using signal detection theory. *Perceptual and Motor Skills*, *67*, 101–102.

Luce, R. D. (1993). *Sound & hearing: A conceptual introduction*. Hillsdale, NJ: Erlbaum.

Luce, R. D., & Krumhansl, C. L. (1988). Measurement, scaling, and psychophysics. In R. C. Atkinson, R. J. Herrnstein, G. Lindzey, & R. D. Luce (Eds.), *Stevens' handbook of experimental psychology* (2nd ed., Vol. 1, pp. 3–74). New York: Wiley.

Lusk, S. L., Ronis, D. L., & Kerr, M. J. (1995). Predictors of hearing protection use among workers: Implications for training programs. *Human Factors*, *37*(3), 635–640.

Lynch, M. P., Eilers, R. E., Oller, D. K., & Urbano, R. C. (1990). Innateness, experience, and music perception. *Psychological Science*, *1*, 272–276.

Maccoby, E. E. (1990). Gender differentiation: Explanatory viewpoints. Paper presented at the meeting of the American Psychological Society, Dallas, TX.

Mack, A. (1986). Perceptual aspects of motion in the frontal plane. In K. R. Boff, L. Kaufman, & J. P. Thomas (Eds.), *Handbook of perception and human performance* (pp. 17.1–17.38). New York: Wiley.

Mack, A., Tang, B., Tuma, R., Kahn, S., & Rock, I. (1992). Perceptual organization and attention. *Cognitive Psychology*, *24*, 475–501.

MacLaury, R. E. (1992). From brightness to hue: An explanatory model of color-category evolution. *Current Anthropology*, *33*, 137–186.

MacLeod, D. I. A., Chen, B., & Stockman, A. (1990). Why do we see better in bright light? In C. Blakemore (Ed.), *Vision: Coding and efficiency* (pp. 169–174). Cambridge: Cambridge University Press.

MacLeod, D. I. A., & Willen, J. D. (1995). Is there a visual space? In R. D. Luce, M. D'Zmura, D. Hoffman, G. J. Iverson, & A. K. Romney (Eds.), *Geometric representations of perceptual phenomena: Papers in honor of Tarow Indow on his 70th birthday* (pp. 47–60). Mahwah, NJ: Erlbaum.

Macmillan, N. A., & Creelman, C. D. (1991). *Detection theory: A user's guide*. Cambridge: Cambridge University Press.

Mahar, D. P., & Mackenzie, B. D. (1993). Masking, information integration, and tactile pattern perception: A comparison of the isolation and integration hypotheses. *Perception*, *22*, 483–496.

Mair, R. G., Harrison, L. M., & Flint, D. L. (1995). The neuropsychology of odor memory. In F. R. Schab & R. G. Crowder (Eds.), *Memory for odors* (pp. 39–69). Mahwah, NJ: Erlbaum.

Makous, J. C., & Middlebrooks, J. C. (1990). Two-dimensional sound localization by human listeners. *Journal of the Acoustical Society of America*, *87*, 2188–2200.

Maloney, L. T. (1993). Color constancy and color perception: The linear-models framework. In D. E. Meyer & S. Kornblum (Eds.), *Attention and performance XIV: Synergies in experimental psychology, artificial intelligence, and cognitive neuroscience* (pp. 59–78). Cambridge, MA: MIT Press.

Maloney, L. T., & Wandell, B. A. (1986). Color constancy: A method for recovering surface spectral reflectance. *Journal of the Optical Society of America (A)*, *3*, 29–33.

Marean, G. C., Werner, L. A., & Kuhl, P. K. (1992). Vowel categorization by very young infants. *Developmental Psychology*, *28*, 396–405.

Marks, L. E. (1992). The contingency of perceptual processing: Context modifies equal-loudness relations. *Psychological Science*, *3*, 285–291.

Marks, L. E. (1993). Contextual processing of multidimensional and unidimensional auditory stimuli. *Journal of Experimental Psychology: Human Perception and Performance*, *19*, 227–249.

Marks, L. E. (1994). "Recalibrating" the auditory system: The perception of loudness. *Journal of Experimental Psychology: Human Perception and Performance*, 20, 382–396.

Marks, L. E., Borg, G., & Westerlund, J. (1992). Differences in taste perception assessed by magnitude matching and category-ratio scaling. *Chemical Senses*, 17, 493–506.

Marks, W. B., Dobelle, W. H., & MacNichol, E. F., Jr. (1964). Visual pigments of single primate cones. *Science*, 143, 1181–1183.

Marr, D. (1982). *Vision: A computational investigation into the human representation and processing of visual information*. San Francisco: Freeman.

Marr, D., & Nishihara, H. K. (1978). Representation and recognition of the spatial organization of three-dimensional shapes. *Proceedings of the Royal Society of London B*, 200, 269–294.

Martin, F. N. (1994). *Introduction to audiology* (5th ed.). Englewood Cliffs, NJ: Prentice-Hall.

Masin, S. C., & Vidotto, G. (1983). A magnitude estimation study of the inverted-T illusion. *Perception & Psychophysics*, 33, 582–584.

Masland, R. H. (1986). The functional architecture of the retina. *Scientific American*, 255(6), 102–111.

Massaro, D. W. (1987). *Speech perception by ear and eye: A paradigm for psychological inquiry*. Hillsdale, NJ: Erlbaum.

Massaro, D. W., & Cohen, M. M. (1983). Evaluation and integration of visual and auditory information in speech perception. *Journal of Experimental Psychology: Human Perception and Performance*, 9, 753–771.

Massaro, D. W., & Cohen, M. M. (1990). Perception of synthesized audible and visible speech. *Psychological Science*, 1, 55–63.

Masters, I. G. (1990–1991). The basics. *Stereo Review*.

Masterson, F. A., & Ellins, S. R. (1974). The role of vision in the orientation of the echolocating bat, Myotis lucifigis. *Behaviour*, 51, 88–98.

Mather, G., O'Halloran, A., & Anstis, S. (1991). The spacing illusion: A spatial aperture problem? *Perception*, 20, 387–392.

Mather, G., & West, S. (1993). Recognition of animal locomotion from dynamic point-light displays. *Perception*, 22, 759–766.

Matlin, M. W. (1994). *Cognition* (3rd ed.). New York: Holt, Rinehart & Winston.

Mattingly, I. G., & Liberman, A. M. (1988). Specialized perceiving systems for speech and other biologically significant sounds. In G. M. Edelman, W. E. Gall, & W. M. Cowan (Eds.), *Auditory function: Neurobiological bases of hearing* (pp. 775–793). New York: Wiley.

Mattingly, I. G., & Studdert-Kennedy, M. (Ed.). (1991). *Modularity and the motor theory of speech perception: Proceedings of a conference to honor Alvin M. Liberman*. Hillsdale, NJ: Erlbaum.

May, M. (1991). Aerial defense tactics of flying insects. *American Scientist*, 79, 316–328.

May, M. (1994). Three-dimensional mammography. *American Scientist*, 82, 421–422.

McAdams, S. (1993). Recognition of sound sources and events. In S. McAdams & E. Bigand (Eds.), *Thinking in sound: The cognitive psychology of human audition* (pp. 146–198). Oxford: Clarendon.

McAdams, S., & Bigand, E. (1993a). Introduction to auditory cognition. In S. McAdams & E. Bigand (Eds.), *Thinking in sound: The cognitive psychology of human audition* (pp. 1–9). New York: Oxford University Press.

McAdams, S., & Bigand, E. (Eds.). (1993b). *Thinking in sound: The cognitive psychology of human audition*. New York: Oxford University Press.

McBurney, D. H. (1978). Psychological dimensions and perceptual analysis of taste. In E. C. Carterette & M. P. Friedman (Eds.), *Handbook of Perception* (pp. 125–155). New York: Academic Press.

McBurney, D. H., & Gent, J. F. (1979). On the nature of taste qualities. *Psychological Bulletin*, 86, 151–167.

McBurney, D. H., & Shick, T. R. (1971). Taste and water taste of twenty-six compounds for man. *Perception & Psychophysics*, 10, 249–252.

McCann, J. J., & Benton, J. L. (1969). Interaction of the long-wave cones and the rods to produce color sensations. *Journal of the Optical Society of America*, 59, 103–107.

McClellan, P. G., Bernstein, I. H., & Garbin, C. P. (1984). What makes the Mueller a liar: A multiple-cue approach. *Perception & Psychophysics*, 36, 234–244.

McClintock, M. K. (1971). Menstrual synchrony and suppression. *Nature*, 229, 244–245.

McCloskey, M., Rapp, B., Yantis, S., Rubin, G., Bacon, W. F., Dagnelie, G., Gordon, B., Aliminosa, D., Boatman, D. F., Badecker, W., Johnson, D. N., Tusa, R. J., & Palmer, E. (1995). A developmental deficit in localizing objects from vision. *Psychological Science*, 6(2), 112–117.

McClurkin, J. W., Optican, L. M., Richmond, B. J., & Gawne, T. J. (1991). Concurrent processing and complexity of temporally encoded neural messages in visual perception. *Science*, 253, 675–677.

McCready, D. W., Jr. (1985). On size, distance, and visual angle perception. *Perception & Psychophysics*, 37, 323–334.

McCready, D. W., Jr. (1986). Moon illusions redescribed. *Perception & Psychophysics*, 39, 64–72.

McFadden, D. (1982). *Tinnitus: Facts, theories and treatments*. Washington, DC: National Academy Press.

McFadden, D., & Plattsmier, H. S. (1983). Aspirin can potentiate the temporary hearing loss induced by intense sounds. *Hearing Research, 9,* 295–316.

McFadden, D., & Wightman, F. L. (1983). Audition: Some relations between normal and pathological hearing. *Annual Review of Psychology, 34,* 95–128.

McGurk, H., & McDonald, J. (1976). Hearing lips and seeing voices. *Nature, 264,* 746–748.

McKee, S. P. (1993). Editorial: Psychophysics and perception. *Perception, 22,* 505–507.

McKee, S. P., & Welch, L. (1992). The precision of size constancy. *Vision Research, 32,* 1447–1460.

McKelvie, S. J. (1984). Effect of psychophysical method on measurement of the Müller–Lyer illusion. *Perceptual and Motor Skills, 58,* 822.

McLaughlin, S., & Margolskee, R. F. (1994). The sense of taste. *American Scientist, 82,* 538–545.

McLin, L. N., Schor, C. M., & Kruger, P. B. (1988). Changing size (looming) as a stimulus to accommodation and vergence. *Vision Research, 28,* 883–898.

McNaughton, P. A. (1990). The light response of photoreceptors. In C. Blakemore (Ed.), *Vision: Coding and efficiency* (pp. 65–73). Cambridge: Cambridge University Press.

McNeil, J. E., & Warrington, E. K. (1991). Prosopagnosia: A reclassification. *Quarterly Journal of Experimental Psychology, 43A,* 267–287.

McNeil, J. E., & Warrington, E. K. (1993). Prosopagnosia: A face-specific disorder. *Quarterly Journal of Experimental Psychology, 46A,* 1–10.

Mehler, J., Jusczyk, P., Lambertz, G., Halsted, N., Bertoncini, J., & Amiel-Tison, C. (1988). A precursor of language acquisition in young infants. *Cognition, 29,* 143–178.

Melara, R. D., Marks, L. E., & Potts, B. C. (1993). Primacy of dimensions in color perception. *Journal of Experimental Psychology: Human Perception and Performance, 19,* 1082–1104.

Melzack, R. (1973). *The puzzle of pain.* London: Penguin.

Melzack, R. (1990). The tragedy of needless pain. *Scientific American, 262*(2), 27–33.

Melzack, R. (1992a). Human versus pain: The dilemma of morphine. In F. Sicuteri, L. Terenius, L. Vecchiet, & C. A. Maggi (Eds.), *Advances in pain research and therapy: Pain versus man* (pp. 149–159). New York: Raven.

Melzack, R. (1992b). Phantom limbs. *Scientific American, 266,* 120–126.

Melzack, R. (1994). Folk medicine and the sensory modulation of pain. In P. D. Wall & R. Melzack (Eds.), *Textbook of pain* (pp. 1209–1217). Edinburgh: Churchill Livingstone.

Melzack, R., & Casey, K. L. (1968). Sensory, motivational, and central determinants of pain: A new conceptual model. In D. Kenshalo (Ed.), *The skin senses* (pp. 423–443). Springfield, IL: Thomas.

Melzack, R., & Katz, J. (1992). The McGill Pain Questionnaire: Appraisal and current status. In D. C. Turk & R. Melzack (Eds.), *Handbook of pain assessment* (pp. 152–168). New York: Guilford.

Melzack, R., & Wall, P. D. (1962). On the nature of cutaneous sensory mechanisms. *Brain, 85,* 331–356.

Melzack, R., & Wall, P. D. (1965). Pain mechanisms: A new theory. *Science, 150,* 971–979.

Melzack, R., & Wall, P. D. (1982). *The challenge of pain.* New York: Basic Books.

Melzack, R., Wall, P. D., & Ty, T. C. (1982). Acute pain in an emergency room clinic: Latency of onset and descriptor patterns related to different injuries. *Pain, 14,* 33–43.

Merigan, W. H., & Maunsell, J. H. R. (1993). How parallel are the primate visual pathways? *Annual Review of Neuroscience, 16,* 369–402.

Merry, C. J., Sizemore, C. W., & Franks, J. R. (1992). The effect of fitting procedure on hearing protector attenuation. *Ear and Hearing, 13,* 11–18.

Mershon, D. H., Jones, T. A., & Taylor, M. E. (1993). Organizational factors and the perception of motion in depth. *Perception & Psychophysics, 54,* 240–249.

Merskey, H. (1986). Classification of chronic pain: Descriptions of chronic pain syndromes and definitions of pain terms. *Pain, Suppl. 3,* S1–S226.

Merzenich, M. M., Nelson, R. J., Stryker, M. P., Cyander, M. S., Schoppman, A., & Zook, J. M. (1984). Somatosensory cortical map changes following digit amputation in adult monkeys. *Journal of Comparative Neurology, 224,* 591–605.

Metelli, F. (1982). Some characteristics of Gestalt-oriented research in perception. In J. Beck (Ed.), *Organization and representation in perception* (pp. 219–234). Hillsdale, NJ: Erlbaum.

Meyer, G. E., & Petry, S. (1987). Top-down and bottom-up: The illusory contour as a microcosm of issues in perception. In S. Petry & G. E. Meyer (Eds.), *The perception of illusory contours* (pp. 3–26). New York: Springer-Verlag.

Meyer, L. B. (1994). Emotion and meaning in music. In R. Aiello & J. A. Sloboda (Eds.), *Musical perceptions* (pp. 3–39). New York: Oxford University Press.

Michaels, C. F., & Carello, C. (1981). *Direct perception.* Englewood Cliffs, NJ: Prentice-Hall.

Middlebrooks, J. C., & Green, D. M. (1991). Sound localization by human listeners. *Annual Review of Psychology, 42,* 135–159.

Midkiff, E. E., & Bernstein, I. L. (1985). Targets of learned food aversions in humans. *Physiology & Behavior, 34,* 839–841.

Miles, F. A., & Busettini, C. (1992). Ocular compensation for self-motion: Visual mechanisms. In B.

Cohen, D. L. Tomko, & F. Guedry (Eds.), *Sensing and controlling motion: Vestibular and sensorimotor function* (pp. 220–232). New York: The New York Academy of Sciences.

Miller, I. J., Jr., & Bartoshuk, L. M. (1991). Taste perception, taste bud distribution, and spatial relationships. In T. V. Getchell, R. L. Doty, L. M. Bartoshuk, & J. B. Snow, Jr. (Eds.), *Smell and taste in health and disease* (pp. 205–233). New York: Raven.

Miller, J. D. (1978). Effects of noise on people. In E. C. Carterette & M. P. Friedman (Eds.), *Handbook of perception* (pp. 609–640). New York: Academic Press.

Miller, J. L. (1990). Speech perception. In D. N. Osherson & H. Lasnik (Eds.), *Language: An invitation to cognitive science* (pp. 69–93). Cambridge, MA: MIT Press.

Miller, R. J., & LeBeau, R. C. (1982). Induced stress, situationally-specific trait anxiety, and dark focus. *Psychophysiology, 19*, 260–265.

Miller, R. J., & Takahama, M. (1987). Effects of relaxation and aversive visual stimulation on dark focus accommodation. *Ophthalmological and Physiological Optics, 7*, 219–223.

Miller, R. J., & Takahama, M. (1988). Arousal-related changes in dark focus accommodation and dark vergence. *Investigative Ophthalmology & Visual Science, 29*, 1168–1178.

Mills, A. W. (1958). On the minimum audible angle. *Journal of the Acoustical Society of America, 30*, 237–246.

Minnaert, M. (1968/1993). *Light and color in the outdoors* (L. Seymour, Trans.). New York: Springer-Verlag.

Miskiewicz, A., Scharf, B., Hellman, R., & Meiselman, C. (1993). Loudness adaptation at high frequencies. *Journal of the Acoustical Society of America, 94*, 1281–1286.

Mitchison, G. J., & McKee, S. P. (1985). Interpolation in stereoscopic matching. *Nature, 315*, 402–404.

Mitchison, G. J., & McKee, S. P. (1987a). Interpolation and the detection of fine structure in stereoscopic matching. *Vision Research, 27*, 295–302.

Mitchison, G. J., & McKee, S. P. (1987b). The resolution of ambiguous stereoscopic matches by interpolation. *Vision Research, 27*, 285–294.

Mitchison, G. J., & Westheimer, G. (1984). The perception of depth in simple figures. *Vision Research, 24*, 1063–1073.

Miyashita, Y. (1993). Inferior temporal cortex: Where visual perception meets memory. *Annual Review of Neuroscience, 16*, 245–263.

Miyazaki, K. (1993). Absolute pitch as an inability: Identification of musical intervals in a tonal context. *Music Perception, 11*, 55–71.

Mogil, J. S., Sternberg, W. F., Kest, B., Marek, P., & Liebeskind, J. C. (1993a). Sex differences in the an-

tagonism of swim stress-induced analgesia: Effects of gonadectomy and estrogen replacement. *Pain, 53*, 17–25.

Mogil, J. S., Sternberg, W. F., & Liebeskind, J. C. (1993b). Studies of pain, stress, and immunity. In C. R. Chapman & K. M. Foley (Eds.), *Current and emerging issues in cancer pain: Research and practice* (pp. 31–47). New York: Raven.

Moir, H. C. (1936). Some observations on the appreciation of flavour in foodstuffs. *Chemistry & Industry, 55*, 145–148.

Molins, J. V. (1991). Some thoughts on impossible figures. *Perceptual and Motor Skills, 73*, 107–114.

Mollon, J. D. (1982a). Color vision. *Annual Review of Psychology, 33*, 41–85.

Mollon, J. D. (1982b). Colour vision and colour blindness. In H. B. Barlow & J. D. Mollon (Eds.), *The senses* (pp. 165–191). Cambridge: Cambridge University Press.

Montag, E. D., & Boynton, R. M. (1987). Rod influence in dichromatic surface color perception. *Vision Research, 27*, 2153–2162.

Moody, D. B., Stebbins, W. C., & May, B. J. (1990). Auditory perception of communication signals by Japanese monkeys. In W. C. Stebbins & M. A. Berkley (Eds.), *Comparative perception: Complex Signals* (pp. 311–343). New York: Wiley.

Moore, B. C. J. (1982). *Introduction to the psychology of hearing* (2nd ed.). New York: Academic Press.

Moore, D. (1989). Sound localization mechanisms. *Nature, 337*, 208–209.

Moore, P. A. (1994). A model of the role of adaptation and disadaptation in olfactory receptor neurons: Implications for the coding of temporal and intensity patterns in odor signals. *Chemical Senses, 19*, 71–86.

Morais, J., Cary, L., Alegria, J., & Bertelson, P. (1979). Does awareness of speech as a sequence of phones arise spontaneously? *Cognition, 7*, 323–331.

Morgan, M. J. (1992). On the scaling of size judgments by orientational cues. *Vision Research, 32*, 1433–1445.

Morgan, M. J., Hole, G. J., & Glennerster, A. (1990). Biases and sensitivities in geometrical illusions. *Vision Research, 30*, 1793–1810.

Morse, P. A., & Cowan, N. (1982). Infant auditory and speech perception. In T. M. Field, A. Huston, H. C. Quay, L. Troll, & G. E. Finley (Eds.), *Review of human development* (pp. 32–61). New York: Wiley.

Morton, J., & Johnson, M. H. (1991). CONSPEC and CONLERN: A two-process theory of infant face recognition. *Psychological Review, 98*, 164–181.

Morton, J., & Long, J. (1976). Effects of word transitional probability on phoneme identification. *Journal of Verbal Learning and Verbal Behavior, 15*, 43–51.

Moskowitz, H. R. (1978a). Food and food technology: Food habits, gastronomy, flavors, and sensory evaluation. In E. C. Carterette & M. P. Friedman (Eds.), *Handbook of perception* (pp. 349–382). New York: Academic Press.

Moskowitz, H. R. (1978b). Taste and food technology: Acceptability, aesthetics, and preference. In E. C. Carterette & M. P. Friedman (Eds.), *Handbook of perception* (pp. 157–194). New York: Academic Press.

Mountain, D. C., & Cody, A. R. (1989). Mechanical coupling between inner and outer hair cells in the mammalian cochlea. In J. P. Wilson & D. T. Kemp (Eds.), *Cochlear mechanisms: Structure, function, and models* (pp. 153–160). New York: Plenum.

Mountcastle, V. B. (1957). Modality and topographic properties of single neurons of cat's somatic sensory cortex. *Journal of Neurophysiology, 20,* 408–434.

Mountcastle, V. B. (1978). An organizing principle for cerebral function: The unit module and the distributed system. In G. M. Edelson & V. B. Mountcastle (Eds.), *The mindful brain: Cortical organization and the group selective theory of higher brain function* (pp. 7–50). Cambridge, MA: MIT Press.

Movshon, J. A., & Newsome, W. T. (1992). Neural foundations of visual motion perception. *Current Directions in Psychological Science, 1,* 35–39.

Movshon, J. A., & Van Sluyters, R. C. (1981). Visual neural development. *Annual Review of Psychology, 32,* 477–522.

Mozell, M. M. (1971). Olfaction. In J. W. Kling & L. A. Riggs (Eds.), *Woodworth & Schlosberg's experimental psychology* (pp. 193–222). New York: Holt, Rinehart & Winston.

Mullenix, J. W., & Pisoni, D. B. (1989). Some effects of talker variability on spoken word recognition. *Journal of the Acoustical Society of America, 85,* 365–378.

Mullenix, J. W., & Pisoni, D. B. (1990). Stimulus variability and processing dependencies in speech perception. *Perception & Psychophysics, 47,* 379–390.

Mundt, J. C. (1988). Object-motion sensitivity loss due to motion in the peripheral visual field. *Bulletin of the Psychonomic Society, 26,* 225–228.

Murphy, B. J. (1978). Pattern thresholds for moving and stationary gratings during smooth eye movement. *Vision Research, 18,* 521–530.

Murphy, C. (1995). Age-associated differences in memory for odors. In F. R. Schab & R. G. Crowder (Eds.), *Memory for odors* (pp. 109–131). Mahwah, NJ: Erlbaum.

Murphy, C., & Cain, W. S. (1980). Taste and olfaction: Independence vs. interaction. *Physiology & Behavior, 24,* 601–605.

Murphy, C., & Cain, W. S. (1986). Odor identification: The blind are better. *Physiology & Behavior, 37,* 177–180.

Murphy, C., Cain, W. S., & Bartoshuk, L. M. (1977). Mutual interaction of taste and olfaction. *Sensory Processes, 1,* 204–211.

Murray, D. J. (1993). A perspective for viewing the history of psychophysics. *Behavioral and Brain Sciences, 16,* 115–186.

Murray, J. E. (1995). Imagining and naming rotated natural objects. *Psychonomic Bulletin & Review, 2*(2), 239–243.

Musicant, A. D., & Butler, R. A. (1984). The influence of pinnae-based spectral cues on sound localization. *Journal of the Acoustical Society of America, 75,* 1195–1200.

Myers, A. K. (1982). Psychophysical scaling and scales of physical stimulus measurement. *Psychological Bulletin, 92,* 203–214.

Nafe, M. P., & Wagoner, K. S. (1941). The nature of pressure adaptation. *Journal of General Psychology, 25,* 323–351.

Naj, A. K. (1986, November 25). Hot topic: Chilies cause pleasant pain, even mild euphoria. *The Wall Street Journal,* p. 20.

Nakayama, K. (1994). James J. Gibson—An appreciation. *Psychological Review, 101,* 329–335.

Nakayama, K., & Shimojo, S. (1990). Da Vinci stereopsis: Depth and subjective occluding contours from unpaired image points. *Vision Research, 30,* 1811–1825.

Nathan, P. (1982). *The nervous system* (2nd ed.). Oxford: Oxford University Press.

Nathans, J. (1989). The genes for color vision. *Scientific American, 260*(2), 42–49.

Nathans, J., Merbs, S. L., Sung, C.-H., Weitz, C. J., & Wang, Y. (1992). Molecular genetics of human visual pigments. *Annual Review of Genetics, 26,* 403–424.

Neils, J., Newman, C. W., Hill, M., & Weiler, E. (1991). The effects of rate, sequencing, and memory on auditory processing in the elderly. *Journal of Gerontology: Psychological Sciences, 46,* P71–P75.

Neisser, U. (1981). Obituary: James J. Gibson (1904–1979). *American Psychologist, 36,* 214–215.

Neisser, U., & Hirst, W. (1974). Effect of practice on the identification of auditory sequences. *Perception & Psychophysics, 15,* 391–398.

Neitz, J., Neitz, M., & Jacobs, G. H. (1993). More than three different cone pigments among people with normal color vision. *Vision Research, 33,* 117–122.

Newman, C. G., Whinham, E. A., & MacRae, A. W. (1973). The influence of texture on judgments of slant and relative distance in a picture with suggested depth. *Perception & Psychophysics, 14,* 280–284.

Noble, W. (1983). Hearing, hearing impairment, and the audible world: A theoretical essay. *Audiology, 22,* 325–338.

Nordmark, J. O. (1978). Frequency and periodicity analysis. In E. C. Carterette & M. P. Friedman

(Eds.), *Handbook of perception* (pp. 243–282). New York: Academic Press.

Norman, J. F., & Todd, J. T. (1993). The perceptual analysis of structure from motion for rotating objects undergoing affine stretching transformations. *Perception & Psychophysics*, *53*(3), 279–291.

North, R. B. (1994). Neural stimulation techniques for chronic pain. In C. D. Tollison (Ed.), *Handbook of pain management* (pp. 74–84). Baltimore: Williams & Wilkins.

O'Day, W. T., & Young, R. W. (1978). Rhythmic daily shedding of outer segment membranes by visual cells in the goldfish. *Journal of Cell Biology*, *76*, 593–604.

Ohzawa, I., DeAngelis, G. C., & Freeman, R. D. (1990). Stereoscopic depth discrimination in the visual cortex: Neurons ideally suited as disparity detectors. *Science*, *249*, 1037–1041.

Oldfield, S. R., & Parker, S. P. A. (1984). Acuity of sound localisation: A topography of auditory space: I. Normal hearing conditions. *Perception*, *13*, 581–600.

Oldfield, S. R., & Parker, S. P. A. (1986). Acuity of sound localisation: A topography of auditory space: III. Monaural hearing conditions. *Perception*, *15*, 67–81.

O'Leary, A., McMahon, M. L., & Wallach, H. (1988). Perception of complex motion paths under three conditions of stimulation. *Perception & Psychophysics*, *43*, 339–345.

Oliver, D. L., & Huerta, M. F. (1991). Inferior and superior colliculi. In D. B. Webster, A. N. Popper, & R. R. Fay (Eds.), *The mammalian auditory pathway: Neuroanatomy* (pp. 168–221). New York: Springer-Verlag.

Olsho, L. W., Koch, E. G., Carter, E. A., Halpin, C. F., & Spetner, N. B. (1988). Pure-tone sensitivity of human infants. *Journal of the Acoustical Society of America*, *84*, 1316–1324.

Olson, H. F. (1967). *Music, physics, and engineering* (2nd ed.). New York: Dover.

Olzak, L. A., & Thomas, J. P. (1986). Seeing spatial patterns. In K. R. Boff, L. Kaufman, & J. P. Thomas (Eds.), *Handbook of perception and human performance* (pp. 7.1–7.56). New York: Wiley.

O'Mahony, M. (1978). Smell illusions and suggestion: Reports of smells contingent on tones played on television and radio. *Chemical Senses and Flavor*, *3*, 183–187.

O'Mahony, M. (1984). Alternative explanations for procedural effects on magnitude-estimation exponents for taste, involving adaptation, context, and volume effects. *Perception*, *13*, 67–73.

O'Mahony, M., & Ishii, R. (1986). A comparison of English and Japanese taste languages: Taste de-

scriptive methodology, codability and the unami taste. *British Journal of Psychology*, *77*, 161–174.

O'Mahony, M., & Thompson, B. (1977). Taste quality descriptions: Can the subject's response be affected by mentioning taste words in the instructions? *Chemical Senses and Flavor*, *2*, 283–298.

Oman, C. M. (1991). Sensory conflict in motion sickness: An Observer Theory approach. In S. R. Ellis (Ed.), *Pictorial communication in virtual and real environments* (pp. 362–376). London: Taylor & Francis.

Orchik, D. J., Schumaier, D. R., Shea, J. J., & Moretz, W. H. (1985). Intensity and frequency of sound levels from cordless telephones. *Clinical Pediatrics*, *24*, 688–689.

Ordy, J. M., Brizzee, K. R., & Johnson, H. A. (1982). Cellular alterations in visual pathways and the limbic system: Implications for vision and short-term memory. In R. Sekuler, D. Kline, & K. Dismukes (Eds.), *Aging and human visual function* (pp. 79–114). New York: Alan R. Liss.

O'Regan, J. K., & Humbert, R. (1989). Estimating psychometric functions in forced-choice situations: Significant biases found in threshold and slope estimations when small samples are used. *Perception & Psychophysics*, *46*, 434–442.

O'Toole, A. J., & Kersten, D. J. (1992). Learning to see random-dot stereograms. *Perception*, *21*, 227–243.

Owens, D. A., Antonoff, R. J., & Francis, E. L. (1994). Biological motion and nighttime pedestrian conspicuity. *Human Factors*, *36*(4), 718–732.

Owsley, C., Sekuler, R., & Siemsen, D. (1983). Contrast sensitivity throughout adulthood. *Vision Research*, *23*, 689–699.

Paap, K. R., & Partridge, D. (1988). Visual perception. In M. F. McTear (Ed.), *Understanding cognitive science* (pp. 69–101). New York: Wiley.

Palmer, S., & Rock, I. (1994a). On the nature and order of organizational processing: A reply to Peterson. *Psychonomic Bulletin & Review*, *1*(4), 515–519.

Palmer, S., & Rock, I. (1994b). Rethinking perceptual organization: The role of uniform connectedness. *Psychonomic Bulletin & Review*, *1*, 29–55.

Palmer, S. E. (1975a). The effects of contextual scenes on the identification of objects. *Memory & Cognition*, *3*, 519–526.

Palmer, S. E. (1975b). Visual perception and world knowledge: Notes on a model of sensory–cognitive interaction. In D. A. Norman & D. E. Rumelhart (Eds.), *Explorations in cognition* (pp. 279–307). San Francisco: Freeman.

Palmer, S. E. (1991). Goodness, Gestalt, groups, and Garner: Local symmetry subgroups as a theory of figural goodness. In G. R. Lockhead & J. R. Pomerantz (Eds.), *The perception of structure: Essays in honor of Wendell R. Garner* (pp. 23–39). Washington, DC: American Psychological Association.

Palmer, S. E. (1992a). Common region: A new principle of perceptual grouping. *Cognitive Psychology, 24,* 436–447.

Palmer, S. E. (1992b). Modern theories of Gestalt perception. In G. W. Humphreys (Ed.), *Understanding vision: An interdisciplinary perspective* (pp. 39–70). Oxford: Blackwell.

Paloski, W. H., Reschke, M. F., Black, F. O., Doxey, D. D., & Harm, D. L. (1992). Recovery of postural equilibrium control following spaceflight. In B. Cohen, D. L. Tomko, & F. Guedry (Eds.), *Sensing and controlling motion: Vestibular and sensorimotor function* (pp. 747–754). New York: The New York Academy of Sciences.

Pang, X. D., & Peake, W. T. (1986). How do contractions of the stapedius muscle alter the acoustic properties of the ear? In J. B. Allen, J. L. Hall, A. Hubbard, S. T. Neely, & A. Tubis (Eds.), *Peripheral auditory mechanisms* (pp. 36–43). Berlin: Springer-Verlag.

Pantev, C., Hoke, M., Lütkenhöner, B., & Lehnertz, K. (1989). Tonotopic organization of the auditory cortex: Pitch versus frequency representation. *Science, 246,* 486–488.

Paramei, G. V., Izmailov, C. A., & Sokolov, E. N. (1991). Multidimensional scaling of large chromatic differences by normal and color-deficient subjects. *Psychological Science, 2,* 244–248.

Parkes, A. S., & Bruce, H. M. (1961). Olfactory stimuli in mammalian reproduction. *Science, 134,* 1049–1054.

Parks, T. E. (1984). Illusory figures: A (mostly) atheoretical review. *Psychological Bulletin, 95,* 282–300.

Parks, T. E. (1986). Illusory figures, illusory objects, and real objects. *Psychological Review, 93,* 207–215.

Parks, T. E. (1993). The effect of extraneous elements surrounding a Kanizsa-like illusory pattern. *Perception, 22,* 1093–1097.

Parks, T. E., & Rock, I. (1990). Illusory contours from pictorially three-dimensional inducing elements. *Perception, 19,* 119–121.

Pastalan, L. A. (1982). Environmental design and adaptation to the visual environment of the elderly. In R. Sekuler, D. Kline, & K. Dismukes (Eds.), *Aging and human visual function* (pp. 323–333). New York: Alan R. Liss.

Pastore, R. E., Li, X.-F., & Layer, J. K. (1990). Categorical perception of nonspeech chirps and bleats. *Perception & Psychophysics, 48,* 151–156.

Patterson, D. R., Everett, J. J., Burns, G. L., & Marvin, J. A. (1992a). Hypnosis for the treatment of burn pain. *Journal of Consulting and Clinical Psychology, 60,* 713–717.

Patterson, R., & Martin, W. L. (1992). Human stereopsis. *Human Factors, 34,* 669–692.

Patterson, R., Moe, L., & Hewitt, T. (1992b). Factors that affect depth perception in stereoscopic displays. *Human Factors, 34,* 655–667.

Penfield, W., & Rasmussen, T. (1950). *The cerebral cortex of man.* New York: Macmillan.

Peper, L., Bootsma, R. J., Mestre, D. R., & Bakker, F. C. (1994). Catching balls: How to get the hand to the right place at the right time. *Journal of Experimental Psychology: Human Perception and Performance, 20,* 591–612.

Perrett, D. I., & Mistlin, A. J. (1990). Perception of facial characteristics by monkeys. In W. C. Stebbins & M. A. Berkeley (Eds.), *Comparative perception: Complex signals* (pp. 187–215). New York: Wiley.

Perrott, D. R. (1993). Auditory and visual localization: Two modalities, one world. *Audio Engineering Society Proceedings, 12,* 221–231.

Perrott, D. R., Costantino, B., & Cisneros, J. (1993). Auditory and visual localization performance in a sequential discrimination task. *Journal of the Acoustical Society of America, 93,* 2134–2138.

Perrott, D. R., & Saberi, K. (1990). Minimum audible angle thresholds for sources varying in both elevation and azimuth. *Journal of the Acoustical Society of America, 87,* 1728–1731.

Perrott, D. R., Sadralodabai, T., Saberi, K., & Strybel, T. Z. (1991). Aurally aided visual search in the central visual field: Effects of visual load and visual enhancement of the target. *Human Factors, 33,* 389–400.

Peterhans, E., & von der Heydt, R. (1989). Mechanisms of contour perception in monkey visual cortex: II. Contours bridging gaps. *Journal of Neuroscience, 9,* 1749–1763.

Peterhans, E., von der Heydt, R., & Baumgartner, G. (1986). Neuronal responses to illusory contour stimuli reveal stages of visual cortical processing. In J. D. Pettigrew, K. J. Sanderson, & W. R. Levick (Eds.), *Visual neuroscience* (pp. 343–351). New York: Cambridge University Press.

Petersik, J. T. (1989). The two-process distinction in apparent motion. *Psychological Bulletin, 106,* 107–127.

Peterson, M. A. (1994a). Object recognition processes can and do operate before figure-ground organization. *Current Directions in Psychological Science, 3,* 105–111.

Peterson, M. A. (1994b). The proper placement of uniform connectedness. *Psychonomic Bulletin & Review, 1*(4), 509–514.

Peterson, M. A., & Gibson, B. S. (1993). Shape recognition inputs to figure–ground organization in three-dimensional displays. *Cognitive Psychology, 25,* 383–429.

Peterson, M. A., & Gibson, B. S. (1994a). Must figure–ground organization precede object recognition? An assumption in peril. *Psychological Science, 5,* 253–259.

Peterson, M. A., & Gibson, B. S. (1994b). Object recognition contributions to figure–ground organization: Operations on outlines and subjective contours. *Perception & Psychophysics, 56,* 551–564.

Peterson, M. A., Harvey, E. M., & Weidenbacher, H. J. (1991). Shape recognition contributions to figure–ground reversal: Which route counts? *Journal of Experimental Psychology: Human Perception and Performance, 17,* 1075–1089.

Petrosino, L., Fucci, D., Harris, D., & Randolph-Tyler, E. (1988). Lingual vibrotactile/auditory magnitude estimation and cross-modal matching: Comparison of suprathreshold responses in men and women. *Perceptual and Motor Skills, 67,* 291–300.

Pfaffmann, C. (1978). The vertebrate phylogeny, neural code, and integrative processes of taste. In E. C. Carterette & M. P. Friedman (Eds.), *Handbook of perception* (pp. 51–123). New York: Academic Press.

Phillips, D. P., & Brugge, J. F. (1985). Progress in neurophysiology of sound localization. *Annual Review of Psychology, 36,* 245–274.

Pick, A. D., & Palmer, C. F. (1993). Development of the perception of musical events. In T. J. Tighe & W. J. Dowling (Eds.), *Psychology and music: The understanding of melody and rhythm* (pp. 197–213). Hillsdale, NJ: Erlbaum.

Pickles, J. O. (1988). *An introduction to the physiology of hearing* (2nd ed.). London: Academic Press.

Pickles, J. O. (1993a). Early events in auditory processing. *Current Biology, 3,* 558–562.

Pickles, J. O. (1993b). A model for the mechanics of the stereociliar bundle on acousticolateral hair cells. *Hearing Research, 68,* 159–172.

Pickles, J. O., & Corey, D. P. (1992). Mechanoelectrical transduction by hair cells. *Trends in Neurosciences, 15*(7), 254–259.

Pierce, J. R. (1983). *The science of musical sound.* New York: Freeman.

Pinel, J. P. J. (1993). *Biopsychology* (2nd ed.). Boston: Allyn & Bacon.

Pinker, S. (1984). Visual cognition: An introduction. *Cognition, 18,* 1–63.

Pirenne, M. H. (1975). Vision and art. In E. C. Carterette & M. P. Friedman (Eds.), *Handbook of perception* (pp. 434–490). New York: Academic Press.

Plaut, D. C., & Farah, M. J. (1991). Visual object representation: Interpreting neurophysiological data within a computational framework. *Journal of Cognitive Neuroscience, 2,* 320–342.

Plude, D. J. (1990). Aging, feature integration, and visual selective attention. In J. T. Enns (Ed.), *The development of attention: Research and theory* (pp. 467–487). Amsterdam: North-Holland.

Plug, C., & Ross, H. E. (1989). Historical review. In M. Hershenson (Ed.), *The moon illusion* (pp. 5–27). Hillsdale, NJ: Erlbaum.

Podd, J. (1990). The effects of memory load and delay on facial recognition. *Applied Cognitive Psychology, 4,* 47–59.

Pokorny, J., Shevell, S. K., & Smith, V. C. (1991). Colour appearance and colour constancy. In P. Gouras (Ed.), *The perception of colour* (pp. 43–61). Boca Raton, FL: CRC Press.

Pokorny, J., & Smith, V. C. (1982). New observations concerning red–green color defects. *Color Research and Application, 7,* 159–164.

Pokorny, J., & Smith, V. C. (1986). Colorimetry and color discrimination. In K. R. Boff, L. Kaufman, & J. P. Thomas (Eds.), *Handbook of perception and human performance* (pp. 8.1–8.51). New York: Wiley.

Pola, J., & Matin, L. (1977). Eye movements following autokinesis. *Bulletin of the Psychonomic Society, 10,* 397–398.

Pollack, I. (1978). Decoupling of auditory pitch and stimulus frequency: The Shepard demonstration revisited. *Journal of the Acoustical Society of America, 63,* 202–206.

Pollack, I., & Pickett, J. M. (1964). The intelligibility of excerpts from conversational speech. *Language & Speech, 6,* 165–171.

Pollak, G. D. (1989). The functional organization of the auditory brainstem in the mustache bat and mechanisms for sound localization. In R. N. Singh & N. J. Strausfeld (Eds.), *Neurobiology of sensory systems* (pp. 469–497). New York: Plenum.

Pollick, F. E. (1994). Perceiving shape from profiles. *Perception & Psychophysics, 55,* 152–161.

Pollino, D. (1993). Personal communication.

Pomerantz, J. R. (1986). Visual form perception: An overview. In E. Schwab & H. Nusbaum (Eds.), *Pattern recognition by humans and machines: Visual perception* (pp. 1–30). Orlando, FL: Academic Press.

Pomerantz, J. R., & Kubovy, M. (1981). Perceptual organization: An overview. In M. Kubovy & J. R. Pomerantz (Eds.), *Perceptual organization* (pp. 423–456). Hillsdale, NJ: Erlbaum.

Pomerantz, J. R., & Kubovy, M. (1986). Theoretical approaches to perceptual organization. In K. R. Boff, L. Kaufman, & J. P. Thomas (Eds.), *Handbook of perception and human performance* (pp. 36.1–36.46). New York: Wiley.

Pomerantz, J. R., Sager, L. C., & Stoever, R. J. (1977). Perception of wholes and of their component parts: Some configural superiority effects. *Journal of Experimental Psychology: Human Perception and Performance, 3,* 422–435.

Pons, T. P., Preston, E., Garraghty, A. K., Kaas, J., Taub, E., & Mishkin, M. (1991). Massive cortical reorganization after sensory deafferentation in adult macaques. *Science, 252,* 1857–1860.

Porter, R. H. (1991). Human reproduction and the mother–infant relationship: The role of odors. In T. V. Getchell, R. L. Doty, L. M. Bartoshuk, & J. B. Snow, Jr. (Eds.), *Smell and taste in health and disease* (pp. 429–442). New York: Raven.

Porter, R. H., Cernoch, J. M., & Balogh, R. D. (1985). Odor signatures and kin recognition. *Physiology & Behavior, 34*, 445–448.

Porter, R. H., Cernoch, J. M., & McLaughlin, F. J. (1983). Maternal recognition of neonates through olfactory cues. *Physiology & Behavior, 30*, 151–154.

Porter, R. H., & Moore, J. D. (1981). Human kin recognition by olfactory cues. *Physiology & Behavior, 27*, 493–495.

Posner, M. I., & Keele, S. W. (1968). On the genesis of abstract ideas. *Journal of Experimental Psychology, 77*, 353–363.

Post, R. B., & Leibowitz, H. W. (1985). A revised analysis of the role of efference in motor perception. *Perception, 14*, 631–643.

Post, R. B., Leibowitz, H. W., & Shupert, C. L. (1982). Autokinesis and peripheral stimuli: Implications for fixational stability. *Perception, 11*, 477–482.

Poulton, E. C. (1970). *The environment at work.* Springfield, IL: Thomas.

Poulton, E. C. (1989). *Bias in quantifying judgments.* Hove, UK: Erlbaum.

Prak, N. L. (1977). *The visual perception of the built environment.* Delft: Delft University Press.

Prazdny, K. (1986). What variables control (long-range) apparent motion? *Perception, 15*, 37–40.

Predebon, J. (1992). The influence of object familiarity on magnitude estimates of apparent size. *Perception, 21*, 77–90.

Preisler, A. (1993). The influence of spectral composition of complex tones and of musical experience on the perceptibility of virtual pitch. *Perception & Psychophysics, 54*, 589–603.

Pressey, A. W., & Epp, D. (1992). Spatial attention in Ponzo-like patterns. *Perception & Psychophysics, 52*(2), 211–221.

Price, D. D., & Harkins, S. W. (1992). Psychophysical approaches to pain measurement and assessment. In D. C. Turk & R. Melzack (Eds.), *Handbook of pain assessment* (pp. 111–134). New York: Guilford.

Price, D. D., McHaffie, J. G., & Stein, B. E. (1992). The psychophysical attributes of heart-induced pain and their relationship to neural mechanisms. *Journal of Cognitive Neuroscience, 4*, 1–14.

Priest, H. F., & Cutting, J. E. (1985). Visual flow and direction of locomotion. *Science, 227*, 1063–1064.

Prinzmetal, W. (1995). Visual feature integration in a world of objects. *Current Directions in Psychological Science, 4*(3), 90–94.

Prkachin, K. M. (1992a). The consistency of facial expressions of pain: A comparison across modalities. *Pain, 51*, 297–306.

Prkachin, K. M. (1992b). Dissociating spontaneous and deliberate expressions of pain: Signal detection analyses. *Pain, 51*, 57–65.

Prkachin, K. M., Berzins, S., & Mercer, S. R. (1994). Encoding and decoding of pain expressions: A judgement study. *Pain, 58*, 253–259.

Probst, T., Krafczyk, S., & Brandt, T. (1987). Object-motion detection affected by concurrent self-motion perception: Applied aspects for vehicle guidance. *Ophthalmological and Physiological Optics, 7*, 309–314.

Probst, T., Krafczyk, S., Brandt, T., & Wist, E. R. (1984). Interaction between perceived self-motion and object motion impairs vehicle guidance. *Science, 225*, 536–538.

Proffitt, D. R. (1991). Perceiving environmental properties from motion information: Minimal conditions. In S. R. Ellis (Ed.), *Pictorial communication in virtual and real environments* (pp. 47–60). London: Taylor & Francis.

Pugh, E. N., Jr. (1988). Vision: Physics and retinal physiology. In R. C. Atkinson, R. J. Herrnstein, G. Lindzey, & R. D. Luce (Eds.), *Stevens' handbook of experimental psychology* (2nd ed., Vol. 1, pp. 75–163). New York: Wiley.

Purghé, F. (1993). Illusory contours from pictorially three-dimensional inducing elements: Counterevidence for Parks and Rock's example. *Perception, 22*, 809–818.

Quinlan, P. T. (1991). Differing approaches to two-dimensional shape recognition. *Psychological Bulletin, 109*, 224–241.

Quittner, A. L., Smith, L. B., Osberger, M. J., Mitchell, T. V., & Katz, D. B. (1994). The impact of audition on the development of visual attention. *Psychological Science, 5*(6), 347–353.

Rabin, M. D., & Cain, W. S. (1984). Odor recognition: Familiarity, identifiability, and encoding consistency. *Journal of Experimental Psychology: Learning, Memory, and Cognition, 10*, 316–325.

Rabin, M. D., & Cain, W. S. (1986). Determinants of measured olfactory sensitivity. *Perception & Psychophysics, 39*, 281–286.

Ramachandran, V. S. (1986). *Utilitarian theory of perception.* Paper presented at the meeting of the American Psychological Association, Washington, DC.

Ramachandran, V. S. (1988). Perceiving shape from shading. *Scientific American, 259*(2), 76–83.

Ramachandran, V. S. (1990). Interactions between motion, depth, color and form: The utilitarian theory of perception. In C. Blakemore (Ed.), *Vision: Coding and efficiency* (pp. 346–360). Cambridge: Cambridge University Press.

Ramachandran, V. S. (1992a). Blind spots. *Scientific American, 266*, 86–91.

Ramachandran, V. S. (1992b). Filling in the gaps in perception: Part 1. *Current Directions in Psychological Science, 1*, 199–205.

Ramachandran, V. S. (1992c). Perception: A biological perspective. In G. A. Carpenter & S. Grossberg (Eds.), *Neural networks for vision and image processing* (pp. 45–91). Cambridge, MA: MIT Press.

Ramachandran, V. S. (1993). Filling in gaps in perception: Part II. Scotomas and phantom limbs. *Current Directions in Psychological Science, 2*, 56–65.

Ramachandran, V. S., & Anstis, S. M. (1986). The perception of apparent motion. *Scientific American, 254*(6), 102–109.

Ramachandran, V. S., & Gregory, R. L. (1991). Perceptual filling in of artificially induced scotomas in human vision. *Nature, 350*, 699–702.

Rasmussen, P., & Jensen, T. S. (1992). Phantom pain and phenomena after amputation. In F. Sicuteri, L. Terenius, L. Vecchiet, & C. A. Maggi (Eds.), *Advances in Pain Research and Therapy: Pain versus Man* (pp. 167–176). New York: Raven.

Ratliff, F. (1984). Why Mach bands are not seen at the edges of a step. *Vision Research, 24*, 163–165.

Ratliff, F. (1992). *Paul Signac and color in Neo-Impressionism*. New York: Rockefeller University Press.

Rayner, K. (1992a). Eye movements and visual cognition: Introduction. In K. Rayner (Ed.), *Eye movements and visual cognition: Scene perception and reading* (pp. 1–7). New York: Springer-Verlag.

Rayner, K. (Ed.). (1992b). *Eye movements and visual cognition: Scene perception and reading*. New York: Springer-Verlag.

Rechschaffen, A., & Mednick, S. A. (1955). The autokinetic word technique. *Journal of Abnormal and Social Psychology, 51*, 346.

Reddy, R. (1976). Speech recognition by machine: A review. *Proceedings of the IEEE, 64*, 501–531.

Reed, E. S. (1988). *James J. Gibson and the psychology of perception*. New Haven: Yale University Press.

Reeves, A. (1983). Distinguishing opponent and non-opponent detection pathways in early dark adaptation. *Vision Research, 23*, 647–654.

Regan, D. (1985). "How do we avoid confounding the direction we are looking and the direction we are moving?" Response. *Science, 227*, 1064–1065.

Regan, D. (1992). Visual judgements and misjudgements in cricket, and the art of flight. *Perception, 21*, 91–115.

Regan, D., Beverley, K., & Cynader, M. (1979). The visual perception of motion in depth. *Scientific American, 241*(1), 136–151.

Regan, D., & Beverley, K. I. (1982). How do we avoid confounding the direction we are looking and the direction we are moving? *Science, 215*, 194–196.

Regan, D., & Beverley, K. I. (1984). Figure–ground segregation by motion contrast and by luminance contrast. *Journal of the Optical Society of America A, 1*, 433–442.

Regan, D., Frisby, J. P., Poggio, G. F., Schor, C. M., & Tyler, C. W. (1990). The perception of stereodepth and stereomotion. In L. Spillmann & J. S. Werner (Eds.), *Visual perception: The neurophysiological foundations* (pp. 317–347). San Diego: Academic Press.

Reichel, F. D., & Todd, J. T. (1990). Perceived depth inversion of smoothly curved surfaces due to image inversion. *Journal of Experimental Psychology: Human Perception and Performance, 16*, 653–664.

Reicher, G. M. (1969). Perceptual recognition as a function of meaningfulness of stimulus materials. *Journal of Experimental Psychology, 81*, 275–280.

Reinhardt-Rutland, A. H. (1988). Induced movement in the visual modality: An overview. *Psychological Bulletin, 103*, 57–71.

Remez, R. E., Rubin, P. E., Pisoni, D. B., & Carrell, T. D. (1981). Speech perception without traditional speech cues. *Science, 212*, 947–950.

Renouf, D. (1989). Sensory function in the harbor seal. *Scientific American, 260*(4), 90–95.

Restle, F. (1970). Moon illusion explained on the basis of relative size. *Science, 167*, 1092–1096.

Riccio, G. E., & Stoffregen, T. A. (1990). Gravitoinertial force versus the direction of balance in the perception and control of orientation. *Psychological Review, 97*, 135–137.

Richards, W. (1975). Visual space perception. In E. C. Carterette & M. P. Friedman (Eds.), *Handbook of perception* (pp. 351–386). New York: Academic Press.

Richards, W. (1988). The approach. In W. Richards (Ed.), *Natural computation* (pp. 3–13). Cambridge, MA: MIT Press.

Richards, W., Nishihara, H. K., & Dawson, B. (1988). CARTOON: A biologically motivated edge detection algorithm. In W. Richards (Ed.), *Natural computation* (pp. 55–69). Cambridge, MA: MIT Press.

Richardson, J. T. E., & Zucco, G. M. (1989). Cognition and olfaction: A review. *Psychological Bulletin, 105*, 352–360.

Riddoch, M. J., & Humphreys, G. W. (1992). The smiling giraffe: An illustration of a visual memory disorder. In R. Campbell (Ed.), *Mental lives: Case studies in cognition* (pp. 161–177). Oxford: Blackwell.

Riggs, L. A. (1971). Vision. In J. W. Kling & L. A. Riggs (Eds.), *Woodworth & Schlosberg's experimental psychology* (pp. 273–314). New York: Holt, Rinehart & Winston.

Riggs, L. A., Ratliff, F., Cornsweet, J. C., & Cornsweet, T. N. (1953). The disappearance of steadily fixated visual test objects. *Journal of the Optical Society of America, 43*, 495–501.

Riordan-Eva, P. (1992a). Anatomy & embryology of the eye. In D. Vaughn, T. Asbury, & P. Riordan-Eva (Eds.), *General ophthalmology* (pp. 1–29). Norwalk, CT: Appleton & Lange.

Riordan-Eva, P. (1992b). Blindness. In D. Vaughn, T. Asbury, & P. Riordan-Eva (Eds.), *General ophthalmology* (pp. 404–409). Norwalk, CT: Appleton & Lange.

Risset, J. C., & Wessel, D. L. (1982). Exploration of timbre by analysis and synthesis. In D. Deutsch (Ed.), *The psychology of music* (pp. 25–58). New York: Academic Press.

Robles, L., Ruggero, M. A., & Rich, N. C. (1986). Mossbauer measurements of the mechanical response to single-tone and two-tone stimuli at the base of the chinchilla cochlea. In J. B. Allen, J. L. Hall, A. Hubbard, S. T. Neely, & A. Tubis (Eds.), *Peripheral auditory mechanisms* (pp. 121–128). Berlin: Springer-Verlag.

Rock, I. (1983). *The logic of perception.* Cambridge, MA: MIT Press.

Rock, I. (1986). Cognitive intervention in perceptual processing. In T. J. Knapp & L. C. Robertson (Eds.), *Approaches to cognition: Contrasts and controversies* (pp. 189–221). Hillsdale, NJ: Erlbaum.

Rock, I. (1987). A problem-solving approach to illusory contours. In S. Petry & G. E. Meyer (Eds.), *The perception of illusory contours* (pp. 62–70). New York: Springer-Verlag.

Rock, I. (1988). On Thompson's inverted-face phenomenon (Research Note). *Perception, 17*, 815–817.

Rock, I., & Anson, R. (1979). Illusory contours as the solution to a problem. *Perception, 8*, 665–681.

Rock, I., & Ebenholtz, S. (1959). The relational determination of perceived size. *Psychological Review, 66*, 387–401.

Rock, I., & Kaufman, L. (1962). The moon illusion, II. *Science, 136*, 1023–1031.

Rock, I., & Linnett, C. M. (1993). Is a perceived shape based on its retinal image? *Perception, 22*, 61–76.

Rock, I., Linnett, C. M., Grant, P., & Mack, A. (1992a). Perception without attention: Results of a new method. *Cognitive Psychology, 24*, 502–534.

Rock, I., & Mack, A. (1994). Attention and perceptual organization. In S. Ballesteros (Ed.), *Cognitive approaches to human perception* (pp. 23–41). Hillsdale, NJ: Erlbaum.

Rock, I., Nijhawan, R., & Palmer, S. (1992b). Grouping based on phenomenal similarity of achromatic color. *Perception, 21*, 779–789.

Rock, I., & Palmer, S. (1990). The legacy of Gestalt psychology. *Scientific American, 263*(6), 84–90.

Rodgers, J. E. (1982). The malleable memory of eyewitnesses. *Science Digest, 3*, 32–35.

Rodieck, R. W., Brening, R. K., & Watanabe, M. (1993). The origin of parallel visual pathways. In R. Shapley & D. M.-K. Lam (Eds.), *Contrast sensitivity: Proceedings of the Retina Research Foundation Symposia* (pp. 117–144). Cambridge, MA: MIT Press.

Rogel, M. J. (1978). A critical evaluation of the possibility of higher primate reproductive and sexual pheromones. *Psychological Bulletin, 85*, 810–830.

Rogers, B. J., & Collett, T. S. (1989). The appearance of surfaces specified by motion parallax and binocular disparity. *Quarterly Journal of Experimental Psychology, 41A*(4), 697–717.

Rogers, T. B., Kuiper, N. A., & Kirker, W. S. (1977). Self-reference and the encoding of personal information. *Journal of Personality and Social Psychology, 35*, 677–688.

Rollman, G. B. (1977). Signal detection theory measurement of pain: A review and critique. *Pain, 3*, 187–211.

Rollman, G. B. (1980). Letter to the editor: On the utility of signal detection theory pain measures. *Pain, 9*, 375–379.

Rollman, G. B. (1991). Pain responsiveness. In M. A. Heller & W. Schiff (Eds.), *The psychology of touch* (pp. 91–114). Hillsdale, NJ: Erlbaum.

Rollman, G. B. (1992). Cognitive effects in pain and pain judgments. In D. Algom (Ed.), *Psychophysical approaches to cognition* (pp. 515–574). Amsterdam: North-Holland.

Rollman, G. B., & Harris, G. (1987). The detectability, discriminability, and perceived magnitude of painful electrical shock. *Perception & Psychophysics, 42*, 257–268.

Rolnick, A., & Lubow, R. E. (1991). Why is the driver rarely motion sick? The role of controllability in motion sickness. *Ergonomics, 34*, 867–879.

Rosch, E. (1977). Human categorization. In N. Warren (Ed.), *Studies in cross-cultural psychology* (pp. 1–49). London: Academic Press.

Rose, J. E., Brugge, J. F., Anderson, D. J., & Hind, J. E. (1967). Phase locked response to low-frequency tones in single auditory nerve fibers of the squirrel monkey. *Journal of Neurophysiology, 30*, 769–793.

Rose, J. E., Gross, N. B., Geisler, C. D., & Hind, J. E. (1966). Some neural mechanisms in the inferior colliculus of the cat which may be relevant to localization of a sound source. *Journal of Neurophysiology, 29*, 288–314.

Rosen, S., & Howell, P. (1991). *Signals and systems for speech and hearing.* London: Academic Press.

Rosenblum, L. D., & Saldaña, H. M. (1992). Discrimination tests of visually influenced syllables. *Perception & Psychophysics, 52,* 461–473.

Rosenblum, L. D., Saldaña, H. M., & Carello, C. (1993). Dynamical constraints on pictorial action lines. *Journal of Experimental Psychology: Human Perception and Performance, 19,* 381–396.

Rosenblum, L. D., Wuestefeld, A. P., & Saldaña, H. M. (1993). Auditory looming perception: Influences on anticipatory judgments. *Perception, 22,* 1467–1482.

Rosenzweig, S. (1987). The final tribute of E. G. Boring to G. T. Fechner: Concerning the date October 22, 1850. *American Psychologist, 42,* 787–790.

Rosowski, J. J., Carney, L. H., Lynch, T. J., & Peake, W. T. (1986). The effectiveness of external and middle ears in coupling acoustic power into the cochlea. In J. B. Allen, J. L. Hall, A. Hubbard, S. T. Neely, & A. Tubis (Eds.), *Peripheral auditory mechanisms* (pp. 3–12). Berlin: Springer-Verlag.

Ross, H. E., & Ross, G. M. (1976). Did Ptolemy understand the moon illusion. *Perception, 5,* 377–385.

Ross, J. (1976). The resources of binocular perception. *Scientific American, 234*(3), 80–86.

Rossing, T. D. (1990). *The science of sound.* Reading, MA: Addison-Wesley.

Rossing, T. D., & Houtsma, A. J. M. (1986). Effects of signal envelope on the pitch of short sinusoidal tones. *Journal of the Acoustical Society of America, 79,* 1926.

Rowe-Boyer, M. M., & Brosvic, G. M. (1990). Procedure-specific estimates of structural and strategic factors in the horizontal–vertical illusion. *Perceptual and Motor Skills, 70,* 571–576.

Rubin, E. (1915/1958). Synoplevede Figurer [Figure and ground]. In D. C. Beardslee & M. Wertheimer (Eds.), *Readings in perception* (pp. 194–203). Princeton, NJ: Van Nostrand.

Rubin, P., Turvey, M. T., & Van Gelder, P. (1976). Initial phonemes are detected faster in spoken words than in nonspoken words. *Perception & Psychophysics, 19,* 394–398.

Ruff, H. A. (1982). The development of object perception in infancy. In T. M. Field, A. Huston, H. C. Quay, L. Troll, & G. E. Finley (Eds.), *Review of human development* (pp. 93–106). New York: Wiley.

Ruff, H. A. (1985). Detection of information specifying the motion of objects by 3- and 5-month-old infants. *Developmental Psychology, 21,* 295–305.

Runeson, S., & Frykholm, G. (1983). Kinematic specifications of dynamics as an informational basis for person-and-action perception: Expectation, gender-recognition, and deceptive intention. *Journal of Experimental Psychology: General, 112,* 585–615.

Rushton, W. A. H. (1958). Kinetics of cone pigments measured objectively in the living human fovea. *Annals of the New York Academy of Sciences, 74,* 291–304.

Rushton, W. A. H. (1975). Visual pigments and color blindness. *Scientific American, 232*(3), 64–74.

Russell, I. J., & Kössl, M. (1992). Sensory transduction and frequency selectivity in the basal turn of the guinea-pig cochlea. In R. P. Carylon, C. J. Darwin, & I. J. Russell (Eds.), *Processing of complex sounds by the auditory system* (pp. 317–324). Oxford: Clarendon.

Russell, M. J. (1976). Human olfactory communication. *Nature, 260,* 520–522.

Russell, M. J., Switz, G. M., & Thompson, K. (1980). Olfactory influences on the human menstrual cycle. *Pharmacology, Biochemistry, & Behavior, 13,* 737–738.

Rutherford, W. (1886). A new theory of hearing. *Journal of Anatomy and Physiology, 21,* 166–168.

Sachs, M. B., & Blackburn, C. C. (1991). Processing of complex sounds in the cochlear nucleus. In R. A. Altschuler, R. P. Bobbin, B. M. Clopton, & D. W. Hoffman (Eds.), *Neurobiology of hearing: The central auditory system* (pp. 79–98). New York: Raven.

Sacks, O. (1985). *The man who mistook his wife for a hat, and other clinical tales.* New York: Summit Books.

Sacks, O. (1995). *An anthropologist on Mars: Seven paradoxical tales.* New York: Alfred A. Knopf.

Sacks, O., & Wasserman, R. (1987, November 19). The case of the color-blind painter. *The New York Review of Books,* pp. 25–34.

Saldaña, H. M., & Rosenblum, L. D. (1993). Visual influences on auditory pluck and bow judgements. *Perception & Psychophysics, 54,* 406–416.

Saldaña, H. M., & Rosenblum, L. D. (1994). Selective adaptation in speech perception using a compelling audiovisual adaptor. *Journal of the Acoustical Society of America, 95,* 3658–3661.

Salter, D. (1988). How spectacles improve your hearing. *New Scientist, 120,* 83–84.

Salthouse, T. A. (1991). *Theoretical perspectives on cognitive aging.* Hillsdale, NJ: Erlbaum.

Samuel, A. G. (1981). Phonemic restoration: Insights from a new methodology. *Journal of Experimental Psychology: General, 110,* 474–494.

Samuel, A. G. (1987). Lexical uniqueness effects on phonemic restoration. *Journal of Memory and Language, 26,* 36–56.

Samuel, A. G., & Ressler, W. H. (1986). Attention within auditory word perception: Insights from the phonemic restoration illusion. *Journal of Experimental Psychology: Human Perception and Performance, 12,* 70–79.

Savage, J. E., & Slepecky, N. B. (1993). Involvement of different isoforms of actin in outer hair-cell motility. In R. T. Verrillo (Ed.), *Sensory research: Multimodal perspectives* (pp. 233–248). Hillsdale, NJ: Erlbaum.

Scatena, P. (1990). Phantom representations of congenitally absent limbs. *Perceptual and Motor Skills, 70*, 1227–1232.

Schab, F. R. (1990). Odors and the remembrance of things past. *Journal of Experimental Psychology: Learning, Memory, and Cognition, 16*, 648–655.

Schab, F. R. (1991). Odor memory: Taking stock. *Psychological Bulletin, 109*, 242–251.

Schab, F. R., & Crowder, R. G. (Eds.). (1995). *Memory for odors*. Mahwah, NJ: Erlbaum.

Scharf, B. (1978). Loudness. In E. C. Carterette & M. P. Friedman (Eds.), *Handbook of perception* (pp. 187–242). New York: Academic Press.

Scharf, B., & Buus, S. (1986). Audition I. In K. R. Boff, L. Kaufman, & J. P. Thomas (Eds.), *Handbook of perception and human performance* (pp. 14.1–14.71). New York: Wiley.

Scharf, B., Canévet, G., & Ward, L. M. (1992). On the relation between intensity discrimination and adaptation. In Y. Cazals, L. Demany, & K. Horner (Eds.), *Auditory physiology and perception* (pp. 289–295). Oxford: Pergamon.

Scharf, B., & Houtsma, A. J. M. (1986). Audition II. In K. R. Boff, L. Kaufman, & J. P. Thomas (Eds.), *Handbook of perception and human performance* (pp. 15.1–15.60). New York: Wiley.

Scherer, K. R. (1986). Vocal affect expression: A review and a model for future research. *Psychological Bulletin, 99*, 143–165.

Schiff, W. (1980). *Perception: An applied approach*. Boston: Houghton Mifflin.

Schiffman, S. S. (1991). Drugs influencing taste and smell perception. In T. V. Getchell, R. L. Doty, L. M. Bartoshuk, & J. B. Snow, Jr. (Eds.), *Smell and taste in health and disease* (pp. 845–850). New York: Raven.

Schiffman, S. S. (1992). Aging and the sense of smell: Potential benefits of fragrance enhancement. In S. Van Toller & G. H. Dodd (Eds.), *Fragrance: The psychology and biology of perfume* (pp. 51–62). London: Elsevier.

Schiffman, S. S., & Erickson, R. P. (1980). The issue of primary tastes versus a taste continuum. *Neuroscience and Biobehavioral Reviews, 4*, 109–117.

Schiller, P. H. (1986). The central visual system. *Vision Research, 26*, 1351–1386.

Schiller, P. H. (1994). Area V4 of the primate visual cortex. *Current Directions in Psychological Science, 3*, 89–92.

Schiller, P. H., & Lee, K. (1991). The role of the primate extrastriate area V4 in vision. *Science, 251*, 1251–1253.

Schirillo, J., Reeves, A., & Arend, L. (1990). Perceived lightness, but not brightness, of achromatic surfaces depends on perceived depth information. *Perception & Psychophysics, 48*, 82–90.

Schleidt, M. (1992). The semiotic relevance of human olfaction: A biological approach. In S. Van Toller & G. H. Dodd (Eds.), *Fragrance: The psychology and biology of perfume* (pp. 37–50). London: Elsevier.

Schum, L. K., & Tye-Murray, N. (1995). Alerting and assistive systems: Counseling implications for cochlear implant users. In R. S. Tyler & D. J. Schum (Eds.), *Assistive devices for persons with hearing impairment* (pp. 86–122). Boston: Allyn & Bacon.

Scialfa, C. T., Garvey, P. M., Tyrrell, R. A., & Leibowitz, H. W. (1992). Age differences in dynamic contrast thresholds. *Journal of Gerontology: Psychological Sciences, 47*, P172–P175.

Scott, T. R., & Plata-Salaman, C. R. (1991). Coding of taste quality. In T. V. Getchell, R. L. Doty, L. M. Bartoshuk, & J. B. Snow, Jr. (Eds.), *Smell and taste in health and disease* (pp. 345–368). New York: Raven.

Sedgwick, H. A. (1986). Space perception. In K. R. Boff, L. Kaufman, & J. P. Thomas (Eds.), *Handbook of perception and human performance* (pp. 21.1–21.57). New York: Wiley.

Sekuler, R. (1975). Visual motion perception. In E. C. Carterette & M. P. Friedman (Eds.), *Handbook of perception* (pp. 387–430). New York: Academic Press.

Sekuler, R. (1995). Motion perception as a partnership: Exogenous and endogenous contributions. *Current Directions in Psychological Science, 4*(2), 43–47.

Sekuler, R., Anstis, S., Braddick, O. J., Brandt, T., Movshon, J. A., & Orban, G. (1990). The perception of motion. In L. Spillmann & J. S. Werner (Eds.), *Visual perception: The neurophysiological foundations* (pp. 205–230). San Diego: Academic Press.

Sekuler, R., Ball, K., Tynan, P., & Machamer, J. (1982a). Psychophysics of motion perception. In A. H. Wertheim, W. A. Wagenaar, & H. W. Leibowitz (Eds.), *Tutorials on motion perception* (pp. 81–100). New York: Plenum.

Sekuler, R., Kline, D., & Dismukes, K. (Eds.). (1982b). *Aging and human visual function*. New York: Alan R. Liss.

Sereno, M. E. (1993). *Neural computation of pattern motion: Modeling stages of motion analysis in the primate visual cortex*. Cambridge, MA: MIT Press.

Sergent, J. (1988). An investigation into perceptual completion in blind areas of the visual field. *Brain, 111*, 347–373.

Sewall, L., & Wooten, B. R. (1991). Stimulus determinants of achromatic constancy. *Journal of the Optical Society of America A, 8*, 1794–1809.

Shallenberger, R. S. (1993). *Taste chemistry*. London: Blackie.

Shapiro, P. N., & Penrod, S. (1986). Meta-analysis of facial identification studies. *Psychological Bulletin, 100*(2), 139–156.

Shapley, R. (1992). Parallel retinocortical channels: X and Y and P and M. In J. R. Brannan (Ed.), *Applica-*

tions of parallel processing in vision (pp. 3–36). Amsterdam: North-Holland.

Shapley, R., Kaplan, E., & Purpura, K. (1993). Contrast sensitivity and light adaptation in photoreceptors or in the retinal network. In R. Shapley & D. M.-K. Lam (Eds.), *Contrast sensitivity: Proceedings of the Retina Research Foundation Symposia* (pp. 103–116). Cambridge, MA: MIT Press.

Shelton, B. R., Rodger, J. C., & Searle, C. L. (1982). The relation between vision, head motion and accuracy of free-field auditory localization. *Journal of Auditory Research, 22,* 1–7.

Shepard, R. N. (1964). Circularity in judgments of relative pitch. *Journal of the Acoustical Society of America, 36,* 2346–2353.

Shepard, R. N. (1982). Structural representations of musical pitch. In D. Deutsch (Ed.), *The psychology of music* (pp. 343–390). New York: Academic Press.

Shepard, R. N. (1993). On the physical basis, linguistic representation, and conscious experience of colors. In G. Harman (Ed.), *Conceptions of the human mind: Essays in honor of George A. Miller* (pp. 217–245). Hillsdale, NJ: Erlbaum.

Shepard, R. N., & Cooper, L. A. (1992). Representation of colors in the blind, color-blind, and normally sighted. *Psychological Science, 3,* 97–104.

Sherrick, C. (1991). Vibrotactile pattern perception: Some findings and applications. In M. A. Heller & W. Schiff (Eds.), *The psychology of touch* (pp. 189–217). Hillsdale, NJ: Erlbaum.

Sherrick, C. E., & Cholewiak, R. W. (1986). Cutaneous sensitivity. In K. R. Boff, L. Kaufman, & J. P. Thomas (Eds.), *Handbook of perception and human performance* (pp. 12.1–12.58). New York: Wiley.

Sherrick, C. E., Cholewiak, R. W., & Collins, A. A. (1990). The localization of low- and high-frequency vibrotactile stimuli. *Journal of the Acoustical Society of America, 88,* 169–179.

Shiffrar, M. (1994). When what meets where. *Current Directions in Psychological Science, 3,* 96–100.

Shiffrar, M., & Freyd, J. J. (1990). Apparent motion of the human body. *Psychological Science, 1,* 257–264.

Shiffrar, M., & Freyd, J. J. (1993). Timing and apparent motion path choice with human body photographs. *Psychological Science, 4,* 379–384.

Shock, J. P. (1992). Lens. In D. Vaughn, T. Asbury, & P. Riordan-Eva (Eds.), *General ophthalmology* (pp. 169–178). Norwalk, CT: Appleton & Lange.

Shreeve, J. (1993). Touching the phantom. *Discover, 14,* 34–42.

Siegel, R. M., & Andersen, R. A. (1991). The perception of structure from visual motion in monkey and man. *Journal of Cognitive Neuroscience, 2,* 306–319.

Siegel, S., & Petry, S. (1991). Evidence for independent processing of subjective contour brightness and sharpness. *Perception, 20,* 233–241.

Simmons, J. A., & Chen, L. (1989). The acoustic basis for target discrimination by FM echolocating bats. *Journal of the Acoustical Society of America, 86,* 1333–1350.

Simpson, W. A. (1989). The step method: A new adaptive psychophysical procedure. *Perception & Psychophysics, 45,* 572–576.

Sinclair, S. (1985). *How animals see.* New York: Facts on File Publications.

Sivak, M., Olson, P. L., & Pastalan, L. A. (1981). Effect of driver's age on nighttime legibility of highway signs. *Human Factors, 23,* 59–64.

Sivian, L. S., & White, S. D. (1933). On minimum audible sound fields. *Journal of the Acoustical Society of America, 4,* 288–321.

Sjoberg, W., & Windes, J. (1992). Recognition times for rotated normal and "Thatcher" faces. *Perceptual and Motor Skills, 75,* 1176–1178.

Sloan, L. L. (1980). Need for precise measures of acuity. *Archives of Ophthalmology, 98,* 286–290.

Sloboda, J. A. (1985). *The musical mind.* Oxford: Clarendon.

Smith, D. V., & Frank, M. E. (1993). Sensory coding by peripheral taste fibers. In S. A. Simon & S. D. Roper (Eds.), *Mechanisms of taste transduction* (pp. 295–338). Boca Raton, FL: CRC Press.

Smith, R. S., Doty, R. L., Burlingame, G. K., & McKeown, D. A. (1993). Smell and taste function in the visually impaired. *Perception & Psychophysics, 54,* 649–655.

Soechting, J. F., & Flanders, M. (1992). Moving in three-dimensional space: Frames of reference, vectors, and coordinate systems. *Annual Review of Neuroscience, 15,* 167–191.

Soken, N. H., & Pick, A. D. (1992). Intermodal perception of happy and angry expressive behaviors by seven-month-old infants. *Child Development, 63,* 787–795.

Soli, S. D. (1994). Hearing aids: Today and tomorrow. *Echoes: The Newsletter of The Acoustical Society of America, 4*(3), 1–5.

Solomon, G. D. (1994). Analgesic medications. In C. D. Tollison (Ed.), *Handbook of pain management* (pp. 155–164). Baltimore: Williams & Wilkins.

Solso, R. L. (1994). *Cognition and the visual arts.* Cambridge, MA: MIT Press.

Solso, R. L. (1995). *Cognitive psychology* (4th ed.). Boston: Allyn & Bacon.

Solso, R. L., & McCarthy, J. E. (1981). Prototype formation of faces: A case of pseudomemory. *British Journal of Psychology, 72,* 499–503.

Spangler, K. M., & Warr, W. B. (1991). The descending auditory system. In R. A. Altschuler, R. P. Bobbin, B. M. Clopton, & D. W. Hoffman (Eds.), *Neurobiology of hearing: The central auditory system* (pp. 27–45). New York: Raven.

Spanos, N. P., Carmanico, S. J., & Ellis, J. A. (1994). Hypnotic analgesia. In P. D. Wall & R. Melzack (Eds.), *Textbook of pain* (pp. 1349–1366). Edinburgh: Churchill Livingstone.

Sparks, D. L., & Mays, L. E. (1990). Signal transformations required for the generation of saccadic eye movements. *Annual Review of Neuroscience, 13*, 309–336.

Spector, A. (1982). Aging of the lens and cataract formation. In R. Sekuler, D. Kline, & K. Dismukes (Eds.), *Aging and human visual function* (pp. 27–43). New York: Alan R. Liss.

Spelke, E. S. (1985). Preferential-looking methods as tools for the study of cognition in infancy. In G. Gottlieb & N. A. Krasnegor (Eds.), *Measurement of audition and vision in the first year of postnatal life* (pp. 323–361). Norwood, NJ: Ablex.

Spelke, E. S. (1987). The development of intermodal perception. In P. Salapatek & L. Cohen (Eds.), *Handbook of infant perception* (pp. 233–273). Orlando, FL: Academic Press.

Sperling, G., Landy, M. S., Dosher, B. A., & Perkins, M. E. (1989). Kinetic depth effect and identification of shape. *Journal of Experimental Psychology: Human Perception and Performance, 15*, 826–840.

Srinivasan, M. V. (1992). Distance perception in insects. *Current Directions in Psychological Science, 1*, 22–26.

Stebbins, W. C. (1983). *The acoustic sense of animals.* Cambridge, MA: Harvard University Press.

Steiman, H. (1988, July 31). The mystery of taste. *The Wine Spectator*, pp. 15–17.

Stein, B. E., & Meredith, M. A. (1993). *The merging of the senses.* Cambridge, MA: MIT Press.

Steiner, J. E. (1979). Human facial expressions in response to taste and smell stimulation. In H. W. Reese & L. P. Lipsitt (Eds.), *Advances in child development and behavior* (v. 13, pp. 257–295). New York: Academic Press.

Stephens, B. R., & Banks, M. S. (1987). Contrast discrimination in human infants. *Journal of Experimental Psychology: Human Perception and Performance, 13*, 558–565.

Sternbach, R. A. (1978). Psychological dimensions and perceptual analyses, including pathologies of pain. In E. C. Carterette & M. P. Friedman (Eds.), *Handbook of perception* (pp. 231–261). New York: Academic Press.

Sternbach, R. A. (1983). Ethical considerations in pain research in man. In R. Melzack (Ed.), *Pain measurement and assessment* (pp. 259–265). New York: Raven.

Stevens, J. C. (1979). Variation of cold sensitivity over the body surface. *Sensory Processes, 3*, 317–326.

Stevens, J. C. (1991). Thermal sensitivity. In M. A. Heller & W. Schiff (Eds.), *The psychology of touch* (pp. 61–90). Hillsdale, NJ: Erlbaum.

Stevens, J. C., & Cain, W. S. (1986). Smelling via the mouth: Effect of aging. *Perception & Psychophysics, 40*, 142–146.

Stevens, J. C., & Dadarwala, A. D. (1993). Variability of olfactory threshold and its role in assessment of aging. *Perception & Psychophysics, 54*, 296–302.

Stevens, J. C., Marks, L. E., & Simonson, D. C. (1974). Regional sensitivity and spatial summation in the warmth sense. *Physiology & Behavior, 13*, 825–836.

Stevens, J. K., Emerson, R. C., Gerstein, G. L., Kallos, T., Neufeld, G. R., Nichols, C. W., & Rosenquist, A. C. (1976). Paralysis of the awake human: Vision perceptions. *Vision Research, 16*, 93–98.

Stevens, S. S. (1955). The measurement of loudness. *Journal of the Acoustical Society of America, 27*, 815–829.

Stevens, S. S. (1962). The surprising simplicity of sensory metrics. *American Psychologist, 17*, 29–39.

Stevens, S. S. (1986). *Psychophysics: Introduction to its perceptual, neural and social prospects.* New Brunswick, NJ: Transaction.

Stevens, S. S., & Newman, E. B. (1936). The localization of actual sources of sound. *American Journal of Psychology, 48*, 297–306.

Stevens, S. S., Volkman, J., & Newman, E. B. (1937). A scale for the measurement of the psychological magnitude of pitch. *Journal of the Acoustical Society of America, 8*, 185–190.

Stillings, N. A., Feinstein, M. H., Garfield, J. L., Rissland, E. L., Rosenbaum, D. A., Weisler, S. E., & Baker-Ward, L. (1987). *Cognitive science: An introduction.* Cambridge, MA: MIT Press.

Stillman, J. A. (1989). A comparison of three adaptive psychophysical procedures using inexperienced listeners. *Perception & Psychophysics, 46*, 345–350.

Stoddart, D. M. (1990). *The scented ape: The biology and culture of human odour.* New York: Cambridge University Press.

Stoffregen, T. A., & Riccio, G. E. (1988). An ecological theory of orientation and the vestibular system. *Psychological Review, 95*, 3–14.

Stokes, D. (1985, Summer). The owl and the ear. *The Stanford Magazine*, pp. 24–28.

Stoner, G. R., & Albright, T. D. (1993). Image segmentation cues in motion processing: Implications for modularity in vision. *Journal of Cognitive Neuroscience, 5*, 129–149.

Storandt, M. (1982). Concepts and methodological issues in the study of aging. In R. Sekuler, D. Kline, & K. Dismukes (Eds.), *Aging and human visual function* (pp. 269–278). New York: Alan R. Liss.

Storr, A. (1992). *Music and the mind.* New York: Ballantine.

Stromeyer, C. F. (1978). Form–color aftereffects in human vision. In R. Held, H. W. Leibowitz, & H.

L. Teuber (Eds.), *Handbook of sensory physiology: Vol. 8 Perception* (pp. 97–142). Berlin: Springer-Verlag.

Stryer, L. (1987). The molecules of visual excitation. *Scientific American, 257*(1), 42–50.

Stryker, M. P. (1992). Elements of visual perception. *Nature, 360,* 301.

Suga, N. (1990). Biosonar and neural computation in bats. *Scientific American, 262*(6), 60–68.

Sullivan, W. (1984, March 20). Bats find offspring even in cave's chaos. *The New York Times,* p. C1.

Summerfield, Q. (1987). Some preliminaries to a comprehensive account of audio-visual speech perception. In B. Dodd & R. Campbell (Eds.), *Hearing by eye: The psychology of lip reading* (pp. 3–51). Hillsdale, NJ: Erlbaum.

Summerfield, Q. (1991). Visual perception of phonetic gestures. In I. G. Mattingly & M. Studdert-Kennedy (Eds.), *Modularity and the motor theory of speech perception* (pp. 117–143). Hillsdale, NJ: Erlbaum.

Summerfield, Q. (1992). Lipreading and audio-visual speech perception. In V. Bruce, A. Cowey, A. W. Ellis, & D. I. Perrett (Eds.), *Processing the facial image* (pp. 71–78). Oxford: Clarendon.

Sunday, S. R., & Halmi, K. A. (1991). Taste hedonics in anorexia nervosa and bulimia nervosa. In R. C. Bolles (Ed.), *The hedonics of taste* (pp. 185–197). Hillsdale, NJ: Erlbaum.

Süskind, P. (1987). *Perfume: The story of a murderer* (J. E. Woods, Trans.). New York: Pocket Books.

Swets, J. A. (1986a). Form of empirical ROCs in discrimination and diagnostic tasks: Implications for theory and measurement of performance. *Psychological Bulletin, 99,* 181–198.

Swets, J. A. (1986b). Indices of discrimination or diagnostic accuracy: Their ROC's and implied models. *Psychological Bulletin, 99,* 100–117.

Takahashi, T. T. (1989). The neural coding of auditory space. *Journal of Experimental Biology, 146,* 307–322.

Takeuchi, A. H., & Hulse, S. H. (1993). Absolute pitch. *Psychological Bulletin, 113,* 345–361.

Talbot, J. D., Marrett, S., Evans, A. C., Meyer, E., Bushnell, M. C., & Duncan, G. H. (1991). Multiple representations of pain in human cerebral cortex. *Science, 251,* 1355–1358.

Tan, H. S., Shelhamer, M., & Zee, D. S. (1992). Effect of head orientation and position on vestibuloocular reflex adaptation. In B. Cohen, D. L. Tomko, & F. Guedry (Eds.), *Sensing and controlling motion: Vestibular and sensorimotor function* (pp. 158–165). New York: The New York Academy of Sciences.

Tanaka, J. W., & Farah, M. J. (1993). Parts and wholes in face recognition. *Quarterly Journal of Experimental Psychology, 46A,* 225–245.

Tarr, M. J. (1995). Rotating objects to recognize them: A case study on the role of viewpoint dependency in the recognition of three-dimensional objects. *Psychonomic Bulletin & Review, 2*(1), 55–82.

Tarr, M. J., & Pinker, S. (1990). When does human object recognition use a viewer-centered reference frame? *Psychological Science, 1,* 253–256.

Tarr, M. J., & Pinker, S. (1991). Orientation-dependent mechanisms in shape recognition: Further issues. *Psychological Science, 2,* 207–209.

Taus, R. H., Stevens, J. C., & Marks, L. E. (1975). Spatial location of warmth. *Perception & Psychophysics, 17,* 194–196.

Taylor, I., & Taylor, M. M. (1983). *The psychology of reading.* New York: Academic Press.

Taylor, W., Pearson, J., Mair, A., & Burns, W. (1965). Study of noise and hearing in jute weaving. *Journal of the Acoustical Society of America, 38,* 113–120.

Teas, D. C. (1989). Auditory physiology: Present trends. *Annual Review of Psychology, 40,* 405–429.

Teghtsoonian, M. (1974). The doubtful phenomenon of over-constancy. In H. R. Moskowitz (Ed.), *Sensation and measurement* (pp. 411–420). Dordrecht, Holland: D. Reidel.

Teghtsoonian, M. (1983). Olfaction: Perception's Cinderella. *Contemporary Psychology, 28,* 763–764.

Teghtsoonian, R. (1973). Range effects in psychophysical scaling and a revision of Stevens' law. *American Journal of Psychology, 86,* 3–29.

Teghtsoonian, R., Teghtsoonian, M., Berglund, B., & Berglund, U. (1978). Invariance of odor strength with sniff vigor: An olfactory analogue to size constancy. *Journal of Experimental Psychology: Human Perception and Performance, 4,* 144–152.

Teller, D. Y., & Bornstein, M. H. (1987). Infant color vision and color perception. In P. Salapatek & L. B. Cohen (Eds.), *Handbook of infant perception: Vol. 1 From sensation to perception* (pp. 185–236). New York: Academic Press.

Teller, D. Y., & Lindsey, D. T. (1993). Motion nulling techniques and infant color vision. In C. E. Granrud (Ed.), *Visual perception and cognition in infancy* (pp. 47–73). Hillsdale, NJ: Erlbaum.

Thompson, J. W., & Filshie, J. (1993). Transcutaneous electrical nerve stimulation (TENS) and acupuncture. In D. Doyle, G. W. C. Hanks, & N. MacDonald (Eds.), *Oxford textbook of palliative medicine* (pp. 229–243). Oxford: Oxford University Press.

Thompson, P. (1980). Margaret Thatcher—a new illusion. *Perception, 9,* 483–484.

Thompson, R. F. (1985). *The brain: An introduction to neuroscience.* New York: Freeman.

Thurlow, W. R. (1971). Audition. In J. W. Kling & L. A. Riggs (Eds.), *Woodworth and Schlosberg's experimental psychology* (pp. 223–271). New York: Holt, Rinehart & Winston.

Tittle, J. S., & Braunstein, M. L. (1993). Recovery of 3-D shape from binocular disparity and structure from motion. *Perception & Psychophysics, 54,* 157–169.

Todd, J. T., & Akerstrom, R. A. (1987). Perception of three-dimensional form from patterns of optical texture. *Journal of Experimental Psychology: Human Perception and Performance, 13,* 242–255.

Todd, J. T., & Reichel, F. D. (1990). The visual perception of smoothly curved surfaces from double-projected contour patterns. *Journal of Experimental Psychology: Human Perception and Performance, 16,* 665–674.

Touchette, N. (1993). Estrogen signals a novel route to pain relief. *Journal of NIH Research, 5,* 53–58.

Toufexis, A. (1983, July 18). The bluing of America. *Time,* p. 62.

Trainor, L. J., & Trehub, S. E. (1992). A comparison of infants' and adults' sensitivity to Western musical structure. *Journal of Experimental Psychology: Human Perception and Performance, 18,* 394–402.

Trehub, S. E. (1985). Auditory pattern perception in infancy. In S. E. Trehub & B. A. Schneider (Eds.), *The anatomy of the developing ear* (pp. 183–195). New York: Plenum.

Trehub, S. E. (1990). The perception of musical patterns by human infants: The provision of similar patterns by their parents. In M. A. Berkley & W. C. Stebbins (Eds.), *Comparative perception: Basic mechanisms* (pp. 429–459). New York: Wiley.

Trehub, S. E. (1993). The music listening skills of infants and young children. In T. J. Tighe & W. J. Dowling (Eds.), *Psychology and music: The understanding of melody and rhythm* (pp. 161–176). Hillsdale, NJ: Erlbaum.

Trehub, S. E., & Trainor, L. J. (1993). Listening strategies in infancy: The roots of music and language development. In S. McAdams & E. Bigand (Eds.), *Thinking in sound: The cognitive psychology of human audition* (pp. 278–327). New York: Oxford University Press.

Trehub, S. E., Trainor, L. J., & Unyk, A. M. (1993). Music and speech processing in the first year of life. In H. W. Reese (Ed.), *Advances in child development and behavior* (pp. 1–35). San Diego: Academic Press.

Treisman, A. (1986). Features and objects in visual processing. *Scientific American, 255,* 114B–125.

Treisman, A., Cavanagh, P., Fischer, B., Ramachandran, V. S., & von der Heydt, R. (1990). Form perception and attention: Striate cortex and beyond. In L. Spillmann & J. S. Werner (Eds.), *Visual perception: The neurophysiological foundations* (pp. 273–316). San Diego: Academic Press.

Treisman, A., & Gelade, G. (1980). A feature-integration theory of attention. *Cognitive Psychology, 12,* 97–136.

Treisman, A., & Schmidt, H. (1982). Illusory conjunction in the perception of objects. *Cognitive Psychology, 14,* 107–141.

Treisman, A., & Souther, J. (1985). Search asymmetry: A diagnostic for preattentive processing of separable features. *Journal of Experimental Psychology: General, 114,* 285–310.

Ts'o, D. Y., Frostig, R. D., Lieke, E. E., & Grinvald, A. (1990). Functional organization of primate visual cortex revealed by high resolution optical imaging. *Science, 249,* 417–420.

Turk, D. C. (1994). Perspectives on chronic pain: The role of psychological factors. *Current Directions in Psychological Science, 3*(2), 45–48.

Turk, D. C., & Meichenbaum, D. (1994). A cognitive-behavioural approach to pain management. In P. D. Wall & R. Melzack (Eds.), *Textbook of pain* (pp. 1337–1348). Edinburgh: Churchill Livingstone.

Turk, D. C., & Rudy, T. E. (1994). A cognitive-behavioral perspective on chronic pain: Beyond the scalpel and syringe. In C. D. Tollison (Ed.), *Handbook of pain management* (pp. 136–151). Baltimore: Williams & Wilkins.

Turner, J. A., Deyo, R. A., Loeser, J. D., Von Korf, M., & Fordyce, W. E. (1994). The importance of placebo effects in pain treatment and research. *JAMA, 271,* 1609–1614.

Tuttle, M. D., & Ryan, M. J. (1981). Bat predation and the evolution of frog vocalizations in the neotropics. *Science, 214,* 677–678.

Tversky, B. (1991). Distortions in memory for visual displays. In S. R. Ellis (Ed.), *Pictorial communication in virtual and real environments* (pp. 61–75). London: Taylor & Francis.

Tyler, C. W. (1991a). Cyclopean vision. In D. Regan (Ed.), *Binocular Vision* (pp. 38–74). New York: Macmillan.

Tyler, C. W. (1991b). Disambiguation of objects by stereopsis and motion cues. In G. Obrecht & L. W. Stark (Eds.), *Presbyopia research: From molecular biology to visual adaptation* (pp. 223–233). New York: Plenum.

Tyler, C. W. (1991c). The horopter and binocular fusion. In D. Regan (Ed.), *Binocular vision* (pp. 19–37). New York: Macmillan.

Tyler, C. W., & Cavanagh, P. (1991). Purely chromatic perception of motion in depth: Two eyes as sensitive as one. *Perception & Psychophysics, 49,* 53–61.

Tyler, C. W., & Clarke, M. B. (Eds.). (1990). *The autostereogram.* Bellingham, WA: The Society of Photo-Optical Instrumentation Engineers—The International Society for Optical Engineering.

Ubell, E. (1995, January 15). New devices can help you hear. *Parade Magazine,* pp. 14–15.

Uchikawa, K., Uchikawa, H., & Boynton, R. M. (1989). Partial color constancy of isolated surface colors examined by a color-naming method. *Perception, 18,* 83–91.

Ullman, S. (1983). The measurement of visual motion. *Trends in Neurosciences, 6*, 177–179.

Ullman, S. (1993). The visual representation of three-dimensional objects. In D. E. Meyer & S. Kornblum (Eds.), *Attention and performance XIV: Synergies in experimental psychology, artificial intelligence, and cognitive neuroscience* (pp. 79–98). Cambridge, MA: MIT Press.

Uttal, W. R. (1981). *A taxonomy of visual processes*. Hillsdale, NJ: Erlbaum.

Uttal, W. R. (1988). *On seeing forms*. Hillsdale, NJ: Erlbaum.

Vallbo, Å. B. (1981). Sensations evoked from the glabrous skin of the human hand by electrical stimulation of unitary mechanosensitive efferents. *Brain Research, 215*, 359–363.

Van Damme, W. J. M., Oosterhoff, F. H., & Van de Grind, W. A. (1994). Discrimination of 3-D shape and 3-D curvature from motion in active vision. *Perception & Psychophysics, 55*, 340–349.

van den Brink, G. (1982). On the relativity of pitch. *Perception, 11*, 721–731.

van Erning, L. J. T. O., Gerrits, H. J. M., & Eijkman, E. G. J. (1988). Apparent size and receptive field properties. *Vision Research, 28*, 407–418.

Van Essen, D. C., Anderson, C. H., & Felleman, D. J. (1992). Information procession in the primate visual system: An integrated systems perspective. *Science, 255*, 419–422.

van Kruysbergen, N. A. W. H., & de Weert, C. M. M. (1993). Apparent motion perception: The contribution of the binocular and monocular systems: An improved test based on motion aftereffects. *Perception, 22*, 771–784.

Van Toller, S., & Dodd, G. H. (Eds.). (1988). *Perfumery: The psychology and biology of fragrance*. London: Chapman and Hall.

van Tuijl, H. (1980). Perceptual interpretation of complex line patterns. *Journal of Experimental Psychology: Human Perception and Performance, 6*, 197–221.

Vaughn, D., Asbury, T., & Riordan-Eva, P. (Eds.). (1992). *General ophthalmology* (13th ed.). Norwalk, CT: Appleton & Lange.

Vaughn, D., & Riordan-Eva, P. (1992). Glaucoma. In D. Vaughn, T. Asbury, & P. Riordan-Eva (Eds.), *General ophthalmology* (pp. 213–230). Norwalk, CT: Appleton & Lange.

Verrillo, R. T. (1993). The effects of aging on the sense of touch. In R. T. Verrillo (Ed.), *Sensory research: Multimodal perspectives* (pp. 285–298). Hillsdale, NJ: Erlbaum.

Virshup, A. (1985, November 18). Restaurant loudness. *New York*, pp. 32–37.

Vogel, J. M., & Teghtsoonian, M. (1972). The effects of perspective alterations on apparent size and distance scales. *Perception & Psychophysics, 11*, 294–298.

Vokey, J. R., & Read, J. D. (1985). Subliminal messages: Between the Devil and the media. *American Psychologist, 40*, 1231–1239.

von der Heydt, R., & Peterhans, E. (1989). Mechanisms of contour perception in monkey visual cortex: I. Lines of pattern discontinuity. *Journal of Neuroscience, 9*, 1731–1748.

von der Heydt, R., Peterhans, E., & Baumgartner, G. (1984). Illusory contours and cortical neuron responses. *Science, 224*, 1260–1262.

Von Holst, E. (1954). Relations between the central nervous system and the peripheral organs. *British Journal of Animal Behaviour, 2*, 89–94.

von Winterfeldt, D., & Edwards, E. (1982). Costs and payoffs in perceptual research. *Psychological Bulletin, 91*, 609–622.

Wagemans, J. P. (1988). Modules in vision: A case study of interdisciplinarity in cognitive science. *Acta Psychologica, 67*, 59–93.

Wagner, M., Baird, J. C., & Fuld, K. (1989). Transformation model of the moon illusion. In M. Hershenson (Ed.), *The moon illusion* (pp. 147–165). Hillsdale, NJ: Erlbaum.

Walker-Andrews, A. S. (1986). Intermodal perception of expressive behaviors: Relation of eye and voice? *Developmental Psychology, 22*, 373–377.

Walker-Andrews, A. S., Bahrick, L. E., Raglioni, S. S., & Diaz, I. (1991). Infants' bimodal perception of gender. *Ecological Psychology, 3*, 55–75.

Wall, P. D. (1979). On the relation of injury to pain. *Pain, 6*, 253–264.

Wall, P. D. (1993). Pain and the placebo response. In G. R. Bock & J. Marsh (Eds.), *Experimental and theoretical studies of consciousness* (pp. 187–216). Chichester: Wiley.

Wall, P. D., & Melzack, R. (Eds.). (1994). *Textbook of pain* (3rd ed.). Edinburgh: Churchill Livingstone.

Wallach, H. (1948). Brightness constancy and the nature of achromatic colors. *Journal of Experimental Psychology, 38*, 310–324.

Wallach, H. (1959). Perception of motion. *Scientific American, 201*, 56–60.

Wallach, H. (1985a). Learned stimulation in space and motion perception. *American Psychologist, 40*, 399–404.

Wallach, H. (1985b). Perceiving a stable environment. *Scientific American, 252*(5), 118–124.

Wallach, H. (1987). Perceiving a stable environment when one moves. *Annual Review of Psychology, 38*, 1–27.

Wallach, H., & Marshall, F. J. (1986a). Shape constancy and polar perspective. *Journal of Experimental Psychology: Human Perception and Performance, 12,* 338–342.

Wallach, H., & Marshall, F. J. (1986b). Shape constancy in pictorial representation. *Perception & Psychophysics, 39,* 232–235.

Wallach, H., & O'Connell, D. N. (1953). The kinetic depth effect. *Journal of Experimental Psychology, 45,* 205–217.

Wallach, H., & O'Leary, A. (1979). Adaptation in distance perception with head-movement parallax serving as the veridical cue. *Perception & Psychophysics, 25,* 42–46.

Walton, G. E., Bower, N. J. A., & Bower, T. G. R. (1992). Recognition of familiar faces by newborns. *Infant Behavior and Development, 15,* 265–269.

Wandell, B. A. (1987). Computational models for color constancy. In *Frontiers of visual science: Proceedings of the 1985 Symposium* (pp. 109–118). Washington, DC: National Academy Press.

Wandell, B. A. (1995). *Foundations of vision.* Sunderland, MA: Sinauer.

Ward, L. M., Porac, C., Coren, S., & Girgus, J. (1977). The case for misapplied constancy scaling: Depth association elicited by illusion configurations. *American Journal of Psychology, 90,* 609–620.

Warren, D. H., & Rossano, M. J. (1991). Intermodality relations: Vision and touch. In M. A. Heller & W. Schiff (Eds.), *The psychology of touch* (pp. 119–137). Hillsdale, NJ: Erlbaum.

Warren, R. M. (1982). *Auditory perception: A new synthesis.* Elmsford, NY: Pergamon.

Warren, R. M. (1983). Auditory illusions and their relation to mechanisms normally enhancing accuracy of perception. *Journal of Audio Engineering Society, 31,* 623–630.

Warren, R. M. (1984). Perceptual restoration of obliterated sounds. *Psychological Bulletin, 96,* 371–383.

Warren, R. M. (1993). Perception of acoustic sequences: Global integration versus temporal resolution. In S. McAdams & E. Bigand (Eds.), *Thinking in sound: The cognitive psychology of human audition* (pp. 37–68). New York: Oxford University Press.

Warren, R. M., Bashford, J. A., Healey, E. W., & Brubaker, B. S. (1994). Auditory induction: Reciprocal changes in alternating sounds. *Perception & Psychophysics, 55,* 313–322.

Warren, R. M., & Warren, R. P. (1970). Auditory illusions and confusions. *Scientific American, 223*(6), 30–36.

Warren, W. H., Jr., & Hannon, D. J. (1988). Direction of self-motion is perceived from optical flow. *Nature, 336,* 162–163.

Warren, W. H., Jr., & Hannon, D. J. (1990). Eye movements and optical flow. *Journal of the Optical Society of America (A), 7,* 160–169.

Warren, W. H., Jr., Morris, M. W., & Kalish, M. (1988). Perception of translational heading from optical flow. *Journal of Experimental Psychology: Human Perception and Performance, 14,* 646–660.

Warren, W. H., Jr., & Whang, S. (1987). Visual guidance of walking through apertures: Body-scale information for affordances. *Journal of Experimental Psychology: Human Perception and Performance, 13,* 371–383.

Warrington, E. K., & Taylor, A. M. (1978). Two categorical stages of object recognition. *Perception, 7,* 695–705.

Wasserman, G. S. (1978). *Color vision: An historical introduction.* New York: Wiley.

Watson, A. B. (1986). Temporal sensitivity. In K. R. Boff, L. Kaufman, & J. P. Thomas (Eds.), *Handbook of perception and human performance* (pp. 6.1–6.43). New York: Wiley.

Watson, C. S., & Foyle, D. C. (1985). Central factors in the discrimination and identification of complex sounds. *Journal of the Acoustical Society of America, 78,* 375–380.

Watson, J. S., Banks, M. S., Hofsten, C., & Royden, C. S. (1992). Gravity as a monocular cue for perception of absolute distance and/or absolute size. *Perception, 21,* 69–76.

Watt, D. G. D., Bouyer, L. J. G., Nevo, I. T., Smith, A. V., & Tiande, Y. (1992). What is motion sickness? In B. Cohen, D. L. Tomko, & F. Guedry (Eds.), *Sensing and controlling motion: Vestibular and sensorimotor function* (pp. 660–667). New York: The New York Academy of Sciences.

Watts, R. G., & Bahill, A. T. (1990). *Keep your eye on the ball: The science and folklore of baseball.* San Francisco: Freeman.

Weale, R. A. (1982). *A biography of the eye.* London: Lewis.

Webster, D. B. (1991). An overview of mammalian auditory pathways with an emphasis on humans. In D. B. Webster, A. N. Popper, & R. R. Fay (Eds.), *The mammalian auditory pathway: Neuroanatomy* (pp. 1–22). New York: Springer-Verlag.

Wegener, B. (1982). *Social attitudes and psychophysical measurement.* Hillsdale, NJ: Erlbaum.

Weinstein, S. (1968). Intensive and extensive aspects of tactile sensitivity as a function of body part, sex, and laterality. In D. R. Kenshalo (Ed.), *The skin senses* (pp. 195–218). Springfield, IL: Thomas.

Weisenberg, M. (1984). Cognitive aspects of pain. In P. D. Wall & R. Melzack (Eds.), *Textbook of pain* (pp. 162–172). Edinburgh: Churchill Livingstone.

Weiskrantz, L. (1986). *Blindsight: A case study and implications*. Oxford: Clarendon.

Weiskrantz, L. (1992, September/October). Unconscious vision: The strange phenomenon of blindsight. *The Sciences*, pp. 23–28.

Weisstein, N. (1980). Tutorial: The joy of Fourier analysis. In C. S. Harris (Ed.), *Visual coding and adaptability* (pp. 365–380). Hillsdale, NJ: Erlbaum.

Weisstein, N., & Harris, C. S. (1974). Visual detection of line segments: An object-superiority effect. *Science, 186*, 752–755.

Weisstein, N., Maguire, W., & Brannan, J. R. (1992). M and P pathways and the perception of figure and ground. In J. R. Brannan (Ed.), *Applications of parallel processing in vision* (pp. 137–166). Amsterdam: North-Holland.

Weisstein, N., Maguire, W., & Williams, M. C. (1982). The effect of perceived depth on phantoms and the phantom motion aftereffect. In J. Beck (Ed.), *Organization and representation in perception* (pp. 235–249). Hillsdale, NJ: Erlbaum.

Welch, R. B., & Warren, D. H. (1980). Immediate perceptual response to intersensory discrepancy. *Psychological Bulletin, 88*, 638–667.

Weller, L., & Weller, A. (1993). Human menstrual synchrony: A critical assessment. *Neuroscience and Biobehavioral Reviews, 17*, 427–439.

Wenger, M. A., Jones, F. N., & Jones, M. H. (1956). *Physiological psychology*. New York: Holt, Rinehart & Winston.

Werker, J. F. (1994). Cross-language speech perception: Development change does not involve loss. In J. G. Goodman & H. C. Nusbaum (Eds.), *The development of speech perception: The transition from speech sounds to spoken words* (pp. 93–120). Cambridge, MA: MIT Press.

Werker, J. F., & Desjardins, R. N. (1995). Listening to speech in the 1st year of life: Experiential influences on phoneme perception. *Current Directions in Psychological Science, 4*(3), 76–81.

Werker, J. F., & Tees, R. C. (1984). Cross-language speech perception: Evidence for perceptual reorganization during the first year of life. *Infant Behavior and Development, 7*, 49–63.

Werner, H. (1935). Studies on contour. *American Journal of Psychology, 37*, 40–64.

Wertheim, A. H. (1994). Motion perception during self-motion: The direct versus inferential controversy revisited. *Behavioral and Brain Sciences, 17*, 293–355.

Wertheimer, M. (1923). Untersuchungen zür Lehre von der Gestalt, II. (Translated as Laws of organization in perceptual forms.). In W. D. Ellis (Ed.), *A source book of Gestalt psychology* (pp. 71–88). London: Routledge & Kegan Paul.

Westheimer, G. (1986). The eye as an optical instrument. In K. R. Boff, L. Kaufman, & J. P. Thomas (Eds.), *Handbook of perception and human performance* (pp. 4.1–4.20). New York: Wiley.

Wever, E. G. (1949). *Theory of hearing*. New York: Wiley.

Wever, E. G., & Bray, C. W. (1930). Action currents in the auditory nerve in response to acoustical stimulation. *Proceedings of the National Academy of Sciences USA, 16*, 344–350.

Whalen, D. H., & Liberman, A. M. (1987). Speech perception takes precedence over nonspeech perception. *Science, 237*, 169–171.

Whitbourne, S. K. (1985). *The aging body: Physiological changes and psychological consequences*. New York: Springer-Verlag.

Whitbourne, S. K., & Powers, C. B. (1996). Psychological perspectives on the normal aging process. In L. L. Carstensen, B. A. Edelstein, & L. Dornbrand (Eds.), *The practical handbook of clinical gerontology*. Thousand Oaks, CA: Sage.

Whittle, P. (1994). The psychophysics of contrast brightness. In A. Gilchrist (Ed.), *Lightness, brightness, and transparency* (pp. 35–110). Hillsdale, NJ: Erlbaum.

Wichman, H. (1991). *Color vision* (NLA News, Vol. 8, No. 4). Claremont, CA: Claremont McKenna College.

Wideman, M. V., & Singer, J. E. (1984). The role of psychological mechanisms in preparation for childbirth. *American Psychologist, 39*, 1357–1371.

Wier, C. G., Norton, S. J., & Kincaid, G. E. (1984). Spontaneous narrow-band oto-acoustic signals emitted by human ears: A replication. *Journal of the Acoustical Society of America, 76*, 1248–1250.

Wiesel, R. N., & Raviola, E. (1986). The mystery of myopia. *The Sciences, 26*, 46–52.

Wiesel, T. N., Hirsch, J. A., & Gilbert, C. D. (1992). Dynamic aspects of visual cortical function. In D. M.-K. Lam & G. M. Bray (Eds.), *Regeneration and plasticity in the mammalian visual system: Proceedings of the Retina Research Foundation symposia* (pp. 223–232). Cambridge, MA: MIT Press.

Wightman, F. L. (1981). Pitch perception: An example of auditory pattern recognition. In D. J. Getty & J. H. Howard, Jr. (Eds.), *Auditory and visual pattern recognition* (pp. 3–26). Hillsdale, NJ: Erlbaum.

Wightman, F. L., Kistler, D. J., & Perkins, M. E. (1987). A new approach to the study of human sound localization. In W. A. Yost & G. Gourevitch (Eds.), *Directional hearing* (pp. 26–48). New York: Springer-Verlag.

Wildes, R. P. (1990). Computational vision with reference to binocular stereo vision. In K. N. Leibovic (Ed.), *Science of vision* (pp. 332–364). New York: Springer-Verlag.

Williams, D. (1992). Cooperative parallel processing in depth, motion and texture perception. In J. R.

Brannan (Ed.), *Applications of parallel processing in vision* (pp. 167–225). Amsterdam: North-Holland.

Williamson, S. J., & Cummins, H. Z. (1983). *Light and color in nature and art.* New York: Wiley.

Wilson, H. (1992). A critical review of menstrual synchrony research. *Psychoneuroendocrinology, 17,* 565–591.

Wilson, J. P. (1992). Cochlear mechanics. In Y. Cazals, L. Demany, & K. Horner (Eds.), *Auditory physiology and perception* (pp. 71–84). Oxford: Pergamon.

Wilson, M. A., & McNaughton, B. L. (1993). Dynamics of the hippocampal ensemble code for space. *Science, 261,* 1055–1057.

Wilson, P. G. (1994). Phantom pain. In C. D. Tollison (Ed.), *Handbook of pain management* (pp. 497–502). Baltimore: Williams & Wilkins.

Winckelgren, I. (1992). How the brain "sees" borders where there are none. *Science, 256,* 1520–1521.

Wolfe, J. M. (1986). Stereopsis and binocular rivalry. *Psychological Review, 93,* 269–282.

Worthey, J. A. (1985). Limitations of color constancy. *Journal of the Optical Society of America, 2,* 1014–1026.

Wright, R. W. (1982). *The sense of smell.* Boca Raton, FL: CRC Press.

Wright, W. D. (1972). Colour mixture. In D. Jameson & L. M. Hurvich (Eds.), *Handbook of sensory physiology: Vol. 7. Visual psychophysics* (pp. 434–454). Berlin: Springer-Verlag.

Wurtz, R. H., Duffy, C. J., & Roy, J.-P. (1993). Motion processing for guiding self-motion. In T. Ono, L. R. Squire, M. E. Raichle, D. I. Perrett, & M. Fukuda (Eds.), *Brain mechanisms of perception and memory* (pp. 141–165). New York: Oxford University Press.

Wurtz, R. H., Goldberg, M. E., & Robinson, D. L. (1982). Brain mechanisms of visual attention. *Scientific American, 246*(6), 124–135.

Wynn, V. T. (1993). Accuracy and consistency of absolute pitch. *Perception, 22,* 113–121.

Wysocki, C. J., Beauchamp, G. K., Todrank, J., & Pierce, J. D., Jr. (1992). Individual differences in olfactory ability. In S. Van Toller & G. H. Dodd (Eds.), *Fragrance: The psychology and biology of perfume* (pp. 91–112). London: Elsevier.

Wyszecki, G. (1986). Color appearance. In K. R. Boff, L. Kaufman, & J. P. Thomas (Eds.), *Handbook of perception and human performance* (pp. 9.1–9.57). New York: Wiley.

Yamamoto, T., Yuyama, N., & Kawamura, Y. (1981). Central processing of taste perception. In Y. Katsuki, R. Norgren, & M. Sato (Eds.), *Brain mechanisms of sensation* (pp. 197–207). New York: Wiley.

Yellott, J. I. (1981). Binocular depth inversion. *Scientific American, 245*(1), 148–159.

Yin, T. C. T., & Kuwada, S. (1983). Binaural interaction in low-frequency neurons in inferior colliculus of the cat. Effects of changing frequency. *Journal of Neurophysiology, 50,* 1020–1042.

Yonas, A., Goldsmith, L. T., & Hallstrom, J. L. (1978). Development of sensitivity to information provided by cast shadows in pictures. *Perception, 7,* 333–341.

Yonas, A., Granrud, C., Arterberry, M., & Hanson, B. (1986). Infants' distance perception from linear perspective and texture gradients. *Infant Behavior and Development, 9,* 247–256.

Yonas, A., Granrud, C., & Pettersen, L. (1985). Infants' sensitivity to relative size information for distance. *Developmental Psychology, 21,* 161–167.

Yonas, A., & Owsley, C. (1987). Development of visual space perception. In P. Salapatek & L. Cohen (Eds.), *Handbook of infant perception* (pp. 79–122). Orlando, FL: Academic Press.

Yost, W. A. (1991). Auditory image perception and analysis: The basis for hearing. *Hearing Research, 56,* 8–18.

Yost, W. A. (1992). Auditory perception and sound source determination. *Current Directions in Psychological Science, 1,* 179–184.

Yost, W. A., & Dye, R. H. (1991). Properties of sound localization by humans. In R. A. Altschuler, R. P. Bobbin, B. M. Clopton, & D. W. Hoffman (Eds.), *Neurobiology of hearing: The central auditory system* (pp. 389–410). New York: Raven.

Yost, W. A., & Hafter, E. R. (1987). Lateralization. In W. A. Yost & G. Gourevitch (Eds.), *Directional Hearing* (pp. 49–84). New York: Springer-Verlag.

Yost, W. A., & Nielsen, D. W. (1985). *Fundamentals of hearing: An introduction* (2nd ed.). New York: CBS College.

Young, F. A. (1981). Primate myopia. *American Journal of Optometry and Physiological Optics, 58,* 560–566.

Young, M. P., & Yamane, S. (1992). Sparse population coding of faces in the inferotemporal cortex. *Science, 256,* 1327–1331.

Young, M. P., & Yamane, S. (1993). An analysis at the population level of the processing of faces in the inferotemporal cortex. In T. Ono, L. R. Squire, M. E. Raichle, D. I. Perrett, & M. Fukuda (Eds.), *Brain mechanisms of perception and memory* (pp. 47–70). New York: Oxford University Press.

Zatorre, R. J., & Jones-Gotman, M. (1990). Right-nostril advantage for discrimination of odors. *Perception & Psychophysics, 47,* 526–531.

Zeki, S. (1990). The motion pathways of the visual cortex. In C. Blakemore (Ed.), *Vision: Coding and efficiency* (pp. 321–345). Cambridge: Cambridge University Press.

Zeki, S. (1992). The visual image in mind and brain. *Scientific American, 267*(3), 69–76.

Zeki, S. (1993). *A vision of the brain.* Oxford: Blackwell.

Zellner, D. A. (1991). How foods get to be liked: Some general mechanisms and some special cases. In R. C. Bolles (Ed.), *The hedonics of taste* (pp. 199–217). Hillsdale, NJ: Erlbaum.

Zellner, D. A., Bartoli, A. M., & Eckard, R. (1991). Influence of color on odor identification and liking ratings. *American Journal of Psychology, 4,* 547–561.

Zellner, D. A., & Kautz, M. A. (1990). Color affects odor intensity. *Journal of Experimental Psychology: Human Perception and Performance, 16,* 391–397.

Zellner, D. A., Stewart, W. F., Rozin, P., & Brown, J. M. (1988). Effect of temperature and expectations on liking for beverages. *Physiology & Behavior, 44,* 61–68.

Zenatti, A. (1993). Children's musical cognition and taste. In T. J. Tighe & W. J. Dowling (Eds.), *Psychology and music: The understanding of melody and rhythm* (pp. 177–196). Hillsdale, NJ: Erlbaum.

Zihl, J., von Cramon, D., & Mai, N. (1983). Selective disturbance of movement vision after bilateral brain damage. *Brain, 106,* 313–340.

Zimmer, C. (1993). Making senses. *Discover, 14,* 78–85.

Zrenner, E., Abramov, I., Akita, M., Cowey, A., Livingstone, M., & Valberg, A. (1990). Color perception: Retina to cortex. In L. Spillmann & J. S. Werner (Eds.), *Visual perception: The neurophysiological foundations* (pp. 163–204). San Diego: Academic Press.

Zurek, P. M. (1981). Spontaneous narrowband acoustic signals emitted by human ears. *Journal of the Acoustical Society of America, 69,* 514–523.

Zurek, P. M. (1985). Acoustic emissions from the ear: A summary of results from humans and animals. *Journal of the Acoustical Society of America, 78,* 340–344.

Zwicker, E., & Schloth, E. (1984). Interrelation of different oto-acoustic emissions. *Journal of the Acoustical Society of America, 75,* 1148–1154.

Zwislocki, J. J. (1981). Sound analysis in the ear: A history of discoveries. *American Scientist, 69,* 184–192.

Zwislocki, J. J. (1991). What is the cochlear place code for pitch? *Acta Otolaryngologica (Stockh), 111,* 256–262.

Author Index

Subject Index

Research, 33, 1993. Reprinted by permission of the author.

Fig 7.9 From "A Multi-Stage Color Model" by by R. L. De-Valois and K. K. DeValois, *Vision Research*, 33, 1993. Reprinted by permission of the author.

Fig 7.10 From *A Vision of the Brain*, by S. Zeki published by Blackwell Science Ltd. Reprinted by permission.

Fig 7.11 From "Partial Color Constancy of Isolated Colors Examined by a Color-Naming Method" by K. Uchikawa, H. Uchikawa, and R. M. Boynton, 1989, *Perception*, 18, p. 85 (Fig 1). Reproduced by permission of Pion, London.

Fig 7.12 From *Current* by Bridget Riley, 1964. Synthetic polymer paint on composition board, 58-3/8 x 58-7/8. Collection, The Museum of Modern Art, New York. Philip Johnson Fund. Reproduced by permission.

Demo 8.2 From "Dynamical Constraints on Pictorial Action Lines" by L. D. Rosenblum and H. M. Saldana, and C. Carello, *Journal of Experimental Psychology: Human Perception and Performance*, 19, 1993. Copyright © 1993 by the American Psychological Association. Reprinted with permission.

Fig 8.3 From "Masking the Motions of Human Gait" by J. E. Cutting, C. Moore, and R. Morrison, 1988, *Perception & Psychophysics*, 44, pp. 339–347 (Fig 1 and 2). Reprinted by permission of Psychonomic Society, Inc. and the authors.

Fig 8.5 From "The Perception of Apparent Motion" by Vilaynaur S. Ramachandran and Stuart M. Anstis, June 1986, *Scientific American*. Copyright © 1986 by Scientific American, Inc. All rights reserved.

Fig 8.6 Photographs courtesy of Dr. M. Shiffrar.

Fig 8.9 From "The Perception of Apparent Motion" by Vilaynaur S. Ramachandran and Stuart M. Anstis, June 1986, *Scientific American*. Copyright © 1986 by Scientific American, Inc. All rights reserved.

Fig 8.12 From *An Introduction to the Physiology of Hearing* (2nd ed.) by J. O. Pickles, 1988, London: Academic Pess. Copyright © 1987 J. O. Pickles. Reprinted by permission of the author.

Fig 9.4 Adapted from *Hearing: Physiological Acoustics, Neural Coding, and Psychoacoustics* (Fig 7.3) by W. L. Gulick, G. A. Gescheider, and R. D. Frisina, 1989, New York: Oxford University Press. Copyright © 1988 by the Oxford University Press. Reprinted by permission.

Fig 9.10 From *A Textbook of Histology* (10th ed.) by W. Bloom and D. W. Fawcett, 1975, Philadelphia: Saunders. Reprinted by permission of the author.

Fig 9.13 Adapted from *Hearing: Physiological Acoustics, Neural Coding, and Psychoacoustics* (Fig 7.3) by W. L. Gulick, G. A. Gescheider, and R. D. Frisina, 1989, New York: Oxford University Press. Copyright © 1988 by the Oxford University Press. Reprinted by permission.

Fig 10.2 From "Stimulus Representation in the Discharge Patterns of Auditory Nerves" by N. Y. S. Kiang, 1975, in E. L. Eagles (Ed.), *The Nervous System*, New York: Raven. Reprinted by permission.

Fig 10.3 From *Listening: An Introduction to the Perception of Auditory Events* (Fig 2.6) by S. Handel, 1989, Cambridge, MA: MIT Press. Copyright 1989 by the Massachusetts Institute of Technology. Reprinted by permission.

Fig 10.4 Adapted from "Loudness, Its Definition, Measurement, and Calculation" by H. Fletcher and W. A. Munson, 1933, *Journal of the Acoustical Society of America*, 5, pp. 82–108. Reprinted by permission of the American Institute of Physics.

Fig 10.6 Adapted from *Hearing: Physiological Acoustics, Neural Coding, and Psychoacoustics* (Fig 13.8), by W. L. Gulick, G. A. Gescheider, & R. D. Frisina, 1989. New York: Oxford University Press. © Oxford University Press.

Fig 10.7 Adapted from "Localization of High-Frequency Tones" by W. E. Fedderson, T. T. Sandel, D. C. Teas, and L. A. Jeffress, 1957, *The Journal of the Acoustical Society of America*, 29, p. 989. Reprinted by permission.

Fig 10.9 From "The Hearing of the Barn Owl" by Eric I. Knudsen, December 1981, *Scientific American*. Copyright © 1981 by Scientific American, Inc. All rights reserved.

Fig 11.1 From "Perception of Complex Auditory Patterns by Humans" by B. Espinoza-Vargas and C. S. Watson, in *The Comparative Psychology of Audition: Perceiving Complex Sounds*, Fig 3.1, 1989, Hillsdale, NJ: Erlbaum. Reprinted by permission of the authors and publisher.

Fig 11.2 From *The Science of Musical Sounds* by John R. Pierce. Copyright © 1983 Scientific American Books. Adapted from a figure in *Musical Acoustics: An Introduction* by Donald E. Hall, Belmont, CA: Wadsworth. Reprinted by permission.

Fig 11.4 From "Perceiving Tonal Structure in Music" by C.L. Krumhansl, 1985, *American Scientist*, 73, pp. 371–378 (Fig 2). Reprinted by permission of the author and publisher.

Fig 11.5 From *Music, Physics, and Engineering* (2nd ed.) by H. F. Olson, 1967, New York: Dover. Reprinted by permission.

Fig 11.7 From "Illusions for Stereo Headphones" by D. Deutsch, 1987, *Audio*, 71, pp. 36–48 (Fig 2). Reprinted by permission of the author and publisher.

Fig 11.8 From "Pitch Proximity in the Grouping of Simultaneous Tones" by D. Deutsch. © 1991 by The Regents of the University of California. Reprinted from *Music Perception*, Vol. 9 (2), pp. 187, by permission.

Fig 11.9 From "A Musical Paradox" by D. Deutsch, 1986, *Music Perception*, 3, pp. 275–280 (Fig 4). Reprinted by permission.

Fig 11.12 From "Selective Adaptation of Linguistic Feature Detectors" by P. D. Eimas and J. D. Corbit, *Cognitive Psychology*, 4, 99–109. Reprinted by permission of Academic Press, Inc.

Fig 11.13 From "On the Finding That Speech Is Special" by A. M. Liberman, 1982, *American Psychologist*, 37, pp. 148–167. Copyright © 1982 by the American Psychological Association. Reprinted by permission.

Fig 12.4 Adapted from *The Challenge of Pain* (Fig 33), by R. Melzack & P. D. Wall, 1982, New York: Basic Books. © Penguin Books, Ltd.

Fig 12.5 Reprinted with permission of Simon and Schuster from *The Cerebral Cortex of Man* by W. Penfield and T. Rasmussen, 1950, New York: Macmillan. Copyright 1950 by Macmillan Publishing Co., renewed 1978 by Theodore Rasmussen.

Fig 12.7 From "Picture and Pattern Perception in the Sighted and the Blind: The Advantage of the Late Blind" by M. A. Heller, 1989, *Perception*, 18, pp. 379–389 (Fig 2). Reproduced by permission of Pion, London.

Fig 13.4 From "Invariance of Odor Strength with Sniff Vigor: An Olfactory Analogue to Size Constancy" by R. Teghtsoonian, M. Teghtsoonian, B. Berglund, and U. Berglund, 1978, *Journal of Experimental Psychology: Human Perception and Performance*, 4, pp. 144–152 (Fig 4). Copyright © 1963 by the American Psychological Association. Reprinted by permission.

Fig 14.1 From "Movement-Produced Stimulation in the Development of Visually Guided Behavior" by R. Held and A. Hein, 1963, *Journal of Comparative and Physiological Psychology*, 56, pp. 872–876. Copyright © 1963 by the American Psychological Association. Reprinted by permission.

Fig 14.2 From "CONSPEC and CONLERN: A Two-Process Theory of Infant Face Recognition" by J. Morton and M. H. Johnson, *Psychological Review*, 98, 1991, 164–181, Fig 1. Copyright © 1991 by the American Psychological Association. Reprinted by permission.

Fig 14.3 From "Perception of Partly Occluded Objects in Infancy" by P. J. Kellman, and E. S. Spelke, *Cognitive Psychology*, 15, 483–524. Reprinted by permission of Academic Press, Inc. and the author.

Fig 14.4 From "Cross-Language Speech Perception: Evidence for Perceptual Reorganization During the First Year of Life" by J. F. Werker and R. C. Tees, 1984, *Infant Behavior and Development*, 7, pp. 49–63 (Fig 4). Reprinted by permission.

Fig 14.8 From "Age-Related Decrement in Hearing for Speech. Sampling and Longitudinal Studies" by M. Bergman, V. G. Blumenfeld, D. Cascardo, B. Dash, H. Levitt, and M. K. Margulies, 1976, *Journal of Gerontology*, 31, p. 534 (Fig 1). Reprinted by permission.

An example of the Ishihara test for color deficiency

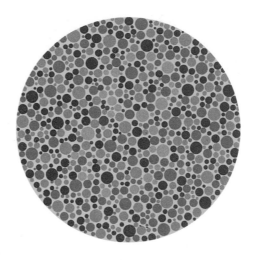

Reprint authorized by Graham-Field Surgical Co., Inc., 415 Second Avenue, New Hyde Park, NY 11040. Sole Distributors.

An example of simultaneous color contrast